ANTINET ZETTELKASTEN

ANTINET ZETTELKASTEN

A KNOWLEDGE SYSTEM THAT WILL TURN YOU INTO A PROLIFIC READER, RESEARCHER AND WRITER

SCOTT P. SCHEPER

Greenlamp
CALIFORNIA

Published in the United States by
Greenlamp, an imprint and division of
Greenlamp LLC, San Diego, California

Greenlamp, LLC
600 W. Broadway, Suite 700
San Diego, CA 92101

Copyright © 2022 by Scott P. Scheper

All rights reserved

No portion of this book may be reproduced
in any form without permission from the publisher.
For permissions contact: copyright@greenlamp.com

Diagrams and illustrations by Arianna Zabriskie

ISBN: 979-8-9868626-0-6 (paperback: alk. paper)

I would like to thank
my co-author,
my Antinet, Stewie.

CONTENTS

PART 3: **KNOWLEDGE DEVELOPMENT**

PART 4: **THE NATURE OF THE ANTINET**

AUTHOR'S NOTE

DURING THE YEAR I WROTE this book, every day I woke up and deliberately chose faith over fear.

I had recently come off a lucrative venture where I co-founded a cryptocurrency. I quit that venture in not the most pleasant fashion. My friends and family expected me to start a newer, bigger, and better cryptocurrency. The stage was set for me to "get back" at my old business partners who I had a falling out with...

And there I was, assembling boxes of notecards and writing about it. There I was, dedicating my life to a thing that flies over the heads of most people. There was no clear path to recouping my time spent exploring the system you're about to learn in this book. Yet, I chose faith. *There's something here,* I told myself. *There's something that is bigger than a mere box of notecards.* After reading this book, I know you'll find this to be true.

This book is for those who value the intellectual pursuit in life. It's for those who wish to unlock their inner-genius so that they can contribute something to the world. It's for those committed to growth and learning.

Thank you for joining me on this journey.

Just remember one thing—actually two: First, always choose faith over fear. And second: always remember...to stay crispy, my friend.[1]

Scott P. Scheper
Sunday, 7:36 am
St. Thomas, Virgin Islands

1 This phrase is a funny joke I started saying when I was doing a daily podcast in early 2021. The phrase stuck and you can find me using it in my highly entertaining emails. You can join my email list at https://scottscheper.com.

PREFACE (DO NOT SKIP)

THE SUBJECT OF THIS BOOK concerns itself with a knowledge development system created entirely out of notecards. I call this system the Antinet Zettelkasten (or simply, the "Antinet").

THE TRIPLE-ENTENDRE OF THE ANTINET

The Antinet is a triple-entendre.

First off, it's a tongue-in-cheek jab at the digitally obsessed world we live in. There's no debating that digital technologies have changed our world, mostly for the better. Digital technologies are better than their analog counterparts for many things: navigation, an open encyclopedia, information sharing, and so on. However, the one thing I contend that digital is *not* great for is this: *thinking*. Deep, deliberate thinking. Both short-term development of thought and long-term development of thought are best procured using analog tools.

This being the case, the Antinet doesn't mean "anti-internet." In fact, in this book, I introduce an *option* for using a digital reference manager. Therefore, the Antinet is not purely analog in nature. After all, digital reference managers require the internet.

The second meaning behind the term Antinet refers to its use as an acronym. The Antinet is an acronym that maps to four principles (detailed later on). The four principles the acronym maps to are the same four principles employed by Niklas Luhmann, the main originator of the Antinet. I'll introduce you to the acronym of the Antinet later in this book. And I'll introduce you to Luhmann shortly. But first, let me tell you about the third entendre.

The third meaning behind Antinet refers to Antonin Sertillanges. This Catholic intellectual and writer built his own Antinet-like system and wrote about it in his book *The Intellectual Life*. I talk about Sertillanges throughout this book. The "Ant" in Antinet also serves as an ode to Antonin.

ANTINET VS. ZETTELKASTEN

The Antinet most directly originated from the work of a German scholar named Niklas Luhmann, a man who gained popularity for his genius-level theoretical work in the field of sociology. Luhmann referred to his Antinet as a *Zettelkasten*, which in American English means *notebox*, and in European English translates to *slip box*. Throughout the rest of this book, I'll use the terms *Antinet, Zettelkasten, analog Zettelkasten*, and *Luhmann's notebox*, interchangeably. And for any grammarians out there: I use the German singular form of *Zettelkasten* as both singular and plural in English, rather than trying to work in the German plural form of *Zettelkästen*. *The Chicago Manual of Style*, on which this book's format relies, dictates one should not pluralize foreign words as though they were English.

I must caution you that outside of this book, the term *Zettelkasten* does not refer to the same concept I'm referring to. When I use the term Zettelkasten, I'm referring to the version of the Zettelkasten that Niklas Luhmann himself used: an analog one. I am not referring to the abstracted interpretations that the term has found itself cloaked in today. This so-called "cloaked" version stems from the metamorphosis of a physical thinking system into a metaphysical one. The embodiment of this new version is akin to that of digital notetaking apps with note-linking capabilities. Such apps (which are themselves *digital Zettelkasten* systems) merely link notes. I consider such apps to operate in an entirely different realm altogether. Get ready to enter the world of the Antinet. It's a trip.

A NOTE ON THE SUBTITLE OF THIS BOOK

The initial subtitle for this book was, *The Secret Knowledge Development System Evolved by History's Greatest Minds.* After I finished writing this book, I decided to change its subtitle to the one you find on its cover: *Uncovering the True Magic of the Notebox System That Will Turn You into a Research and Writing Machine.* I believe this new version better emphasizes two "core aspects" of the book, which I will detail now:

The first core aspect of this book centers around *uncovering the true magic of Niklas Luhmann's notebox system (the Zettelkasten).* You will learn how the modern (digital) interpretations of Niklas Luhmann's Zettelkasten are quite different from its true (original) nature. These modern interpretations of Zettelkasten lack the most important principles of the system. As a result, the modern interpretations are *far less effective* when it comes to achieving its main goal (genius-level creative output).[1] In this book, we will uncover the true magic of Niklas Luhmann's Zettelkasten so that you can experience its fullness (and avoid wasting your time with the modern, less-effective digital interpretations).

The second core aspect of this book centers around directing us towards the end goal. What is the end goal? The end goal is to become *a research and writing machine.* You see, a common misconception regarding Zettelkasten is that it is a subfield of *Personal Knowledge Management* ("PKM"). PKM has largely come to refer to digital notetaking apps for *storing information.* With each passing year, new digital notetaking apps emerge with more and more features (linking notes, tagging notes, creating pre-built templates for notes, metadata conventions for notes, etc.). The one thing digital notetaking apps seemingly *do not* focus on is...helping you develop knowledge! Luhmann's sole purpose for building his Zettelkasten centered on helping him become a research and writing machine. It was a system that helped him *develop knowledge.* It was a system that helped him *evolve*

---

1 In fact, the modern interpretations of Zettelkasten can be even worse than 'less effective.' They end up being time-suck activities that revolve around linking digital files and farting around with tags and metadata (when you should be developing knowledge). As a result, not only are you left with 'less effective' creative output, you're left with a mess of thousands of digital notes that cause you to quit the project you set out to work on.

the many thoughts that emerged from his readings (over four decades). All of this was done with a sole focus on becoming a prolific research and writing machine (which is what he became). In brief, the true nature of Zettelkasten is not an information storage system; it's a *Knowledge Development System*—more specifically, it's an *Analog Knowledge Development* system (an "AKD").[2]

Am I saying that the Zettelkasten is *only* for those interested in becoming a research machine or a writing machine? Not quite. Even if you're interested in becoming a reading machine (i.e., learning machine), an Antinet Zettelkasten can help you. However, it is important to adopt the mindset of approaching the books you read *as if* you'll be writing a book about the material. Paradoxically, adopting this mindset (as if you were going to *teach* the material), helps you *learn* the material.[3] In brief, by adopting the *writing machine* mindset, you will become a better *learning machine.*

After I determined this was the better subtitle, I let things sit for a week or so. To recap, the subtitle I was left with was, *Uncovering the True Magic of the Notebox System That Will Turn You into a Research and Writing Machine.* However, when looking at the length of the subtitle, I found it to be too wordy. Therefore, I decided to condense it to what you find on the cover: *A Knowledge System That Will Turn You Into a Prolific Reader, Researcher and Writer.* That cuts straight to the heart of the matter (even though uncovering the *true* nature of Niklas Luhmann's Zettelkasten remains a core theme of this book).

While the new subtitle better encompasses the two core aspects of this book, I think the very first subtitle is also worth diving into (aka, the "legacy subtitle"). The reason why is that much of this book touches on the rich history of the Zettelkasten. This adds important seasoning to the book. Let's dive into this now.

---

2 I hear you. The last thing the world needs right now are more acronyms, but whatever.

3 This is something we'll discuss throughout this book. It touches on the mindset of *growth* vs. the mindset of *contribution.*

THE RICH HISTORY OF ZETTELKASTEN

The legacy subtitle of this book is *The Secret Knowledge Development System Evolved by History's Greatest Minds*. Please take note of a few things:

First, note the phrase *History's Greatest Minds*. This touches on the idea that it was not Luhmann *alone* who produced the Antinet Zettelkasten. After all, in 1786, Johann Friedrich Blumenbach described the usage of slip boxes (*Zettelkästchen*).[4] Indeed, some of history's greatest minds used systems closely resembling the Antinet. Luhmann was intimately familiar with many of these scholars[5]. In turn, they have had a hand in evolving the Antinet as we know it.

Those who evolved the Antinet include the following individuals:[6]

- Georg Philipp Harsdöffer
- Jacob and Wilhelm Grimm
- Siegfried Kracauer
- Roland Barthes
- Reinhart Koselleck
- Georg Wilhelm Friedrich Hegel
- Walter Benjamin
- Aby Warburg
- Hans Blumenberg
- Friedrich Kittler
- Jean Paul (Johann Paul Friedrich Richter)
- Heinrich Heine
- Arno Schmidt
- Ernst Jünger
- Vladimir Nabokov
- Niklas Luhmann
- Jules Verne
- Walter Kempowski
- Michael Ende
- Antonin Sertillanges

Second, note the phrase *Evolved by*. The historical genealogy of the Antinet was "perhaps first mentioned in 1548 by Conrad Gessner." It was then expanded by Georg Philipp Harsdöffer (1607–1658), Joachim Jungius (1587–1657), and Gottfried Wilhelm Leibniz (1646–1716). The Catholic

4 Helmut Zedelmaier, Christoph Just Udenius and the German Ars Excerpendi around 1700: On the Flourishing and Disappearance of a Pedagogical Genre (Brill, 2016), 102.

5 For instance, Georg Wilhelm Friedrich Hegel.

6 Markus Krajewski, Note-Keeping: History, Theory, Practice of a Counter Measure- ment against Forgetting (Brill, 2016), 324.

intellectual and philosopher Antonin Sertillanges outlines a similar system to the Antinet. His book, *The Intellectual Life*, published in 1921, contains the instructions in explicit detail.[7]

The Antinet was developed by the likes of many learned scholars throughout time. Yet, the Antinet's "non-electronic completion" is viewed by scholars as stamped by Niklas Luhmann.[8]

In the early 1950s, when Luhmann began building his Zettelkasten, he was working at the Lüneburg Higher Administrative Court. It was there that he spent his time "organizing a reference system for administrative court decisions."[9] When asked by an interviewer what he did after getting off work at five o'clock in the evening, Luhmann replied that he read a lot and, "above all I started to work with a Zettelkasten."[10] From this, one infers that whatever Luhmann learned while organizing the reference system for the Lüneburg Higher Administrative Court ended up helping him *evolve* the Zettelkasten into what it is today.

For this reason, the Antinet is not *a secret knowledge development system created by one individual*; rather, it's *a secret knowledge development system evolved by history's greatest minds*. The overhyped digital notetaking systems of today have rendered the old way of developing knowledge almost completely lost. Analog knowledge development has become a secret. Its methods are a secret known only to a small collection of people. For instance, scholars who study the evolution of notetaking in Early Modern Europe.[11] Even though the legacy subtitle is admittedly sensationalistic, I hold that there is at least sensational substance to support its sensationalism.

---

7 OP A. G. Sertillanges, *The Intellectual Life: Its Spirit, Conditions, Methods*, trans. Mary Ryan, Reprint edition (Washington, D.C.: The Catholic University of America Press, 1992), 195–7.

8 Krajewski, Note-Keeping, 319.

9 Niklas Luhmann, *Short Cuts* (*English Translation*) (Frankfurt am Main: Zweitau sendeins, 2002), 10.

10 Luhmann, Short Cuts, 11.

11 For instance, the scholars who authored individual chapters in the collection, *Forgetting Machines: Knowledge Management Evolution in Early Modern Europe*.

In summary, you can see by the depth of both subtitles how robust this book is. It touches on many aspects of the Zettelkasten: its true nature, its modern misconceptions, its key principles, its history, its magic, its scientific underpinnings, and more. This additional context gives you a greater respect for the journey you're about to embark on in reading this book. But before you do, let's talk about the goal of this book.

THE GOAL OF THIS BOOK

The goal of this book is both simple *and* complex. My goal is to help people who are committed to growth and learning to create genius-level work. I hope the genius-level work created lasts for two hundred years or more. The reason any piece of work might last for two hundred years or more is related to the contribution it makes to other people.

That is my *why*.

My *what* is this system: the Antinet. The Antinet is a *knowledge development system*. It's a tool that enables one to develop *thoughts*. I also contend that it develops thoughts better than its digital imitators. The Antinet enables one to unlock brilliant insights. It's built on fundamental principles that help develop one's mind. It's built on both order and chaos. In turn, it reveals accidental associations and unconventional interactions between ideas. There are other properties of the system I will introduce in the book as well.

My *how* is the way that I preach this system. Spoiler alert: I'm not an academic.

I couldn't care less about ascribing to academic conventions (i.e., academic jargon).

Anyway, I intend to write using my own voice. I intend to speak in a way that discusses complex ideas in an as simple manner as possible, without being simplistic. That is *how* I intend to deliver the message of the Antinet Zettelkasten to you.

My *why*, my *what* and my *how* are both simple *and* complex. An Antinet is a system founded on simple laws yet morphs into something quite complex.

The theory behind why it works is also simple yet has very deep implications in the field of knowledge. Get ready for a fun ride.

THE DIFFICULTY LEVEL OF THIS TEXT

This book is intended for the general reader; however, it is not trivial. It's quite challenging in parts and quite theoretical in parts. In summation, it's just as theoretical as it is practical, yet its theoretical contents contain practical implications that cannot be reproduced by a mere "how-to guide" on this subject.

By becoming acquainted with the theoretical depth of the Antinet, you will come away with a richer understanding of a system that, upon first glance, seems rather simple. After reading this book, you will have a fuller understanding of the system and the deep-rooted rationale for its structure. As a result, I believe you will have a higher likelihood of sticking with the system in the long term.

THIS PROBABLY WILL NOT BE THE LAST TIME YOU READ THIS BOOK

While writing this book, I began uploading YouTube videos demonstrating how an Antinet works. As a result, I began receiving feedback, questions, and comments. One comment, in particular, stuck out to me. It was from an Antinetter named Kathleen, who specializes in the field of linguistics. In a comment on one of my videos, Kathleen wrote:

> "I just watched this again and finally, this being my third time through this particular video, it made sense from start to finish. I don't envy the challenge you have taken on to describe this system. It's so nebulous until you have the cards in front of you… The video hasn't changed, but this time through it was a totally different video for me. How will you convey to your readers that they might have to spiral back to chapters previously covered once they start getting an inkling of what's going on with an Antinet?"

The answer to that question is simple: you will likely need to revisit this book and review it after you have some experience building an Antinet. However, don't let this fact stop you from proceeding. If you value developing your mind, developing your thoughts, and creating genius-level work, understanding and building an Antinet is worth it.

The fact that you may need to revisit this book regularly through the years is a good thing. It means the content is important enough to actually revisit! I have several books that I keep on my shelf in my office. They're staring at me right now from across the room as I write this. I revisit them from time to time, and I keep them on my shelf to remind me that I ought to reread them if I encounter a lull in my work.

In summary, you must be prepared to do two things when engaging this book: (1) actively apply the knowledge and techniques (as Kathleen has), and (2) revisit the information at various stages in your journey.

A NOTE ON HOW TO READ THIS BOOK

A curious thing happens when one develops knowledge using the techniques you're about to learn. In-depth context often accompanies each thought. Other thoughts oftentimes inspire each paragraph. These inspired thoughts can derive from your thoughts, or these inspired thoughts can come from others' thoughts. As a result, paragraphs and sentences end up so deep that one's writing begins to reflect this. It reflects this in the form of footnotes.

I have written this book using my own Antinet. As such, I have been quite judicious in attaching comments and sources in the form of footnotes. This text is ripe with footnotes. My recommendation is to read the book once without worrying about the footnotes.

Do not get stuck on the idea that you must read every single footnote. If a sentence with a footnote truly sparks your curiosity, certainly feel free to read the footnote. Otherwise, do not get bogged down.

ADVICE FOR THOSE WHO WANT TO USE THEIR OWN ANTINET WHILE READING THIS BOOK

If you want to use (and build out) your own Antinet while reading this book, then pay attention: do not read this book linearly.

Here's what you should do: First, read *Chapter 11: The Hitchhiker's Guide to the Antinet.* This chapter will give you a good base version for your own Antinet. Follow the instructions in detail.

Second, within *Chapter 14: Extraction,* there's a section titled *The 2-Step Luhmannian Bibcard Method.* Read this section. Then, while reading this book, use a bibcard and create brief *bib notes.* You can use multiple bibcards (you don't need to fit all your bib notes from this book onto one bibcard). After you read that section, you'll understand what bibcards are and what bib notes are.

Last, if you're ever confused about a term, you'll find a helpful *Glossary* in the back of the book.

After you complete the steps outlined, you can begin reading this book, starting from *Chapter 1* and proceeding linearly.

A FINAL PIECE OF ADVICE

With this book, you have stumbled upon something special. It's unique, quirky, and—dammit—it's downright crazy! You are embarking on a journey in learning the old way to develop knowledge. With the recent over-hyped popularity of digital tools, *the old way* of developing knowledge has become *the secret way*. This revolves around using just your brain, pen, and paper. I contend this secret way is the best way.

The greatest thinkers and writers of all time did not need a computer to develop genius-level work, and neither do you. I'm going to show you how to start thinking again, using a pen, notecards, and...your brain! Get ready for the ride of your intellectual life.

CHAPTER ONE

THE JOURNEY THAT LED ME TO PUBLISH A BOOK ON THE ANTINET

THERE I WAS, LYING ON MY COUCH one weekday afternoon during the pandemic of 2020. I had just finished a three-hour binge of the show *Billions.*

It's a weekday, I said to myself. *I should be doing something productive. Look at me, I'm a single 34-year-old with nothing to live for besides my cat* (a ragdoll named Brodus Maximus). I felt like a complete slouch, a freaking loser. I was empty and unfulfilled.

Roughly a year prior, I had left the cryptocurrency company I had co-founded. For two years, I worked eight days a week to launch the company. In record-breaking time, I helped take the company from $2.14 million in debt to becoming one of the most exciting high-growth companies out there.[1] We raised roughly $10 million via what is known as an ICO (Initial Coin Offering). We then raised over $14.1 million in equity during the next six months.[2]

Things were looking great. I was helping people, is what I thought. I was raising money to build ground-breaking technology that would re-shape

1 "PART II," accessed February 15, 2022, https://www.sec.gov/Archives/edgar/data/1577351/000119312518143726/d579201dpartii.htm.

2 "PART II," accessed February 15, 2022, https://www.sec.gov/Archives/edgar/data/1577351/000119312519133301/d689828dpartii.htm#fin689828_5. This was done through making use of the U.S. Security & Exchange Commission's Program for startup companies that was enacted as part of the Jumpstart Our Business Startups Act (JOBS Act), known as a Reg A+ Offering.

the way GPS works, using cryptocurrency to incentivize individuals. We then held an exciting conference in downtown San Diego, and I spoke to over a thousand excited investors and customers who were diehard fans.

Over the next year, however, the market proceeded down a slow death march. Cryptocurrency prices across the entire industry dropped significantly. My investment and investments made by my family and friends who trusted me were down over 95%. The thousands of customers and investors who had once declared their love for the company were disgruntled. They were now practically threatening to bring pitchforks to our offices!

Since I was the face of the company, I took the brunt of it. It felt awful; I was called a scammer and every other awful thing you can think of. Things got even worse. We had to lay off almost half our company in a day (totaling over forty people).[3]

On the day of the layoff, I observed my relationships with now-former employees transform from some of my closest to my most contentious ones. I felt depleted, yet I couldn't show it because I still needed to lead the rest of the team out of the mess. I pressed on for another six months. When we got the company to a stable point, I knew deep down that I needed to take a break, and I had to step away for personal reasons. I was empty inside. On top of this, the technology really hadn't panned out; it needed more time to develop. Meanwhile, the vision was redirected into something I wasn't proud of. Yet, because I was not the majority partner or shareholder, I didn't have the legal control required to do anything about it. Nor did I possess the energy to fight it. I was physically, emotionally, and mentally burnt out.

Fast-forward a year later, and there I was, on my couch, lying down in a vegetative coma of indolence, watching *Billions*. I wasn't necessarily suicidal,

3 "San Diego Blockchain Startup XY Lays off 40 People, Losing Half Its Staff," San Diego Union-Tribune, June 4, 2019, https://www.sandiegouniontribune.com/business/technology/story/2019-06-04san-diego-blockchain-startup-xy-lays-off-40-people-losing-half-its-staff.

but I was sad; I had thoroughly lost my excitement for life. Plus, on top of this, my other ragdoll cat, Mr. Bigglesworth (Brodus's brother), passed away from stomach cancer. He was only two years old. After watching him suffer for months, I decided to pull the plug. It may seem ridiculous writing about this; there are definitely more severe travesties in life. But I was single at the time, with only two cats for company. Yet there I found myself, holding one of them in my arms as the veterinarian injected him with something to make his breathing stop forever.

I was depressed; I came down with a major case of black ass, as Samuel Johnson would call it (his phrase for melancholy). On the surface, I wished to create even more significant success than what I had engineered at the cryptocurrency company. This time, however, I wanted more control over the product and the company's direction so that, in my mind, we wouldn't compromise on the vision.

Yet what I really desired was to serve people worth serving. Sure, there were some excellent people I got to serve at the cryptocurrency company; but, let's face it, the vast majority of those involved were in it to make money without having to do anything. The people interested in cryptocurrency were there for one thing, and one thing only: to get rich doing nothing. When the market is up, you're Jesus Christ himself; when the market is down, you're the reason for all their problems.

I would rather not serve people who were *get-rich-quickers*, and I wanted to avoid being in the business of wasting my energy with wasteful products. Sure, I wanted to have a significant impact, but I also wanted to provide a product that actually leaves future generations with something useful.

After finishing the entire season of *Billions*, I decided to sell my 72-inch big screen TV and spend time brainstorming my next venture. I was still fascinated with cryptocurrency, and I was intrigued by decentralized finance. I saw innovation coming out of that space. But I was leaning toward creating something in my craft of marketing and copywriting. Specifically, I was intrigued by the idea of creating a newsletter, and it would be in a format inspired by my mentor, the late, great copywriter Gary Halbert. I began to grow inspired by the idea of creating a newsletter related to marketing, copywriting, cryptocurrency, and whatever else I was interested in.

In this state, I began to form a habit. For the next several months, I would sit on my patio in the sun, smoking cigars and reading. I ended up smoking far too many cigars. I got up to four per day, and it was so bad my lymph nodes kept flaring up, screaming at me to quit (which I finally did).

Anyway, I began to read all day on my patio. I read psychology and philosophy books. I would sit there in the sun and shade, take a few puffs of a cigar, read, and then use a commonplace book to take notes. I had used a commonplace book in the past to store notes, but I ran into limitations. After a few days, I was reminded of those limitations.

I also had used notecards in the past. I began writing notes on notecards roughly fifteen years prior, and I had been pretty consistent at taking notes for books using 3 x 5 inch notecards. Yet, these notes had become numerous and unruly because they were organized in "silos." Each concept on the card was difficult to find because they were clustered by the title of the book. Nevertheless, even with these limitations, I inexplicably found notecards to be the best tool for learning and retaining information.

Yet, using notecards proved difficult. I was on the patio smoking cigars in the sun during this time. It was hard enough to read a book with the wind constantly blowing, flipping the pages. Using notecards was even more annoying, and they flew everywhere. For this reason, I stuck with using a commonplace book.

The problem I was running into with the commonplace book was that the silos of information I was creating were disconnected. I read books and then wrote my thoughts out and came up with great ideas; however, the thoughts were not connected. It was turning into a swamp of excellent knowledge, turned mucky because it wasn't connected to a source of clean water.

If I read something new that would develop and evolve a previous concept, my previous ideas would remain locked inside a random page in the middle of my commonplace book, requiring that I dig around to find it (or otherwise forget it). The idea would become stale and disconnected.

Yet, while reading, I felt there was an incommunicable power in taking notes by hand—whether that be in my commonplace book or on notecards. Writing things down by hand developed my understanding of what I was reading. It increased my retention of the concepts I wrote down and evolved my thinking. It helped me form new ideas in a way that was far better than typing notes into my laptop. Plus, a laptop workflow doesn't work so well when you read in the sun while smoking cigars. It gets hot and ashy and dirty. And then there's the glare factor.

I was aiming to begin organizing my thoughts and knowledge to turn them into something that helped me create my next venture. I felt the urge to connect my ideas as I spotted many patterns in my readings. These were patterns across the disciplinary fields of psychology, philosophy, and marketing. At this point, I turned to a surprising tool that, in retrospect, yielded some surprisingly good results. I started using Microsoft Excel to link my ideas. I also used it to diagram concepts and connections between them. It proved handy in organizing information at a high level.

Over the years, I have tried out every tool you can think of. This includes notetaking apps like Evernote, mind-mapping software, the reMarkable Tablet, and many other tools. The closest tool I found for helping me organize my knowledge was Trello. Yet, even Trello was lacking compared to good ol' Microsoft Excel.

Several months went by, and I continued along in this way, settling for a mishmash workflow: using my commonplace book, Microsoft Excel, and sometimes notecards.

One morning, I woke up and did what I usually did—I checked a website called *Hacker News*.[4] This site serves as a hub of user-submitted stories, in which the best ones get upvoted. That morning, at the top of the page,

4 **https://news.ycombinator.com**

was a submission titled, "Foam: A personal knowledge management and sharing system for VSCode." I clicked on the link and began exploring. I learned that Foam was a "personal knowledge management sharing system," and it was for "organizing your research, [and] keeping re-discoverable notes."[5] I learned that all of this is just a fancy way of saying it's an application for creating markdown files and linking to other markdown files within the text of the notes. This is done by using two square brackets in a method known as *wikilinks*, for instance: [[**Example Link to Some Note**]].

I also learned from Foam's website that it was based on something called Roam Research ("Roam"). Yet unlike Roam, and unlike something called "Zettelkasten," one could "use Foam without joining a cult."[6]

I had no idea what Roam or Zettelkasten was, nor did I care. I had enough on my plate (like trying to figure out what to do with my life). Plus, the idea of joining a cult didn't sound appealing. And after Googling "Zettelkasten" and coming across the website zettelkasten.de, I found the content way over my head. With that, I continued experimenting with Foam without bothering to understand all the other stuff.

After downloading Foam, I recall picking it up quickly. The lightbulb went on in my mind. It became clear how novel it was to create notes and then link them together. My enthusiasm continued to grow when Foam presented me with a nifty-looking bubble graph showing how my notes connected to one another. I was blown away. *It was official,* I thought to myself, *I've entered the Matrix, and there's no going back.*

At this point, I ditched the mashup of my commonplace book, Excel, and notecards. I was convinced I had discovered the new and better world of linked notes.

---

5 "Foam," Foam, accessed February 10, 2022, https://foambubble.github.io/foam/.

6 "Principles," Foam, accessed August 27, 2021, https://foambubble.github.io/foam/principles.html.

After a short stint using Foam, I stumbled across a similar tool called *Obsidian*. After using Obsidian for a brief time, it became apparent that this tool was better than Foam. It was slick and packed with more features. For me, the killer feature was its ability to dynamically update all links. With this feature, if you changed the filename of a note, the other links pointing to the file wouldn't break.

I found myself so enthusiastic about Obsidian that I would spend my evenings watching YouTube videos on its best practices. In doing this, I came across a particular YouTube channel with professional, well-produced videos. Its creator was a sharp guy in his mid-to-late twenties who spoke clearly. After watching a series of these videos, I learned that he had created a six-week-long online course purporting to teach his methods.

I signed up for the course's most premium package: $1,322 for a six-week course with a 90-minute one-on-one session with its creator. I spent the next six weeks learning the principles. Not only that, but I learned things like how one should *not* copy-and-paste things into notes. I learned that folders were "rigid" and "bad." I learned that one should instead embrace tags and create files that act as a "map of content" for notes. I learned more advanced things like the concept of workflows and using templates for creating new notes. I began exploring all the plugins Obsidian came with and I installed new community plugins and began enhancing my Obsidian editor's color scheme and layout. I continued to learn the ins and outs of notetaking best practices. I learned about the concept of taking something called "atomic notes" and laboriously breaking apart my monolithic notes into individual components. I learned about setting up different hotkeys and macros to speed up my "notemaking" process.

After several months, I became a pretty advanced user of Obsidian. I had custom commands and macros that were fed inputs and spat out nicely formatted starter templates for my notes. I used these features extensively. I had dozens of hotkeys I would use for various things to save time. I became what I now call a "hotkey junkie."

Nevertheless, discouraging thoughts would arise in my mind now and then.

The thoughts revolved around the fear that all I was really doing was busy work. Deep down, I felt like I was just majoring in the minor. "Never mistake activity for achievement," as John Wooden would say.

At this point, I was looking at a folder size of 105 MB, with 1,272 items in it. Almost all the files were notes, though there were a few images and template files. After this much work, I imagined I would feel more tranquil and organized—or at the very least, closer to what I was trying to accomplish.

I had set out to use Obsidian to map out all the concepts from the books I was reading. My goal was to organize them into a cohesive whole that would become greater than the sum of its parts. I hoped to use the concepts to produce a book or a newsletter on marketing, copywriting, and cryptocurrency. Yet, I had ended up with what amounted to a rat's nest of 1,272 linked files, and a nifty diagram presenting me with a bubble graph of the mess!

I felt hopeless, and like I had ventured further away from making sense of my readings. Even the mishmash of my commonplace book and Excel felt more helpful than the mess I had created with Obsidian.

At this point, a book showed up in the mail. I had heard about the book in the online course I had taken. The book, *How to Take Smart Notes*, was written by an academic named Sönke Ahrens. I began reading the book and soon encountered the same term, which I recall coming across on Foam's website, where it had been implied that this term had a cultish following—the term was *Zettelkasten*.

Yet as I read the book *How to Take Smart Notes* and learned more about *Zettelkasten* and its creator, Niklas Luhmann, I started to gain a clearer understanding of what it was actually all about.

Ahrens provided more explicit detail on how a Zettelkasten worked compared with what I had found researching online. In addition, Ahrens explained how an analog Zettelkasten worked. Although it provided a very sparse description, it was the only description I had come across that explained how an analog Zettelkasten works.

Oddly, however, Ahrens seemed less interested in the functions of the analog Zettelkasten. Instead, he spent most of his time preaching that Luhmann's system could be refitted for the digital age by using digital apps possessing note-linking capabilities. In this spirit, Ahrens seemed to invent new concepts for doing this, coining terms like *fleeting notes, literature notes* and *permanent notes.*

Although Ahrens's notion sounded intriguing, from my previous experiences, it created a digital mess. Instead, I decided to give the analog version—the original version—a good solid try first.

As soon as I began using the Zettelkasten in analog form, I recall saying to myself, *"Ahhh…so this is how all this stuff is supposed to work!"* I remember thinking how different it was compared to the digital apps I had used—and how much better the analog version was! The next day, I wrote by hand for nearly twelve hours straight. I wanted to stop, but simply couldn't. I had so many ideas I felt needed to be developed. In the previous months, I had spent most of my energy linking notes, formatting them, and making them "atomic." Now my thoughts were pouring out. I remember writing so much that a callous formed on my index finger. Thoughts were being developed on paper and flowing from my mind. Yet, I could actually see myself using the knowledge and internally developing it over the long term. This experience was exciting.

Yet, Ahrens's description of how an analog Zettelkasten worked was rather wanting. It was missing a ton of detail and was vaguely outlined in several paragraphs.[7] But to Ahrens's credit, his vague description was perhaps the best out there of how an analog Zettelkasten worked. To compensate for the vagueness of Ahrens's description, I began researching online. Soon, I came across something fascinating: a special project had commenced at Bielefeld University in Germany, the same university where Luhmann was tenured.

7 Sönke Ahrens, *How to Take Smart Notes: One Simple Technique to Boost Writing, Learning and Thinking: For Students, Academics and Nonfiction Book Writers* (North Charleston, SC: CreateSpace, 2017), 18-20.

The project entailed digitizing Luhmann's entire Zettelkasten (roughly ninety thousand notecards) and uploading it online for all to view.[8]

I began to scan Luhmann's Online Archive and even started writing out the translated versions of his notes by hand. Using Luhmann's actual Zettelkasten as a guide, I began building out my analog Zettelkasten over the following months.

I also began porting over the notecards I had taken for the previous fifteen years. I had been building out a notecard box off and on over the previous fifteen years. These cards were not addressed, but just free-floating notecards. The thing I was missing was the infinite internal branching brought forth by the Antinet's tree structure.

I started installing the old cards into my analog Zettelkasten by giving them numeric-alpha addresses in the top-right corner, and then branching them with similar cards. I began to observe how the notecards I had created for over a decade began to reveal patterns I would have otherwise not seen if they'd remained organized by book title. It was very exciting to observe the power of such a system.

The experience and the journey I went through helped me realize that the magic of a Zettelkasten—and indeed the magic of knowledge management—rests not in the idea of creating notes; just as important is the medium one uses to create the notes. The magic of Zettelkasten does not come from taking atomic notes and linking them together using sexy software. Rather, the magic rests in the analog thinking system Luhmann created. One built of a pen, paper, and...a brain.

Over the following months, I began to see some encouraging results using the analog Zettelkasten. From studying Luhmann's archives, I discovered there were four key principles that serve as the foundation of Luhmann's

8 **Johannes Schmidt, "Niklas Luhmann's Card Index: Thinking Tool, Communication Partner, Publication Machine," Forgetting Machines. Knowledge Management Evolution in Early Modern Europe 53 (2016), 292.**

system. These four principles comprise the acronym "ANTI." From there on, I began using the term "Antinet" to describe the system.

Meanwhile, I was progressing on the project related to marketing, copywriting, and cryptocurrency. I began to see my knowledge compounding, and this helped me produce content.

I was gaining a ton of momentum and making progress. I also began using an analog weekly planner to manage my to-do's and my goals. I found my productivity skyrocketing during this period. These practices also helped me detach myself from the digital distractions brought forth by phone and laptop.

More importantly, my mind felt like it was actually being stretched, and like it was growing again. If I'm not learning and growing, I'm not the happiest person to be around. This system started bringing me happiness and joy again.

I've since introduced the magic of the Antinet to my Little Brother, who I mentor (initially, we met through the Big Brothers Big Sisters mentorship program, and I've continued mentoring him beyond). I've seen him go from starting fights in clubs to literally bring his Antinet into the library and growing his mind all day. He reads and develops his notes from his readings well past the time the sun goes down. He's learning copywriting and marketing with my help. He'll also soon be the first in his family to graduate from college. Like me, he has named his Antinet (he named his "Huncho"; mine is named "Stewie"), in recognition of what Luhmann himself described as the magic of the Antinet: it functions as "an alter ego with whom we can constantly communicate."[9]

After discovering the power of the analog Zettelkasten (aka, the Antinet), I began sharing my material online with people. I've met some incredible people through my website, and through Reddit, YouTube, and Twitter. I've started to see the transformation of others who use analog thinking systems.

---

9 Niklas Luhmann, "Communication with Noteboxes (Revised Edition)," trans. Manfred Kuehn, https://daily.scottscheper.com/zettelkasten/.

There are some fascinating people out there who are having success with this tool. For instance, Stephanie Williams uses an Antinet to teach her deaf son, who has a unique learning style.[10]

The Antinet helped me achieve what I was missing—a system that possessed the power of thinking on paper. It helped me retain the power of writing by hand without it turning into a disconnected knowledge swamp (which is what commonplace books create). It helped me to finally make some progress in my projects and develop them to fruition.

Yet something odd happened early on in my project related to marketing, copywriting, and cryptocurrency. It fell to the wayside because I felt this compelling desire to share the power of the Antinet. After all, I had to discover the system the hard way, and I knew others would have to go through the same slog I experienced to discover the true power of the Zettelkasten (in all its analog glory). At this point, I stopped and listened to my heart, not my head. If I had learned anything from my previous cryptocurrency experience, true fulfillment comes not from chasing money but from genuinely creating a product one can be proud of. Sure, there's more money in creating a newsletter or book that provides money-making insights for entrepreneurs, marketers, and crypto speculators. Yet, in my heart, I felt less passionate about doing such a thing and more compelled to explore the seemingly absurd idea of teaching people about an analog thinking system.

Let's be clear, getting passionate about an analog Zettelkasten is quite absurd. It's a seemingly outdated system of notecards devised by some dead academic whose books are nearly impossible to read! Yet I couldn't resist. I felt drawn to sharing what I had discovered. I remembered the fascinating people I interacted with in the online course I had taken on Obsidian. I weighed these feelings and then decided. To hell with taking the safe route and creating some crypto project to serve entitled speculators (who want to get rich without lifting a finger)!

---

10 Stephanie Williams,...Filing the Courses I Plan to Take into My Analogue Zettelkasten Aka #Antinet," Twitter, January 30, 2022, https://twitter.com/utheol/status/1487584728064606208.

I decided to do the risky thing—some would say the crazy thing. That is, I decided to spend a year of my life reading and writing all day about an analog notebox system—the Antinet. I've worked on this book like a dog; however, I've done so without burning myself out.

I am energized writing about something that I know can help driven people, academics, and knowledge workers develop their minds. It hasn't been easy. I've been living off my investments and savings, without making a penny off this work. But I don't care; I sleep soundly at night knowing I haven't sold my soul, or wasted people's lives with wasteful, speculative products that bilk other people out of money. Somehow I ended up doing what I wanted to do all along—and I found it in quite an odd vehicle. I decided to do something that was missing in my previous ventures, and that is this: helping people worth helping.

It's an honor for me to serve you and help you read more effectively, take useful notes from readings, and transform them into powerful long-term material that makes an impact in your field.

However, I would like to point something out: what you've signed up for won't be easy. You're choosing to do things the hard way—the only way—the best way.

CHAPTER TWO

THE WHO AND WHY OF THE ANTINET

IN THE EARLY DAYS OF WRITING this book, I recorded a podcast every day.[1] In the podcast, I mainly discussed items related to what I was discovering about the Antinet.

One day, my father, who has served his community as a mortgage broker for over thirty-five years, visited me in San Diego, California. I learned that he had listened to a lengthy episode about the Antinet recorded the previous day. Yet instead of feeling grateful, I felt a bit uneasy. This prompted me to clarify who should bother investing their finite life energy into learning about the Antinet. Sure, my dad probably listened to the podcast because he loves me. But should he really invest his time learning about the Antinet?

Attention is the most valuable asset you have. You must not waste it learning something that you really shouldn't bother with. I love my dad and would hate to think he'd waste his time learning about the Antinet when he really should be spending it on his craft. Even though I don't know you, I'd hate for you to waste your time as well. For this reason, before you even begin getting too deep into this book, I would like to provide some context and reasons for why you should or shouldn't read this book.

---

1 **I have since discontinued the podcast, yet I continue to publish a piece of content every day as part of a deliberate commitment. You can still listen to the podcast here: https://podcast.scottscheper.com/**

WHY YOU SHOULD BOTHER READING THIS BOOK

Here are three reasons why you should read this book:

1. You're a writer, author, or person who wants to create genius-level work in your field—the type of work that will last for over two hundred years.

2. You already have experience writing by hand, and you're aware of its power—yet you ran into the same wall I once ran into stemming from notecard systems organized by category.

3. You wish to use a system that develops the two most essential skills you'll need for thriving in the future: (1) the skill of getting to know your mind (self-awareness) and (2) the skill of developing your mind's flexibility.[2]

WHO SHOULD EVEN BOTHER READING THIS BOOK

As mentioned in the preface, Niklas Luhmann was the originator of the Antinet, and you will be learning more about him in this book. Luhmann himself held that the Antinet was a "universal tool." A tool that could capture any thought and potentially provide value to anyone, as long the thought could be written on a notecard.[3]

Although Luhmann held that one "can place almost everything in [the notebox]," so long as it can be "noted down," I hold a closer view to that of several scholars, that an Antinet is primarily beneficial for researchers and

2 According to Yuval Noah Harari, a bestselling author, and profoundly independent thinker, "We need to know ourselves better and we need to develop this mental flexibility. Not as a kind of hobby for the side. This is really the most important quality or skill to just survive the upheavals in the coming decades." See Clay Skipper, "The Most Important Survival Skill for the Next 50 Years Isn't What You Think," GQ, September 30, 2018, https://www.gq.com/story/yuval-noah-harari-tech-future-survival.

3 Niklas Luhmann, "Communicating with Slip Boxes," accessed May 5, 2021, https://luhmann.surge.sh/communicating-with-slip-boxes. "The slip box becomes a universal instrument. You can place almost everything in it, and not just ad hoc and in isolation, but with internal possibilities of connection with other contents." Also, "It becomes a sensitive system that internally reacts to many ideas, as long as they can be noted down."

writers who wish to notate thoughts and ideas from their readings.[4] It's mainly useful for non-fiction writers who do much reading, thinking, and processing of ideas. The Antinet develops thoughts both in the short term and long term. Thoughts serve as the raw material for non-fiction writers, and thoughts stand as the raw material for the Antinet.

The purpose of the Antinet is to develop your thoughts so that they are more thoroughly evolved and supported by the time they make their way to your manuscript.

The Antinet is primarily a tool for researchers and writers. However, do note the use of the term *primarily*. The Antinet is *primarily* useful for non-fiction writers; yet, it's not *exclusively* useful for such individuals.

A MORE PESSIMISTIC ANSWER

A pessimistic answer to the question of who should bother learning the Antinet is this: most people shouldn't bother with this book.

Here's why—there are 1.65 million writers in the world.[5] There are at least 7.8 million researchers in the world.[6] For good measure, let's throw in an extra twenty million more individuals who are aspiring writers, professional researchers, graduate students, and independent intellectuals. That's 29.45 million people. Divide that into 7.9 billion people on earth, and you get 0.37%. In other words, there's a 0.37% chance that an Antinet is helpful for any given person. Therefore, there's only a small chance that you should bother with this book. However, you're not an average person. Being that you found yourself here and are reading this right now, perhaps I've already filtered out the other 99.63% of people. And, in that case, I'm honored to have you here!

---

4 Luhmann, "Communicating with Slip Boxes." "The slip box becomes a universal instrument. You can place almost everything in it, and not just ad hoc and in isolation, but with internal possibilities of connections with other contents."

5 Devon Delfino, "20 Writing Statistics." Writer, November 11, 2020. https://writer.com/blog/professional-writing-salary-statistics/.

6 "UNESCO: Facts and Figures: Human Resources," UNESCO: Facts and figures: Human resources, n.d., https://en.unesco.org/node/252277.

A MORE OPTIMISTIC ANSWER TO WHO SHOULD EVEN BOTHER WITH LEARNING ABOUT THE ANTINET

The Antinet is a system that serves as a *ruminant* for your thoughts. The idea that only non-fiction writers can benefit from such a system is somewhat limiting and probably inaccurate. Indeed, mathematicians who construct proofs that require rumination over months (or perhaps years) would most certainly find value in a system such as an Antinet.

Richard Feynman and many physicists would find their success watered down if it were not for their analog devices that serve as a form of short-term thought development and long-term rumination.

It appears that non-fiction writers and deep researchers are *primarily* those who will benefit from thinking systems such as an Antinet.

If you're an entrepreneur, an artist, a software engineer, a business professional, etc., here's the cold hard truth: an Antinet will likely be less helpful to you—unless you intend to publish and ship content. This goes for any Zettelkasten system (even the digital knockoffs).

Regardless of what camp you fall into, there's one thing you cannot forego. And that is, a commitment over the long term to developing your knowledge using an Antinet. Think decades, not years.

WHY NOTETAKING IS IMPORTANT TO LEARN IN THE FIRST PLACE

It's been put forth by scholars that "reading without noting" yields "superficial knowledge." This is because reading, as an act alone, is "not accompanied by the attention and thought required to make a well-considered note."[7]

Notetaking serves as the mechanism that enables a contradictory paradox. One initially considers notetaking to be a *memory replacement tool*. That is,

---

7 Richard Yeo, *Notebooks, Recollection, and External Memory: Some Early Modern English Ideas and Practices*. (Brill, 2016), 138.

you don't have to memorize anything because you can just dump it all in an archive of notes; in other words, you can replace the need to memorize. However, something else occurs entirely. Notetaking, if done via writing by hand, acts as a *memory enhancement tool.*

Notetaking was thought to aid memory in two different ways, observes Ann Blair in her work on the subject. First, it creates a written record to return to. Second, and more interestingly, by forcing the mind to dwell on the material, the act of writing excerpts and the thoughts they generate enables one to retain better what was read or heard.[8]

Jeremias Drexel (1581—1638) observes that if one takes notes, their memory becomes far from being neglected; in fact, their memory becomes "substantially more effective." As the scholar Alberto Cevolini reflects, notetaking promotes better *understanding* of material. The reason why centers around the time and attention devoted to the reading. "The reader," observes Cevolini, "reflects longer on what he is reading, and the matter becomes more clearly understood."[9]

In addition, notetaking procures long-term knowledge storage by setting up the required material for *maintenance rehearsal* and *elaborative rehearsal*—critical components of human memory that will be covered later in the book.

Simply stated, if developing deep, long-term *non-superficial knowledge* from the books you read is of essential value to you, then notetaking is the most critical skill you must master.

WHY A NOTETAKING SYSTEM IS IMPORTANT

One reason to build a notetaking system centers on the simple idea that one should follow in the footsteps of history's greatest scholars and thinkers: "In light of [notetaking's] (literally) rich tradition, one would be well-advised

8 Ann Blair, *Early Modern Attitudes toward the Delegation of Copying and Note-Taking* (Brill, 2016), 276.

9 Alberto Cevolini, Storing Expansions: Openness and Closure in Secondary Memories (Brill, 2016), 168.

to mind the recommendations of the scholars, and set about the construction of [a notetaking system] as soon as possible."[10]

Another reason is that a notetaking system allows one to offload the cognitive processing work that memory requires for later recall. Cognitive processing can then be used to think, develop, and reflect on ideas instead of developing mnemonic memorization tricks, such as the method of loci used by ancient Greek thinkers.

Yet, as previously touched upon, a notetaking system is primarily best suited for writers and researchers who "ingest" and produce much content. Scholars agree that a notetaking system is a valuable tool for those who mainly wish to "work with information gleaned from reading."[11]

WHY USE AN ANTINET

An Antinet is a strict interpretation of the already niche field of Zettelkasten, which many believe to exist within the niche field of personal knowledge management (PKM).[12] PKM is a niche field within knowledge management, which stands already as a rather niche field itself. In brief, the Antinet is believed to reside in the deep alcoves of an already very niche field.

Chances are, you're a nerd like me who geeks out over learning, growth, reading, and the development of your mind. If that's not you, then you're in the wrong place. If this describes you, then carry on reading.

The question then becomes, *why should you invest your time learning about the Antinet in the first place?*

There are several reasons, which I'll outline throughout the book; however, the short answer is this: it's the purest, hardest, most-time-intensive,

---

10 Markus Krajewski, *Note-Keeping: History, Theory, Practice of a Counter-Measurement against Forgetting* (Brill, 2016), 322.

11 Krajewski, *Note-Keeping*, 312.

12 This is a common misconception. In reality, Zettelkasten does not fall under the field of PKM. The *true* nature of Zettelkasten revolves around *knowledge development*. It does not revolve around storing and managing *information* (which is what PKM is really about).

but most rewarding way to develop your knowledge. Digital apps and other new tools cut corners that produce stunted thoughts. Life's too short. If you're going to produce work, do it the hard way. The result will show signs of your commitment to this.

The Antinet is for those who aim to produce thought-provoking content, even if it's at the expense of being easy. Digital tools, I contend, are easier and more convenient than building an analog knowledge system; however, the output digital systems produce is of lesser quality than systems that force one to *think on paper.*

THE ANTINET EVOLVES YOUR MIND

Another reason one ought to adopt and learn the Antinet centers around *evolution.* If you wish to evolve as a person and evolve your mind, an Antinet is the most full-bodied tool for doing such.

Akin to the concept of human evolution happening by way of *externalization* (i.e., creating tools like axes, spears, vehicles for transport), a theory "that was very successful in the second half of the twentieth century states that evolution implies an increasing 'exteriorization' of individual memories."[13] This means that to evolve, we must externalize our memories and move from the structural coupling of *communication from consciousness* to *communication with machines.*

Yet, there's a problem with this evolutionary leap. The issue is that when one moves toward communication with machines (such as using digital notes to interact with one's own internally-sourced thoughts), one's consciousness becomes watered down and stripped of its individualism.

The Antinet Preserves One's Consciousness Better Than Digital Tools Because of Its Analog Nature

Your handwriting is a mighty powerful thing. Something covered later in

---

13 Cevolini, Alberto, ed. *Forgetting Machines: Knowledge Management Evolution in Early Modern Europe.* Library of the Written Word, volume 53, (Boston: Brill, 2016), 12.

this book is the concept of an *internal ghost, internal monologue,* and *internal dialogue.* Niklas Luhmann referenced this concept as well. The idea of the internal ghost has been observed and studied by scholars as the interaction between (1) external memory systems like the Antinet and (2) internal memory (which is the so-called wetware memory that resides inside your skull).

After studying John Boyle, John Locke, and Robert Hooke, one researcher found that "annotations that are stored in the external memory can function only in tandem with internal memory, so excerpts and notes prompt recollection of more than what they actually contain."[14] The magic that's happening here is that when one interacts with notes written in one's own handwriting and with other external contextual details attached to it (like the color and shape of the notecards), one's consciousness and memory fills in the details and other thoughts that serve as a cue for one's consciousness.

In other words, the notes in your Antinet set off a chain reaction—a conversation, internally, that becomes an internal *dialogue* (not an internal monologue). This experience is a powerful phenomenon generated in analog knowledge systems such as the Antinet.

Unlike digital notes, which can multiply endlessly due to virtually unlimited storage-space limits, notes in an Antinet serve as a cue for generating the *recall* process in your mind. Digital notes take a different form; they tend to be all-encompassing and thorough, which gets overwhelming. Your notes should be a communication experience that takes place when you use them to write your book, essay, blog post, or paper.

Evolution via Communication and Artificial Consciousness

Evolution and human progress will emerge from the transition of the structural coupling of *communication and consciousness* to the structural coupling of *communication and artificial consciousness* (by way of *externalization*).

---

14 Cevolini, *Forgetting Machines,* 12.

The best tools are the ones that lead to artificial consciousness—by which I mean a communication partner that seems to have its own externalized *personality.*[15]

Thus far, digital notetaking apps have proven useful as information storage systems, not as artificial consciousness storage systems. The Antinet is a better artificial consciousness storage system, and it serves as a better cue for the internal mental dialogue when it comes time to write. Moreover, I contend that an Antinet is, paradoxically, closer to enabling human evolution than digital tools even though digital tools are perceived as being more evolved.

WHY YOU SHOULD EVEN CARE ABOUT LEARNING A SYSTEM THAT STRICTLY ADHERES TO NIKLAS LUHMANN'S ZETTELKASTEN

Among scholars—and one in particular who has surveyed nearly all knowledge development systems used throughout history—Niklas Luhmann's Zettelkasten system is decidedly one that "stands out." Alberto Cevolini points out that Luhmann's paper outlining his Zettelkasten can be regarded as modern society's most advanced result of a long-lasting reflection performed on knowledge management.[16]

I contend that history's physical analog thinking systems evolved to their most advanced level with Luhmann's Zettelkasten system. Instead of being carried forth and developed from there, it has essentially been replaced with digital notetaking tools, which I suggest are worse in many ways. The popularity of analog thinking tools has dwindled as a consequence, and their popularity has been supplanted with the usage of digital tools. Additionally, the actual evolution of analog thinking systems has seemingly stopped. I can only hope that my book will bring back some innovation in this space.

---

15 Niklas Luhmann, "Communication with Noteboxes (Revised Edition)," trans. Manfred Kuehn, https://daily.scottscheper.com/zettelkasten/. Luhmann referred to this personality as an "alter ego."

16 Cevolini, *Forgetting Machines*, 26.

Each Component of Luhmann's Principles is Unique and They Combine to Create a Whole Greater Than the Sum of Its Parts

In this book, I'll detail the four principles that make Luhmann's system unique. The four principles combine to create the Antinet. When you interpret Luhmann's system loosely, it loses its luster and impact. One of its key impacts is its proclivity to transform from a memory replacement tool to a system that actually ends up enhancing memory—a so-called *memory aid.*

The four principles of the Antinet force something called *neuro-associative recall.* Together, each aspect of the Antinet transforms it from a memory-storage system to a memory-supercharging system.

Luhmann echoes this notion. He suggests that the Antinet forces one to *file* thoughts ("placing of the notes"). While it "takes time," according to Luhmann, it also does two things: (1) it helps enliven the "sheer monotony of reading," and (2) it "incidentally trains the memory."[17]

WHY YOU SHOULD NOT BOTHER READING THIS BOOK

Luhmann's notebox system has become surprisingly popular recently with the publication of several books, and it's also become popularized through online communities.[18] Myths about Luhmann's system have also emerged. One such myth is that Luhmann's system produces prolific amounts of writing—without the process of writing being difficult.

The author of perhaps the most popular book on Luhmann's Zettelkasten writes that Luhmann's productivity is impressive, yet even more amazing is that "[Luhmann] seemed to achieve all this with almost no real effort."[19]

---

17 Niklas Luhmann, Short Cuts (English Translation) (Frankfurt am Main: Zweitausendeins, 2002), 83. See the last chapter of "Short Cuts" (available in German).

18 Sönke Ahrens, *How to Take Smart Notes: One Simple Technique to Boost Writing, Learning and Thinking: For Students, Academics and Nonfiction Book Writers.* (North Charleston, SC: CreateSpace, 2017); also https://zettelkasten.de.

19 Ahrens, *How to Take Smart Notes,* 15.

This is a false notion that will be explored later in the book, but the result of its proliferation is that the Zettelkasten finds itself presented as a system that causes many people to overlook the actual realities of using it: the truth is that Luhmann worked night and day, and his writing and theoretical work were his life. To a large degree, he produced so much because his wife passed away, and he had a caretaker who cooked his meals and helped him raise his children. This allowed Luhmann to focus almost exclusively on writing. In brief, the Zettelkasten does not replace hard work; rather, it greatly enhances the depth of thought in one's work output; however, there's one caveat. Those who wish to use such a system must not shy away from the prospect of *hard work.*

Another thing that must be considered is that an Antinet is something you should investigate if, and only if, you have adequate time. If you're under constant deadlines, for instance—daily deadlines, such as those experienced by a newspaper writer—an Antinet is probably not for you. Paradoxically, unlimited time is also not ideal either. You must have short-term projects as milestones. Luhmann had this in the form of peer-reviewed articles. While the number of books Luhmann published is impressive (seventy), just as impressive is that he published 550 articles.[20] These served as short-term projects which helped him develop his thirty-year undertaking to devise a *theory of everything* in the field of sociology.

After Luhmann passed away, two hundred more unpublished manuscripts were found among his possessions.[21] The sheer volume of Luhmann's output stands as one of the main selling points for the Zettelkasten system. It's a big part of what has attracted many people to the concept. Further, Luhmann continued to be productive even after he passed away with a half-dozen of his books published posthumously. Sönke Ahrens writes that he knows

20 Johannes Schmidt, "Niklas Luhmann's Card Index: Thinking Tool, Communication Partner, Publication Machine." In *Forgetting Machines. Knowledge Management Evolution in Early Modern Europe,* edited by Alberto Cevolini (Boston: Brill2016), 289; Vanderstraeten, Raf. "Luhmann on Socialization and Education." Educational Theory 50 (January 25, 2005): 1–23.

21 Undisciplined, "Archiving Luhmann w/ Johannes Schmidt," 2021, accessed May 11, 2022, https://www.youtube.com/watch?v=kz2K3auPLWU, 24:30.

more than a few colleagues who would give a lot to be as productive as Luhmann—even as productive as Luhmann was after he died![22]

However, here's the reality: Luhmann's books were poorly written (due to academic German conventions still practiced today). Luhmann's writings are packed with very deep ideas, yet, reading Luhmann's work is a sleep-inducing experience. His books are extremely and unapologetically challenging to understand. They're convoluted with academic jargon and unnecessarily large words. Even Luhmann himself acknowledged the issues with his writing style that caused him to have difficulty getting his work translated. From observing beginners and translators who tried reading his texts, Luhmann once remarked, "I have noticed how haphazardly I write—despite considerable care in preserving and refining theoretical coherences."[23]

Hans-Georg Moeller considers Luhmann's social theory to be the best analysis of contemporary society presently available. Yet, he observes that Luhmann's work remains "far less prominent" than it ought to be. The reason? Luhmann's books were so difficult to read.[24] This same scholar wrote an entire book dedicated to exploring Niklas Luhmann's theoretical work. Before even beginning the book, he allocates a section dedicated to how and why Luhmann produced books that were so challenging. Luhmann's word selection, style, and tone were that of an academic who gave lectures so dense that you left feeling like you didn't understand a thing. This gives you a glimpse of what reading Luhmann's work feels like. Luhmann's writing style is so thickly drenched in doctrinaire academic-prose that the scholar who wrote a book on Luhmann refers to his writing style as *soporific*.[25]

WHY LUHMANN'S BOOKS WERE SO BAD

The reason Niklas Luhmann's books were so bad centers around the following aspects:

---

22 Ahrens, *How to Take Smart Notes*, 14.

23 Niklas Luhmann, *Short Cuts* (English), 82.

24 Hans-Georg Moeller, *The Radical Luhmann* (New York: Columbia University Press, 2011), 3.

25 Moeller, *The Radical Luhmann*, 3.

Academic Pretentiousness Described the German Academic Climate of His Time

Luhmann's dense academic writing style was almost a requirement in his field if he wished to be taken seriously. It was an "environment of academically pretentious soporific authors."[26] The greatness of one's work correlated directly with how inaccessible and difficult it was to penetrate.[27] In other words, the more ridiculously challenging it was to read a person's work, the more respect the one who wrote it received—assuming the ideas weren't pure gibberish. Luhmann's work most certainly was not gibberish; it was deep, brilliant, unconventional, cross-disciplinary, and, astoundingly, quite valid.

Luhmann operated within the academically pretentious standard of Germany's academic environment. As a result, his books reflect his environment. One scholar states, "Luhmann (or rather, his writing) suffered from being too closely associated with the German academic elite at the time."[28]

Luhmann Barely Edited His Work

"Once I've written [a manuscript]," Luhmann stated in an interview, "I don't usually revise it."[29] In brief, he was not a perfectionist. He did not have a writing process like F. Scott Fitzgerald, wherein he would write books in longhand using a pencil in a notebook before typing the manuscript using a typewriter. Luhmann wrote his texts by hand on notecards, but he put little effort into making them cohesive and flow naturally. Luhmann was more concerned with just getting his work shipped, as imperfect as it was. "I don't have any notion of perfection when it comes to books and essays," Luhmann said, "like some people who think they have to write a definitive work with their first book."[30] Luhmann considered nearly all of his roughly seventy books, 550 articles, and two hundred unpublished manuscripts

---

26 Hans-Georg Moeller, The Radical Luhmann (New York: Columbia University Press, 2011), 15.

27 Hans-Georg Moeller, The Radical Luhmann (New York: Columbia University Press, 2011), 14.

28 Hans-Georg Moeller, The Radical Luhmann (New York: Columbia University Press, 2011), 14.

29 Niklas Luhmann, *Short Cuts* (English), 17.

30 Niklas Luhmann, *Short Cuts* (English), 17.

as "version zero." The only book he did not hold as "version zero" was his *Theory of Society* (which took him some thirty years to write).[31] He created major versions of this book every decade: one each in the 1960s, 1970s, 1980s, and 1990s.[32]

It may be overstating things to insinuate Luhmann *never* revised his manuscripts. In fact, he did insert new pages between existing pages of his drafts, similar to how he made his notes branch in his Zettelkasten. For instance, one finds manuscripts with pages *1, 2, 2A, 2B,* 3. The pages *2A* and *2B* were inserted as an afterthought.[33] Therefore, clearly, Luhmann did some editing after writing a manuscript.

Luhmann Desired to Be Impenetrable by the General Public in Fear of His Career Being Threatened

There's a dark secret in Luhmann's life that isn't talked about much.[34] I will cover it later in this book; however, it provides a perfectly understandable reason why Luhmann would want to remain impenetrable to the general public. Because his positions in sociology are so complex, it is conceivable that the public would have placed him in an ideologically dangerous category, thereby threatening his career. To mitigate such a risk, one can suppose Luhmann erred on the side of being highbrow so that only well-read intellectuals could decipher what he was saying. This risked fewer opportunities of mischaracterization from untrained readers in the social sciences.

Luhmann's writing style helped ensure that only academics proficient and trained in such a style would be capable of *even attempting* to understand his work. To illustrate this point, we can refer to an interview with Luhmann from 1973. The interviewer asks Luhmann what critics he fears most, and his reply

31 Niklas Luhmann, *Short Cuts* (English), 17.

32 Undisciplined, Archiving Luhmann w/ Johannes Schmidt, 2021, https://www.youtube.com/watch?v=kz2K3auPLWU, 21:40 and 28:58.

33 Undisciplined, Archiving Luhmann w/ Johannes Schmidt, 2021, https://www.youtube.com/watch?v=kz2K3auPLWU, 48:30.

34 This "dark secret" of Luhmann's life is omitted from Sönke Ahrens' book *How to Take Smart Notes*, as well as from popular websites like zettelkasten.de

is classic: "The stupid ones."[35] Luhmann's writing style prevented the stupid ones from reading his work, and it's continued to do so long after he's passed.

Luhmann's Zettelkasten System Created a Deep Spider-Like Network That Was Hard to Disentangle Using a Typewriter

Even academics trained in reading dense prose have found themselves challenged by Luhmann's writing style, stemming from the complex, multidisciplinary webs of thought Luhmann's books dump onto the page. Luhmann proclaimed, in a seemingly proud manner, that "there's no linearity, but a spider-web-like system that can be started anywhere."[36] Such a non-linear structure makes Luhmann's work something that is "not reader-friendly," according to one scholar.[37] Luhmann asserts that the non-linear nature of his work is a feature, not a bug. It enables one to pick up one of his books and start reading anywhere–such as the beginning or end of the book. Yet this assumes some familiarity with Luhmann's work. As Moeller points out, anyone can indeed begin reading anywhere, but they can't start understanding anywhere.[38] One can begin reading anywhere, assuming they're already well-versed in Luhmann's work. Becoming well-versed in Luhmann is hard to achieve if you start with Luhmann's books, though it's been said that his lectures were easier to comprehend.[39]

There's no friendly initiation when you begin trying to read Luhmann's work. You're quickly confronted with unconventional, intimidating terminology. This terminology is packed with sudden, chaotic shifts between ideas.[40] Want to know the best part about all this? Luhmann doesn't even bother to explain the unconventional terminology he introduces. He leaves you to embark

---

35 holgersen911, "Niklas Luhmann—Observer in the Crow's Nest" (Eng Sub), 2012, https://www.youtube.com/watch?v=qRSCKSPMuDc, accessed May 11, 2022, 12:40.

36 Hans-Georg Moeller, *The Radical Luhmann* (New York: Columbia University Press, 2011), 11.

37 Niklas Luhmann, *Short Cuts* (English), 11.

38 Moeller, *The Radical Luhmann*, 11-12.

39 Undisciplined, "Archiving Luhmann w/ Johannes Schmidt," 4:00.

40 Moeller, *The Radical Luhmann*, 11ff.

on a mental journey down the complex jungle of intellectual self-discovery. One thing is certain: you'd better be prepared to bring your own map.

Judging the books that contained such complex webs of ideas, one may be quick to blame Luhmann's Zettelkasten; however, that's jumping to conclusions too quickly. Luhmann's environment certainly influenced the complex style Luhmann strived for in his texts, but there are a few other reasons Luhmann's work is web-like: one is out of principle, and the other is that Luhmann perhaps enjoyed being a troll. Let's cover such aspects now.

Luhmann Desired to Be Impenetrable for The Sake of Principle

Luhmann brings forth the idea that *not everything ought to be easy to understand*. He once posed the question: "Should everything that is said be equally forced under the rod of comprehensibility?... Comprehensibility without effort? Understandable without any preparation, without any time thinking and deciphering?"[41] From this, Luhmann implied that one shouldn't expect all knowledge to be in a format that could be spoon-fed to those who are not committed to the work involved in understanding advanced thought. Advanced knowledge is something that must be earned, in other words. It does one an injustice to make such knowledge so easily digestible; doing such a thing waters down the impact knowledge can have on one's mind.

Perhaps this is just a cop-out by Luhmann. After all, it's easier to offload the cognitive work involved in simplifying ideas. But maybe Luhmann does have a point. It would degrade some of the world's magic if all knowledge were trivial to ingest. Perhaps Luhmann's right in this respect.

Indeed, the more complex and impenetrable a subject is, the more attractive it can become for those with a thirst for knowledge. The difficulty of deciphering Luhmann stands as the very thing that initially attracted Johannes Schmidt (the scholar heading up the digitization of Luhmann's literary estate). When Schmidt first came across Luhmann's work, he did not understand a word of it.

---

41 **Niklas Luhmann, *Short Cuts* (English), 6.**

In making his texts challenging to decipher, Luhmann essentially filtered out and disqualified those he could not care less about—that is, people who weren't serious and committed to putting in the work required to engage with theoretical sociology.

For those serious about social theory, the complexity of Luhmann counter-intuitively seemed to serve as the key attraction. From there, his writing sucked people into *The Matrix of Sociology*, if you will.

In an interview with Johannes Schmidt conducted by a man who runs a podcast covering complex philosophical and social concepts, they both shared the same experience upon first encountering Luhmann: "When you first read Luhmann, on the one hand, you don't understand at all, but on the other hand that makes you want to!"[42]

We could refer to this as the phenomenon of *complexity attraction*—referring to the event wherein complexity serves as an attraction mechanism for those passionate about a field.

Another example of *complexity attraction* is illustrated by the author of the book, *The Radical Luhmann*. He recounts a story in which an academic friend of his missed a talk by a guest lecturer in philosophy. When the friend asked another academic who attended the conference how it was, the person replied in all seriousness, "It was awesome—I did not understand a word!"[43]

LUHMANN DESIRED TO BE IMPENETRABLE FOR THE SAKE OF BEING AN IRREVERENT TROLL

Luhmann's character is described as an obscure, ironic, radical thinker.[44] Perhaps today we'd consider him a bit of a troll. Luhmann has some trollish tendencies, covered later in the book. His theories were often quite paradoxical and, after long explanations, pointed back to them-

42 Undisciplined, "Archiving Luhmann w/ Johannes Schmidt,", 6:50.

43 Moeller, *The Radical Luhmann*.

44 Moeller, *The Radical Luhmann*.

selves and the beginning of where they started. He was fascinated with self-referential systems wherein the beginning is the end, and the end is the beginning. His Zettelkasten system reflected such ideas, which is somewhat unsurprising.

In brief, one should not get caught up in the idea that the Zettelkasten will magically enable you to spit out a massive number of books or papers that are instant classics and perfect. It can undoubtedly produce excellent work; however, the sizable amount of work Luhmann produced largely also came from the fact that he only lightly edited his work. Furthermore, his work was tangled in a spider-like web. Some of this is due to his Zettelkasten, which is due to the aforementioned variables.

In my opinion, there's a healthy balance for how to use a Zettelkasten system. It centers around the age-old balance of *quality vs. quantity*. The Antinet's main benefit is its ability to develop thoughts thoroughly. It truly does help create profound ideas; however, you must also be prepared to take the time to edit your work and make it readable for your audience—if, that is, you wish to appeal to general readers. Instead of publishing seventy books, if Luhmann had instead focused on making, say, ten books (and thus had taken the additional time to make his ideas easier to digest) perhaps his theoretical work would be much more popular than it remains today.

Using an Antinet will enable you to develop and put all the crazy, otherworldly thoughts from your mind into a rumination system that allows it to grow. From there, their complexity will grow. You can certainly decide to forego simplifying your text for the general reader. Or, you can use such a system to enable you to offload the complexity that usually lives in your mind so that you can then create a more reader-friendly, more straightforward version for your audience. It's entirely up to you.

It's essential to keep all of this in mind when deciding whether you wish to build your own Antinet. When using an Antinet, your ideas and thoughts will indeed be developed to a greater degree than they otherwise would. Yet, it also means that the complexity and entanglements of your ideas will also grow, thus requiring much editing to make your work digestible.

In brief, Luhmann's pedantic, and overly-complex writing style can be attributed to several things. Primarily it stems from the German academic climate of his day. It also stems from his carnivalesque and trollish nature. He purposely sought to be impenetrable by "stupid" critics. Yet, the Antinet itself isn't to blame for Luhmann's writing voice.

On the opposite end of the spectrum, we find Umberto Eco, an Italian scholar who used his own Antinet-like system. Eco's notecard system, like the Antinet, possessed web-like cross-references. However, Eco wrote in a way that both *entertained* and *informed* his readers at the same time.[45] Just because one uses a web-like analog system doesn't mean their writing style magically becomes arrogant.

Now, should you write in the trollishly pedantic academic style of Luhmann? Or, should you opt for the *entertaining* and *informative* style of Umberto Eco? My opinion is to follow the advice of Hemingway: *write the truth*. Write the truest sentence you can. Write with your 100% authentic voice. Your readers can smell it on you. People are more perceptive than you think. If writing like a trollish academic pleases you, and *if it is you*, then by all means write that way! Otherwise, err on the side of writing to *communicate*, instead of writing to confuse.

Assuming I haven't scared you away at this point, let's now move on to why one would opt for an Antinet in the first place. Let's talk about where the Antinet shines.

WHERE THE ANTINET TRULY SHINES

The entire point of using an Antinet centers around producing unconventional, deeply evolved thoughts. Certain aspects of an Antinet ensure unconventional, deeply evolved thoughts emerge from the system, and these areas are where it shines in comparison to other knowledge systems.

---

45 Umberto Eco, How to Write a Thesis, trans. Caterina Mongiat Farina and Geoff Farina, Translation edition (Cambridge, Massachusetts: The MIT Press, 2015), xiv.

PRODUCING GENIUS-LEVEL WORK THROUGH CREATIVE INSIGHTS AND UNCONVENTIONAL INTERACTIONS

Let's start from the end result of what an Antinet aims to produce, and then work backward from there.

An Antinet aims to produce *genius-level work*. Plain and simple.

To produce genius-level work, one must unlock creative insights that otherwise would remain disconnected in disparate fields. As a thinker, your goal centers not on hitting targets that others find difficult to hit, but to hit targets that others can't even see. This comes about by unlocking *creative insights.*

Nassim Nicholas Taleb observes that the primary reason for America's dominance in the global economy (with companies like Apple, Amazon, Nike, Google, Facebook, etc.) all stems from one key strength: *creativity.*[46]

The question then becomes: *how does one unlock creative insights?*

Unlocking creative insights stem from one thing: *unconventional interactions.* For something to be unconventional requires some degree of randomness and thc paradoxical quality of being true, with the insight often inspiring a sense of awe and wonder. The requirement for interactions is *comparison.* That is, one must be able to relate and associate concepts. This primes similar ideas to be nested and neighbored around one another so that when an unconventional link is connected to a "neighborhood" in the Zettelkasten, it creates unexpected ideas that emerge from viewing it in context with its neighboring cards.

At the center of innovation rest two seemingly different concepts, from two seemingly different contexts, that interact to create something greater than either of those two concepts individually. This is a central idea of commu-

46 Nassim Nicholas Taleb, *The Black Swan: The Impact of the Highly Improbable*, 2nd ed., Random (New York: Random House Trade Paperbacks, 2010), 64.

nication theory—a field Luhmann's work was deeply rooted in and that he understood quite well. Innovation and breakthroughs in thinking happen when two different ideas, with different goals and perspectives, *communicate* and create *new meaning*.[47] This is related to the concept of *emergence* in systems theory, in which new properties and behaviors emerge when individual parts interact in a broader whole.

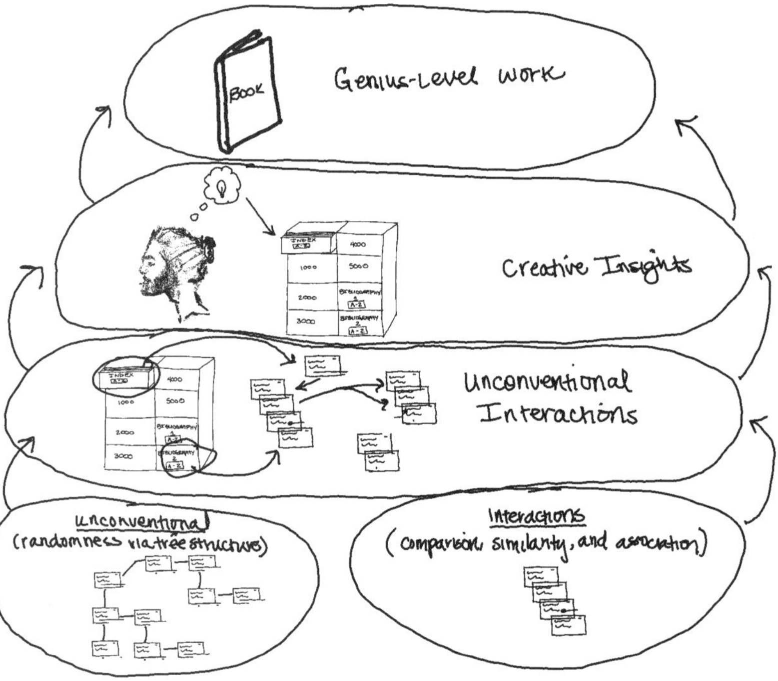

Such phenomena appear to occur more profoundly within a system such as an Antinet. Unlike digital systems (which have the tendency of being flooded with too much information), an analog thinking system seems

---

47 See Luhmann "Communicating with Slip Boxes": "Information, accordingly, originates only in systems which possess a comparative schema—even if this amounts only to: "this or something else." For communication, we do not have to presuppose that both parties use the same comparative schema. The effect of surprise even increases when this is not the case and when we believe that a message means something (or is useful) against the background of other possibilities."

to generate fewer yet much more meaningful interactions, which, in turn, generate creative insights that are not replicable by the system's digital cousins.

THE ANTINET SHINES WHEN ONE DESIRES TO DEVELOP A LONG-TERM THESIS OR SERIES OF WORKS IN AN AREA (SUCH AS A THIRTY-YEAR THESIS)

The reason Luhmann created his Zettelkasten in the first place is two-fold.

First, Luhmann set out to create a system for retrieving things forgotten by memory. Yet after a certain point, as early as 1981, he discovered its true power—his Zettelkasten became a thinking tool and communication partner that emerged almost as if it were its own mind, a *ghost in the box*. More on this will be covered later. More pertinent right now, however, is the second reason Luhmann started his Antinet.

The second reason relates to his main objective: to embark upon a thirty-year-long quest to excavate a *theory of everything* as it relates to human society.

Authors like Robert Greene and Ryan Holiday have publicly shared their notecard systems, yet their systems are quite trivial compared to an Antinet. They're organized by topic or book title. They were created primarily for writing one book, which are projects lasting one to several years. Their notebox systems were not architected for projects with a time span of three decades. A short-term project is more straightforward in scope than a thirty-year theory of everything. This likely explains why Greene's and Holiday's notebox systems don't seem to restrict them. However, when you're trying to categorize and prepare for a project that will last thirty years, you must embrace chaos. You cannot hope to have the categories you start out with be perfectly ordered and arranged by topic forever. You can't expect to have the notebox adhere to the original set of organized sections over the long term. The thoughts and ideas must emerge as your research grows. Knowledge will emerge from the trees and branches of thought in unconventional places.

This raises some problems with category-based notebox systems, however. Each time you finish a book, the cards live only in the silo of that project.

A great wall is seemingly hoisted around the project, preventing future work from smoothly referencing its parts. It's forever walled off from the other future projects you embark upon. Its fruitful and potent ideas are blocked off from colliding with ideas related to any future work you create. As a result, you cannot experience the cumulative *compounding* miracle the Antinet seems innately built for.

The *compounding* miracle cannot be unleashed if you have to start over from scratch every time you start a new project, as evidence suggests Holiday does each time he starts a new book.[48]

Luhmann recognized this, which is one reason he architected his Antinet in such a way. "I started the index card file," Luhmann explained, "because it was obvious to me I would have to plan for a lifetime not for a book."[49]

In brief, the Antinet is best for long-term projects and also if you intend to leverage the miracle of compounding your ideas over a thirty-year-plus timeframe. That doesn't mean you must commit to working on one project for thirty years; instead, it means you must commit to having your work compound and interact with itself over thirty years (this is made possible by way of the Antinet's structure).

Other problems with categorical-based notebox systems will be outlined later on in the book.

THE ANTINET SHINES IN REVEALING STRUCTURED ACCIDENTS

The Antinet enables users to slow down their minds and develop their thoughts. It also excels in stimulating one to think of associated ideas and then

48 Ryan Holiday, "The Notecard System: The Key For Remembering, Organizing And Using Everything You Read," RyanHoliday.Net (blog), April 1, 2014, https://ryanholiday.net/the-notecard-system-the-key-for-remembering-organizing-and-using-everything-you-read/. For instance, one can observe a dedicated box of notecards being created for Holiday's book, *The Obstacle is The Way*.

49 Schmidt, "Niklas Luhmann's Card Index: Thinking Tool," 290.

link to those ideas in the note. Some confuse this (the concept of linking) as the unique benefit of Luhmann's system; however, this is not the case.

The practice of reading something and writing the idea immediately into a digital markdown file, and then linking that file to some other idea is not what is meant by *unconventional interactions*. For something to be an *unconventional interaction*, it must genuinely be unconventional. Nearly anyone can search their digital notes to find keywords related to the current idea they just wrote down and link that idea. The idea of simply linking your notes in this way is a misinterpretation that plagues countless numbers of people in the digital Zettelkasten world.

For instance, David Kadavy's book about digital Zettelkästen outlines the advantage of the system, stating that you activate your mind's "associative" machine when you think of a related concept in your mind, which "collides" with another related idea.[50] While this is true to a degree, it largely misses the mark. Here's why:

The point of the Antinet is its ability to serve as a thinking machine, as a knowledge development system, and as an *extended memory*. The system forces the user to think of the keyterm they would use to describe a concept. Only after this critical step do you look up the concept and go through your notes and compare and remind yourself of the things you've forgotten in the process. The magic of an Antinet does not center on one's ability to think about what a new concept you've read relates to (as that's a conventional interaction, not an unconventional interaction). Rather, as Luhmann puts it, its magic stems from "interactions that were never planned, never preconceived, or conceived" by your *current* way of thinking.[51]

---

50 David Kadavy, *Digital Zettelkasten: Principles, Methods, & Examples*, Kindle Edition (Kadavy, Inc.), 35. "By trying to think of how to describe the passage in my own words, I activate the associative machine, which often causes the current idea to collide with some other idea in my mind. Associative thinking promotes a positive mood, so it shouldn't be a surprise how fun this task is. If writing a passage makes me think of something related, I write it in parentheses."

51 Luhmann, "Communicating with Slip Boxes": "The slip box provides combinatorial possibilities which were never planned, never preconceived, or conceived in this way."

The magic of innovation and of unlocking creativity stems from the possibility of (1) making relations using the term you're currently thinking of, but more importantly (2) the analog nature of the system with its tree-structure (which you'll learn about later in the book), ends up inducing *structured accidents* that are otherwise impossible to replicate.[52]

This is why it's critical, in Luhmann's words, that your "selection and comparisons are not identical with the schema of searching for them."[53] Why is this the case? Because simply searching for a keyword, digitally, robs the potential for innovation to occur *not* through seeing what you felt was *related* in that moment, but through the ingenious, unconventional discoveries you make along the way navigating to the nearby cards, and nearby branches of thought that have emerged and evolved around the cards you're looking for. This tree-like structure, of which the Antinet is comprised, is what helps unlock truly *unconventional interactions*. The concept of the tree-like structure is something to be covered in detail later in this book.

---

52 Luhmann, "Communicating with Slip Boxes": "The communication with the slip box becomes fruitful only at a high level of generalization, namely that of establishing communicative relations of relations. And it becomes productive only at the moment of evaluation, and is thus bound to a certain time and is to a high degree accidental."

53 Luhmann, "Communicating with Slip Boxes": "This effect of innovation is based on the one hand on the circumstance that the query provokes possibilities of making relations which could not be traced prior to it. On the other hand, it is based also on the fact that the internal horizons of selection and comparisons are not identical with schema of searching for them."

CHAPTER THREE

THE CURRENT ZETTELKASTEN LANDSCAPE

WHY I DECIDED TO WRITE THIS BOOK

Let's first start with why I am *not* writing a book about the Antinet (i.e., an analog Zettelkasten).

I am not writing a book on the Antinet to sell a massive number of books. As mentioned, I started out working with an Antinet because I desired to write about my interests in other fields (specifically: marketing, copywriting, philosophy, and psychology). While working on a book in these fields, I decided to use an analog Zettelkasten to help me. In doing this, I discovered how wrong the conventional wisdom is about Zettelkasten. I had to learn this the hard way. In order to figure out the truth, I went straight to the original source: Luhmann's online archive. I spent many months reverse-engineering Luhmann's Zettelkasten. I wrote out many of his notecards by hand to understand how it truly works. I discovered that the Zettelkasten is much different than how it's described everywhere else.

I think it's important to publish this book on the Antinet because there's already a wealth of wonderful books in the field of marketing, copywriting, and psychology. Within the realm of Zettelkasten, there's really only one dominant book out there right now: *How to Take Smart Notes* by Sönke Ahrens.

This would be fine if the book was excellent; however, there are two issues with the book. First, it contains information that gets the most critical pieces of the Zettelkasten wrong. And second, many people don't even realize Ahrens's book exists. This becomes problematic because the online environment for gaining an accurate understanding of a Zettelkasten is even worse. I surveyed the top nine search engine results for the term "Zettelkasten." In brief, every one of them contains flaws in their description of what a Zettelkasten is.

When searching for the term "Zettelkasten" on Google, the first result is Wikipedia's entry for Zettelkasten. This entry gets it wrong in several ways. First, it describes the Zettelkasten as a hierarchical structure.[1] This is wrong. A Zettelkasten is a tree-like structure wherein each leaf is of the same importance as any other. Each leaf, like each note, just lives in a different location on a tree. Second, Wikipedia posits a Zettelkasten as something built in digital format using "specialist knowledge management software." The entry then reluctantly admits that it "can be done on paper using index cards."[2] In reality, the true power of Zettelkasten revolves around the fact that it is—in its very essence—an actual notebox!

The second result I was given was the website zettelkasten.de.[3] When I first began surveying the top search results for Zettelkasten, I landed on a "Lessons Learned" post on the home page of zettelkasten.de. The post was written by a machine-learning researcher who shared his journey using a Zettelkasten. This researcher mentioned the frustration using *tags*. The site owners responded, sharing their frustrations with tags, saying that the "mess" it creates resonated with them. Yet as a solution, they referenced a

---

1 "Zettelkasten," in Wikipedia, June 8, 2021, https://en.wikipedia.org/w/index.php?title=Zettelkasten&oldid=1027589556. "The notes are numbered hierarchically, so that new notes may be inserted at the appropriate place, and contain metadata to allow the note-taker to associate notes with each other."

2 "Zettelkasten," in Wikipedia.

3 I am grateful for this website and its owners and operators. They have done much to proselytize the idea of Zettelkasten. I have since become friends with the two individuals who operate the website. I find them very open-minded and receptive to my views. Still, I possess different philosophical views, and I disagree with them on several fronts (when it comes to Zettelkasten). Naturally, this is the case as I'm a fervent adopter of the analog Zettelkasten in its purest form.

post that discusses a distinction between *good and bad tags*.[4] To me, this just seems like complexity built on unnecessary complexity. Remember, I was very new to the field of Zettelkasten at the time. I soon discovered that the creator of Zettelkasten, Niklas Luhmann, never used *tags*. This illustrates what I believe happens to many people who are new to Zettelkasten. They end up stumbling across these types of online posts and find themselves unnecessarily confused.

The search engine's third result on the term "Zettelkasten" also came from zettelkasten.de. It was the *Getting Started Overview* page where one finds advice such as "Don't use categories. Use tags instead."[5] The problem here is twofold. First, as stated previously, Luhmann never used *tags* (as the concept was not yet invented). And second, Luhmann didn't even subscribe to this notion in spirit. Luhmann used categories and top-level sections for his Zettelkasten. They weren't strict categories like the Dewey Decimal system. They were more like *rough* starting points. Nonetheless, they were indeed categories. In Luhmann's first Zettelkasten, he had 108 categories. His second Zettelkasten was more narrowly focused on his sociological work, yet it still contained 11 top-level categories.[6]

The next handful of search engine results suffers similar inaccuracies. They contain material overly focused on the digitized—and in my opinion, compromised—version of the Zettelkasten. They also include complete inventions first devised by Sönke Ahrens. They also confuse Luhmann's numeric-alpha notecard address system by telling readers to use dates for

---

4 @boxcariii, "Field Report #2: Lessons Learned From Processing," Zettelkasten Method, 57:36 100AD, https://zettelkasten.de/posts/field-report-2-lessons-learned/. "...Oh man, the "my tags are a mess" part resonated with me. I still have notes from almost a decade ago, before Sascha brought up the useful distinction of topic-vs.-object tags in our discussions. I guess we all must suffer from experiences like this at least once :)..."

5 "Getting Started • Zettelkasten Method," accessed June 28, 2021, https://zettelkasten.de/posts/overview/.

6 Johannes Schmidt, "Niklas Luhmann's Card Index: Thinking Tool, Communication Partner, Publication Machine," Forgetting Machines. Knowledge Management Evolution in Early Modern Europe 53 (2016), 292.

their notecard IDs.[7] The best information source on the Zettelkasten doesn't even make it into the first five pages of the search results.[8]

Simply stated, learning what a Zettelkasten is by searching the term online is like walking into a minefield of misinformation.

I believe there are only a handful of sources the inquisitive are left with if they wish to gain an accurate understanding of Zettelkasten in its purest form (the analog form). Those sources are (1) the online archive of Niklas Luhmann's actual Zettelkasten, (2) the paper outlining Zettelkasten written by Niklas Luhmann himself, titled, *Communication with Noteboxes,* (3) the works of Johannes Schmidt, a scholar at Bielefeld University who heads up Luhmann's archive project, and who has studied Luhmann's materials closest.[9]

These three sources are difficult to penetrate and understand. With pen and notecards in hand, I spent one month reading Luhmann's paper, *Communication with Noteboxes*. When printed out, this paper totals a mere four pages. It's so densely written it requires very careful reading in order to grasp what is being said. I spent over a month reading this paper! Yet, my careful review was worth it; there is so much to learn by reading the paper. I spent about six weeks doing the same thing with Johannes Schmidt's in-depth article on Luhmann's Zettelkasten.[10] This, too, was a very dense read.

---

7 "A Beginner's Guide to the Zettelkasten Method," *Zenkit* (blog), April 29, 2021, https://zenkit.com/en/blog/a-beginners-guide-to-the-zettelkasten-method/; Rebecca Williams, "The Zettelkasten Method: Examples to Help You Get Started.," Medium, October 5, 2020, https://medium.com/@rebeccawilliams 9941/the-zettelkasten-method-examples-to-help-you-get-started-8f844fa9ae6; David B. Clear, "Zettelkasten—How One German ScholarWasSoFreakishlyProductive,"Medium,January17,2021,https://writingcooperative.comzettelkasten-how-one-german-scholar-was-so-freakishly-productive-997e4e0ca125.

8 The best source is Niklas Luhmann's online archive (https://niklas-luhmann-archiv.de/).

9 (1)https://daily.scottscheper.com/zettelkasten/; (2) https://niklas-luhmann-archiv.de/bestand/zettelkasten/tutorial; (3) Johannes F.K. Schmidt, "Niklas Luhmann's Card Index: The Fabrication of Serendipity," Sociologica Vol 12 (July 26, 2018): 53-60; and Schmidt, "Niklas Luhmann's Card Index: Thinking Tool."

10 Schmidt, "Niklas Luhmann's Card Index: Thinking Tool."

I tell you all of this not necessarily to encourage you to do the same. Instead, I tell you this in case you're curious and want to venture down the rabbit-hole of Zettelkasten knowledge yourself. These are the primary sources. They're difficult. Thankfully, however, you don't have to spend weeks trying to piece together a Zettelkasten from those few articles. That's why I'm here—to introduce to you the world of the *real* Zettelkasten (without boring the heck out of you with dense academic prose). Even if I do bore the heck out of you in some parts, just know that it could be worse, much worse. If you doubt that, just try reading Luhmann's paper!

Before moving on, let me first outline my intent in describing the misinterpretations others hold in regards to Zettelkasten. I am not doing this because I'm motivated by some sadistic pleasure gained from criticizing the well-intentioned work of others.[11] In fact, I feel bad about calling to light what I see as the errors and misinterpretations of such people. Every individual I've come across in the personal knowledge management and Zettelkasten fields are well-intentioned. Granted these people often sell online courses, or online consulting, and have agendas related to those sales; yet it's not disguised. It's quite apparent what the catch is. Every one of them believes he or she is teaching material that will help people produce better knowledge. Moreover, much of the proselytizers of Zettelkasten knowledge come close to getting things right. Indeed, some authors share useful principles that even Luhmann himself did not bother mentioning.[12]

As I was learning Luhmann's Zettelkasten myself, I observed something that reminded me of a cognitive error called the *availability cascade.* Even if you're unfamiliar with the term, you're undoubtedly familiar with its concept. An *availability cascade* describes the phenomenon of an idea spreading

---

11 I'll leave that to people like Nassim Nicholas Taleb!

12 Much of the material in Ahrens's book is interesting. See his more qualitative material relating to the concept of *flow,* and his other related readings. See also "10 Principles to Revolutionize Your Note-Taking and Writing," *Forte Labs,* February 4, 2020, https://fortelabs.co/blog/how-to-take-smart-notes/. "Principle #1: Writing is not the outcome of thinking; it is the medium in which thinking takes place... Principle #6: Our work only gets better when exposed to high-quality feedback... Principle #7: Work on multiple, simultaneous projects... Principle #10: Save contradictory ideas."

rapidly and creating a self-reinforcing cascade of information. It occurs as the result of encapsulating a novel and complex concept into a simplified version—and here's the key part—the simplified version is slightly less accurate. This creates a waterfall of incorrect information that re-circulates itself and spreads rapidly. Why? Because simpler ideas spread more easily.

Recently, a study at UC San Diego was published showcasing the *availability cascade*. The study found that research that is less likely to be true is cited 153 times more if the material is interesting. Implicit in this is the following idea: research spreads more if it's *simplified* enough to be *interesting* in the first place (regardless of its accuracy).

The phenomenon of the *availability cascade* finds itself ever-so-present within the land of Zettelkasten. It's negatively affecting every well-intentioned knowledge worker who becomes hopeful and excited about Zettelkasten. Here's why: a second wave of teachers of the Zettelkasten finds itself emerging right now. Most of them do not use the primary sources as their material for teaching others about what a Zettelkasten is. Instead, this new wave of Zettelkasten evangelists use Sönke Ahrens's work, namely his book *How to Take Smart Notes*, as the primary material on which they rely.[13] The problem with these new Zettelkasten evangelists is not just their misunderstanding of how the Zettelkasten truly works, but also the contradictions they introduce.[14]

For instance, one self-declared bestselling author published a book recently on how the Zettelkasten works.[15] His book not only preaches Ahrens's work, it appends new inventions onto it. As a result, one is left with inventions

13"10 Principles to Revolutionize Your Note-Taking and Writing" ; David Kadavy, *Digital Zettelkasten: Principles, Methods, & Examples* (Kadavy, Inc., 2022), 7; "A Beginner's Guide to the Zettelkasten Method," *Zenkit* (blog); Williams, "The Zettelkasten Method.

14 For instance, you find authors asserting things like the analog Zettelkasten has a "slow rate" of exposing users to information, and thus "reduces your focus." Whereas, in reality the exact opposite is found to be as true. For the source of such contradictions, see: Kadavy, *Digital Zettelkasten*: "You may find it easier to sort through digital notes than paper, or you may find the slow rate with which you're exposed to new information with paper notes reduces your focus."

15 Kadavy, *Digital Zettelkasten*, 64.

built on top of an already sizable list of inventions. I will introduce you to these inventions shortly. They derive from a new quasi-religion that has developed a rather malignant growth inside the world of Zettelkasten. I call this quasi-religion, *Ahrensianity*.

AHRENSIANITY

Mark Twain once wrote to himself privately in his notebook, "If Christ were here there is one thing he would not be—a Christian."[16] This indeed may be true. After all, Jesus referred to himself as Jewish and never called himself a "Christian," for one. Second, he was a poor Galilean who was illiterate and didn't speak Greek (the language the New Testament was written in). Where did "Christian" come from then? From the early Hellenic-Jewish Apostle named Paul—a man who never met nor knew Jesus, yet who served as a forceful voice in the formative decades after the death of Jesus. Paul's teachings and writings formed the core beliefs and doctrines of Christianity. In brief, his interpretations of a remote Jew he didn't even know are what ended up giving birth to Christianity as we know it.[17]

Since the 1700s, scholars have been publishing arguments that show how Paul's teachings differ from and contradict Jesus's teachings. Furthermore, Paul's teachings add inventions to Jesus's preachings that were never held by Jesus. This has given rise to the term "Pauline Christianity," or "Paulism," which the world today knows as Christianity. Yet, again, this body of teachings finds itself profoundly different from that of the founder—Jesus of Nazareth.[18] I don't know about you, but I'm a much bigger fan of Jesus of Nazareth and his teachings, than I am of religious dogma.

It may seem absurd, but the phenomenon of Paul learning of Jesus and then inventing the notion of Christianity is similar to that of Sönke Ahrens learning of Niklas Luhmann and inventing the notion of Zettelkasten. Yet

---

16 "Mark Twain Quotations—Christianity," accessed July 1, 2021, http://www.twainquotes.com/Christianity.html.

17 Reza Aslan, *Zealot: The Life and Times of Jesus of Nazareth*, Reprint edition (New York: Random House Trade Paperbacks, 2014), 171, 186–7.

18 Aslan, *Zealot*, 190.

what Ahrens teaches is not the Zettelkasten system as Luhmann conceived of it; rather it contains its own flavor and spin. Yet, with Ahrens's insistence on the idea that the power of the Zettelkasten revolves around the mere linking of notes (in digital form), it's perhaps been taken even further away from the original form than what Paul did to Jesus's teachings.

In brief, Ahrens's *interpretations of Zettelkasten* should not be called *Zettelkasten*. It should be called *Ahrenskasten*, or perhaps...Ahrensianity!

The doctrine of Ahrensianity is composed, primarily, of three types of notes: (1) fleeting notes, (2) literature notes, and (3) permanent notes. All three of these notes stand as an invention and were never terms Niklas Luhmann used. Of the three, perhaps literature notes are closest to what Luhmann actually did; however, there are even issues with the description of such notes in Ahrens's book.

THE LATTER-DAY AHRENSIANS

In a newly released book with Zettelkasten in its title, David Kadavy proceeds to illustrate the doctrine of Ahrensianity in his chapter, "Anatomy of a Zettelkasten."[19] He then adds his own inventions by adding three more components to the mix: "inbox," "someday/maybe," and "raw." This leaves us with even more complexity built on top of something not even based entirely on Zettelkasten in the first place (but rather based on the interpretations of Sönke Ahrens).[20] This is an example of *interpretations piling on top of interpretations*. Meet the latter-day Ahrensians.

As mentioned briefly, there exist confusion and contradictions within this new wave of Zettelkasten interpretation. After exposure to the lessons of Sönke Ahrens and observing confusing and contradictory reasoning brought

---

19 Kadavy, *Digital Zettelkasten*, 25.

20 Perhaps this is why the Bible's Book of Revelations began implementing the first crude form of copyright law in warning copyists and scribes who were liberal with their interpretations of their texts! For more on this, see Revelations 22:18-19. See also Bart D. Ehrman, *Misquoting Jesus: The Story Behind Who Changed the Bible and Why*, Reprint edition (New York: HarperOne, 2007).

forth by the new wave of Ahrensian devotees, it becomes clear why it's so crucial to properly understand Zettelkasten.

For instance, one finds authors both touting the benefits of digital notes for enabling search functionality, and devaluing the analog method. Kadavy does this by stating that because an analog Zettelkasten possesses a "slow rate" of exposing users to information while using it, it consequently "reduces your focus."[21] In brief, this notion is absurd. It even conflicts with what Ahrens would admit as a primary benefit of analog.

This demonstrates something that is happening at a more rapid pace within the field of Zettelkasten. We have Kadavy, an Ahrensian follower, providing an example of why digital-based thinking and notetaking may be better because of *search* functionality. We also have him adding his own spin on top of the Ahrensian spin and advocating for digital search functionality of a notetaking system because, he asserts, more exposure to information will increase one's focus.[22] Again, this is absurd. But the contradictions get worse: ten pages after asserting this, Kadavy advises readers to *not worry* about being "efficient."[23] He goes on to declare that the "bottleneck" of great ideas does not stem from the speed and quantity of writing and thinking, but from slow, consistent, hard, and deliberate thought.[24]

In essence, an author who wrote a book on digital Zettelkasten finds himself really an advocate of the analog Zettelkasten—yet perhaps he's too blind to see its power. He's blinded by the digital age we live in, and seems so convinced of the technologies it's yielded. Yet he discounts the technology of the organ that resides inside one's skull. This technology, the human brain,

---

21 Kadavy, *Digital Zettelkasten*, 19.

22 There are several reasons the notion that *being exposed to more information causes one's focus to increase is absurd*. One reason comes from the findings of Nobel Prize winner, Herbert Simon, who observed that more information exposure is directly and negatively correlated with one thing—you guessed it!—focus. In brief, information exposure kills attention.

23 Kadavy, *Digital Zettelkasten*, 29.

24 Kadavy, *Digital Zettelkasten*, 29.

seems to do better in environments where its allowed to slow down and think on paper (when it comes to writing, at least).

A Lesson from Robert Caro

Where does slow, consistent, hard, and deliberate thought come from? Let's ask two-time Pulitzer Prize winning author, Robert Caro. In an interview, Caro was asked why he wrote out all of his books long-hand first, and then by typewriter. Caro responded, "It's to slow myself down." He concludes, "If I write by hand it's a little bit slower and I think things through."[25]

How did Caro learn the power of such a method? He learned it early in his writing career. One of Caro's writing professors once imparted advice to him. The advice ended up exposing Caro's writing methods at the time. As Caro recounts of the experience: "You know, sometimes you know when someone has seen right through you." Right then and there Caro knew his professor had seen through him. What Caro was referring to was the advice he received from his professor: "Mr. Caro, you're never going to achieve what you want to achieve unless you learn to stop thinking with your fingers." By this, Caro's professor meant that Caro must stop just writing papers directly using his typewriter. Instead Caro ought to slow down and think on paper, with a pen. When Caro wrote his first book, he changed up his process. At the time he was still not heeding his professor's advice. Why? Because he was "a newspaper man" and time was of the essence. Yet, when he set out to write his book, he switched. When he set out to write his book, he first wrote the draft in longhand, and then he wrote it out via typewriter.[26]

In summary, slow, consistent, deliberate thought comes from the world of analog. Specifically, it comes from writing by hand. This is something built

---

25 Democracy Now!, "From LBJ to Robert Moses: Robert Caro on Writing About Political Power & Its Impact on the Powerless," 2019, https://www.youtube.com/watch?v=R4j1h71xVG4, Minute 38.

26 New-York Historical Society, "Inside the Robert A. Caro Archive, Episode 1: Electra 210 Typewriter," 2021, https://www.youtube.com/watch?v=ORf1AhUhQPQ.

into the Antinet. Trust me, it will transform the way in which you think. It will transform your research. And it will transform your writing.

Those Who Teach Zettelkasten Don't Even Know What a Zettelkasten Truly Is

Unless you're a careful and scrutinizing reader, these seemingly contradictory positions may go unnoticed. However, since you're now privy to Ahrensianity, you are better equipped for two things. First, you'll find it easier to spot such contradictions when you read an article about Zettelkasten that, in reality, is teaching the Ahrensian interpretation of Luhmann's Zettelkasten (and not the real authentic Zettelkasten); and second, you will understand *why* the author is confused in the first place. The reason the author is confused about what a Zettelkasten is, is simply this: a Zettelkasten isn't merely a notetaking methodology. A Zettelkasten is a method to build your own person—a second version of yourself with whom you can communicate—a *second mind*. More on this will be explored in detail later in the book.

An Example Contradiction: Dynamically Updating Links

A key feature of digital Zettelkasten apps is the dynamic updating of links across all files when you update the filename. In other words, when you edit a note's filename, all other notes that link to that filename dynamically update as well (so that the links don't break). This is an important feature because the majority of digital "Zettelkasten" are not truly Zettelkasten. A true Zettelkasten system has numeric-alpha filenames (**e.g. 2701/1A**). Apps without the dynamic-updating function instead utilize filenames that are typically a human-readable concept name. For instance, a note that outlines *confirmation bias* would typically be named **confirmation bias.md**. If one were to, for instance, change the filename from **confirmation bias.md** to **confirmation fallacy.md**, then all of the links pointing to the original would break. One would have to use the *find-and-replace-all* text feature to fix the broken links. This is not the case with the dynamic updating feature in certain notetaking apps. As a result, much time is saved with the valuable dynamic updating feature.

In essence, the ability to dynamically update links is quite useful for those who use digital Zettelkasten. Yet, one finds authors writing about these apps contradicting the value of such a feature. Kadavy flat out states that it is an "overrated feature" for digital Zettelkasten.[27] I don't even use a digital Zettelkasten, nor do I wish to, yet even I can see how poorly informed this opinion is! Such an assertion could be understandable if one were using numeric-alpha addresses (that is, is using Zettelkasten in its truer form), as there would be no reason for the filenames to ever change in the first place.

The numeric-alpha naming convention Luhmann devised enables one to infinitely internally branch thoughts and link all entries anywhere. In fact, the reason one ought *never* to update filenames is that mistakes or odd conventions (and old naming of concepts) prove quite valuable. Moreover, they form odd clusters that order themselves in unique ways allowing one to observe the evolution of one's thinking. This is invaluable for the *knowledge development system* that a Zettelkasten is.

Another Contradiction: Linking Notes vs. Rewriting Ideas

The very same author who undermines the value of dynamic links in a digital Zettelkasten makes an even more absurd statement that introduces confusion for those wishing to become more effective knowledge creators. Kadavy states that *linking* is overrated and he supports rewriting instead of linking. Why? He reasons that it's easier to just rewrite things by typing.[28] I find this rather absurd because it diminishes the major premise of a digital Zettelkasten: the attractiveness of a digital Zettelkasten, in comparison with a digital note database, centers on the benefit of linking thoughts. One rationale for this is that by linking, users need not constantly rewrite everything. Instead, they can revise and develop the thought that they link to. Many first-generation Ahrensian followers base their biggest idea around that of linking thoughts.[29] For this reason, it becomes a bit of a mess when one digital Zettelkasten follower promotes one idea and the other promotes the exact opposite notion. At the center of this mess rests the core of it all: basing one's teachings on someone other than the system's creator (Niklas Luhmann).

---

27 Kadavy, *Digital Zettelkasten*, 30.

28 Kadavy, *Digital Zettelkasten*, 31.

29 "Linking Your Thinking," accessed July 7, 2021, https://www.linkingyourthinking.com/.

Instead, when you base your opinion on an early Zettelkasten apostle (Sönke Ahrens), you're left with contradictions. You'll find one digital Zettelkasten teacher advocating for one thing, and a different digital Zettelkasten teacher advocating for the exact opposite. The key lesson here? Start with Luhmann, start with the original source, and then work backwards from there.

Another Contradiction: Highlighting Books

Advising readers to highlight books while reading is something Luhmann never did. Yet we find such advice from Kadavy, the teacher of digital Zettelkasten methods. This author advises readers to highlight text in their e-readers.[30] This goes against even Sönke Ahrens's advice. Further, Kadavy then advises readers to "highlight the highlights."[31]

On the matter of highlighting texts, I will say this: highlighting is not advisable. It is not a good method for focused reading of challenging and complex information. For challenging material, it's best to invest the time required to reformulate it, and reflect on it in the form of notes. There are no shortcuts.

While highlighting does not possess the cognitive-development power of reformulating and reflecting on information, it is not "completely pointless," as one cognitive scientist, Fiona McPherson, points out. The reason it's not *completely pointless* is that highlighting books can have the helpful effect of forcing one to actually read the words.[32]

But look at what the cognitive scientist is really admitting here. Her main point is that highlighting is not *completely pointless*; it's just barely above *completely pointless*. In other words, it's *mostly pointless*.

I'd advise you to stay away from the practice of highlighting. If the material is familiar to you, and especially if it's complicated, highlighting won't help

---

30 Kadavy, *Digital Zettelkasten*, 31.

31 Kadavy, *Digital Zettelkasten*, 33.

32 Fiona McPherson, *Effective Note-taking*, revised edition (Wellington: Wayz Press, 2018), 17.

much. Furthermore, research shows that highlighting may even "harm" your ability to recall information in certain scenarios.[33]

As McPherson observes, the main value of highlighting does not intrinsically add much value to your understanding of the material. Its main benefit centers on its ability to motivate one to spend *more time* with the material.[34] This effect caused by spending *more time* with material will resurface throughout this book. Perhaps not so ironically, the reason the analog Zettelkasten outweighs the effectiveness of digital Zettelkasten is because the analog form forces users to spend *more time* developing thoughts.

Direct Contradictions of Luhmann's Teachings

I've laid out several contradictions that have emerged within recent digital Zettelkasten teachings. Unfortunately, many more continue to rise to the surface. Some contradictions are even more severe than others.

There are also direct contradictions of Luhmann's teachings. For instance, Luhmann calls the Zettelkasten a "universal instrument" which accepts any keyterm one wishes to create in the index.[35] Even the simple, isolated basic keyterm of "*Picasso*" is fine, as Luhmann says, because it may unlock accidental insights.[36] According to Luhmann, it's more fruitful to create keyterms that generalize different things, and relate heterogeneous things to a larger theme or observation. More on this will be explained later in this book. However, we find Kadavy citing Ahrens on how one ought to select keyterms for tagging.[37] Note that he cites Ahrens instead of the creator of the Zettelkasten, Niklas Luhmann. He then prescribes to the reader the

33 McPherson, *Effective Note-taking*, 23; James H. Crouse and Peter Idstein, "Effects of Encoding Cues on Prose Learning," Journal of Educational Psychology 63, no. 4 (1972): 309–13.

34 McPherson, *Effective Note-taking*, 24.

35 Niklas Luhmann, "Communication with Noteboxes (Revised Edition)," trans. Manfred Kuehn, https://daily.scottscheper.com/zettelkasten/.

36 Plus, thinking of the keyterm "*Picasso*" may help you recall the idea, and then travel down the branch of thought you're looking for.

37 Kadavy, *Digital Zettelkasten*, 47.

following directive: "avoid generic keywords, such as 'psychology.'" [38] This directly conflicts with Luhmann describing the Zettelkasten as a "universal instrument" into which one can place almost any keyterm and get back *unconventional insights*.

Unfortunately, those who accept such advice may never experience the magic and accidental insights generated by working with an analog thinking system. While the analog route may seem difficult at first, the alternative isn't that nice and pretty. Furthermore, it's rather vague. For instance, toward the end of Kadavy's book on digital Zettelkasten, there's a section that debates "linking vs. tagging vs. both."[39] Luhmann never found himself bothered with such drivel because, as I've already stated, the concept of tagging notes didn't exist. Kadavy's solution to this topic remains to be decided by the reader as he concludes, "there's no right answer." [40] Actually, there is a right answer. Do what Luhmann did, and use an analog thinking system and stop worrying about such irrelevant things!

Stripping Away The Importance of The Numeric-Alpha Card Addresses

Within the Latter-day Ahrensian Zettelkasten school, there exists a more pernicious contradiction of the original form that promotes downplaying the importance of numeric-alpha card addresses.

If you wish to take Luhmann seriously, then you must accept his notion that an alter ego arises out of an analog Zettelkasten. A *ghost in the box* arises in the form of a *second mind* (if you structure your analog Zettelkasten properly). This creates an entity that allows you to *communicate* with it in the first place.

As Luhmann makes clear, the numeric-alpha card addresses are a key component that "makes possible its ability to communicate in the first place."[41]

---

38 Kadavy, *Digital Zettelkasten*, 48.

39 Kadavy, *Digital Zettelkasten*, 50.

40 Kadavy, *Digital Zettelkasten*, 50.

41 Luhmann, "Communicating with Slip Boxes."

It becomes, therefore, quite confusing when digital Zettelkasten proponents take a nonchalant approach to this concept—if they even decide to mention it at all, that is![42]

For instance, Kadavy's book that supposedly teaches digital Zettelkasten starts off the chapter on file identification with, "A big debate among Zettelkasten practitioners is file-naming convention."[43] In reality, there is no debate if one is to subscribe to the Zettelkasten in its truest form. Yet the author of this book carries on and lists out four options to choose from.

Here are the recommendations described by the author:

The first option this author lists is to use "phrases" in the filename. This practice is precisely what Luhmann says one *should not* do! Luhmann explicitly advises that the Zettelkasten must not *rely on a structure that uses content-based order.*[44]

The second option Kadavy lays out for IDs is that of an ugly date-timestamp number.[45] This makes very little sense, as the magic of Zettelkasten revolves around the idea that you branch internally, in an infinite manner based on the idea—not the time and date in which that idea formed. Date-time IDs destroy the beauty of the numeric-alpha convention Luhmann used. It adds complicated bloat to something that is otherwise so simple.

The third option for IDs Kadavy mentions is, in his words, "the most complicated naming convention."[46] He references the naming convention called

---

42 Kadavy, *Digital Zettelkasten*; "Building a Second Brain: An Overview," *Forte Labs*, February 20, 2019, https://fortelabs.co/blog/basboverview/.

43 Kadavy, *Digital Zettelkasten*, 38. Mind you, the author's discussion of what Luhmann deemed a "most important [decision]" in constructing a Zettelkasten, doesn't arrive until chapter eleven of this author's book on digital Zettelkasten.

44 Luhmann, "Communicating with Slip Boxes." "Fixed numbers, abstracted from any content-based order relying on the entire structure has a number of advantages which, taken together, enable us to reach a higher type of order."

45 Kadavy, *Digital Zettelkasten*, 39.

46 Kadavy, *Digital Zettelkasten*, 40.

Folgezettel. This is a term that has, for some odd reason, gained popularity amongst the new digital Zettelkasten school (note: Luhmann actually never used the term). What this term means is essentially an address affixed to each card that is numeric-alpha and that can be branched, and internally evolved (e.g. 2412/1A/1). I will not go into detail on this now, as it's a core component of the Antinet and will be discussed in great length later on. The author goes on to declare it as "unnecessary" for building a digital Zettelkasten. But something that is even more unnecessary in a digital Zettelkasten is... the digital part!

Where Kadavy goes from bad to worse, however, is in his misunderstanding of what numeric-alpha card addresses actually are. He states that it forces a "hierarchical arrangement of notes in a system supposed to be non-hierarchical."[47] This notion is absurd. Each note in the Antinet is like a leaf on a tree. Every leaf on a tree is of the same class as other leaves; they just live in a different location on the tree. As Johannes Schmidt points out "the position of a special subject or card says nothing of the theoretical importance of the card." As far as hierarchy, "there's no bottom and there's no top."[48] Secondly, who stated that the Zettelkasten is "supposed to be non-hierarchical?" Even though an analog Zettelkasten (and its numeric-alpha card addresses) is not hierarchical (which the author gets wrong), the notion that a Zettelkasten is "supposed to be non-hierarchical" stands as a myth.

Kadavy outlines the final option for how to identify one's notes: *use a combination of mixing up all three of these options.*[49] This is fine advice if you wish to spend your days reading and spinning your wheels in the mud trying to make use of what you've just read.

From this one starts to get a glimpse of how much of a mess the current landscape is for English-speaking people who dare do an internet search for the term "Zettelkasten." Just as an illustration, if you end up searching

---

47 Kadavy, *Digital Zettelkasten*, 43.

48 Undisciplined, "Archiving Luhmann w/ Johannes Schmidt," 2021, https://www.youtube.com/watch?v=kz2K3auPLWU, 37:20.

49 Kadavy, *Digital Zettelkasten*, 46.

for "Zettelkasten," you end up with an 80% or greater chance of selecting an article that does not teach the ID system Luhmann used for his Zettelkasten (the numeric-alpha address version).

This misinformation continues to spread at a rapid pace. The *availability cascade* of inaccurate but simplistic Zettelkasten information exacerbates the issue, and it's getting harder for potential users to grasp what the Zettelkasten system actually was, and is.

The Problem with Latter-Day Ahrensian Teachings

The problem with the teachings of those basing their source material off of Sönke Ahrens's publications is the fact that all of the subtleties and magic of the Zettelkasten are discarded. There exists a magic in building a pen-and-paper-based system, a communication partner, an alter-ego, a *second mind.* This type of system creates accidents and randomness that are invaluable. Its essence is watered down, if not altogether nuked by its digital, inbred, cousins.

It's unfortunate that those who teach the Zettelkasten system have missed out on the true underlying magic of Luhmann's system in its purest form. Going in search of the magic requires a person to be rather crazy (like yours truly). You must take a risk and purchase the materials required and go through the long slog of creating your own analog Zettelkasten (using only pen and notecards). Furthermore, it's a lonely journey as there's not much information out there about how to build an analog Zettelkasten (though hopefully I'll help make the road less lonely). It's also one that may be filled with missteps that are hard to correct given the fact that there's no *find-and-replace-all* functionality. Yet it's worth the investment. Sure, it's unfortunate that these digital Zettelkasten teachers never discovered the true magic of Zettelkasten. But it's more unfortunate that they end up unintentionally misleading others who may have otherwise put in the work to build a true Zettelkasten (if they had only known how it really works and what is to be gained by it).

WHY I DECIDED TO WRITE A BOOK ABOUT THE ZETTELKASTEN

Even though the information landscape pertaining to Zettelkasten is riddled with inaccurate information, it's not the reason I decided to publish a book on the Zettelkasten. I mean, there's a massive amount of misinformation in many other fields. The field I spent much time in several years ago was that of cryptocurrency. There are massive sums of inaccurate information in that field. Yet, this didn't drive me to publish a book on cryptocurrency. Why? It's simple. Because that audience is primarily filled with speculators who want to make money without lifting a finger.

The reason I decided to publish my views and findings related to the Zettelkasten system stems from the following:

First, the misinformation connected with Luhmann's Zettelkasten is multiplying due to the *availability cascade* phenomenon.

Second, if I don't write about what I've learned about Zettelkasten now (while my passion for it is still fresh), then I probably never will.

Third, and most importantly, I actually care about sharing this information because I care about the people who would potentially waste their lives learning the wrong methods and techniques to build a Zettelkasten. I believe that many people have, are, and will waste their precious life energy learning the ins-and-outs of digital apps instead of creating the genius-level work they're capable of.

Why do I care to publish my findings on the Zettelkasten? I'd like to think it's because I'm a saint, and that it's simply just *the right thing to do*. But seriously, I think the reason why I care about such people like yourself is because I was once in your shoes.

I very clearly recall the confusion I experienced and even the suffering I experienced from not knowing *how* to organize all the thoughts floating around in my head.

I care to share with you what I've learned because I've seen the faces of those in the community of people who are eager to learn. When I took an online course on personal knowledge management, I interacted with people like you—people who are committed to growth and learning. That course humanized the need for the information I learned, and so too has interacting with people like yourself on my YouTube channel.[50]

In brief, I'm publishing this book because as I've demonstrated, I believe the landscape of accurate information pertaining to the Zettelkasten system is bad and it's getting worse, and it's worth sharing my views with this community because the people it's comprised of are people worth serving.

Now, before we get into the core of the Antinet, let's first dive into the mind of its creator: Niklas Luhmann. Understanding the mind of its creator provides tremendous value in understanding the nature of what we'll be building together: the Antinet Zettelkasten.

50 **https://www.youtube.com/channel/UCnvMBVMXMPKA4Lmy5Ihd-FQ**

CHAPTER FOUR

NIKLAS LUHMANN, THE MAN

BEFORE WE BEGIN DIVING into Niklas Luhmann's notebox system, there's one area worth first exploring: Niklas Luhmann, the man. That is, Luhmann's background, his theories, his beliefs, and his attitudes.

WHY IT'S IMPORTANT TO GAIN FAMILIARITY WITH NIKLAS LUHMANN

The structure, spirit and personality of the Antinet carries imprints of its biggest contributor, Niklas Luhmann.

The Antinet enables one to be "light of mind" amidst the complexity of knowledge. This type of state reflects Niklas Luhmann's tendency toward being abstract, vague, trollishly carnivalesque and—at the same time—brilliant. The Antinet carries with it such a demeanor. It is one of order, disorder, absurdisms, and brilliance—yet the Antinet also contains imperfections. Its order is not perfect either. A system of perfect order is seen in the digital realm—with its deterministic, orderly execution of programs that subscribe to a uniform, predictable protocol. For a glimpse of imperfections and chaos, one need only review the archive of Luhmann's notebox, or view his private home office.[1] In brief, Luhmann's theoretical work was not developed in an environment of pure order.

---

1 holgersen911, Niklas Luhmann—Beobachter Im Krähennest (Eng Sub), 2012, https://www.youtube.com/watch?v=qRSCKSPMuDc.

Simply stated, the Antinet is not for OCD-individuals who can't sleep at night unless their workflow follows some made-up *atomic* protocol.[2]

Because Luhmann's writing was so dry and complex, it leads to confusion and misinterpretations of what his system actually is. This confusion of what a Zettelkasten *actually is* continues to spread to this day.

Up until now, those who desired to understand Luhmann's Zettelkasten in its purest form were faced with disentangling the prose of Luhmann's paper "Communication with Noteboxes." This paper took me about three weeks to read and extract into my own Antinet. I spent almost six days a week doing this; I then spent another month doing the same with Johannes Schmidt's paper on Luhmann's Zettelkasten, and another month perusing the digital Zettelkasten archives.

Like Luhmann's books and papers, he left his Zettelkasten system to be understood only by those who invest the time and energy into disentangling his prose. Most people have not done this. As a result they've been left with a surface-level understanding of what he built. However, if you venture deeper and dig into what Luhmann really said, one discovers the system to be quite profound.[3]

A BRIEF BACKGROUND OF NIKLAS LUHMANN

Niklas Luhmann was born in Lüneburg, Germany on December 8, 1927. He was the son of a brewer, though Luhmann himself was disinterested in drinking.[4]Drinking beer at festivals and the local *Biergarten* was (and still is)

---

2 By "atomic" I'm referring to the interpretation that Luhmann's notes were perfectly containerized units of thought. This is a myth. Luhmann's notes were streams of thought that carried over across multiple notecards.

3 One example of this is the fact that Luhmann created the system to use a multiple-storage architecture—something that has become the dominant model for computers to manage memory. Luhmann devised this in the early 1950s before computers were dominant and before the notion of multiple-storage was widely-accepted. For more, see: Johannes Schmidt, "Niklas Luhmann's Card Index: Thinking Tool, Communication Partner, Publication Machine," Forgetting Machines. Knowledge Management Evolution in Early Modern Europe 53 (2016), 309.

4 Hans-Georg Moeller, The Radical Luhmann (New York: Columbia University Press,

seen as "a social virtue" in Germany.[5] Abstaining from such events, which offered invaluable networking opportunities, likely contributed to Luhmann becoming an outsider. This also created a barrier to his advancement in his early career as a civil servant, working for the government.

According to Luhmann's youngest son, Clemens, Luhmann avoided drinking alcohol throughout his life. Yet, on very, *very* rare occasions, Luhmann would drink alcohol. When he did it was one glass of red wine. According to Clemens, the reason his father avoided alcohol was simply this: he didn't want to appear stupid![6]

Back to young Luhmann: After a year working at the Lüneburg Higher Administration Court, Luhmann took another bureaucratic job in Hanover, Germany. After a year there, and after "problems had arisen, especially in the area of Nazi reparations," Luhmann took a different job at the Lower Saxony Ministry of Culture.[7]

It soon became clear Luhmann did not wish to be a mere government employee. He desired an easy job where he could immediately go home at five o'clock sharp. He desired this type of work-life balance so that he could pursue his true passions in the evenings. When asked by an interviewer what those true passions were, Luhmann replied that his interests at night revolved around two things: first, reading books, and second, his notebox system (that is, his Antinet).

During this time Luhmann recalls that he "read a lot."[8] He read sociology and philosophy—mainly Descartes and Husserl. In sociology, he was absorbed by a concept that would stand as a core component of his social theoretical

---

2011), 121-2.

5 Hans-Georg Moeller, The Radical Luhmann (New York: Columbia University Press, 2011), 153.

6 Clemens Luhmann, Interview by Scott P. Scheper, April 27, 2022.

7 Niklas Luhmann, Short Cuts (English Translation) (Frankfurt am Main: Zweitausendeins, 2002), 10.

8 Niklas Luhmann, Short Cuts (English Translation) (Frankfurt am Main: Zweitausendeins, 2002), 11.

work. The concept is called *functionalism*. One can browse the notes from those readings in Luhmann's online archive.[9]

Yet Luhmann spent most of his time in the evenings working with his Antinet. He did this "above all" other activities.[10]

Luhmann's paradise was reading and conversing with the greatest minds of humanity. He would read philosophy and sociology, and then reformulate and reflect on the readings by expressing them on paper via writing by hand with a pen. After this he would install into his Antinet the thoughts from these conversations between him and the author he was reading.

Yet one day, early in his career, Luhmann's paradise would come under attack. His job became more demanding. Nights spent with his books and his Antinet were "no longer possible with growing tasks."[11]

One day a senior member of his company sat Luhmann down. Hoping to advise Luhmann and help advance Luhmann's career as a civil servant, he proffered some advice. "You should look into doing some extracurricular volunteering, and work in a district." Luhmann replied that he wouldn't. "Why?" the senior employee asked. Luhmann replied, "I am reading Hölderlin."[12] Luhmann was referring to Friedrich Hölderlin, a German philosopher and poet. It was a higher priority for Luhmann to expand his mind than to expand his career prospects playing the conventional games of bureaucratic advancement. A short while later, Luhmann would leave the government job and attend Harvard University.

A brief lesson can be learned from this important point: Luhmann's vocation

---

9 "ZK I: Note 80.6 - Niklas Luhmann Archive," accessed June 1, 2022, https://niklas-luhmann-archiv.de/bestand/zettelkasten/zettel/ZK_1_NB_80-6_V.

10 Niklas Luhmann, Short Cuts (English Translation) (Frankfurt am Main: Zweitausendeins, 2002), 11.

11 Niklas Luhmann, Short Cuts (English Translation) (Frankfurt am Main: Zweitausendeins, 2002), 11.

12 Niklas Luhmann, Short Cuts (English Translation) (Frankfurt am Main: Zweitausendeins, 2002), 11.

was reading, thinking, and writing. He turned his *vocation* into his *vacation*. The Antinet did not serve Luhmann as a tool to *replace* this line of work; instead, it was a tool to *aid* and *enhance* it.

❋ ❋ ❋

Later on in life, when Luhmann did finally get his dream job working as a professor at Bielefeld University, he was able to spend his time doing what he loved: reading, thinking, and writing. At that point Luhmann didn't desire fame from his work. He didn't desire wealth or riches so that he could spend days bronzing on Caribbean beaches. He instead desired one thing: "more time."[13]

Luhmann desired more time so he could spend it doing more of what he loved: reading, writing, and working. When asked of his ultimate Utopia, Luhmann replied, "I could imagine that for me, the day has thirty hours."[14] He wanted thirty-hour-long days spent mostly reading, writing, and thinking.

As for Luhmann's family life, in 1960 at the age of thirty three, Luhmann married his wife, Ursula. They had three children together and a nice life. Sadly, she died in 1977, when Luhmann was fifty years old. After she died, Luhmann never married again. He had a caretaker cook meals and help him take care of his three children. This enabled Luhmann to focus and continue spending time on his true passions: reading and his Antinet.

Luhmann's professional life was a successful one—albeit a rather quiet one. He is referred to as "the most important German sociologist in the twentieth century."[15] Yet he lived a rather simple lifestyle. His routine and workflow will be covered later in the book. His life revolved around his intellectual

---

13 Niklas Luhmann, Short Cuts (English Translation) (Frankfurt am Main: Zweitausendeins, 2002), 15.

14 Niklas Luhmann, Short Cuts (English Translation) (Frankfurt am Main: Zweitausendeins, 2002), 15.

15 Undisciplined, Archiving Luhmann w/ Johannes Schmidt, 2021, https://www.youtube.com/watch?v=kz2K3auPLWU, 19:16.

pursuits. His life was dedicated to his grand theory of everything as it pertains to society.

Luhmann's publication footprint is sizable and impressive. The "sheer number [of publications] is unprecedented," writes one scholar.[16] Luhmann produced 550 academic papers and seventy books in approximately forty years.[17] In his literary estate, Johannes Schmidt uncovered three thousand manuscripts, two hundred of which were previously unpublished.[18] As Schmidt puts it, Luhmann was (with the help of his Antinet) "a publication machine."[19]

LUHMANN'S PHILOSOPHICAL AND POLITICAL VIEWS

Luhmann was misconceived to be a conservative, right-wing thinker because he debated Jürgen Habermas, a popular left-wing liberal ideologue. Those who attended the event say Luhmann dismantled Habermas's positions, which resulted in Luhmann becoming "rather famous" in Germany.[20]

Yet Luhmann was not a right-wing conservative. His views could be likened to a *laissez faire* approach to politics and the economy. He could more be likened to a Libertarian (to use American political terminology). Luhmann was an ironic character with a stoic demeanor. So too were his political positions. Perhaps a better description of Luhmann's political position could be that of *absurdism*, with a trend toward being *carnivalesque*. Luh-

16 Johannes Schmidt, "Niklas Luhmann's Card Index: Thinking Tool, Communication Partner, Publication Machine," Forgetting Machines. Knowledge Management Evolution in Early Modern Europe 53 (2016), 289.

17 Johannes Schmidt, "Niklas Luhmann's Card Index: Thinking Tool, Communication Partner, Publication Machine," Forgetting Machines. Knowledge Management Evolution in Early Modern Europe 53 (2016), 289; Raf Vanderstraeten, "Luhmann on Socialization and Education," Educational Theory 50 (January 25, 2005): 1–23.

18 Undisciplined, Archiving Luhmann w/ Johannes Schmidt, 2021, https://www.youtube.com/watch?v=kz2K3auPLWU, 24:30.

19 Johannes Schmidt, "Niklas Luhmann's Card Index: Thinking Tool, Communication Partner, Publication Machine," Forgetting Machines. Knowledge Management Evolution in Early Modern Europe 53 (2016), 311.

20 Hans-Georg Moeller, The Radical Luhmann (New York: Columbia University Press, 2011), 102.

mann's philosophical views were a unique blend of stoicism, Spinozism, and Daoism.[21] He was always careful to not fall into the trap of moralizing issues, and practiced being one step removed from established positions on matters. He desired to avoid the trap of dogmatism, which first starts with a strong belief in one side being *good*, and the other side being *bad*. Luhmann spent a lot of time disciplining his mind so that it could always remain one thing: detached.

As one author puts it, "[Luhmann was] quite disturbed by ideological attempts at taking democracy too seriously and thought that such attempts may paradoxically pose a danger for its existence."[22]

The same could be said of Luhmann's views toward nationalism (or "love for one's country," as some would deem it). In his opinion, passion could turn into dogma, which then could turn into storming the United States Capitol. Having learned from a childhood experience (which will be revealed shortly), Luhmann was quite reticent about allowing dogma to influence his thinking. Thus, he remained disciplined in a rational, detached thinking style. This is worth noting because it would have been quite easy for him to have gone a different route. One of Luhmann's greatest influences, Georg Hegel, was quite an enthusiastic ideologue.[23] It would be easy to conceive of Luhmann trying to further the ideologies of his mentor; yet, he did not do such a thing.

Of what can be said of Luhmann's religious views remains rather brief: he was not very religious.[24]

---

21 Hans-Georg Moeller, The Radical Luhmann (New York: Columbia University Press, 2011), 116.

22 Hans-Georg Moeller, The Radical Luhmann (New York: Columbia University Press, 2011), 103.

23 Hans-Georg Moeller, The Radical Luhmann (New York: Columbia University Press, 2011), 37.

24 Hans-Georg Moeller, The Radical Luhmann (New York: Columbia University Press, 2011), 37.

LUHMANN'S THEORETICAL CONCEPTS

There are a series of concepts that continually resurface in Luhmann's writings. These concepts were of great importance to his work, and they will be covered in further detail throughout the book.

One of Luhmann's cornerstone concepts revolves around *communication*. One of his more frequently quoted statements suggests that "Humans cannot communicate; not even their brains can communicate; not even their conscious minds can communicate. Only communication can communicate."[25]

In light of this, it's worth considering that the Antinet revolves around communication. Ideas communicate through being stored in contextual branches and stems of thoughts. The ideas also communicate with one another through remote linking to other leaves of thought in the internally-constructed tree of knowledge.

Communication was not only a pillar of Luhmann's theoretical work; it also stands as a pillar of his Antinet. This is why Luhmann titled his paper, "*Communication* with Noteboxes" [emphasis mine].

Another cornerstone of Luhmann's theoretical work is *systems theory*. This relates to the field of *cybernetics* and *self-referential systems*, which houses itself in the term *autopoeiesis*.[26] This concept is a very interesting one. It's a biological concept that Luhmann applied to social sciences. Later on in the book, I'll unpack these concepts and explain them in further detail.

SYSTEMS THEORY 2.0

Luhmann's take on systems theory was not conventional. It could be better likened to *systems theory 2.0*.

---

25 Hans Ulrich Gumbrecht and Karl Ludwig Pfeiffer, Materialities of Communication (Stanford University Press, 1994), 371.

26 Niklas Luhmann, Short Cuts (English Translation) (Frankfurt am Main: Zweitausendeins, 2002), 26.

Systems theory 1.0 revolves around the mereological notion of *whole-part-theory*. In this model, the system equals the whole. The parts are like organs in a body yet are thought of as more modular and static in nature. When you think of systems theory 1.0, think simple *input-output* machines (like a vending machine). You put a dollar in, and it spits out a snack (assuming it doesn't get stuck)!

Systems theory 2.0 finds itself in a world of complex interdependent subsystems. *Complexity* serves as a cornerstone of Luhmann's theoretical work and as such it strongly influenced his notion of systems. The 'system', in Luhmann's systems theory 2.0, consists of an internal environment that houses subsystems. The 'parts' are actually subsystems, each with their own complex processes and interactions with their environment. Whereas the parts in systems theory 1.0 are thought of as modular and static organs, the parts in systems theory 2.0 are themselves systems, like the cardiovascular system and immune system in a human body. The parts are essentially their own complex systems, which are comprised of their own complex systems, which are comprised of their own complex systems, and on and on. It's essentially one big complex fractal of systems and subsystems.

LUHMANN'S NOTION OF SYSTEM'S THEORY (system's theory 2.0)
SHOULD BE CALLED "SYSTEM-ENVIRONMENT THEORY"

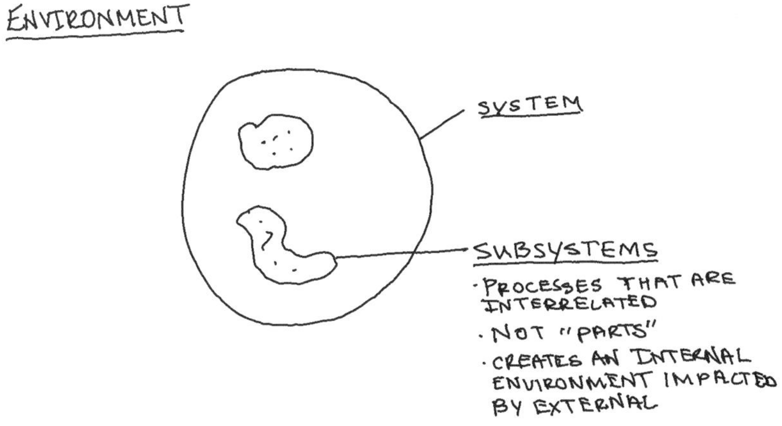
ENVIRONMENT
SYSTEM
SUBSYSTEMS
· PROCESSES THAT ARE INTERRELATED
· NOT "PARTS"
· CREATES AN INTERNAL ENVIRONMENT IMPACTED BY EXTERNAL

Systems theory 2.0 suggests that the *environment* of the subsystems is provided by other systems: "Within a complex system, such as the human body, there are a large number of subsystems that mutually provide the environment for one another."[27] One scholar observes that Luhmann's work in systems theory raises the question of whether it should be more appropriately named, "system-environment theory."[28]

In the world of the Antinet, the subsystems are essentially contextual stems of thought that form around notes. Each of these subsystems cluster together to form themselves as a subsystem. They also can link to and connect with other subsystems in remote parts of the Antinet. These clusters of subsystems create an internal environment in the Antinet that mirrors the chain-linked structure of how human memory works.

Luhmann devised radical theories that were not conventional and that were not based on classic sociological concepts. As mentioned previously, Luhmann's intellectual rival, Jürgen Habermas, aimed for his theoretical work to "improve society by making it communicate more rationally."[29] Habermas subscribed to Karl Marx's famous dictum that philosophy and theory must not merely analyze the world; it must set out to change it.[30]

Luhmann thought such notions futile. In his opinion, ideology packed into theory and science result in bad science—namely, confirmation bias. His opinion was colored by the social unrest of the time (1968), and the tendency of packing ideological political agendas into sociological theories.

Luhmann sought to de-anthropocentrize sociology by exploring what the field would look like if it did not revolve around people. Rather, he conceived

---

27 Hans-Georg Moeller, The Radical Luhmann (New York: Columbia University Press, 2011), 128.

28 Hans-Georg Moeller, The Radical Luhmann (New York: Columbia University Press, 2011), 62.

29 Hans-Georg Moeller, The Radical Luhmann (New York: Columbia University Press, 2011), 135.

30 Hans-Georg Moeller, The Radical Luhmann (New York: Columbia University Press, 2011), 25.

a social system centered on concepts and systems. Luhmann called his theoretical work "radically anti-humanist," and "radically anti-regionalist."[31]

By anti-humanist, Luhmann was not implying that he was against human beings. Rather, he held that anthropocentric models of reality are "unfit to theoretically describe and analyze communication."[32] By anti-regionalist, Luhmann desired for his theoretical work to be like mathematics; i.e., a science that works across cultures. For example, math works in Japan, and it works just the same in America.

These terms, *anti-humanism* and *anti-regionalist* provide a nice summary of Luhmann's thought.[33] The terms are rather alarming at first; yet, when you peel away the layers and truly understand what they mean, they're rather concise and quite profound.

After conducting a comprehensive analysis of Luhmann's work, one scholar labeled his theories as *metabiological*. "Just as Greek metaphysics explained the world beyond the physical by applying physical concepts," one scholar writes, "Luhmann applied biological concepts for a descriptive analysis of the nonbiological world and, in particular, society and communication."[34] In sum, Luhmann's theoretical work was deep, radical, and widely researched, spanning many disciplinary fields. By understanding this, one begins to understand why he structured the Antinet the way he did. It allowed him to link together and pull from many sources to illustrate his ideas in great depth.

Understanding this provides ideas for how you yourself may wish to apply such a methodology to your own disciplinary field. You are undoubtedly

31 Hans-Georg Moeller, The Radical Luhmann (New York: Columbia University Press, 2011), 19.

32 Hans-Georg Moeller, The Radical Luhmann (New York: Columbia University Press, 2011), 131.

33 This serves as yet another reason why the term *Antinet* encapsulates the essence of Luhmann's system. It was Anti-convention!

34 Hans-Georg Moeller, The Radical Luhmann (New York: Columbia University Press, 2011), 124.

unique in the way you think, and in your understanding of the material from which you pull ideas together. The Antinet serves as a fantastic system to assemble this wide-ranging material in such a way to make it more straightforward so as to communicate thoughts from your own uniquely genius ways of thinking.

LUHMANN, THE TROLL

Luhmann was polite, respectful, and sharp; yet he was also a trollish, ironical character.

One scholar describes Luhmann's writing style as using "dry, technical, and conceptual language frequently interspersed with bits of sarcasm, satire, and parody."[35]

INSTANCES OF LUHMANN'S TROLLISHNESS

Luhmann's work tends to provoke others and give off a trollish air; yet upon closer review, it packs wisdom and poses very good points.

As mentioned, Luhmann held that society is composed of internal subsystems that can affect one another (as they're related)—like the way a human body includes the cardiovascular system and immune system. He likens these to the economic system and political system.

However, Luhmann also held that the subsystems themselves cannot control one another. Therefore, organizations like the International Monetary Fund (IMF), and the G8 Summit, which deem themselves to have influence and control over the economic system function, in Luhmann's view, in a similar way to the members of tribal groups who do rain dance rituals. This, according to Luhmann, helps the tribe "spread the impression that something is being done rather than merely waiting until things change by themselves."[36]

35 Hans-Georg Moeller, The Radical Luhmann (New York: Columbia University Press, 2011), 50.

36 Hans-Georg Moeller, The Radical Luhmann (New York: Columbia University Press, 2011), 28.

That Luhmann posed such an idea was quite the controversial thing to do. The notion is quite unsettling, especially for the members of the IMF and G8 Summit who might come across this assertion.

Luhmann, however, was not presenting this notion to divide and humiliate the people and members of the IMF and G8 Summit (or the tribal members who dance for rain). He is not claiming they're irrational or silly, or that such things should be abolished. Rather, what Luhmann asserted is that such organizations serve a function in modern society, just as they did in tribal society. They provide optimism and hope to its members. Even if the organizations cannot control the future, they give its citizens the impression they do, which provides optimism for people to press forward.[37]

Although Luhmann introduced radical notions (even at the expense of offending established institutions), he was described as distanced, but "extremely polite."[38]

Luhmann would politely wait for people to finish making their point, no matter how confused or absurd the question was. Instead of flatly telling a person that they were wrong, Luhmann's replies were softer in manner: "Of course you can do it that way," Luhmann would start, "but I would prefer to start with a different distinction." Luhmann was very polite in delivering his message, yet he was also very clear and precise.

THE IRONIC, CARNIVALESQUE SIDE OF LUHMANN

The philosophy underneath the foundation of Luhmann's troll-like ironic and smirky demeanor can be described as something I mentioned earlier: he tended toward the *absurdist* and *carnivalesque*.

Yet the result of being an absurdist does not connote becoming filled with despair (after accepting the notion that life and reality are absurd, even point-

37 Hans-Georg Moeller, The Radical Luhmann (New York: Columbia University Press, 2011), 28.

38 Undisciplined, Archiving Luhmann w/ Johannes Schmidt, 2021, https://www.youtube.com/watch?v=kz2K3auPLWU, 57:45 and 58:55.

PHOTO CREDIT: "Carnivalesque Luhmann," accessed January 25, 2022
https://miro.medium.com/max/940/0*eMW-vEwe5E56raEs.jpg

less). Rather, the reasonable reaction is to be filled with a lightness, knowing that the world's complexity is something uncontrollable and unknowable. One may even feel a sense of joy in knowing this.

Enlightenment thinkers were not of the type to accept such notions. They possessed comparatively serious dispositions—"Cartesian scientific 'certainty'"—with regard to their beliefs in right and wrong. Yet when one adopts a more open, curious, and awe-filled view of the absurd complexities that compose reality, one can achieve a lightness of being.[39]

Irony is the art and science of paradoxes, that is, dichotomies that arise in our perceptions of truth. Irony is when something is, at the same time, and to the same extent, both serious and not serious—both valid and invalid. It's when something makes sense, and at the same time, it also "makes nonsense."[40] Luhmann's theories, and even the Antinet itself, can be reflected in

39 Hans-Georg Moeller, The Radical Luhmann (New York: Columbia University Press, 2011), 50.

40 Hans-Georg Moeller, The Radical Luhmann (New York: Columbia University Press, 2011), 113.

this notion. Here rests a system that enables one to be a publication machine by slowing down. It rapidly produces large amounts of well-formed text by undertaking the comparatively non-rapid process of writing thoughts by hand. Like Luhmann's theories, the Antinet is rather ironic and paradoxical in nature.

LUHMANN, THE BEATLES FAN?

Luhmann wasn't just a pedantic academic with a certain trollish predisposition. He was plugged in and 'in-touch' with popular culture.

For instance, he would use lyrics from *The Beatles* to illustrate his points (citing "Everybody's got something to hide, except me and my monkey" and "Your inside is out, and your outside is in"). He used such quotes to illustrate the social unrest movement of 1968.[41]

Although Luhmann mentioned Beatles lyrics every now and then, according to Luhmann's youngest son, Luhmann wasn't a fan. Luhmann primarily listened to Louis Armstrong and classical music.[42] For Luhmann, a large part of being in-touch with popular culture is thanks to the fact that he lived with his children after his wife passed. "My children are an essential part of my life," Luhmann said. "I live here with them and the whole youth culture around them."[43]

LUHMANN, THE JOKER

A final example of Luhmann's character can be found in his own Antinet. On one of his cards, one finds the following note:

> In the notebox is a note containing the argument that refutes the claims on all the other notes. But this note disappears as

41 Niklas Luhmann, Short Cuts (English Translation) (Frankfurt am Main: Zweitausendeins, 2002), 38.

42 Clemens Luhmann, Interview by Scott P. Scheper, April 27, 2022.

43 Niklas Luhmann, Short Cuts (English Translation) (Frankfurt am Main: Zweitausendeins, 2002), 20.

> soon as you open the notebox. I.e., he assumes a different number, disguises himself and then cannot be found. A joker.[44]

I haven't been able to figure out this riddle. Perhaps the card Luhmann is talking about is his own internal monologue; his own inner voice, Luhmann himself—a joker.

CONCLUSION

You now have a taste of the type of character Niklas Luhmann was. You also have a sense for the theories underlying Luhmann's research. These are important aspects to understand. As you'll soon find out, these properties are felt within the architecture and nature of the Antinet Zettelkasten.

44"ZK II: Zettel 9/8j—Niklas Luhmann-Archiv," accessed February 23, 2022, https://niklas-luhmann-archiv.de/bestand/zettelkasten/zettel/ZK_2_NB_9-8j_V.

CHAPTER FIVE

WHAT IS AN ANTINET?

"HEY BOY!" A SOLDIER SHOUTED at 17-year-old Niklas Luhmann, "stick out your arm!"

Young Luhmann complied. He stuck out his arm.

Luhmann stood as a prisoner captured along with his friends. They ranged from fifteen to eighteen years old. One expects they were scared. Yet, instead of being frightened, Luhmann was one thing: he was hopeful.

"Finally," one imagines Luhmann thinking to himself, "I'll be freed of the glorified slave labor I've been forced into for the past several years!"

What happened next would be stamped onto Niklas Luhmann's psyche—and also stamped onto his body—for the rest of his life.

The soldier who shouted at Luhmann approached him and got into Luhmann's face. Next, the soldier ripped away Luhmann's wristwatch from his arm. He then threw Luhmann to the ground. Luhmann was kicked and beaten for what felt like hours—viciously beaten by the soldier—an American soldier—who had just hauled in his latest herd of Nazi captives, which included Luhmann.

A detail not often mentioned of Niklas Luhmann, the godfather of the Zettelkasten notetaking system, is the following fact: **Niklas Luhmann was, technically, a Nazi**.

Yet before wishing upon him *Inglorious Basterds* forehead-carving treatment, I ought provide you with an additional bit of information: serving in the Nazi ranks was not Luhmann's choice.

On January 22, 1943, following the implementation of a decree, the Nazis enacted an order. The order called for drafting entire school classes of male students born in 1926 and 1927 into military units. Supervising this program were two institutions: the Hitler Youth organization and the infamous Nazi air force, the *Luftwaffe*. Because of this order, fifteen-year-old Niklas Luhmann (born on December 8, 1927) was forced to join the Nazi ranks of the *Luftwaffenhelfer*. These were assistants to the infamous air force of the Nazis.[1] However, at the desperate end of World War II, Luhmann was sent to the front lines of the war. Shortly after this assignment, he and his comrades were captured by American soldiers.

Note that Luhmann was *conscripted* into Nazi service. The word, *conscripted,* basically means one is given the so-called "early honor" to serve their country, for free, and without pay. It was a government order. They had no say in this matter.

Toward the end of World War II, the Nazis realized things looked bleak for them. For this reason, they forced their citizen's children into slave labor for their '*just*' cause. These children were *supposed to* have been between the ages of fifteen to eighteen years. Yet American soldiers reported capturing Nazi children as young as eight years old carrying guns.[2]

---

1 "*Luftwaffenhelfer*." In *Wikipedia,* April 13, 2021. https://en.wikipedia.org/w/index.php?title=Luftwaffenhelfer&oldid=1017572660.

2 Though there were reports that those conscripted into service by the Nazis were even of much younger age—during World War II, as the Nazi party grew desperate, American soldiers found children enlisting as young as eight-years-old, and that the Nazis were equipping them with guns. See, "The History Place—Hitler Youth: Hitler's Boy Soldiers 1939–1945," April 22, 2015. https://web.archive.org/web/20150422044533/http://www.historyplace.com/worldwar2/hitleryouth/hj-boy-soldiers.htm: "American troops reported capturing armed 8-year-olds at Aachen in Western Germany and knocking out artillery units operated entirely by boys aged twelve and under."

Luhmann did not elect to serve the Nazi cause, and he was not a fan of the Nazi ideology; however, that didn't matter. Luhmann had no choice but to serve the Nazis.

When the American soldiers captured Luhmann, he was beaten as if he were a Third Reich soldier of the highest-rank.

Yet this most unfortunate experience transformed Luhmann's thinking process in an invaluable way. You see, what made Luhmann such a profound thinker stems from one thing, *perspective.*

As we'll discuss more in a later chapter, perspective derives from the Latin roots, *per*, meaning "thoroughly and fully," and *specere*, meaning "to observe, and see, and spectate." Combined, *perspective* means thoroughly observing, seeing, and spectating.

Luhmann's theories encompass some of the most radical perspectives in the social sciences. His perspectives were shaped by his experience of being tortured at the hands of American soldiers.

Many people, including myself, tend towards the simplicity of dualistic philosophies. We prefer the simplicity of *good vs. evil.* We love *Hero's Journeys*—stories like *Star Wars* and the light side vs. the dark side. Yet, as Luhmann learned very early and painfully, reality is not so simple. Reality is often quite complex.

Luhmann discovered this when the Americans captured him and beat him during the final moments of World War II. On that day, Luhmann (and his fellow glorified slave-laborers) found themselves hopeful. They were hopeful that the "coercive apparatus"—the Nazi regime—would wither away once the Nazis were defeated.[3] Luhmann believed the world reflected that of *good vs. evil.* Even though Luhmann was working for the Nazi party,

3 **Niklas Luhmann, *Short Cuts.* Orig.-Ausg., 4. Aufl. Short Cuts 1. Frankfurt am Main: Zweitausendeins, 2002. Page 11.**

he believed the Nazis to be the evil side. After all, they coercively enslaved him into service, and the Allied powers were thought to be the good side.

Luhmann and his colleagues were quite elated when they were captured. They were now captured by the good side, soon freed of the Nazi evil they had found themselves chained to. Once Luhmann and his colleagues were captured, however, they were ushered like cattle into a room. When the soldier shouted at Luhmann to hold his arm out, Luhmann extended his arm as if to embrace his American savior. Luhmann wished to clasp hands and thank the soldier for rescuing him from the Nazi's forced labor.

Yet, instead of being embraced with the clasping of hands, the American soldier ripped off Luhmann's watch, threw Luhmann to the ground, and proceeded to beat him viciously. Luhmann's friends looked on in dismay.

"What the hell's happening?!" we can imagine Luhmann asking himself in a state of distress. "I thought the Americans were here to rescue me and to free me!" Luhmann thought Americans—aka, the good guys—were rescuing him.

It's rather heartbreaking to imagine the young 17-year-old Luhmann in such a state. Imagine the painful thoughts racing through Luhmann's mind. It's sad to think of other children like him who experienced the same; children scared for their lives, suddenly being thrown to the ground and beaten. Luhmann's experience was not isolated, either. It happened to many POWs—children and adults.

Luhmann realized the world was not as simple as the paradigm of *good vs. evil* during this moment. The world was complex, and the world was sometimes rather sad.

This life experience led Luhmann to realize that political regimes "could not run along the axis of "good/evil, but rather that one must judge the figures in their limited reality."[4] To be clear, the beatings of Luhmann and his friends were not permitted by the Allied powers. The preventative mechanism for

4 **Luhmann.** ***Short Cuts,*** **11.**

such abuse was supposed to be the Geneva Convention. The Geneva Convention outlined provisions for properly treating prisoners of war ("POWs"). Its goal centered on protocols designed to treat POWs with *honor and respect.*[5] Apparently, the terms *honor* and *respect* were loosely interpreted by the American soldiers. These soldiers were presumably emotionally exhausted by the war. Seeing friends suffer and die (in physical form) weighed more heavily than the Geneva Convention's rules (which were of metaphysical form). The Geneva Convention's *metaphysical* rules seemed purely imaginary compared to *physical* death.

From the abuse and violence inflicted on Luhmann and his fellow Nazi-slave-children, Luhmann saw reality as the murky picture it is, perhaps for the first time in his life.

The lesson in all of this? Simply this: no system is impenetrable to evil acts.

Luhmann viewed Americans as the lesser evil, saying, "The American system, for example, seems to me the most good." Nevertheless, Luhmann was not blind to the systematic problems ingrained in any political system.

Luhmann recognized reality as a complex system mixed with a lot of good and a lot of bad. He later declared that non-Nazi systems of governance possess "more positive features and more negative features than any previous society. So today is both better and worse."[6]

The experience shaped Luhmann so profoundly that he devised a thinking system for himself, and made sure to architect it in such a way as to challenge others' perennial tendency of drifting back into an overly simplistic view of the world. He needed a system to deter the common tendency of drifting into simple dualistic suppositions of *good* vs. *evil.*

---

5 "Treaties, States Parties, and Commentaries - Geneva Convention (III) on Prisoners of War, 1949–14—Respect for the Persons and Honour of Prisoners." Accessed January 4, 2022. https://ihl-databases.icrc.org/applic/ihl/ihl.nsf/ART/375-590018?OpenDocument.

6 Luhmann. *Short Cuts*, 30–31.

It's "increasingly rare," Luhmann said, that thoughts or disagreements can be developed in a useful way if you "moralize" them.[7] Luhmann needed a system to constantly adapt his *perspective* in such a way as to filter out the tendencies and biases conducive to falling into the simplicity fallacy—that of oversimplifying reality.

THE ZETTELKASTEN AS AN ADAPTIVE OPTIC SYSTEM FOR RAW AND DISTORTED THOUGHTS

Luhmann needed a tool similar to something called an *adaptive optic system* (in the world of astronomy). This technology is built into telescopes, and it converts blurry, distorted pictures of the universe into crisp and clear images. It achieves this by sending the initial light waves it receives, which are raw and distorted, into a self-correcting feedback loop that measures the distortions. Next, a critical step happens: the system generates an *inverse* wavefront to compensate for the initial distorted light waves.

The Zettelkasten system works much like an *adaptive optic system*. Except instead of crystallizing raw and distorted light waves, *raw and distorted thoughts* serve as the materials crystallized.

❋ ❋ ❋

Now, back to Luhmann's experience of being tortured by American soldiers. Let's wrap up this part of the story.

Shortly after being held in captivity, Luhmann was released. He was one of the luckier ones simply because he was still seventeen years old. He was not technically an adult yet. However, the nightmare of American captivity was not yet over for his friends who had recently turned eighteen. They were sent to French mines and forced into slave labor and even more beatings.[8]

---

7 **holgersen911, "Niklas Luhmann - Observer in the Crow's Nest (Eng Sub)," 2012, https://www.youtube.com/watch?v=qRSCKSPMuDc, 18:00.**

8 ***Niklas Luhmann: Society as a System of Communication HANS-GEORG MOELLER 367. Philosophical Profiles in the Theory of Communication*. Accessed August 20, 2021. https://**

In his later adult life, Luhmann held these memories in his mind. His theory of society proposes radical notions—such as sociology not necessarily being about people, but of environmental factors. That is, society is more ecological than sociological. Also, he held that polar extremes in society are necessary. These radical views are but one reason Luhmann's writings were so complicated and hard to understand. I cover this in more detail at another point in the book, but in sum, Luhmann's antithetical ideas were at risk of triggering uproar; therefore, he was incentivized to package his complex views with difficult prose. He did this to shield himself from being read by casual readers.

Luhmann's Zettelkasten served a critical function in doing this (among many other things), and would later assist his ideas in gaining notoriety. Eventually Luhmann became one of the greatest modern social theory thinkers of our time. His system for managing his theories—the Zettelkasten—informs and inspires knowledge workers to this day.

Yet there's one issue emerging today which risks watering down the impact of the Zettelkasten system Luhmann devised. That's what we shall talk about next.

SPECIFIC PRINCIPLES VS. GENERAL PRINCIPLES

It is my belief that there is a risk to Luhmann's Zettelkasten system becoming misinterpreted and thereby morphed into something it is not.

A *principle* is defined as a fundamental truth that serves as the foundation for a system.[9] Seems straightforward, right? The problem today is that the *specific principles* of the Zettelkasten system that Luhmann himself specified in his own paper are being cast as *general principles*.[10] The *specific principles* of

---

www.peterlang.com/view/9781453902028/9781453902028.00019.xml.

9 Angus Stevenson, and Christine A. Lindberg, eds. *New Oxford American Dictionary 3rd Edition*. Oxford ; New York: Oxford University Press, 2010.

10 Luhmann, "Communicating with Slip Boxes," accessed May 4, 2021, https://luhmann.surge.sh/communicating-with-slip-boxes; Niklas Luhmann, "Communication with Noteboxes (Revised Edition)," trans. Manfred Kuehn, https://daily.scottscheper.com/zettelkasten/.

Luhmann's Zettelkasten system were cast aside and written off as unnecessary and archaic. Luhmann's system is built entirely of physical, not digital, parts. With those parts of Luhmann's system stripped away, deleted, and morphed from physical form to metaphysical form, the critical essence of the Zettelkasten system has been demoted. The parts have been deleted and replaced with analogous abstractions, with the belief that the original parts were non-critical. In reality, these substituted *parts* are indeed *very critical* to the *whole*!

This entirely different system I'm alluding to is that of digital notetaking apps. These apps possess functionality enabling one to link notes. Even though such apps are thought of as a Zettelkasten, the magic that Luhmann built into his system is lost. Or at the very least, much of the Zettelkasten magic is replaced by something else entirely.

Digital notetaking apps with note-linking capability are often thought of as Zettelkasten systems. This is not the case. As a result, people who are newly curious about Zettelkasten end up hopelessly lost and confused. Or people end up *thinking* they understand what a Zettelkasten is. They proceed to take thousands of digital notes before they realize they're lost and confused. They're left with a mess of digital information, and they have no idea why they even began to take notes in the first place.

I'm not against progress; however, it becomes confusing when a new concept (i.e. digital notetaking apps with linking capabilities) ensconces itself in a term used by an entirely different concept (i.e. Niklas Luhmann's Zettelkasten).

At the core of this situation rests the delineation of *specific* vs. *general principles.*

Let's first discuss *general principles.*

I am not a fan of creating your own instantiation of a system and then referring to it as if it's identical to that which it was inspired by.

Take a deep breath, and reread that paragraph.

OK, now let me give you an example of this. Let's start with a *wiki*. A wiki is an information source developed collaboratively by a community of users. It allows any user to add and edit content.[11] If I were to create my own version of a wiki in physical form, and if, as a result of the different medium, I were forced to alter and change the essence of how it works, I would hope that I wouldn't do one thing—and that is this: I hope I wouldn't call it a wiki! Doing so would confuse everyone; I would term the new system (inspired by a wiki) differently, since it's new. It is (only) inspired by the concept of wiki. I also would not force those who still use digital wiki systems to forever specify that they use *digital wikis* (as opposed to my new *analog wiki*). Yet this rather absurd illustration is precisely what has taken place with regards to the Zettelkasten. If you use a physical Zettelkasten system today, with the same principles that Luhmann used, one is forced to specify that they're using an *analog Zettelkasten*, or a *Luhmannian Zettelkasten* (as opposed to a *Zettelkasten*—that is, a digital notetaking app with linking functionality).

Look, I am not against identifying *general principles* and adapting such principles into more convenient forms in support of your own personal preferences and goals. Research in knowledge science espouses the view that "general principles should be adapted by individuals." Even ancient learned scholars believed this to be necessary. Early modern Europe produced strict doctrinaire thinkers. One such thinker was the Jesuit pedagogue, Jeremias Drexel (1570–1625). Drexel once asserted, "If [the] precepts and rules of notetaking do not please you, draw up other precepts for yourself, fewer in number, shorter, suited to your studies, just as long as you take notes."[12]

The question then becomes: in Niklas Luhmann's Zettelkasten, what stands as a *general principle* and what stands as a *specific principle*? That is, what could be altered and eliminated in the name of inspiration, and what is a *specific principle* that must be strictly adhered to if one were to strive to use the same system Luhmann used when he used the term *Zettelkasten*?

---

11 Stevenson and Lindberg, eds. *New Oxford American Dictionary 3rd Edition.*

12 Richard Yeo. *Notebooks, Recollection, and External Memory: Some Early Modern English Ideas and Practices.* Brill, 2016, 139.

On this matter, I have two beliefs:

First, I believe that *general principles* in a Zettelkasten system are processes—such as how one takes notes from the materials one reads. So-called *literature notes* are an example of a *general principle* in a Zettelkasten. Relatedly, the term *literature notes* is suboptimal. *Literature notes* was a term never used by Niklas Luhmann, but was popularized by modern authors who loosely interpret Luhmann's system. Furthermore, the term *literature note* renders the types of notes Luhmann took as ambiguous.[13]

The bottom line is that the manner in which you take notes while reading is an example of adhering to a *general principle.* Reason being, the process of taking notes while reading is a *highly personalized activity.* The content you select while reading, and the manner and style in which you *choose* to extract that selection is highly personalized. How you do it must be adapted by you. As the scholar, Alberto Cevolini, puts it, "what attracts attention and is deemed memorable in a book may not be the same for all readers. By definition, information retrieval is a *selective performance*; in turn, selection is a highly personalized activity."[14]

My second belief concerns itself with what constitutes *specific principles* in a Zettelkasten system.

I suggest that there are four principles which are *specific principles* in a Zettelkasten.

I am not the first to propose that a Zettelkasten consists of four principles. The first person to do so was Niklas Luhmann himself. He referred to the principles as *requirements.* The second individual to outline its four principles was Johannes Schmidt, the scholar who perhaps knows Luhmann's work best.[15]

---

13 **Luhmann took different types of notes. Some were word-for-word excerpts (i.e. quotes), some were notes that were brief observations, and some were summaries in his own words of what he read. I'll discuss these types of notes in detail later.**

14 **Alberto Cevolini, ed. *Forgetting Machines: Knowledge Management Evolution in Early Modern Europe.* Library of the Written Word, volume 53. Leiden; Boston: Brill, 2016, 4.**

15 **Undisciplined, "Archiving Luhmann w/ Johannes Schmidt," 2021, https://www.youtube.**

The principles I'm presenting are mapped onto Luhmann's four principles; however, in my perfectly biased opinion, they are more simple and useful in understanding the Zettelkasten. Plus, they form a cool acronym!

Three of the four principles I introduce are referred to by Luhmann as *internal requirements*. One of the four principles he specified was referred to as an *external requirement*.[16]

It's worth noting that my views on what stands as a *general principle* vs. *specific principle* remain an area in which I hold different opinions than others. Sascha Fast, a leading educator of the Zettelkasten system and who operates perhaps the most visited website pertaining to the Zettelkasten (zettelkaste.de), quotes the Israeli fitness trainer, Ido Portal who says, "Principles are higher than techniques. Principles produce techniques in an instant."[17] This quote implies that the four specific principles outlined by Niklas Luhmann are merely *techniques* that could be adapted and adjusted freely without worry of compromising the whole.

Fast goes on to outline several principles, such as the "Principle of Atomicity" which pertains to the idea that one should "put things that belong together into a single note, give it an ID, but limit its content to that single topic." [18] Fast's second principle, labeled the "Principle of Connectivity," argues for alternative techniques for implementing two of the principles Luhmann specifies as internal requirements for a Zettelkasten system, that of (1) "the possibility of arbitrary internal branching," and (2) "possibility of linking" via the numeric-alpha addressing scheme used by Luhmann.[19]

---

com/watch?v=kz2K3auPLWU, 34:00. Johannes Schmidt's version of Luhmann's principles is as follows: (1) a "specific system of organization", (2) "rules of numbering", (3) "internal system of linking", and (4) a "Comprehensive keyword index."

16 Luhmann, "Communicating with Slip Boxes."

17 "Getting Started • Zettelkasten Method," accessed June 28, 2021, https://zettelkasten.de/posts/overview/.

18 "Getting Started • Zettelkasten Method." Accessed June 28, 2021. https://zettelkasten.de/posts/overview/.

19 Luhmann, "Communicating with Slip Boxes," accessed May 4, 2021, https://luhmann.surge.sh/communicating-with-slip-boxes; Niklas Luhmann, "Zettelkasten,", accessed

I do not hold the first principle (the "Principle of Atomicity") as a *general principle* because Luhmann *generally* did not abide by such a principle. One idea per note is a convenient idea espoused by many people, but it is largely a myth as it pertains to Luhmann's system.[20] Yet, for digital Zettelkasten, I agree with Fast in that it's probably a useful practice.

The same applies to Fast's "Principle of Connectivity." Perhaps it's a useful practice for digital Zettelkasten; however, it essentially demotes two of Luhmann's core principles (the "internal branching" tree-like structure of notes, and the numeric-alpha addressing of notes) and passes them off as mere "techniques."

The reason this is important to know, and why it's worthy of your time, centers on the fact that when too many aspects of a system are relegated to abstractions, you generalize it so severely that it transforms the original system into something it is not. It strips away a system's unique, rough personality and smooths it down into a watered-down, blurry image of what it once was. The image you see when you squint your eyes at the Mona Lisa: is it the Mona Lisa you're seeing? Or a blurred-out version? More directly, if you define the principles of a Zettelkasten as something that is founded on *atomicity*, and *connectivity*, then thousands of systems could qualify as a Zettelkasten. Wikipedia could be considered a Zettelkasten by these principles (even though it's not). A website could be regarded as a Zettelkasten in that case. A thesaurus (with its *See also* references) could be considered a Zettelkasten. Or, as most people believe, a digital notetaking app with note-linking functionality (via something popularized with the term *wikilinks*), yes definitely this, could even be considered a Zettelkasten. In the considerable amount of time I've spent working with an analog Zettelkasten—one which adheres to Luhmann's four principles—I can say that such a system operates much

---

August 3, 2021, https://daily.scottscheper.com/zettelkasten/.

20 This idea was popularized by Sönke Ahrens in his book, and has since been spread rapidly throughout Personal Knowledge Management communities online. For the source of this myth, one may consult his book *How to Take Smart Notes: One Simple Technique to Boost Writing, Learning and Thinking: For Students, Academics and Nonfiction Book Writers*. North Charleston, SC: CreateSpace, 2017.

differently than any of these things. In other words, Luhmann's Zettelkasten system stands apart as an entirely different entity compared with Wikipedia, websites, thesauri, and digital "Zettelkasten."

These are but philosophical views; however, I consider it essential to present the idea that one ought to take seriously the requirements that Luhmann himself specified. One should take these requirements seriously enough to at least try them out. I've found the four principles to be pivotal in my experience working with a Zettelkasten.

For the time being, I'll continue referring to the analog Zettelkasten as a Zettelkasten; however, in a little bit I'll introduce the four specific principles adopted by Niklas Luhmann. After I do this, I'll be introducing a new term that I believe encompasses Luhmann's system more accurately. In the meantime, the term Zettelkasten shall suffice.

In brief, a Zettelkasten possesses four specific principles. These four principles define what a Zettelkasten is. However, before I share these principles with you, I'd like to turn to what a Zettelkasten *is not*. Why? Because it helps demystify the essence of a Zettelkasten in preparation for being introduced to what it actually is.

Let's dive into this now.

THE TERM ZETTELKASTEN

I lied. Before I tell you what a Zettelkasten is not, let's hone in on the term *Zettelkasten* itself.

The term Zettelkasten in American English translates to *notebox*. The term *notebox* is the shortened form of a "notecard box." *Zettel* is the German word for *note*, and *kasten* is the German word for *box*.

The reason this is worthy of mention is because of the widespread misinterpretation of the term Zettelkasten. When searching the web, one finds references of it as a "slipbox."

The reason *slip* is translated from *zettel* stems from a translation defining it as a *slip of paper*. In popular English-German translation dictionaries, *slip of paper* remains listed but is no longer used as the preferred definition.[21] The most widely used and arguably the "best among all" translation sources is one that does not hold *slip* as the most correct term for *zettel*.[22] It holds that the most correct translation for the term *zettel* is simply a *note*.

The mix-up with *slip* vs. *note* stems from specifications provided by the American National Standards Institute ("ANSI") and the European paper standards, International Organization for Standardization ("ISO").[23]

The type of paper used by Luhmann is not commonly found in the US. I know this, of course, because it's the first thing I tried getting my hands on after learning what type of paper Luhmann used. It's tricky to find, but more tricky is finding cabinets with drawers that can properly store such paper. The paper size used by Luhmann is ISO's paper size, *A6*, which is 4.1 inches by 5.8 inches. According to ISO standard 2784, the American equivalent of A6 paper is paper sized 4 inches by 6 inches, which are notecards (or blank index cards).[24]

In brief, Luhmann used *zettel* (i.e. *note*) to refer to a *notecard*. In other words, a *zettel* is a *notecard*; Luhmann never used *zettel* in the manner in which people use it today—which is to connote a digital document containing text, usually in markdown format.

---

21 "Zettel—English translation in English—Langenscheidt dictionary German-English." Accessed July 17, 2021. https://en.langenscheidt.com/german-english/zettel.

22 "(4) Is Google Translator the Best among All?" Quora. Accessed July 17, 2021. https://www.quora.com/Is-Google-Translator-the-best-among-all; "Google Translate." Accessed July 17, 2021. https://translate.google.com/?sl=de&tl=en&text=zettel&op=translate.

23 Printleaf's Blog for Design and Printing Solutions. "Standard U.S vs European Paper Sizes Infographic," January 18, 2018. https://blog.printleaf.com/standard-us-vs-european-paper-sizes-what-you-need-to-know.

24 "Paper Size." In *Wikipedia*, July 9, 2021. https://en.wikipedia.org/w/index.php?title=Papersize&oldid=1032765899.

In Luhmann's formative article on his Zettelkasten system, "Communication with Noteboxes," Luhmann meant *notebox* as in *notecard box*; he did not refer to a note as some metaphysical instantiation of a notecard; he would otherwise refer to that as a *thought*.

From this one ought not to discount the importance of notecards—with their physical properties that include having a static fixed place in space, and limitations on character-length which they strictly enforce by their size. One also must not discount the effect these properties had in shaping and forming Luhmann's thoughts. Why? Because the medium one uses not only *is* the message, it develops the message.[25]

This may seem like dry material, but I assure you, it's necessary knowledge if you wish to properly adopt and use a Zettelkasten system and avoid the landmines you'll face the second you begin exploring the concept of Zettelkasten outside this clear canvas I'm about to paint for you. It's straightforward that *Zettelkasten* means *notebox* if you've read what I've written here. Be forewarned, however; as soon as you begin surfing the web or watching YouTube videos, you'll begin to come upon descriptions of Zettelkasten that are outdated, misguided, or flat-out wrong (unless you've stumbled onto my YouTube videos, of course)!

Now that you know that *Zettelkasten* translates to *notebox*, it's time to belabor this matter further by exploring the next topic: *what a Zettelkasten is not.*

WHAT A ZETTELKASTEN IS NOT

Zettelkasten does not refer to *any* notebox system. For instance it does not connote a notebox organized by human-readable top-level concepts or names, such as the system described by the author Ryan Holiday (which he adapted from the author Robert Greene).[26]

25 "The Medium Is the Message." In *Wikipedia*, November 25, 2021. https://en.wikipedia.org/w/index.php?title=Themediumisthemessage&oldid=1057037064.

26 For instance, a Zettelkasten is not the equivalent found in Ryan Holiday, "The Notecard System: The Key For Remembering, Organizing And Using Everything You Read." *RyanHoliday.net* (blog), April 1, 2014. https://ryanholiday.net/the-notecard-system-the-key-for-remembering-organizing-and-using-everything-you-read/.

Luhmann makes it clear that what he means by the term *notebox* is not a "mere container from which we can retrieve what we put in."[27] When Luhmann writes of "communication with noteboxes," he's not really communicating with noteboxes but *with what the notebox becomes*. What he's communicating with, he says, is a system that can "communicate" in the first place. The benefit of a communication partner is the learning that comes through not only new information, but through *accidents* and *surprises*. We'll cover these in detail later on in this book. Accidents and surprises emerge not via dynamically-structured notecards ordered by topic; rather, the magic Luhmann writes about emerges from the interplay of four specific principles he outlines. This is but one reason why *just any* notebox system does not connote a Luhmannian notebox system.

In brief, a Ryan Holiday notebox system is not a Zettelkasten.

A Zettelkasten is also not the equivalent of a *commonplace book*, which is essentially a notebook organized by topic. The limitations of commonplace books centers around the following: they only enable short-term knowledge development. They do not cater to allowing thoughts to evolve over time, infinitely. They do not allow for the infinite internal branching and expansion of ideas. One of the four principles of the Zettelkasten (the true Zettelkasten) enables this expansion. This sets the Zettelkasten system apart from all others.

Let's hone in for a moment on commonplace books.

I find the people who prefer analog thinking systems are oftentimes those who greatly value commonplace books. Actually, I think commonplace books are fantastic thinking systems; yet they pale in comparison to the Antinet over the long haul.

Commonplace books are closely related to florilegia. These were notebooks containing religious verses and excerpts grouped by theme. When I refer to this type of knowledge system I refer to commonplace books. These types of tools were incredible tools for advancing science and knowledge—

---

27 Luhmann, "Communicating with Slip Boxes"; Luhmann, "Zettelkasten."

especially during the Renaissance. One scholar refers to these tools as "the person-plus-notebook-system."[28]

There are many great thinkers throughout history who used commonplace books. Thomas Jefferson was an avid user of commonplace books. Dutch humanist, Desiderius Erasmus (1446-1536) was an ardent advocate of commonplace books.[29] Sigmund Freud used a "new kind of notebook, the 'wunderblock' or (magic notepad)."[30] Behind the cool name is the same thing: a commonplace book.

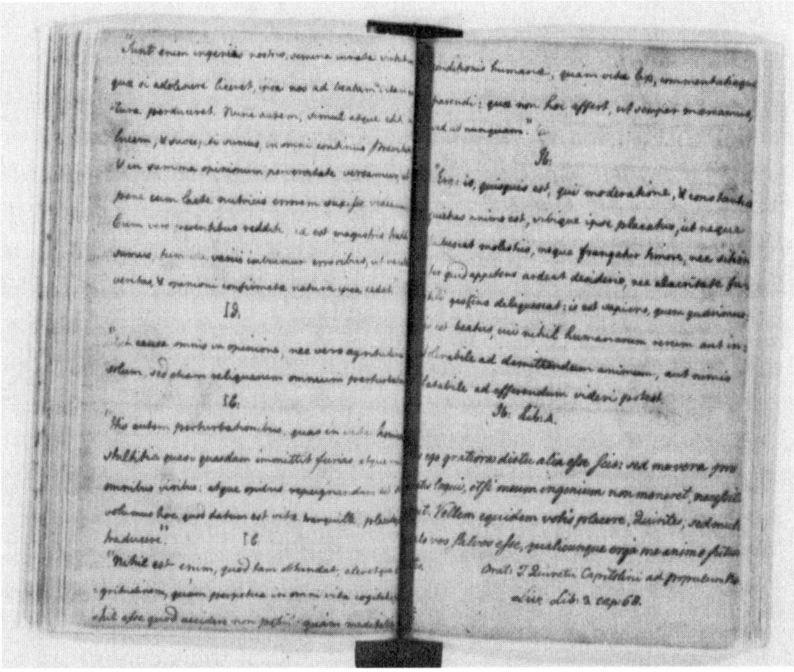

An image of one of Thomas Jefferson's commonplace books.
PHOTO CREDIT: "Image 36 of Thomas Jefferson, 1758-1772, Literary Commonplace Book," image, Library of Congress, Washington, D.C. 20540 USA, accessed May 4, 2022.

---

28 Richard Yeo, *Notebooks, Recollection, and External Memory: Some Early Modern English Ideas and Practices* (Brill, 2016), 131.

29 Richard Yeo, *Notebooks, Recollection, and External Memory: Some Early Modern English Ideas and Practices* (Brill, 2016), 135.

30 Richard Yeo, *Notebooks, Recollection, and External Memory: Some Early Modern English Ideas and Practices* (Brill, 2016), 129.

Yet, there are shortcomings of commonplace books. They embody that of a "subsidiary memory," whereas the Antinet is more than this. The Antinet is a *second mind*, an equal. In fact, you'll oftentimes find yourself humbled by the knowledge the Antinet surfaces. The idea of the Antinet as something greater than a subsidiary memory, does not come from myself. It actually originates from scholars who analyzed both commonplace books and Antinet Zettelkasten systems. "The florilegium was a type of 'double memory' to which scholars could resort anytime their personal memory failed, the filing cabinet behaves as a true communication partner with its own idiosyncrasies and its own opinions."[31]

As one scholar observes, florilegium and commonplace books act as just another *ego*, whereas an Antinet behaves as an *alter ego*. It's no surprise to learn that Luhmann referred to his own Antinet as an *alter ego*.[32]

An *ego* is the conscious sense of *self*. It's what you think of when you use the word 'I'.[33]

When you write down your thoughts in commonplace book or Moleskine notebook, you see yourself in them. It's a linear version of yourself. It's less chaotic in nature usually because each page is closely related in time.

An *alter ego* is a second identity. It's a second mind that exists metaphorically.[34] The alter ego exists either as a substitute or a representative of your mind, yet it possesses unique characteristics. It possesses its own unique personality. Think of Superman, compared with his alter ego, Clark Kent.

---

31 Alberto Cevolini, ed., Forgetting Machines: Knowledge Management Evolution in Early Modern Europe, Library of the Written Word, volume 53 (Leiden ; Boston: Brill, 2016), 28-29.

32 Niklas Luhmann, "Communication with Noteboxes (Revised Edition)," trans. Manfred Kuehn, https://daily.scottscheper.com/zettelkasten/.

33 "Ego—APA Dictionary of Psychology," accessed December 13, 2021, https://dictionary.apa.org/ego.

34 "Alter Ego—APA Dictionary of Psychology," accessed December 13, 2021, https://dictionary.apa.org/alter-ego.

The Antinet is more of an alter ego. It develops its own unique personality whom you communicate with.

An Antinet is not a collection of excerpts, quotes, kindle highlights, or florilegia. It's something more complex than these types of devices. The Antinet is not a subsidiary memory; it's a second mind.

In brief, if you've ever kept a notebook containing your thoughts and readings, and organized them by category, that's not a Zettelkasten system, nor is it something which I believe you'll ever want to go back to once you begin using a Zettelkasten.

I won't cover the advantages and disadvantages of such systems here; just for now, know that they're quite different from a Zettelkasten system.

WHAT A ZETTELKASTEN SYSTEM IS

I hold, like Niklas Luhmann held, that his notebox system is built on four specific principles. One of the principles (or requirements) is *external* according to Luhmann, which means it lives in physical reality. The other three principles are *internal* concepts, which means that they are more metaphysical in nature—though they are present within the physical principle.

THE FOUR PRINCIPLES OF A (TRUE) ZETTELKASTEN

Principle #1: Analog

The first principle is what Luhmann referred to as an *external* requirement for a Zettelkasten. By *external,* Luhmann meant it's something that is physical in nature: "Wooden boxes, which have drawers that can be pulled open, and pieces of paper."[35]

Luhmann referred to this principle as a *mere externality*; however, he referred to it as *mere* for good reason. At the time there was no metaphysical, internal way of memorizing knowledge other than resorting to the mnemonic techniques. Such techniques were used by ancient Greek thinkers like Socrates. This involved mapping metaphysical thoughts onto physical items present

---

35 Luhmann, "Communicating with Slip Boxes"; Luhmann, "Zettelkasten."

in either a literal or an imagined room or space. The physical objects acted as *cues* allowing one to better *recall* any *thought* stored in memory.

Believe it or not, at the time when learned scholars and thinkers began to transition from such mnemonic techniques (which are metaphysical in nature) to notes stored in physical materials (such as was tablets, and later on, paper), it was met with much resistance—even Socrates himself, we learn by way of his followers, derided the emerging popularity of taking physical notes.[36] Plato echoed the same sentiment as Socrates: "According to Plato, the true learned man should rather be autonomous. He should not ask for help coming from the outside; instead, he should be able to help himself, especially in face-to-face interactions."[37] Yet Plato also began adopting the idea of storing thoughts in physical materials. His tool of choice was the wax tablet.[38]

In my opinion, using physical materials to work with knowledge unlocks some of the most powerful results. Later in the book, I detail why I believe the analog component to be so important. I will also share research and specific illustrations showing why physical materials are so critical to developing knowledge. To that end, Luhmann did not need to specify *analog* as a requirement over *digital*. Why? Because digital tools were not an option when he started building his Zettelkasten. I have reason to believe that if Niklas Luhmann were alive today he would continue using his analog Zettelkasten. There's magic within the analog medium incapable of being reproduced in digital tools. I will share why I believe this to be the case later on in this book.

---

36 Ann M. Blair, *Too Much to Know: Managing Scholarly Information before the Modern Age*, First Edition (New Haven, Conn.: Yale University Press, 2011), 78.

37 Cevolini, ed., *Forgetting Machines*, 1.

38 Related note: I ended up purchasing a wax tablet to experience what it would've been like for Plato in developing his knowledge. I found it surprising how useful the tool is; it's almost like a portable whiteboard. However its key differences are: 1) its more painful to write knowledge down so you must be very deliberate in thinking before you write, 2) the limitation of space forces you to be very concise (and thus err on the side of writing down short words, or *cues*, that trigger a longer thought).

Principle #2: Numeric-alpha Notecard Addresses

Perhaps the most important principle in Luhmann's notebox system is that of the *numeric-alpha* notecard addresses. *Numeric-alpha* refers to card addresses which start with a number and then are combined with alphabetical characters to branch down and internally expand to an infinite degree. This simple practice creates a self-referential object for every single one of your *thoughts*. This enables what Luhmann phrased, "the possibility of linking."[39] Linking thoughts is the very thing which enables the system to become self-referential in nature, a *cybernetic* network as Luhmann thought of it.[40]

What is meant by *addresses* should also not be overlooked. In the first Zettelkasten Luhmann created in the 1950's, he used a convention that employed commas for separating his different branches of thought in his Antinet. For instance, his notecard "5,1A" contained an excerpted quote by an author.[41] In Luhmann's second Zettelkasten, which was built specifically to help him with his thirty-year-long undertaking to create a unified theory of everything as it applies to society, he used a mix of slashes and periods and commas. For instance: '21/1,1'.[42] I simply use the numeric-alpha scheme combined with slashes (I do not use commas or periods as separators). For instance: '27/2A/12'. I've yet to find it necessary or natural to use periods or commas. Regardless, we'll explore in detail the specific schemes and practices of building your own Antinet later in the book. The beauty of the system is that there's not a strict computer science protocol. There's no scheme you must adhere to in order to work with the system. You can mold it and work with it in the way your brain most prefers (as long as you operate within the framework of the four principles I'm introducing now)!

Now back to the concept of *card addresses* for a moment. When people first see a card address like, '27/2A/12' they immediately think it adheres to a

---

39 Luhmann, "Communicating with Slip Boxes."; Luhmann, "Zettelkasten."

40 "ZK II: Note 9/8—Niklas Luhmann Archive." Accessed January 10, 2022. https://niklas-luhmann-archiv.de/bestand/zettelkasten/zettel/ZK_2_NB_9-8_V.

41 "ZK I: Note 5.1a—Niklas Luhmann Archive"" accessed January 11, 2022, https://niklas-luhmann-archiv.de/bestand/zettelkasten/zettel/ZK_1_NB_5-1a_V.

42 "ZK II: Zettel 21/1,1—Niklas Luhmann-Archiv," accessed January 11, 2022, https://niklas-luhmann-archiv.de/bestand/zettelkasten/zettel/ZK_2_NB_21-1-1_V.

hierarchical structure. The address does not indicate a hierarchy, however. It's merely the *location* of where the leaf lives on a branch of your tree. Think of it more like a *geographic coordinate system,* like latitude and longitude (for instance '-77.0364,38.8951'). The periods do not connote a hierarchy; the address '27/2A/12' could simply be represented as '27.2A.12', and that would be just fine. It's a matter of personal preference.

Anyway, we're in the weeds here. Much about numeric-alpha addresses will be covered later on in this book. For now, just know that this is perhaps the most important principle of Luhmann's four principles. It also happens to be the principle that people *overthink* the most, too! Assigning a numeric-alpha address to a notecard paralyzes people. It can be the thing that kills your progress. This all stems from one's internal tendency towards perfectionism. Digital notetaking tools have trained many to be perfectionists (even at the expense of being productive). This tendency is something we'll be fixing. With the Antinet you'll learn to focus on what really matters: developing knowledge (not cutesy bubble graphs displaying connected digital notes). I'll be teaching you to major in the major (instead of majoring in the minor). Don't worry, I'm here to help in your recovery.

Again, the importance of numeric-alpha addresses cannot be emphasized enough. It not only enables linking, it enables the self-referential composition of the Zettelkasten which gives it a unique *personality*. Luhmann holds this as one of the most important aspects of the system. The unique personality stands as the raw material which will help the Zettelkasten morph into an unexpected structure allowing you to *communicate* with the *second mind,* the *doppelgänger,* the *ghost (or spirit, or mind) in the box,* as Luhmann referred to it.[43] This is the entity Luhmann was suggesting would communicate when he titled his paper, "*Communication with Noteboxes.*" Numeric-alpha addresses make this possible.

---

43 "ZK II: Note 9 / 8.3 - Niklas Luhmann Archive," accessed January 11, 2022, https://niklas-luhmann-archiv.de/bestand/zettelkasten/zettel/ZK_2_NB_9-8-3_V.

Principle #3: Tree

The third principle Luhmann specifies is a structure that allows for "the possibility of arbitrary internal branching."[44]

Luhmann realized early on in life—thanks partly to his experiences being tortured by the so-called *good guys* at the end of World War II—that the world is not so simple. It's quite complex. Reality resolves to nature, which resolves to chaos. If scientists seek to discover and publish the truth, then it's necessary to accept chaos. Life is not a simple dualistic affair, as Luhmann discovered. It's not always one of *good vs. evil.* The world is complex, and so is the human mind.

With this understood, the question then becomes: how can one devise a system built on that which best models reality? Reality is chaos, yet it also emerges from ordered and simplistic rules (think the laws of thermodynamics). Reality (chaos) also emerges from simplistic parts (for instance, the atomic theory posits that matter is composed of particles called atoms). Reality is chaos built out of simple laws of order, and units of order. These simple laws and units of order bind the system together, allowing one to navigate complexity. It was with this in mind that Luhmann crafted his notebox system.

Within the current popularity of communities forming around Personal Knowledge Management ("PKM") systems, it's become a popular idea to embrace so-called *dynamic* systems—ones that are *fluid* and are built on things like *wikilinks,* and *tags.* An idea taught in the popular PKM course, *Linking Your Thinking,* preaches this idea in dogmatic fashion: "Folders are rigid and exclusionary by their nature. Whatever is in a folder lives separated from the main collection. It's a rigid hierarchy that imposes order."[45] This notion, however, is mere pop-productivity opinion. Luhmann's Zettelkasten

44 Niklas Luhmann, "Communicating with Slip Boxes by Niklas Luhmann," trans. Manfred Kuehn, accessed May 4, 2021, https://luhmann.surge.sh/communicating-with-slip-boxes.

45 "1c.3 Using Folders—LYT Curriculum / Unit 1—PKM & Idea Emergence," Linking Your Thinking, accessed October 25, 2021, https://forum.linkingyourthinking.com/t/1c-3-using-folders/142/2.

was not *dynamic,* nor was it *fluid.* It could be argued that it was built entirely of folders (in the digital computer directory sense). The reason why a dynamic, fluid structure is one you ought not to strive for centers on the following fact: such a structure would be lacking in rough, unique conventions. It would lack a unique personality, which is what Luhmann's system optimized for. In brief, it would not mirror the systems found in nature.

Simply stated, Luhmann's Zettelkasten structure was not *dynamic* or *fluid* in nature. Yet, it was not *rigid,* either. Examples of a *rigid* structure are classification systems like the Dewey Decimal System, or Paul Otlet's massive notecard world museum known as *The Mundaneum.* These types of systems are useful for *interpersonal knowledge systems;* however, they're not illustrative of what Niklas Luhmann's system was: an *intrapersonal knowledge system.* Luhmann's notebox system was not logically or neatly organized in a way that allowed for convenient public access. It was pure chaos to anyone (other than its creator) who perused its contents. In other words, Luhmann's Zettelkasten was not a structure that could be characterized as one of *order.*

In brief, Luhmann's notebox system was not *dynamic* and *fluid.* Yet it was not one of *order,* either.

So what are we to think of Luhmann's notebox system? In my experience using it, I find it to be more *organic* in nature. Like nature, it has laws and rules by which it operates; yet, it's also subject to complete and total *random* choice. We know this because in describing it, Luhmann uses the word *arbitrary* to describe its *arbitrary internal branching.* Defined, *arbitrary,* means something that is decided *randomly* on personal whim.[46] This *arbitrary, random* structure contributes to one of its greatest aspects—the aspect of *surprises.* Even though I'd call it an *organic* structure, that term seems rather trite. Other ways you can think of it is as a *molecular* structure, or an *atomic* structure. Yet, in recent time, concepts like *atomicity,* as I've touched on, have been overused and abstracted unnecessarily. Sure, *atomicity* could be considered a property of the Zettelkasten, but it could be argued *atomicity* is a property of nearly everything that is composed of matter!

46 Stevenson and Lindberg, eds., *New Oxford American Dictionary 3rd Edition.*

Let's not get carried away, however. Let's jump back to the question: how are we to think of Luhmann's notebox system?

It's actually quite simple, and I'll share with you precisely how you should think of the Zettelkasten in just a moment. Until then, it's important to close the loop on the characteristic which describes it.

One of the scholars who studied Luhmann's Zettelkasten closest is the researcher Johannes Schmidt from Bielefeld University in Germany. Bielefeld is the same university Luhmann worked at, and where he used his Zettelkasten to devise his impressive social theoretical work. It's no coincidence that Schmidt knows Luhmann's system so well. Schmidt has spent countless hours sifting through Luhmann's notebox card-by-card in person. He's currently the scientific coordinator of the project to digitize Luhmann's notebox and publish its contents online for all to explore.[47] According to Schmidt, Luhmann's notebox system is "a rough structure."[48] It's organized "by subject areas, which is reflected in the first number assigned to the card."[49] The characteristic which describes a Zettelkasten is simply this: it's a *rough structure* that consists of both "order and disorder."[50]

Now that we know the characteristic of a Zettelkasten not as a *dynamic, fluid* structure, nor a structure of complete *order*, we can think of it as a *rough* structure. Yet, knowing this gets us only so far. Knowing the abstract characteristic of a system is nice, yes, but not really that useful in practice. For this reason, I'll share with you what I've found to be the best illustration of what type of structure a Zettelkasten is.

---

47 "PEVZ: Johannes Schmidt - Contact (Bielefeld University)," accessed January 11, 2022, https://ekvv.uni-bielefeld.de/perspubl/publ/PersonDetail.jsp?personId=25653450.

48 Johannes Schmidt, "Niklas Luhmann's Card Index: Thinking Tool, Communication Partner, Publication Machine," *Forgetting Machines. Knowledge Management Evolution in Early Modern Europe* 53 (2016), https://pub.uni-bielefeld.de/record/2942475, 295.

49 Schmidt, "Niklas Luhmann's Card Index: Thinking Tool," 295.

50 Luhmann, "Communicating with Slip Boxes," accessed May 4, 2021, https://luhmann.surge.sh/communicating-with-slip-boxes; Luhmann, "Communication with a Notebox (Revised Edition)," accessed August 3, 2021, https://daily.scottscheper.com/zettelkasten/.

Think of a Zettelkasten as a tree. A real tree. Not a tree that is platonic in nature. Not a diagram of a tree. Not a tree directory structure that you think of in computer science. Rather think of the Zettelkasten as an actual tree. What does an actual tree contain? It contains a trunk, branches, stems, vines, and leaves. We'll go into detail on this later on in the book; but for now, think of each individual leaf as a notecard. With a Zettelkasten, you'll be building trees of knowledge, one that has different trunks, different branches, different stems of thoughts, and even vines that link to other branches, allowing you to explore and swing between branches and trees.

The importance of the Zettelkasten's tree-like structure should not be overlooked. Human memory works in a way that closely models tree-like structures. Even physically, the human brain, neurons, and neural networks follow branching structures. Some of the most beautiful tree-like images are the networks of the human brain: "If each nerve cell enlarged a thousand fold looks like a tree, then a small region of the nervous system at the same magnified scale resembles a gigantic, fantastic forest."[51]

The structure of your second mind (which is what a Zettelkasten, if built properly, will create) is critically important. It's not just about storing information and creating cool bubble graphs of notes that link together (that's what digital tools focus on); rather, it's about *exploration,* as one scholar put it. The tree structure of the Zettelkasten enables meaningful exploration, as Alberto Cevolini points out: "secondary memories themselves have an inner order that allows for *exploration*."[52]

Later we'll be exploring the *tree* structure of Luhmann's Zettelkasten in more detail. We'll be exploring how to think of it. More practically, we'll be exploring how to *leverage it* to help you develop and evolve your knowledge over time.

---

51 For beautiful images and more exploration on this subject, see: Giorgio A. Ascoli, *Trees of the Brain, Roots of the Mind* (Cambridge, MA: MIT Press, 2015).

52 Cevolini, ed., *Forgetting Machines,* 16. Emphasis added.

Principle #4: Index

The last principle in Luhmann's notebox system is the *index*. Luhmann calls this concept a "Register."[53] I prefer *index*, but you're welcome to use whatever terminology you like best. You can think of the index as a *map*. It's your map for exploring your own *tree of knowledge*.

Say you're traveling, staying in a new location and suddenly you realize you haven't eaten all day. You're starving. You think to yourself, *I'm really craving In-N-Out Burger right now*. You recall seeing an In-N-Out Burger the previous day, but since you're traveling, you're not sure how to get there. You pull out your phone, open your maps app, and then what do you do? Do you type in the latitude-longitude coordinates '32.7794303,-117.242262'? Or, instead, do you type in the human-memorable name known as 'In-N-Out Burger'? Chances are you opt for the human-memorable name. This is precisely how to think of the index for your Zettelkasten. The index is a key-value associative array. They *keyterm* is the human-readable name, and the *value* is the location of the leaf on a tree in your Zettelkasten. For instance, here's an example taken directly from my Zettelkasten: "Truth": '5455/1'.

If you're a software developer or programmer, and you're familiar with data structures like JSON, or Python dictionaries, or YAML arrays, you can get pretty advanced with your index. You can create nested items of key-value pairs. If you're not a nerd (or a wannabe nerd, like me), then don't worry about this stuff. We'll cover keyterms and the index in detail later on (and you won't have to be a computer nerd to understand it).

The bottom line is this: think of the index as your own map that enables you to swing onto a certain leaf, on a certain branch of a certain tree. From there, you can then continue *exploring* by reviewing the nearby stems of thoughts and the individual cards which, themselves, contain remote links. These remote links enable you to swing around to other leaves on other branches of your tree of knowledge. More on this will be revealed later in the book. But for now, you're ready to be introduced to what an Antinet is composed of.

53 Luhmann, "Communicating with Slip Boxes."; Luhmann, "Zettelkasten."

INTRODUCING "THE ANTINET"

To summarize, these are the four principles of a Luhmannian Zettelkasten:

1. it is **A**nalog;
2. it uses **N**umeric-alpha Addresses;
3. it has a **T**ree Structure;
4. and an **I**ndex.

The first letters of each of those four things ("**A**", "**N**", "**T**", "**I**") are what make it an ***Antinet.***

Many people, when first coming across the term *Antinet,* may mistake it for being *anti-digital,* or *anti-technology*. This misinterpretation is something I understand, and frankly, something I take delight in. I snicker at the idea of ruffling people's feathers because there's a part of me that is a troll, just as Niklas Luhmann himself was.

The consequences of this aren't the most pleasant, however. In my very early days sharing this knowledge, I was met with much resistance. In online forums whenever I answered Zettelkasten questions (from an analog perspective), I received polarized reactions. That is, I tended to receive a healthy supply of upvotes, and a heavy supply of downvotes. That's fine with me. I deserved it; however, if you spent some time reading what I actually said, I was not as anti-digital as one would think.

To be clear, I am anti-digital when it comes to a knowledge development system such as the Antinet; but within reason. I understand that some people may operate and think better with digital tools. That's fine. In my book you'll find a section for those who refuse to give up digital media for working with knowledge. It's a compromised version—I strongly believe that—but it may be useful for some. However after you read the science and rationale for an *analog* knowledge development system, I'm confident you'll at least give such a system your best shot first.

Now that I've explained what *Antinet* stands for, I will be using the term *Antinet* as the primary term through the remainder of this book (instead of

Zettelkasten). Here and there I'll drop in the term Zettelkasten; but my preferred term is Antinet. I choose to do this because today the term *Zettelkasten* connotes digital notetaking apps with linking capabilities. Also, the reason I don't just use the term *notebox system* is because it's already used for systems that simply store notecards categorically.[54]

Before we move on, there's one last thing you should know. It pertains to the *net* in *Antinet*.

The "Net" in "Antinet"

The *net* in *Antinet* refers to *network*. To Luhmann, the system he built was a *cybernetic network*. It was *self-referential* in nature because of its ability to cross-reference its contents through the *numeric-alpha* addresses.[55]

Luhmann, familiar with how human memory worked, understood how the brain is structured—as a network, just as we know it today—*a network that possesses approximately 100 billion neurons and 200 trillion connections.*[56]

✻ ✻ ✻

Now that you know the four principles of the notebox network Luhmann designed, you're closer to understanding it. But there's only one problem: you now know *what* an Antinet is, but you still have no idea what an Antinet *really* is. The four principles describe the *parts* of Luhmann's system. They describe its fundamental raw "atomic" material. They do not describe the *whole* it creates—and trust me, the four parts do combine to create a whole greater than the sum of its parts.

---

54 As, for instance, seen in Holiday, "The Notecard System." *RyanHoliday.Net* (blog), April 1, 2014. https://ryanholiday.net/the-notecard-system-the-key-for-remembering- organizing-and-using-everything-you-read/.

55 "ZK II: Note 9/8 - Niklas Luhmann Archive." Accessed January 10, 2022. https://niklas-luhmann-archiv.de/bestand/zettelkasten/zettel/ZK_2_NB_9-8_V.

56 Michael Jacob Kahana, *Foundations of Human Memory.* (New York: Oxford University Press, 2014), 30.

When the four principles are combined into a system, the Antinet becomes a *thinking tool*, a *communication partner*, and a *second mind*. They combine to produce many other novel phenomena, such as insightful *surprises* by way of ordered *randomness*. The Antinet becomes a system where *thought* is developed—both in the short term (by way of writing by hand, and thinking on paper) as well as the long term (by its branched architecture that stamps things in time that are most useful later on: this includes mistakes in your own thinking that are stamped in time, which will prove valuable). Also stamped in time is your own mind, and its own context, with its own links (that one thinks of at the time of writing and developing *thought*). In brief, there's a *temporal* context which is stamped and installed into your Antinet. This context, this inner voice, if you will, then develops into a *second mind* enabling you to communicate with it, and in Luhmann's terms, to ask it questions. It is the combination of all four principles which transform the Antinet from a mere notebox into a *second mind*.[57]

Magic takes place when the four principles interact in the Antinet. Johannes Schmidt observes that, when the four principles of an Antinet are combined, "all of them together create a complex cognitive system."[58] This is accomplished, through the four principles, in several ways:

1. The *neuroimprinting* on the mind via its *analog* medium of writing by hand.
2. The "(selective) relations" between notes enabled via the *numeric-alpha addresses*.[59]
3. The "special filing technique", with its *infinite internal branching* via the tree structure.[60]
4. The *index*, which enables you to neuro-imprint ideas and cues in human-memorable language.

57 **It's become a marketing idea of late to refer to a system that stores information as a *second brain*; yet, that's not really what you want, nor is that even a good term for what you're developing with an Antinet. What you're building is a second *mind*. In the scholarly field, this idea is often referred to as an *extended mind*. More on this concept later.**

58 **Undisciplined, "Archiving Luhmann w/ Johannes Schmidt."**

59 **Schmidt, "Niklas Luhmann's Card Index: Thinking Tool," 309.**

60 **Schmidt, "Niklas Luhmann's Card Index: Thinking Tool," 309.**

All of these four elements interact and create unexpected effects, including *reverberation—as it's called* in the science of human memory—allowing you to retain more knowledge and connections than you ever thought possible. You'll begin to notice yourself reading differently. Certain index keyterms arise while reading; all you have to do is write the keyterm down on a notecard (called a "bibcard"). This is what Luhmann did.

As it relates to the four principles, *this structure,* as Johannes Schmidt observes, *demonstrates how quickly* the Antinet sets you on a path away from what one would deem *ordered* (and taxonomically sound). Although seemingly nonsensical, to the creator—that is, to you—the Antinet becomes perfectly natural to understand. One is *led away from the original topic and to a variety of other subjects—ones that would not have initially been associated with one another.*[61] All of these incommunicable experiences are formed by the structure of the Antinet's four principles.

The *whole* of an Antinet is incommunicable—meaning, you'll need to understand it yourself by experiencing it yourself. Don't worry, though. I'll be showing you *precisely* how to build your own Antinet a few chapters from now. Until then, I'd like to share with you a little bit more about what an Antinet *really* is.

WHAT AN ANTINET REALLY IS

An *Antinet,* defined, is composed of four principles which form a *knowledge system* (as well as other systems) which in turn, transforms itself into a *second mind.*

From this definition, it may not seem like much, but there's a lot to unpack here. Unpacking this definition is what I'll be doing in this section. My goal centers on two things: first, to give you a glimpse of the metaphysical experience in working with an Antinet; and second, to do so in a way that isn't boring as hell. Sound good? Let's get started.

---

61 Schmidt, "Niklas Luhmann's Card Index: Thinking Tool," 309.

THE FUNDAMENTALS OF KNOWLEDGE DEVELOPMENT

We'll be discussing the concept of *knowledge development* later. First, though, we need to understand the fundamental raw material of what we're even working with as *knowledge developers*. The best place to start is merely with the question, *What is a thought?*

What Is a "Thought"?

The best way to understand what an Antinet *really* comes from asking what it *contains*.

What does an Antinet actually contain? Notes, yes. But what does a note contain? There are many types of notes, yes. But for all intents and purposes, a note contains one thing: a *thought*.

The latest research in cognitive neuroscience shows that the average person experiences 6,200 thoughts per day.[62] Many of these thoughts are useful, yet they need some time to develop. They need what Luhmann referred to as *rumination* in order to sprout and grow. Unfortunately, most thoughts never have the chance to ruminate. Even if captured digitally, thinkers rarely undertake the practices necessary to sort and make use of all the information they encounter. Why? Simply because they quickly find themselves drowning in too much information (and as a result, too many thoughts). In other words, we experience *thought overload*—and this is especially the case for thoughts enmeshed in digital workflows.

The problem of *thought overload*, however, is the very thing Luhmann figured out how to solve. By way of metaphor, Luhmann's Antinet transforms one's mind into a persistent, supercharged version of itself. Luhmann devised a knowledge structure for his thoughts which transformed his mind—and he admitted he was not naturally very proficient at remembering thoughts.

---

62 "Discovery of 'Thought Worms' Opens Window to the Mind," Queen's Gazette | Queen's University, July 13, 2020, https://www.queensu.ca/gazette/stories/discovery-thought-worms-opens-window-mind.

Luhmann desired to create a *marcescent* tree of knowledge. A *marcescent* tree is one which never loses any of its leaves. It's a phenomenon in nature. Like the leaves of a marcescent tree, Luhmann created a mind that never loses thoughts. Indeed, the Antinet is a mind that never loses its thoughts. It's a marcescent tree. The only risk is if it catches on fire or is destroyed (which is something I'll address later in this book).

OK, let's now address the question: *What actually is a thought in the first place?!* For this answer, let's turn to the dictionary for help.

Perhaps the world's biggest trolls are those working at Merriam-Webster who devised the definition for the word *thought*. By their definition, a thought is *something that comes from thinking.*[63] How profound. If you look up the word *thinking*, you'll learn that it's *something a mind does to produce thoughts.*[64] What we're left with is a circular reference that doesn't tell us very much.

Thankfully from the land of psychology emerges a definition of *thought* that is of more use: a *thought* is simply a representation of reality.[65] In other words, a thought is a reflection or observation of reality. Such things are what you write down on a notecard. Its aim is to represent some aspect of reality (physical or metaphysical reality).

Your thoughts do not live in an isolated universe. They're shaped by several dimensions, which are constantly changing over the course of your life. Thoughts are a product of *self, space, time, reverberation* (recent behaviors and interests), and *content* (current context). These five dimensions stand essentially as a *container* which shapes a *thought*. More on this will be written about later in the book. For now it's worth knowing that one of the core

---

63 "What Actually Is a Thought? And How Is Information Physical? | Psychology Today, "accessed July 29, 2021, https://www.psychologytoday.com/us/blog/finding-purpose/201902/what-actually-is-thought-and-how-is-information-physical.

64 "Definition of THINKING," accessed July 29, 2021, https://www.merriam-webster.com/dictionary/thinking.

65 Ralph Lewis, "What Actually Is a Thought? And How Is Information Physical? | Psychology Today," accessed July 29, 2021, https://www.psychologytoday.com/us/blog/finding-purpose/201902/what-actually-is-thought-and-how-is-information-physical.

strengths of an Antinet is its ability to preserve not just the *thought* itself, but the *container* of dimensions in which a thought is formed.

What Is a 'Memory'?

Great, now you know that a *thought* is. It's your mind's representation of reality. You also know that it's shaped by several dimensions.

The next question is, *what's a memory*?

Before answering this question, one must delineate between *a memory*, and *memory* (as in *human memory*). We'll start with what *a memory* is.

Put simply, *a memory* is a stored representation of a *thought*. Like a *thought*, your memories are also a function of several dimensions which shape it. Scientific experiments in the study of human memory show that different brain regions process different dimensions attributed to a memory. This model of memory is called the *attribute model of memory*. To reiterate, the attribute model of memory asserts a view in which different brain regions process different dimensions of a memory. Like the dimensions of *thought*, the dimensions attributed to a memory include variables like space, time, sensory perceptions, and emotional aspects.[66]

What Is 'Human Memory'?

Now we know what a *thought* is, and what *a memory* is. There's only one more thing we ought to get on the same page about before trying to understand what an Antinet *really* is.

But first, now is a good time to take a step back for a moment. Let's answer the question of why it's even important to understand what an Antinet *really* is.

The reason it's important is that by learning how *knowledge development* works, your own thinking, researching, and publishing output will be greatly enhanced. Even if you decide that building an Antinet is not for you, you

---

66 "Attribute Model of Memory—APA Dictionary of Psychology," accessed November 8, 2021, https://dictionary.apa.org/attribute-model-of-memory.

can still greatly benefit from learning these concepts. Got it? Good. Let's jump back into the fundamentals of knowledge development (*thought, a memory,* and *human memory*).

The last thing you ought to know centers around what *human memory* is.

The reason *memory* can be a confusing concept centers on the fact that *a* memory is different from plain ol' *memory.* **The term *memory* refers to the collective process of encoding, storing, and retrieving *a memory*.**

Now that we know that *a memory* is a stored representation of a *thought,* and a *thought* is your mind's representation of *reality,* effectively, ***human memory* is your mind's ability to encode, store, and retrieve representations of reality.**

This is a greatly simplified conceptualization of *human memory.* Why? Simply because human memory is one of the last major unknowns in the field of neuroscience. Human memory is still a mystery.[67] In my opinion, this is very exciting. Richard Feynman, the revered American theoretical physicist, observed it as "a very important problem which has not been solved at all."[68]

Luhmann was familiar with how human memory works. He understood it not as something composed of one thing; rather, he knew it as something composed of trillions of connections built on *association.* The concept of *association* shall be discussed later in the book. According to Richard Yeo, memory isn't something that happens in the brain alone. It's more complex than that. Memory is "often distributed across heterogenous systems combining neural, bodily, social, and technological resources."[69]

There are different lenses and models scholars use to study human memory. I won't get into them now, nor will I get into the pros and cons of each. The tendency to overcomplicate things plagues the disciplinary field of human

67 Kahana, *Foundations of Human Memory,* 31.

68 Kahana, *Foundations of Human Memory,* ix.

69 Cevolini, ed., *Forgetting Machines,* 129.

memory studies (and, let's be honest, many academic fields as well). Often, scholars fall prey to the complexity cognitive fallacy. They overcomplicate ideas, filling them with unnecessary technobabble when trying to explain something even they don't understand yet.[70] This is why, for now, and for our purposes, the simple definition of human memory I laid out previously will more than suffice in aiding our understanding of what an Antinet *really* is.

Before moving on, here's a summary of the three fundamental components of *knowledge development* we've just learned:

- A *thought* is your mind's representation of *reality*.
- A *memory* is a stored representation of a *thought*.
- *Human memory* is the collective process of encoding, storing, and retrieving *a memory*.

What Is "Reality"?

For the sake of moving forward, I'm tempted to dive right into addressing what an Antinet *really* is; however, I simply can't.

Here's why: if you review the definitions of the three concepts I've laid out previously, there's one concept I haven't properly addressed yet. That concept is, *reality*.

I bet you didn't think you'd be faced with the question *what is reality?* when you began reading about something called an 'Antinet'; but alas, here we are. I'm not going to dive too deeply into the solving of the question of *reality* right now, but I'll give you a better understanding than you might otherwise have had. In brief, no two people share the same reality (*it's, like, relative, man*). In all seriousness, Einstein proved reality is not one fixed state. Reality is really an infinite number of unique realities that depend on *where* you are, and how fast you're moving in spacetime.[71] More pragmatically, there are

70 For an example of this, one need only read academic textbooks on computational theories of human memory. Specifically, see Kahana, *Foundations of Human Memory*, 35–7.

71 Scott Adams, *God's Debris: A Thought Experiment* (Kansas City: Andrews McMeel Publishing, 2004), 85.

three types of reality: (1) *objective reality,* which are things like gravity that we all experience, (2) *subjective reality,* such as pain or another sensation one might experience, and (3) *inter-subjective reality,* which include shared beliefs and sociological concepts (like money, politics, and power).[72]

From a philosophical perspective, the concept of reality has been debated for aeons. There are different ontological positions describing reality. These positions include monism, dualism, pluralism, and my favorite—dialectical monism. I'm not going to continue any further down the philosophical discussion of reality, but for now, think of reality as *any physical or metaphysical truth you experience.* By *physical truth,* this refers to that which your sensory system detects in your environment (sight, smell, taste, touch, sound). By *metaphysical truth,* this refers to that which your mind (or body—via intuition) detects, experiences, and believes to be true. These sensations and insights are your *reality,* and they're represented in *thought.*

OK, whew! We've now successfully gone down the metaphysical and theoretical rabbit-hole. We've addressed what *thought* is, what *a memory* is, what *human memory* is, and what *reality* is. Here's a full summary of four fundamental components involved in *knowledge development*:

- A *thought* is your mind's representation of *reality.*
- A *memory* is a stored representation of a *thought.*
- *Human memory* is the collective process of encoding, storing, and retriev ing *a memory.*
- *Reality* is any physical or metaphysical *truth* you experience.

Your Ultimate Task When Working with an Antinet

What we could technically do next is chase down the definition and our understanding of *truth.* Ultimately this exercise is never-ending. Like the *Antinet,* the *truth* of the cosmos is a *self-referential, recursive* beast. It's filled with seemingly never-ending paradoxes that point back to its *self.*[73] For an

72 Yuval Noah Harari, *Homo Deus: A Brief History of Tomorrow,* Illustrated edition (New York, NY: Harper, 2017), 144.

73 For advanced Antinetters: Here's a sign that you're on the right track when developing

example of what I mean by *self-referential*, let's take the dictionary's definition of *truth*. *The Oxford English Dictionary* defines *truth* as "the quality or state of being true."[74] That's as *self-referential* as it gets right there, and that's the *truth* (I couldn't help it). In brief, we can define truth simply as *that which we believe as true*. From there we can explore the concept of *belief*, but I'm going to stop now before someone gets hurt.

Ultimately, as *knowledge developers*, and *knowledge creators*, we're all in the business of *truth*. When using an Antinet and writing down your *thoughts* in the form of notes, the ultimate goal is to write down *your truth*—and to do it *honestly*. This directive is deathly serious. One of the most critical factors that will make your time building an Antinet worthwhile is to write down as honestly as possible, your *truth*. For example, "The author mentions *rumination* and *surprise*, but I fail to see the significance of such things." Or, "I honestly have no idea what my goal is with learning an Antinet at this point, and the reason why is *x*." Or, "What the author says makes a lot of sense; however, I've already invested so much time building thousands of digital notes using tool *x*. If I switch now, who's to say I won't just switch again to a new knowledge tool three months from now!"[75]

Writing your honest truth results in you taking your Antinet seriously. It will mitigate the risk of ever abandoning it. Perhaps most importantly, it will result in creating and publishing genius-level work built to inspire others for centuries.

We humans have a very keen sense of bullshit. People are better than you think at detecting bullshit. We can tell when someone's writing the truth, and

---

knowledge using an Antinet: if you notice contradictions in your knowledge; if you notice seemingly absurd paradoxes. If you notice one piece of insight, but can link to the seemingly exact opposite insight (yet both ideas are true); All of these events are a signal that you're using the Antinet properly. They're signals that you're developing knowledge properly. In fact, I have a section in my Antinet dedicated to such paradoxes ("1609"). This is something you'll want to create as well.

74 Stevenson and Lindberg, eds., *New Oxford American Dictionary*, s.v. "truth."

75 The Antinet will be the very last knowledge development system you'll ever need to learn and use (*if* you stick to the knowledge development process I teach in Part III)!

when someone's writing something just to sell books. The way to sell books is, paradoxically, to *not try to sell books*! The way to sell books is to write the truth—your truth. And that starts by writing the truth in the form of notes. This doesn't only apply to writing books, it applies to any form of creative output (e.g. music, plays, songwriting, etc.). The bottom line is that, with the Antinet, the name of the game is writing *your truth*, as honestly as possible.

In Ernest Hemingway's fantastic non-fiction book, *Death in the Afternoon*, he takes the reader through the world of bullfighting. While it's a seemingly grotesque sport—especially in modern times—it is a book I highly recommend reading if one wishes to observe what I mean by writing the truth. It's a master-course for what good writing is. In the book he writes of bullfighting, "I should not try to defend it now, only to tell honestly the things I have found true about it."[76] Like Hemingway, your ultimate task when developing your thoughts in the Antinet concerns itself with one thing: it's to tell honestly the things you find to be *true*.

WHY AN ANTINET IS NOT ABOUT STORING NOTES

An Antinet is *not* an analog note database. It's not even about storing notes. The Antinet concerns itself with the dualistic emergence of a *second mind*. A second mind is formed by properly integrating the four principles of the Antinet, and implementing an effective workflow enabling it to operate as a *thinking system*.

An Antinet is not a *notetaking system*; it's not a notetaking app based on the functionality of linking notes (that is, *wikilinks*). To its creator (Niklas Luhmann), the Antinet was not "just an analog database," writes Johannes Schmidt.[77] It was not a container for storing notes; it was not chaotic for its creator either. The Antinet "was not a maze but a thinking tool, a communication partner, and a publication machine."[78]

---

76 Ernest Hemingway, *Death in the Afternoon* (London: Vintage Books, 2000).

77 Johannes Schmidt, "Niklas Luhmann's Card Index: Thinking Tool, Communication Partner, Publication Machine," Forgetting Machines. Knowledge Management Evolu- tion in Early Modern Europe 53 (2016), https://pub.uni-bielefeld.de/record/ 2942475, 310.

78 Johannes Schmidt, "Niklas Luhmann's Card Index: Thinking Tool, Communication Partner, Publication Machine," Forgetting Machines. Knowledge Management Evolution

The problem with thinking of the Antinet as a *notetaking system* is that, well, it's *not* a notetaking system! The term *notetaking* connotes the idea that you're writing down facts or thoughts that are already formed. Luhmann's Antinet was not a notetaking system. Hell, even the principles of an Antinet are not that important if the only thing they yield is the better *taking* of notes. The reason why an Antinet is important centers on the benefits it yields for one's mind and thoughts. The Antinet is a *thinking system* because it transforms the way one thinks. It also is a *thought system* because it develops thought, both in the short term and the long term.

The key differentiator between an Antinet and a digital notetaking app is precisely that the Antinet is a *thinking system.*

The Antinet, when used properly, and when its four principles are involved, results in one's *thinking* being transformed. The way you read books and recall thoughts changes in the course of using the Antinet. It's an incommunicable experience, and something I'll be touching on throughout the book.

Digital notetaking apps, on the other hand, can perhaps be employed to develop thought. In that respect they can be thought of as *thought systems*; however, they cannot be characterized as a *thinking system* (unless they are properly structured by way of the four principles of the Antinet). Even then, a digital notetaking app's effectiveness is watered down because it naturally omits the first principle of the Antinet (*analog*).

The analog principle is critical because it involves writing by hand. This practice results in neuroimprinting thoughts on the mind, which is a critical element involved in a process called *neuro-associative recall,* which we'll discuss next.

From using the Antinet, it could be postulated that Luhmann's mind grew in two areas: (1) memory span of thought (or *thought-span*), and (2) *neuro-associative recall.*

Let's explore both of these concepts now.

---

in Early Modern Europe 53 (2016), https://pub.uni-bielefeld.de/record/2942475, 311.

The Antinet's Effect on the "Memory Span" of Thoughts ("Thought-Span")

Within the field of memory research, scientists use the term *memory span* to refer to the minimum number of items one can recall.

Related experiments traditionally focus on more rudimentary recall tasks. They entail asking participants to recall a list of words, letters, or digits.[79] The goal with an Antinet is to develop your memory span not for words, letters, or digits; but to develop your memory span for *thought*. That is, the goal is to develop the mind to instantly recall thoughts, and to recall as many thoughts as possible. This is what is meant by *thought-span*.[80]

How is it possible to develop the memory span of thoughts? This is achieved through *neuroimprinting* thoughts on your mind via something called *elaborative rehearsal* in the field of human memory. Also involved is *maintenance rehearsal*. Both of these processes are procured by a feature innate to the Antinet by way of its first principle (*analog*). Before moving on, let's take a moment to address what is meant by the term *neuroimprinting*.

NEUROIMPRINTING IN THE ANTINET

Within the world of copywriting (which is the profession of writing compelling advertisements), one of the greatest copywriters who ever lived is Gary Halbert.[81] This self-proclaimed, "Prince of Print," used a method called *neuroimprinting* by which he taught copywriters how to become the best in their field. The simple practice is to write down, by hand, every single word (word-for-word) of the best advertisements ever written.

By trade, I was a copywriter in my previous professional life. Today, I am more generally, a writer. I was a good copywriter—scratch that—I was really

---

79 On a related note, the average memory span of most people is five words, six letters, and seven digits. This is why phone numbers in the United States consist of seven digits.

80 Kahana, *Foundations of Human Memory*, 271.

81 Sir Gary C. Halbert, "The Prince of Print". For his website, see: "The Gary Halbert Letter," accessed January 13, 2022, https://thegaryhalbertletter.com/.

good. My experience as a copywriter provided me with the greatest gift one could ask for: a lime green Lamborghini.

Just kidding![82] Success as a copywriter has given me the gift of *time*. It's given me time to concentrate on writing about things I become fascinated with. For the past year, this fascination became an obsession with the powerful physical thinking system used by Niklas Luhmann. I had been writing and developing a notecard database from readings over the course of sixteen years. It wasn't until fifteen years into this that I discovered the secret magic of Niklas Luhmann's Antinet. My notebox has since been transformed and transitioned into an Antinet. How to transition a legacy notebox isn't something I'll cover right now, just know that it is indeed possible.

Here's the point: I've had a lot of success as a copywriter, which has gifted me with the time of writing right now, to you. The secret to how I developed such skills as a copywriter can be found inside my own Antinet. Inside of it, I have over three hundred hand-written notecards of the best headlines ever written in advertising. I have personally experienced the magic of *neuroimprinting*. I won't belabor this point. *Neuroimprinting* is a critical tool for developing one's skills, mind, and thoughts. I have not found this magic to translate into the digital medium in a lossless way.

If you write out a great poem by keyboard, it will be imprinted on your screen. If you write out a great poem by hand, it will be imprinted on your soul.

THE DEEP ROOTS OF NEUROIMPRINTING

It can be argued that *neuroimprinting* is a biological term observed to occur in infant birds, such as geese, ducks, and chickens.[83] However I believe the concept to be less formal in nature (scientifically). Regardless, I hold the concept of *neuroimprinting* to be true because of empirical evidence.

---

82 I've since sold the Lamborghini. It was fun for a while, but I'm happier with a more simple life. Plus, my other car is great. It's a Tesla Model S Plaid. It's wrapped in a beautiful lime green. And, oh yeah, it's faster than the Lambo. The Italians have a lot of catching up to do!

83 Hiroko Ohki-Hamazaki, "Neurobiology of imprinting," *Brain and Nerve = Shinkei Kenkyu No Shinpo* 64, no. 6 (June 2012): 657–64.

The concept of neuroimprinting has rich and deep roots in scholarship. The scholar Francesco Sacchini (1570–1625) cites ancients who copied down texts. He explains they did such a practice not in order to have copies of them, but in order to better retain the knowledge.[84]

Sacchini recounts a story of Demosthenes copying down Thucydides eight times in order to understand the ideas more thoroughly. Sacchini also asserts that Saint Jerome (342–420 AD) wrote many volumes by hand, "not due to the weakness of his library but out of desire to profit from the exercise."[85]

The New England preacher Richard Steele wrote in 1682: "The very writing of any thing fixes it deeper in the mind."[86]

At Harvard College in the late seventeenth century, students were taught in the following manner. They were given the assignment to write down textbooks bought in England, by hand.[87] It may sound like a lazy way of teaching; however, there remains a serious argument for the power of teaching students by making them write out knowledge by hand. We have moved away from the practice in modern times, but it's something that may warrant revisiting.

The Antinet's Effect: Neuro-Associative Recall

By *neuroimprinting* thoughts on your mind, via writing by hand, you're primed to develop the most important muscle for recognizing and installing important thoughts from the books you read. The "muscle" I'm referring to is the *neuro-associative recall "muscle"* of your brain. The strength of your *neuro-associative recall muscle* is predicated on the *analog* principle of the Antinet. It's also predicated on the *index* principle of the Antinet. The *index* principle forces you to imprint a term onto your mind. That term then maps to a specific *numeric-alpha address*. Without these two principles, you lose the ability to exercise and strengthen the *neuro-associative recall muscle*. In other words, when using an Antinet you're training your memory by

84 Ann Blair, *Early Modern Attitudes toward the Delegation of Copying and Note-Taking*, 277.

85 Blair, *Early Modern Attitudes*, 277.

86 Ann Blair, *Early Modern Attitudes*, 277.

87 Ann Blair, *Early Modern Attitudes*, 278.

lengthening the memory span in which to recall a *thought*. You're doing so by *neuroimprinting* a cue (in the form of a keyterm). This cue acts as a way to immediately recall thoughts to your mind. This exercises your *neuro-associative recall muscle*, which transforms your brain. While reading you'll suddenly spot an idea or a thought. Instead of thinking of this thought as something new, you'll immediately think of the keyterm it relates to in the Antinet. This better allows you to classify the idea, associate the idea, and then develop the current knowledge that you have of the thought. All of this, again, is founded on the four key principles of the Antinet. It's specifically founded on two of those principles working together (*analog* and *index*). If it's not apparent by now, it should start to become more obvious why the four principles are so critical for developing the type of system Luhmann used. When you strip the system of such functionality (which is what digital Zettelkasten do), you prevent such phenomena from happening.

When you use a physical thinking tool like the Antinet, you end up exercising your brain and its various "muscles," and its various pathways. There's no easy-way out; no lazy search mechanism that enables you to avoid thinking and associating ideas. It may seem outdated at first, but I assure you, a system that requires you to think and exercise your mind beats the latest and greatest digital app every time. Why? Because the best computer you'll ever have is the one already operating inside your skull. Using an Antinet results in developing this organ; it could be argued that digital tools work in the opposite direction—perhaps they even tend to degrade your thinking.

The Antinet Is Not in the Same Category as "Notetaking Apps"

Notetaking apps primarily concern themselves with storing information that is *mostly* developed already. With an Antinet system you're developing thoughts primarily through the process of writing them down by hand. It is a thinking system because it produces thoughts. It's not the best tool for storing already thought-about information; though that does indeed have major benefits (*neuroimprinting* the great ideas and work of others on your mind). Primarily, the Antinet is a tool for developing information into knowledge—knowledge being your own thoughts.

The primary benefit of a digital notetaking app is its *storage capacity*. People seem to find comfort in digitally storing notes and syncing them across devices. They prefer this, without realizing they are prioritizing *storage* over the more crucial benefit: *developing and evolving thought*. It is my belief that a system that develops and evolves thought into *developed thought* is preferable to a system that merely stores (and links) *undeveloped thought*. Paradoxically, it seems that digital notetaking apps ultimately do a worse job of storing thoughts. Why? Because information is encountered less frequently, and thus recalled less frequently by the user than the knowledge stored in an Antinet. Why? Because digital information faces the perennial issue of generating a black hole of too much information.

WHY AN ANTINET IS NOT A "MEMORY SYSTEM"

While an Antinet is a *thinking system*; it's not only that type of system. It comprises other systems: it is a *memory system*, but not *only* a memory system; it's also a *sorting system*, and a *search system*. Markus Krajewski has observed that an Antinet is not just a "memory aid" for recalling thoughts. It's also, (1) a "sorting aid" (for sorting through thoughts), (2) a "search engine" (by way of *index*), and (3) a "computer" (in German, *Rechenmaschine*), "in the strict etymological sense of *rechnen* as 'to organize', 'to guide' and 'to prepare.'"[88]

Another way of phrasing it is that an Antinet acts as a pre-processing engine allowing your thoughts to become *ruminated* on, fixed, corrected, recorrected, and matured. All of this happens before even writing the first word of your book, paper, essay, dissertation, blog post, or anything else. The way in which a thought forms and evolves is also different compared to how it would otherwise evolve in digital notetaking apps.

A key reason the Antinet is not a memory system, but more of a thinking system, centers on its proficiency in bringing to the surface parts of your thinking that are, upon further rumination, potentially not entirely correct. The Antinet, thanks to its structure and analog design, allows for *proactive interference*. It does this in a manner that is different—if not entirely impos-

88 Markus Krajewski, *Note-Keeping: History, Theory, Practice of a Counter-Measurement against Forgetting* (Brill, 2016), 319.

sible–for digital tools to achieve. What is meant by *proactive interference* will be covered next.

Human memory is complex, important, and still a mystery.[89] When Luhmann began building his Antinet, it was in reaction to his "poor memory."[90] Yet he discovered the issue to be much more complex, in part because his understanding of memory was incomplete. What he referred to as a "poor memory" when he began building his Antinet in the 1950s related to *retroactive interference*, the interference caused by losing thoughts you've already previously learned.

Another type of interference in human memory prevents one from thinking clearly. It's called *proactive interference*.[91] You've probably heard the expression involving the notion of *being your own worst enemy*. This expression is founded on the idea that your own false-beliefs and cognitive fallacies can end up harming you more than any other person could. This isn't an imaginary notion; much of the time it perfectly describes reality.

Wherever you go in life, you carry something with you. You carry information, facts, knowledge, and beliefs. These are stored in your mind. These things rely on your *memory* for their encoding, storage, and retrieval. There's a problem, however: your memory may have filled in gaps or assumptions with an oversimplified representation of reality to support the encoding, storage, and retrieval of thought(s). These parts proceed to go unquestioned; they're never analyzed or consciously recognized by yourself. The core problem with this is that these memory shortcuts, if you will, end up preventing you from assimilating new, deeper, and more profound ways to think about things. In brief, it is not the *inability to recall thoughts* that is the problem; rather it's the inability to *learn and evolve current thoughts* that becomes a problem. This is what is meant by *proactive interference*.

---

89 Kahana, *Foundations of Human Memory*, ix.

90 Johannes Schmidt, "Niklas Luhmann's Card Index: Thinking Tool, Communication Partner, Publication Machine," Forgetting Machines. Knowledge Management Evolution in Early Modern Europe 53 (2016), https://pub.uni-bielefeld.de/record/2942475, 290.

91 Kahana, *Foundations of Human Memory*, 7.

Why does *proactive interference* happen? It happens because thoughts remain in a fixed state; not in a state where they can evolve—and just as important—not where the trail of a thought's evolution can be clearly viewed. This is one of the benefits of *analog* notecards. When notecards combine with the evolving branching and stemming *tree structure* component of the Antinet, it is possible to observe knowledge growth. This prevents thoughts from being subject to *proactive interference* by forcing the thinker to constantly review and recall thoughts they stumble across—this happens more frequently in an Antinet because users are forced to swing from card to card, guided by the index, instead of simply searching the collection by keyword (like in digital notetaking apps).

Thinking systems that mitigate *proactive interference* are a critical component to improving the intelligence of one's work. "Intelligence is traditionally viewed as the ability to think and learn. Yet, in a turbulent world, there's another set of cognitive skills that might matter more: the ability to rethink and unlearn."[92] A system that mitigates *proactive interference* is a system that helps one *rethink and unlearn*. This type of system is precisely what the Antinet allows with its third principle, the *tree structure*.

In summary, the Antinet is *not* a memory system, alone. Memory systems imply helping solve for one type of *interference* in human memory (that is, the interference that causes one to forget something). The Antinet solves for both types of interference in thought development (including the interference caused by thinking you know something that you don't really know).

WORKING WITH AN ANTINET DEVELOPS YOUR MEMORY FACULTIES

An Antinet is not an external system that enables you to simply offload the energy you'd otherwise rely on for your brain to recall thoughts. It acts as a system that exercises and enhances your brain's memory faculties. That is, the Antinet enhances your brain's ability to encode, store, and recall

92 Adam Grant, *Think Again: The Power of Knowing What You Don't Know* (New York, New York: Viking, 2021), 2.

thought(s). The Antinet, with its neuroimprinting process, develops your mind's capabilities for *recollecting* and *recognizing* interesting patterns when you read. This enables you to make connections to material *ruminating* in your Antinet. In the field of human memory studies, this involves a process called *recognition*.[93] Let's cover this briefly now.

In the field of human memory studies, when you *recognize* a concept, two processes occur in the mind:

1. Familiarity: this process involves placing a confidence value on how familiar you are with the content you encounter. This includes what those who study human memory call *strength theory*.

2. Recollection: this process involves the recall of *contextual* information related to the content you encounter while reading.

It's critical to *recognize* a concept while reading because it provides for two things: (1) it enables you to create information via *comparison*, and (2) it allows you to relate this information to a *selective* set of other *relations*. This is a necessary precursor for creating knowledge, and ultimately, achieving wisdom. The concept of *selective relations* will be discussed at length later in this book.

Let's jump back to the two processes occurring in the mind during *recognition: familiarity* and *recollection*. The question becomes *How does the Antinet serve to enhance these two processes?*

The Antinet enhances the process of *familiarity* (familiarity with a concept) through the practice of two of its principles: (1) its *analog* principle, which spawns *neuroimprinting*, and (2) its *index* component, which results in consistent reviewing of information while searching for previously-noted thoughts.

The Antinet also enhances the process of *recollection* through forcing users to *develop thoughts within contexts*. This emerges via the third principle of the

93 Kahana, *Foundations of Human Memory*, 102.

Antinet, its *tree structure*. Users create different *contexts* by organizing their knowledge around *branches*, or *stems of thought* in their Antinet.

As scholars have observed, both variables (*familiarity* and *recollection*) paradoxically transform a notetaking system from something designed to replace human memory into a system that both replaces *and* enhances human memory. Alberto Cevolini points out that *handwritten notetaking, due to the repetition that helps the mind retain passages, and the respective construction of a card index, serve as both a substitute for personal memory and a memory aid.*[94]

The Antinet structures itself in a way that enhances the *familiarity* and *recollection* processes involved in *recognition*. This allows you to *recognize* thoughts from readings, and better *encode* and *store* those thoughts for later *recall*. In short, the Antinet achieves this from doing one thing: developing your mind and its memory.

AN ANTINET IS PRIMARILY A THINKING SYSTEM

By now it should be apparent that an Antinet is not a notetaking app centered on the convenient storage of and access to thoughts. Its primary concern is in the developing and evolving of *thought*. An *Antinet* is not a notetaking system. What an Antinet really is, is quite apparent: it's a *thinking system*. If you want a *memory system*, there are tools like *Anki*.[95] If you want a notetaking system, perhaps one of the digital notetaking apps (or supposed digital Zettelkasten) would be of value. The Antinet, on the other hand, is a *thinking system*. It's a *thought development system*, as well. It falls under the all-encompassing concept of a *knowledge development system*. It naturally improves your memory, but it does more: (1) it strengthens your *neuro-associative recall ability*, which was touched upon previously, and (2) the Antinet improves your ability to *learn* faster, and at a deeper level.

Specifically, in human memory, there are several critical processes we've discussed already: (1) *recognition*, (2) *recall*, and (3) *familiarity*. However,

---

94 Cevolini, ed., *Forgetting Machines*, 24.

95 "Anki—Powerful, Intelligent Flashcards," accessed January 14, 2022, https://apps.ankiweb.net/.

there's another process that is just as critical. That process is known as *association*.[96] This concept will be further explored later in the book.

In brief, a traditional notetaking system is more like a *personal information storage system*. Again, an Antinet is a *thinking system*. It's also a *thought development system*. It's something that develops thought in both the *short term* and the *long term* because of what memory is. Sure, human memory's raw material consists of memories, which are representations of thought; however, the process of memory itself is an *active* process, an "active operation."[97]

Now that you know what an Antinet *primarily* is, you're starting to get a clearer idea of what an Antinet *really* is, which we'll be diving into next. Be forewarned, however, that we're about to get *metaphysical*. Don't worry, it's not spiritual woo-woo stuff. There will be no tarot cards read, or astrological birth-charts to explain what an Antinet really is. However, we are getting more and more into the land of empirical productivity. And this land, as Luhmann himself expressed, is filled with incommunicable truth. Let's proceed into this land now.

INTRODUCING YOUR SECOND MIND

The magic inherent in the system Niklas Luhmann built did not center on its features. Many think the key defining magic in Luhmann's system is its ability to link notes (that is, to create so-called *wikilinks*). Or, thanks to some authors, some are led to believe the magic centers on Luhmann's proclivity to elaborate on notes, as opposed to collecting excerpts from books.[98] Both of these notions do not encapsulate the magic of Luhmann's system.

---

96 Kahana, *Foundations of Human Memory*, 112.

97 Markus Krajewski, *Note-Keeping: History, Theory, Practice of a Counter-Measurement against Forgetting* (Brill, 2016).

98 Such as Sönke Ahrens and his book, *How to Take Smart Notes*; also, the notion that Luhmann did not excerpt passages from books is false. Luhmann most definitely did quote texts in both of his Zettelkasten.

The Two "Magical" Effects That Emerge from an Antinet

The magic of Luhmann's system stems from two effects that emerge *when* the four principles of the Antinet are implemented properly.

The first magical effect is what happened to Luhmann's mind (and by extrapolation, what can happen to yours). Luhmann's mind essentially morphed from using the Antinet. This metamorphosis of Luhmann's brain, I contend, would not have taken place if he used digital tools (which lack the four principles of the Antinet).

We've already discussed the ways in which the mind changes from using an Antinet. This includes the impact of *neuroimprinting*, and how one's reading changes due to the exercising of one's *neuro-associative recall* muscle. For this reason I won't go into detail on such now.

The second magical effect is what happened after a "number of years" working with his Antinet. Until the emergence of the second magical effect, the Antinet "functions as a mere container from which we can retrieve what we put in," writes Luhmann.[99] After Luhmann outlines the four principles of the Antinet in his paper, Luhmann explains that something else emerges: "an alter ego with who we can constantly communicate."[100] In other words, it is a *second mind*. Luhmann writes that such an entity emerges "as a result of extensive work with this technique."[101]

HOW DOES THIS SECOND MIND EMERGE?

The *second mind* emerges thanks to (1) long-term thought evolution, as well as (2) short-term thought development, which happen on paper via writing by hand. These aspects of the Antinet effectively transform it from a *mere container* of notes, into a different metaphysical entity altogether. Similar to the human phenomenon of *consciousness*, and related to the *whole-part theory*

---

99 "Communicating with Slip Boxes by Niklas Luhmann," accessed May 4, 2021, https://luhmann.surge.sh/communicating-with-slip-boxes.

100 Luhmann, "Communicating with Slip Boxes."

101 Luhmann, "Communicating with Slip Boxes."

and *mind-body duality*, the Antinet proceeds through a similar metamorphosis. The nature of this *mind-body duality* is what we'll venture into next.

The Mind-Body Duality of the Antinet

One of the most intriguing fields in philosophy studies the *mind-body problem.* The philosophical branch called *philosophy of mind* studies this phenomenon. In brief, it all centers on these questions: *What is the mind? What is consciousness? Does the mind even exist? Are your thoughts formed by your brain, which is a whole system made up of individual parts (for example, neurons)?*

If one subscribes to a *materialist* view of the world, then there is no mind. There's only your brain, with its neurons that connect to other neurons. We're just one big blob of biochemical processes, according to some pop-science authors.[102]

In other words, the interaction of neurons connecting to other neurons, is the illusion we call the mind. But is this all there is? Or is there a whole created by these neurons that is greater than the sum of its parts? This summarizes the mind-body debate which has stumped the greatest thinkers for hundreds of years.

As an aside, according to Hans-Georg Moeller, who studies Luhmann's theoretical work, Niklas Luhmann apparently introduced a solution to this problem, deeming it "the most obvious, and yet most overlooked achievement of the Luhmannian shift to theory."[103] But I won't take you down that rabbit-hole right now. I'm interested in helping you create genius-level work that shakes up the field you're in for two hundred years. The system which will help you do this is the Antinet, so I'll focus on that.

In summary, only you can decide whether or not you have a mind. Your experience of the mind is just that—an experience. It's empirical, but you're

---

102 For instance, in *Homo Deus*, Yuval Noah Harari claims the mind does not exist. Such an entity has never been identified. As far as we can tell, Harari asserts, it's just neurons connecting new neurons in the brain.

103 Hans-Georg Moeller, *The Radical Luhmann* (New York: Columbia University Press, 2011), xi.

the only subject that can observe the phenomenon of your own mind. This is why Luhmann prefaced his paper on the Antinet as *empirical sociology*. Luhmann grants that the usual research methods of empirical sociology would fail; yet, "still, it is empirical, as this case really obtains."[104]

THE BRAIN OF THE ANTINET

The one prerequisite for creating a second mind, and even forming and devising the mind-body problem is one thing: it's called...a brain!

Think of the brain of your Antinet as the raw material, the notecards, and the four principles applied within the notebox. The brain of the Antinet is composed of analog notecards, numeric-alpha addresses, the tree structure, the index, and the network. The brain one creates using this structure is unique, and thus will create a unique second mind. The second mind that emerges from a different brain will by nature be quite different. For instance, a compilation of notecards organized by author or category is much more conventional than an Antinet. The Antinet is a structure of both order and disorder. This is why it is so critical to pay attention to how Luhmann built his Antinet. It is why it's critical to not abstract away its parts into whatever you deem more convenient or modern. Luhmann structured the brain of his Antinet with an intimate understanding of how human memory works. Only by building a system composed of the same parts of the human brain can one effectively create one of the magical effects of the Antinet—a second mind.

Does the idea of creating a metaphysical entity (a *second mind*) out of a box of notecards sound questionable? If so, that's fine! Again, Luhmann prefaced his paper with the assertion that this whole subject area is empirical. In other words, you can't spend your time just reading about it, or asking questions in Zettelkasten forums online. There's only one way you can decide whether or not there's any *truth* in the concept of a *second mind*, and that is to test it out yourself.

---

104 Luhmann, "Communicating with Slip Boxes." Luhmann writes, "What follows is a piece of empirical sociology. It concerns me and someone else, namely my slip box or index card file. It should be clear that the usual methods of empirical sociology would fail in this special case. Still, it is empirical, as this case really obtains."

Later in the book I'll be taking you through, in detail, precisely how you go about testing out the Antinet yourself. Until then, let's dive into more detail and research on the concept of the *second mind*, or, what Luhmann once referred to it as, the *ghost in the box*.

The Ghost in the Antinet

When you peruse the thoughts written in the hand of someone who has died, it's almost as if there's a ghost-like quality to it. Ann Blair observes that handwriting gives readers a "privileged point of access to the person writing."[105]

This phenomenon is experienced with the Antinet. Yet unlike Blair's example, when it's just you and your Antinet, you experience this sensation by reading your own thoughts, written in your own hand. When working with an Antinet, you begin communicating with yourself in a unique fashion. Instead of an *internal monologue*, you begin to experience something called *internal dialogue*. More on this will be discussed later.

John Locke realized the advantages of having an *internal dialogue*. He experienced the advantages of viewing a historical record of his own thinking. It "carried the possibility of him reading it, in the future, as a historical record of his thinking."[106] It allowed him to have a dialogue with himself, and to see where his thinking went wrong.

Reading Johannes Schmidt's account of perusing the contents of Luhmann's Antinet, one pictures Schmidt having a similar experience. It's an experience of perusing the "backstage" and inner thoughts of one's own mind. Of Luhmann's Antinet, Schmidt observes that it "is more than just an analog database of Luhmann's theory." Schmidt likens it to "the backstage" of Luhmann's grand theory and scholarly work, "and therefore [as] Niklas Luhmann's intellectual autobiography."[107]

---

105 Blair, *Early Modern Attitudes*, 265.

106 Yeo, *Notebooks, Recollection, and External Memory*, 149.

107 Schmidt, "Niklas Luhmann's Card Index: Thinking Tool," 310.

Of the *mind in a box* or *ghost in the box* concept, Niklas Luhmann himself put forth an interesting illustration. Recognizing that this concept is difficult to communicate, Luhmann chose to illustrate this by comparing reading notes without access to the second mind, with the difference between viewing porn and having sex.

In one of the infamous notecards in the Zettelkasten section he used for preparing the paper *Communication with Noteboxes,* Luhmann wrote:

> **Ghost in the box?**
>
> Spectators come. You get to see everything and nothing but that—like porn movies. And so is the disappointment.[108]

What Luhmann means is that the voyeur sees everything, just as people get to see all of Luhmann's thoughts when perusing his Antinet. However, in reality, they're seeing *nothing.* They're not seeing the internal dialogue and experience Luhmann himself has when he (as its creator) peruses his own Antinet. Like watching porn, you get to see everything; yet, you don't experience the incommunicable connection and internal/communal dialogue two lovers are having during sex. Granted, perhaps the internal dialogue isn't as prevalent when two porn stars are going at it, but you get the point.

Modern day scientists agree with Luhmann's notion of a *mind in a box* emerging from Antinets (and other physical external memory devices). "The effectiveness of [Antinets] does not lie in the sporadic access that it provides to single entries, or in what these entries, once selected, may teach the user. A card index is a true secondary memory when…inquiries become an opportunity to trigger a network of associative references and links which give birth to 'collaborative' reasoning that had not been previously designed."[109] The scholar, Alberto Cevolini, confirms this notion. "To argue that the filing cabinet simply stores records would be to give a too short (and

108 "ZK II: Note 9 / 8.3—Niklas Luhmann Archive," accessed January 11, 2022, https://niklas-luhmann-archiv.de/bestand/zettelkasten/zettel/ZK_2_NB_9-8-3_V.

109 Cevolini, ed., *Forgetting Machines,* 19–20.

therefore misleading) description of the interplay of user and machine."[110] The *interplay of user and machine* provides an external glimpse into what's really going on—internal dialogue with yourself, and an instantiation of yourself in external form (your second mind).

The concept of this *second mind,* and the internal dialogue which emerges as a result of its presence, has been observed and studied by scholars as the interaction between the following items: (1) *external memory* (that is, the Antinet), and (2) *internal memory* (the memory biologically stored inside your brain and body).

After studying John Boyle, John Locke, and Robert Hooke, Alberto Cevolini confirms "that annotations that are stored in the external memory can function only in tandem with internal memory, so excerpts and notes prompt recollection of more than what they actually contain."[111]

In other words, the notes in your Antinet set off a chain-reaction of thought-connections; that is, the notes in your Antinet act as a cue that precipitates a chain-reaction of communication and internal dialogue.

This generates the *recall* process in your mind.

In their paper *The Extended Mind,* Andy Clark and David J. Chalmers, assert that the memories contained in external form (like the Antinet) are not merely memory systems, and therefore, they're not really external memories.[112] Rather, they're *extended minds.*

THE TERM "SECOND MIND"

In the field of knowledge, a term that is increasingly popular is *extended mind.* The scholar, Richard Yeo, argues that the term *extended mind* is problematic because confusion arises between *consciousness* and *communication.* "Consequently, memory is seen as a psychic phenomenon." Yeo further points

110 Cevolini, ed., *Forgetting Machines,* 19.

111 Cevolini, ed., *Forgetting Machines,* 12.

112 Andy Clark and David J. Chalmers, "The Extended Mind," Analysis 58, no. 1 (1998): 7–19.

out an issue with the word *extended,* asking *What does "extended" actually mean?* And by *mind,* he asks whether it should be termed *cognition,* which refers to the mental action of acquiring knowledge and understanding.[113]

The problem with the term *extended cognition* centers on the fact that it misses the *ghost in the box* quality or phenomenon Luhmann, and other scholars have described. However, there may be some validity to the issue Yeo points out concerning the term *extended.* For this reason, I choose to retain the term *mind* (in order to encapsulate the ghost-like spirit and the experience of having internal dialogue). However, I opt to drop *extended,* and prefer *second* in its place. Why? Because as Yeo points out, *extended* is a rather vague term. *Is it truly extended thought since it's really my own thought? Or is it rather a second storage mechanism for my own thought?* As a result, I opt for *second.*

Finally, we get to the point of what an Antinet really is: a *second mind.*

SECOND MIND VS. SECOND BRAIN

You may be wondering about the recent popularity of the term *second brain* used by Tiago Forte.

Forte runs a business which sells online courses that aim to "train knowledge workers in how to use technology to radically improve their productivity."[114] Forte's material centers on upgrading David Allen's *Getting Things Done method.* He teaches people how to capture material they read online, and how to process that material to get things done. He proposes the concept of organizing content into explicit areas like *projects* and *resources.*

As far as knowledge development goes, Forte doesn't have too much to say. I believe this to be the case because, "[Forte's course] Building A Second Brain started out as a course on using Evernote more effectively."[115] Evernote is

113 Cevolini, ed., *Forgetting Machines,* 12.

114 "About Forte Labs," Forte Labs, accessed January 17, 2022, https://fortelabs.co/about-forte-labs/.

115 "Building A Second Brain," Fernando Gros, June 24, 2020, https://fernandogros.com/building-a-second-brain/.

an app that does not prioritize the linking of notes, nor does it promote knowledge development. Rather it focuses on cross-device digital storage of *information*.

In brief, Forte's usage of the term, *second brain* really relates to processes inspired by David Allen's *Getting Things Done* ("GTD"). Forte's primary application of the term *second brain* revolves around productivity (not knowledge development). And this is fine! I have nothing against this, even though I don't subscribe to it.

Forte moves David Allen's *Getting Things Done* into the digital age. He does this by proposing strategies for organizing digital information into seemingly logical categories on your computer (for instance a folder for *projects*). This really isn't a *brain*; it's more of a philosophy on being more productive with digital information.

Regardless of Forte's *second brain* not really being a *second brain* (but more a digital productivity philosophy), I hold that a *second brain* isn't really what you want anyway (if your goal is knowledge creation).

YOU WANT A SECOND MIND, NOT A SECOND BRAIN

With Forte teaching how to record information (using apps like Evernote), he's essentially promoting a system that cannot communicate with itself. Evernote is not a system that contains parts that can self-reference in a fixed, permanent state. It's essentially a brain comprised of a blob of neurons—a blob of neurons that cannot communicate with one another and that cannot connect with one another to create new entities. Many digital Zettelkasten are second brains; however, they're not *second minds*. Digital Zettelkasten are a hodge-podge of parts that don't communicate. Instead of a tree of knowledge, they're a pile of leaves. If a person's brain were constructed in the same manner, the person would not be alive. They'd be a vegetable.

In brief, you want a *second mind*, not a *second brain*. A brain is a materialistic blob of biochemical gunk. A *second mind* is a system wherein the whole has become greater than the sum of its parts. While I could continue down this metaphorical road, I won't belabor this too much.

One last thing, before we move on: I believe Tiago Forte's content is helpful and valuable for those who wish to be more productive working with digital information. If that's what you're looking for, this book is not for you. We're concerned with knowledge development. We're concerned with developing and evolving your thoughts (both in the short term and long term). The reason we're concerned with such centers around one thing: creating genius-level knowledge. **The goal with the Antinet is to turn you into a learning machine, a content machine, a research machine, and a writing machine. Bottom line: if you do what I outline in this book, you'll become all of these things. You'll become *an unstoppable knowledge machine.***

THE PROBLEM IN TRYING TO EXPLAIN A SECOND MIND

Niklas Luhmann was one of the major thinkers involved in the establishment of *systems theory,* especially within the sociological sphere.[116] It is therefore rather intriguing that he did not use *systems theory* as the basis for his explanation of the Antinet; rather, he used *communication theory* to explain it. One problem with Luhmann using communication theory, however, is that a core part of human experience and knowledge is more than that which is acquired through theory. Rather, truth and reality, at least for humanity, are also influenced by the metaphysical realm. Both Eastern and Western philosophies share one common assumption: that there is such a thing as *incommunicable truth.*[117] This concept suggests that in order to truly understand the power of the second mind, it cannot be taught; rather, it can only be experienced.

Another issue with trying to explain an Antinet is the fact that it could take a number of years of working with it before the *second mind* emerges. This is

---

116 Rudolf Stichweh, *Systems Theory*; "Since its beginnings the social sciences were an important part of the establishment of systems theory. Jürgen Ruesch and Gregory Bateson were in 1951 the first who tried to base a social science discipline on an information and communication theory coming from cybernetics ("Communication. The Social Matrix of Psychiatry"). But the two most influential suggestions were the comprehensive sociological versions of systems theory which were proposed by Talcott Parsons since the 1950s and by Niklas Luhmann since the 1970s."

117 Joseph Campbell, The Hero with a Thousand Faces, 3rd ed, Bollingen Series XVII (Novato, Calif: New World Library, 2008), 25.

one factor all too conveniently omitted from books like *How to Take Smart Notes*. Again, for better or worse, Luhmann declares in his paper that it will be a number of years before the *second mind* emerges; until then the Antinet operates as a mere container for storing notes.

In my experience, however, the emergence of the *second mind* comes sooner than several years into the practice. It is likely to emerge several months after regular and committed use. For me, it emerged perhaps three or four months after I began working with it. However, it should be noted that I worked with it five days a week. In addition, the presence of the second mind grows stronger every single day.

The bottom line is this: the more time you spend with a thing, the more of you it becomes, and, the more of it becomes of you.

The Nature of the Second Mind

The Antinet is a unique type of system; more so than the novelties preached in digital-Zettelkasten-land which over-emphasize its features, yet overlook the magic.[118] An Antinet is an *intrapersonal knowledge system*. It possesses a unique proclivity for inducing internal dialogue (as opposed to internal monologue). Its evolution over time happens in a self-organized fashion that cannot be pre-planned. It's also consciousness-oriented, instead of comprehension-oriented. It works in tandem with its creator and is not designed to be a stand-alone system that is easily comprehensible to the public eye. The material and content it contains stem from deep-thinking, from working out ideas on paper, through rumination, and in the seeking of deep understanding. The ideas that emerge from it will surprise you. What makes it even more surprising is seeing how the ideas stem from you—from your own handwriting. The nature of the Antinet is founded on a *communication theory* because *it really is* a communication relationship between you, and your past self. When you try and transition such a system to digital, you're destroying a core aspect of the Antinet. You're destroying

118 These include features like linking notes, atomic notes, and other flavor-of-the-month ideas.

a key piece of the second mind—you're ripping away that person, and its personality, before it even has a chance to be born.

When I read my handwritten notes, and observe the material of the notecards it was written on from fifteen years ago, it communicates something to me—something special that cannot be communicated in digital-file format. *I see myself in my handwriting.* I see the state of my life I was in at the time. I see the state of my mind at the time. Sometimes I have a reverence and respect for what I've written. *Did I really write that and come up with that?* And sometimes I see something where I think, *Geez, I've really developed my thinking, and my mind, and have grown a lot since then.* This is one aspect and one experience you'll have when working with your *second mind*. I'm excited for you to experience it, but that's really all I'm going to say for now. I'll share more in detail later in the book; however, as I've mentioned before, much of it is *incommunicable*.

The reason one ought to take the four principles Luhmann outlined so seriously is that they're key ingredients for transforming an Antinet into what it *really* is, which is a *second mind*.

I've touched on the importance of the four principles already; however, it's worth restating how intentional Luhmann was in the construction of the Antinet. One scholar observed Luhmann's system is "clearly constructed as a cybernetic machine."[119] Luhmann was influenced by cybernetics, the field concerned with the study of goal-oriented systems founded on *communication* and *feedback*. Ultimately, Luhmann's Antinet "reproduces itself recursively" in order to produce knowledge.[120]

The Antinet also relates to another concept Luhmann introduced to the field of sociology—*autopoiesis*.[121] This term stems from two Greek terms (1) αὐτο- (*auto*), which translates to *self*, and (2) ποίησις (*poiesis*), which means

---

119 Cevolini, ed., *Forgetting Machines*, 26.

120 Cevolini, ed., *Forgetting Machines*, 26.

121 "Autopoiesis—an Overview | ScienceDirect Topics," accessed January 18, 2022, https://www.sciencedirect.com/topics/social-sciences/autopoiesis.

creation. In brief, autopoiesis means *self-creation* and concerns the study of systems which create themselves.

While it could be argued the Antinet exhibits *autopoiesis*, it technically doesn't create other Antinets; rather, it creates a different entity altogether—a metaphysical *second mind* with whom you communicate. While the Antinet itself may not be autopoietic, the second mind that emerges from the system, and specifically its memory, could be said to "function as an autopoietic system," observes the scholar, Alberto Cevolini.[122]

CONCLUSION

By now, you're starting to understand the depth of this seemingly-simple system of notecards. Before moving forward let's recap what we've covered.

As you may recall, we defined an *Antinet* as a system comprising four principles which form a *thinking system*. This *thinking system* transforms itself into a *second mind*.

You know what the four principles of the Antinet are (*analog, numeric-alpha, tree, index*). You understand the Antinet is a *network*. You know what is meant by the Antinet as a *thinking system*. You are also familiar with the concept of the *second mind*.

What we're going to cover next concerns the scientific reasoning for devoting so much energy and commitment to such a system. We're going to explore this by taking a closer look at the explicitness in Luhmann's design of the Antinet. We'll be doing this by diving into each of the principles of Luhmann's Antinet individually. We'll be starting where the magic of the Antinet really begins: its analog nature.

Let's go.

---

122 Alberto Cevolini, Storing Expansions: Openness and Closure in Secondary Memories (Brill, 2016), 163.

CHAPTER SIX

ANALOG

"The technical requirements of slip boxes involve wooden boxes, which have drawers that can be pulled open, and pieces of paper in octavo format (about half of a letter-size sheet [4 x 6 inch notecards or A6 paper slips]). We should only write on one side of these papers so that in searching through them, we do not have to take out a paper in order to read it. This doubles the space, but not entirely (since we would not write on both sides of all the slips). This consideration is not unimportant as the arrangement of boxes can, after some decades, become so large that it cannot be easily be used from one's chair. In order to counteract this tendency, I recommend taking normal paper and not card stock."

—Niklas Luhmann, *Communication with Noteboxes*[1]

DISCOVERING THE ANALOG IMPLEMENTATION OF ZETTELKASTEN

I STUMBLED UPON THE ANALOG version of the Zettelkasten purely by accident. At the time, I was fully committed to the digital version. I actually came upon the idea of the analog Zettelkasten through Sönke Ahrens's book *How to Take Smart Notes*. It was a brief mention, but it was enough to get me started on the path. A path that would become my life for the following year: reverse-engineering how the analog Zettelkasten *actually* worked.

1 Niklas Luhmann, "Communication with Noteboxes (Revised Edition)," trans. Manfred Kuehn, https://daily.scottscheper.com/zettelkasten/.

Initially I tried using the analog version of the Zettelkasten merely to implement anything I was not currently doing using the digital notetaking app, Obsidian.

I hoped that Ahrens's book could help me mitigate my fear of stopping the current streak I was on (of creating and publishing content consistently). I had some good momentum, which finally seemed to have pulled me out of a lull of just *consuming* knowledge (instead of producing it).

I was on day forty-eight of my commitment to my daily practice (which entailed things like reading every morning, installing the right mental mindset, working out, actually getting out of my house, and going to my office).

It was a Sunday in early March at 2:16 pm. Before getting down to work in my office in downtown San Diego, I wrote the following:

One thing I will say is this: I had the thought today that I really wish and hope that I [do] not make [my daily writing practice] a chore by going insane [using] an atomic workflow.

Atomic workflow is a term that refers to a trend in web development. The aim is to simplify components of websites by creating representations of different website parts analogous to biological concepts (atoms, molecules, organisms, etc.). For instance, a button on a website is likened to an atom. An input field is another atom. When both atoms are combined, they create a search box (which is likened to a molecule). The search molecule provides search functionality.[2]

Novel, though this idea may appear, it adds yet another layer of abstraction (and distraction) to the already overly complex field of web development.

The temptation to apply the concept of *atomicity* to fields is not new. In fact, in the field of human memory studies, one researcher proposed that human memory, too, adheres to the atomic composition principle. In other words,

2 "Atomic Design Methodology | Atomic Design by Brad Frost," accessed July 15, 2021, http://atomicdesign.bradfrost.com/chapter-2/.

an item in memory is not one single thing; rather, it's composed of many smaller subunits like protons, neutrons, and electrons.

The problem with this is the fact that atomicity can be loosely applied to almost anything. This sentence is atomic. Each sentence is an organelle, comprising molecules (words) that themselves comprise atoms (individual letters). This whole abstraction really doesn't do much. It's just a trendy fad to break things apart into *atomic* components. It distracts from the really important stuff, that is, your actual writing output.

The atomic design ideology seems to have gripped the imaginations of those enthralled with the world of personal knowledge management ("PKM"). The PKM folk end up spending much of their time on forums debating workflows and best practices which, paradoxically, results in less productivity. As a result, less knowledge is developed for PKM folk to "manage."

Back to the story: on that Sunday afternoon in my office, I felt myself falling into the trap of *majoring in the minor*. I've fallen into this trap thousands of times. I was worried and fearful that all of my recent hard work and progress in getting out of my creative lull and into a productive lifestyle was at risk. The reason why comes down to one word: *complexity*. The whole *atomic workflow* concept became a distraction. It led me into the land PKM people habitually become infatuated with: templates, workflows, layouts, plugins, CSS styles, etc.

Yet, I held out *hope* that the solution to not falling into the trap of complexity would be resolved by reading Sönke Ahrens's book on notetaking.

When I started reading *How to Take Smart Notes* I got a glimpse of how to actually build out an analog Zettelkasten. Every other place online, including the most visited website promoting Zettelkasten, only taught the digital version of the system.

I remember the realization and thoughts I had shortly after trying out the analog form of the Zettelkasten. I said to myself, *Ohhh, so this is what the Zettelkasten is actually supposed to be like*! Mind you, this was after I had spent months learning what a Zettelkasten *supposedly* was (according to people who taught the digital Zettelkasten).

At this point I had already gone through a six-week-long course on linking digital notes, and a ninety minute one-on-one session with the creator of the course. Yet, the lightbulb didn't turn on until I actually tried using a Zettelkasten in analog form. Side note: It makes me wonder if the people teaching digital notetaking courses are even aware of what working with a Zettelkasten is *actually* supposed to feel like!

Anyway, at the time I thought I knew what a Zettelkasten was, but after trying an analog Zettelkasten, it became clear to me that I didn't. At most I knew 10% of what a Zettelkasten really was all about. I didn't realize how little I knew about the system until much later. It also took me a while after that to discover that Ahrens's interpretation of Luhmann's system was actually quite different from what Luhmann actually did.

It was very soon into my working with the analog Zettelkasten that I realized how much better the physical version was. I thought it took me about a week to realize this; however, after reviewing my notes later on, I realized it was even sooner than a week that I realized the power of analog. I felt a sense that analog was more powerful than digital not by a little bit, but by a lot!

It was important that the benefits of analog needed to outweigh the benefits of digital by a large margin because I had spent many months of my life building out an extensive digital Zettelkasten (with over a thousand notes).

However, even with the extensive amount of work I put into the digital Zettelkasten system, I simply couldn't deny the truth: the analog version of the Zettelkasten was simply better than the digital.

Two days after I had started reading *How to Take Smart Notes*, I wrote the following down in my journal: "I can't help but feel like it may be best to move towards analog completely." I then added the following admission: "To be honest, the primary thing that makes me want to stick with my digital notetaking app is the beautiful font and layout and style I spent this weekend creating."

The truth was apparent: the digital Zettelkasten system resulted in me *not* producing genius-level creative output. Instead the digital Zettelkasten system resulted in me distracting myself with the bells and whistles of the tool. The most recent time-sucks had included restructuring the directory structure and folders of my notes into an atomic format. It also included me spending an entire weekend creating a nifty theme for my notes. I sometimes just can't help but get distracted with things that don't matter!

Anyway, I found myself still resistant to switching over completely to analog because of the *sunk cost fallacy*. I was committed to digital because of how much time I had already spent building out my digital notes. Plus, I had no idea about the power of analog yet. As one Antinetter put it to me, "When you use digital notetaking apps, you have no idea how lost you are *until* you switch to analog."

Anyway, to help me through this process, I did the ole Benjamin Franklin tactic. I created a pros and cons list.

Here's what I wrote down in my journal:

Pros of Analog:

- Simple
- Fewer distractions
- Makes use of my beautiful Montblanc pens
- More freedom and creativity
- Past success (writing by hand really helped my results in college)
- Academic research backing improved *understanding* while learning by writing by hand
- Constraints breed creativity
- Feynman said "thinking is writing," and by this he meant, writing longhand.

Cons of Analog:

- Cannot quickly search for keywords. Though to be fair, I don't even use this feature too extensively right now with [my digital notetaking app]. In addition, the results are rarely *that* relevant to what I'm looking for).
- Misses out on training me to write quickly and freely on the keyboard. Though, to be fair, is this really a con? It may be good to slow down and write via longhand because it forces me to actually *think* deeply before I write.
- Cannot share or publish my notes easily online. Though, who even wants half-developed information? It's best to publish work that has already been *deeply* processed and structured.

These were my initial pros and cons, and they are largely still true today; however, I've learned more since writing that list. There are more cons to consider, of course (like the risk of fire or water damage to notes, which I'll address). Yet I discovered later that the initial cons of analog actually are some of its greatest pros.

Let's now dive into a more in-depth look at the pros and cons of analog I've since realized.

THE PROS OF ANALOG

ANALOG CREATES A BETTER COMMUNICATION PARTNER THAN DIGITAL

A thing people seem to overlook in regards to Luhmann's Zettelkasten is that, to Luhmann, his Zettelkasten was not a tool. It was a person.

Animism centers on the belief that certain objects, places, plants, and creatures possess a distinct spiritual essence—a soul, if you will. The Antinet serves as a perfect example for such an idea. The Antinet becomes its own unique entity with its own unique personality with whom you communicate.

This type of system is watered-down in the world of digital notetaking apps. Digital notetaking apps rarely retain a core structure. Their arms, legs, and feet (i.e., notes, directories, and tags) can be deleted on a whim. They have nothing to build on or stand on. Digital Zettelkasten systems end up looking like a massive interlinked graph of notes, with no personality.

The Antinet, on the other hand, does indeed retain a core structure. Its branches, stems of thoughts and notes are never deleted. They evolve and they grow with you throughout your life. They are *real*, they are *physical*, they are an extension of you, and they become a part of you. The Antinet becomes your *second mind* with whom you can *communicate* with. Again, this is something missing in digital notetaking apps.

The *communication* component of the Zettelkasten is critical. Luhmann believed this himself, which is why he titled his paper "*Communication with Noteboxes.*" As one of the inventors of systems theory, Luhmann said he regards both himself and his Zettelkasten as "systems" and joked that "no one will be surprised [by this]."[3] He says this jokingly because he's one of the first and major proponents of applying systems theory to the field of sociology. Yet, Luhmann goes on to explicitly say that "systems theory" is not his choice to begin explaining the Zettelkasten system. Rather, he chooses a "communication theory" to explain what his Zettelkasten actually is.

The idea of a notebox system emerging into an external instantiation of one's own communication partner did not originate with Niklas Luhmann. Rather, "this idea actually dates back to a situation already described in 1805 by Heinrich von Kleist in his impressive analysis of the 'midwifery of thought.'"[4]

If you're going to create something valuable, it requires deep thought, sophisticated ideas, and deep connections. This type of thinking is achieved through writing. Period.

Since the hardest part is the actual writing (and thinking) it is useful to then transform the process into something that will grow and evolve forever.

---

3 Niklas Luhmann, "Communicating with Slip Boxes," accessed May 4, 2021, https://luhmann.surge.sh/communicating-with-slip-boxes.

4 Markus Krajewski, *Note-Keeping: History, Theory, Practice of a Counter-Measurement against Forgetting* (Brill, 2016), 325.

It also becomes worthwhile for your structure to grow and develop its own unique personality.

Writing this book on the Antinet Zettelkasten would be a much different experience and would yield different ideas if I were to write it using the same section of my notes ten years from now. In other words, due to the internal branching nature, my current Antinet will inevitably evolve and grow internally over the years. The Antinet, just like a person, grows in unique ways, and there's so much richly packed knowledge that it will yield surprising ideas for years to come. This is exciting, as the Antinet presents itself as a goldmine of knowledge waiting to be stumbled upon and used some time in the future, whether that be a year from now or ten years from now.

As Luhmann observed, one of the greatest benefits of communication is that each partner can mutually surprise the other with unexpected insight.[5] When you're using an Antinet, you're essentially having a conversation with it as you're perusing its contents. After you look up the location of an idea in the index, you then embark upon the process of sifting through the cards in the area your index pointed you to. From there, you're reading your own thoughts in your own handwriting and trying to decipher what that internal voice is saying. Along the way, you're challenging one another. You come across a card and question its bold claims; yet, upon a closer look you actually realize that its claims are right and you're wrong! This is like any high-yielding real-life communication experience. You debate one another and are sometimes proven wrong, which is a good thing!

In the several companies I've started, I've found some of the greatest innovations to come about through just random conversation. My former business partner and I would have lengthy and profound discussions. We would both end up revising and updating our initial perspectives and come up with truly brilliant ideas. This type of experience is something that seems to happen when using an analog Zettelkasten. It's one of those incommunicable truths that one must experience for themselves to truly grasp.

---

5 "Communicating with Slip Boxes by Niklas Luhmann," accessed May 4, 2021, https://luhmann.surge.sh/communicating-with-slip-boxes.

What Luhmann meant by *communication with noteboxes* relates to having a conversation with one's Antinet. This concept is similar to having a conversation with the author of a book that you read. As Mortimer Adler points out in his classic work titled *How to Read a Book*, reading a book is very much a *communication experience*. In the book Adler lays out an analogy of a pitcher and catcher in baseball.[6] The pitcher (the book author) is throwing you a *thought* (which is the baseball). You, the reader, are the catcher. A baseball catcher is active, *not* passive. He's actively anticipating the pitch, ready to adjust to it and adjusts in order to receive it. Communication is not a vegetative experience. The same holds true for reading. It's not like sitting down on the couch, binge watching whatever is popular on Netflix. It's a very alert process. This is what it's like working with an Antinet.

ANALOG CAPTURES ONE'S CONSCIOUSNESS BETTER THAN DIGITAL

Another instance of analog serving as a pro over digital revolves around *capturing consciousness.*

The Antinet Zettelkasten unlocks the type of communication relationship Luhmann referenced in "*Communication with Noteboxes*." The Antinet Zettelkasten captures your own consciousness, your own past self, in a way that outshines digital Zettelkasten systems because it is truly a partner in a communication relationship between *your current self* and *your past self.*

Alberto Cevolini writes: "Compared with the rhetorical storehouse, the card index preserves a knowledge—we could also say, *a past*—that not only continually changes but also can be recalled in a highly selective manner."[7]

When you go digital, you're quite literally destroying the magic of the Antinet, stripping the system of the person and personality that lives inside it.

---

6 Mortimer Jerome Adler and Charles Van Doren, How to Read a Book, Rev. and updated ed (New York: Simon and Schuster, 1972), 5.

7 Alberto Cevolini, ed., Forgetting Machines: Knowledge Management Evolution in Early Modern Europe, Library of the Written Word, volume 53 (Leiden; Boston: Brill, 2016), 32. Emphasis added.

When I read my handwritten notes from fifteen years ago, they feel much more *real* than any digital notes I took fifteen years ago (which, believe it or not, are harder for me to find than my physical notes). When I come across handwritten notes from fifteen years ago, I see myself in the handwriting. I see a different version of myself. A past version of myself. My mind is transported into that state, much like a song transports you into some state you were in when you first heard it.

For instance, take the album by Coldplay titled *X&Y* (yes, I admit, I once listened to Coldplay). Anyway, when I hear a song from the album today, it transports me to the summer of 2005 when I was listening to it on vacation with my family in Hawaii. A similar phenomenon happens when you interact with handwritten notes. You're transported to the time and place you first read the book and took the note. With each handwritten note, you also transcribe a piece of your own consciousness—your own state and self-awareness—onto the card. This does not seem to happen in the same way with digital systems.

This argument may sound like woo-woo mysticism, but I assure you it's not. Scholars are familiar with this notion and Luhmann himself certainly felt this was true.[8] This is noteworthy since Luhmann's "*Communication with Noteboxes*" is heralded as "the most advanced result of a long-lasting reflection performed by modern society."[9]

In a thorough and deeply cogent paper on Luhmann's Zettelkasten, Johannes Schmidt "investigates the origins and development of Luhmann's filing technique in detail, also availing himself of first-hand information about the content of this exceptional filing cabinet."[10] From this paper, Alberto Cevolini concludes that Schmidt's paper "demonstrates that Luhmann did

8 "ZK II: Note 9 / 8.3 - Niklas Luhmann Archive," accessed January 11, 2022, https://niklas-luhmann-archiv.de/bestand/zettelkasten/zettel/ZK_2_NB_9-8-3_V.

9 Alberto Cevolini, ed., Forgetting Machines: Knowledge Management Evolution in Early Modern Europe, Library of the Written Word, volume 53 (Leiden ; Boston: Brill, 2016), 26.

10 Alberto Cevolini, ed., Forgetting Machines: Knowledge Management Evolution in Early Modern Europe, Library of the Written Word, volume 53 (Leiden; Boston: Brill, 2016), 26.

not regard his filing cabinet as a simple slip box, rather *he interacted with it as if it were a true communication partner.*"[11]

The reason handwritten notes produce the *ghost in the box effect* (that is, preserving your past self) seems to emanate from one thing: consciousness. Handwritten notes capture your own experience, sentiments, and sentience at the time you wrote your thoughts on the card.

Knowledge = meaning x information. Knowledge is dependent on internal dialogue between you and your past self. That is, knowledge deepens during the intrapersonal communication process with your past self's consciousness. When you read your old notes, in your own handwriting, oftentimes there is *meaning* that is communicated through the notes that only *you*, its creator, can understand. This transitions the note from being just *information* to being a unit of *knowledge* (*information* combined with *meaning*). Analog systems with handwritten notes seem to retain their meaning better than commoditized, non-unique digital typefaces. With digital systems, you can never be 100% absolutely certain that it was indeed you who wrote the text. After all, the content could have been copied and pasted. With your own longhand handwriting, the spirit of your past self is much harder to spoof.

ANALOG TRANSFORMS THE ZETTELKASTEN INTO A THINKING TOOL (BOTH SHORT-TERM AND LONG-TERM)

> [Luhmann's Zettelkasten] served him as a thinking tool. This is not only true in terms of the proposition that the file acted as a communication partner in the research process but also in regard to the fact that in Luhmann's mind the process of writing things down enables disciplined thinking in the

11 Alberto Cevolini, ed., Forgetting Machines: Knowledge Management Evolution in Early Modern Europe, Library of the Written Word, volume 53 (Leiden; Boston: Brill, 2016), 26. Emphasis added.

> first place: "Underlying the filing technique is the experience that without writing, there is no thinking."
>
> —Johannes Schmidt in *Niklas Luhmann's Card Index: Thinking Tool, Communication Partner, Publication Machine*

Johannes Schmidt regards Luhmann's Zettelkasten as a *thinking tool.*[12] There are really two components to this thinking tool: (1) it enhances immediate short-term thinking, and (2) it helps thoughts evolve over the long term.

The tool enhances thoughts in the short term through the process of forcing one to think by writing by hand. As Nobel-Prize-winning physicist Richard Feynman once said, "you have to work on paper."[13] Or take Alexander Grothendieck, a leading figure in the creation of modern algebraic geometry. In watching Grothendieck work, one person observed, "[Grothendieck] was improvising, in his fast and elegant handwriting. He said that *he couldn't think without writing.*"[14]

In the long term, the Antinet (the *thinking tool*) grows by way of its tree-like internal branching structure, with more and more handwritten thoughts linking together and creating new related stems. As mentioned, this essentially transforms the Antinet into a new entity altogether—a second mind.

Both the short term component of the thinking tool, and the long-term component of the thinking tool rely on the analog nature of the Antinet.

---

12 Johannes Schmidt, "Niklas Luhmann's Card Index: Thinking Tool, Communication Partner, Publication Machine," Forgetting Machines. Knowledge Management Evolution in Early Modern Europe 53 (2016), https://pub.uni-bielefeld.de/record/2942475.

13 "Many Eminent Thinkers Need a Writing Surface to Think," Andy's working notes, accessed March 19, 2022, https://notes.andymatuschak.org/z5WDNZizsbAzE1p2BLwr339fV4TCpzNvaztP2.

14 "Many Eminent Thinkers Need a Writing Surface to Think," Andy's working notes, accessed March 19, 2022, https://notes.andymatuschak.org/z5WDNZizsbAzE1p2BLwr339fV4TCpzNvaztP2. Emphasis added.

NOTECARDS' LIMITED SPACE FORCE UNLIMITED COMBINATIONS OF THOUGHT

I'm not a fan of *synthetic* atomicity. Take for instance, the previously mentioned *atomic design methodology* which entails thinking of website components as atoms, molecules, organisms, etc.[15] Such a paradigm overcomplicates the already overcomplicated field of web development. Digital Zettelkasten workflow warriors have jumped on this bandwagon, with people synthetically trying to make their notes *atomic* by arbitrarily breaking them into smaller parts. However, with most digital Zettelkasten systems, there's no actual size constraint, such as a character limit, like one would find in Twitter.

For instance, Sönke Ahrens in *How to Take Smart Notes* writes, "I highly recommend treating a digital note as if the space were limited... Each note should fit onto the screen and there should be no need of scrolling."[16] The problem with such advice is that, after some time, it's too easy to forget to follow it.

Notecards are different. There is an actual, physically limited, space into which one must condense thoughts. The limited notecard space forces true atomicity, unlike inadequately implemented digital notetaking apps.

Here's why this is important: scholars studying the field of knowledge argue that atomic knowledge ("dismembered" into notecards) creates combinatory power by way of "links and cross-references" that allow users to "shift their cognitive energies (newly relieved of the burden of memorization) to processing information."[17]

The *shift* in cognitive energies does not happen because one is completely relieved of having to memorize anything (as in the case of storing thoughts in a digital notetaking app). Rather, with analog systems, the *shift* happens

15 "Atomic Design Methodology | Atomic Design by Brad Frost," accessed July 15, 2021, http://atomicdesign.bradfrost.com/chapter-2/.

16 Sönke Ahrens, How to Take Smart Notes: One Simple Technique to Boost Writing, Learning and Thinking: For Students, Academics and Nonfiction Book Writers (North Charleston, SC: CreateSpace, 2017), 129-130.

17 Alberto Cevolini, ed., Forgetting Machines: Knowledge Management Evolution in Early Modern Europe, Library of the Written Word, volume 53 (Leiden ; Boston: Brill, 2016), 16.

because you've actually stamped the knowledge into your mind by way of neuroimprinting the knowledge on your mind. This provides you with a working memory of knowledge you can carry with you as you read more material. The name of the game isn't about offloading thoughts; it's about neuroimprinting thoughts. This feature, combined with the character limits of notecards, is a great advantage of analog systems.

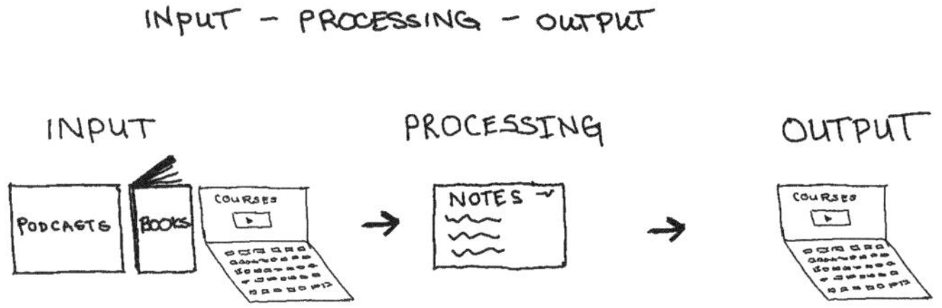

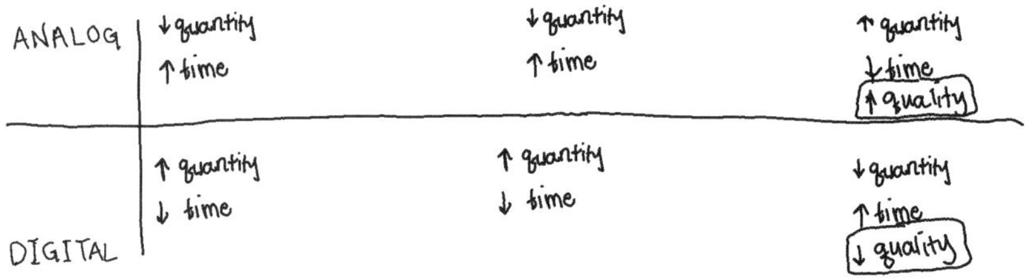

It's a paradox. The slower pace required to use an analog Zettelkasten results in a decrease in the number of items put into the system; it simply takes longer to add the same amount of information one might add to a digital system. The same applies to the processing of the information put into each system. With the analog system, more time is required to convert the material you read into knowledge by adding your own reformulations and reflections—something not commonly undertaken in the digital versions.

Yet here's where the paradox emerges. The workflow of the analog system (which takes more time to consume and process less information), actually results in producing a greater *quantity* of output in less time, compared with digital systems. Also, the *quality* of the output outshines output produced by digital notetaking systems.

There are two key factors that enable the paradoxical occurrence of greater work output from an analog system that slows work down: (1) neuroimprinting enables a more robust working memory when writing and creating output, and (2) the character limit of analog systems enable combinatorial possibilities in perpetuity that thereby enable more content to be generated from the same units of knowledge (namely, from the same notecards).

ANALOG PREVENTS HYPER-SELECTION OF IRRELEVANT MATERIAL WHILE READING

The most critical aspect of notetaking is not what to select from the material you read; it's what *not* to select from the material you read. According to Fiona McPherson, a cognitive scientist specializing in the study of Notetaking, the "most crucial" part of the entire process revolves around *selection.* By selection she is referring to determining what information is important, and just as critically, *not selecting information that is not important.*[18]

For this reason, tools that help you to *not* select irrelevant information prove advantageous. The Antinet shines in this respect due to the time and effort required to select material by writing it down by hand (in the process of extracting worthwhile notes and writing them down on a bibcard). This takes much more effort than merely highlighting somewhat interesting passages on a Kindle (something I did before discovering the Antinet). This extraction and selection process ends up increasing your focus while reading, so that you soon adopt a habit of selecting only the most truly meaningful ideas from the material you read.

Analog systems are "highly selective," as the scholar Alberto Cevolini points out. Its selectivity is a feature, not a bug. Handwriting text is harder than typing text. It takes longer. It forces "selectivity" in the system. "It would be meaningless to move the whole content of a book into [a Zettelkasten]," writes Cevolini.[19]

With digital systems, it's trivial to extract and store information from the

---

18 Fiona McPherson, *Effective Note-taking,* revised edition (Wellington: Wayz Press, 2018), 13.

19 Alberto Cevolini, ed., Forgetting Machines: Knowledge Management Evolution in Early Modern Europe, Library of the Written Word, volume 53 (Leiden; Boston: Brill, 2016), 31.

material you read. This is not a good thing. Very quickly you accumulate and collect way too much information. Before you know it, you're drowning. The bad information crowds out the good. This is another reason analog systems outshine digital.

ANALOG ENABLES ONE TO COMPARE, CONTRAST, AND ORGANIZE THOUGHTS BETTER THAN DIGITAL

As Sönke Ahrens observes, "to have concrete notes in front of our eyes and be able to compare them directly makes differences, even small ones, much easier to spot."[20]

I couldn't have written this book without the aid of laying out all of the different sections on my desk. I created a hub of cards that had collective cardlinks on them. Each card was organized by topic and contained subtopics that pointed me to various card addresses in my Antinet. I then moved them around a large table to create the perfect logical layout for this book. Here's a picture of it:

20 Sönke Ahrens, *How to Take Smart Notes: One Simple Technique to Boost Writing, Learning and Thinking: For Students, Academics and Nonfiction Book Writers* (North Charleston, SC: CreateSpace, 2017), 122.

To write the book, I simply proceeded card-by-card and column-by-column. Each card contained its own numeric-alpha address in the top-right corner so that they could later be refiled in my Antinet. Here's a closer look:

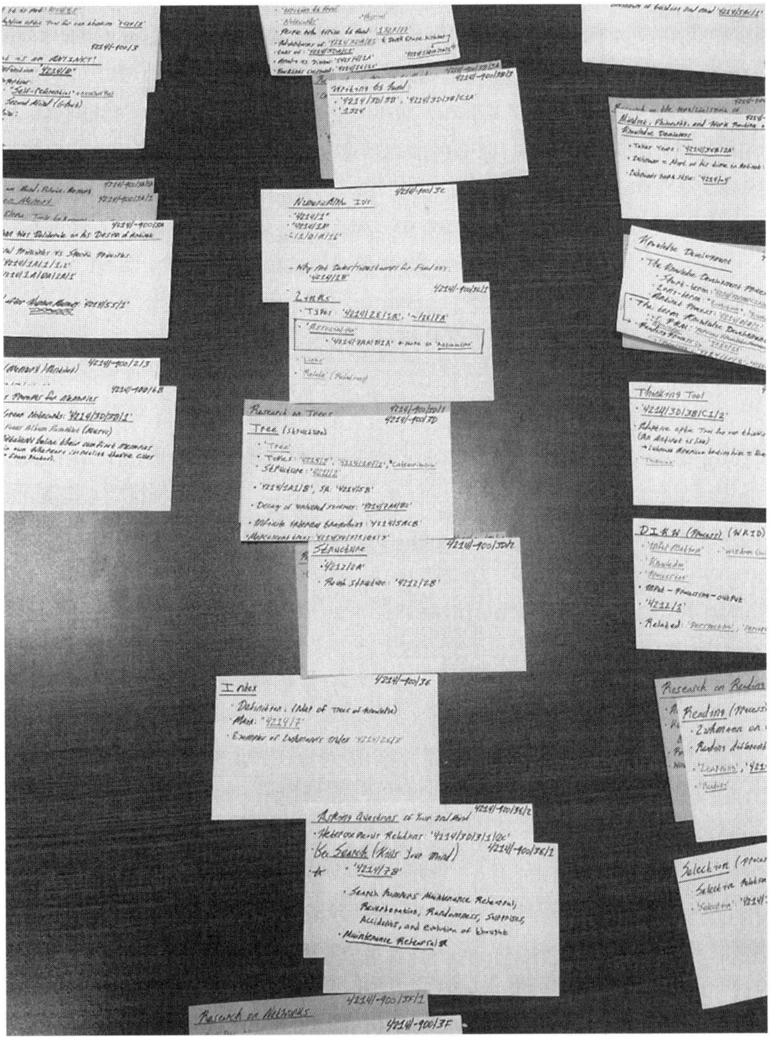

In the past, I've used analogous digital tools like Trello, Scrivener and others to organize information. None came close to my experience of physically working with knowledge. By moving around the individual units on a table, writing my book became a much easier task. This is but another overlooked advantage of analog knowledge systems.

ANALOG FORCES ONE TO FOLLOW BEST PRACTICES

One of the other benefits of an analog system centers on the fact that it forces one to follow best practices and guidelines brought forth by digital Zettelkasten teachers. For instance, one author teaching digital Zettelkasten recommends linking and rewriting notes in order to make notetaking less boring.[21] This advice is a *recommendation* for digital Zettelkasten users. For analog Zettelkasten users, it's a *requirement.* There's no other choice. There seems to be confusion among digital Zettelkasten practitioners about this. Every single time you install a card in the Antinet, you're effectively linking it to all other cards in the system. You give it a numeric-alpha address that provides it with a chained location in your tree of knowledge. It's essentially linked to its closest neighbors, and their closest neighbors, and their closest neighbors, and on and on.

With digital Zettelkasten systems, developers devise synthetic rules and methodologies to improvise for their own best practices. Digital Zettelkasten systems have jury-rigged guidelines and principles that are all but impossible to follow because they require near-perfect self-discipline to stick with. With the Antinet, no self-discipline is required. The best practices of linking every note and rewriting and rephrasing ideas is built into the core protocol of analog systems.

In brief, Digital Zettelkasten systems rely on willpower to function. If you're using a system that relies on personal willpower, it's inevitable that a breakdown will occur at some point. With the Antinet, this is not an issue.

ANALOG EXPOSES YOUR OWN MISTAKES AND SELF-DECEPTIONS MORE EFFECTIVELY THAN DIGITAL

Modern society's most fundamental metaphorical symbol for *good vs. evil* is the biblical *tree of knowledge.* Like the biblical tree of knowledge, your own tree of knowledge that you create in the Antinet is susceptible to *evil*

21 David Kadavy, Digital Zettelkasten: Principles, Methods, & Examples (Kadavy, Inc., 2022), 14-15.

information. Actually, let's not call it *evil* information, but *unwise* information. The unwise information I speak of does not derive from cunning serpents tempting you to eat a fruit.[22] Rather, the *unwise* information I speak of derives from a different beast altogether: yourself!

Indeed, when you review the thoughts of your mind and happen upon a view or opinion you no longer hold as true, it's extremely difficult to delude yourself into believing you never held such an opinion. Why? Because it's staring you in the face—*in your own handwriting.*

You see, your Antinet, your own tree of knowledge, contains *both* wise fruit and unwise fruit (or good fruit vs. evil fruit).

On one hand, it's important to express your thoughts and ideas *truly* with conviction and self-belief. As Charlie Munger says, "Never underestimate the man who overestimates himself."[23] As Gary Halbert, the best copywriter who ever lived puts it, "Nothing is impossible for the man who refuses to listen to reason."[24] While certainly containing some truth, both Munger's and Halbert's statements communicate the jocoserious reality implanted within their words. At one level, Munger and Halbert were advocating for their readers to believe in themselves; yet, at another level they were warning of the power wielded in doing so.

Taken to the extreme, self-belief quickly can transform into self-delusion. "The simple truth," as Munger puts it, "is that we aren't adapted to face the world as it is today." He goes on to outline how critical the *environment* was for shaping the traits of our ancestors. "We can learn to push our minds into

---

22 Robert Alter, ed., The Hebrew Bible: A Translation with Commentary, First edition (New York; London: W. W. Norton & Company, 2018), 90-91.

23 Taylor Locke, "Charlie Munger on Elon Musk: 'Never Underestimate the Man Who Overestimates Himself,'" CNBC, February 14, 2020, https://www.cnbc.com/2020/02/14/charlie-munger-shares-opinion-of-tesla-ceo-elon-musk.html.

24 "A Quote from The Boron Letters," accessed March 21, 2022, https://www.goodreads.com/quotes/7317468-nothing-is-impossible-for-a-man-who-refuses-to-listen.

alternative ways of thinking, but it isn't easy." Why's that? It comes down to one thing, according to Munger: "self-deception."[25]

Systems that expose us to our own self-deception and mistakes in thinking are far more valuable than systems that conceal such things.

Analog Stamps Your Mistakes In Time (And This is a Good Thing)

There is a saying dating back to at least 1915, "Everybody makes mistakes—that's why they put erasers on pencils."[26] I first heard this saying from my dad. However, when he recited it to me, I found myself disagreeing with a small but important component of it. My position is that, while it's useful to erase mistakes, there is an even more valuable exercise *in not using an eraser at all*! Instead, it's better to append new, corrected information behind or under the initial mistake. That way, you can view a history of your mistakes and see your growth. It also serves as a useful tool in the future for reviewing your past mistakes.

Why are mistakes valuable? Because they curb the risk of a grandiosity. Charlie Munger says it best: "I like people admitting they were complete stupid horses' asses. I know I'll perform better if I rub my nose in my mistakes. This is a wonderful trick to learn."[27]

After stating my case against erasers, my mom chimed in and backed me on this. Of course my dad wasn't arguing for the literal idea of forgetting about your mistakes. Neither was the original quote stating this. The quote about erasers argues that you should be OK making mistakes. This is 100% accurate. But if you want to experience next-level growth, you need to append

25 "Charlie Munger on The Psychology of Human Misjudgment," 25iq, February 2, 2013, https://25iq.com/2013/02/02/charlie-munger-on-the-psychology-of-human-misjudgment/.

26 Barry Popik, "Barry Popik," accessed May 23, 2021, https://www.barrypopik.com/index.php/newyorkcity/entry/everybodymakesmistakesthatswhytheyputerasersonpencils.

27 "Charlie Munger on Mistakes," 25iq, November 16, 2012, https://25iq.com/2012/11/16/charlie-munger-on-mistakes/.

revisions to your mistakes behind or beneath the initial mistake. Don't erase them. More, you need to rub your nose in your mistakes! It's humbling, it's deflating, but after a while, you start to develop a thick skin.

The power of the Antinet is that it stamps your mistakes in a capsule of time. You then view the evolution of your own self-deception in order to not fall into the trap of making similar mistakes again.

With digital systems, it's all-too-easy to simply overwrite or delete your own mistakes.

As Johannes Schmidt observes of Luhmann's Antinet:

> It contains not only validated knowledge but also reflects the thought process, including potential mistakes and blind alleys that were later revised but not removed from the file as the original cards always remained in Luhmann's file and perhaps a new card with revisions was added if needed.[28]

As the scholar, Markus Krajewski, writes of using an analog Zettelkasten, "The reader is not only reading his own memory, but rather also his shifting frame of reference over time."[29] Thus, when you review your own notes (in your own handwriting), you have changing perspectives that shift over time. You can view your "less complex" thoughts and how they've changed, developed and internally *evolved* over a long period.

Most surprising are the links stamped onto the cards at the moment you wrote them that shed light on what the past version of you was thinking at the time when you wrote them. "What is more surprising are the references listed."[30]

---

28 Johannes Schmidt, "Niklas Luhmann's Card Index: Thinking Tool, Communication Partner, Publication Machine," Forgetting Machines. Knowledge Management Evolution in Early Modern Europe 53 (2016), 309.

29 Markus Krajewski, *Note-Keeping: History, Theory, Practice of a Counter-Measurement against Forgetting* (Brill, 2016), 331.

30 Markus Krajewski, *Note-Keeping: History, Theory, Practice of a Counter-Measurement against Forgetting* (Brill, 2016), 331.

Here's an example from my own life. I once confused the terms *prospection* and *proprioception*.

Prospection is the concept of creating mental representations about the future (or possible future scenarios). Proprioception refers to your body's ability to sense movement, action, or its location.

This is one of my older notes (on a 3 x 5 inch card; for newer notes I use 4 x 6 inch cards). It's a *reformulation* note I took from reading the book, *Sapiens*. The card address is 2714/4:

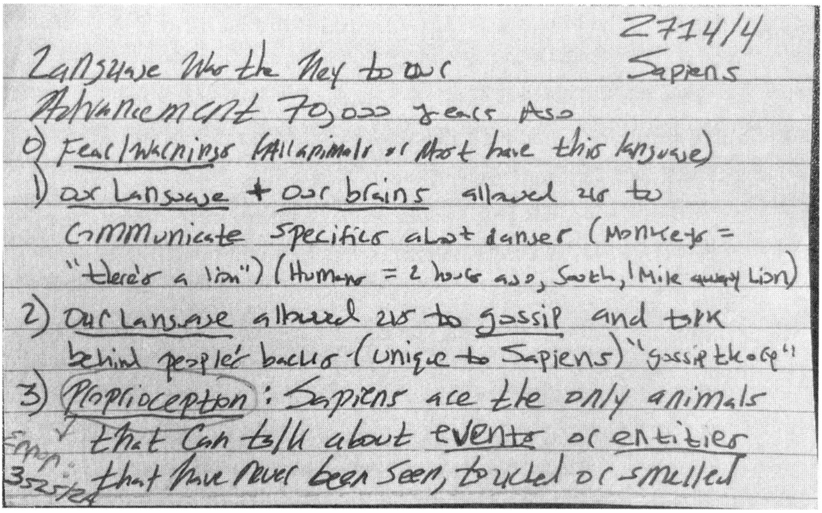

In the bottom left-hand corner I added an update in green ink (which tells me it's a new comment I added long after making the card): "Error," and in blue ink I include the cardlink: 3525/2A.[31] If we navigate to card 3525/2A, we find the following:

31 Note: I don't use blue ink anymore; I only use black ink (for main notes), red ink (for references), and green ink (for *both* comments and cardlinks).

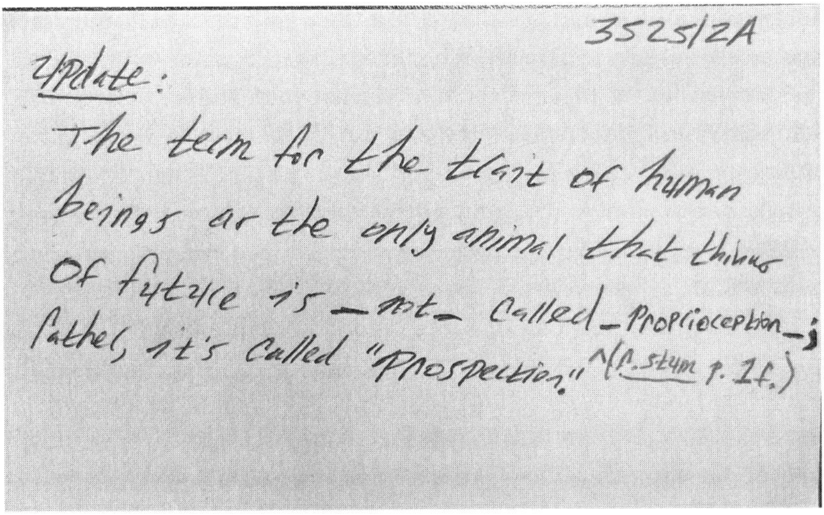
3525/2A

Update:

The term for the trait of human beings as the only animal that thinks of future is not called proprioception; rather, it's called "Prospection." (S. Stum p. 1f.)

Immediately linked to this card (by way of the tree internal branching structure), I find an old card 3525/2.

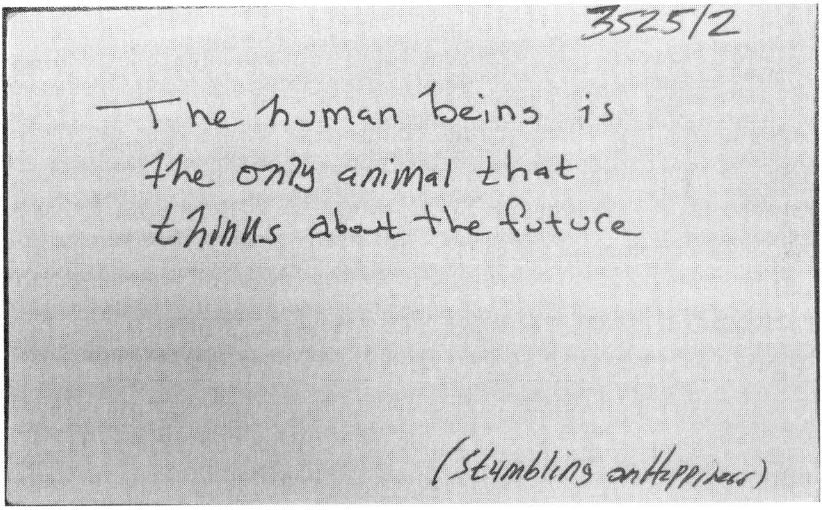
3525/2

The human being is the only animal that thinks about the future

(Stumbling on Happiness)

Aha! This is what I thought of originally when I wrote the first card (2714/4), but I couldn't quite recall where the idea came from, or what the term I was thinking of was. When I initially wrote 2714/4, I made the mistake of confusing the term *proprioception* with *prospection*, a concept I first learned about in the book *Stumbling on Happiness*.

Locking this mistake into a permanent state then allows me to communicate that such terms are sometimes confused. For instance, when writing a piece that happens to use the concept of *prospection* in the future, I could start with something like, *A term sometimes confused with proprioception is that of prospection, which means X, whereas proprioception means Y.* Stamping such a mistake permanently in the Antinet helps me refresh and re-remind myself of the confusion in order to prevent the mistake from occurring again. Even more powerful, however, is the opportunity this creates for an accidental breakthrough and creative insight. For instance, I could ask myself, *How are the concepts of proprioception related?* Interestingly enough, they are somewhat related. Proprioception involves the mental representation of your *present self*; whereas prospection relates to the mental representation of your *future self*. We can then explore why this may be the case by digging into the etymology of the terms. Before you know it, you're embarking on a journey of going deep into a field of knowledge that fascinates you. Inevitably you'll end up with much richer insights than is typically found taking digital notes.

There are ways to jury-rig such a system in digital form (using Git, for instance). However, I find that such solutions are an afterthought. They may expose the "change history" of a note or a document; however the feature is usually placed to the side of the screen of the main note. Even then, it requires manual digging and clicking to reveal the commit history (or change historyo of the note. With an Antinet, such a feature is baked into the core protocol of the system.

ANALOG ENABLES YOU TO GAIN BETTER FAMILIARITY WITH YOUR KNOWLEDGE

Another key property of the Antinet is revealed by Luhmann's familiarity with his own tree of knowledge. Luhmann knew his Zettelkasten like the back of his hand. His knowledge was permanently stamped onto his mind. One critical aspect of becoming a "publication machine" is how well you know your way around your knowledge. Johannes Schmidt does not overlook this factor, observing Luhmann "engaged in an ongoing process of tending to his file."[32] The extensive time he spent doing this resulted in him gaining

32 Johannes Schmidt, "Niklas Luhmann's Card Index: Thinking Tool, Communication

a deep understanding of his knowledge. For a thirty-plus year repository of information, one would think there would be a detailed table of contents to help him navigate; however, "Luhmann never created a detailed table of contents."[33]

Luhmann benefitted greatly by being essentially forced to work with his knowledge as it accumulated (due to the Zettelkasten's analog nature, and there being no search feature). This critical property allowed him to store deeply interconnected and complex information. It helped him integrate new ideas, all while gracefully navigating his mind and memory (past and present). He would insert newly acquired information into the appropriate place which resulted in deeply evolved thoughts.

How did Luhmann achieve such a deeply imprinted "groove" of his thoughts? There's several ways. First, his ideas were neuroimprinted on his mind due to the analog nature of the system. Second, he developed rapid recall of information from the deep web-like network embedded in the analog system. He developed this faculty by *engaging in the ongoing process of tending to his Antinet.*[34] When you partake in this process, it's very much distinct from the process of reviewing digital files. Reviewing digital files can cause your eyes to glaze over. You forget what you're searching for and soon become distracted by other things.

With the Antinet, searching for notes becomes a fun, active process, during which you think about and have a conversation with the material. You often find yourself challenging your notes, or, trying to understand the context that led you to write a particular thought. Most important, the process builds your memory in such a way that you and all of your thoughts and learnings

---

Partner, Publication Machine," Forgetting Machines. Knowledge Management Evolution in Early Modern Europe 53 (2016), https://pub.uni-bielefeld.de/record/2942475, 305.

33 Johannes Schmidt, "Niklas Luhmann's Card Index: Thinking Tool, Communication Partner, Publication Machine," Forgetting Machines. Knowledge Management Evolution in Early Modern Europe 53 (2016), https://pub.uni-bielefeld.de/record/2942475, 305.

34 Johannes Schmidt, "Niklas Luhmann's Card Index: Thinking Tool, Communication Partner, Publication Machine," Forgetting Machines. Knowledge Management Evolution in Early Modern Europe 53 (2016), https://pub.uni-bielefeld.de/record/2942475, 305.

reverberate in your mind. You effectively prime your mind for compounding growth, which emerges in your output.

For me, this was an unexpected hidden benefit of analog. In retrospect, however, it's pretty obvious. You build out your brain's memory constantly without feeling like it's a chore.

In my time using digital notetaking apps, I forced such a practice upon myself using a plugin that opened a random note. This didn't last long. Opening a random note every day felt like a chore, and I quickly dropped the practice.

A more effective method, which I've stuck with for over a decade, is the practice of reviewing a random chunk notecards. I would randomly sift through my reading notes and allow the concepts I had previously read to reverberate through my mind.

Still, it requires self-discipline and seems to wane after some time. However, in working with an Antinet, one reviews thoughts automatically while searching for ideas. It's a lot more fun. It's less of a chore, and it always introduces opportunities for surprises.

The ability to rapidly learn and later retrieve novel associations, memories, and information is an important ability. In fact, it's a core part of what makes us human. This is why such a feature is so important in the Antinet. As Michael Kahana states, one's ability to recall and associate ideas is "an important tool in coping effectively with one's environment."[35]

Yet in our era of rapidly expanding digital technology, with regard to human memory, people seem to throw logic and rationality out the window. That same Kahana also points out that having a good memory may not be all that important for the ultimate survival of the species due to our "present era of personal-data assistants and Google's vast searchable databases."[36]

---

35 Michael Jacob Kahana, Foundations of Human Memory. (New York: Oxford University Press, 2014), 112.

36 Michael Jacob Kahana, Foundations of Human Memory. (New York: Oxford University

This logical jump misses one thing: actual logic. Developing your memory and your ability to recognize patterns when learning new information *is* critical—and likely will remain critical—at the least for noteworthy success in your field. Analog systems enhance this faculty; digital systems seem less effective in doing so.

OTHER PROS OF ANALOG SYSTEMS

One concept you'll learn about in this book is what is termed *external context* in the field of human memory studies. External context introduces properties that can later help you recall information and knowledge. These things include parts of your sensory system—sounds, tastes, textures, etc.[37] These properties are found in analog systems; they are not native to digital systems. In a later section I talk about how I retrieve certain memories and ideas based on the external context and cues generated by certain notecards. Digital systems do not possess such features.

The Science Behind Analog Systems Developing Knowledge

The premise of analog systems aiding in the development of your mind (compared with digital systems) can be explained by the latest research in the study of human memory. With analog systems, you're constantly in a state of *recognition,* reviewing thoughts found in your own system and trying to *recognize* the core idea behind the concept. When you read new information you're also trying to recognize the core idea behind the concept.

When you recognize a concept, thought, or idea, two processes occur within your mind.

First, the *familiarity process* kicks into gear. When you think of the concept or idea, a value of your confidence in the familiarity of the content that arises emerges. It's essentially a *confidence value* of how confident you are and how

Press, 2014), 112.

37 Michael Jacob Kahana, Foundations of Human Memory. (New York: Oxford University Press, 2014), 12.

familiar you are with a thought. This concept comprises something called *strength theory* in human memory.

The second process is the *recollection process*. The recollection process involves the recall of *contextual information* related to the content of the thought.

For exceptional knowledge work, it's critical to exercise your mind's recognition ability—that is, the faculty for recognizing concepts, thoughts, and ideas. This is critical because it allows you to do two things when reading a text:

First, it enables you to create *information* by way of *comparison*. As Luhmann writes:

> Information is an intra-systematic event. It results when one compares one message or entry with regard to other possibilities. Information, accordingly, originates only in systems which possess a comparative schema—even if this amounts only to: "this or something else."[38]

By neuroimprinting concepts in your mind, you're effectively enabling a working memory store of knowledge to *compare* with new ideas that you come across in your reading. You then set off a process of comparing the idea from your readings with the knowledge already stored in your Antinet. You cannot install a new piece of knowledge in your Antinet without comparing it to your current knowledge. You're forced to find *the most similar* location wherein that knowledge should be installed. With digital systems, this is not a requirement. Digital does not force the *comparison* process into every single note before it's created.

Second, by exercising your ability to recollect concepts, you are forced to relate information to a *selective* set of other *relations* (a process necessary to create knowledge, and through action, wisdom).

---

38 "Communicating with Slip Boxes by Niklas Luhmann," accessed May 4, 2021, https://luhmann.surge.sh/communicating-with-slip-boxes.

To summarize, the analog nature of the Antinet develops the mind's faculties for *recollecting* and *recognizing* interesting patterns while reading. This allows you to make connections to material ruminating in your second mind.

Familiarity is developed through writing longhand, and it is furthered due to the system not having a search feature. There's no other choice but to actively review and work with your knowledge.

Recollection emerges through developing your thoughts *within contexts* (i.e., branches, stems and areas within your tree of knowledge).

As some scholars have observed, both of these variables paradoxically transform notetaking from a system designed to store memories into a system that both stores *and* enhances memories. "[Handwritten] notetaking [due to repetition that helped the mind retain passages] and the respective construction of a card index were considered both a substitute for personal memory and a memory aid."[39]

This phenomenon may not be exclusive to analog systems, however I argue that it's more common in analog systems because analog systems *force* the occurrence of familiarity and recollection, even if it's inconvenient (it's much more convenient to use the search box of a digital notetaking app).

Luhmann talked about *generalizing* concepts and abstracting them out in such a way as to create containers of insight later on. He highlighted the practice of creating answers to specific questions that he could ask his Antinet. For instance, Luhmann posed the following question: *why are museums empty, whereas exhibits of paintings by Monet, Picasso, or Medici are too crowded?* The answer seems to revolve around exhibits being short-term events—they're "temporally limited." Luhmann then created the following index entry: "preference for what is temporally limited." This allowed Luhmann to accumulate more cards that exhibit a *preference for what is temporally*

39 **Alberto Cevolini, ed., Forgetting Machines: Knowledge Management Evolution in Early Modern Europe, Library of the Written Word, volume 53 (Leiden ; Boston: Brill, 2016), 24.**

limited.[40] Later, when more cards accumulated under this entry, Luhmann could compare the different phenomena that correlated with a *preference for what is temporally limited*. From there he could spot patterns and propose a theory for why certain things occur.

This is a deliberate process. It takes work and effort to create. There's no *magical future* to surface such insights. Cutesy bubble graphs of notes won't magically surface such insights. Neither will the so-called "power of digital search."

Let's talk briefly about the notion concerning the power of digital search. In reality, the power of digital search is a myth. Due to search functionality, digital notetaking systems possess less impetus to exercise the recognition faculty of one's mind. With analog, you're forced to deliberately create patterns in your mind as well as shortcuts for concepts to spot later on. This is yet another advantage of analog systems.

These are the pros of working with an analog system. These strengths have emerged from my own experience working with an Antinet for over a year, and from my research into analog thinking systems. There are other positive aspects that are more obvious; however, I won't bother going into the obvious ones in detail. It's best to experience them for yourself by testing the Antinet for yourself. That's the fun part, anyway!

Let's now discuss the cons of analog.

THE CONS OF ANALOG

There are no cons of analog.

Just kidding! There are a number of negative aspects that arise while working with analog systems. Let's go through them now.

---

40 "Communicating with Slip Boxes by Niklas Luhmann," accessed May 4, 2021, https://luhmann.surge.sh/communicating-with-slip-boxes.

ANALOG FACES THE RISK OF DESTRUCTION DUE TO FIRE, FLOOD, OR OTHER DISASTER

At least once a week I get the following type of comment on Reddit or my YouTube channel: *Yeah, sounds great Scott, but what about a fire or flood?*

It's a valid question. Many of history's greatest minds who used analog knowledge systems suffered the downside of losing their archive to fire or flood. For instance, Thomas Jefferson's personal library and notes were the casualty of a house fire, causing him great despair.[41] The same happened to Aldous Huxley in his later years when a brushfire broke out at his California home. He rushed in and saved his manuscript of the book he was working on at the time (*The Island*).[42] Unfortunately his personal library of four thousand books was engulfed by the flames.

There's no denying that a downside of analog centers around its risk of destruction (due to fire, flood, or other natural disaster). But is it really enough risk to warrant opting for digital over analog? I think not.

Here's one way to think of this: would you rather live a life possessing something extremely valuable that can be lost, or, would you rather possess something that is worth less without risk of loss? Note: I contend that digital notes are not *worthless*; but they are *worth less* in that they contain *less worth* than analog notes. The reason centers on the thought that is poured into notes written by hand. They are worth more. They take more time, they require more attention, and they are created at greater expense than digital notes.

Like any good hero's journey, after you spend months or years building your own Antinet, you'll experience the moment of realizing where the value truly resides. The value of the Antinet and its analog notes does not reside in the cabinets in which you store your thoughts. Rather, the value resides in how your brain develops and changes. Working with an analog system like the Antinet transforms the way that you think. In essence, the true value of

---

41 Jon Meacham, Thomas Jefferson: The Art of Power, Illustrated edition (New York, NY: Random House Trade Paperbacks, 2013).

42 Dana Sawyer, Aldous Huxley: A Biography (Trillium Press, 2015), 182.

the Antinet is not its physical material, it's the metaphysical material that it creates. The value is in what the analog system does to your mind, not the actual contents of the box itself.

This mirrors that moment in the hero's journey wherein the hero has victory in his or her sights. Yet the hero foregoes crossing the finish line because his friend who had helped him on the journey (and who the hero may be in conflict with) is suddenly in trouble. In this moment, the hero realizes the physical prize is *worth less* than the fulfillment and love of relationships and connection with others (i.e., the metaphysical prize). In other words, the hero chooses fulfillment over achievement. With this realization, the hero comes to understand that life isn't about struggling for the external physical item signifying achievement. Rather, life is about the fulfillment of internal metaphysical qualities (such as virtue, growth, challenge and self-respect).

I realize this may sound sappy and ridiculous, especially in the context of reading a book about developing knowledge using notecards, but I assure you there's truth in this notion. The true value of the Antinet journey is not in the external physical knowledge; it's what the process of developing the knowledge does to your mind. If my Antinet burned down, I'd do two things: (1) I'd sit down and write furiously to finish the project I was in the middle of, while the knowledge was still fresh, and (2) I'd start a new Antinet. It's that simple.

That's a metaphysical solution to analog's risk of destruction due to disaster. However, there's also a physical solution. Fireproof and waterproof cabinets exist and they're quite effective. However, they aren't cheap. They're in the same price range as a computer. Still, they are an option. If you live in an area where you greatly fear the risk of damage and destruction, you can certainly go this route.

For myself, I have not gone this route. I have thought about looking into fireproof and waterproof cabinets built specifically for the Antinet's notecards; however I have not done this yet at the time of this writing. For me, I sleep soundly at night knowing my Antinet is stored in a safe office in a nice building. It's not without risk, yet it doesn't keep me up at night.

Now, I would like to pose a counter-intuitive idea: the risk of destruction is a good thing. I think there's a subconscious component to my notes being analog whereby I'm more motivated to turn my notes into a published product. Because my notes stare me in the face (and there is a sizable amount of notes to stare me in the face), I'm more motivated to actually sit down at the computer and type them into my text editor. When my notes are converted into text, it extinguishes the risk of fire (pun intended). The risk of fire or water damage actually forces me to publish my work faster, and to turn it into something useful more immediately.

To wrap things up, the risk of damage and destruction of notes due to fire, flood, or other natural disaster is real—yet it's also not real. It's real in that it can physically happen; yet it's not real in that it cannot physically happen unless your mind is destroyed by the fire, flood, or other disaster—and that's a different problem altogether! That's a problem digital systems cannot account for either.

ANALOG IS HARDER THAN DIGITAL

Another con of analog is that it's harder than digital. It requires more effort, time, and deliberate attention. More, it requires a greater quantity of work to produce less. With digital notetaking systems, knowledge is easier to create. It's also cheaper to create. However, I contend that the extra effort and the deeper thought processing is worth it. Oftentimes, the hard way is the best way. In fact, it can be argued that it's the only *true* way.

Writing by hand was valued by writers in the early modern period precisely for the reason that it was hard. It sharpened not only their faculties for controlling their *attention*, but also improved their *retention* of material. As scholar Anne Blair observes, writers used the process of writing by hand as "a mental and physical discipline that sharpened attention and retention." [43]

For myself, using an analog system helps cure my ADHD-tendencies. When I begin writing a main note (i.e., reformulating or reflecting on material),

---

43 Ann Blair, *Early Modern Attitudes toward the Delegation of Copying and Note-Taking* (Brill, 2016), 265.

I feel almost sucked into the experience. I cannot pry myself away from my desk until I finish the thought. This practice is certainly not exclusive to analog; however, I find it more prevalent in analog. I also find my thoughts to be better developed and processed when writing by hand. Much of this book was written by hand using my Antinet. This sentence and this section you're reading right now, however, were not written by hand. I'm thinking by typing on my computer (hypocrite)! While I do not think this is necessarily a bad section, I do think it would have been much better and had a stronger impact if I had taken the time to deliberately write it out by hand first. The reason I have not done so is because the content backing much of what I'm writing here will be covered in another section of this book (a section on the power of writing by hand). So, essentially I have indeed written out the core idea of this section (the power of writing by hand), yet I have not specifically handwritten *this section*. Still, I have deeply thought through the core idea I'm writing about in this section. How so? Because I developed it elsewhere through writing by hand.

Analog is harder than digital not only in terms of the effort it requires, but in other ways as well. With an analog system, you must buy a variety of materials. Blank notecards, boxes, containers, Wite-Out, pens, rulers, and other items. That's not too difficult, yet it does indeed require more space.

Analog systems also result in quizzical regard from others who see you using such. They may question your sanity for investing so much time and energy into boxes of physical notecards. If you aren't strong-minded, you may even end up questioning your own sanity!

Here's The Truth: The Hard Way Is Better

One of the biggest myths about Zettelkasten centers around the tradeoff between ease vs. effort. Here's the truth: you must be prepared to do things the hard way if you wish to produce great work. The paradox, however, is that the hard way turns out to be the easy way. The up front hard work of writing notes by hand later turns into the greatest benefit of the system.

As Mortimer Adler outlines in his classic *How to Read a Book,* one must be prepared to go about processing books the hard way. "That is the only way,"

Adler writes. "Without external help of any sort, you go to work on the book. With nothing but the power of your own mind."[44]

After Ryan Holiday wrote a piece outlining his notebox system, he responded to a question he is frequently asked: "Wouldn't digital be easier?" Here's Holiday's response:

> Yes. But I don't want this to be easy. Writing them [notes] down by hand forces me to take my time and to go over everything again (taking notes on a Kindle is too easy and that's the problem). Also being able to physically arrange stuff is crucial for getting the structure of your book or project right. I can move cards from one category to another. As I shuffle through the cards, I bump into stuff I had forgotten about, etc.[45]

Holiday makes three important points here. One is the benefit of an analog system enabling him to better develop his thoughts. The other is the benefit of haptic factors utilized in knowledge management (that is, being able to lay the cards out in front of you to physically rearrange). The last benefit Holiday touches on is bumping into stuff he had forgotten about. Here Holiday is describing *maintenance rehearsal* in human memory.

All of these aspects, admittedly the *hard way to do this,* end up producing better work. The hard way, paradoxically, becomes the best way.

The bottom line is that analog thinking systems are hard. They take more time and energy investment than digital systems. They're also less conventional than digital systems, and thus suffer from an implicit bias that digital systems are used by smarter people who are geeky enough to know shortcuts

---

44 Mortimer Jerome Adler and Charles Van Doren, How to Read a Book, Rev. and updated ed (New York: Simon and Schuster, 1972), 7.

45 Ryan Holiday, "The Notecard System: The Key For Remembering, Organizing And Using Everything You Read," RyanHoliday.Net (blog), April 1, 2014, https://ryanholiday.net/the-notecard-system-the-key-for-remembering-organizing-and-using-everything-you-read/.

and hotkeys (rubbish). This is a false notion. There are no shortcuts. In fact, the shortcuts end up falling far short of the desired destination: excellence.

ANALOG IS LESS MOBILE THAN DIGITAL (OR IS IT?)

Another con of analog centers around the perceived immobility of the system. Its roots, once again, trace back to Sönke Ahrens. In *How to Take Smart Notes*, Ahrens says he chose to use a digital Zettelkasten for "mobility."[46] His presumption is that a laptop storing his notes is easier to carry than a filing cabinet full of notecards. While this may be true, he's actually making the wrong comparison. Sure, a laptop carrying notes is more mobile than carrying around filing cabinets full of notecards. However, they are not equivalent. He mistakenly believes that the two are equal when, in reality, they are not.

An analog system like the Antinet contains thoughts and a structure of knowledge that are irreplicable in a digital notetaking system. The knowledge Ahrens carries with him on his laptop is of lesser value and worth than the knowledge contained in a robust analog system.

In addition, the material you carry with you when using an analog system does not just reside in the card boxes. The knowledge resides in your mind. Such knowledge, when digitally managed, would otherwise not be stamped in your mind in such a way. In effect, with the Antinet you carry knowledge with you, wherever you go. Whether you're in the shower (where breakthroughs in thinking actually happen), or whether you're on your couch reading, you carry with you knowledge that would otherwise be missing if you used digital systems. In this way, it can be argued that digital systems are *less* mobile than *analog* systems. Why? Because with analog systems, you can carry more knowledge, internally, than you can with digital systems. Plus digital notes result in cheaper, less processed knowledge stored in the depths of a notetaking app.

46 Sönke Ahrens, How to Take Smart Notes: One Simple Technique to Boost Writing, Learning and Thinking: For Students, Academics and Nonfiction Book Writers (North Charleston, SC: CreateSpace, 2017), 31.

ANALOG KNOWLEDGE SYSTEMS VS. DIGITAL KNOWLEDGE SYSTEMS

As the data scientist John Foreman observes, machines can help us measure the correlations and proximities between clusters of groups or individuals who buy a particular item; however, they cannot tell us *why people do not buy*.[47] There is an internal experience (a *theory of mind*) that is invisible to computers. Computers do not know what it's like to be human. Humans do, and there's no replacement for this missing feature. I'd like to propose that analog systems retain *humanness* better than digital systems. They seem to also introduce the *understanding* of the internal human experience better than digital systems.

Many people inappropriately compare digital and analog Zettelkasten systems. Even learned scholars deeply familiar with knowledge systems make such a mistake. For instance, Markus Krajewski writes: "A critical advantage lies in the fact that software based literary databases are not simply able to remember, but can also be employed as *productive assistants* in the production of arguments."[48] The problem with this scholar's assertion centers around two things: First, Luhmann himself described his Zettelkasten as a personal productive assistant.[49] And second, Krajewski does not explain *why* he holds the view that a digital Zettelkasten can be a productive assistant whereas an analog Zettelkasten cannot.[50]

---

47 John W. Foreman, Data Smart: Using Data Science to Transform Information into Insight (Indianapolis, IN: Wiley, 2014). There are a lot of reasons why someone does *not* take an action, but only a few reasons why someone does. This introduces the concept of cosine distance, a mathematical method for determining the similarity between two documents or vectors. Yet the problem still remains for computers: determining why someone *did not* buy. These are creative problems that involve understanding the human experience, which computers are not as capable of solving (compared with a marketer who studies psychology, at least).

48 Markus Krajewski, *Note-Keeping: History, Theory, Practice of a Counter-Measurement against Forgetting* (Brill, 2016), 322.

49 "ZK II: Zettel 9/8,1—Niklas Luhmann-Archiv," accessed March 21, 2022, https://niklas-luhmann-archiv.de/bestand/zettelkasten/zettel/ZK_2_NB_9-8-1_V.

50 Although perhaps it can be explained by the fact that he created a piece of software that proposes to replace the need for an analog Note-taking system. Along these lines, the scholar could be simply seeing his software through rose-colored glasses.

THE DOWNSIDES OF DIGITAL

Many seem to overlook the downsides of digital. We have a vague sense that digital environments are distracting; however research is starting to show us how distracting they actually are. For instance, one study tracked the anonymous digital activity of fifty-thousand users. The results illustrated that half of the users checked communication apps (like Slack and email) "every six minutes or less."[51]

When you're working, even if you have notifications turned off, a distracting app is just a click away. This environment is not optimal for deep work or writing.

Furthermore, the digital work environment has been shown to result in suboptimal health. *The International Archives of Occupational and Environment Health* published a study that observed long-term trends of nearly five thousand Swedish workers. The results showed a trend of suboptimal health outcomes associated with high information and digital technology usage. Other research shows that email is connected with unhappiness. In other words, every six minutes or so when you're looped into checking email, you're also looped into an activity that has been shown to cause unhappiness.[52]

In brief, the digital environment appears to be more distracting and also leads to less happiness and suboptimal health. Yet the digital work environment is the very thing I find myself having to convince the majority of knowledge workers to escape!

IF LUHMANN WERE ALIVE TODAY

One might be tempted to think that if Luhmann were alive today, he would opt for a digital notetaking system. I have several reasons why I think he would not.

---

51 Cal Newport, A World Without Email: Reimagining Work in an Age of Communication Overload (New York: Portfolio, 2021), 11.

52 Cal Newport, A World Without Email: Reimagining Work in an Age of Communication Overload (New York: Portfolio, 2021), 37.

First and foremost, Luhmann lived until 1998. Personal computers were introduced in 1977 and became common in the 1980s.[53] It's likely that an academic who was familiar with information science and systems theory would be savvy enough to learn how a personal computer works. Yet Luhmann never seemed to move to the digital medium for managing his knowledge.

In fact, later in his life (when computers were a more accessible option) Luhmann wrote a piece titled *Learning to Read*. In it, Luhmann introduced various best practices for reading. He advised the taking of notes (not excerpts, but reformulation notes), and he also advises readers to store those notes in a computer or an analog Zettelkasten.[54] Even after parting with this advice, Luhmann continued to use his analog Zettelkasten. Therefore, perhaps the question is not whether Luhmann would choose digital if he were alive today—after all, he already had that option. Rather the question becomes, why did Luhmann choose to stick with his analog Zettelkasten? The primary reason centers on what his analog Zettelkasten became for Luhmann: it became his *second mind*.

There's a continual fallacy that arises in confusing systems storing information for others vs. systems that store knowledge for oneself. The same scholar who calls digital systems *productive assistants* also asserts that slipboxes, noteboxes (and Antinets), are for "internal use only."[55]

Luhmann's goal, quite literally, centered on creating a productive assistant to bounce ideas off of, and guess what…he achieved it with his analog Zettelkasten. When given the choice to discard the second mind he created (and opt for digital instead), Luhmann clearly made the right choice: he chose his Antinet.

❋ ❋ ❋

53 "Home Computer," in Wikipedia, July 15, 2021, https://en.wikipedia.org/w/index.php?title=Homecomputer&oldid=1033746593.

54 Niklas Luhmann, Niklas Luhmann Short Cuts (English Translation), 2002, 83.

55 Markus Krajewski, *Note-Keeping: History, Theory, Practice of a Counter-Measurement against Forgetting* (Brill, 2016), 319.

The physical, external properties that make such systems like the Antinet more powerful than digital are becoming increasingly recognized by scholars for their powerful features (when they're not shockingly overlooked). The best advertisement for an analog Zettelkasten is perhaps an article titled "*Rank and File*," in which the author professes awe for the intellectual prowess of a professor who inspired him.[56] It turns out that this revered professor used an analog system of notecards. The author attempted to employ such a notetaking system in digital form, only to realize its shortcomings. It's rather head-scratching, but the author doesn't then try an analog Zettelkasten system. Instead, after his failure in making use out of a digital Zettelkasten, the author gives up on the idea completely. It's unfortunate. The only thing he got wrong in his digital Zettelkasten was the digital part.

PEOPLE OF ANALOG

My uncle is an attorney based in Los Angeles, California. He was born to be an attorney. He's one of the rarer attorneys who is passionate, charming (in his own mind), and most shocking of all, he's an attorney who is not a complete a-hole! He also has a steel trap for a memory. According to him, it's not that he has a good memory, it's just that he can't seem to forget things! The things he remembers aren't legal cases and practical stuff. They're things like football stats, player's names and numbers, Heisman trophy winners by year, the scores of every Super Bowl ever played, and more. He knows every single winner of the Indianapolis 500, dating back to the year 1911. You simply give him a year, and he'll instantly tell you the name of the winner and any other contextual details about the event.

On a recent Super Bowl Sunday we decided to watch the football game at my parent's home. A few hours before the game started, I decided to take a break from being around company, and I found a quiet place in my father's home office where my father was working as well. At a separate desk, I began making main notes from the bibcard I had created while reading Luhmann's book *Short Cuts*. After some time, my uncle walked in to see what me and my dad were up to.

---

56 "Rank and File," Real Life, accessed January 14, 2022, https://reallifemag.com/rank-and-file/.

My dad was up to his usual stuff: paying bills, returning emails from clients, etc. However, my uncle turned to me and saw six notecards of main notes scattered on my desk. "What the hell are you doing?" he asked. "Whoa, that's actually pretty good handwriting!" After giving him a surface-level explanation of the notecard system and professing the power of writing by hand, he replied, "That's been my secret to success. Every opening statement I've ever done in my legal career, I've written out by hand."

I wouldn't be surprised if writing things out by hand also stands key to his steel trap memory.

The more I share the power of analog methods, of notecards, and writing by hand, the more people I discover who use such tools. I get information sent to me from my fellow Antinetters attesting to this. I also keep an eye out while reading. I frequently spot people who reveal their secrets to revolve around analog knowledge tools. When I do, I usually note them down.

For instance, take Ted Nelson, the godfather of hypertext documents and hyperlinks who inspired the internet as we know it. One would expect him to arrive at meetings with a laptop. Yet, he uses analog tools like notebooks, notecards, sticky notes, and tape recorders. In a humorous account by Kevin Kelly, the creator of Wired magazine, Kelly shares how Nelson arrived at their meeting to outline the future with such tools.[57]

One of the best marketers of all time is an old curmudgeon named Dan Kennedy. He's a character who sports a horseshoe mustache and a "No B.S." attitude (which also serves as the title for his book series). A central point in his book *No B.S. Time Management for Entrepreneurs* focuses on creating a "success environment" for oneself. This environment is to be stocked with analog tools. He lists off tools including clocks, symbols of wealth, folders, massive Ziploc bags for each project, and, of course, notecards.[58]

---

57 Kevin Kelly, The Inevitable: Understanding the 12 Technological Forces That Will Shape Our Future (New York, New York: Penguin Books, 2017).

58 Dan S. Kennedy, No B.S. Time Management for Entrepreneurs: The Ultimate No Holds Barred Kick Butt Take No Prisoners Guide to Time Productivity and Sanity, 3rd edition

On the very first page of *The Journals of Abraham Maslow* we find Maslow stating the importance of managing his knowledge using analog tools and 3 x 5 inch notecards.[59]

Indeed, the "soul" of Umberto Eco's classic book, *How to Write a Thesis,* is his analog notecard system.[60]

And then there's John August, the screenwriter behind movies like *Big Fish, Charlie's Angels, Titan A.E.* and *Charlie and the Chocolate Factory*. What's the secret to August's success? Writing his story down on notecards and laying them out on a table. From there he organizes the story and develops the screenplay.[61]

F. Scott Fitzgerald wrote his novels by hand using paper and super sharp pencils. He didn't even erase his mistakes, preferring to cross them out.[62] His personal assistant later in his life observed how Fitzgerald would write by hand every day (presumably even after recovering from his epic gin-induced hangovers)![63]

Other people who use analog tools, including notecards, and who write by hand include the following people: comedian Jerry Seinfeld, author Elizabeth Gilbert, author Ryan Holiday, author Robert Greene, novelist Anne Lamott, and writer Robert Caro (whom I talk about elsewhere in this book).[64] The list goes on and on.

(Irvine, California: Entrepreneur Press, 2017).

59 Richard Lowry, ed., The Journals of Abraham Maslow, First Thus edition (Lexington, Mass: Penguin Books, 1982), 1.

60 Umberto Eco, How to Write a Thesis, trans. Caterina Mongiat Farina and Geoff Farina, Translation edition (Cambridge, Massachusetts: The MIT Press, 2015), xvii.

61 "Hollywood Screenwriter John August's 10 Best Index Card Practices," ScreenCraft, December 30, 2019, https://screencraft.org/blog/hollywood-screenwriter-john-augusts-10-best-index-card-practices/.

62 "The Great Gatsby," SP Books, accessed March 22, 2022, https://www.spbooks.com/67-the-great-gatsby-9791095457428.html.

63 Frances Kroll Ring, Against the Current: As I Remember F. Scott Fitzgerald (Figueroa Press, 2005), 34.

64 The New York Times, Jerry Seinfeld Interview: How to Write a Joke | The New York Times,

HISTORY'S GREATEST MINDS USED ANALOG THINKING SYSTEMS LIKE THE ANTINET

A great many intellectuals of the past used tools like the Antinet, including the German philosopher and mathematician Gottfried Wilhelm Leibniz (1646–1716). Around 1676 he built a so-called excerpt cabinet (*scrinium literatum*). He was inspired by the Swiss physician and naturalist, Conrad Gessner (1516–1565), who built a "humble paper-slip" system.[65] Gessner is known as possibly the first person in history who is mentioned using an Antinet-like system.[66] Other early adopters of an Antinet-like system include Georg Philipp Harsdörffer (1607–1658) and Joachim Jungius (1587–1657).

The first English dictionary, famously built by Samuel Johnson, was assembled using notecards. He sorted the dictionary entries into alphabetical order and then glued them into a master manuscript.[67]

I won't risk boring you with a comprehensive history of people who used Antinet-like systems. The list of people who did is rather robust and can be found in many books dedicated entirely to the scholarship of analog thinking systems.

2012, https://www.youtube.com/watch?v=itWxXyCfW5s; Tim Ferriss, "Elizabeth Gilbert's Creative Path: Saying No, Trusting Your Intuition, Index Cards, Integrity Checks, Grief, Awe, and Much More (#430)," The Blog of Author Tim Ferriss, May 8, 2020, https://tim.blog/2020/05/08/elizabeth-gilbert/; Ryan Holiday, "The Notecard System: The Key For Remembering, Organizing And Using Everything You Read," RyanHoliday.Net (blog), April 1, 2014, https://ryanholiday.net/the-notecard-system-the-key-for-remembering-organizing-and-using-everything-you-read/; London Real, HOW I WRITE MY BOOKS: Robert Greene Reveals His Research Methods When Writing His Latest Work, 2020, https://www.youtube.com/watch?v=2ueMHk-GljKo; Anne Lamott, Bird by Bird: Some Instructions on Writing and Life, 1st edition (Anchor, 2007), 133.

65 Alex Wright, Cataloging the World: Paul Otlet and the Birth of the Information Age, 1st edition (Oxford; New York: Oxford University Press, 2014), 30.

66 Markus Krajewski, *Note-Keeping: History, Theory, Practice of a Counter-Measurement against Forgetting* (Brill, 2016), 319.

67 Alex Wright, Cataloging the World: Paul Otlet and the Birth of the Information Age, 1st edition (Oxford; New York: Oxford University Press, 2014), 32.

If you're interested in exploring the history of analog thinking systems, I'll provide the following list. The list makes no claim of being exhaustive, however the books listed certainly serve as a fine jumping-off point for those interested in the history of knowledge systems.

- Blair, Ann M. *Too Much to Know: Managing Scholarly Information before the Modern Age*. First Edition. New Haven, Conn.: Yale University Press, 2011.

- Cevolini, Alberto, ed. *Forgetting Machines: Knowledge Management Evolution in Early Modern Europe*. Library of the Written Word, volume 53. Leiden ; Boston: Brill, 2016.

- Krajewski, Markus. *Paper Machines: About Cards & Catalogs, 1548-1929*. Translated by Peter Krapp. History and Foundations of Information Science. Cambridge, MA, USA: MIT Press, 2011.

- Wright, Alex. *Cataloging the World: Paul Otlet and the Birth of the Informa tion Age*. 1st edition. Oxford ; New York: Oxford University Press, 2014.[68]

- Yeo, Richard. *Notebooks, English Virtuosi, and Early Modern Science*. 1st edition. Chicago ; London: University of Chicago Press, 2014.

THE POWER OF WRITING BY HAND

MY JOURNEY DISCOVERING THE POWER OF WRITING BY HAND

One of the secrets to my success in college can be attributed to one thing: writing by hand.

Many of my other peers brought their laptops to class. When the professor began talking, they'd flip it open and take notes for a while, never looking up to engage with the professor. After some time, they'd open up a new

68 For Antinet-like systems and the people who used them, see pages: 30–33, 41–42, 49, 78, and 230. For the power of analog notecards and paper slips, see: 80–81, 229–30, 223, 239, 251, 253, and 286.

tab, surf the web for news, check email, respond to messages, and be taken away from class.

I never experienced the temptations that would lead me to fall into this trap. I always had only one thing in front of me. Actually, two: a Five Star spiral notebook, and a pen.

One reason why I never brought a laptop to class was that it felt disrespectful to the professor. They can't see what you're doing, and they have no way of telling if you're just flat-out ignoring them. There you have a person dedicating their life to teaching you something, and you're staring into a screen, seemingly ignoring them. It just didn't sit right with me.

That said, the feeling of being disrespectful to the professor wasn't the only reason I didn't bring a laptop. I didn't bring a laptop to class for several other reasons.

First, by taking notes by hand, you end up *understanding* the material better (as research now confirms).[69] When you write by hand, you're thinking and understanding in a way that is more effective than taking notes using a laptop.

Second, when you write by hand, you end up paying very close attention to the physical cues of the professor or lecturer. You're better able to filter out what's truly important.

Third, when you write by hand, your selection skills and your ability to select important material improve. Why? Because you're more *constrained* by what you can actually write down. Writing by hand is harder, it takes more time. You have to *slow down* and select only the most important pieces of information, and you must do it in a concise way that captures the concept.

69 Pam A. Mueller and Daniel M. Oppenheimer, "The Pen Is Mightier Than the Keyboard: Advantages of Longhand Over Laptop Note Taking," Psychological Science 25, no. 6 (June 1, 2014): 1159–68.

Fourth, when I wrote by hand in class, I was more present. This resulted in two things: first, time flew by. And second, I enjoyed class much more than I would have if my laptop had been open. In fact, research suggests that those who write by hand end up experiencing much more joy than those who type away at their keyboard.[70]

Last, when you write by hand, you simply get better results.

In a college environment, one might assume it to be socially acceptable to be perceived as *studious* or a *hard worker* by peers. Yet, this wasn't always the case. I'd often find myself faced with direct questions from my peers. For instance, my friends would say to me, point-blank: *The lecture material is posted on the class website. Why are you taking notes?* I found myself having to answer this question more often than one would imagine.

I recall a fellow student bragging, *I don't need to take notes.* He then pointed to his head and said, *I keep everything in here.*

In these situations I was faced with a choice. *Should I stick with taking notes by hand, or should I try to appear smarter by holding it all in my head?* I decided to press forward with my practice of taking notes by hand (even though it was hard work and slow).

Thankfully I stuck to the hard way, because every single time, in every single class, I outperformed my other classmates who didn't take notes. I also outperformed everyone who took notes by typing. Oh, and the guy claiming to keep everything in his brain? He almost flunked out.

THE PARADOXICAL HISTORY OF LONGHAND

The power of writing by hand isn't something realized only in modern times; there's rich history behind the practice of writing by hand.

70 Aya S. Ihara et al., "Advantage of Handwriting Over Typing on Learning Words: Evidence From an N400 Event-Related Potential Index," Frontiers in Human Neuroscience 15 (2021): 679191.

Something counterintuitive happened during the Renaissance among learned scholars and thinkers. During this period, the typographic industry exploded in growth (the so-called *ars artificialiter scribendi*).[71] Previous to this, scholars relied on "helpers" and scribes to do their writing for them. After the typographic machines came onto the scene, however, scholars read texts via typographic medium by themselves. They also began to write their own thoughts in commonplace books. Soon after, the scholars began parting ways with their scribes and helpers. Instead of dictating their thoughts to them, they "chose to handwrite."[72] Why? Because writing by hand developed their thoughts to a far greater degree than simply dictating their thoughts to their helpers.

WRITING BY HAND ENABLES A COMMUNICATION PARTNER TO EMERGE IN THE ANTINET

At the time of his death, Luhmann's literary estate contained three thousand of his manuscripts, two hundred of which were previously unpublished. The starting point for these manuscripts was Luhmann's Antinet, where he developed the foundation through writing by hand.

> Writing is not what follows research, learning or studying, it is the *medium* of all this work.[73]

> Writing is not the pharmakon of memory; instead, it is a hypomnematic device that encourages scholars to use their mental energies for more abstract—that is, context-detached operations.[74]

---

71 Alberto Cevolini, ed., Forgetting Machines: Knowledge Management Evolution in Early Modern Europe, Library of the Written Word, volume 53 (Leiden; Boston: Brill, 2016), 24.

72 Alberto Cevolini, ed., Forgetting Machines: Knowledge Management Evolution in Early Modern Europe, Library of the Written Word, volume 53 (Leiden; Boston: Brill, 2016), 24.

73 Sönke Ahrens, How to Take Smart Notes: One Simple Technique to Boost Writing, Learning and Thinking: For Students, Academics and Nonfiction Book Writers (North Charleston, SC: CreateSpace, 2017), 2.

74 Alberto Cevolini, ed., Forgetting Machines: Knowledge Management Evolution in

Writing does not come *after* research. It is the very thing that develops the research. Writing is the process by which you actually *understand* research. And as the scientific literature shows, writing by hand promotes this understanding better than typing on a keyboard.[75] Sönke Ahrens points this out as well: in terms of *understanding* what they had been taught, students who write by hand outshine those who write by keyboard.[76]

This illustrates an important point: developing your thoughts through writing by hand builds the foundation for your thinking and is the starting point from which thoughts can be developed into something even greater. It is not the end itself. If someone believes that an Antinet alone spits out great work, they're dreaming. This seems to be the belief of digital notetaking bubble graph boiz. For an Antinet to truly bear fruit, the initial thought that is developed with the Antinet must continue to be processed in manuscript form.

This seems to be less of a likelihood with digital tools. It's all too easy to copy-and-paste notes and then try developing them from there. When you use an Antinet, there's no other choice but to rewrite the knowledge from your cards into your text editor (and thereby, you reprocess your already processed thoughts). You're essentially reprocessing the thoughts you've already processed when you originally wrote them down by hand. This is hugely advantageous and should not be overlooked.

Luhmann's Antinet put his thoughts through an intense process so that, by the time they were included in a manuscript or book, the thought was developed to a far deeper degree than just thinking while typing. Luhmann

---

Early Modern Europe, Library of the Written Word, volume 53 (Leiden ; Boston: Brill, 2016), 1.

75 Pam A. Mueller and Daniel M. Oppenheimer, "The Pen Is Mightier Than the Keyboard: Advantages of Longhand Over Laptop Note Taking," Psychological Science 25, no. 6 (June 1, 2014): 1159–68. In addition, more scientific literature backing the power of writing by hand is explored elsewhere in this book.

76 Sönke Ahrens, How to Take Smart Notes: One Simple Technique to Boost Writing, Learning and Thinking: For Students, Academics and Nonfiction Book Writers (North Charleston, SC: CreateSpace, 2017), 78.

found himself in a fantastic position to develop his thoughts even further. He started with a "leg up" compared to the alternative of thinking on the fly while writing a manuscript.

When writing a manuscript with your Antinet, you have your notecards to guide you, and it begins to feel like a true partnership.

I've experienced this myself by writing this book. The notes from my Antinet have already gone through development in two ways: (1) short-term development through writing by hand, and (2) long-term development by way of engaging new, supporting evidence and further calcifications of an idea (backed by more examples, reflections, reformulations and excerpts).

When it comes down to typing the notes into a manuscript, it's boring to just type things word-for-word from your notes; instead, the experience is a lot more active and fun if thinking is involved while typing and while trying to fully decipher what is being said. You end up developing thoughts to further clarity. Right now, I'm writing this paragraph you're reading right now with my notecards sitting to the left of my keyboard. Oftentimes, I'll find myself arguing with what I've written on the notecards and sometimes phrase what I've written very differently. I question what I've written on the notecards and feel compelled to re-check sources. *Did the author who I'm quoting, really say that?!* I say to myself. I then check, and more often than not, I find that the author did indeed say it.

This entire experience enables me to connect with the reader more and communicate the idea properly by sharing with the reader my own initial skepticisms when presented with an idea. For instance, *I know what you're about to read may sound suspect. I realize the concept of 'communicating with a ghost in a box of notecards' sounds like woo-woo mysticism. Yet, this is precisely how the greatest social scientist of the 20th century explained the Antinet.*

In this respect, the Antinet becomes a true communication partner, a true writing partner. At the foundation of such an emergent experience is the technology of analog notes…written by hand.

WRITING BY HAND SPARKS AN EVOLUTIONARY ADVANCE THAT DEVELOPS WORKING MEMORY CAPACITY

The deliberate process of writing by hand, observes Harvard University researcher Ann Blair, "produced a somewhat odd effect." The system, which was supposed to simply replace the cognitive overhead of having to memorize information both, (1) replaced cognitive overhead of memorizing, and unexpectedly, (2) it enhanced one's ability to retain almost everything learned Renaissance scholars had read. The handwritten notetaking system and "the respective construction of a card index were considered both a substitute for personal memory and a memory aid."[77]

What Blair describes is a *contradiction. Contradictions,* such as a method that *both* replaces the cognitive process of memorization and, at the same time, enhances it, serves as a sign of a "transitional" phase towards progress in evolution.[78] In effect, the practice of writing things down by hand, and thereby building a thinking system that enhances one's ability to retain information, serves as an evolutionary jump for humans who possess this faculty. This scholar observed the phenomenon of a thinking system (built of hand-written notes and indexes) replacing and enhancing memory, and observed that such a system "may be understood as signs of evolutionary advance."[79]

Central to evolutionary advances sits one key concept: *contradictory phenomena*. Therefore, it's rather puzzling that the world of notetaking today finds the majority of its practitioners opting for digital systems. These systems have not proven themselves to possess the contradictory phenomenon of analog systems. Indeed, science proves digital systems to be less effective than analog systems for learning *and* understanding (which will be covered shortly). Digital systems may serve as an adequate *memory replacement* tool; however, they are not *memory enhancement* tools. Analog systems are both.

77 Alberto Cevolini, ed., Forgetting Machines: Knowledge Management Evolution in Early Modern Europe, Library of the Written Word, volume 53 (Leiden; Boston: Brill, 2016), 24.

78 Alberto Cevolini, ed., Forgetting Machines: Knowledge Management Evolution in Early Modern Europe, Library of the Written Word, volume 53 (Leiden; Boston: Brill, 2016), 24.

79 Alberto Cevolini, ed., Forgetting Machines: Knowledge Management Evolution in Early Modern Europe, Library of the Written Word, volume 53 (Leiden; Boston: Brill, 2016), 24.

The seemingly contradictory nature of being both a memory replacement tool *and* a memory enhancement tool points to analog systems as the more *evolutionarily advanced* medium (as absurd as that may seem).

The practice of writing by hand, as pointed out by Ann Blair, results in the enhancement of memory. This is of supreme importance because one of the most critical elements involved in learning is the development of one's *working memory capacity*.[80]

Let's talk briefly about the science of human memory now.

Working Memory, Short-term Storage, and Long-term Storage

Working memory refers to the process in which information is stored in your short-term memory, where it is actively worked on and encoded. After this stage, memories can then be stored in long-term storage for later retrieval.

Luhmann wrote of *multiple storage* memory systems being around the corner, yet the computing power of his era wasn't able to produce such a thing.[81] However, we also know that Luhmann wasn't convinced that computer memory would replace the need for systems relying on human memory. From Luhmann's notecard we can see Luhmann was familiar with W. Ross Ashby's view that "our scientific thinking [of human memory] tends to be grossly misled by the example of the big digital computer."[82]

80 Fiona McPherson, Effective Note-taking, revised edition (Wellington: Wayz Press, 2018), 7-8.

81 "ZK II: Note 9 / 8b2—Niklas Luhmann Archive," accessed September 21, 2021, https://niklas-luhmann-archiv.de/bestand/zettelkasten/zettel/ZK_2_NB_9-8b2_V; "ZK II: Zettel 9/8,2—Niklas Luhmann-Archiv," accessed March 3, 2022, https://niklas-luhmann-archiv.de/bestand/zettelkasten/zettel/ZK_2_NB_9-8-2_V; Johannes Schmidt, "Niklas Luhmann's Card Index: Thinking Tool, Communication Partner, Publication Machine," Forgetting Machines. Knowledge Management Evolution in Early Modern Europe 53 (2016), https://pub.uni-bielefeld.de/record/2942475, 299.

82 "ZK II: Sheet 9/8b - Niklas Luhmann Archive," accessed March 17, 2022, https://niklas-luhmann-archiv.de/bestand/zettelkasten/zettel/ZK_2_NB_9-8b_V; W. Ross Ashby, "The Place of the Brain in the Natural World," Biosystems 1, no. 2 (May 1, 1967): 95–104, 103.

By referencing the concept of *multiple storage,* Luhmann seems to be more in-tune with how the concept worked in abstract models of human memory (rather than the abstractions of abstractions of human memory, which computer science devised).

What Luhmann may have been alluding to was something one scientist in human memory refers to as "the most influential computational model of memory."[83] The model referred to was proposed by Atkinson and Shiffrin in 1968—during Luhmann's prime theoretical working days—and was known as *dual storage.*[84]

The conception of dual storage systems became popular in the 1970s because of its analogy to computer systems that have separate short-term and long-term storage components.[85] It does not seem coincidental that Luhmann wrote of both in such a close proximity to one another.[86] In brief, he was likely aware of the dual storage memory model.

Today the dual storage memory model is encompassed under the term *Search of Associative Memory,* or *"SAM"*. According to SAM, remembered information is stored in two different types of "containers" within your mind: (1) short-term storage ("STS"), and (2) long-term storage ("LTS").[87]

SHORT-TERM STORAGE (STS) AND THE ANTINET

Short-term storage is thought of as a "buffer." In a computing context,

---

83 Michael Jacob Kahana, Foundations of Human Memory. (New York: Oxford University Press, 2014), 223.

84 Michael Jacob Kahana, Foundations of Human Memory. (New York: Oxford University Press, 2014), 223.

85 Michael Jacob Kahana, Foundations of Human Memory. (New York: Oxford University Press, 2014), 225.

86 "ZK II: Zettel 9/8,2—Niklas Luhmann-Archiv," accessed March 3, 2022, https://niklas-luhmann-archiv.de/bestand/zettelkasten/zettel/ZK_2_NB_9-8-2_V; "ZK II: Note 9 / 8b2—Niklas Luhmann Archive," accessed September 21, 2021, https://niklas-luhmann-archiv.de/bestand/zettelkasten/zettel/ZK_2_NB_9-8b2_V.

87 Michael Jacob Kahana, Foundations of Human Memory. (New York: Oxford University Press, 2014), 224.

a buffer is a temporary memory-storage area where data is stored before being processed and installed into long-term storage.[88]

STS has limited capacity for the number of items it can store.

Think of it like writing a bullet point list of ideas on a card and then shortly thereafter elaborating on each of those bullet point ideas on a dedicated card.

STS is the phase in which you write main notes. You write excerpts, reformulations, or reflections from your readings or source material. It's the RAM, in computer terms. It's the working memory, which is developed through writing by hand.

LONG-TERM STORAGE ("LTS") AND THE ANTINET

In a later chapter, I'll be teaching you the core components of the Antinet. The primary box in which knowledge is developed happens in something called "the main box." Think of long-term storage as the main box of your Antinet, the area where your developed thoughts are then stored for the long term.

Memory scientists liken LTS to a variant of associative neuro network models, yet LTS comprises the following features: (1) it stores associations *among* items, and (2) it stores associations *between* items and context.

The Antinet's tree structure, with proximity-based associations built into its protocol, as well as its context branches, are a perfect instantiation of LTS.

Both the architecture of short-term storage and long-term storage are perfectly represented in the Antinet—much more perfectly than a collection of mere bubbles linked together in a digital graph (*cough,* digital notetaking apps, *cough*).

Let's jump back to working memory.

---

88 Angus Stevenson and Christine A. Lindberg, eds., New Oxford Amerian Dictionary 3rd Edition, 3rd edition (Oxford ; New York: Oxford University Press, 2010), s.v. "Buffer."

Before information can be installed into long-term storage (the main box of your Antinet), it must first be encoded and then processed. You encode and process the thoughts by *writing by hand*.[89]

A popular factoid related to working memory is the idea that it can only hold seven chunks of information in it.[90] However the latest research argues that working memory can only hold four items during the processing phase.[91]

When doing knowledge work, and when thinking, it's advantageous to possess the ability to hold multiple ideas in your mind simultaneously. Often I'll create a card that states four or five *hypotheses*.[92] Each individual one then will get a dedicated card to be built out individually.

We find instances of Luhmann doing this as well. For instance, take the following note from Luhmann's archived Zettelkasten:

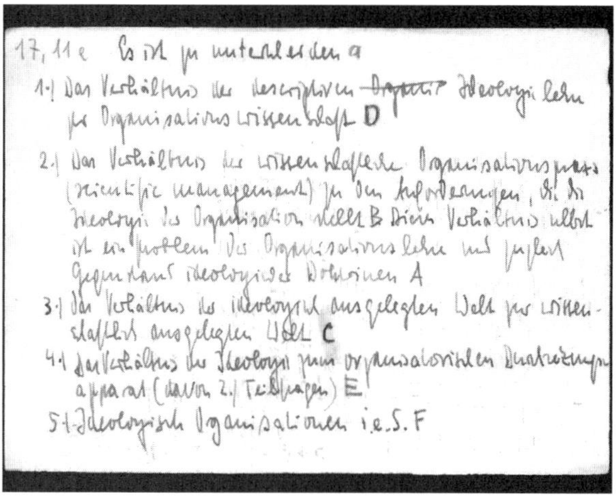

PHOTO CREDIT: "ZK I: Note 17,11e—Niklas Luhmann Archive," accessed March 23, 2022, https://niklas-luhmann-archiv.de/bestand/zettelkasten/zettel/ZK_1_NB_17-11e_V.

---

89 Fiona McPherson, Effective Note-taking, revised edition (Wellington: Wayz Press, 2018), 8.

90 Fiona McPherson, Effective Note-taking, revised edition (Wellington: Wayz Press, 2018), 7.

91 Fiona McPherson, Effective Note-taking, revised edition (Wellington: Wayz Press, 2018), 8.

92 Note how I use the term hypotheses instead of theses. A hypothesis is a proposed explanation made on the basis of limited evidence. A thesis is a statement that is put forward as a premise to be proved. When you're developing your knowledge using an Antinet, you're putting forth an idea for further investigation (usually on limited evidence). For this reason, it's more fitting to refer to such as a hypothesis

Luhmann lists out five hypotheses to be further developed. Each has a corresponding letter which represents the dedicated card on which the individual hypothesis is to be explored.

The parent card housing the hypothesis possesses the card address 17,11e. The other cards are explored according to the red letter accompanying them. For instance, 17,11ea, 17,11eD, 17,11eB, 17,11eA, etc.

The graph view of the tree looks like this:

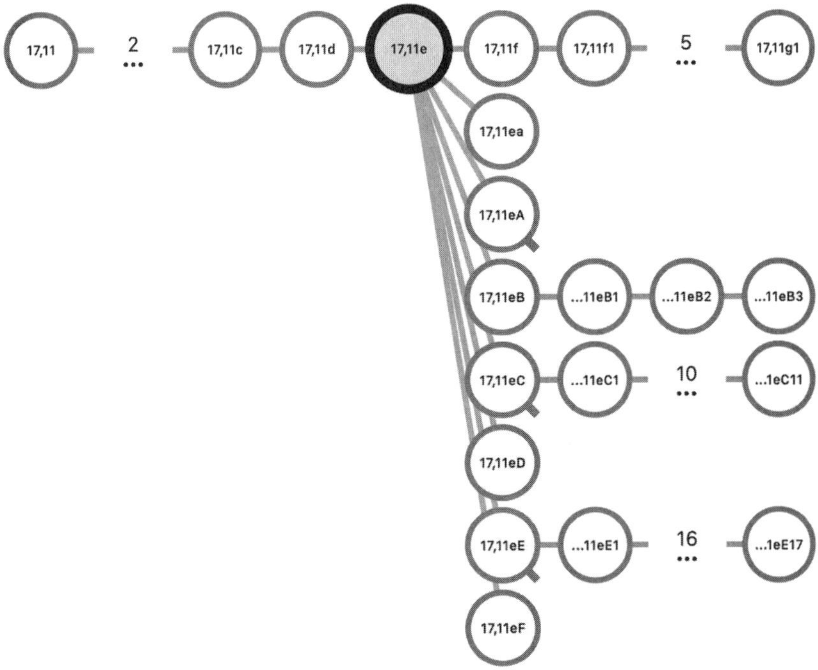

PHOTO CREDIT: "ZK I: Note 17,11e - Niklas Luhmann Archive," accessed March 23, 2022, https://niklas-luhmann-archiv.de/bestand/zettelkasten/zettel/ZK_1_NB_17-11e_V.

Being able to hold a handful of hypotheses in your mind at the same time (as opposed to to one or two) becomes advantageous. It is valuable to exercise and build up your *working memory capacity* because it is critical in developing truly insightful thoughts.

In addition, there is an important subcomponent within working memory called "executive control," which factors into your ability to control your *attention*.[93]

Writing by hand and working in an analog system generates "less distractions and less competing demands," compared with the digital environments (where you're blasted with notifications, for example). Even for those who profess to have self-discipline, are faced with the reality that they're just one click away from lost time. Even for those who claim to wield total self-discipline, with digital notetaking, you're just one click away from lost time. And as Benjamin Franklin pointed out, "Lost time is never found again."

WRITING BY HAND DISENTANGLES THOUGHTS

Dawson Trotman's statement that *thoughts disentangle themselves when they pass through your fingertips* certainly rings true for me, and other authors have expressed similar sentiments. For instance, clinical psychologist and bestselling author, Jordan Peterson. Peterson writes his books by coming up with a skeleton framework of his thesis. He places the "skeleton framework" in a Microsoft Word document and creates a mental image of the framework, which he refers to as a *memory palace*.[94] Yet even with Peterson's techniques, he ran into difficulties while finishing his book *12 Rules for Life*. What helped Peterson during this time was a certain pen with a light affixed to it that allowed him to write in the dark. The *Pen of Light* is how he referred to it. Instead of slogging away at his keyboard, he decided to write by hand. He underwent the act of disentangling his thoughts by getting them out on paper with a pen, enabling him to "find the words to properly close [the] book."[95]

WRITING BY HAND EXERCISES NEURO-ASSOCIATIVE RECALL

In your quest to create genius-level work, you must exercise *neuro-associative*

---

93 Fiona McPherson, Effective Note-taking, revised edition (Wellington: Wayz Press, 2018), 9.

94 "Jordan Peterson Reveals His Thought Process and Writing Techniques –YouTube," accessed February 25, 2022, https://www.youtube.com/watch?v=DKc4-iVJsLo.

95 Jordan B. Peterson, 12 Rules for Life: An Antidote to Chaos, Later prt. edition (Toronto: Random House Canada, 2018), 368.

recall to uncover unconventional insights. [96] This entails recognizing a cue (in the form of a keyterm), and recalling a concept, thought or idea that you've associated with the cue.

I refer to this as *neuro-associative recall,* and I hold that the Antinet develops this ability much more than digital systems do.

For instance, I've employed the neuroimprinting process of writing by hand and creating dedicated keyterms in my index for certain ideas, which has resulted in my being able to instantly recall a concept or set of thoughts. For instance, when presented with the concept of *power law,* or the *pareto principle* or the *80/20 principle,* I instantly think of the keyterm *big impact.* The phrase *big impact* comes from a principle outlined by Nassim Nicholas Taleb in *The Black Swan.* He discusses the tradeoff between the *big picture* of things and *micro theory.* That is, the *big events* vs. *micro events.* He advises one to focus on the *big picture* items that have a *big impact.*[97]

I've stamped this concept into my mind so that whenever I read something new, I can instantly recall the thought. I know where in my Antinet to place such similar thoughts that I come across while reading. This involves a strong neuro-associative recall ability.

Neuro-associative recall involves the process of (1) consuming information and inputs, and (2) *recalling* a concept *associated* with the new information.

This simple two-part process allows one to *compare* new information with previous information to *learn* from and *recognize* surprising realizations. Thus, it enables the Antinet to truly turn into a surprise-generator (one of its core functions).

Let's hone in on the second component of this process: "recall."

---

96 Michael Jacob Kahana, Foundations of Human Memory. (New York: Oxford University Press, 2014), 112. Kahana points out that the technical term is "associative recall."

97 Nassim Nicholas Taleb, The Black Swan: The Impact of the Highly Improbable, 2nd ed., Random trade pbk. ed (New York: Random House Trade Paperbacks, 2010), 142ff.

Memory researchers, when analyzing the critical process between an item's concept and a thought moving from short-term storage (such as in developing thoughts on main notes) to long-term storage (such as installing the cards into your main box) demonstrate that the manner in which you *encode* a concept turns out to have a *substantial impact on recall.*[98] In other words, speaking thoughts into a voice recorder, as opposed to typing them out or writing them out by hand, has a drastically different result for how well you'll recall that item. Not only this, it has a drastically different result for how well you will *think through* the ideas in the first place.

Scientists specializing in human memory have identified two mechanisms for encoding thoughts. These items have an impact on your ability to later recall the thoughts. I go into these concepts in more detail elsewhere in the book, but suffice it to say that these concepts are maintenance rehearsal (refreshing on the notecards by reviewing them), and elaborative rehearsal (thinking through the thoughts by writing them out by hand).

Encompassing both of these mechanisms that increase the strength of recall is the following observation: recall critically depends on the amount of *time* an item has spent being processed in short-term storage.[99] In other words, the more time you spend processing ideas (as is involved in writing by hand compared to typing digitally), the greater your ability to recall the thought or concept later on.

If you still aren't convinced in the power of writing by hand, I would like to turn to two resources right now who will back me in this: (1) Science, and (2) God.

HOW RESEARCH SUPPORTS WRITING BY HAND

There have been numerous studies outlining the benefits and power of writing by hand. Let's go through them now:

---

98 Michael Jacob Kahana, Foundations of Human Memory. (New York: Oxford University Press, 2014), 246.

99 Michael Jacob Kahana, Foundations of Human Memory. (New York: Oxford University Press, 2014), 246.

One group of researchers conducted an experiment that tested subjects' ability to recognize characters. One segment of subjects copied down the characters by hand; the other segment typed the characters on a keyboard.

> Results showed that when the characters had been learned by typing, they were more frequently confused with their mirror images than when they had been written by hand. This handwriting advantage did not appear immediately, but mostly [appeared] three weeks after the end of the training.[100]

In another study, a group of researchers studied the process of learning new words. They compared three groups of people: those who wrote by hand with pen, those wrote by hand with a digital pen, and those who typed on a keyboard.

Some interesting results emerged from this study. First, "positive mood during learning was significantly higher during handwriting than during typing."[101]

Second, the researchers found that "movements involved in handwriting allow a greater memorization of new words."[102]

Last, "handwriting with a digital pen and tablet can increase the ability to learn compared with keyboard typing once the individuals are accustomed to it."[103] This last finding may prompt one to consider using a digital pen

---

100 Marieke Longcamp et al., "Remembering the Orientation of Newly Learned Characters Depends on the Associated Writing Knowledge: A Comparison between Handwriting and Typing," Human Movement Science, Advances in Graphonomics: Studies on Fine Motor Control, Its Development and Disorders, 25, no. 4 (October 1, 2006): 646–56.

101 Aya S. Ihara et al., "Advantage of Handwriting Over Typing on Learning Words: Evidence From an N400 Event-Related Potential Index," Frontiers in Human Neuroscience 15 (2021): 679191.

102 Aya S. Ihara et al., "Advantage of Handwriting Over Typing on Learning Words: Evidence From an N400 Event-Related Potential Index," Frontiers in Human Neuroscience 15 (2021): 679191.

103 Aya S. Ihara et al., "Advantage of Handwriting Over Typing on Learning Words: Evidence From an N400 Event-Related Potential Index," Frontiers in Human Neuroscience 15 (2021): 679191.

or reMarkable table. I contend, however, that those routes miss the other benefits of analog systems. That is, laying out the cards in front of you, considering the external context associated with sifting through your cards, and the other benefits outlined in this book. Regardless, let's call a spade a spade: even digital handwriting outshines typing in terms of learning new concepts, words, and stamping such information on your mind.

Another study by a group of researchers compared the memory process for subjects who wrote by hand vs. typed. Here's what they found:

> A comparison of recall and recognition for common words demonstrates that memory is better for words when they have been written down rather than when they are typed. This provides additional support for the hypothesis that the additional context provided by the complex task of writing results in better memory. With the recent trend towards electronic note taking, the educational and practical implications of these findings would suggest that performance may be improved by using traditional paper-and-pen notes.[104]

Another researcher went deeper in exploring how handwriting seems to positively impact the recognition process of memory. Here's what she found:

> My colleagues and I showed that early handwriting practice affects visual symbol recognition because it results in the production of variable visual forms that aid in symbol understanding.[105]

One of the more popular studies on handwriting vs. typing using a keyboard is titled, *The Pen Is Mightier than the Keyboard: Advantages of Longhand over*

104 Timothy J. Smoker, Carrie E. Murphy, and Alison K. Rockwell, "Comparing Memory for Handwriting versus Typing," Proceedings of the Human Factors and Ergonomics Society Annual Meeting 53, no. 22 (October 1, 2009): 1744–47

105 "The Importance of Handwriting Experience on the Development of the Literate Brain —Karin H. James, 2017," accessed August 13, 2021, https://journals.sagepub.com/doi/abs/10.1177/0963721417709821.

Laptop Note Taking. Sönke Ahrens himself cites this research paper in his book *How to Take Smart Notes*; yet puzzlingly enough, he seems to discard such findings and explains to his readers that he opts for a digital Zettelkasten due to *mobility*. I won't get into my gripe with this right now. Let's talk about the study itself.

The researchers, Pam A. Mueller and Daniel M. Oppenheimer conducted a study involving two groups of students. One group took notes using a laptop; the other group of students took notes by hand.

What the researchers discovered was that taking notes digitally may be "impairing learning because their use results in shallower processing."[106]

Here is what the researchers discovered:

> In three studies, we found that students who took notes on laptops performed worse on conceptual questions than students who took notes longhand. We show that whereas taking more notes can be beneficial, laptop note takers' tendency to transcribe lectures verbatim rather than processing information and reframing it in their own words is detrimental to learning.[107]

While this study from 2014 supports my thesis that writing by hand is more effective than writing digitally, I must share the latest research, which discredits this finding (for sake of intellectual integrity). This brings us to a 2021 study titled, *Don't Ditch the Laptop Just Yet: A Direct Replication of Mueller and Oppenheimer's (2014) Study 1 Plus Mini Meta-Analyses Across Similar Studies*. In this study, researchers replicated Mueller and Oppenheimer's

---

106 Pam A. Mueller and Daniel M. Oppenheimer, "The Pen Is Mightier Than the Keyboard: Advantages of Longhand Over Laptop Note Taking," Psychological Science 25, no. 6 (June 1, 2014): 1159–68.

107 Pam A. Mueller and Daniel M. Oppenheimer, "The Pen Is Mightier Than the Keyboard: Advantages of Longhand Over Laptop Note Taking," Psychological Science 25, no. 6 (June 1, 2014): 1159–68.

experiment. However, the results did not "support the idea that longhand note taking improves immediate learning via better encoding of information."[108]

So, what do we make of this? Which one is mightier: pen or keyboard? On this matter, I will say this: the only right answer is test. Experiment for yourself. For many, the pen is indeed mightier than the keyboard; however, the popularity and cultural stigma of using pen and paper prevents many from adopting longhand. There's an underlying pressure to use digital tools. There's an implicit sense that in order to "be smart" (and technically sophisticated), one must embrace the supposed superpower of digital notetaking apps (with their illusive bubble graphs). I think this is incorrect. Many people use digital tools for thinking when, in reality, they should be using analog tools. The most recent research appears to support this conclusion. In a study titled, *Make a Note of It: Comparison in Longhand, Keyboard, and Stylus notetaking Techniques,* researchers found that "students performed better using their preferred note-taking method."[109] The moral of the story? Experiment for yourself. Determine your preferred notetaking method (and don't be surprised to find that it is, indeed, writing by hand)!

Before we conclude this section, let's briefly turn to a different practice: reading. Not only has writing on a digital device been shown to hamper learning and comprehension, a recent study found that even *reading comprehension* is reduced when using a digital device.[110] Even if you hold that writing digitally is better for you, that doesn't mean reading digitally is better for you. In fact, reading digitally is probably *not* better for you (at least in terms of comprehension).

108 Heather L. Urry et al., "Don't Ditch the Laptop Just Yet: A Direct Replication of Mueller and Oppenheimer's (2014) Study 1 Plus Mini Meta-Analyses Across Similar Studies," Psychological Science 32, no. 3 (March 1, 2021): 326–39.

109 Madelynn D. Shell, Maranda Strouth, and Alexandria M. Reynolds, "Make a Note of It: Comparison in Longhand, Keyboard, and Stylus Note-Taking Techniques," Learning Assistance Review 26, no. 2 (2021): 1–21.

110 Motoyasu Honma et al., "Reading on a Smartphone Affects Sigh Generation, Brain Activity, and Comprehension," Scientific Reports 12, no. 1 (January 31, 2022): 1589.

In sum, the research makes it apparent: not only is the pen mightier than the keyboard, the physical book is, too (at least, for many of us)!

HOW GOD SUPPORTS WRITING BY HAND

If you won't take my word for it, and if you don't care about the scientific literature supporting the process of writing by hand, well, then I suppose you can take the word of another entity. He goes by the name of...*GOD*!

For the LORD said, "Write the vision; make it plain on tablets" (Habakkuk 2:2 [NRSV]), or Isaiah 8:1 (NRSV): "Then the LORD said to me, take a large tablet and write on it in common characters."

There you have it. God espouses the power of writing by hand.

I lay forth this reason slightly tongue-in-cheek. I'd prefer you adopt the practice of writing by hand by testing it out yourself (or from reading the scientific literature). After all, I may have ever-so-slightly taken these quotes from God out of context. But since these two verses were presented to me while attending church with my family one day, I figured I might as well extract them onto a bibcard and share them with you here.

CONCLUSION

There you have it. I've laid out in detail the power of analog, the power of writing by hand, the people who write by hand, and the science behind analog. Heck, I've even thrown in God as a reason to take writing by hand seriously. If you're still not convinced by the power of analog, well then, that means only one thing: even God can't help you. I'm kidding, of course, but seriously: try the Antinet yourself. Only after that should you determine if it's truly as powerful as what I (and others) say.

CHAPTER SEVEN

NUMERIC-ALPHA

"Since all notes have fixed numbers, you can add as many references to them as you may want. Central concepts can have many links which show on which other contexts we can find materials relevant for them. Through references, we can, without too much work or paper, solve the problem of multiple storage."

—Niklas Luhmann, *Communication with Noteboxes*[1]

NUMERIC-ALPHA ADDRESSES ARE ARGUABLY THE MOST IMPORTANT COMPONENT OF THE ANTINET

ALBERTO CEVOLINI, A SCHOLAR WHO has studied a vast amount of knowledge systems throughout history, observes that Luhmann's numbering of entries is too important to brush over too quickly. In the scholar's view, Luhmann's numeric-alpha scheme represents one of the most interesting evolutionary transitions in the field of knowledge management systems.[2]

The most important feature of the Antinet is the one that generates its most important results. To Luhmann the most important result of the Antinet concerns its *inner life*.

1 Niklas Luhmann, "Communication with Noteboxes (Revised Edition)," trans. Manfred Kuehn, https://daily.scottscheper.com/zettelkasten/.

2 Alberto Cevolini, ed., Forgetting Machines: Knowledge Management Evolution in Early Modern Europe, Library of the Written Word, volume 53 (Leiden; Boston: Brill, 2016), 27.

The inner life of the Antinet is brought about by two things.

First, it revolves around creating a *communication partner* (a second mind, a *ghost in the box,* and an alter-ego).

In the beginning of his paper on his Antinet, Luhmann states something rather radical: he says that "it is easy to think of systems theory" as the way to describe the Antinet. After all, "we consider ourselves to be systems." But he goes on to explain that he chooses "communication theory" to describe his system. "One of us listens to the other." He continues, "This needs to be explained."[3]

The radical notion centers on his usage of the terms *us* and *we*. What he's referring to is the communication and dialogue that takes place between him and his Antinet, yet the way in which he's referring to it makes him sound more like a schizophrenic than the most important German sociologist of the twentieth century!

But if we decide to take Luhmann's word for it, perhaps we could learn something from this. Perhaps there really is something to the idea of creating a communication partner out of an analog notebox.

How do we go about experiencing such a phenomenon of creating a communication partner?

According to Luhmann, it requires giving each card a *firm fixed place* through use of a numeric-alpha address. "This decision about structure..." according to Luhmann, "makes possible the creation of high complexity in the card file and *thus makes possible its ability to communicate in the first place.*"[4]

---

3 Niklas Luhmann, "Communication with Noteboxes (Revised Edition)," trans. Manfred Kuehn, https://daily.scottscheper.com/zettelkasten/.

4 Niklas Luhmann, "Communication with Noteboxes (Revised Edition)," trans. Manfred Kuehn, https://daily.scottscheper.com/zettelkasten/. Emphasis added.

The second component of the inner life of the Antinet is its ability to become a *surprise-generator* through its ability to produce fortunate *accidents*. "The role of accidents in the theory of science is not disputed," writes Luhmann. "If you employ evolutionary models, accidents assume a most important role."[5] These *accidents* are really *accidental insights* that come about by stumbling upon ideas or thoughts while exploring the physical form and nature of your knowledge (by sifting through your cards by hand).

These two components describe the most important aspect of Luhmann's system, its "inner life." As Luhmann writes:

> For the inner life of the card index, for the arrangement of notes or its mental history, it is most important that we decide against the systematic ordering in accordance with topics and sub-topics and choose instead a firm fixed place (Stellordnung).[6]

The most important component for establishing the *inner life* of this system, and giving it a *firm fixed place,* revolves around one thing: numeric-alpha addresses.

This makes it quite puzzling when so-called Zettelkasten experts, productivity experts, PKM experts, and second-brain proselytizers take a nonchalant approach to explaining numeric-alpha addresses.

THE HISTORY OF NUMERIC-ALPHA ADDRESSES IN NOTECARD SYSTEMS

Niklas Luhmann was not the first person to devise the notion of using numeric-alpha addresses on notecards. Fridericus Sidelius and Paulus Sigismundus recommended notecards (*excerpta schedacea*) in a booklet they published in 1713. In the booklet they stated "it would be sufficient to preserve index cards in distinguished files and number them consecutively, while leaving

5 Niklas Luhmann, "Communication with Noteboxes (Revised Edition)," trans. Manfred Kuehn, https://daily.scottscheper.com/zettelkasten/.

6 Niklas Luhmann, "Communication with Noteboxes (Revised Edition)," trans. Manfred Kuehn, https://daily.scottscheper.com/zettelkasten/.

a margin [for] later gluing or stitching together all cards belonging to the same entry."[7]

A novel knowledge development system was devised by Thomas Harrison more than fifty years prior to the publishing of the booklet by Sidelius and Sigismundus. Harrison's system was called the "Ark of Studies." Harrison advised that the notecard-like slips of paper in the Ark of Studies could be arranged in alphabetical order, or, could be numbered.[8]

At the beginning of the eighteenth century, Johann Benedict Metzler recommended numbering notecards because "compared with alphabetical order, numerical order is clearer and avoids the inconvenience of empty spaces."[9]

The history of numeric-alpha notes stands quite rich. Many thinkers stumbled onto the system because it simply makes sense. John Locke even devised his own numeric-alpha system for his notes.[10] In Antonin Sertillanges's Antinet, which he outlines in his 1921 book, *The Intellectual Life*, he advises that each slip should be numbered in the corner or in the middle of the slip.[11]

Luhmann never shared specifically where he got the idea for his Antinet. Nor did he state where the idea for using numeric-alpha addresses came from. However, I believe much of the system's essence derived from the first job he held during his short legal career. The first job he took after law school was at the Lüneburg Higher Administrative Court. His task was to organize a reference system for administrative court decisions. According to Luhmann, "the court should be able to see what higher court decisions

7 Alberto Cevolini, ed., Forgetting Machines: Knowledge Management Evolution in Early Modern Europe, Library of the Written Word, volume 53 (Leiden ; Boston: Brill, 2016), 27.

8 Alberto Cevolini, ed., Forgetting Machines: Knowledge Management Evolution in Early Modern Europe, Library of the Written Word, volume 53 (Leiden ; Boston: Brill, 2016), 28.

9 Alberto Cevolini, ed., Forgetting Machines: Knowledge Management Evolution in Early Modern Europe, Library of the Written Word, volume 53 (Leiden ; Boston: Brill, 2016), 28.

10 Alberto Cevolini, ed., Forgetting Machines: Knowledge Management Evolution in Early Modern Europe, Library of the Written Word, volume 53 (Leiden; Boston: Brill, 2016), 28.

11 OP A. G. Sertillanges, The Intellectual Life: Its Spirit, Conditions, Methods, trans. Mary Ryan, Reprint edition (Washington, D.C.: The Catholic University of America Press, 1992), 196.

were available at any given time."[12] It is there, I believe, that Luhmann either developed or learned the reference system that gave birth to the Zettelkasten. He worked at the Lüneburg Higher Administrative Court precisely around the time he created his first Zettelkasten system (1952–1953).

Recently, a group of researchers gathered on Luhmann's ninetieth birthday to discuss Luhmann's time at the Lüneburg Higher Administrative Court. Of Luhmann's work during that time, one scholar noted that there are no longer any physical traces; all traces of it were destroyed in accordance with regulations.[13] However, from personnel notes about Luhmann at the time, we learn several things, including that Luhmann built out a notebox in the court's library.

The scheme used in the German legal administration system relies on each document having a "file number" (*Aktenzeichen*).[14] This number is, separated by a slash (/), is unique (no file can have the same number), and can be combined with alphabetical characters. An example *Aktenzeichen* is 211321/37A.

In brief, Luhmann's work at Lüneburg Higher Administrative Court greatly shaped the origins of the numeric-alpha address. If Luhmann didn't learn about *Aktenzeichen* at the Lüneburg Higher Administrative Court, then at the very least, it derived from his time studying law and using such a reference system.

THE ANATOMY OF NUMERIC-ALPHA ADDRESSES

The anatomy of numeric-alpha addresses is quite simple. Each address starts with a number and can be combined with an alphabetical character that serves as a *variant* of the idea. From there, the addresses "branch-down," and

12 Niklas Luhmann, Niklas Luhmann Short Cuts (English Translation), 2002, 11.

13 Timon Beyes et al., eds., Niklas Luhmann am OVG Lüneburg: zur Entstehung der Systemtheorie, Soziologische Schriften, Band 86 (Berlin: Duncker & Humblot, 2021), 15.

14 "Aktenzeichen (Deutschland)," in Wikipedia, February 3, 2022, https://de.wikipedia.org/w/index.php?title=Aktenzeichen(Deutschland)&oldid=219821207.

allow users to create more cards by adding a forward slash (/), a period (.), a comma (,), or even by just appending the address with alternating numbers and alphabetical characters. Personally, I prefer forward slashes (/).

Let's use a hypothetical example. Here is an example of an arbitrary set of branches:

- `3000`–Natural Science
    * `3100`–Biology
        * `3110`–Zoology
            * `3118`–Specific Animals of Interest
                * `3118/1`–Horses
                * `3118/2`–Donkeys
                * `3118/3`–Turtles (I like turtles)

Now, let's say later on you want to add a card for a mule (the offspring of a male donkey and a female horse).

You're faced with a few options. In fact, you can really do anything (as long as you link to the *Mule* card). However let's say you wish to place the *Mule* card after *Donkey* and before *Turtles*. What do you do? It's simple. You create a card 3118/2A for *Mules*.

It then looks like this:

- `3118/1`–Horses
- `3118/2`–Donkeys
- `3118/2A`–Mules
- `3118/3`–Turtles

The 3118/2A is the numeric-alpha address for mules. It never changes. As Luhmann writes, it has a *fixed position*, which is a core element that gives your Antinet its inner life. It's such a simple discipline and practice yet, over time, you'll see that this simple concept turns your Antinet into a *communication partner* and a brilliant system for generating breakthroughs (by way of *accidents*).

NUMERIC-ALPHA ADDRESSES IN REAL LIFE

When you start looking for them, you'll start to see numeric-alpha addresses everywhere; for instance, freeway exit numbers.

Numeric-alpha addresses in the Antinet operate much like the addresses allotted to freeway exits. Instead of having to remember full names, one can simply look for a numeric-alpha address like 9B. The 9B simply routes you to a location. It does not indicate a hierarchical relationship with exits 9 or 9A; it just indicates that the exit will take you to a different location in the world. This is precisely how such addresses work in the Antinet; they route you to different locations in your tree of knowledge.

NUMERIC-ALPHA ADDRESSES UNLOCK THE SELF-REFERENTIAL NATURE OF THE ANTINET

The concept of *self-reference* refers to the notion of a sentence, idea, formula, function, or a system that refers to its *self* (or itself). For instance, the term "I" in English is a self-reference to oneself. Or take the concept def init(self): in the Python programming language used in computing). It enables a class to create objects that refer to itself and that *call* itself (reference itself). Self-referential statements are often paradoxical and can be considered *recursive*.

The scholar Alberto Cevolini observes that an numeric-alpha address "ensures utmost autonomy, i.e. *self-referential closure of the machine*."[15]

The *self-referential closure of the machine* is a critical piece of the Antinet's architecture. It's the key piece that transforms the Antinet into a *cybernetic system* (a system that achieves a goal through feedback and communication).

The numeric-alpha addresses enable the Antinet to refer to itself and its own individual parts. It's a key piece for creating the *personality* (the *ghost*, the *alter ego*). As a result, observes Cevolini, "interaction" with the Antinet, becomes "a type of communication"—an internal dialogue.[16]

Luhmann was intimately familiar with the power of self-referential systems. His magnum opus social theory was largely predicated on society as a self-referential system.[17] As such, Luhmann designed the Antinet with the capability to refer to itself. Just as a human can refer to its own parts (like the left hand), the Antinet can refer to its own parts (its thoughts identified by its unique numeric-alpha card addresses).

---

15 Alberto Cevolini, ed., Forgetting Machines: Knowledge Management Evolution in Early Modern Europe, Library of the Written Word, volume 53 (Leiden ; Boston: Brill, 2016), 28. Emphasis added.

16 Alberto Cevolini, ed., Forgetting Machines: Knowledge Management Evolution in Early Modern Europe, Library of the Written Word, volume 53 (Leiden; Boston: Brill, 2016), 28.

17 Cf. Jan-Peter Vos, The Making of Strategic Realities: An Application of the Social Systems Theory of Niklas Luhmann, ECIS Dissertation Series 11 (Eindhoven: Eindhoven Centre for Innovation Studies, 2002).

Luhmann was also greatly influenced by the idea of *self-description*. He was inspired by the work of Georg Wilhelm Friedrich Hegel, a German philosopher who wrote extensively about self-description by way of making the case for philosophy as the apotheosis of science.[18] Luhmann's theories attempted to adhere to the idea of self-description. He sought to devise a theory of society that explained itself through itself.[19]

For a fun illustration of self-referential systems, let's take an example from my own Antinet. I have a card at the very beginning (card address 0).

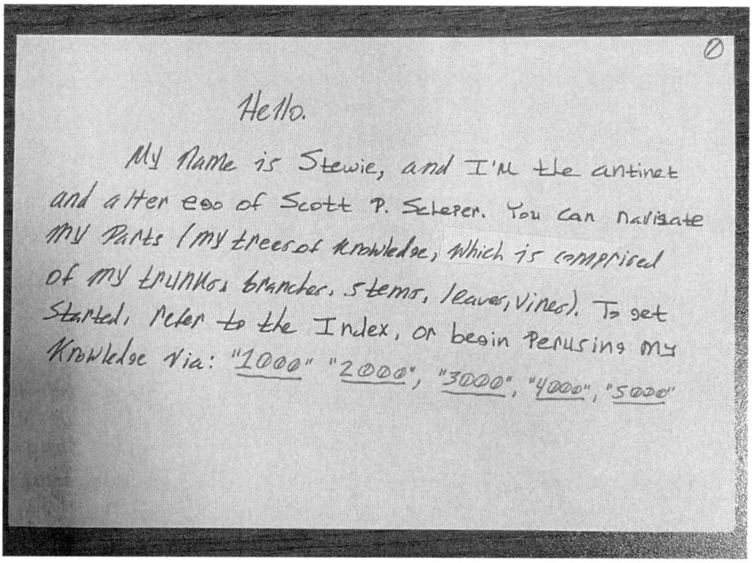

My own Antinet essentially introduces himself and refers to his own parts.

This may seem absurd, but Luhmann did similar things in his own Antinet.[20] It keeps things light and fun!

18 Hans-Georg Moeller, The Radical Luhmann (New York: Columbia University Press, 2011), 35.

19 Hans-Georg Moeller, The Radical Luhmann (New York: Columbia University Press, 2011), 37.

20 "ZK II: Zettel 9/8j—Niklas Luhmann-Archiv," accessed February 22, 2022, https://niklas-luhmann-archiv.de/bestand/zettelkasten/zettel/ZK_2_NB_9-8j_V.

THE SCIENCE BEHIND NUMERIC-ALPHA ADDRESSES

Throughout this book I emphasize over and over that Luhmann's system was a deliberate creation. It mirrors how human memory works to a surprisingly close degree.

The numeric-alpha addresses transform the Antinet's network into something akin to *auto-associations* discussed in memory science. An auto-association is built on *content-addressable memory*, similar to how computes work: "the bits themselves are meaningless, and the bytes made out of them have arbitrary addresses, like houses on a street, which have nothing to do with their contents."[21]

This is also how the Antinet works thanks to the numeric-alpha addresses. "Memory locations are accessed by their addresses."[22] The way in which you explore these addresses is through the keyterms which are housed in the index, serving as a cue to light up areas of your mind.

Multi-storage models posited by those who study human memory indicate why numeric-alpha addresses are critical. Johannes Schmidt explains that, "embedding a topic in various *contexts* gives rise to different lines of information by means of opening up different realms of *comparison* in each case."[23]

THE CONCEPT OF COMPARISON

Let's talk about the concept of *comparison* briefly. Steven Pinker points out an important point relating to the concept of *comparison* in his book *How the Mind Works*. Pinker writes that without specifying a goal, "the very idea of intelligence is meaningless."[24]

---

21 Steven Pinker, How the Mind Works, Norton pbk (New York: Norton, 2009), 104.

22 Steven Pinker, How the Mind Works, Norton pbk (New York: Norton, 2009), 104.

23 Johannes Schmidt, "Niklas Luhmann's Card Index: Thinking Tool, Communication Partner, Publication Machine," Forgetting Machines. Knowledge Management Evolution in Early Modern Europe 53 (2016), 299. Emphasis added.

24 Steven Pinker, How the Mind Works, Norton pbk (New York: Norton, 2009), 61.

And what is *intelligence*? It's something that comes from *information*, thus bringing up the question, *What is information?* According to Pinker, "information is a correlation between two things that is produced by a lawful process."[25] For instance, the rings of a tree stump *compared* with the age of the tree. The Antinet is constructed around this concept. Before you install anything into the Antinet, it *forces* comparison and correlation. As Luhmann puts it, "Information, accordingly, originates only in systems which possess a comparative schema—even if this amounts only to: 'this or something else.'"[26]

THE CONCEPT OF RELATIONS

"Life is just one damn relatedness after another."
—Julian Huxley[27]

When you install anything in the Antinet, you're *relating* the concept on the note to the *most similar* concept already installed in your Antinet. You're comparing, contrasting, and correlating the thought with all other thoughts in long-term storage.

This introduces us to the concept that the Antinet is really a relation of "(selective) relations," as Johannes Schmidt puts it.[28] For instance, when you read, there's a relation between the book and your mind.[29] These are what one would call *selective relations*. You're selecting information from a book that you relate to another thought in your mind. From here, you *relate* this information to other thoughts already installed in your Antinet. You do

25 Steven Pinker, How the Mind Works, Norton pbk (New York: Norton, 2009), 65.

26 Niklas Luhmann, "Communication with Noteboxes (Revised Edition)," trans. Manfred Kuehn, https://daily.scottscheper.com/zettelkasten/.

27 Charles T. Munger, Poor Charlie's Almanack: The Wit and Wisdom of Charles T. Munger, Expanded Third Edition, ed. Peter D. Kaufman, 3rd edition (Walsworth Publishing Company, 2005).

28 Johannes Schmidt, "Niklas Luhmann's Card Index: Thinking Tool, Communication Partner, Publication Machine," Forgetting Machines. Knowledge Management Evolution in Early Modern Europe 53 (2016), 309.

29 Mortimer Jerome Adler and Charles Van Doren, How to Read a Book, Rev. and updated ed (New York: Simon and Schuster, 1972), 7.

this by assigning them a numeric-alpha address and placing them next to, or under, the most similar card.

At this point we have a *relation of selective relations.*

However, with *remotelinks,* which will be detailed later, we can link to other *relations of selective relations* on other branches of our Antinet.

In effect, we have a *relation of relations of selective relations.* Basically, the Antinet is a spider-like web of knowledge you've selected from your readings.

If you find this a bit confusing, don't worry. You're not the only one. I'll explain it in a clearer manner later in this book—specifically, in the chapter on *selection.*

In brief, the Antinet and its numeric-alpha address scheme models itself after the science of human memory. Creating a note in a stream of consciousness state mirrors the *short-term storage* concept in human memory. In turn, this opens up different realms of information when the card is installed in your Antinet (the *long-term storage* component of human memory). The different realms of information are powered by the core process built into the Antinet: comparing thoughts and deciding what they're *related* to (*this or something else,* as Luhmann says).[30]

THE RESISTANCE OF NUMERIC-ALPHA ADDRESSES

For some reason, numeric-alpha addresses never took off within the land of digital Zettelkasten. Why? Probably because it was perceived as unnecessary.[31]

I've brought up Johannes Schmidt's statement that numeric-alpha addresses serve as *an essential prerequisite for creativity* in Luhmann's system.[32] Yet

30 Niklas Luhmann, "Communication with Noteboxes (Revised Edition)," trans. Manfred Kuehn, https://daily.scottscheper.com/zettelkasten/.

31 In reality, the only thing unnecessary in digital Zettelkasten is the 'digital' part!

32 Johannes Schmidt, "Niklas Luhmann's Card Index: Thinking Tool, Communication

I'm met with resistance to this assertion. Some object that my reasoning is "an appeal to authority and not a proper argument."[33] This objection is puzzling because the entire premise of using a Zettelkasten in the first place comes from an appeal to authority.[34] Regardless, there's not much that can be accomplished through theoretical debate on this front. In reality, one must investigate the power of numeric-alpha addresses for oneself. This is only achieved through experimenting with the system and experiencing it first-hand.

With that said, I'd like to caution against the common convention used in digital Zettelkasten systems today: *human-readable note titles*. For instance, in writing a note on the definition of self-reference, many digital Zettelkasten practitioners would name the note or filename Definition of Self-reference, or Self-reference (Definition), or some other scheme. However, in an Antinet, the note would receive a numeric-alpha address like 4214/1A/0.

Here's why this is important:

A numeric-alpha card address instantiates a *thought*. A thought is an incommunicable event that takes place in the mind. You can do your best to represent a thought by communicating it as clearly as possible; however, you cannot "losslessly" export that thought and perfectly install it in the mind of the receiver.

As such, a thought is encompassed by many things, including words, images, and other elements of reality. Giving it a numeric-alpha address is a way of treating it properly. When you try to encapsulate the entire thought in

---

Partner, Publication Machine," Forgetting Machines. Knowledge Management Evolution in Early Modern Europe 53 (2016), 299.

33 sscheper, "Luhmann's Antinet Zettelkasten Was Not Forced Into Its Structure Due to 'Technological Limitations,'" Reddit Post, R/Zettelkasten, September 22, 2021, www.reddit.com/r/Zettelkasten/comments/psysso/luhmanns*Antinet*zettelkasten*was*not*forced*into/.

34 sascha, "Introduction to the Zettelkasten Method," Zettelkasten Method, 54:00 100AD, https://www.zettelkasten.de/introduction/. "The Zettelkasten, as we know it today, really took off with Niklas Luhmann, the godfather of the Zettelkasten Method, the most powerful tool for thinking and note taking out there… Niklas Luhmann was a highly productive social scientist. He published 50 books and over 600 articles.(1) He didn't achieve this on his own. He had quite a companion…"

a human-readable note title, you're watering it down into a mere artificial phrase. The artificial phrase can never encapsulate the true nature of the thought (which includes the associations that also arise when thinking of it). This is why giving the thought a numeric-alpha address is preferred.

The thought *is* the thought. It is not, and should not, be watered down by artificial phrases (aka, a note title).

In human memory, a thought is a collection of many things; and it's melded together with links. A thought does not come packed with a pretty human-readable title name, and neither should be the product of your thought, in written form.

NUMERIC-ALPHA ADDRESSES ENABLE LINKS

> *"Possibility of linking (Verweisungsmöglichkeiten). Since all notes have fixed numbers, you can add as many references to them as you may want."*
> – Niklas Luhmann, *Communication with Noteboxes*[35]

The numeric-alpha addresses make it possible to do another critical thing: *linking*.

THE TWO CLASSES OF LINKS

There are two classes of links in an Antinet:

1. Internal Links
2. External Links

You can think of it like this: *internal links* refer to links within your own mind (i.e., within the Antinet). *External links* refer to links to another's mind (i.e., external to your Antinet).

---

35 Niklas Luhmann, "Communication with Noteboxes (Revised Edition)," trans. Manfred Kuehn, https://daily.scottscheper.com/zettelkasten/.

I. Internal Links

An *internal link* is a link to an area or card in your Antinet. There are several types of internal links:

1. MAINCARD LINKS (AKA, "CARDLINKS")

The majority of internal links in your Antinet are *maincard links* (aka, *cardlinks*). These are links to cards in the main box of your Antinet. Such links look like 5425/2A, 1337/1B, etc.

There are several types of cardlinks: (1) Stemlinks, (2) Branchlinks, and (3) Remotelinks. We'll briefly cover these now.

I. STEMLINKS

Stemlinks are links that are relative to the current stem of thought that you're on. For instance, say the current card you're on is 4214/2E/3A. If you see a link on the card that simply reads /1, this tells you the link is to card 4214/2E/3A/1. The /1 is a stemlink.

Stemlinks are similar to the concept *relative links* within the world of web development. Luhmann employed this concept in his own Antinet, which Johannes Schmidt refers as "single references."[36]

For instance, on the card 17.1b9, you'll see the red numbers 1 and 2.

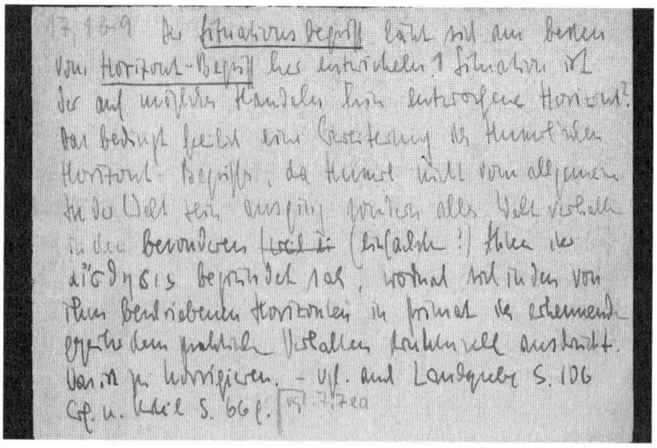

PHOTO CREDIT:
"ZK I: Zettel 17,1b9 -Niklas Luhmann-Archiv," accessed July 15, 2021, https://niklas-luhmann-archiv.de/bestand/zettelkasten/zettel/ZK_1_NB_17-1b9_V.

36 Johannes Schmidt, "Niklas Luhmann's Card Index: Thinking Tool, Communication Partner, Publication Machine," Forgetting Machines. Knowledge Management Evolution in Early Modern Europe 53 (2016), 303.

The red 1 and 2 are stemlinks. They are links to the cards 17.1b9.1 and 17.1b9.2.

This is helpful when you're writing in a stream of consciousness manner. It sends a signal in the form of a reminder that you intend to elaborate on certain sentences by giving them a dedicated card in the following stem of thought.

II. BRANCHLINKS

Branchlinks are a concept I started using for the sake of saving space. For instance, say I'm writing a note on the card 5218/2A. If I want to link to another card, say 5218/1/1A/2B/1, instead of writing out the 5218, I'll use the tilde character (~). In computing, the tilde character typically refers to the current user's home directory. Within the world of the Antinet, it refers to the current card's branch. Therefore, instead of writing 5218/1/1A/2B/1, I write ~/1/1A/2B/1, which is a link within the current branch I'm in (5218). The ~/1/1A/2B/1 is a branchlink, which is shorthand for 5218/1/1A/2B/1.

III. REMOTELINKS

Say you're writing a note within the card 4214/5A/2 and you create a link to the card 1334/2A/4. What you have just created is a *remotelink*. You're linking to a card in a remote area in your tree of knowledge. Remotelinks are essentially the full card address of another card that resides in a relatively remote part of your Antinet.

Think of remotelinks kind of like vines on a tree. A vine will take you from one branch of a tree, to a more remote branch of the tree.

THE SCIENCE OF MAINCARD LINKS

Given that Luhmann was deliberate in the design of the Antinet's structure, we can begin to see the brilliance in how it mirrors the way human memory works.[37] In the field of memory science, stemlinks are what are called *forward*

37 Johannes Schmidt, "Niklas Luhmann's Card Index: Thinking Tool, Communication Partner, Publication Machine," Forgetting Machines. Knowledge Management Evolution in Early Modern Europe 53 (2016), 300. As covered in this book, Luhmann was not forced into the Antinet's architecture. There were other options at his disposal. He could have chosen a commonplace book structure, or a categorically-organized notecard system. As Schmidt says, "At first glance, Luhmann's organization of his collection appears to lack

and backward associations.[38] The branchlinks are items located nearby, and in one's general neighborhood. Yet, like human memory, the further away and the more items there are in between each memory, the association decreases.[39] Remotelinks mimic "remote associations" as understood in the study of human memory.[40] Again, the further away the memories are from one another, the further their association is (unless they're connected via remotelinks).

WHEN IN DOUBT, USE FULL CARDLINKS

Both stemlinks and branchlinks are shorthand and can save time. When in doubt, the safest bet is to write the full card address. Regardless, it's nice to have stemlinks and branchlinks at your disposal when creating notes.

2. KEYTERM LINKS

Keyterm links are links that point you to a keyterm in the index box. For instance, on some of my notes I'll have a keyterm written and underlined in green or blue ink. This tells me to refer to the index and look up that term.

For instance, here's a collective of links for the section I'm writing about right now (on the concept of links).

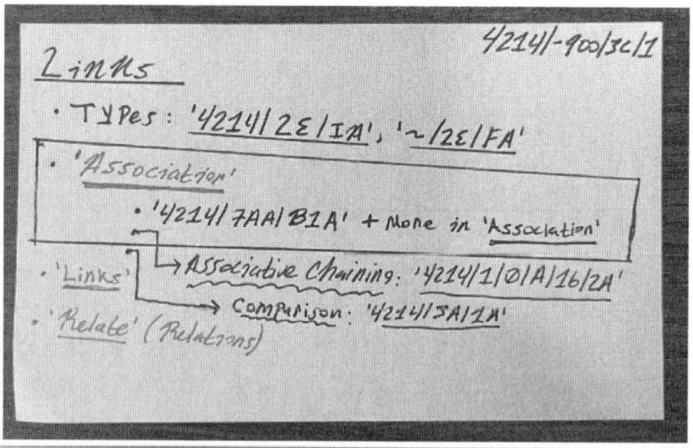

any clear order; it even seems chaotic. However, this was a deliberate choice."

38 Michael Jacob Kahana, Foundations of Human Memory. (New York: Oxford University Press, 2014), 11.

39 Michael Jacob Kahana, Foundations of Human Memory. (New York: Oxford University Press, 2014), 11.

40 Michael Jacob Kahana, Foundations of Human Memory. (New York: Oxford University Press, 2014), 7, 11.

You'll see the following keyterm links in green: Association, Links, and Relate (Relations). This tells me to go look up those keyterms in the index. When I look them up, I can then build out more content for this section from those keyterm cards.

For instance, here's the keyterm for Association found in my index box:

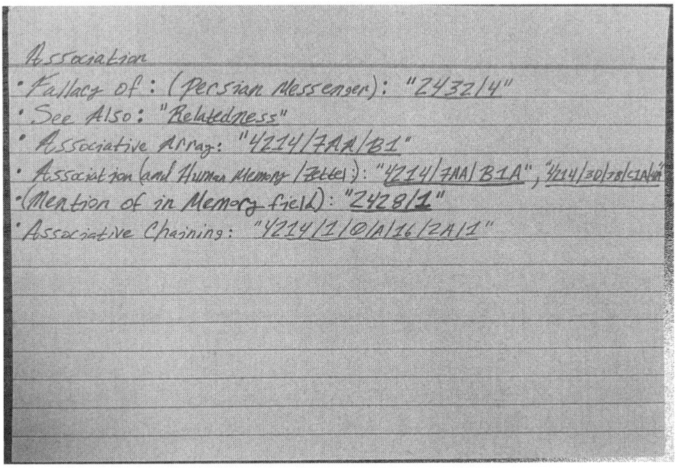

From here, I can then add any sections related to this section on *Links* as I see fit.

II. External Links (aka, ExRefs)

External links (aka, ExRefs) are external references to an outside source of knowledge (like a book, YouTube video, podcast, etc.). Also included in the external link is the page number (or timestamp) from the source.

My ExRefs are always written in red pen, and they resemble that of a footnote. There are two formats of an ExRef. They either begin with a b. or an r.. We'll cover both types of ExRefs now.

1. BIBLIOGRAPHY BOX EXREFS

The Antinet's bibliography box is an analog reference manager. It enables one to organize and manage their bibliography references using "bibcards." More on bibcards will be covered later. Basically, they're cards that contain the details of the book you engage with (or podcast, video, website, etc.).

The first type of ExRef begins with a lowercase-b, followed by a period (b.). Here's an example from the card 4214/4/1BD/1.

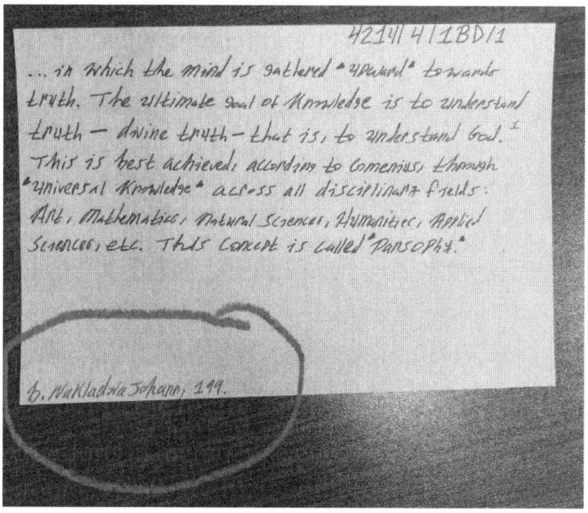

Note the red 1 on the card resembling a footnote. This points to the item circled in red: b.NakladovaJohann, 199. This is an ExRef. It signals that the idea originated from the bibcard, b.NakladovaJohann, and from the page number 199. Think of the b.NakladovaJohann kind of like a *tag* (in digital speak). It's a short phrase that enables one to quickly navigate to the reference in the bib box. If we look up b.NakladovaJohann in the bib box, we find the full details of this reference:

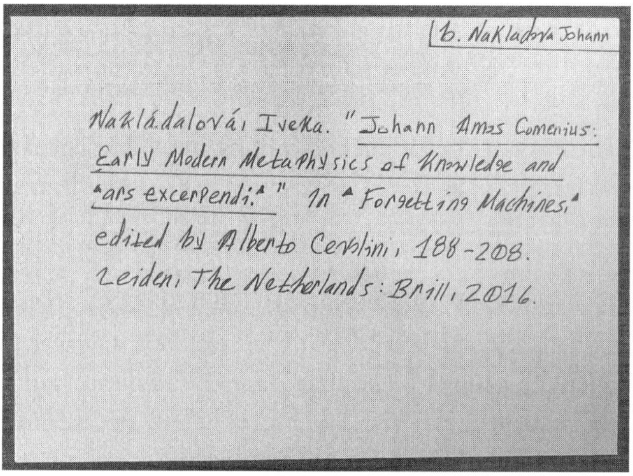

In brief, this tells us that the idea on the card 4214/4/1BD/1 originated from page 199 in the chapter, "Johann Amos Comenius: Early Modern Metaphysics of Knowledge and Ars Excerpendi," by Iveta Nakládalová, which is found in the book titled, *Forgetting Machines.*

2. DIGITAL REFERENCE MANAGER EXREFS

When people talk about a *reference manager,* they really mean a *digital reference manager.* This is a digital tool for storing bibliographic references. These encompass books, articles, papers, videos, podcasts, or other media.

While I am a major proponent of using the analog medium as a thinking system, I am not a luddite. There are clear advantages in using a digital reference manager, as well. First, digital reference managers allow you to store local copies of web pages. This ensures that you'll have the source even if the web page is later deleted. And second, digital reference managers are convenient in that they automatically format references in whatever style guide you use (AP Style, Chicago Style, MLA Style, etc.).

There are a number of digital apps to choose from when it comes to a reference manager. I've tried a handful of them, yet the one I always go back to is called *Zotero.*[41] It's simple, it's free and it has all the features you'll need.

There are cases in which I'll read a web page that is brief enough that it's unnecessary to create a dedicated hand-written bibcard for it. Yet, at the same time, there will be ideas in it that I'll want to reference in a maincard. In such instances, I first add the article to Zotero using a one-click browser extension. Then, I create a *tag* for the referenced article that begins with a lowercase-r, followed by a period (r.). Unlike the b., the r. tells me the item is stored in my *digital* reference manager.

Here's an example of a digital reference manager ExRef from my own Antinet:

41 https://www.zotero.org/

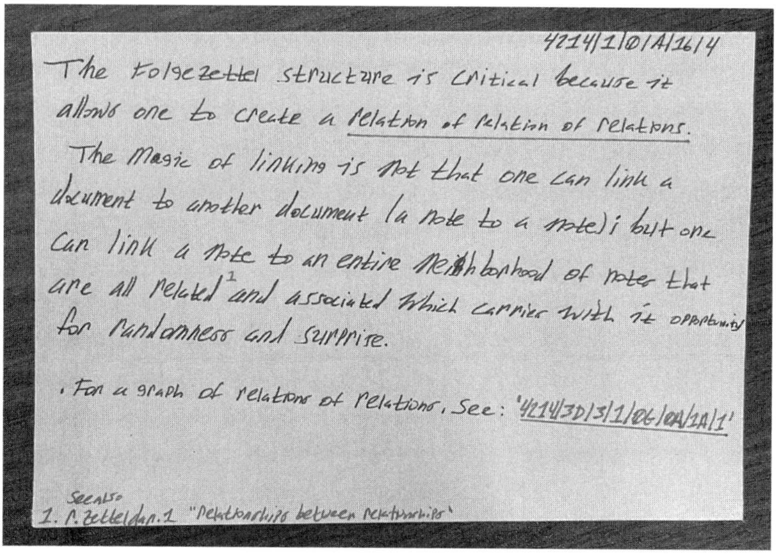

The r.Zetteldan.1 tells me to look this tag up in Zotero. When I do this, I'm pointed to a blog post about the Zettelkasten written by a software developer named Daniel Lüdecke.[42] The r.Zetteldan.1 is an ExRef stored in Zotero. Such ExRefs are quite useful. Digital reference manager ExRefs are yet another tool you have at your disposal.

Now that you know the fundamentals of links in the Antinet, let's jump back into the land of theory. We'll cap this chapter off by discussing the real-life memory science of links.

The Science and Importance of Links

> *"Each note is only an element that derives its quality from the web of references and cross references within the system. A note that is not linked to this web becomes lost in the file; the file forgets it."*
>
> —Niklas Luhmann[43]

---

42 "Luhmanns Arbeitsweise Im Elektronischen Zettelkasten," Strenge Jacke! (blog), September 8, 2015, https://strengejacke.wordpress.com/2015/09/08/luhmanns-arbeitsweise-im -elektronischen-zettelkasten/.

43 Johannes Schmidt, "Niklas Luhmann's Card Index: Thinking Tool, Communication

> *"As discussed by philosophers since ancient times, our memories appear to be organized in terms of associative structures formed between items that are contiguous in space and time. Two items are said to be associated if presentation of one leads to thinking of (or responding with) the other."*
>
> —Michael J. Kahana, *Foundations of Human Memory*[44]

In memory-science terminology, links are *associations*. When trying to think of a memory, you're undergoing something called the process of *retrieval*. The most widely accepted theories of how retrieval works revolve around *association*.[45]

Association is the raw material powering two things: (1) biological learning, and (2) artificial learning (specifically, deep learning).[46]

The manner in which associations are built within digital notetaking apps look nice and pretty. They create nifty-looking graphs and visualizations. However, such tools are not structured in a way to optimize *learning*. Antinets, on the other hand, are built entirely around association. You cannot install a note in the Antinet without associating it with the neighboring notes. As a result a chain-reaction takes place in the system. All notes are essentially chain-linked to every other note in the system. This is the concept of *associative chaining*, which I detail later in this book.

Partner, Publication Machine," Forgetting Machines. Knowledge Management Evolution in Early Modern Europe 53 (2016), 306.

44 Michael Jacob Kahana, Foundations of Human Memory. (New York: Oxford University Press, 2014), 111. Emphasis added.

45 Michael Jacob Kahana, Foundations of Human Memory. (New York: Oxford University Press, 2014), 27.

46 "What Are Neural Networks?," August 3, 2021, https://www.ibm.com/cloud/learn/neural-networks. "Neural networks, also known as artificial neural networks (ANNs) or simulated neural networks (SNNs), are a subset of machine learning and are at the heart of deep learning algorithms. Their name and structure are inspired by the human brain, mimicking the way that biological neurons signal to one another."

It seems like a rather fringe area of focus, yet the study of *how association occurs in the brain* ended up revolutionizing the world. This field of study sparked the discovery of neural networks in the 1970s.[47] Artificial neural networks sit at the heart of deep learning, which is a subfield of machine learning.[48] If you use Facebook, Instagram, Pinterest, Google, Amazon, Netflix—and really almost any large-scale consumer internet product—there's a high probability you're interacting with an artificial neural network.[49] Even if you're in a car, there's a chance you're interacting with a neural network.[50] All of these technologies are powered by the science that emerged from the question of how linking works in the human brain. This is why I'm bothering to spend time emphasizing the power and importance of links and associations!

To recap, the raw material of deep learning is a neural network, and the raw material of neural networks are the thing the Antinet is built on: *associations.*

If you're aiming to build a knowledge development system that increases learning and unconventional insights, then it's important to understand how associations work (and how they're structured within the Antinet). The human memory operates with concepts analogous to the types of associations in the Antinet (stemlinks, branchlinks, and remotelinks). Digital notetaking apps are not structured in such a way. The digital notetaking preachers seem to treat such a structure as a matter of personal preference which, I hold, is a grave mistake.[51]

---

47 Michael Jacob Kahana, Foundations of Human Memory. (New York: Oxford University Press, 2014), 142.

48 "What Are Neural Networks?," August 3, 2021, https://www.ibm.com/cloud/learn/neural-networks.

49 "Neural Networks: Applications in the Real World," upGrad blog, February 6, 2018, https://www.upgrad.com/blog/neural-networks-applications-in-the-real-world/.

50 "Artificial Intelligence & Autopilot," Tesla, accessed November 9, 2021, https://www.tesla.com/AI.

51 For instance digital Note-taking preachers hold note titles, like numeric-alpha addresses as a personal choice and not critically important. See: David Kadavy, Digital Zettelkasten: Principles, Methods, & Examples (Kadavy, Inc., 2022), 38ff.

Even though digital notetaking preachers get a lot of things wrong, they do get some things correct. One author gets it correct by emphasizing the importance of *association* in an abstracted information network, yet he still under-represents the depth of its importance.[52]

You see, associations in a neural network are not *opt-in*. They're not just a clever strategy. They're not some hip, new workflow method. They're not a *best-practice* one ought to follow for good knowledge work. *Associations are not optional in an Antinet,* they are a *requirement*. Like a neural network, associations are a requirement in an Antinet. Before you can install anything into your Antinet, it must be associated with, and installed near, its most related note.

The association composition in an Antinet is not one of mere opinion. It ought to mirror the two properties related to how *long-term storage* in human memory works. The Antinet stores associations among items, and it stores associations *between* items and context.

The Antinet's tree structure, with proximity-based associations as well as context-based associations (in terms of stems and branches), serves as a perfect model for how human memory works. It's the model the Antinet is built on.

The concept the Antinet forces is that of working out your neuro-associative recall "muscle." It does this by forcing you to *think* and *associate*. It requires that you compare information you happen upon in your reading with the knowledge stored in the long-term location within your second mind (your Antinet). Only after this exercise of comparison can you actually install information in your Antinet. Again, this process is not some best-practice principle by which one might manually integrates information (such as in a digital Zettelkasten workflow). Rather, it's built into the core foundation of the analog system. Every time you develop new knowledge, the Antinet forces a process that models how the human brain works. To tie the Antinet

---

52 David Kadavy, Digital Zettelkasten: Principles, Methods, & Examples (Kadavy, Inc., 2022), 14.

in with physiological neural networks one last time, we can point to the process of comparing new and old information, which is impaired with some patients suffering anterograde amnesia.[53] Basically those with impaired neuro-associative recall ability are able to create new maincard notes. However, they do not possess the ability to install those new notes. They do not have the ability to exercise neuro-associative recall and delineate *where* each new idea they encounter should be stored. Basically, they have no index box which enables them to navigate their tree of knowledge.

CONCLUSION

We've covered quite a bit in this chapter. We've surveyed the history of numeric-alpha addresses. We've also explored the science and fundamental components of such. Numeric-alpha addresses unlock a critical aspect of the Antinet: links. We've gone into detail on the different types of links, as well as the memory science behind links.

At this point you're beginning to understand the depth of the Antinet. This isn't some trivial notebox system. It's much greater than that. In the next chapter, we'll dive deeper into the depths of the Antinet. We'll cover another critical component which makes the Antinet the ultimate system for developing knowledge: its tree structure.

53 Michael Jacob Kahana, Foundations of Human Memory. (New York: Oxford University Press, 2014), 225.

CHAPTER EIGHT

TREE

"[The Antinet has] the possibility of arbitrary internal branching. We do not need to add notes at the end, but we can connect them anywhere—even to a particular word in the middle of a continuous text."

–Niklas Luhmann, *Communication with Noteboxes*[1]

IN THIS SECTION I DETAIL the structure of the Antinet. In brief, I hold that the best representation of the Antinet's structure is a *tree*. The idea of using a tree as a metaphor of Antinet-like knowledge systems is not new. In fact, it's a rather ancient idea. Early modern scholars referred to their Antinet systems as *sylva,* which in Latin means "forest." It was described in this manner due to an Antinet's characteristic of "arranged chaos."[2]

I contend that the very best systems possess tree-like structures. For instance, Github is built on a tree-like structure called *Git*. When Github arrived to the version-control arena (i.e., the arena of managing different software versions), Git quickly blew away the other systems. The other systems were rife with horrid version conflicts and syncing issues.

---

1 Niklas Luhmann, "Communication with Noteboxes (Revised Edition)," trans. Manfred Kuehn, https://daily.scottscheper.com/zettelkasten/.

2 Alberto Cevolini, *Storing Expansions: Openness and Closure in Secondary Memories* (Brill, 2016), 184.

The tree structure of the Antinet creates many of the system's irreplaceable benefits. Benefits include increasing the likelihood of breakthrough insights by way of surprise, and many more benefits.

In addition, there's a metaphysical power to the idea of tree-like structures. Not only do tree structures have applications of the practical sort, trees serve as a very powerful symbol. Indeed, trees stand as the central motif for some of humankind's most moving belief systems. All of these items, and more, will be explored in detail in this chapter.

TYPES OF KNOWLEDGE STRUCTURES

Before we dive into the structure of the Antinet, let's survey a few types of knowledge structures.

THE "RIGID" STRUCTURE

The so-called "rigid" knowledge structure is reflected in systems that are organized by hierarchical taxonomy. This type of structure can be represented in folders and sub-folders in a computer file system.

The basic structure looks like this:

- Topic 1
    * Subtopic 1
        * Sub-subtopic 1
            * Etc.
- Topic 2
- Etc.

Examples of systems that use this structure include (1) the Dewey Decimal Classification System, (2) the Library of Congress Classification System, and (3) notebox systems organized by topic or category.

It's become commonplace for personal knowledge management ("PKM") experts to advise against these rigid structures.[3] However, it is unfair to write

3 "1c.3 Using Folders—LYT Curriculum / Unit 1 - PKM & Idea Emergence," Linking Your

off such structures completely. They're useful in that they keep things simple and easy to understand. Still, rigid structures lack the features that make the Antinet great: linking thoughts, developing thoughts, and creating a unique *personality* out of your system that evolves over time.

THE "FLUID" STRUCTURE

When rigid structures are introduced by PKM experts, they're implied as being "bad." The "good" structure is then introduced: so-called *fluid* structures.

Fluid structures are types of systems built with tags, keyword search, and wikilinks. These structures allow users to create linked bubble graphs that give the illusion of viewing your mind.

For instance, a graph like this:

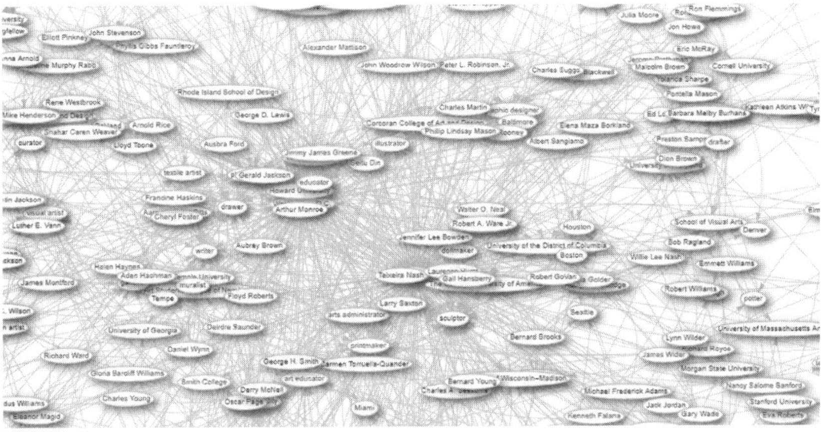

PHOTO CREDIT: Sbae2020, English: Knowledge Graph for Evans-Tibbs Artists, August 2021, August 2021, Own work, https://commons.wikimedia.org/wiki/File:KnowledgeGraph02.png.

However, these structures are a mere illusion. They're pretty to look at; however they are not the best structure for developing and evolving thought.

Thinking, accessed October 25, 2021, https://forum.linkingyourthinking.com/t/1c-3-using-folders /142/2.

Rather than being a useful representation of your brain, think of such structures as a pile of leaves on the ground with vines that connect them.

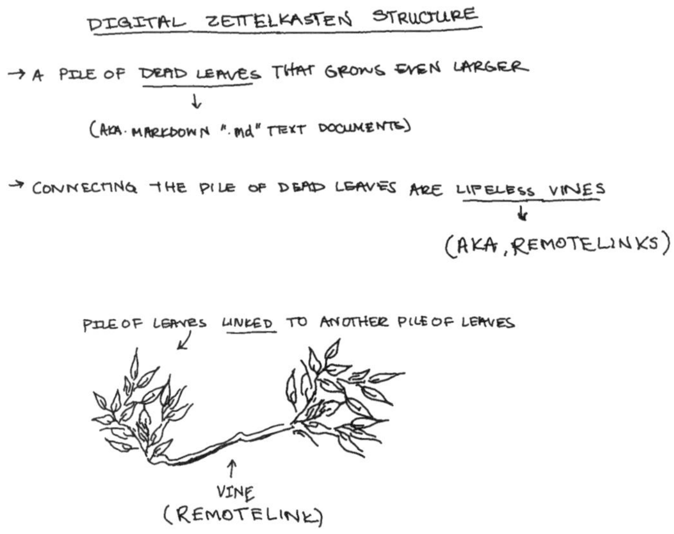

Digital Zettelkasten systems look much like this structure. You're left with either a blob of loosely connected spoke-wheel bubbles, or a needlessly long document of notes. This is not the best way for your brain to process information. Nor is it the best way to create knowledge. It's not representative of how human memory works, either.

Your memory, and more specifically, each individual memory, is akin to a tree. Yes, a tree. A tree wherein certain leaves, attached via vines, are lit up with a lightning bolt of activity (kind of like Christmas tree lights).

In the science of human memory, this is known as *distributed representation*.[4] The Antinet's structure is built with *distributed representation* in its core. Digital Zettelkasten apps do not possess such a structure. They are based on surface-level *wikilinks*, not on a branched and chain-linked structures of associations (generated by numeric-alpha addresses). This is one of many

4 Michael Jacob Kahana, Foundations of Human Memory. (New York: Oxford University Press, 2014), 26.

reasons I hold the Antinet as a superior knowledge system compared to digital notetaking apps (with wikilink capabilities).

With the Antinet, the structure is different. It's not a pile of leaves. It's a rough anti-fragile *tree*.

THE ROUGH STRUCTURE OF THE ANTINET

The magic of the Antinet is not in how *rigid* or how *fluid* it is. The magic is in the *roughness* of the structure.

This seems to run counter to the ideology propped up by PKM practitioners and so-called "Note-taking experts." Such people propose systems more analogous to what's currently trendy. The sexy buzzwords of today are things like *decentralization, openness, atomicity* and *dynamic* systems. Naturally, every PKM expert seemingly integrates such terms into their gospel of notetaking.

Yet Luhmann's system does not reflect the popular buzzwords of today. It's not a *decentralized, open, atomic, dynamic* system.

The Antinet is closer to being the exact opposite, in fact.

It's centralized—in that you, its creator, make all of the decisions.

It's closed—in that it's a cybernetic system wherein each card has its own numeric-alpha address; therefore, the cards containing numeric-alpha addresses are effectively closed inside the system. The system can expand and evolve, yet the expansion and branching happens *internally*. The roots, stems, and branches of the system grow deeper.

It's *molecular* more than atomic. Each note can run onto the next note. The whole *one idea per note* notion is a myth propagated by Sönke Ahrens. The Antinet is made up of many chain-linked structures, and they do not subscribe to the idea of strict *atomicity*.

It's not a dynamic system. You can't find-and-replace-all. You can't updated and delete your thoughts freely on a whim. You can't refactor your notes (and thereby procrastinate on actually doing work). The Antinet's structure, including the notes within it, is more marcescent in nature than dynamic (which we'll cover shortly).

THE ROUGH TREE STRUCTURE GIVES THE SYSTEM PERSONALITY

> *"Natural and diagrammatic representations of trees come in many varieties, each with its own charm, virtues, and uses. Some trees are broad and shallow, others are narrow and deep; some trees are balanced with fixed depth, others have varying branching factors and erratic depth."*
>
> —Ben Shneiderman, *The Book of Trees*[5]

The reason it's important that the Antinet possesses such *rough* properties is because it gives the system *personality*. As previously mentioned, the unique structure enables the system to transform into a *second mind*. It enables it to develop an *alter ego*, as Luhmann calls it.[6]

The Antinet's structure gives it a sense of uniqueness and distinction. It's a system that cannot be freely reorganized and edited. You cannot rename every file on a whim based on whatever new convention you fall in love with. The digital notetaking apps suffer from this freedom. Unlike digital systems, the Antinet does not allow for refactoring of notes en masse. You cannot waste time dragging and dropping notes into different subfolders at a later date. You cannot dynamically update all of the links in files. You cannot retroactively integrate some new metadata or front-matter scheme that you delude yourself into believing will make you more productive.

---

5 Manuel Lima, The Book of Trees: Visualizing Branches of Knowledge, Illustrated edition (New York: Princeton Architectural Press, 2014), 8.

6 Niklas Luhmann, "Communication with Noteboxes (Revised Edition)," trans. Manfred Kuehn, https://daily.scottscheper.com/zettelkasten/. "As a result of extensive work with this technique a kind of secondary memory will arise, an alter ego with who we can constantly communicate."

Rather, the Antinet forces you to do two things: first, to think, and second, to evolve thoughts. If you're looking for a system that focuses on everything else, then digital notetaking apps serve as a better alternative.

All of the things the Antinet cannot do are in fact the very elements which contribute to its most important function: *to generate breakthrough creative insights.*

These creative insights are generated through the element of *surprise,* which the Antinet's structure is uniquely positioned to provide. More on *surprises* and the surprise-generating functions of the Antinet will be discussed in a later chapter.

Suffice it to say, the *rough* structure of the Antinet forces—or actually, encourages—users to ask questions they otherwise would never ask. A digital system, with fully-indexed file searching, only enables the lazy act of searching for a keyterm the user is thinking of *at that precise time.*

With the Antinet, things aren't that simple.

The Antinet forces you to ask: *What's the name of the concept I'm thinking of?* And if an answer is not forthcoming, then a process kicks into gear wherein you ask another set of questions: *What is the concept I'm thinking of related to? Where else would it make sense for the concept to be? What other variant terms point to the concept?* If that's unsuccessful, you may then wish to create a new stem of thought for the concept. And because it was so hard to find the concept, you are then incentivized to create a keyterm in the index. That way, you'll be able to find it more quickly in the future.

What about the original concept you were looking for that you never found? In my experience, any concept, if it's important enough, always turns up one way or another. Your Antinet is less of a black hole than digital notetaking apps are. Whenever you do stumble across the concept again, you can then create a remotelink to it, thereby connecting the two disparate stems of thought. In turn this creates an even richer structure of knowledge.

This entire exercise results in several things taking place in the brain. First, you approach the concept in a fun way, using *associative thinking,* which actually improves mood.[7] Second, during this process you stumble upon profound surprises you now recognize as connected. Last, you trigger *internal dialogue.* Your current mind, with its own active present memory and consciousness, communicates with your *past self* (your past mind) as revealed on the note-cards. This process, like communication, results in surprises.

If nothing else, the core process of the Antinet centers on this communication process that allows the Antinet to become a "surprise generator," as Johannes Schmidt refers to it.[8]

ORDER VS. CHAOS

A critical thing to keep in mind is that *pure order* is undesirable (as is pure chaos). While the Dewey Decimal Classification System makes sense in theory, it and other such rigid systems also stand problematic. How so? They do not accurately reflect reality. The categories of such systems are static; they do not evolve, morph, or grow.

Luhmann's system started with *rough* categories and then evolved from there.

The reason I do not refer to the Antinet as a *rigid* structure is because the Antinet is more *organic* in nature. Johannes Schmidt, who is most familiar with Luhmann's system, also refers to it as "a rough structure."[9] Like nature, the Antinet is rough. It's antifragile, as Nassim Nicholas Taleb would say.[10] It gets stronger with randomness, volatility and disorder. It follows certain laws and adheres to certain conventions. It's also a structure subjected to

---

7 Moshe Bar, "A Cognitive Neuroscience Hypothesis of Mood and Depression," Trends in Cognitive Sciences 13, no. 11 (November 2009): 456–63.

8 Johannes Schmidt, "Niklas Luhmann's Card Index: Thinking Tool, Communication Partner, Publication Machine," Forgetting Machines. Knowledge Management Evolution in Early Modern Europe 53 (2016), 295.

9 Johannes Schmidt, "Niklas Luhmann's Card Index: Thinking Tool, Communication Partner, Publication Machine," Forgetting Machines. Knowledge Management Evolution in Early Modern Europe 53 (2016), 295.

10 Farnam Street, "A Definition of Antifragile and Its Implications," Farnam Street, April 7, 2014, http://fs.blog/antifragile-a-definition/.

complete accidents, random chance, and surprise. The system, in brief, mirrors reality. It mirrors both order and chaos.

Early on in life, Niklas Luhmann realized the world isn't a simple dualistic affair (*good vs. evil*). Recall, he learned this particularly from being captured and tortured by the supposed "good guys" at the end of World War II. The world is complex, and so is the human mind.

The question becomes *How can one devise a system built on that which reflects chaos, yet also possess some physical laws of order binding it together, in order to navigate such complexity?*

It was with this question in mind that Luhmann crafted the structure of the Antinet.

THE ANTINET AS AN ACTUAL TREE

> *"The distributions and partitions of knowledge are not like several lines that meet in one angle, and so touch but in a point; but are like branches of a tree, that meet in a stem, which hath a dimension and quantity of entireness and continuance, before it comes to discontinue and break itself into arms and boughs."*
>
> –Francis Bacon[11]

While it's accurate to describe the structure of the Antinet as *rough*, roughness is a *property* of the system, and not the actual structure.

Instead of thinking of the Antinet as a *fluid* structure, or *rigid* structure, or even a hybrid of that dichotomy (a *rough* structure), I hold that the best way to think of the Antinet is as a *tree*—a *real tree.*

---

11 Manuel Lima, The Book of Trees: Visualizing Branches of Knowledge, Illustrated edition (New York: Princeton Architectural Press, 2014), 14.

The idea of using a tree to metaphorically represent the structure of human knowledge is not new. The first metaphorical tree used to represent human knowledge dates back to sometime between AD 268 and 270.[12] This first metaphorical tree of knowledge is known as the Porphyrian tree, named after Greek philosopher and logician Porphyry. The Porphyrian tree reframed and developed Aristotle's classification scheme by presenting it in tree form.

12 Manuel Lima, The Book of Trees: Visualizing Branches of Knowledge, Illustrated edition (New York: Princeton Architectural Press, 2014), 44.

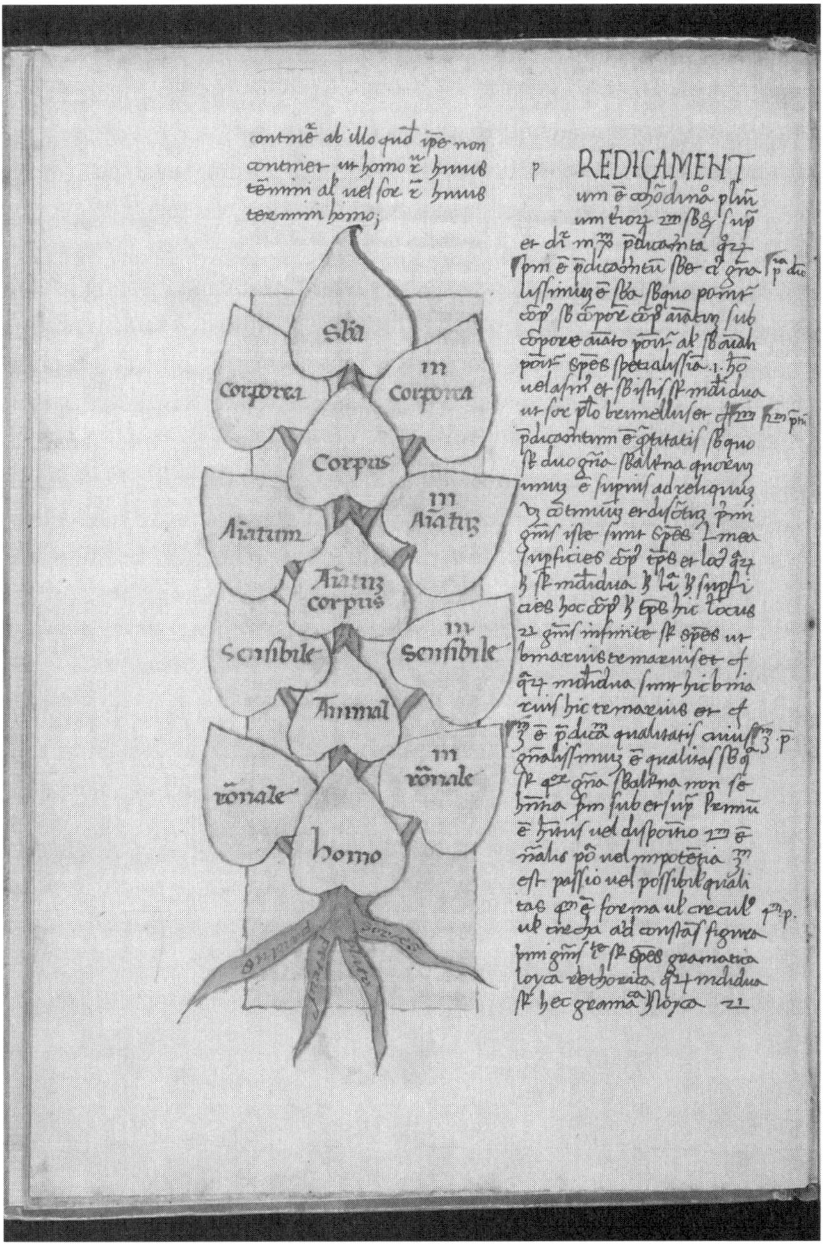

PHOTO CREDIT: Penn Libraries Manuscripts, March 2018, https://upennmanuscripts.tumblr.com/post/171413737213/ljs-457-loyca-parva-etc-written-in-the-abbey-of.

It's important to look to nature as our primary source in forming our understanding of reality. "I think that I shall never see a poem as lovely as a tree," writes Aldous Huxley.[13] By this Huxley was referring to the concept that platonic abstractions can only do so much. True beauty and reality are best represented by nature itself. It's best to think of the Antinet as an *actual* tree, and not merely as a computer science representation of one.

Looking first to nature—and specifically trees—results in creating useful abstractions for managing knowledge. It's important to first look to nature for inspiration, as opposed to looking at some other platonic abstraction for information. Looking to nature first is actually what inspired a useful visual innovation in computer science called rectangular treemaps. Its originator, Ben Shneiderman writes, "The recursive branching structure of trees, which provides a compelling metaphor for organizing knowledge, was at the forefront of my mind as I developed the rectangular treemap as a means to display the nested structure of folders on a computers hard drive."[14] The lesson is that actual, real trees, are the best metaphor to think of when devising the structure of your own Antinet.

Trees are not only useful, but also fundamentally critical in explaining the truth of reality. Charles Darwin writes, "The affinities of all the beings of the same class have sometimes been represented by a great tree. I believe this simile largely speaks the truth."[15] In fact, in Darwin's seminal book *On The Origin of Species*, the only illustration in the entire book is a tree structure.[16]

---

13 Dana Sawyer, Aldous Huxley: A Biography (Trillium Press, 2015), 161.

14 Manuel Lima, The Book of Trees: Visualizing Branches of Knowledge, Illustrated edition (New York: Princeton Architectural Press, 2014), 7.

15 Charles Darwin and Julian Huxley, The Origin of Species: 150th Anniversary Edition, Reprint, Anniversary edition (Signet, 2009), 126.

16 Manuel Lima, The Book of Trees: Visualizing Branches of Knowledge, Illustrated edition (New York: Princeton Architectural Press, 2014), 39.

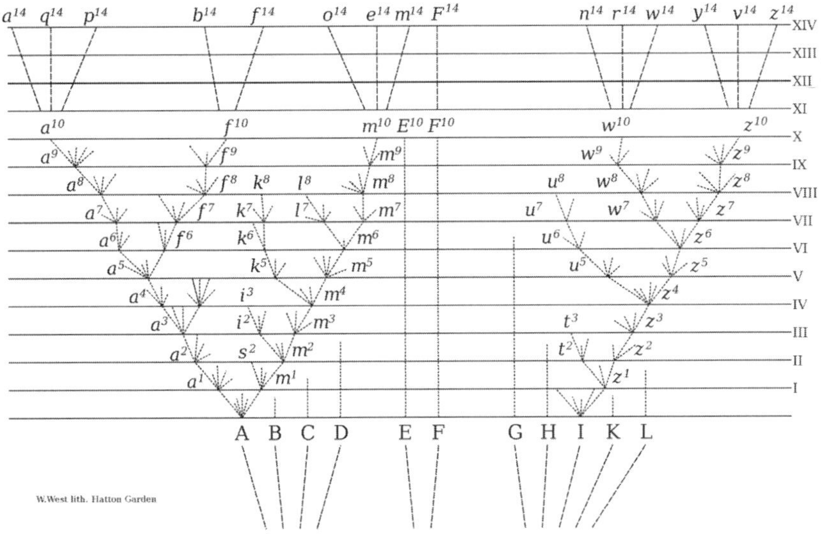

PHOTO CREDIT: *On the Origin of Species* (London: Murray, 1859), 116ff.

Darwin used this model, called the *tree of life,* to explain his theory of evolution.

So critical was this diagram that Darwin wrote the following letter to his publisher a few months before the release of his book: "Enclosed is the Diagram which I wish engraved on Copper on folding out Plate to face latter part of volume. It is an odd looking affair, but is *indispensable* to show the nature of the very complex affinities of past & present animals. I have given full instructions to Engraver, but must see a Proof."[17]

Many applications have been built around trees as metaphors for representing knowledge. For instance, an interesting tree-like application is that of the *Thompson Chain Reference Bible.*

---

17 "Https://Www.Darwinproject.Ac.Uk/Letter/DCP-LETT-2465.Xml," Darwin Correspondence Project, accessed April 19, 2022, https://www.darwinproject.ac.uk/letter/DCP-LETT-2465.xml.

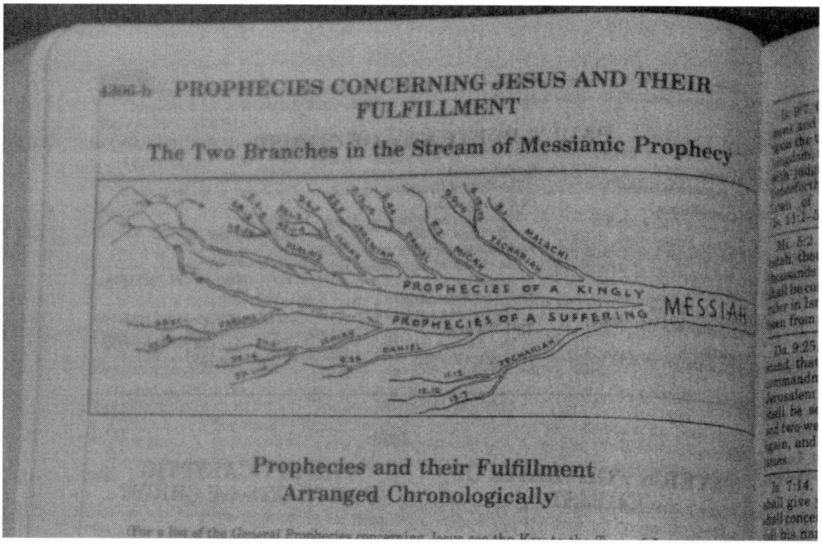

PHOTO CREDIT: "Handy Size Thompson Chain Reference Bible KJV (186)," Bible Buying Guide (blog), accessed April 19, 2022, https://biblebuyingguide.com/wp-content/uploads/2016/05/Handy-Size-Thompson-Chain-Reference-Bible-KJV-186.jpg.

This version effectively breaks apart the Bible into branches and stems of thought. You essentially follow one branch's verse. When you get to the verse, in the page margin is a chain-link to another verse somewhere else in the Bible. For instance, if you follow the verse of a prophecy in the Old Testament, the structure then takes you to a verse in the New Testament wherein Jesus references the prophecy.

The Thompson Chain Reference Bible is actually quite similar to the Antinet. However, the leaves of the Antinet aren't verses, they're notecards.

In sum, using an actual tree as inspiration for knowledge has been proven throughout history to be a powerful metaphor. Luhmann's Antinet embodied this tree-like structure, and it only makes sense we continue to fully embrace it.

Components of the Antinet's Tree Structure

To illustrate how an Antinet reflects a tree structure, think of it like this:[18]

18 Keep in mind, the numbers provided are only illustrative, every Antinet will differ in its

- The *tree* is the entire Antinet. It is your *tree of knowledge.*

- The *branches* are the main top-level sub-sections. For instance: 4000 which represents *Formal Sciences,* and 4212 which represents *Information Science.*

- The *stems* are the individual collections and streams of thoughts that usually are created together. For instance: 4214/1A/1, 4214/1A/2, 4214/1A/3. In this case, the *stem* is 1A.

- The *leaves* are the individual notecards. For instance, 4214/1A/1, 4214/1A/2, 4214/1A/3. These three cards represent three individual leaves.

- The *vines* are *remotelinks* that allow you to swing from one area in your tree of knowledge to another. In the field of human memory science, they're akin to *remote associations.* For instance, within 4214/1A/2 you can link to a remote area like 2431/2A. When you do this, you're effectively swinging from a vine on 4214/1A/2 to 2431/2A.

MARCESCENT THOUGHTS

In the fields of botany and zoology, the term *persistence* refers to the part of a plant or animal that is of a nature wherein it remains attached to the animal. Yet there are some phenomena in nature where plants or animals keep parts of themselves you'd expect them to shed. For instance, one normally expects trees to shed their dead leaves. However, have you ever noticed that certain trees do not do so? This is a phenomenon called *marcescence.* It's a rarity among all of the species of trees, yet certain trees—like beech trees—do not shed spent leaves.[19]

Like literal trees, each person's tree of knowledge residing in their mind does not shed *leaves,* but *thoughts.* Some leaves, like some thoughts, grow brown and stale before they are shed. Other leaves are useful. For instance,

---

morphology. The numbers you use are arbitrary.

19 Tom Oder, "Why Do the Leaves of Some Trees Turn Brown but Not Drop?," Treehugger, accessed August 11, 2021, https://www.treehugger.com/marcescence-why-leaves-some-trees-turn-brown-not-drop-4863742.

producing food (with chlorophyll) by way of photosynthesis, which helps it survive.[20] Yet even valuable leaves—like one's valuable thoughts—are destined to be shed, never to be seen again.

Indeed, shedding some types of thoughts are certainly welcomed by many of us! Yet the latest research in cognitive neuroscience shows that the average person experiences about 6,200 thoughts per day.[21] Many of these thoughts are useful, yet they need some time in the sun to fully sprout and develop.

Unfortunately, most of your thoughts never have the time to sprout and develop. They never have the chance to be ruminated on and await their time to shine.

Productivity junkies try to address this problem by devising systematized digital workflows. The goal centers around capturing *more* information, and storing such in a single repository. Yet, this isn't the solution. Capturing more information is not the solution. Rather, capturing less information, and developing more knowledge is.

Information overload is the very thing Luhmann figured out how to avoid. By way of metaphor, Luhmann's system transforms one's mind into a persistent, supercharged version of itself. Luhmann devised a knowledge structure for his thoughts which transformed his mind into something capable of marcescence, able to retain its key thoughts persistently—forever.

You see, over the course of the days, weeks, months, years, and even decades, your Antinet transforms. It evolves naturally and slowly thanks to the marcescent phenomenon of never shedding its leaves. Its ultimately indescribable, unforeseeable structure corresponds not just to your mind—but to every instance of your mind's thoughts. This is made possible by way of the unique

20 "Leaf | Definition, Parts, & Function," Encyclopedia Britannica, accessed August 11, 2021, https://www.britannica.com/science/leaf-plant-anatomy.

21 "Discovery of 'Thought Worms' Opens Window to the Mind," Queen's Gazette | Queen's University, July 13, 2020, https://www.queensu.ca/gazette/stories/discovery-thought-worms-opens-window-mind.

combination of its components and structure which, if used together, result in a tree that retains its leaves. Your tree of knowledge does not shed its thoughts, it grows and evolves them, thereby enabling you to evolve with your marcescent mind. By constantly communicating with your Antinet, you natively structure thoughts based on where it makes the most sense at the time. You retain your thoughts and evolve them for as long as you communicate with the system.

This illustration largely relies on metaphor but it reflects the truth of using an Antinet in practice. You'll begin to understand the more you use it.

ON HIERARCHIES

Your tree of knowledge is the Antinet. The leaves on the tree of knowledge represent notecards. Each of these notecards is of the same class and status in terms of their theoretical importance.

In an Antinet, there is no hierarchical superiority. As Johannes Schmidt says, "the position of special subject or card says nothing of the theoretical importance of the card."[22] As far as hierarchy goes, as Schmidt says, "there's no bottom and there's no top."[23]

One thing people have difficulty comprehending is how the Antinet *does not* employ a hierarchical taxonomy.

Taxonomy comes from the Greek roots *taxis* and *nomos. Taxis* means *order,* and *nomos,* means *science.* Essentially, taxonomy refers to the science of order. However, the Antinet, as Luhmann writes, is a system of both "order and disorder."[24] It's a system not trying to make a *science* of *order.* It's not trying to make order out of chaos. Rather it's a system that embraces chaos without becoming overwhelmed by it. The mechanisms preventing users

---

22 Undisciplined, Archiving Luhmann w/ Johannes Schmidt, 2021, https://www.youtube.com/watch?v=kz2K3auPLWU, 37:20.

23 Undisciplined, Archiving Luhmann w/ Johannes Schmidt, 2021, https://www.youtube.com/watch?v=kz2K3auPLWU, 37:20.

24 Niklas Luhmann, "Communication with Noteboxes (Revised Edition)," trans. Manfred Kuehn, https://daily.scottscheper.com/zettelkasten/.

from going crazy with too much chaos are the numeric-alpha addresses and the tree structure.

The numeric-alpha addresses alone are not enough for the system to thrive. That's where the *branch separators* come into play. Branch separators are the special characters that fork off a thought into a new branch or stem. They're characters like forward-slashes, periods, or commas.[25]

Some may interpret that whatever comes *after* the branch separator is somehow of a lower-status on the perceived hierarchy. In reality, this is not the case. In fact, as Luhmann confirms, "the positioning of a subject within this system of organization reveals nothing about its theoretical importance for there exist no privileged positions in this web of notes."[26]

Here's an illustration showing how there are no *privileged positions* in the Antinet's structure: Luhmann's most important work is his *Theory of Society*. In his Antinet, Luhmann placed a section for a major project pertaining to his most important work in a very discrete location: 21/3d7fB.[27] This location falls under several other branches which are seemingly less important. When looking at this, it becomes clear that the rank of the importance of a thought is not reflected in its position within the Antinet.

NOTES ARE IN A POSITION, NOT IN A RANK

Each numeric-alpha address pertaining to each note lives in a specific location indicated by its fixed address. Similar to a latitude-longitude coordinate, notes in an Antinet reside at a certain address that is not a ranked order of contents.

Internal Branching

The position-based scheme in the Antinet's structure allows for *internal*

---

25 Personally, I like forward slashes best ("/").

26 Johannes Schmidt, "Niklas Luhmann's Card Index: Thinking Tool, Communication Partner, Publication Machine," Forgetting Machines. Knowledge Management Evolution in Early Modern Europe 53 (2016), 298.

27 Johannes Schmidt, "Niklas Luhmann's Card Index: Thinking Tool, Communication Partner, Publication Machine," Forgetting Machines. Knowledge Management Evolution in Early Modern Europe 53 (2016), 299.

branching. This is important because it allows the system to shift and evolve in unexpected ways.

The Antinet is composed of thoughts that can be visualized as leaves. Like leaves, some grow stale and some new ones grow between others. They're always changing. Some leaves turn brown and dry up. Other areas on your tree unexpectedly grow and flourish. As Luhmann himself states, "some things fade away; some notes are never seen again."[28] Yet the reason you should allow this to occur centers on the opposite scenario. Ideas you had which were "initially positioned so as to play a minor role [in what you're working on] come to dominate the system."[29]

Alternatively, you'll also have thoughts you initially believed would play a major role in your work. Yet the thoughts end up not evolving or being developed at all. This can happen due to the initial excitement for the idea wearing off. Or, this can happen when thoughts lack additional support from your future readings. Both of these stands as a good thing. You don't want to continue developing an idea that no longer seems relevant or useful. This is something that happens naturally in an Antinet.

This highlights the power of internal branching.

The power of internal branching was not realized by Luhmann alone. Others scholars observed the power of such as well. One scholar writes, "the card index is open-ended not only in a physical sense—new file cards and new entries can be added to existing ones without limits—but also in a structural sense."[30] Yet the numeric-alpha addresses also enclose this open-ended system in a cybernetic network. That is, numeric-alpha addresses create a

---

28 Johannes Schmidt, "Niklas Luhmann's Card Index: Thinking Tool, Communication Partner, Publication Machine," Forgetting Machines. Knowledge Management Evolution in Early Modern Europe 53 (2016), 300.

29 Johannes Schmidt, "Niklas Luhmann's Card Index: Thinking Tool, Communication Partner, Publication Machine," Forgetting Machines. Knowledge Management Evolution in Early Modern Europe 53 (2016), 300.

30 Alberto Cevolini, ed., Forgetting Machines: Knowledge Management Evolution in Early Modern Europe, Library of the Written Word, volume 53 (Leiden; Boston: Brill, 2016), 16.

self-contained border between themselves and the outside world. In essence, the system is open-ended, but only in the sense that it grows more complex inwardly instead of externally. The tree of knowledge gets denser and denser. It becomes filled with more leaves, branches, stems, and vines over time.

The internal branching is made possible through the Antinet's structure: its *fixed order of positioning* each leaf on the tree.

As Johannes Schmidt says, it's best not to think of the system as "an order of contents," but as a "fixed order of positioning."[31] By *fixed order of positioning,* he alludes to the *spatial* implications of a thought. A thought doesn't exist in the ether, but can be assigned to a certain position in physical space.

This mirrors how ancient Greek thinkers implemented mnemonic techniques to aid memorization: "If the recollection of things and words is based on semantic associations triggered by images, *then these images must be placed somewhere.* This arrangement cannot be chaotic; it must follow an order that in turn may be *easily memorized.*"[32] By *must be placed somewhere,* think of numeric-alpha addresses and installing your notes in long-term storage. By *easily memorized,* consider the the tree-like structure of the Antinet, as well as the index. One can logically trace the area where the note should be filed after looking up the keyterm in the index.

Links and Reverberation

Internal branching enables you to be pulled deeper into thoughts that are more developed. Yet, internal branching isn't the only mechanism in the Antinet that facilitates this. Johannes Schmidt points out that the parts of the Antinet that are poorly linked, or not even linked at all, result in becoming isolated later on, in part because isolated elements lack *reverberation.*[33]

---

31 Johannes Schmidt, "Niklas Luhmann's Card Index: Thinking Tool, Communication Partner, Publication Machine," Forgetting Machines. Knowledge Management Evolution in Early Modern Europe 53 (2016), 300.

32 Alberto Cevolini, ed., Forgetting Machines: Knowledge Management Evolution in Early Modern Europe, Library of the Written Word, volume 53 (Leiden; Boston: Brill, 2016), 8. Emphasis added.

33 Johannes Schmidt, "Niklas Luhmann's Card Index: Thinking Tool, Communication

Reverberation, a concept that appears throughout this book, relates to "just-experienced associations" setting off a chain reaction of thought. During this period, the concept and the associations are easier to recall.[34]

After you've triggered a reverberation event, over the next several days, the association and connection is given a new lease on life, opening the possibility of those thoughts colliding with new ideas related to your current thoughts and recent discoveries. This enables ideas to evolve.

Reverberation is a necessary ingredient for the evolution of thoughts. Reverberation is attained through creating and re-experiencing linked thoughts. As can be expected, this experience of reverberation, relying exclusively on links as it is, is significantly wiped away with digital keyword search functionality.

When you navigate around your Antinet by way of using associations (links), you are building your memory. You're building memory in the short term by triggering reverberation events, and you're stamping the potential of re-triggering reverberation events in the long term.

Reverberation is also super-charged and strengthened over time via the practice of writing by hand. You see, reverberation transitions an idea into "supersonic mode" within your mind for months (if not years and decades) by way of neuroimprinting ideas on your mind. The reason why this is important is because it enables you to recall the idea when faced with a new idea that contradicts the one still reverberating in your mind. Reverberation, in turn, serves as a self-deception filter for your thoughts.

The tree structure of the Antinet (with its internal branching), as well as links made possible by way of numeric-alpha addresses, enables reverberation to be elevated to a whole new level. This, again, is something lacking in

---

Partner, Publication Machine," Forgetting Machines. Knowledge Management Evolution in Early Modern Europe 53 (2016), 306.

34 Michael Jacob Kahana, Foundations of Human Memory. (New York: Oxford University Press, 2014), 9.

digital Zettelkasten systems with their automated linking and specific-term search properties.

ASSOCIATIVE CHAINING

Let's take a look at two types of structures for organizing knowledge: (1) Associative Bubbles, and (2) Associative Chaining.

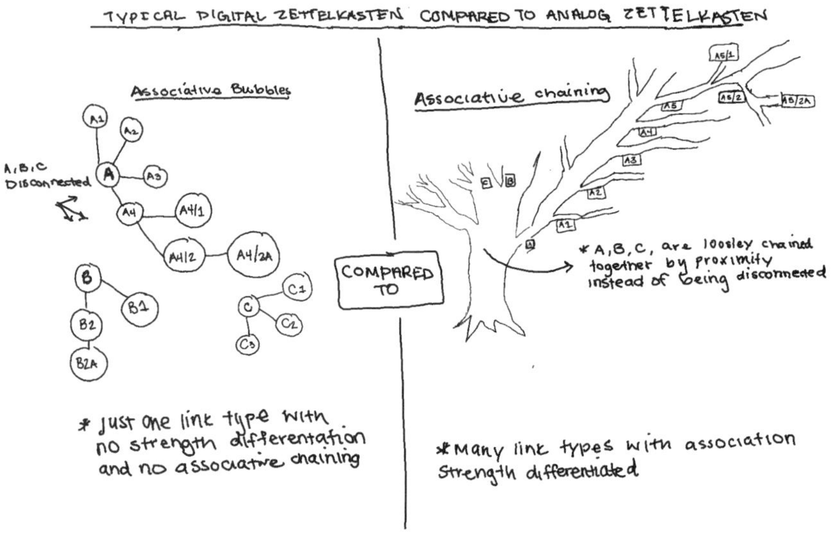

Associative Bubbles

Associative bubble structures contain one link type with no strength differentiation. Think of these as simple links or wikilinks in a typical notetaking app.

These aren't very sophisticated graphs of knowledge, nor are they reflective of how human memory works. The reason centers around the fact that there are no relations between the core branches. For instance, the relations between A, B, and C, are broken in the associative bubble diagram shown. Yet, for some reason, associative bubbles are the most popular structures used in digital notetaking apps today.

Associative Chaining

In comparison, there's *associative chaining*, which stems from the science of human memory. It also reflects the structure of the Antinet.

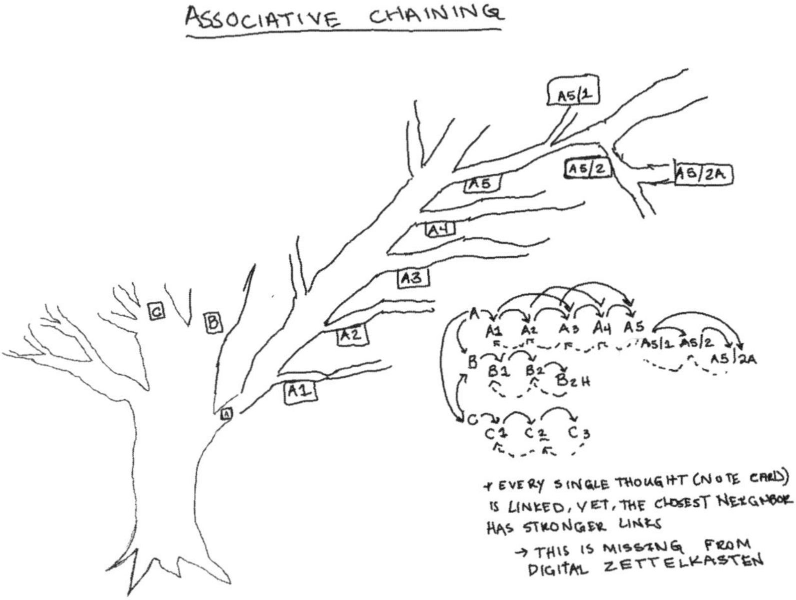

With associative chaining, every single thought is linked by proximity, and the nearest neighbors have the strongest links. There are both forward links, and backward links. However the backwards links are of a weaker association.

HIERARCHICAL ASSOCIATION OF THE ANTINET

If you look closely at the diagram of associative chaining, you'll see that A5 stems into A5/1 and A5/2, which stems into A5/2A. Within the field of memory science, this concept is known as "chunking" or "hierarchical association."[35]

This term *hierarchical association* illustrates a key point. The Antinet's structure is not *hierarchically ordered,* but is rather *hierarchically associated*—with no implication of any special status granted to the order or rank of the note. Merely, notes are organized in a *hierarchical association* based on structure alone (not based on content).

35 **Michael Jacob Kahana, Foundations of Human Memory. (New York: Oxford University Press, 2014), 307.**

Hierarchical association models (aka, *chunking* models) are based on the idea that sequences have *natural breakpoints* dividing words, numbers, and thoughts. By dividing the sequence of items, they're organized into smaller components (aka, *chunks*).[36]

This is not a hierarchical rank indicating importance, however. Within the science of human memory, items correlated with the stem of a tree structure, comprising chunks of more related items, are thought of as "representing more elementary attributes" of the idea. The branches and items found closer to the trunk of the tree are thought of as "representing more abstract structures."[37]

By navigating to one section (or chunk) of leaves on your tree of knowledge, you can navigate *upstem* to other branches, and *downstem* into other sections of leaves.

Within the science of human memory this is referred to as retrieving abstract "superordinate" items from memory and accessing more elemental chunks. In turn you may "retrieve the other items associated [with the memory]" (which is similar in nature to associative chaining).[38]

Though this concept is referred to as a hierarchical associative model, it's not a traditional hierarchy, but one built on "abstract structures" and "more elementary attributes."[39] It's a structure more akin to a *tree* than a hierarchy connoting relative importance.

The latest explorations in memory science have begun to use tree structures in their models.

---

36 Michael Jacob Kahana, Foundations of Human Memory. (New York: Oxford University Press, 2014), 307.

37 Michael Jacob Kahana, Foundations of Human Memory. (New York: Oxford University Press, 2014), 307.

38 Michael Jacob Kahana, Foundations of Human Memory. (New York: Oxford University Press, 2014), 307.

39 Michael Jacob Kahana, Foundations of Human Memory. (New York: Oxford University Press, 2014), 307.

For instance, the concept of chain-structured *long short-term memory* (LSTM) has come to dominate the field of machine learning and data mining. LTSM has proven itself effective at solving a wide-range of problems. This includes problems in the field of speech recognition and machine translation. This model (referred to as S-LSTM) is now being extended by using tree structures, and researchers have found that the performance of this tree-structured model yields better results than LSTM alone.[40]

UNDERSTANDING THE ANTI-HIERARCHY OF THE ANTINET COMES FROM PERSONAL EMPIRICAL EXPERIMENTATION

It's hard to conceive of the Antinet as *not* being a hierarchical system unless you actually experience it yourself (spending time building out your own Antinet and working with it). Until then, it may be helpful to look at hierarchical systems to comprehend the difference.

TOPICS, CATEGORIES AND FUZZY CATEGORIES

An easy way to tell an Antinet system apart from a conventional notebox system is that the notebox system is organized by category alone (without any numerical conventions). If it contains groupings such as Courage, Stoicism, etc., then it's not an Antinet.

With this said, labeling an Antinet as a system *not* organized by category is incorrect. Long story short, the Antinet has an odd relationship with categories.

Indeed, one does organize the Antinet by categories by assigning keyterms to point to a certain numeric-alpha address. However, the Antinet *self-organizes itself* by those numeric-alpha addresses. Basically, *you* organize the Antinet by keyterms and categories, while the Antinet organizes itself by addresses (not by categories).

---

40 Xiaodan Zhu, Parinaz Sobhani, and Hongyu Guo, "Long Short-Term Memory Over Tree Structures," ArXiv:1503.04881 Cs, March 16, 2015, http://arxiv.org/abs/1503.04881, 1.

Luhmann organized his second Antinet by creating eleven top-level categories. However, over the years his system organized itself based on the numeric-alpha addresses.

So, in effect, Luhmann technically *did* organize the system by categories and topics; however, over time, and as more cards were added, it self-organized itself using numeric-alpha addresses, with the addresses going far beyond (and deeper into) the categories and topics Luhmann started with. This allowed his Antinet to morph way beyond any notion of preconceived categories.

That the initial categorizing indicates a hierarchical system is a misconception and myth carried forth and held by many Zettelkasten practitioners.

THE NATURE OF CATEGORY-BASED KNOWLEDGE SYSTEMS

I contend that category-based knowledge systems cater to simpler theories and simpler material (i.e., mass-appeal books). This isn't necessarily a bad thing. I do not wish to impart negative judgment on mass-appeal books; I simply wish to impart a critique that other notebox systems organized by simple and clear topics, end up producing more simplified work.

It's easy to discount category-based notecard systems based on their simplicity, compared with an Antinet system; however, I prefer not to discount them totally.

Category-based systems serve as a more appropriate choice if one wishes to write general books for the general public. For instance, Ryan Holiday, Elizabeth Gilbert, and Robert Greene use topic-organized notebox systems. Their books essentially take simple ideas and concepts and provide useful stories, reflections, and excerpts to support their views.

For instance, an author might take a concept like *courage, make a category in their notebox,* and then add cards with excerpts, stories, and reflections about courage in that category.

This helps produce simpler, easier-to-read books organized by very broad topics; however, it also contributes to several downsides: (1) it risks *over-simplifying* the concept and therefore misinterpreting reality, and (2) it risks steering the author toward saying something that is not groundbreaking or new.

The problem with classification systems built on clear categories and topics is that they do not exist in nature.

As the linguist George Lakoff observed, "Pristine categories are fictions."[41] Categories are artifacts of the human tendency to seek clear definitions of a phenomenon—even if it's too complex to be assigned a clear definition. This tendency was inherited from Aristotle, and we must shed this habit.[42]

Fuzzy Categories

As Steven Pinker points out, when you use a microscope to zoom in on anything, that thing's boundaries turn fuzzy. This introduces a concept Pinker refers to as *fuzzy categories*, a concept that is similar to the idea of the *rough* structure and rough categories the Antinet is built upon.[43]

You cannot create genius-level work if you're confined to thinking about whatever category is popular, or even thinkable.

Moreover, categories tend to induce certain OCD tendencies. One begins to major in the minor. This introduces something I call the *classifier's fallacy*.

The Collector's Fallacy and the Classifier's Fallacy

The *classifier's fallacy* derives its inspiration from something Christian Tietze calls the *collector's fallacy*, the tendency to collet information without actually processing and understanding it through elaboration (such as by making

---

41 Steven Pinker, How the Mind Works, Norton pbk (New York: Norton, 2009), 311.

42 Steven Pinker, How the Mind Works, Norton pbk (New York: Norton, 2009), 311.

43 Steven Pinker, How the Mind Works, Norton pbk (New York: Norton, 2009), 310-2.

main notes that reflect on the content).[44] The collector's fallacy is the tendency to collet information without actually processing and understanding it through elaboration (i.e., making notes that reflect on the content). The Catholic intellectual and philosopher Antonin Sertillanges observed the trap of the collector's fallacy in the early 1920s. "We must beware of a certain craze for collecting which sometimes takes possession of those who makes notes," writes Sertillanges.[45]

Just as harmful as the collector's fallacy is that of the *classifier's fallacy*. With category-based systems, one experiences the tendency to obsess over classifications, notably in deciding which category a note belongs to or over the hierarchical structure of one's classification system. "Excessive attention to classification interferes with use," warns Sertillanges.[46] This is something the Antinet's structure helps stave off. After some time working with the Antinet, users become comfortable enough with the chaos that arises and are able to face the temptations without falling prey to the time-sucking dithering over classifications

Here's the deal. Luhmann did not become "the most important German sociologist in the 20th century" through *thinking conventionally*.[47] He came to be known as such by thinking *unconventionally*. The system Luhmann used promotes *unconventional interactions*. It is a system of chaos founded on simple rules of order. If an author desires to create best-selling books with simplified ideas (at risk of being simplistic), perhaps he or she should opt for a simpler system of organizing his or her knowledge. And experience the tendency of being conventional (rather than unconventional).

44 christian, "The Collector's Fallacy," Zettelkasten Method, 04:32 100AD, https://zettelkasten.de/posts/collectors-fallacy/.

45 OP A. G. Sertillanges, The Intellectual Life: Its Spirit, Conditions, Methods, trans. Mary Ryan, Reprint edition (Washington, D.C.: The Catholic University of America Press, 1992), 194.

46 OP A. G. Sertillanges, The Intellectual Life: Its Spirit, Conditions, Methods, trans. Mary Ryan, Reprint edition (Washington, D.C.: The Catholic University of America Press, 1992), 194.

47 Undisciplined, Archiving Luhmann w/ Johannes Schmidt, 2021, https://www.youtube.com/watch?v=kz2K3auPLWU, 19:16.

The fuzzy categories and structure of the Antinet, on the other hand, prevent it from falling into the trap of oversimplifying reality, leading to deeper, more unconventional, and complex work (for better, or worse).

One of Luhmann's intellectual rivals held a more conventional framework for his theory of society. The man is named Jürgen Habermas. In Robert Greene's book, *The Laws of Human Nature,* its contents are organized by categories like *Irrationality, Narcissism, Shortsightedness, Envy,* and others. Habermas's work is conventionally laid out in a similar manner. One finds a table of contents with ideas which were considered conventional within the dominant school of social theory at the time (known as the Frankfurt School). In the mid-1980s Luhmann was asked whether he thought Habermas used an Antinet system like Luhmann himself did. Luhmann's tart reply is classic: "For [Habermas's] theory, simple [categories] of order seems to be sufficient."[48]

In brief, conventional systems tend to produce conventional thoughts. The Antinet results in a structure that produces thoughts pulled across many contexts and that dances with complexity. The system is built upon similarity and it links ideas that, at first glance, don't seem similar at the time when you go back to write about a section. However, upon closer look, the structure yields some fascinating clusters that would have otherwise been impossible to create if one compartmentalizes every thought into conventional containers.

THE DOWNSIDES OF CATEGORY-BASED SYSTEMS

Now, let's explore some of the downsides of category-based systems.

Duplicating Cards Leads to Diminishing Neuroimprinting Returns

Ryan Holiday uses a notecard system organized by categories (like *Life, Anticipation, Death,* and *Strategy*). His cards are not individually addressed. Rather, you'll find the name of a category in the top-right corner.

---

48 Undisciplined, Archiving Luhmann w/ Johannes Schmidt, 2021, https://www.youtube.com/watch?v=kz2K3auPLWU, 18:27.

When using a category-based system, one often faces the dilemma of a card that can be filed in multiple categories. For instance, a card that fits both into the *Anticipation* category and the *Strategy* category. In such a case, Holiday's advice is simple: "Just make a duplicate card."[49]

While this is not ideal, it's not terribly bad, either. After all, you gain the benefits of neuroimprinting the idea on your mind. However, writing an idea down multiple times does run up against the law of diminishing returns. There's simply *too much to know*, as Ann Blair would say. There's a risk that the excerpt you write down multiple times will prove useless to your work. Also, the idea of copying out reflection notes (which I'll detail later), may span across several cards, is rather impractical in the long term.

Holiday's solution to this problem sheds light on one of the several inadequacies of category-based systems. You see, Luhmann faced the same problem of trying to figure out which keyterm best encapsulated an idea. Yet because of the self-referential nature of the Antinet (made possible by numeric-alpha addresses), all Luhmann had to do was simply create a card that said, *For more on this concept, see card '3411/2A.'* I call this type of card a *hoplink card*, which will be covered later. Oftentimes, however, Luhmann wouldn't create a card with only links on it. There was frequently enough space on any given card to just create a cardlink to the related idea.

DUPLICATING CARDS PREVENTS FEEDBACK SIGNALS IN NOTETAKING SYSTEMS

In addition to the diminishing returns achieved by writing out the same card multiple times, there is something lacking in such a system.

You see, one of the things that has held back notetaking systems is the lack of *feedback*. Whenever you release a new book or piece of work out into the world, you're met with feedback. Sometimes there's an audience for

49 Ryan Holiday, "The Notecard System: The Key For Remembering, Organizing And Using Everything You Read," RyanHoliday.Net (blog), April 1, 2014, https://ryanholiday.net/the-notecard-system-the-key-for-remembering-organizing-and-using-everything-you-read/.

your work, sometimes there's not, and sometimes it's worse: people hate it. However, every single one of those outcomes is fantastic. Feedback, even negative feedback, enables you to learn from your efforts. In the field of artificial intelligence, the entire system relies on feedback. The same holds true for cybernetic networks, which is what an Antinet is. It's a system with a deliberate goal, and it's a system that learns from feedback.

In notetaking systems, you're rarely met with feedback because the system is made for your eyes only (as it should be). It's a system for you to process thoughts, learn thoughts, and reflect on ideas. As such, you do not publish the work, and thus, you don't gain feedback. However, you should not correct the lack of feedback in your notetaking system by publishing your notes. That's a waste of time.

But what are you to do if you wish to evolve your notetaking system, even if you've not yet experienced the *feedback* signals necessary to evolve it?

One way to gain feedback signals relates to duplicate card entries.

When you create a duplicate card in the Antinet, it's a feedback signal. It's not something you want to do, nor is it that likely to happen, because even before you write a maincard, you should first peruse your Antinet to figure out where it's going to fit. Only after that point, do you then begin writing the maincard (which is an excerpt note, a reformulation note, or a reflection note). These will be detailed later. Bottom line: the practice of first figuring out *where* you'll install a new note prevents you from duplicating an already created idea.

When you do create a duplicate card it tells you that your Antinet knows more than you give it credit for. It sends a feedback signal to you that you should spend more time with your Antinet perusing its contents, creating index entries, and getting familiar with it.

Also, when you create a duplicate card it poses an interesting question: were you going to file the duplicate card in a different location? If you were going to file the card in a different location, it sends another signal.

It creates an opportunity to create links across those areas of your Antinet. As a result, it creates an opportunity for accidents or surprises to occur down the road.

THE BENEFITS OF CARDLINKS OVER WRITING OUT COPIES OF DUPLICATE CARDS

Creating cardlinks, instead of copying out a duplicate card possesses several advantages:

First, cardlinks eliminate the wasting of time and the accompanying diminished value of neuroimprinting multiple cards.

Second, cardlinks enrich the cybernetic network of the Antinet because you end up creating a system with more connections. Effectively, the neurons in your brain are enhanced through the making of many connections across the network.

Third, cardlinks enable the Antinet to retain the structure necessary for *compounding* and evolving ideas over the long term. In comparison, category-based systems confine the ideas to silos of information. The cards cannot communicate between silos. At most, they can (merely) reference top-level categories. For instance, they contain references like, *For more on this, see the "Death" category.* The system cannot reference a subsection of cards or even an individual card within the *Death* category, which could contain thousands of cards.

Fourth, cardlinks introduce the possibility of *surprise,* and as a result, the likelihood of inducing breakthrough insights are increased. In an Antinet, when you encounter a remotelink, you're often taken to a completely different branch in the Antinet. In that branch you review stems of thought and leaves that end up serving as the perfect material for what you need.

For instance, right now while writing this section, an accidental surprise occurred. In the following card (4214/5/0/1), you'll see a green snippet of text that says: *For instance, Hoplinks: '4214/3H/4'*

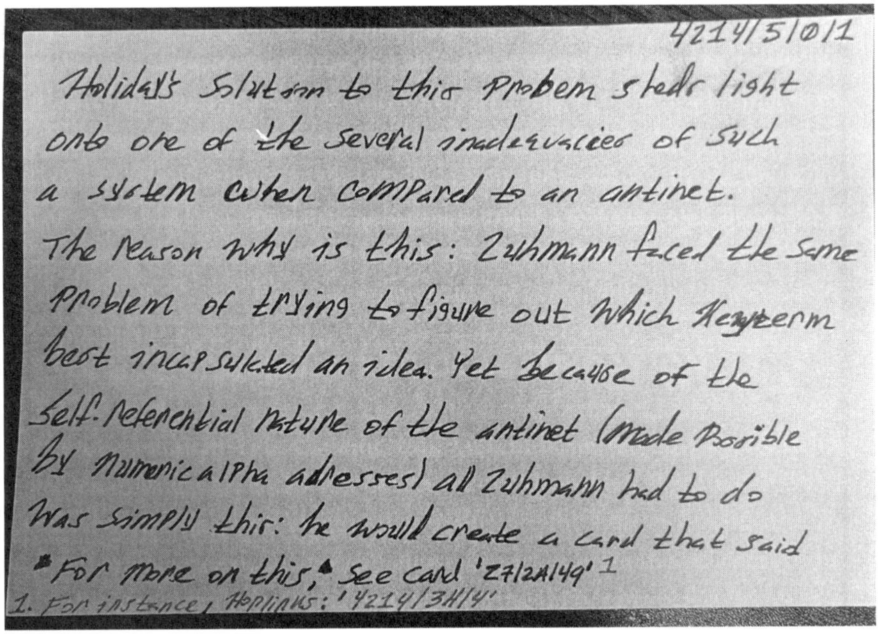
4214/5/0/1

Holiday's Solution to this Problem sheds light onto one of the several inadequacies of such a system when compared to an antinet.

The reason why is this: Luhmann faced the same problem of trying to figure out which keyterm best incapsulated an idea. Yet because of the self-referential nature of the antinet (made possible by numeric alpha adresses) all Luhmann had to do was simply this: he would create a card that said "For more on this, see card 'Z7/2A/49'"[1]

1. For instance, Hoplinks: '4214/3H/4'

When I navigated to 4214/3H/4, I actually stumbled upon a very useful surprise in a few cards placed immediately before 4214/3H/4. The cards were 4214/3H/3B and 4214/3H/3B/1.

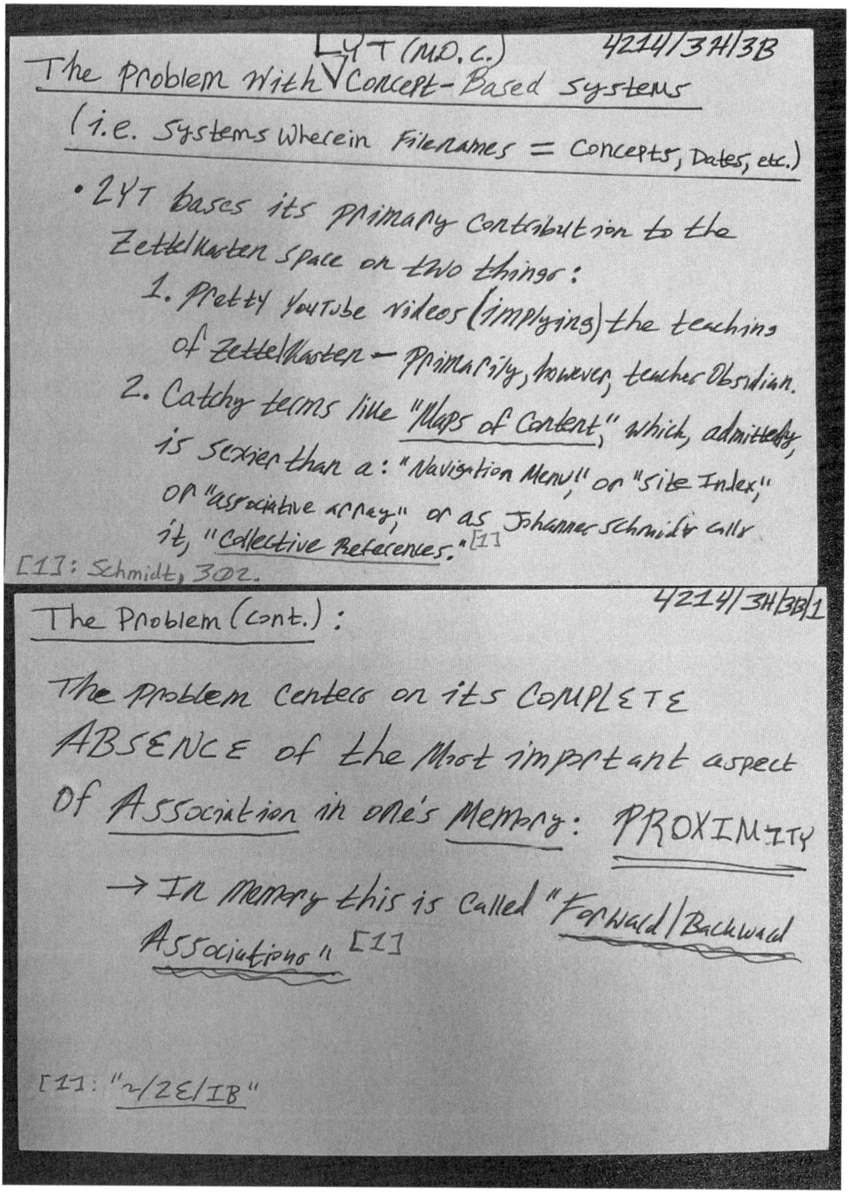

4214/3H/3B

The Problem With LYT (MO.C.) Concept-Based Systems

(i.e. Systems Wherein Filenames = Concepts, Dates, etc.)

• LYT bases its primary contribution to the Zettelkasten space on two things:

1. Pretty YouTube videos (implying) the teachings of Zettelkasten — primarily, however, teaches Obsidian.
2. Catchy terms like "Maps of Content," which, admittedly, is sexier than a: "Navigation Menu," or "Site Index," or "associative array," or as Johannes Schmidt calls it, "Collective References."[1]

[1]: Schmidt, 302.

4214/3H/3B/1

The Problem (cont.):

The problem centers on its COMPLETE ABSENCE of the most important aspect of Association in one's Memory: PROXIMITY

→ In memory this is called "Forward/Backward Associations" [1]

[1]: "2/2E/1B"

These cards pertain to the downsides of category-based systems. I had forgotten about this set of cards. The second card, 4214/3H/3B/1, reminded me of another downside of category-based systems which formed the section you're about to read next. This all came by way of a surprise that generated a breakthrough insight.

Yet even if my (re)discovery of the card 4214/3H/3B/1 didn't come by way of accident (thanks to the tree structure of the Antinet); it would have been discovered by way of linking.

If I continued further along down the branch from the initial card, (4214/5/0/1), I would have happened upon the card 4214/5/B2/1, which points me to 4214/3H/3B/1. See the following note:

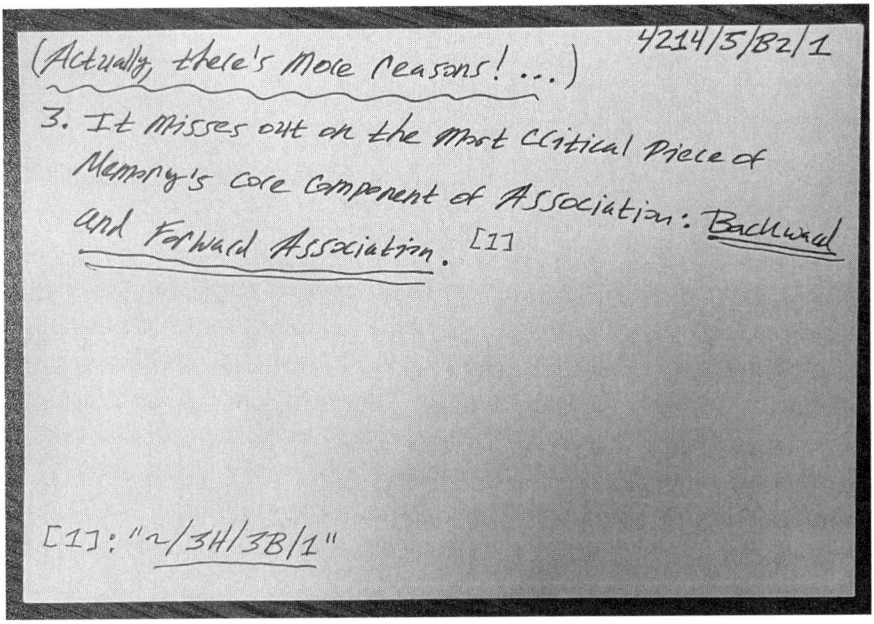

This provides a glimpse into the nature of working with an Antinet. It's a web-like system of chaos and order that introduces surprises. This makes it more fun when it comes time to sit down and write the draft or manuscript of whatever project you're working on.

Category-based Systems Lack the Benefits of Association Based on Proximity

Another problem with category-based systems is the fact that they lack the power of proximal association.

In the Antinet, the closer the cards are to one another, the more *associated* they are. This often comes from, (1) temporal-based creation of the notes, and (2) from years of compounding and installing related notes nearby one another. This mirrors how human memory works. The concept is known as *forward and backward associations.*[50] Because of the numeric-alpha addresses, one can count on building out a system based on *association*. In a category-based notecard system, if your cards ever get shuffled or mixed around, it loses the associations that are evolved and compound over years (even decades) based on proximal associations.

Category-based Systems Lack the Compounding Features of The Antinet

The numeric-alpha addresses (compared with category-based systems), ensure that the external mind you're building models itself after the human brain. The human brain is built around neurons and the connections between them.

As Alberto Cevolini observes, numbering systems do not "mirror the order of the universe," yet they're no more unusual than alphabetically organized systems based on categories.[51] By adopting numeric-alpha addresses, it's possible to shed the notion that the entire universe and reality can be consolidated into easily understood categories. The numeric-alpha addresses compel users to *develop completely different cognitive capacities.*[52] This cognitive capacity results in "a truly *combinatory* ability to manage knowledge."[53] In other words, numeric-alpha addresses combined with the

50 Michael Jacob Kahana, Foundations of Human Memory. (New York: Oxford University Press, 2014), 11

51 Alberto Cevolini, ed., Forgetting Machines: Knowledge Management Evolution in Early Modern Europe, Library of the Written Word, volume 53 (Leiden; Boston: Brill, 2016), 28.

52 Alberto Cevolini, ed., Forgetting Machines: Knowledge Management Evolution in Early Modern Europe, Library of the Written Word, volume 53 (Leiden; Boston: Brill, 2016), 28.

53 Alberto Cevolini, ed., Forgetting Machines: Knowledge Management Evolution in Early

tree structure of the Antinet, allows knowledge to *compound* and *combine* to create breakthrough insights.

Much of this concept was already covered in an earlier chapter discussing the who and why of the Antinet. In that chapter, I touched upon where the Antinet shines, which is when one is developing knowledge for the long term. Category-based systems can certainly work; however, their real power is experienced over the long term.

TREE CLASSIFICATION SYSTEMS

Luhmann's first and second Zettelkasten did indeed contain top-level categories, yet they were not category-based systems. Numeric addresses were affixed to the cards, and they were separated by branch separators (like "/"). This enabled his thoughts to branch internally. The top-level branches were more like *fuzzy categories*. They were good starting points or areas from which knowledge would develop. They retained the rough structure of trees. However, I think it best to think of them as top-level branches instead of top-level categories. Also, instead of calling Luhmann's Antinet architecture a classification system, I like to think of it as a *tree classification system.*

THE LUHMANNIAN TREE CLASSIFICATION SYSTEM

Luhmann started his fist Antinet in early 1950, when he was in his early twenties. He did this to accumulate knowledge and extract concepts from the books he was reading. He used his first Antinet to learn and understand the ideas he was being introduced to in his readings. He had 108 top-level branches in his first Antinet. The list of those branches can be found in *Appendix A.*

Luhmann started his second Antinet with a focus on his sociological research project (which he asserted would take thirty years to complete). In his second Antinet, there were eleven top-level branches. The list of those branches can be found in *Appendix B.*

Modern Europe, Library of the Written Word, volume 53 (Leiden; Boston: Brill, 2016), 28. Emphasis added.

The Luhmannian Tree in Practice

For an example of the tree structure in practice, let's turn to Luhmann's second Antinet, the one that contained eleven top-level branches.

Each of the branches contained subsections (which I call sub-branches). As Johannes Schmidt points out, "each of these subsections was assigned a numerical prefix of up to four digits."[54] For instance, 3411 for *Ideology*.

Here's an example:

- 3 General decision theory
    * 31 Concept of action
    * 32 Models of decision-making
    * 33 Types of decision-making model designs
        * 331 Utilitarian models
        * 332 Optimizing model
        * 333 Satisfying model (theory of acceptable decisions)
    * 34 Simplification of decision-making
        * 341 Anticipatory simplification
            * 3411 Ideology
            * 3412 Authority (organization)
            * 3413 Rules
            * 3414 Legal system
            * 3415 Unplanned structures in the field of decision-making
        * 342 Techniques of decision-making
    * 35 Organization of decision-making

At first glance this structure seems similar to the *rigid* structures. However there are key differences that make it unique.

54 Johannes Schmidt, "Niklas Luhmann's Card Index: Thinking Tool, Communication Partner, Publication Machine," Forgetting Machines. Knowledge Management Evolution in Early Modern Europe 53 (2016), 297.

First off, each has a numeric address between one and four digits long. As Johannes Schmidt writes, "each of these subsections was assigned a numerical prefix of up to four digits."[55] Second, the numeric addresses are arbitrary. They are *roughly* chosen. They are what are known as *fuzzy categories*. Third, each of them contain thoughts organized by numeric-alpha addresses which then can branch down infinitely.

A practice I implement in my own Antinet centers on always using four-digits. For instance, 3 General decision theory would be 3000 General decision theory. Luhmann essentially omitted using zeros; however, for me, it makes sense to employ them.

From each of the branches (or sub-branches), you can then begin *branching down* and creating thoughts on stems under the sub-branches. Each of the thoughts are *leaves* and represent a note. For instance, you'd create 3414/1. This, in turn, can then be branched down even further (3414/1/1), and on and on.

As one software developer who studied Luhmann's archive puts it, "the ability to branch was the central principle" in Luhmann's system.[56] I wholeheartedly agree with this assessment. The Antinet's tree structure makes possible its architecture. It enables it to contain *relations of relations of selective relations.*

THE SCHEPERIAN TREE CLASSIFICATION SYSTEM

The Luhmannian Tree Classification System bases its top-level branches on an arbitrary decision. The creator of decides which branches to create based on the project they intend to build with the system. For instance, in Luhmann's second Antinet, he chose top-level branches relevant to his thirty-year-long undertaking of exploring the theory of society.

---

55 Johannes Schmidt, "Niklas Luhmann's Card Index: Thinking Tool, Communication Partner, Publication Machine," Forgetting Machines. Knowledge Management Evolution in Early Modern Europe 53 (2016), 297.

56 "Luhmanns Arbeitsweise Im Elektronischen Zettelkasten," Strenge Jacke! (blog), September 8, 2015, https://strengejacke.wordpress.com/2015/09/08/luhmanns-arbeits-weise -im-elektronischen-zettelkasten/.

When I built my Antinet, I wanted it to encompass *all* domains of knowledge so that I could move around wherever my interests went over my lifetime. For this reason, I chose to base my classification system on the academic disciplinary fields. The academic disciplinary fields provide a vast domain for one to install their knowledge.

I surveyed various lists of the academic disciplines, including Stanford University's list of academic fields.[57] However, the most robust list I found was Wikipedia's list of academic disciplines.[58]

I base my tree classification system (let's call it the *Scheperian Tree Classification System*) on this robust list.

Here are my top-level branches:

- 1000 – Arts & Humanities
- 2000 – Social Science
- 3000 – Natural Science
- 4000 – Formal Science
- 5000 – Applied Arts & Sciences

The branches are quite broad, and there is a wealth of sub-branches available under each of them. The process entails searching the Wikipedia page of the *Outline of Academic Disciplines* for a given field. From there, you simply choose a number arbitrarily under the parent branch from which to build out a subject area. Material related to life self-development and life philosophy can be added to a section within Applied Arts & Sciences, for instance (5411 – Self-Development).

Luhmann's first Antinet focused on knowledge accumulation. It also focused on generating interesting insights by way of *bisociation*. His second Antinet,

57 Stanford Admitted Students, "Explore Disciplines," Stanford Admitted Students, accessed March 31, 2022, https://admit.stanford.edu/departments-programs/.

58 "Outline of Academic Disciplines," in Wikipedia, March 24, 2022, https://en.wikipedia.org/w/index.php?title=Outlineofacademicdisciplines&oldid=1078952876.

however, was narrower in its focus. The entire thing really could be considered a branch of the sociology branch. It was primarily theory-focused. By using the academic disciplinary fields as detailed previously, the top-level branches can encompass the fields explored in both of Luhmann's Antinets. If he had started building his Antinet out using the academic disciplinary fields as his classification system, there's a good chance he wouldn't have needed to create a second Antinet.

CHOOSING YOUR OWN TREE CLASSIFICATION

According to John Locke, classifications are important for two reasons. First, "it's a great help to the memory." Second, it allows us to "avoid confusion in our thoughts." In other words, it gives us a *map of reality*, or as Locke calls it, "a map as it were of the *mundus intelligibilis*."[59] *Mundus intelligibilis* is the Latin term for *intelligible world*. Classification systems, in other words, create a map of intelligible reality.

When building out the structure of your own Antinet, you're left with several options in choosing a classification system.

You can go the Luhmannian route and create a rough, arbitrary list of sections based on what you think you'll need (like Luhmann's second Antinet containing eleven branches).

Or you can go the route of keeping things more open ended. This seems to be the route Luhmann took with his first Antinet that contains 108 top-level branches.

Sometimes I'm presented with a question like *I'm a data scientist working in the field of machine learning. Why should I adopt the academic disciplinary fields as my classification system? Why do I have to include Arts & Humanities?* The simple answer is that you don't! You don't have to choose the academic disciplinary field classification system. However, you're potentially locking yourself in for life to a small branch. You're betting that you'll be interested in

---

59 Richard Yeo, *Notebooks, Recollection, and External Memory: Some Early Modern English Ideas and Practices* (Brill, 2016), 148.

machine learning for your entire life. I chose the academic disciplines because the system allows me to move around to whatever branch of knowledge I wish to learn about in the future and build out that branch.

The choice is yours. There are many different classifications systems you can gain inspiration from.

You can adopt John Locke's structure: "*Physica*, for medical and scientific subjects, or *Ethica* for moral, philosophical, and political topics."[60]

There are numerous other classification systems to choose from.

Aristotle had his own classification system that categorized every aspect of human understanding into ten categories: substance, quantity, quality, relation, place, time, position, state, action, and affection.[61] Francis Bacon had his own classification system that was divided into (1) *divine learning*, which encompassed the timeless truth of scriptures, and (2) *human learning*, which encompassed history, poetry, philosophy, and other fields.[62] There's also the classification system of Charles Cutter—whose work at the Harvard College library paved the way for the Library of Congress Classification System.[63] There's even classification schemes organized by *space, time,* and *objects*.[64]

There is also, of course, the Dewey Decimal Classification system, which includes ten top-level classes:

---

60 Richard Yeo, *Notebooks, Recollection, and External Memory: Some Early Modern English Ideas and Practices* (Brill, 2016), 147.

61 Alex Wright, Cataloging the World: Paul Otlet and the Birth of the Information Age, 1st edition (Oxford; New York: Oxford University Press, 2014), 27; Manuel Lima, The Book of Trees: Visualizing Branches of Knowledge, Illustrated edition (New York: Princeton Architectural Press, 2014), 44.

62 Alex Wright, Cataloging the World: Paul Otlet and the Birth of the Information Age, 1st edition (Oxford; New York: Oxford University Press, 2014), 27-8.

63 Alex Wright, Cataloging the World: Paul Otlet and the Birth of the Information Age, 1st edition (Oxford; New York: Oxford University Press, 2014), 37.

64 Alex Wright, Cataloging the World: Paul Otlet and the Birth of the Information Age, 1st edition (Oxford; New York: Oxford University Press, 2014), 122, 183.

- 000 – Computer Science, Information, & General Works
- 100 – Philosophy & Psychology
- 200 – Religion
- 300 – Social Sciences
- 400 – Language
- 500 – Science
- 600 – Technology
- 700 – Arts & Recreation
- 800 – Literature
- 900 – History & Geography

I'm sometimes asked why I do not recommend the Dewey Decimal System. There's no really good reason. It's merely preference. I simply like Wikipedia's outline of academic disciplines better. I find it broader and also easier to search. If you like the Dewey Decimal Classification System better, that's fine. Go with what you prefer. Because of the infinite internal branching, it will adjust and evolve to fit your needs.

Remember, these classification systems merely serve as the trunk and broad branches from which your tree of knowledge develops. The true value derives from the many remote stems of thoughts and rich leaves that develop around certain ideas. René Descartes recognized this as well: "It is not from the roots or the trunks of trees that we gather the fruit, but only from the extremities of their branches, so the principal utility of philosophy depends on the separate uses of its parts, which we can only learn last of all."[65]

A more modern classification has emerged called the Johnny Decimal System. It's geared toward managing digital files. It seems we're beginning to come full circle in personal knowledge management. "Nobody can find anything any more," Johnny Decimal's site declares. "Thousands of emails. Hundreds of files. File structures created on a whim and six layers deep. Duplicated

65 René Descartes, Valentine R Miller, and Reese P Miller, Principles of Philosophy: Translated, with Explanatory Notes (Dordrecht: Springer Netherlands, 1982), xxiv.

content, lost content. *We thought search would save us from this nightmare, but we were wrong.*"[66]

I couldn't agree more, yet I think the better solution is found in adopting an analog system over digital, of course!

The bottom line is this: you have several classification system options to choose from, though I'll be teaching Wikipedia's *Outline of Academic Disciplines* in this book. However, whatever system you choose, keep in mind that the classification systems are a *rough* starting point. Because of the tree structure of the Antinet, your system will evolve internally beyond the classification scheme. Classification systems merely assist in creating *a rough starting point* for a branch. They do not serve to encompass everything.

The reason you shouldn't get too hung up the classification system is because of the other component of the Antinet which will be covered next: the index.

When building out an Antinet, you're creating a map for your thoughts, which are *representations of reality*. Classification systems help you create a map of these representations of reality. Yet the index component of the Antinet is a second layer map of your thoughts which enable you to navigate freely across your Antinet without being held back by the limitations of classification systems.

THE METAPHYSICAL POWER OF TREES

> How we long to achieve the growth the tree fosters in itself, the reach and rootage, the sturdiness and balance between high and low, the way it meets each season, holding its ground, spare or blooming.[67]

---

66 John Noble, "Johnny Decimal Home Page," accessed March 31, 2022, https://johnny-decimal.com/.

67 Archive for Research in Archetypal Symbolism, The Book of Symbols. Reflections on Archetypal Images, Illustrated edition (Köln: TASCHEN, 2010), 128.

THE MYTHOLOGY OF TREES

When you begin using an Antinet, you'll be sufficiently supplied with practical knowledge of working with tree structures. Before you're in the thick of this terrain, however, I'd like to supply you with some metaphysical knowledge of tree structures.

Trees are the core symbol of the most important stories ever told in both Eastern and Western theological and philosophical systems.[68]

In the West, the crucifixion of Jesus serves as perhaps the most widely-told story in history. The story's motifs, according to the scholar, Joseph Campbell, center on life after death. This can be thought of as being resurrected or creating a legacy out of one's work.

Within this great story is that of Christ on the *holy rood*. The holy rood is the cross made out of a tree, referred to as the *tree of redemption*.[69]

From The Book of Genesis there's the *tree of life* and the *tree of knowledge*. If you ever wondered why there's evil in the world, here's the answer: It's because of some damn woman named Eve! What did Eve do? She ate from the *tree of knowledge*.

In the West, the metaphorical importance of trees is not exclusively unique to Christianity. The metaphorical significance of trees actually stems from Jewish, Assyrian, and Sumerian traditions.[70]

In the East, we have the foundational story of The Buddha's enlightenment. The motifs of this story center on the once-spoiled aristocrat-turned-ascetic named Siddhartha Gautama. One day, when sitting beneath a bodhi tree (for forty-nine days straight), young Siddhartha became enlightened. The tree,

---

68 Manuel Lima, The Book of Trees: Visualizing Branches of Knowledge, Illustrated edi tion (New York: Princeton Architectural Press, 2014), 16ff.

69 Joseph Campbell, The Hero with a Thousand Faces, 3rd ed, Bollingen Series XVII (Novato, Calif: New World Library, 2008), 25.

70 Manuel Lima, The Book of Trees: Visualizing Branches of Knowledge, Illustrated edi tion (New York: Princeton Architectural Press, 2014), 16.

in turn, became known as the *tree of enlightenment*. The bodhi tree forms the term and figure we know as Buddha.[71]

Not only do we find trees as symbols in the most widely shared Eastern and Western stories, we also see them in our modern mythic stories. *Harry Potter* used his wand as a source of power. The Ents were the tree-people in *The Lord of The Rings, and in The Game of Thrones,* we find *the heart tree, the core symbol of Winterfell, as well as the Three-Eyed Raven, an old man who is enfolded in a tree.*[72]

MORE RESOURCES ON TREES

It may seem rather absurd to be reading about trees in a book about a knowledge system built entirely of notecards. However, there is more to trees than meets the eye.

As I've shown you throughout this chapter, there's applicable power within tree structures and they serve as a fundamental component for how and why the Antinet works so well.

I won't go deeper into tree structures any more than I already have. However, I'd like to leave you with a few resources that may be of interest:

1. **Ascoli, Giorgio A. *Trees of the Brain, Roots of the Mind.* Cambridge, MA, USA: MIT Press, 2015**: This is a fascinating book detailing the tree structures that form the basis of our brain (and mind). The author suggests that the human brain is perhaps the most complex object in the universe. It's comprised of tiny tree-like structures which make up its massive network. Each nerve cell, when enlarged a thousand-fold looks like a tree. It thus follows that regions of the nervous system, when enlarged, resembles a gigantic forest. This book takes a deep dive into the tree-like structures of the brain and explores stunning visualizations of tree networks.

---

71 Joseph Campbell, The Hero with a Thousand Faces, 3rd ed, Bollingen Series XVII (Novato, Calif: New World Library, 2008), 25.

72 "Heart Tree," A Wiki of Ice and Fire, accessed March 30, 2022, https://awoiaf.westeros.org/index.php/Hearttree.

2. **Lima, Manuel. The Book of Trees: Visualizing Branches of Knowledge. Illustrated edition. New York: Princeton Architectural Press, 2014**: This book takes you through the rich history of the metaphorical visualizations of trees. There are a countless number of beautiful photos in this book which show the many different types of tree visualizations. It's not only informative, it's also a wonderful coffee table book!

3. **Wohlleben, Peter, Tim Flannery, and Suzanne Simard. *The Hidden Life of Trees: What They Feel, How They Communicate—Discoveries from A Secret World.* Vancouver, BC, Canada: Greystone Books, 2016**: This book shows that trees are a lot more intelligent than we give them credit for. The author shows how forests are a large social network, including how tree parents live together with their children, communicate with them, support them, how they share nutrients with other trees who are sick or struggling, and even warn nearby trees of impending danger.

These resources are more than enough to appease your basic curiosity about tree structures. However, don't get distracted by them now. We've still got another key component of the Antinet to explore: the index!

CONCLUSION

We've covered a lot in this chapter. You've learned about the *rough* tree structure of the Antinet. You've been introduced to the deep theoretical implications of the tree structure. We touched on the concepts of *order* and *chaos*. We've explored the concept of *hierarchy*, and how the Antinet is *not* a traditional hierarchical structure (but is rather built on *association* and *proximity*). I've taken you into the depths of classification systems. And finally, I capped off this chapter with the mythological magic of trees.

This was a lot to cover. Thanks for sticking with me; I promise you'll be rewarded. You now have a deep theoretical knowledge of the Antinet. This will come in handy in the long term. You'll find yourself more confident in the system because you know the rich depth in which its theory relies. You won't risk yet another instance in your life of getting excited about a new system, only to find yourself quitting (and shifting to whatever the next shiny, new object happens to be). The Antinet *is it*. It's the very best tool for developing deep thought. It's the best system for those who wish to become a *learning machine,* an *online content machine,* a *book-writing machine,* and an *academic research machine.* Keep going.

In the next chapter, we'll be diving into a more "practical" area of the Antinet: the index. Press on.

CHAPTER NINE

INDEX

"Considering the absence of a systematic order, we must regulate the process of rediscovery of notes, for we cannot rely on our memory of numbers. The alternation of numbers and alphabetic characters in numbering the notecards helps memory and is an optical aid when we search for them, but it is insufficient. Therefore we need a [index] of keywords that we constantly update."

–Niklas Luhmann, *Communication with Noteboxes*[1]

WHAT THE INDEX IS

IN THE PREVIOUS CHAPTER, I touched on how classification systems provide utility in that they create a map of *intelligible reality*. The tree, with its organized branches of knowledge, proves useful for managing and perusing your knowledge. Yet classification systems have their limits. They confine information into silos and can be rather broad. Thankfully, the tree structure mitigates some of these downsides. Trees enable thoughts to flow and they create stems into more specific areas for thoughts to evolve (over the long term).

However, the tree structure is not enough. The tool that serves as a second-layer map is the *index*. The index enables one to jump around freely from branch-to-branch, stem-to-stem, and leaf-to-leaf in one's tree of knowledge. The index transforms the system into something that looks like this:

1 Niklas Luhmann, "Communication with Noteboxes (Revised Edition)," trans. Manfred Kuehn, https://daily.scottscheper.com/zettelkasten/.

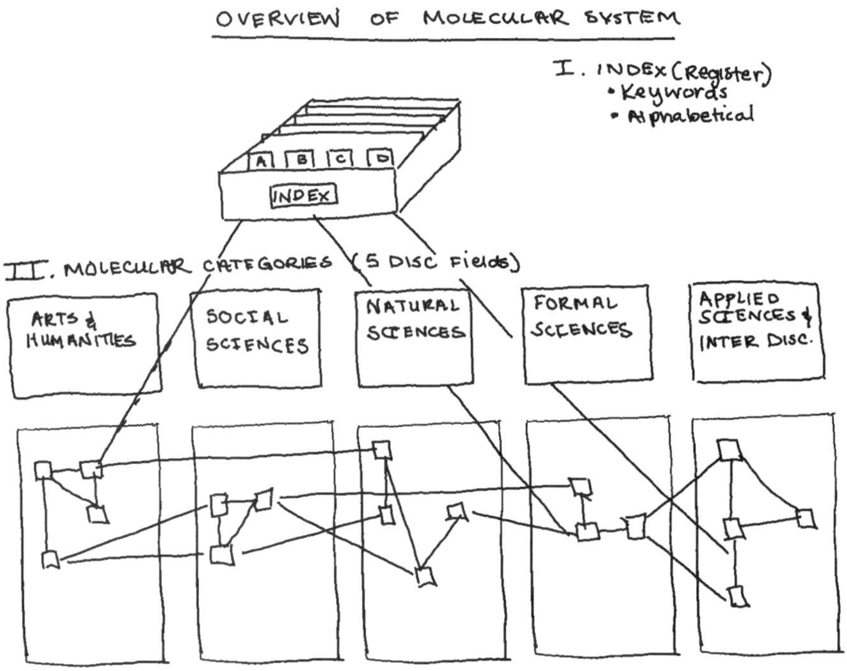

The *index* is composed of a special type of notecard containing two things: (1) a *keyterm,* and (2) a *location.*

As mentioned earlier, a good way to think of the *location* component of the index is to compare it to latitude and longitude coordinates (e.g., 37.2431°N, 115.7930°W). These can be thought of as the place's *global address.*[2] This is why numeric-alpha addresses are *addresses,* opposed to being IDs. But we humans don't think in coordinates, we think in keyterms.

THE KEYTERM

We humans don't spend our time thinking and communicating in the equivalent of latitude/longitude coordinates ("lat/long"). As Luhmann put it, "we cannot rely on our memory of numbers."[3] We need a human-friendly

2 "Understanding Latitude and Longitude," accessed April 4, 2022, https://journeynorth.org/tm/LongitudeIntro.html.

3 Niklas Luhmann, "Communication with Noteboxes (Revised Edition)," trans. Manfred

name to be *associated* with the lat/long coordinates. We need a *key* in other words, of a *term* to associate with the coordinates. This human-friendly *key* and *term* is what we call the *keyterm*.

The keyterm is simply the name of anything your brain *naturally* uses to describe the location of something. It can be anything. It can be a person, place, thing, metaphorical concept, idea, or whatever—*as long as it can be noted down*.[4]

Why the keyterm? Well, I mean, we could try and remember the location of something by memorizing *37.2431°N, 115.7930°W*... or we could remember it by associating it with its more human-friendly name: *Area 51*. I think it's pretty obvious that the keyterm *Area 51* is easier to remember.

With the keyterm, *Area 51*, we can pair it with a *value*. We do this by placing a colon (:) between the keyterm and value. The format looks like this: keyterm: 'value'. For instance, Area 51: '37.2431°N, 115.7930°W'. Within the Antinet, the value is not a lat/long coordinate, but a numeric-alpha address (i.e., Area 51: '2563/27A').

In computer science terminology, this is a type of data structure. It's a *key-value pair*. It's known more familiarly as a *map* or an *associative array*.

I like the term *associative array*, so let's roll with that. A thesaurus is similar to an associative array. Like a thesaurus, which contains multiple synonyms for a word, you can have multiple values for a keyterm. For instance, Area 51: '2563/27A', '5472/3', '3572/22/1/4'). In computer-science geek-speak, this is known as a *multimap, multihash*, or *multidict*.

Kuehn, https://daily.scottscheper.com/zettelkasten/.

4 **Niklas Luhmann, "Communication with Noteboxes (Revised Edition)," trans. Manfred Kuehn, https://daily.scottscheper.com/zettelkasten/. "It becomes a sensitive system that internally reacts to many ideas, as long as they can be noted down."**

THE PURPOSE OF THE INDEX

A system relying on complete random chance (with no index and no tree structure) is an undesirable system. It costs more (effort) than it produces. Yet a system of too much order is lifeless and yields a lower probability of generating breakthrough insights. The perfect middle ground is to have a system that employs an organic tree structure that allows both order and chaos to emerge. The perfect mediator to navigate between order and chaos is the index. This is its single, simple purpose.[5] It's there to provide you with at least one point of entry into your tree of knowledge related to any given keyterm.[6] This allows you to begin stumbling upon other leaves of thought, as well as other stems and branches that have since formed around the term.

Luhmann did not create an exhaustive list of cardlinks for each keyterm. Just because card 5248/3 mentions *complexity*, doesn't mean the indexed keyterm for *complexity* gets a cardlink pointing to 5248/3. Why? Because mentions don't matter. What matters is that the card address to which the *complexity* keyterm points *actually significantly pertains to the concept itself.* Mentions don't matter much. This makes the index more useful than search. When you search your notes digitally, all sorts of irrelevant mentions show up for the search term. This is not so with the index.

The reason Luhmann *did not* create cardlinks for every single card mentioning a keyterm is not because it is technically unfeasible (I mean it is, but it's something that Luhmann wouldn't have preferred even if he possessed the capability). Rather, the reason Luhmann only included a few cardlinks per keyterm can be distilled down to two reasons:

1. The tree structure of the Antinet allows you to follow the stems of thought the notecard rests on. This then takes you on a journey that reveals more cards related to the concept. It then may take you to a *collective* card. This

---

5 Johannes Schmidt, "Niklas Luhmann's Card Index: Thinking Tool, Communication Partner, Publication Machine," Forgetting Machines. Knowledge Management Evolution in Early Modern Europe 53 (2016), 306.

6 Johannes Schmidt, "Niklas Luhmann's Card Index: Thinking Tool, Communication Partner, Publication Machine," Forgetting Machines. Knowledge Management Evolution in Early Modern Europe 53 (2016), 306.

is a card containing a collection of cardlinks to other areas of your Antinet (you'll learn more about collectives later).

2. By creating only a general list of a few cardlinks, it affirms the *rough* tree structure of the Antinet. It re-emphasizes the expectation that the location provides you with a *rough* area of your Antinet. It enables your present conscious mind to interact and communicate with your Antinet. You encounter nearby stems of thoughts in the area that surprise you. When such a communication takes place, breakthrough insights occur which have come about by complete accident. The power of this communication experience will be detailed later in the book.

The reason there are but a few cardlinks for each keyterm entry is that it sets you on a path of exploration. It enables you to explore your tree of knowledge. This also highlights another downside of digital systems. Lacking the nested tree-like structures of the Antinet, digital systems are just a flat-level view of connected bubbles. This knowledge work, however, is not just about storing information and creating cool bubble graphs; it's about *exploration*. The tree structure of the Antinet enables meaningful exploration. As Alberto Cevolini writes, "secondary memories themselves have an inner order that allows for *exploration*."[7]

The Antinet is a long-term storage container of your short-term store of thoughts. In itself, it's a single storage of your mind's thoughts. It transforms your short-term memory and long-term memory into one holistic entity (a second mind). The index is a secondary storage container which allows you to navigate your second mind.

It took a long time for humans to realize that you could create a secondary container (that is, a secondary map) for exploring your own knowledge. It wasn't until the latter half of the sixteenth century that scholars realized

7 **Alberto Cevolini, ed., Forgetting Machines: Knowledge Management Evolution in Early Modern Europe, Library of the Written Word, volume 53 (Leiden; Boston: Brill, 2016), 16. Emphasis added.**

the index could be used as a secondary data storage for navigating the main memory store.[8]

Luhmann was sage in not overlooking the rather new technology of the index. Inspired by The Royal Society of London, Luhmann created his own index, which he called a *register*. In specific notes in his Antinet, Luhmann mentions having paid attention to how the Royal Society developed their register of knowledge.[9] Like Johannes Schmidt, though, I prefer the term *index* to refer to Luhmann's register. You're welcome to use whichever terminology you prefer. Heck, in the beginning I used to refer to it as the *map*. Yet the name that's stuck for me is index, and that's what I shall use from here on.

THE POWER OF THE INDEX

As the scholar who has studied Luhmann's Antinet most closely, Johannes Schmidt, deems the index "a central key to the system."[10] The elimination of a fixed classification system and the lack of table of contents turn the index into a "key tool" for using the file. As Schmidt puts it, "how else should one be able to find certain notes again and thus gain access to the system of references?"[11] In brief, the index is a critical component in using an Antinet.

The index is the conduit by which your brain "structurally couples" itself to the thoughts compiled into an inanimate box. It is the component that breathes life into the Antinet, thereby creating a second mind, an alter ego with which you can communicate.

This isn't woo-woo fuzzy jargon; it's backed by knowledge science. "Memory lies not in the machine," says the scholar, Alberto Cevolini, "but the structural

8 Alberto Cevolini, ed., Forgetting Machines: Knowledge Management Evolution in Early Modern Europe, Library of the Written Word, volume 53 (Leiden; Boston: Brill, 2016), 9.

9 "ZK II: Slip 9/8h - Niklas Luhmann Archive," accessed April 1, 2022, https://niklas-luhmann-archiv.de/bestand/zettelkasten/zettel/ZK_2_NB_9-8h_V.

10 Undisciplined, Archiving Luhmann w/ Johannes Schmidt, 2021, https://www.youtube.com/watch?v=kz2K3auPLWU, 41:48.

11 Johannes Schmidt, "Niklas Luhmann's Card Index: Thinking Tool, Communication Partner, Publication Machine," Forgetting Machines. Knowledge Management Evolution in Early Modern Europe 53 (2016), 302.

coupling of users and machines, that is, in the indexing system."[12] Indeed, the index stands as the core property which transitions the Antinet from merely a container of *others'* thoughts, into "an actual writing generator," observes the scholar Élisabeth Décultot.[13]

CUED RECALL

Cued recall is the modern cognitive scientific term for the no-longer-favored term *recollection*. It occurs when a stimulus (for example a word, sound, or image) elicits a memory of another item with which it is linked.[14] Basically, cued recall works by invoking a memory when presented with a keyterm as the prompt.

When you create a deliberate, hand-written keyterm entry in your index, you are neuroimprinting a *cue* into your mind.

Let's take an example. Say you've read Cal Newport's book, *So Good They Can't Ignore You*. A key idea in that book revolves around something called *deliberate practice*. Deliberate practice is setting aside a deliberately planned time to practice a skill—regardless of whether the activity is enjoyable (oftentimes, it isn't).[15] In the context of the Antinet, if you're interested in this particular concept, you would undertake a time-intensive process. First you would write down the idea on the bibcard related to Newport's book. After that, you would create a maincard for the idea. On the maincard you would either excerpt the idea (by writing down a quote by hand), reformulate the idea (by summarizing it in your own words), or reflect on the idea (by adding your own take, experience, and thoughts on the idea). After this phase, you would then create a keyterm of the idea, consolidating it into a brief word or phrase.

---

12 Alberto Cevolini, ed., Forgetting Machines: Knowledge Management Evolution in Early Modern Europe, Library of the Written Word, volume 53 (Leiden; Boston: Brill, 2016), 32.

13 Élisabeth Décultot, The Art of Excerpting in the Eighteenth Century Literature: Subversion and Continuity of an Old Scholarly Practice (Brill, 2016), 122.

14 Richard Yeo, *Notebooks, Recollection, and External Memory: Some Early Modern English Ideas and Practices* (Brill, 2016), 134.

15 "Deliberate Practice—an Overview | ScienceDirect Topics," accessed April 1, 2022, https://www.sciencedirect.com/topics/psychology/deliberate-practice.

Whenever you begin reading a new book and you come across an idea that relates to *deliberate practice*, you can recall that you already have a keyterm in your Antinet that elaborates on this area. From there, you may either, (1) recall what you already know about *deliberate practice* (thanks to neuroimprinting you can remember what you already know), and (2) you can simply write down the term *deliberate practice* and the page number on the new bibcard. From there you can refer to your Antinet and explore the branches and stems of what you already know about *deliberate practice*. At that point you can develop the thought further by creating a dedicated maincard for it. If you don't feel it is necessary to develop a maincard, you can simply write down the external reference of the book and page number (thereby letting the idea *ruminate*).

In brief, because you've been intentional in creating a keyterm for an idea, you begin to read differently. While reading, when you come across ideas and concepts related to *deliberate practice*, you develop a greater capability to do several things:

1. While reading, the concept you recall may be deemed important enough that you decide to *extract* a new relevant bit of information. As mentioned previously, you may either (1) excerpt it, (2) reformulate it, or (3) elaborate on it.

2. You've deliberately *primed* your mind, and have *selected* the idea of *deliberate practice* as important. Because you've intentionally created a keyterm for the idea, and since you have installed the concept in your Antinet, you may recall the concepts related to it. This is made possible, thanks to the tree structure. You can begin to piece together concepts related to it.

3. Another benefit is that since you *know* you've written something valuable about the keyterm already, you are more motivated to review what you've already written about the concept in your Antinet. I often find myself surprised when I review keyterms. I recall key ideas I've long forgotten about.

DELIBERATE INDEXING IS DIFFERENT FROM TAGGING

As others have observed, so-called "rigid folders" have fallen out of fashion in the modern personal-knowledge-management field. The new popular practice revolves around creating tags (that is, *tagging* notes).[16]

Digital Zettelkasten practitioners may learn of Luhmann's index and deliberate keyterms, and then liken the process to that of tagging notes. They may then proceed to tag every single one of their notes.

There's a difference, however, in how Luhmann used his Antinet. His keyterms served as an entry point into his tree of knowledge (and its branches and stems of thought). Keyterms were used sparingly to get you started on the path of exploring your notes organically by way of exploration. However, as has been observed, tagging is not so central and it's not *intensely necessary* that every note needs to be tagged.[17]

Furthermore, when you tag your notes using digital Zettelkasten tools, it's possible to *over-tag* notes. It naturally follows that it thereby "cheapens" the individual tag. A note with a powerful idea about *truth* is lumped together with other notes tagged with *truth*—even ideas vaguely relating to the concept of *truth*. With digital systems that enable easy and low-cost information collection, the bad ends up drowning out the good.

To understand the different nature of the index system vs. digital tagging, the following diagram helps illustrate the nature of the two:

16 "Luhmanns Arbeitsweise Im Elektronischen Zettelkasten," Strenge Jacke! (blog), September 8, 2015, https://strengejacke.wordpress.com/2015/09/08/luhmanns-arbeitsweise-im-elektronischen -zettelkasten/.

17 "Luhmanns Arbeitsweise Im Elektronischen Zettelkasten," Strenge Jacke! (blog), September 8, 2015, https://strengejacke.wordpress.com/2015/09/08/luhmanns-arbeitsweise-im-elektronischen -zettelkasten/.

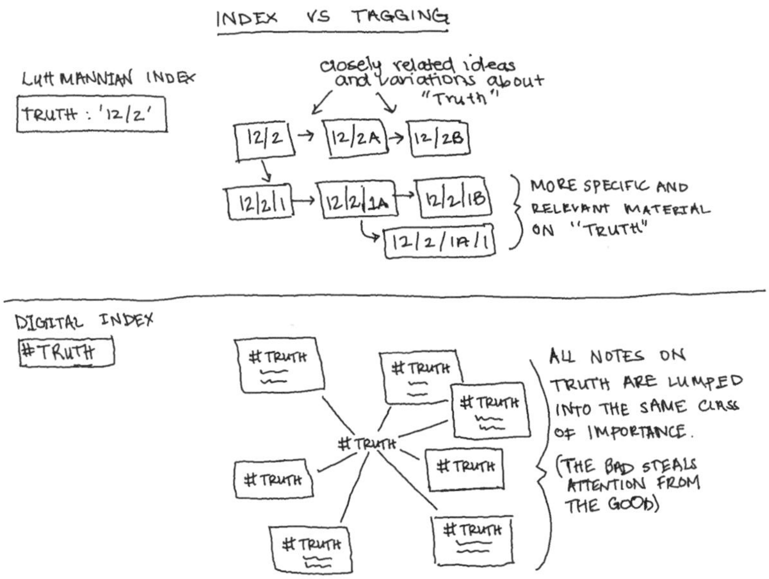

Tagging misses out on the unique branching structure of notes. It results in flat, weak relations and bubble graphs. Because of the tendency to tag anything and everything, a bunch of weak connections and useless material also becomes linked together. Essentially, the tendency to tag every note creates an information swamp. Tagging embodies the typical structure of digital Zettelkasten systems. It creates a pile of leaves on the ground with vines connecting weakly-associated leaves together.

A GUIDE TO THE INDEX

There are three boxes in the Antinet: (1) the bibliography box (the "bib box"), (2) the main box of the Antinet storing thoughts by concept in the numeric-alpha tree structure (the "main box"), and (3) the index box containing keyterms that point one to locations in the Antinet (the "index box").

The index box contains a list of alphabetized cards. There are two types of cards in the index: (1) List Indexcards, and (2) Keyterm Indexcards. Let's cover these now.

LIST INDEXCARDS

List indexcards are cards filed alphabetically, each pertaining to one letter of the alphabet (*A, B, C,* etc.). Under the assigned alphabetical character is a list of keyterms that begin with the letter affixed to the card.

These cards serve as an *associative array* of key-value pairs. The key is the keyterm, and the value is the address of a card in the main box of the Antinet.

When you first start out building your Antinet, you should begin by creating 26 list indexcards (one for each letter in the alphabet).

Examples of List Indexcards

The following list indexcard is from Luhmann (it's a Luhmannian list indexcard):

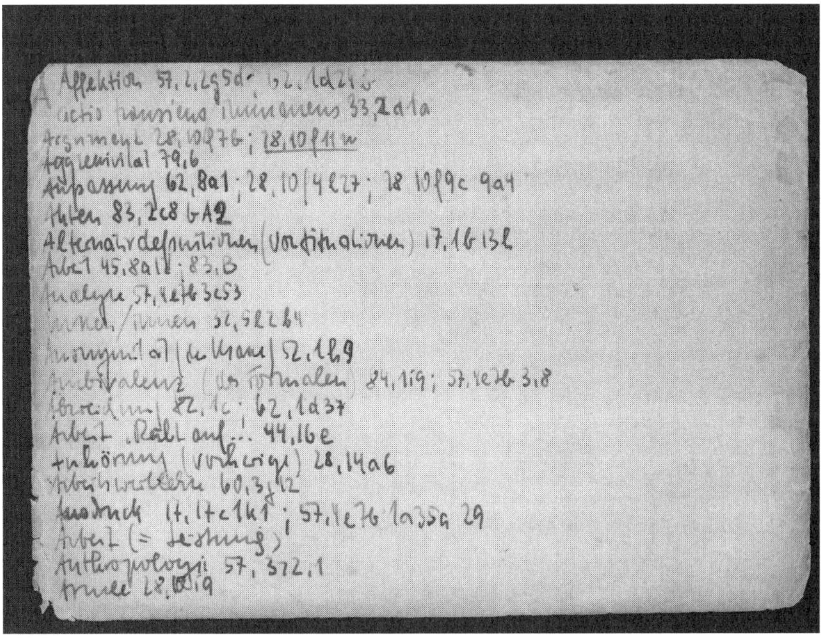

PHOTO CREDIT: "ZK I: Note in the Subject Index (002-A)—Niklas Luhmann Archive," accessed April 1, 2022, https://niklas-luhmann-archiv.de/bestand/zettelkasten/zettel/ZK_2_SW1_002_V.

You'll notice a few things from the card. First, there is a red letter A in the top left corner. This signifies that these are keyterms beginning with A. The second thing you'll notice is that the keyterms in the list *are not* alphabetical. For instance, Argument comes before Aggressivität. The list of keyterms accumulates over time, organically, and in an emergent fashion. The words are organized temporally (by time). The only requirement is that they begin with the letter A.

Here is a list indexcard from my own Antinet (a Scheperian list indexcard):

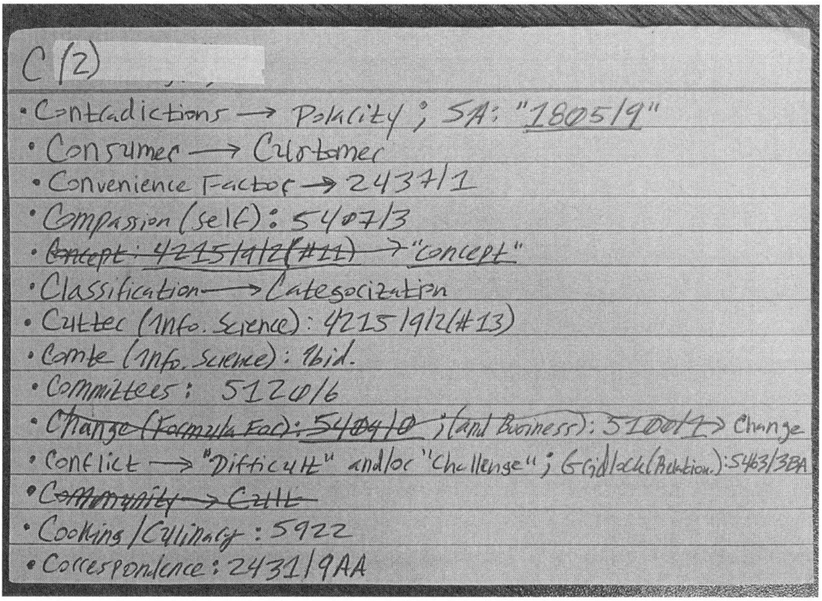

You'll notice a few differences in my own version. First, you'll see there's a convention with arrows. For instance Contradictions → Polarity. This tells me to navigate to the Polarity keyterm in my index box. The second thing you'll notice are conventions like SA: '1805/9'. SA means *See Also*. Third, you'll see that the top of the card reads C (2). This tells me that it's the second list indexcard for the letter C. Fourth, you'll notice that I cross out certain keyterm entries. For instance Change (Formula For)...is crossed out. This tells me to go see the dedicated *keyterm indexcard*, which you'll learn about next.

KEYTERM INDEXCARDS

A keyterm indexcard, as opposed to a list indexcard, is a dedicated card listing multiple links or external references for a given keyterm. Whenever a keyterm entry in a list indexcard accumulates multiple cardlinks, you'll want to create a dedicated keyterm indexcard for it.

Here's an example of a keyterm indexcard:

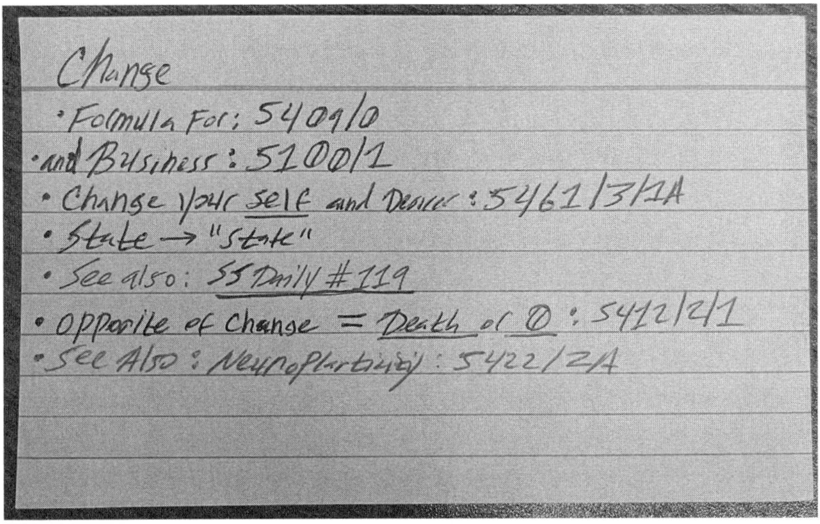

This keyterm indexcard is for the keyterm Change. It displays the crossed-out entries from the list, such as Formula For: '5409/0', which becomes *Formula for Change*; and the listed keyterm and Business; '5100/1' becomes *Change and Business*. The entry State → 'State' refers to *changing state (as in changing one's state of mind), and the arrow prompts me to go see the dedicated keyterm indexcard 'State.'*

THE INDEX BOX

Within the index box, the indexcards should be organized alphabetically. The list indexcards are placed immediately after the letter-dividers, followed by the keyterm indexcards. Each of the following keyterm indexcards starting with the same letter should then be organized alphabetically relative to each other.

To illustrate, on the following page is a picture of my index box. Behind the A divider, you'll first encounter the A (1) list indexcard (note that the yellow A (4) card is visible in this photo).

X
Y
Z
V
W
U
T
S
R
Q
N
O
P
M
K
L
J
I
H
G
F
E
D
Computer Science (4200)
C
B
A(4)
A

Here is another photo. Likewise, the C (1) list indexcard follows the letter C divider; here there are several more list indexcards, which ends with C (4).

Immediately behind C (4) the sequence of my keyterm indexcards begins. The first keyterm indexcard is Candor (Candidness).

Following this card, is the next card in the alphabetical list: Categorization.

This gives you a good practical taste of the components involved in building out an index.

SEARCH IS A BUG, NOT A FEATURE

When you use the index component of the Antinet to search, you're *exploring*. When you search notes digitally, the internal dialogue is different. You're not so much exploring as you are *filtering*. In essence, you are simply trying to recognize and sift through signals. Oftentimes, you spend a great deal of time sifting through keywords that show up in the search results.

Many people who have written about (digital) Zettelkasten miss the fact that *search is a bug, and not a feature*. Why? Perhaps it stems from the perennial human tendency of not recognizing and questioning inaccurate assumptions.

A significant portion of the book *Thinkertoys,* a book focused on improving thinking, centers on challenging assumptions.[18] It's simply difficult and hard work to *invert* and challenge all of your assumptions all the time. It's exhausting. It's no surprise that many digital Zettelkasten practitioners have never stopped to actually question the value of search since we live in the GAMA era: Google, Apple, Meta (Facebook), and Amazon. In this GAMA era, we have a collective bias and acceptance of digital search being a desired feature in all cases.

The assumption that the search function is a universally desirable feature is what plagues digital Zettelkasten systems. For instance, one author declares digital systems to be better because they "allow you to search whole databases."[19] Yet digital search possesses a wealth of insidious negative effects that are difficult to spot with the naked eye. The downsides of such a system become apparent *only after* investing significant time and energy creating a large enough note database in the first place.

---

18 Michael Michalko, Thinkertoys: A Handbook of Creative-Thinking Techniques, Revised edition (Berkeley, Calif: Ten Speed Press, 2006).

19 David Kadavy, Digital Zettelkasten: Principles, Methods, & Examples (Kadavy, Inc., 2022), 17.

As Alberto Cevolini points out, digital search is disappointing for at least two reasons.

The first reason is that search results are "too large."[20] With a digital note-taking app this quickly becomes obvious, and it only gets worse over time. Unfortunately, by the time things get unbearable, you're faced with a massive number of notes. The *sunk-cost dilemma* (sticking with a system that is ineffective just because you've invested so much time and energy in building that system) is a real problem.

Having an app that indexes every single word of your thoughts ends up drowning out the attention you would otherwise spend creating deliberate and carefully selected keyterms.

The second reason digital search is disappointing echoes this issue. "The complete number of results," Cevolini writes, "is never a reliable panorama of what is actually stored in secondary memory and it is not necessarily informative."[21]

The cognitive psychologist and bestselling author Steven Pinker, provides an observation backing this notion. In an "optimally designed" information and knowledge system like the Antinet, search results should only yield items where "the relevance of the item outweighs the cost of retrieving it."[22] The problem with digital systems, however, is that the cost of retrieval is so low that it yields information and knowledge that is of low relevance and low value. I contend that the Antinet does not suffer the same effect.

Although it seems counter-intuitive, human-domain experts outperform search algorithms even today. Take this illustration from Pinker:

---

20 Alberto Cevolini, ed., Forgetting Machines: Knowledge Management Evolution in Early Modern Europe, Library of the Written Word, volume 53 (Leiden; Boston: Brill, 2016), 33.

21 Alberto Cevolini, ed., Forgetting Machines: Knowledge Management Evolution in Early Modern Europe, Library of the Written Word, volume 53 (Leiden; Boston: Brill, 2016), 33.

22 Steven Pinker, How the Mind Works, Norton pbk (New York: Norton, 2009), 142.

> Anyone who has used a computerized library retrieval system quickly comes to rue the avalanche of titles spilling across the screen. A human expert, despite our allegedly feeble powers of retrieval, vastly outperforms any computer in locating a piece of information from its content. When I need to find articles in a topic in an unfamiliar field, I don't use the library computer; I send an email to a pal in the field.[23]

This is something also observed by computer science professor and bestselling author, Cal Newport. He advises his readers to talk to reference librarians. "I'm amazed by how often this resource is overlooked," Newport writes. "Ask the librarian for research help and she will guide you to some amazing sources you would have never found on your own. These extra discoveries make the difference between an average paper and one that shines."[24]

ANTINET SEARCH EQUALS EXPLORATION; DIGITAL SEARCH EQUALS FILTERING IRRELEVANT INFORMATION

When you are trying to find something in your Antinet, think of it like Tarzan swinging through trees. He swings from branch to branch and then along stems and leaves of thought. Every time you swing to a different branch by way of vines (links), you trigger a *reverberation* event. You're reminding yourself not just of the idea, but of the area and stems of thought around the idea. This experience is lost via digital search. You're presented with a plethora of useless information. With the Antinet, you're engaged in the experience of jumping from branch to branch through your knowledge. With digital search, you're not even in the jungle. You're in a dim office somewhere reading about the jungle through a computer screen.

---

23 Steven Pinker, How the Mind Works, Norton pbk (New York: Norton, 2009), 142.

24 "Monday Master Class: The Most Important Paper Research Advice You've Never Heard —Study Hacks—Cal Newport," accessed April 11, 2022, https://www.calnewport.com/blog/2007/12/17/monday-master-class-the-most-important-paper-research-advice-youve-never-heard/.

The Antinet allows you to experience the power of *exploration*. It promotes a way of exploring that is curious, deliberate, and that operates within a general and rough context. This is akin to the experience of being in a library and exploring shelved books. Oftentimes, you happen upon profoundly valuable books by way of *accidental discovery just by* walking down a row in the library that interests you—even if it's somewhat unrelated to your current project. In doing this, you may stumble upon a book that becomes a critical component of the project or book you're working on. Digitally searching your notes eliminates this magical experience.

The digital Zettelkasten proselytizers oftentimes think that *linking* is the core component of Zettelkasten systems. This couldn't be further from the truth. An entire industry of apps and courses revolve around the idea of linking notes. Yet linking does is not the core component of Zettelkasten systems. It is but one property, along with indexing and others, that makes the system work.

For instance, the analog nature of the Antinet makes full-text search impossible. It forces users to *explicitly create* very selective links between thoughts. Why? Because you know there's no full-text search that possesses the illusion of saving you later on. *When you're writing out a note by hand, and you think of a related note, you must create the link right then and there.* There's no safety net. Laziness, in other words, is not an option.

As a result, you invest more energy in creating very selective links. You end up hardcoding cardlinks into your notes with the result that you end up taking them more seriously than you would cheaply created digital wikilinks. After investing that energy, it's more likely that you will follow the cardlinks and *explore* your notes, which then takes you to new places in your Antinet where you might stumble upon other information that would lead to more accidental breakthrough insights.

THE BUGS OF DIGITAL SEARCH

Digital Search Robs You of Maintenance Rehearsal Learning and Association

Manually flipping through your old notes and reviewing them strengths your long-term memory; it gives more opportunities for *maintenance rehearsal* (talked about in detail in this book).

Searching your Antinet relates to the process of reviewing flash cards for an exam. Yet it's not painfully boring like *rote learning* usually is. Rote learning is a memorization technique based on repetition—it's essentially *maintenance rehearsal* that allows you to keep an idea fresh in your mind, then refresh it when your memory lags. Yet, with the Antinet, it's a different flavor of maintenance rehearsal. While you're reviewing your old ideas, you're oftentimes holding a new card idea in your mind. Why? Because you're on a quest to install a new idea that you're probably excited about into your Antinet. The name of the game is similarity. You're on a quest, looking for the most similar idea to install this card next to. This entire quest is a fun process, it even improves mood, which I'll detail shortly. In brief, digital search lacks such a process.

By using a digital Zettelkasten, you thwart the richness of the process of inducing maintenance rehearsal while searching for the most-closely associated idea in the Antinet.

Digital Search Kills the Magic of Structured Accidents

When perusing a library, *structured accidents* often occur. The accidental discovery of an incredible book is not a completely random accident, it's a structured accident. After all, the book is contained within a structured contextual area of the library. It's not completely random.

The magic of the Antinet is not only in how it fosters your thinking of and associating the new concept from the book you've read with what it relates to (that's a conventional interaction). Rather, the magic of the Antinet comes from discoveries "which were never planned, never preconceived, or conceived."[25] Important discoveries come about not so much by way of your current thinking; they come about by realizing the magical connections

---

25 Niklas Luhmann, "Communication with Noteboxes (Revised Edition)," trans. Manfred Kuehn, https://daily.scottscheper.com/zettelkasten/.

you first missed in your old way of thinking. They also come about by way of *structured accidents.*

The power of *accidents* will be covered later in this book, however, let's take a look at a few examples.

The following is an example of a more conventional interaction that reveals somewhat interesting insights.

Here's the keyterm indexcard for Association.

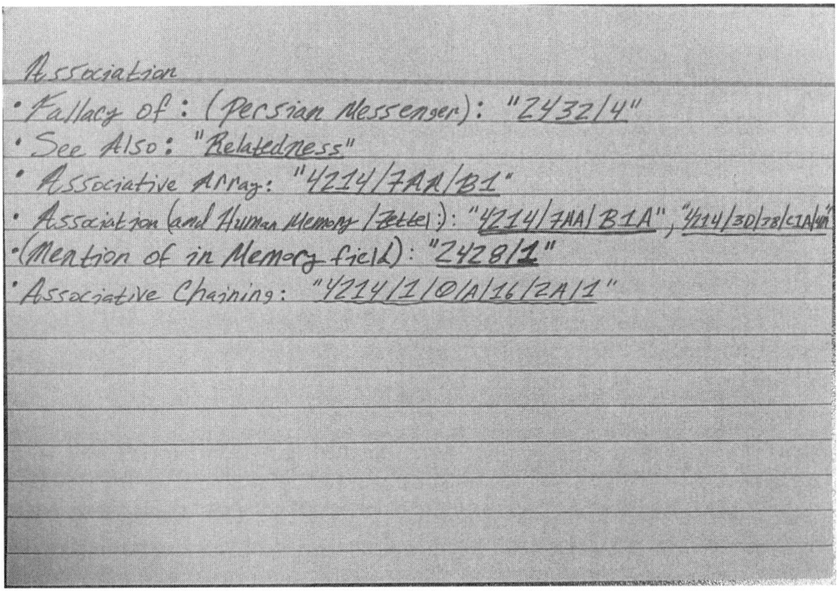

There's one curious entry there written as Fallacy of: (Persian Messenger): '2432/4'. This pertains to the *Persian-messenger* fallacy commonly known as *shooting the messenger* who bears, and is thus associated with, bad news. Because *association* is at the core of the fallacy, the keyterm points me to this area of my Antinet.

This type of thing often occurs in digital search. This, however, is not an unconventional insight. Nor is it something that necessarily produces breakthrough creative insights.

Breakthrough insights come about by way of unconventional interactions. They come about by way of *structured accidents*. This is why it's critical, in Luhmann's words, that your "selection and comparisons are not identical with the schema of searching for them."[26] Simply searching for a keyword robs the potential for innovation to occur. You are only presented with information you feel is related at the time. Ingenious insights come from *unconventional* discoveries you make along the way. The breakthrough ideas that come from flipping through your related past thoughts, *in a structured way*, are what unlock truly unconventional interactions. The tree structure of the Antinet induces these structured accidents.

While the *Persian messenger association fallacy* introduces an interesting interaction, the more compelling ones come about by exploring the items around the area where the concept resides (in this case, exploring around 2432/4). The truly unconventional interactions come about when navigating through and around the tree structure of the Antinet.

Structured accidents are critical for procuring breakthrough insights. The random pieces of information you encounter in your quest of exploring the Antinet create valuable opportunities to experience incidental learning (by way of structured accidents).[27] Digital search mitigates such phenomena from occurring.

Digital Search Robs You of Developing a Unique Structure for Evolving Your Mind

The Antinet's structure allowed Luhmann to store deeply complex and interconnected information, thanks to its tree structure. It allowed him to gracefully navigate his mind and his memory (past and present).

26 Niklas Luhmann, "Communication with Noteboxes (Revised Edition)," trans. Manfred Kuehn, https://daily.scottscheper.com/zettelkasten/.

27 Michael Jacob Kahana, Foundations of Human Memory. (New York: Oxford University Press, 2014), 18-19.

As has been mentioned before, developing his mind and memory came about from two processes. It occurred first by neuroimprinting thoughts by writing by hand. Second, by *engaging in an ongoing process of tending to his file,* Luhmann engaged in constant maintenance rehearsal, eventually developing the ability to recall thoughts without effort.[28]

When you instead review your own thoughts, written in your own handwriting, the process is often very fun. It's also very humbling. You see your thoughts and brilliant ideas written on cards from years ago. It also helps mitigate the sense that you haven't written something. When you see your own handwriting with your own brilliant ideas, you experience a sense of being impressed by your old self! More pertinent, this process builds your memory. It builds it in such a way wherein your thoughts are primed to compound.

With digital search, you're constantly searching for and through documents without any life or personality. They contain your thoughts, yes. But they're in some system-standardized font; the files are not living. They're constantly changing, being deleted, and overwritten. You have no chance to view the changes in your thinking because all traces are erased.

Digital Search Robs You of a Positive Mood

Finally! A simple, easy way to cure depression scientifically proven to cure ass-backward thoughts—INSTANTLY, 100% FREE, DOUBLE-YOUR-MONEY-BACK GUARANTEED!

Sound like a scam?

It's not. As crazy as it may sound, the act of associating concepts helps cure depression. It's a self-referential cycle. A researcher at the Harvard Medical School found that "positive mood promotes associative processing, and

28 Johannes Schmidt, "Niklas Luhmann's Card Index: Thinking Tool, Communication Partner, Publication Machine," Forgetting Machines. Knowledge Management Evolution in Early Modern Europe 53 (2016), 305.

associative processing promotes positive mood."[29] Every single thought in the Antinet can only be installed by embarking upon an associative process.

Every new idea, every new thought, every new extension of thought comes by way of exploring your tree of knowledge (which is a chain-linked set of associations). You then aim to associate any new idea with the concept that most closely resembles the chain of ideas already installed in the Antinet.

The Antinet improves mood, whereas digital search eradicates much of the magic inherent in associative processing. Finally! We have proof. Digital search robs you of a good mood. Digital search worsens your quality of life. If you want a better life, as counterintuitive as it sounds, go analog!

CONCLUSION

In this chapter, we moved through some very important concepts. And we moved through these in rather swift fashion (compared to the previous set of chapters)! We covered the theoretical structure of the index. You learned about the two types of indexcards. You learned how the index box works, and saw several examples. You also learned the truth about digital search: it's a bug, not a feature. Last, we capped off this chapter by covering the negatives of digital search.

The next chapter is very brief, it's the "net" in the Antinet. Keep reading. You've made it through the most challenging part of this book!

---

29 Moshe Bar, "A Cognitive Neuroscience Hypothesis of Mood and Depression," Trends in Cognitive Sciences 13, no. 11 (November 2009): 456–63.

CHAPTER TEN

NETWORK

IN 1956, ON A GRAY EVENING in the padded cell of a mental hospital, W. Ross Ashby sat at his desk. He was putting the finishing touches on his manuscript *Introduction to Cybernetics*. Ashby was not a patient of the mental hospital, however. He was a trained psychiatrist, research pathologist, and at the time, was serving as the Director of Research at Barnwood House Hospital in Gloucester, England.[30] He simply found the padded cells of his patients to be the perfect environment to focus. In this padded cell he published a paper which would greatly influence some of the brightest thinkers in information theory, mathematics, and technology for decades to come.

Ashby was always up to some odd research project. A few years prior, he built what may be the first device in history capable of adapting itself to its environment: the homeostat. For that work, Ashby's wife proffered their kitchen table as the workbench for his experiments that, in the homeostat's case, included Royal Air Force bomb parts.[31]

From this experience Ashby devised his theory of cybernetics.

---

30 William Ross Ashby and Roger Conant, *Mechanisms of Intelligence: Ross Ashby's Writings on Cybernetics* (Seaside, Calif.: Intersystems Publications, 1981), preface.

31 Ashby and Conant, *Mechanisms of Intelligence*, preface.

THE CYBERNETIC NETWORK OF THE ANTINET

On the very first notecard Niklas Luhmann wrote down in preparation for describing the Antinet Zettelkasten, he wrote that it's a *cybernetic* system.[32] We also know that Luhmann was familiar with the work of W. Ross Ashby because we find Luhmann writing of Ashby's work a few cards later.[33] We also know that Luhmann was deeply familiar with a subfield of cybernetics called *autopoiesis* (which is the concept of a system producing and maintaining itself by creating itself).

Cybernetics derives from *kybernetes* (Greek), meaning "steersman," and refers to having a *goal* and achieving the goal through steering in the proper direction by way of the communication of *feedback*. W. Ross Ashby defines it as "the art of steersmanship."[34] One of the pioneers of cybernetics, Norbert Wiener, characterizes it as "control and communication in animal and machine."[35] It arose as a disciplinary field involving information theory, engineering, and computer science, and continues to have a wide-spanning range across many different disciplinary fields.

Luhmann's reference to the structure of his Antinet as a *cybernetic* one makes sense. This field of study centers on *communication*. It's no accident that Luhmann titled his paper on the Antinet, *Communication with Noteboxes*. The communication process arises out of the cybernetic nature of the Antinet, utilizing *control* (by way of a fixed goal), and *feedback*. Cybernetic systems are modeled in both machines and living organisms. In the former, such systems are closely related to machine learning, specifically Q-learning (which artificial intelligence systems use to learn by way of reinforcement).

---

32 "ZK II: Note 9/8—Niklas Luhmann Archive," accessed August 13, 2021, https://niklas-luhmann-archiv.de/bestand/zettelkasten/zettel/ZK_2_NB_9-8_V.

33 "ZK II: Sheet 9/8b—Niklas Luhmann Archive," accessed March 17, 2022, https://niklas-luhmann-archiv.de/bestand/zettelkasten/zettel/ZK_2_NB_9-8b_V.

34 W. Ross Ashby, An Introduction to Cybernetics (Mansfield Centre, CT: Martino Publishing, 1956), 1.

35 "Cyberneticians.com," accessed April 5, 2022, https://cyberneticians.com/cybernetic-quotes.html.

THE NATURE OF THE ANTINET'S CYBERNETIC NETWORK

The cybernetic network structure of the Antinet resembles that of *associationism*.[36] This involves the association of nodes in a network based on *contiguity* (the continuous flow of thought), and on the *similarity* of thoughts causing them to be grouped or linked to one another. These two components (*contiguity* and *similarity*) are what govern *thought*. They're also what comprise the structure of the cybernetic network of the Antinet. In essence, the Antinet is built on associations that are linked together by way of contiguity, in that continuously flowing ideas that overflow across cards are naturally grouped together.

Additionally, the Antinet groups ideas in the long term by way of similarity. The most similar thoughts are naturally grouped together, near one another. The reason for this is that, again, the name of the game is to install notecards closest to their nearest neighbors. This means either an individual notecard, or a new stream of thought that encompasses several notecards which elaborate on an idea.

The cards' numeric-alpha addresses transform the Antinet's network into something akin to *auto-associators* in human memory science. This is something I go into in the chapter on how the Antinet mirrors human memory. In brief, an auto-associator is built on content-addressable memory.[37] That is, every single memory has an address "affixed" to it.

The Antinet's network is essentially composed of individual units of content-addressable memory (thanks to numeric-alpha addresses). How one navigates the network comes by way of the index and tree structure of the Antinet. These two components enrich the network in a powerful way that is absent in digital Zettelkasten systems.

---

36 Steven Pinker, *How the Mind Works* (New York: Norton, 2009), 113.

37 Pinker, *How the Mind Works*, 104.

WHAT CREATES THE CYBERNETIC NETWORK OF THE ANTINET

As already discussed, the Antinet's numeric-alpha addresses "ensure utmost autonomy, i.e. self-referential closure of the machine."[38] The *self-referential closure* of the machine is critical because it serves as the precondition for creating a *cybernetic* network. In brief, the numeric-alpha addresses create the cybernetic network of the Antinet.

This is important because the cybernetic nature of the Antinet is what helps convert it into a network that provides *feedback*. The problem with digital Zettelkasten and many notetaking systems is that they lack feedback mechanisms. With an Antinet, however, the system is enclosed in feedback loops. For example, in your mind you might be looking for an idea or concept. You follow a train of thought, and if you can't find what you're looking for, that is a piece of feedback. The feedback is even more valuable if you're sure that you have the idea stored somewhere in the Antinet. You're forced to have a conversation and to communicate with the Antinet. You ask yourself, *Where else could I have stored the thought I'm looking for? What else is it related to?* In searching for the idea, you're provided with more feedback and you make accidental discoveries. The whole system is a feedback-generating mechanism that brings unexpected new insights to the surface along the way.

CONCLUSION

This chapter is of briefer nature than the others, yet it's no less important. Now you know the nature of the network that characterizes the Antinet: a cybernetic network.

Now we turn to a chapter of more practical nature. In the next chapter you'll be guided through the wild world of building your own Antinet. The first part of the chapter serves as mental preparation in approaching the journey. Then, halfway through the next chapter, you'll be asked to follow a set of guided instructions. Follow them precisely as I outline. Good luck, and Godspeed.

---

38 Alberto Cevolini, ed., *Forgetting Machines: Knowledge Management Evolution in Early Modern Europe*, Library of the Written Word, volume 53 (Leiden ; Boston: Brill, 2016), 28.

CHAPTER ELEVEN

THE HITCHHIKER'S GUIDE TO THE ANTINET

AT THIS POINT YOU HAVE MORE than enough theoretical Antinet knowledge. It's time to roll up your sleeves and build out your own Antinet. For all of the theoretical material you've ingested, you'll be surprised to find its nature to be quite simple.

THE OBSTACLES YOU'LL FACE BUILDING AN ANTINET

Before we dive into the instructions, it's critical for you to understand what to expect. I've found that the biggest thing preventing anyone from building out an Antinet is the false belief in what to expect. We're going to dive into this area now.

HOW TO EVEN BEGIN

The biggest obstacle you'll face in building an Antinet is grasping how to even begin in the first place. At this phase you might think that how you set up your Antinet is critically important to its success. You might have the feeling that if you make a single mistake in the beginning, the whole system is doomed. Forever. Unfortunately, this is the case. Just kidding!

I've seen advice in online forums dedicated to digital Zettelkasten telling people to *just begin* blindly, even randomly. You'll also get advice from the bestselling books that the Zettelkasten just emerges without planning—without trying to create some semblance of organization using categories.

For instance, you'll find authors stating things like: "The trick is that [Luhmann] did not organize his notes by topic, but in a rather abstract way of giving them fixed numbers."[39] Yet, as you learn throughout this book, this notion is false. Luhmann never declared that anyone should start building an Antinet with no idea at all of where they want to go. Luhmann's second Zettelkasten was planned with eleven *fuzzy categories*. Luhmann's first Zettelkasten included 108 top-level categories. Both are included in the appendix of this book.

Luhmann's Antinet categories weren't undetermined; rather, many were *predetermined*. As Johannes Schmidt observes, "The pattern that we see here is very much one of exploring and reflecting on largely predetermined, fairly detailed fields of knowledge."[40]

In brief, you don't want to start with zero idea of how you'd like to structure your Antinet. Ideally, you want to start with a *rough* idea of where you want to take it. You want a fuzzy idea of what you want to build. With that said, the system I'm about to teach you makes use of well-developed disciplinary fields, so even if you don't have a clue about what you want to use your Antinet for, it will still work for you in the long term. The expansive disciplinary fields, plus the internal branching structure of the Antinet, enable the system to evolve in whatever direction your mind wishes to take it.

I realize all this sounds rather abstract and ambiguous; however, once you complete the instructions I'm about to provide, you'll begin to see what I'm talking about. Once you spend a few weeks using the system, you'll get a lot more comfortable with it, and you will be less likely to wonder if you've done something wrong.

---

39 Sönke Ahrens, How to Take Smart Notes: One Simple Technique to Boost Writing, Learning and Thinking: For Students, Academics and Nonfiction Book Writers (North Charleston, SC: CreateSpace, 2017), 19.

40 Johannes Schmidt, "Niklas Luhmann's Card Index: Thinking Tool, Communication Partner, Publication Machine," Forgetting Machines. Knowledge Management Evolution in Early Modern Europe 53 (2016), 296. https://pub.uni-bielefeld.de/record/2942475.

AVOID PERFECTIONISM (ALWAYS EVOLVE, NEVER DELETE)

At the core of what I've just talked about is the tendency of perfectionism. In the beginning of building your Antinet, you must abandon your desire for perfection. One of the most valuable parts of the Antinet is...*mistakes*! Specifically, your mistakes, your own thinking mistakes, and even imperfections in your own numbering conventions of the Antinet.

For instance, in the card I'm using to compose the section you're reading right now, I created what could be called an imperfection in its numbering convention.

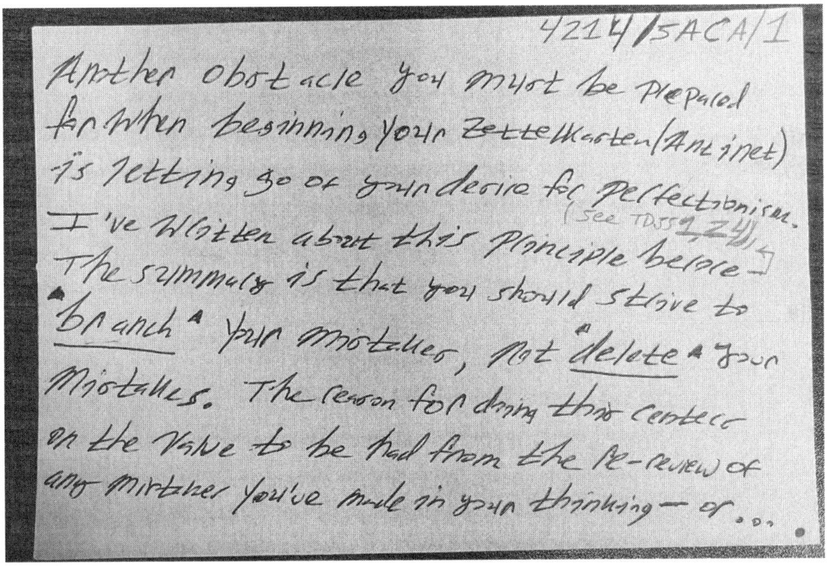
4214/5ACA/1
Another obstacle you must be prepared
for when beginning your ~~Zettelkasten~~ (Antinet)
is letting go of your desire for perfectionism.
I've written about this principle before (See TDSS 4,24)
The summary is that you should strive to
branch your mistakes, not delete your
mistakes. The reason for doing this centers
on the value to be had from the re-review of
any mistakes you've made in your thinking—or...

As you can see from this card, the card address is 4214/5ACA/1. You'll notice that the end part is in green (A/1), whereas the beginning of the card address is in blue. This is because at the time I created the card I hadn't yet figured out where I was going to put it. Therefore, in the beginning I would just write A/1 in green, and once I figured out where to install it, I'd prepend the address with the actual location in blue. Notice that the stem of the cards before 4214/5ACA is 4214/5AC and 4214/5A.

In brief, the structure looks like this:

- 4214/5A
  - 4214/5AC
    - 4214/5ACA
      - 4214/5ACA/1

Note that there's no 4214/5AB. I for some reason, just skip right to using 5AC because I created C before I even knew where I would install the card.

In brief, this isn't the convention I use these days. In my workflow today, I would first figure out *where* I wanted to install the card before I wrote the note. The structure would be something like this instead:

- 4214/5A
  - 4214/5A/1
  - 4214/5A/2
    - 4214/5A/2/1

In spite of the difference, both conventions are fine. The *imperfections* work just as well. It's just that my new conventional way of doing things has changed over time. I find my current convention makes more sense (to me), and it appears cleaner and more logical (again, to me). For instance, today I wouldn't go from 4214/5A to 4214/5AC (thus skipping 4214/5AB). In addition, I also like a more nested structure, which uses slashes (/). For instance, I prefer 'branching down' and creating 4214/5A/1 (opposed to appending letters onto letters, like 4214/5AB).

What counts, though, is the actual thought being developed. I never have the temptation to refactor the addresses of my notes. There's no temptation to make my new notes perfectly backward compatible with my old schemes for numbering. Why? I don't need to. The system just works.

In brief, don't delete your mistakes or imperfections. The reason for this is that there is value in re-reviewing your thoughts or re-reviewing your previous mistakes to see how much you've grown. Or even to see how your previous *corrections* of initially perceived mistakes turned out to also be incorrect! All of these occurrences are valuable.

Here's a secret: even Luhmann didn't get it right the first time. First, Luhmann's thoughts themselves contained mistakes. Yet he never removed them from his Antinet. For instance, Johannes Schmidt writes:

> It [Luhmann's Antinet] contains not only validated knowledge but also reflects the thought process, *including potential mistakes* and blind alleys *that were later revised but not removed from the file as the original cards always remained in Luhmann's file* and perhaps a new card with revisions was added if needed.[41]

Second, Luhmann's conventions, and the components of his Antinet, were never deleted. He never deleted his old indexes, for instance, but continually created more organized versions. After a certain point, his index became messy.[42] Instead of replacing the index with his new one, he simply placed the new index *after* the old one. In total, his second Antinet contains four versions of the index.[43]

Not only did Luhmann modify the index component of his Antinet, he also experimented in other ways. He created an index that was not organized by concepts' keyterms, but by people's names. Luhmann thought that this was a helpful practice because our minds sometimes retrieve ideas by thinking of the name of the author from which they derived.[44]

---

41 Johannes Schmidt, "Niklas Luhmann's Card Index: Thinking Tool, Communication Partner, Publication Machine," Forgetting Machines. Knowledge Management Evolution in Early Modern Europe 53 (2016), 310. Emphasis added.

42 Johannes Schmidt, "Niklas Luhmann's Card Index: Thinking Tool, Communication Partner, Publication Machine," Forgetting Machines. Knowledge Management Evolution in Early Modern Europe 53 (2016), 306.

43 Johannes Schmidt, "Niklas Luhmann's Card Index: Thinking Tool, Communication Partner, Publication Machine," Forgetting Machines. Knowledge Management Evolution in Early Modern Europe 53 (2016), 306.

44 Niklas Luhmann, "Communication with Noteboxes (Revised Edition)," trans. Manfred Kuehn, https://daily.scottscheper.com/zettelkasten/. "This proves to be helpful because our own memory—others will have similar experiences to mine—works in part with key words and in part with author's names."

Yet when Luhmann created a name-based index, he did not attempt to retroactively make it backward compatible. He did not attempt to go through all of his previous notecards and make sure the name-based index comprehensively referenced each of the notes. He did not *systematically pursue* the strategy of adding items to the name index in every case.[45]

What we learn from these examples is to extinguish any sense of perfectionism. That's right. I'm asking you to extinguish the idea that your Antinet is to be a perfectly organized system. There's far more power in creating paths documenting your various mistakes. The stems of thoughts and ideas documenting your mind changing stands as an invaluable property of the Antinet. In addition, you're encouraged to launch experiments (like Luhmann's people-focused index). But at the same time, don't feel like you're bound to systematically pursuing such an experiment forever. Old experiments are valuable in and of themselves, and who knows—maybe you'll pick up where you left off one day and continue developing an experiment you began ages ago.

DOUBTING THE POWER OF ANALOG

When first starting out, you may not realize the sheer power of analog systems. In fact, you may still hold a systemic negative regard for analog systems. Today, society blindly accepts that technology and digital tools are better for everything. However, digital tools are not better for everything. They're certainly not better for thinking and evolving thought.

When you're just starting out, you may find yourself doubting this. You may experience false beliefs and doubts about what you're investing your time and energy into. Please take my word for it until then. In brief, analog is worth it. Developing your mind using analog tools pays off in the long-run; heck, it even pays off in the short-run.

---

45 Johannes Schmidt, "Niklas Luhmann's Card Index: Thinking Tool, Communication Partner, Publication Machine," Forgetting Machines. Knowledge Management Evolution in Early Modern Europe 53 (2016), 306. "However, Luhmann did not systematically pursue this strategy."

DON'T BECOME DISTRACTED BY THE ZETTELKASTEN MYTHS OUT THERE

Perhaps the biggest distraction you'll face in building an Antinet is the misinformation and complete inventions you'll find online about *Zettelkasten.* If you search *Zettelkasten* online, there's a 96% chance you'll come across a myth that misrepresents the system.[46]

The myths you come across about Zettelkasten seem innocuous and quite rational at first. Yet the smallest thing could prevent your notetaking system from becoming an actual *second mind*—a communication partner. For instance, if you buy into the whole idea of creating atomic notes (perfectly organized sets of one idea per card), then you're setting yourself up for failure. The many myths of Zettelkasten will be exposed throughout this book. Until then, just trust me here. Don't get distracted by the stuff about Zettelkasten you find online.

YOU'RE LIKE AN AIRPLANE TAKING OFF

Building an Antinet isn't easy. Especially in the beginning. I'd like to re-emphasize a major point: with the Antinet, you're doing things the old way, the hard way, the true way. Yet, you'll be doing so bit-by-bit, card-by-card. Paradoxically, this turns out to be the easy way in the long-run.

Yet, the major premise in Sönke Ahrens's presentation of Zettelkasten is the notion that it will make writing an easy, "seamless" activity.[47] Ahrens makes it seem like it's a simple system. He misappropriates Luhmann's phrase: "I must tell you that I never force anything. I only do what comes easy to me."[48] Ahrens leaves out the fact that Luhmann said this immediately after

46 I pulled the 96% out of my ass; yet, when I surveyed the search results, I found that roughly 9/10 results regurgitate Sönke Ahrens's interpretation of Zettelkasten, which is *not* how Luhmann's Zettelkasten worked.

47 Sönke Ahrens, How to Take Smart Notes: One Simple Technique to Boost Writing, Learning and Thinking: For Students, Academics and Nonfiction Book Writers (North Charleston, SC: CreateSpace, 2017), 5.

48 Niklas Luhmann, Short Cuts, Orig.-Ausg., 4. Aufl, Short Cuts 1 (Frankfurt am Main: Zweitausendeins, 2002), 37.

outlining his work routine in detail. In brief, Luhmann worked every day from 8:30am until roughly midnight.

Building out an Antinet requires work and a deliberate investment of energy. However, you don't need to work from 8:30am until midnight (for reasons I'll outline shortly).

When starting out, it's best to think of yourself as an airplane taking off. In the beginning it will require more energy. You're about to be introduced to an entirely new way of organizing and evolving your mind, and I'm also introducing you to a new way of reading and developing your thoughts.

Combined with the overhead expenditure of energy required in learning a new system, you're also starting from scratch. You'll face what I call *index fatigue*. In the beginning, you have a completely barren structure. You'll therefore need to spend a considerable amount of time creating new keyterm entries in your index. This is something that decreases and becomes less time-consuming after several months.

Don't get me wrong: you'll always be creating new keyterm entries in your index. But, in the beginning you'll be creating keyterms much more frequently. The important thing is that you manage index fatigue well. Don't get burnt out. Don't land the plane before giving yourself a chance to hit cruise control.

You Only Need Two Hours a Day for Great Intellectual Work

While I do hold it to be true that the Antinet is for those who accept the time investment required, it's important to provide a caveat. The caveat is that *consistency is the goal.* Keep in mind that Luhmann used his Antinet for forty-six years (1951–1997). You should strive for the same.

When I preach hard work, don't interpret my advice as requiring you to work twelve hours a day on your Antinet. Rather two hours of work per day *consistently* over the long term is a good goal. That means reading or writing notes for two hours per day (on average).

The Catholic intellectual Antonin Sertillanges confirms this notion. To do great intellectual work, a person needs only two hours per day of focused study.[49] If you work full-time, you must carve out two hours a day—either before work or after work (or, even split them up). In my early twenties, when I worked a day job full-time, I carved out two hours of work every morning before I left for the office. Luhmann carved out his deliberate focus time with his Antinet in the evenings.[50]

As far as intellectual work goes, the *two-hour a day rule* seems to be a theme. For instance, the scholar Umberto Eco recommends a similar time commitment in his book, *How to Write a Thesis*. One can write a quality thesis, according to Eco, even if "they can only dedicate a few hours each day." Yet Eco hints at an even more important variable: one's *attitude*. Those who gain the most in writing a thesis, it seems, are those who pursue it as a means to attain a "certain intellectual satisfaction."[51] That is, those who approach the process of intellectual work with an attitude that centers *not* on fulfilling an external requirement, but their own internal requirement. I agree.

ON HAVING A GOAL

Richard W. Hamming, an American mathematician who worked at Bell Laboratories and who greatly influenced how computer and telecommunication technology works today once observed how shockingly common it was that his fellow employees were content to work on unimportant problems. They lacked a clear goal or purpose. He noted how it even seemed like they made a *deliberate choice* to work on unimportant problems.

Hamming was a scientist obsessed with truth. He had the tendency of delivering his truth in an unfiltered fashion (often at the expense of other people's feelings). One day Hamming approached a fellow employee and said abruptly, *Why are you even bothering to live if you're not working on an*

49 OP A. G. Sertillanges, The Intellectual Life: Its Spirit, Conditions, Methods, trans. Mary Ryan, Reprint edition (Washington, D.C.: The Catholic University of America Press, 1992), 11.

50 Niklas Luhmann, Niklas Luhmann Short Cuts (English Translation), 2002, 11.

51 Umberto Eco, How to Write a Thesis, trans. Caterina Mongiat Farina and Geoff Farina, Translation edition (Cambridge, Massachusetts: The MIT Press, 2015), 5.

important problem or goal? The employee, understandably, was quite upset. He scoffed at Hamming's offensive words and stormed out of the room.

Later the employee wrote a letter to Hamming thanking him. The letter read: *Thank you. Your words ended up changing my life.*[52]

This brings us to the crux of the matter: goals. Specifically, *your* goals in building an Antinet. This matter is so important that you must explore it in detail before setting out to build your Antinet.

It can be argued that people are too fascinated with Luhmann's Antinet, to the extent that many people overlook the famous declaration Luhmann made. At the beginning of his intellectual career, Luhmann was one of the first professors hired by Bielefeld University. The new administration asked Luhmann what research project he would work on. His response was legendary amongst sociologists: "My project was, and ever since has been, the theory of society; term: thirty years; costs: none."[53]

The Antinet served as the perfect tool for Luhmann because it helped him with his ambitious goal. His goal was a massive undertaking. It was a thirty year project that required a system that would enable him to develop and evolve his thinking over the course of it.

This brings up the question: *what is the goal of an Antinet in the first place?*

In a sense, the ultimate goal of an Antinet centers on "maximizing the number of copies of the genes that created it."[54] Consider this: the goal of Luhmann's Antinet was to maximize the proliferation of his ideas. He intended to do this by packing in evidence from all of his readings. He began by extracting knowledge from books onto their bibcards. From there he would develop

---

52 Richard W. Hamming and Bret Victor, The Art of Doing Science and Engineering: Learning to Learn (Stripe Press, 2020), 386.

53 Niklas Luhmann, Theory of Society, Volume 1, trans. Rhodes Barrett (Stanford: Stanford University Press, 2012), xi.

54 Steven Pinker, How the Mind Works, Norton pbk (New York: Norton, 2009), 43.

that knowledge by elaborating on it (primarily by way of reflection notes). These notes would then chain together and create deeply rich knowledge that supported his theory of society.

In other words, Luhmann was reproducing and creating a legacy from his thoughts as they developed in his Antinet.

The goal of the Antinet, then, is to replicate the thoughts of its creator in the real world. Think of the thoughts as intellectual genetic material encompassed in notecards. Therefore, the goal centers on reproduction—not biological reproduction, but metaphysical reproduction of your thoughts—and metaphysical reproduction of your thinking throughout the world. This is achieved through your thoughts being so well-developed that they end up producing work that reproduces those thoughts and allows them to be spread throughout the world.

Luhmann's Antinet seems to have achieved this. His books are studied by scholars today—or at least studied by the ones with the diligence and motivation to parse his deeply intertwined texts! Yet, ironically, Luhmann's Antinet seems to have the potential to proliferate and live on longer than even Luhmann's actual theoretical work will. Or perhaps it's not so ironic. People are fascinated with how Luhmann became a book-writing academic research machine. The answer? The Antinet.

In essence, the goal of the Antinet is to reproduce the thoughts of its creator by making it easier to create written products with the thoughts it stores.

Let's now turn to the dichotomy of *growth* vs. *contribution*.

GROWTH VS. CONTRIBUTION

There are two *states* one operates in when using the Antinet. One is not necessarily better than the other. In fact, you'll likely move back and forth between each state regularly.

The first state is the *growth* state. This occurs when using an Antinet to *grow* your own knowledge and understanding. Whenever you're venturing into a new disciplinary field, you'll spend the beginning phases learning by reading books in brand new fields and noting down brand new ideas. You'll mostly be writing *reformulation notes* in this phase. You'll be encountering new ideas and reformulating them in your own words.

The second state is the *contribution* state. This occurs when using the Antinet to publish work and the focus is on contributing to others through teaching them material. In this stage your focus will be books that you're creating.

You will often oscillate between the two states. However, I find that it's best to strive and live in the *contribution* state. In other words, you want to write your notes as if they are part of a project or book that you'll be publishing so that you can *teach* others. It's a paradox because the best way to *grow* and learn something is by teaching the material, and the best way to *do that* is through having the mindset of *contribution*.

In the beginning of working on your Antinet, you may not be ready to actually commit to a certain project. I certainly wasn't when I began my journey. However, I would like to nudge you in the direction of moving *toward contribution*.

If Luhmann had not set out with the ambitious goal of creating a theory of society in thirty years, there's a good chance we never would have even heard about the Zettelkasten in the first place. In essence, Luhmann's Antinet wasn't the only thing that helped him create genius-level work. The other thing that helped him was his massive ambitious goal for his Antinet.

The most important step to creating an Antinet that is too easily overlooked is determining what your goal is before writing your first note. It is the overall objective—*the why*—behind what attracted you to the Antinet that is critically important.

You ought to have at least a vague or general direction for what you intend to build with it.

As Steven Pinker points out in his book, *How the Mind Works*, without specifying a goal "the very idea of intelligence is meaningless."[55]

And what is intelligence? It is the phenomenon the Antinet is engineered to create. Intelligence comes from information. Information is a correlation between two things. Before you install anything in your Antinet, you will *compare* and *correlate*. You must decide if a concept is "this or something else," as Luhmann says.[56]

In brief, it helps to specify a goal. To be fair, however, the system works perfectly even when you're in a state in which your goal is to learn and grow.

Luhmann's second Zettelkasten was started when he had a clear goal in mind. His first Zettelkasten, however, was started when he didn't have a clear idea of what his intellectual work would entail in the years he was working for the Higher Administrative Court of Lüneburg. During this time, he spent his nights reading and building his Antinet. He said, "I started my Zettelkasten, because I realized that I had to plan for a life and not for a book."[57]

This statement seems to contradict his reason for starting his second Antinet (the Antinet he created in order to work on his thirty-year book project culminating in his *Theory of Society*).

You might notice, though, that Luhmann did have a goal for his first Zettelkasten: it was to plan for life by learning from many fields of knowledge.

In brief, the Antinet can serve both states. It can assist someone who's in the growth state (without a clear end goal), and it can also assist someone who's in the contribution state (with a clearly defined book or project).

---

55 Steven Pinker, How the Mind Works, Norton pbk (New York: Norton, 2009), 61.

56 Niklas Luhmann, "Communication with Noteboxes (Revised Edition)," trans. Manfred Kuehn, https://daily.scottscheper.com/zettelkasten/.

57 Niklas Luhmann, Niklas Luhmann Short Cuts (English Translation), 2002, 22.

From my experience, I have found the Antinet to *really* shine when one is in the contribution state. When you have a specific project and goal in mind, the Antinet really begins to flex its strength.

In essence, what we're talking about here is the *explore vs. exploit* dilemma. That is, do you approach work as an explorer with an open-mind? Or do you approach your work with a deliberate goal, and exploit an opportunity you see? The explore-exploit tradeoff occurs every single day. It can be as simple as going to your favorite restaurant, or trying out a new one.[58]

In approaching this dilemma, I like a concept introduced by clinical psychologist and bestselling author Jordan Peterson. One ought to define a deliberate goal to limit the chaos of life. Yet one also ought to adopt a *meta goal*. The term *meta*, in Greek, means *above* or *beyond*. Therefore, one ought to have a goal which resides above a concrete project in the physical world. An example of a meta goal is to "live in truth." That is, a meta goal allows one to act diligently toward a defined end in an authentic way that remains in alignment with your soul.[59] Have a defined goal, yes; however, if your soul authentically shifts, shift with it.

BEFORE WRITING YOUR FIRST NOTE

One critical point that rarely gets mentioned may seem rather obvious: it's helpful to have a project in mind for your Antinet. An Antinet is not necessarily something you ought to do with the idea of completely open-ended reading. As Luhmann states, "I first make a plan of what I am going to write, and then take from the note cabinet what I can use."[60] When Luhmann drew from the Antinet the material would use for a new project, that material did not come about through aimless reading. At some point, he made a decision on what project to work on.

---

58 "Explore-Exploit Tradeoff—Definition and Examples," Conceptually, accessed April 12, 2022, https://conceptually.org/concepts/explore-or-exploit.

59 Jordan B. Peterson, 12 Rules for Life: An Antidote to Chaos, Later prt. edition (Toronto: Random House Canada, 2018), 226.

60 Hans-Georg Moeller, The Radical Luhmann (New York: Columbia University Press, 2011), 11.

The key point is that when you decide to work on a project, it doesn't necessarily confine you to that project forever. The material you create in one project will unearth material you can use in your next project.

For instance, when I first started building out my Antinet, I didn't yet realize I was going to write a book on it. I was planning on writing a book that sat at the intersection of copywriting, psychology, and philosophy. My readings included books like *The Hero with a Thousand Faces,* which is about the hero's journey and storytelling. It didn't seem like any of the material would have been relevant to this book; yet, as it turns out, it was relevant! In my section on the tree structure of the Antinet, I used some of the material in discussing the metaphysical power pertaining to the concept of trees. Moreover, reading about the power of trees may have helped spark the light bulb that helped me realize that the Antinet is built on a tree structure.

What I'm trying to say is this: take a goal-oriented approach when building out your Antinet. Do not worry if, later on, you decide to progress to a completely different project. Why? Because it's likely the material you develop will still contribute to the new project. All domains of knowledge are interdisciplinary. Concepts in mathematics can serve one's understanding of philosophical concepts. The great mathematician Bertrand Russell also penned one of the best books ever written on philosophy (*A History of Western Philosophy,* which won him a Nobel Prize in 1950). This is but one of countless examples.

I'll keep hammering this idea into you: having a goal or project in mind is critical when developing notes using an Antinet. Even when reading a book, the goal-oriented nature and intention of reading is paramount.[61] I'll illustrate this principle more in the chapter on reading workflows.

The reason I keep emphasizing this is because the magic of the Antinet really started taking off for me once I shifted to *contribution.* In mid-June 2021, I made a decision to focus on teaching the true Zettelkasten—the Luhmannian version—the Antinet Zettelkasten. Up until that point I was

61 **Mortimer Jerome Adler and Charles Van Doren, How to Read a Book, Rev. and updated ed (New York: Simon and Schuster, 1972), 45.**

resisting the idea of writing a book about the Antinet. I feared it would just be a distraction or procrastination-fueled detour. It also appeared seemingly absurd at the time. My profession and craft was in marketing, copywriting, and cryptocurrency (which are much more lucrative markets). The PKM and productivity market is as niche as it gets. And within that niche almost everyone focuses on teaching the powerful "method" of whatever the latest and greatest digital app is.

Yet, I knew in my heart and soul the truth: analog tools serve as a much more effective system for developing thought. I knew in my heart that people were left with watered down digital Zettelkasten tools. There were no instructions or guides for how to build an analog version—the original version. I couldn't let it go. So, even with doubts in my mind, I made a commitment. *To hell with the copywriting, psychology and philosophy project for now,* I said to myself. *I'm going all in on the Antinet.*

This is when things really started to take off. At this point I began to experience the magic of the Antinet. Yet even before this commitment to the Antinet, I made a *soft* commitment to working on a copywriting, psychology and philosophy project.

Again, commit to an idea or project and don't fret if you decide to shift into a different project altogether. You can shift back to the original project whenever you're done with the new project. You can also shift back to different projects if you hit a wall (figuratively speaking). As Luhmann says (after outlining his twelve-plus-hour work days): "I only write when I know immediately how to do it. If it stops for a moment, I put the thing aside and do something else."[62] However, don't let Luhmann's turn you into someone who switches tasks every other day. Try to start things you'll finish. Commit to them, but also know they can be revisited if you ever decide to switch to something else after a few months.

Johannes Schmidt writes, "at least in the more mature stage of Luhmann's theory-building since the 1970s, [Luhmann's Antinet] *did not serve as a pure archive that he would develop independent of specific publication projects.*"

---

62 Niklas Luhmann, Niklas Luhmann Short Cuts (English Translation), 2002, 19.

Luhmann only installed cards in his Antinet that were related to publication requests he took on.[63]

Yet, as Schmidt points out, the material Luhmann developed during the course of fulfilling publication requests—by writing research papers—ended up serving as the basis for his books. By taking on one project, the new material created unforeseeable developments in his other long-term projects. As Luhmann worked on new publications, "in the process, he would also document the evolution of his thought process," writes Schmidt. "Over the course of producing these publications," his theory developments were *compounded*.[64]

HOW TO BUILD AN ANTINET

OK, now that you know the obstacles to avoid, we can now get into building your Antinet. *Jesus Christ, Scott, it's about time!*

Here is an overview of the system we will be building:

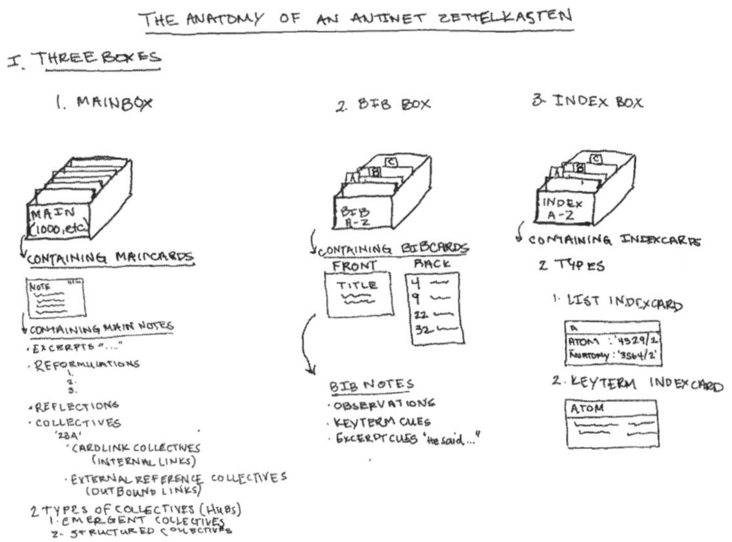

63 Johannes Schmidt, "Niklas Luhmann's Card Index: Thinking Tool, Communication Partner, Publication Machine," Forgetting Machines. Knowledge Management Evolution in Early Modern Europe 53 (2016), 310-11. Emphasis added.

64 Johannes Schmidt, "Niklas Luhmann's Card Index: Thinking Tool, Communication Partner, Publication Machine," Forgetting Machines. Knowledge Management Evolution in Early Modern Europe 53 (2016), 311.

THE SUPPLIES YOU NEED

To help perfect the way I teach the Antinet, I conducted a series of 1-on-1 Antinet coaching sessions (the recordings of which you can find on my YouTube channel).

With each of my Antinet coaching clients, I recommend the following materials for getting started:

1. Three noteboxes that can store 4 x 6 inch notecards (or one box, if you wish to save space for now).

2. A set of blank double-sided 4 x 6 inch notecards.

3. A set of ruled colored 4 x 6 inch indexcards.

4. A set of alphabetical card dividers, wherein each divider label contains a dedicated alphabetical letter (i.e., *A*, *B*, *C*, etc.).

You will also need a badass pen. Use a pen you love to write with. Think of it as an *instrument*. People apply a ton of creativity to what colors they use. You're welcome to use whichever set of colors work best for you. I've experimented with different colored inks over time. My current ink repertoire is black ink for main notes, green ink for cardlinks, and red ink for ExRefs (i.e., citing books and external sources).

BUILDING OUT YOUR MAIN BOX AND INDEX BOX

In my experience coaching people through this process, I find that most people don't have a problem taking notes from the books they read. Taking reading notes is straightforward. Heck, it's even addicting and fun! Those types of notes are filed in the bib box. I'll cover that in the next section which involves reading strategies.

We're going to skip the bib box part for now. Instead we're going to dive right into the heart of the Antinet, the so-called "hard part" of this whole thing. We're going to build out the *main box* and *index box* of your Antinet. Realize that you're not going to really understand why I'm telling you to do certain things in the beginning; but just follow exactly what I say. Don't try and understand it yet. Just proceed step-by-step in a deliberate fashion. Follow every detail. Sound good?

Let's go.

- Take out a pen with black ink.

- Take out a blank white 4 x 6 inch notecard.[65]

- In the top-right corner[66] write 1000.

- In the center write Arts & Humanities.

It should look like this:

65 If you are living in a geographic region adhering to ISO standards, use the A6 paper size. Or, if you do not have access to 4 x 6 inch or A6 notecards, just get creative. Cut out a piece of paper to such a size. Luhmann used old pieces of paper from his father's brewery, as well as paper from his children's old coloring books.

66 Luhmann chose the top-left corner; I prefer top-right corner.

- Take out another notecard.
- In the corner write 2000, and in the middle write Social Sciences.
- Take out another notecard.
- In the corner write 3000, and in the middle write Natural Sciences.
- Take out another notecard.
- In the corner write 4000, and in the middle write Formal Sciences.
- Take out one more notecard.
- In the corner write 5000, and in the middle write Applied Arts & Sciences.
- Now, stack all five of these cards in sequential order from 1000 to 5000 and place them in the first box.

This is your main box.

- On the front of this box create a small label for this box that reads Main.

It should look like this:

▸ Now, pull out 26 ruled indexcards. I like to use colored indexcards for these. Set them in front of you.

It should look like this:

▸ With the first indexcard, in the top-left corner, write A.

It should look like this:

▸ Do the same exact thing for the remaining twenty five letters in the alphabet.

- Now, stack the 26 cards in alphabetical order, from A-Z, then place the stack of 26 cards in the second box.
- On the second box, create a label that reads Index, and place it on the front of the box.

It should look like this:

The first box is your main box. Your Antinet is a tree of knowledge. The tree contains five main branches (1000, 2000, 3000, 4000, and 5000). From these five branches, many other branches will "branch off." Stems will form, and leaves of notecards will fill up the tree. Right now, your tree of knowledge is barren. We'll fix that soon.

The second box containing 26 cards is your index. Your index is the map you create as you build your tree of knowledge.

Now, pull out another blank notecard.

On this notecard, write out the following quote. However, before you write it out, make sure you leave about a centimeter of space at the top of the quote.

> "One of the most basic presuppositions of communication is that the partners can mutually surprise each other. Only in this way can information be produced in the respective other. Information is an intra-systematic event. It results when one compares one message or entry with regard to other possibilities. Information, accordingly, originates only in systems which possess a comparative schema—even if this only amounts to 'this or something else.'"

It should look like this:

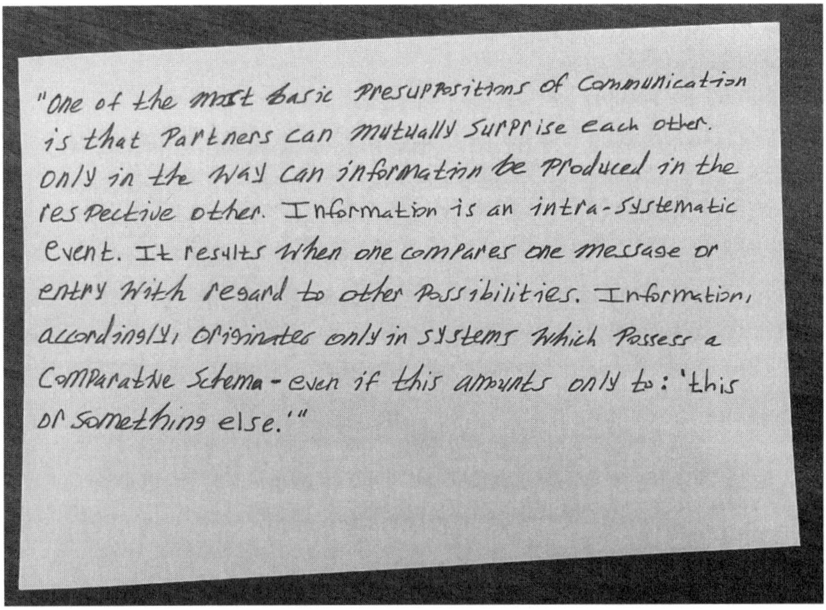

At this point, you're probably wondering why the heck I made you write down this excerpt. After all, your reason for using an Antinet probably won't focus on writing about *communication theory* or *information theory*.

The reason why I chose to start with this is to show the flexibility of the system we're about to create.

You see, in Luhmann's first Antinet, he created 108 top-level categories. They were rough starting points. They included many topics he was interested in. Yet when he created his second Antinet, it was focused primarily on his theoretical sociological work.

If Luhmann had started out with a broader classification system (instead of his arbitrarily chosen 108 categories), I hold that he would never have needed to create a second Antinet. If he had structured his first Antinet to be all-encompassing, he could have created a branch (or set of branches), which nicely encompassed his theoretical sociological work.

The goal with your Antinet is to avoid having to make a second, separate Antinet; to reach that goal, you'll use an all-encompassing structure to house all your knowledge so that you can use the same Antinet for the rest of your life.

This will be made possible by using a well-developed and robust classification system. For this reason, I choose to use the academic disciplinary fields provided by Wikipedia.

Here is a link to Wikipedia's *Outline of academic disciplines*:
https://en.wikipedia.org/wiki/Outline_of_academic_disciplines

This classification system will serve as a *rough* guide for how to structure your Antinet.

You will notice that the contents of the academic disciplines have five top-level branches. These five top-level branches map directly to the five branches you already created. The sub-branches of each of these categories can be created and numbered arbitrarily. The choice of the numbers and whether or not to even create the sub-branch is entirely up to you. Here's a picture (see following page):

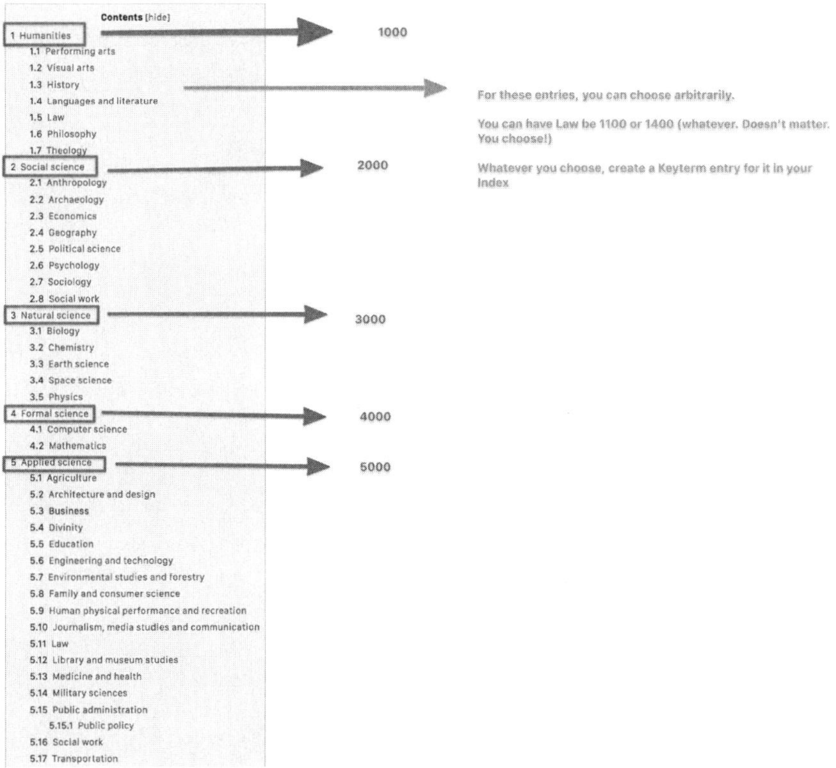

I will now show you how to use the academic disciplines to help you figure out *where* to install your notecards.

OK, so where should we place the notecard we've just created?

The quote I had you write on the notecard is from Niklas Luhmann. He's writing of the Antinet as his communication partner. He's observing that *information* comes about by comparing something to something else. I guess it could be filed in either an *information* branch, or a *communication* branch. But which one? In my opinion, the primary idea in this quote revolves around *information,* so let's go with that.

Now, let's open up the Wikipedia's academic disciplines page, and search the page for the term *information.* What we find are twenty-one search results for the term *information* on the page. We also find that the first three seem irrelevant…

But, aha! The fourth result seems intriguing…it's something called *Information Theory*. What the heck is *Information Theory*? Let's find out.

▸ Pull out another blank notecard. In the middle write:

> **Information Theory**
> Information Theory studies the transmission, processing, extraction, and utilization of information.

It should look like this:

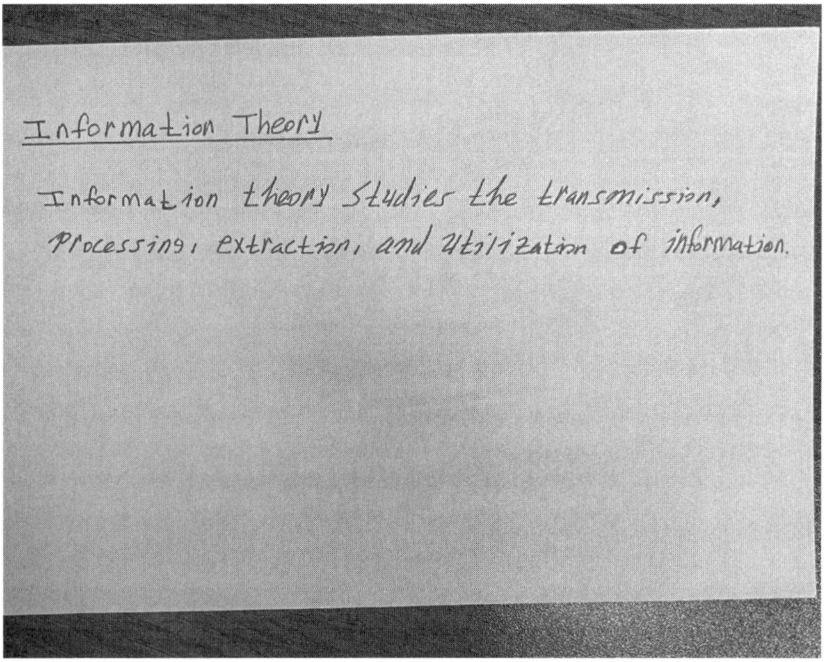

Still with me?

Good.

You now have two cards in front of you. One with the quote written on it, and the other for Information Theory. If you don't, retrace your steps (and get your shit together). Kidding, but seriously.

Let's keep going.

So now we have two cards with handwritten stuff on them.

Where should we file these cards?

Let's start with the second card we wrote. The one that outlines *Information Theory.*

By consulting Wikipedia's academic disciplines, we can see that *Information Theory* falls under the field of *Formal Sciences*. It falls specifically within the subfield of *Computer Science.*

- Still with me? Cool. Now pull out another blank card.

- In the top-corner write, 4200 and in the middle write:

> **<u>Computer Science</u>**
> Computer Science is the study of computation, automation, and information.

It should look like this:

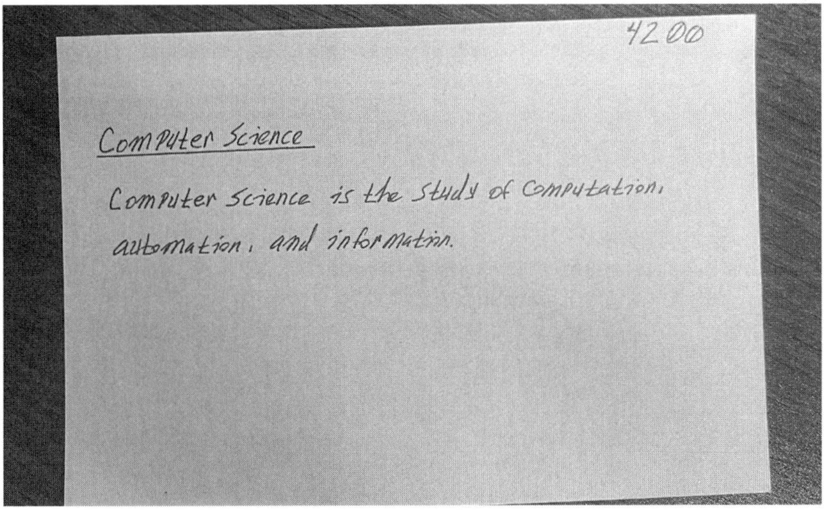

- Now it's time to consult the index. In your index box find the *list indexcard* C and pull it out.

- With the card C, write an entry that reads Computer Science: '4200'.

It should look something like this:

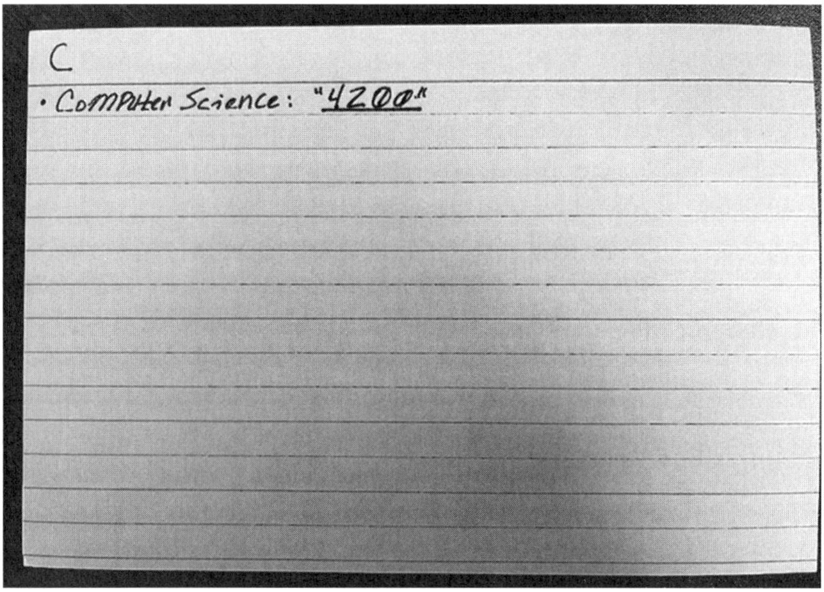

I like to put little quotes around cardlinks so they feel more contained.
It's just a personal preference.

- Now place the C list indexcard back inside the index box. File the card 4200 behind the card 4000 in the main box.

OK, now back to the *Information Theory* card.

Where should we file the *Information Theory* card?

- Let's place it within the *Computer Science* branch. Why? Because according to Wikipedia's *Outline of Academic Disciplines, Information Theory* falls under *Computer Science*. So, let's arbitrarily choose 4212 for *Information Theory*.

▸ In the top-corner of the *Information Theory* card write 4212.

It should look like this:

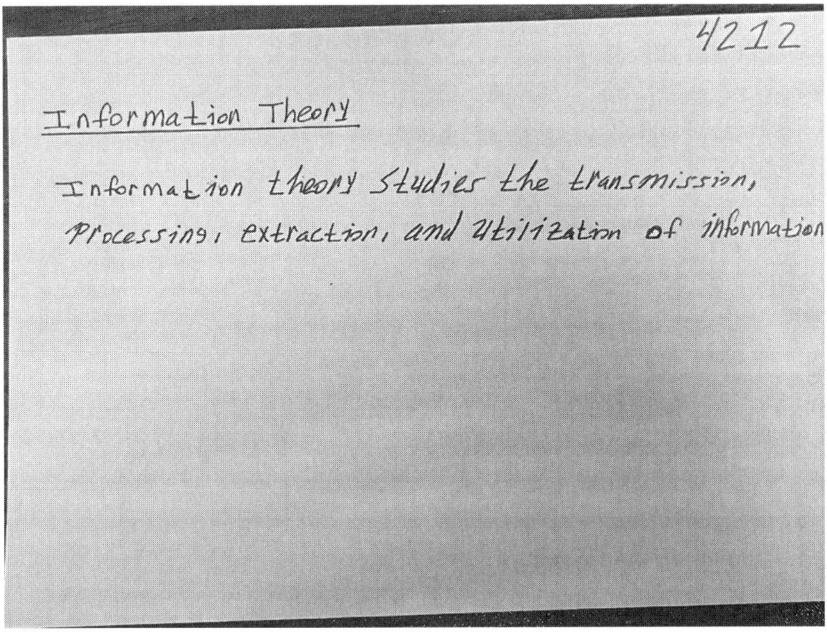

4212
Information Theory
Information theory studies the transmission, processing, extraction, and utilization of information

▸ Now file this card in your main box behind card 4200.

Good job so far!

Now, there should be one remaining card in front of you—the card with the long-quote on it. Let's figure out where to file this card.

In the Antinet, the name of the game is *similarity*. When figuring out where to install a card, you must ask: *What is this card most similar to?*

OK, so what is this card in front of us most similar to? That's easy. It's most similar to the *Information Theory* card. Indeed, it even falls within the *Information Theory* branch.

▸ In the top-right corner of the card write 4212/1.

It should look like this:

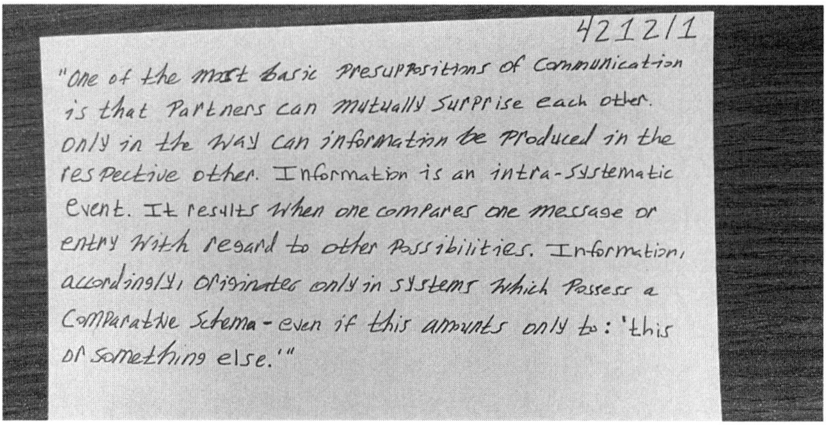
4212/1

"One of the most basic presuppositions of communication is that partners can mutually surprise each other. Only in the way can information be produced in the respective other. Information is an intra-systematic event. It results when one compares one message or entry with regard to other possibilities. Information, accordingly, originates only in systems which possess a comparative schema - even if this amounts only to: 'this or something else.'"

Heck yes! We're all done, right? Almost, but not quite.

There are a few more things we ought to do.

- First, pull out the list indexcard I from your index box.
- Create an entry: Information Theory, and next to that write, 4212

It should look like this:

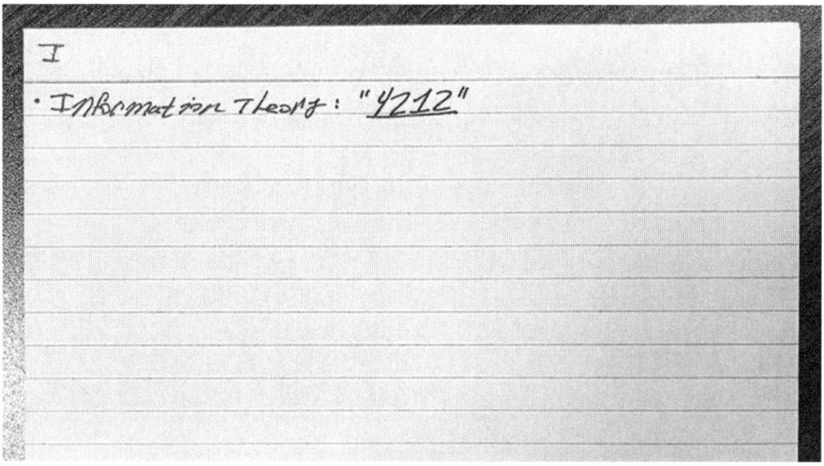
I

• Information Theory: "4212"

There's another thing we ought to do (since we're pros).

- Let's add an entry under list indexcard C for *Communication* within the context of *Information Theory*. Pull out the list indexcard C and write Communication (within Information Theory): '4212/1'.

It should look like this:

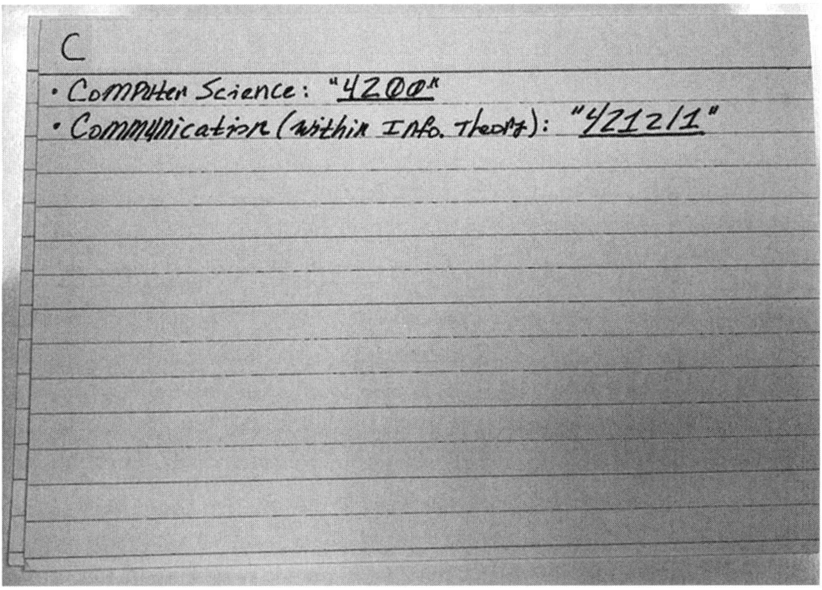

- OK, now file away C by putting it back in your index box.

In front of you, there should be one notecard: 4212/1. Before you install 4212/1 into your main box, we have one more thing we need to do.

On 4212/1, what you did was write down a quote. The notion that Luhmann never wrote down excerpts or quotes is a myth. Luhmann did, indeed, write down quotes from the books he read. That said, you want to err on the side of creating more *reformulation notes* and *reflection notes* (instead of *excerpt notes*). I'll detail those types of notes in a later chapter. For now, it's helpful to start you off with an excerpt note (which is why I had you write down that quote)!

When you create an excerpt note, it requires one thing. It must also provide *the source* from where the quote came from. To answer this, we shall now dive into External Reference Links ("ExRefs").

Stay with me; we're almost done.

- On a computer, download the reference manager called *Zotero* by visiting www.zotero.org.

- After you download and install Zotero on your computer, there is one more step. You must download the Zotero connector for your web browser. Visit the following link and download the connector for the browser that you use: https://www.zotero.org/download/connectors

- Next, open up Zotero.

- Now, using the browser in which you have the Zotero Connector installed, visit the following URL: https://daily.scottscheper.com/zettelkasten/ This URL is where the quote originated from. It is an English translation of a paper titled *Communication with Noteboxes* by Niklas Luhmann.[67]

- While viewing this web page, click the Zotero icon which should now be installed in the panel of your browser. It should capture the page and add it as an entry to your Zotero Desktop application.

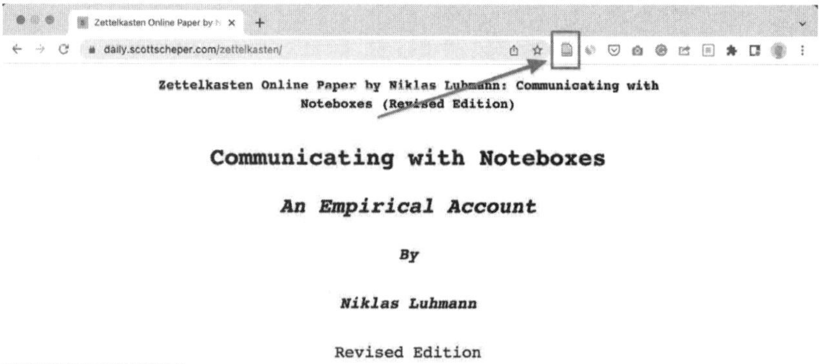
Zettelkasten Online Paper by N
daily.scottscheper.com/zettelkasten/
Zettelkasten Online Paper by Niklas Luhmann: Communicating with Noteboxes (Revised Edition)
Communicating with Noteboxes
An Empirical Account
By
Niklas Luhmann
Revised Edition

67 I host this paper on a website I created while I was releasing daily writing pieces (part of a daily publishing challenge).

- Now, switch over to the Zotero Desktop application. Click on the new entry. It should look something like this:

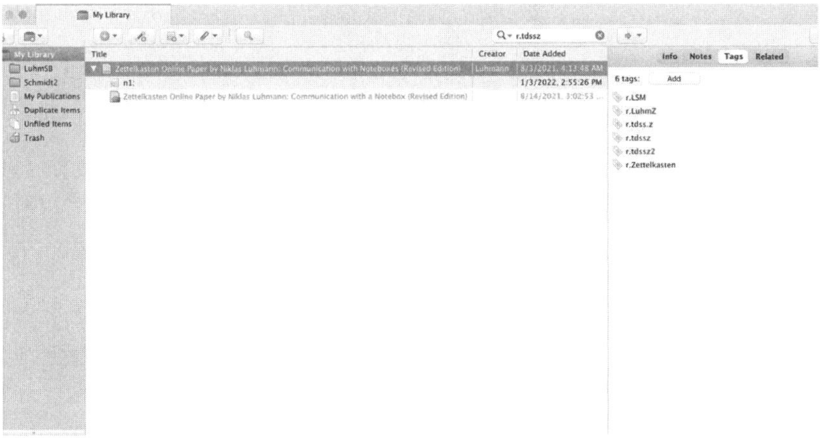

After clicking on the entry, you should see four buttons in the right-hand area: Info, Notes, Tags, and Related.

- Click *Tags*.

- Add a new tag and name it r.TDSSZ.[68]

The "r." prepended to the reference identifier indicates that we're referencing an ExRef stored in Zotero.

Ok, now let's jump back to the card 4212/1.

- Take out a pen. One with red ink.

- Immediately after the quote ends, add a little footnote in red ink by writing [1] after it. In the bottom-left corner, with red ink as well, write the following: 1. r.TDSSZ. This signals to us where this quote originated from.

68 Since the website was created by yours truly, and since it is called The Daily Scott Scheper, and, since it is a page about Zettelkasten, that's where the abbreviation comes from: "TDSSZ."

The card 4212/1 should now look like this:

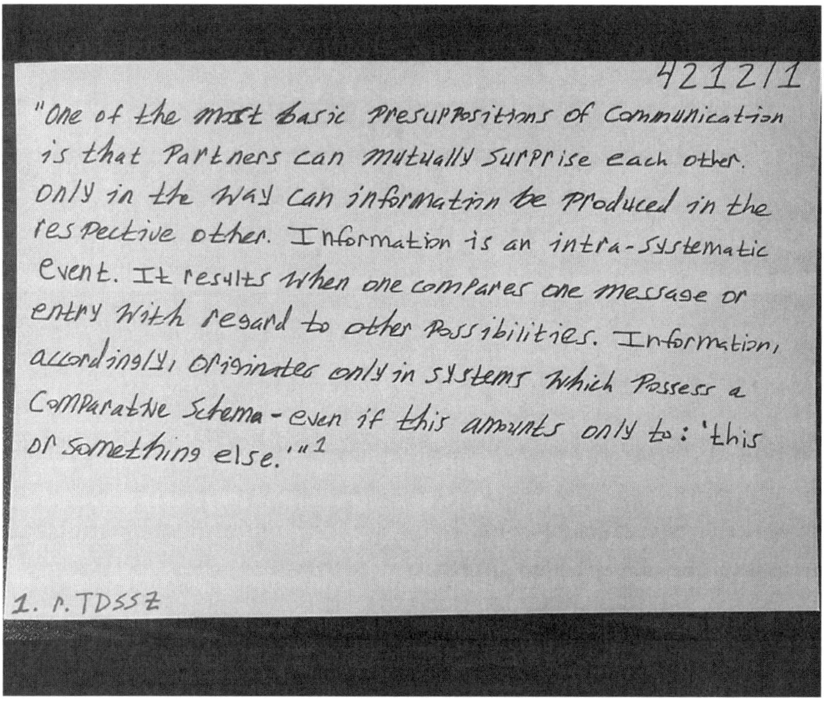
4212/1

"One of the most basic presuppositions of communication is that partners can mutually surprise each other. Only in the way can information be produced in the respective other. Information is an intra-systematic event. It results when one compares one message or entry with regard to other possibilities. Information, accordingly, originates only in systems which possess a comparative schema - even if this amounts only to: 'this or something else.'"1

1. r.TDSSZ

Now take a look at that beautiful card in front of you. Bask in its glory.

▸ Now file it away behind notecard 4212.

That's it for now.

This should give you a taste for what it's like working with an Antinet.

You now have your main box and index box built out.

Eventually, as you build out your Antinet, it will grow significantly. Instead of one main box, you'll have many main boxes. In fact, you'll probably end up with a box for each of the five branches you've created. A box each for 1000, 2000, 3000, 4000, 5000. At that point, your Antinet will have grown to look like this:

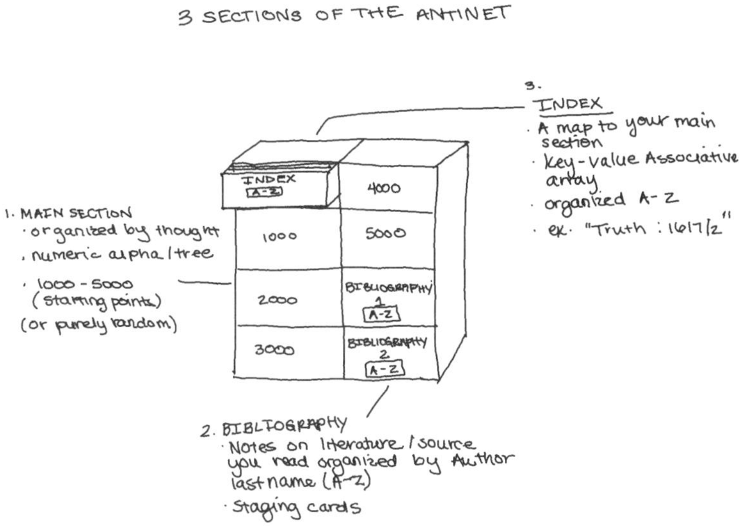

One of the things I recommend picking up is a set of alphabetical card dividers.

The card dividers are useful for when your index box expands. They're also useful for storing bibcards in your bib box (which I'll outline in the chapter on *Extraction*).

Here's a picture of my index box:

The alphabetical dividers are helpful for sorting through the indexcards quickly.

These are mere conveniences. You don't need them to thrive in the beginning, but they're things you'll want to add to your Antinet as it grows.

FREQUENTLY ASKED QUESTIONS

There's a chance you'll have questions come up that I haven't addressed fully. In such a case, a good resource is the Antinet Reddit Community (www.reddit.com/r/Antinet). There's also a good chance the question you may have has been answered there, not just by myself, but by other Antinetters, as well. In addition, I recommend you visit my website as another resource (www.scottscheper.com). On my website, and through my email list, I share a wealth of Antinet resources.

With that said, I'd like to address a few questions I get asked frequently.

WHERE SHOULD I PLACE THIS CARD?

It seems like the most common area where people get hung up is the numeric-alpha addresses. We imagine that there's some *correct* place or area for a card to be filed. That's one of the downsides of using academic disciplines as a classification system. It implies that there's some perfect and correct place for a certain card to be placed.

Let me make it perfectly clear: the correct place for any card is to install it *near its most similar neighbor.*

If you want to install a card in a more remote location, under a branch you feel fits better, simply create a cardlink for it. For instance, my main section where I write about the Antinet resides at 4214. However, there are certain sections related to that topic, which live in other locations.

For example, I have a section about *writing by hand,* which is discussed in 4214/3D/3B. However, I also have a section on the power of writing by hand in section 1323. Why? Because the section 1323 resides closer to my section on *writing.* This isn't a problem. I just have a card within 4214/3D/3B that says, For more on writing by hand, see also: '1323'.

If you're struggling to figure out how to make branches for your cards, remember that there's no correct solution. It's arbitrary. Each scenario will work. If you're trying to figure out whether to create a branch at 4212 vs. 4300, let me offer some guidance: if the area will comprise a significant portion of your work with many sub-branches, then I'd opt for 4300. This grants you the ability to organize a structure like this:

- 4300
    * 4310
        * 4311
        * 4312
    * 4320

However, even if you elected to go with 4212, you'll be fine. You can organize such a branch like this:

- 4212
    * 4212/10
        * 4212/10/1
        * 4212/10/2
    * 4212/20

These are very clean examples. However, in reality, when you use an Antinet, it's never perfectly clean. It's a system of ordered chaos. Embrace it. Stop trying to confine the infinite depths of knowledge to some preconceived set of categories.

Your Antinet, over time, will evolve into a unique structure. This gives it a personality. This is what transforms it into an *alter-ego*, a *second mind*, a *communication partner*.

WHAT IF I ALREADY HAVE A CARD THERE?

Another question I get asked pertains to what you should do if you already have a card installed in the desired location.

For instance, take the following sequence:

- 4214
    * 4214/1
        * 4214/1/1
    * 4214/1A
    * 4214/2

Now, say you want to install a card immediately after 4214/1. The only problem is that 4214/1/1 is already there. What are you to do?

The solution is quite simple. Simply create a card 4214/1/0.

This then naturally brings up a follow-up question. What do you do when you want to install a card before 4214/1/0?

Again, it's simple, move into the negatives. What comes before zero? Why, negative-one comes before zero! Simply create 4214/1/-1

Now, using negative numbers is something Luhmann did not do; however, I've found it to work quite well for me.

As a result you'll have:

- 4214
    * 4214/1
        * 4214/1/-1
        * 4214/1/0
        * 4214/1/1
    * 4214/1A
    * 4214/2

WHAT IF A CARD FITS INTO MULTIPLE CATEGORIES?

Let's go deeper into the question of where to install cards. Again, the game you're playing with the Antinet is *associating* the card next to, or under, its *most similar neighbor*.

This exercises the *comparison faculty* of your brain. Comparison, again, is a critical process for creating *information,* a precursor for knowledge.

If a card fits into multiple categories, first off, do not get anxiety about it. "Every place is adequate," as Johannes Schmidt says. "The card only has to connect with the card before it."[69]

But what happens if you have a card that fits into two different places in your Antinet?

There are three primary ways to handle this: (1) Index Cardlinks, (2) Hoplink Cards, and (3) "See Also" Cardlinks.

Index Cardlinks

In the walkthrough we just went through in building your own Antinet, we encountered a scenario where a card fits into the *information* branch, as well the *communication* branch. What we did was simply choose to install it in the *information* branch. We then created an entry in the list indexcard for C, writing Communication (within Info. Theory): '4212/1'.

This is an index cardlink. Whenever you're ready to create a branch in the main box of the Antinet for *Communication,* you'll also see that you have a card pertaining to *Communication* within the *Information Theory* branch.

Hoplink Cards

Another way of handling this would be to create a new card and place it in the *Communication* branch (whenever it's created). On the card, it would simply say, For Communication in the context of Information Theory, visit '4212/1'. This is what I call a *hoplink card.* Luhmann created these types of cards, as well.

Here's an example hoplink card:

---

69 Undisciplined, Archiving Luhmann w/ Johannes Schmidt, 2021, https://www.youtube.com/watch?v=kz2K3auPLWU, 36:50.

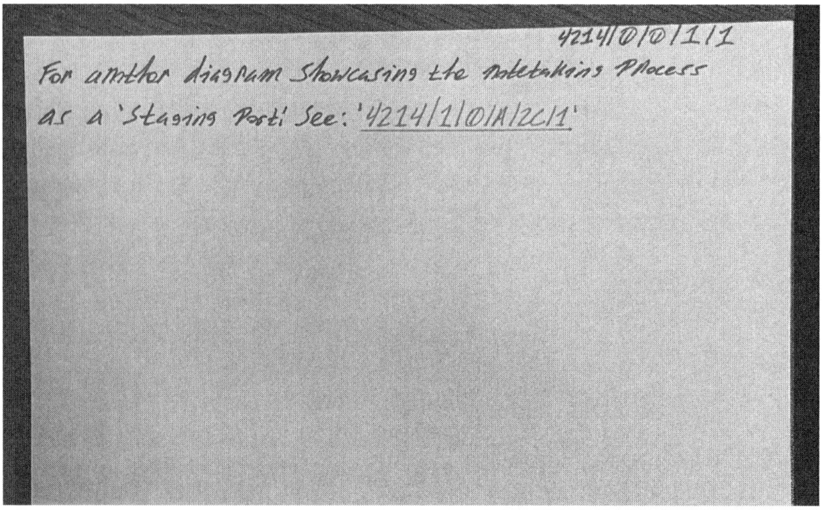

More on hoplink cards are explored in the chapter, *Creation*.

"See Also" Cardlinks

In most cases, you don't need to create a dedicated hoplink card. At the bottom of a card already written about *communication*, you can simply add a bit of text at the bottom that says: See also: '4214/5AE/2'. Here's an example from my own Antinet:

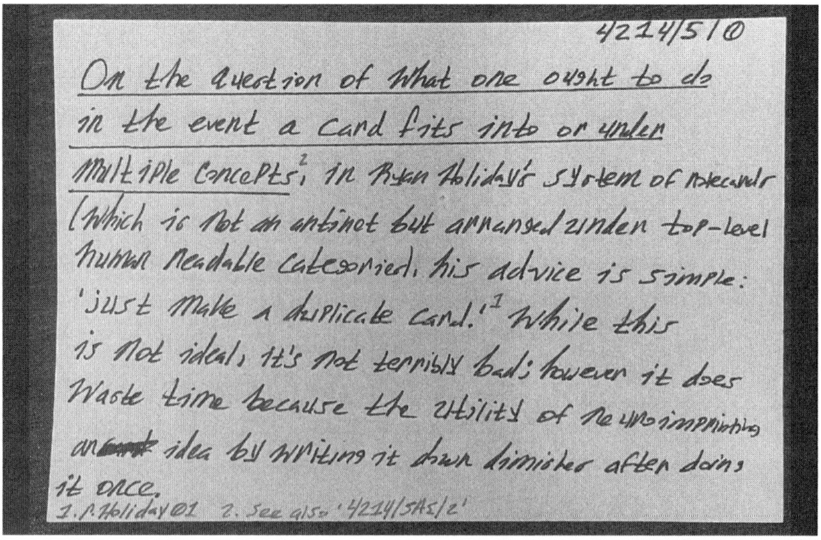

This is a "see also" cardlink.

As you can see (pun intended), numeric-alpha addresses are powerful. They enable a whole wealth of possibilities and ways to link bits of your knowledge together to generate new connections. This is where a system like the Antinet really begins to outshine other systems.

"SEE ALSO" EXREFS

"See also" cardlinks not only pertain to internal cardlinks (which link to cards within your Antinet). They can also be used for ExRefs (external references).

For instance, say you read a book that contains a good passage relating to *Love*. Yet you're not working actively on a project related to *Love*. Instead of developing an elaborate main note on love, for sake of time, you can simply create an entry, which reads See also: r.Moeller, 36. Luhmann did this frequently.

HOW DO I CREATE NOTES FOR COLD HARD FACTS?

While writing the section at the beginning of this book, I received the following question: *How do I install cold hard facts in my Antinet?*

The individual who asked me this question works in the field of French real estate law. He was wondering where to file the following note: "French real estate law requires each condominium to be divided by unit, and each apartment is a unit."

On this matter, I'll say a few things.

I have indeed installed cold hard facts in my own Antinet. They are cards like population size by country, revenue figures of businesses, etc.

However, I created these cold hard fact cards in the pre-Antinet days.[70] So that's one reason they even exist. I have since retroactively gone back and

70 For over a decade, and before discovering the Antinet, I used a notebox system organized

installed many of these cold hard fact cards into my Antinet. In every case, I've found the academic disciplinary fields to accommodate them. There's always a branch for where they can go. And even if there isn't a clear branch within the academic disciplinary fields, you can just create one (and likely place it in branch 5000).

I like to place my cold hard fact cards on 3 x 5 inch cards. I like to consult them from time to time in order to unearth accidental insights.

Yet, as I touched upon in the beginning of this book, the Antinet is *primarily* useful for creators. It's useful for those who wish to elaborate on thoughts and evolve them by *reflecting* on them. You evolve your thoughts by linking them to more thoughts filed behind them.

If you wish to just memorize a bunch of cold hard facts, an Antinet may be overkill. Heck, even digital tools like *Anki* do the trick for this type of thing. Of course, there is certainly value to be obtained from the act of writing facts down by hand.

Typically, those who benefit most from an Antinet are writers, researchers, and creators who wish to *evolve* thought.

After sharing my response with the individual who asked the question about cold hard facts, he provided more clarity. In actuality, his work in French real estate law is for his thesis. In this case, the Antinet will have more use, and provide more value.

To wrap this up, it is possible to use the Antinet to store cold hard facts. For example, you'd place the previously mentioned card in *Real Estate Law* branch. For instance, 1310. Near that branch, you could create a branch for French Real Estate Law at 1312. Within that branch, you can begin creating cards pertaining to specific laws at 1312/1. Again, these numbers are arbitrary and can be chosen by you based on personal whim.

---

by book or category (like Ryan Holiday's notebox system).

CONCLUSION

We've covered a lot in this chapter. We started with important principles involved in building an Antinet. We covered the mindset with which you should approach the beginning phases of building an Antinet. We emphasized that you must not get lost in the trap of perfectionism. We also capped off this preamble with the concept of *goals,* and *growth vs. contribution.*

We then dove headfirst into building out your own Antinet. If you followed the steps (which I hope you did), you now have a solid base. You have the start of your own Antinet!

Now that you have a solid foundation, it's time to embark upon the next phase of our journey: *Knowledge Development.* Get ready. This section of the book is a lot more fun than it sounds. It also serves as the core process for building your knowledge. Let's go.

CHAPTER TWELVE

KNOWLEDGE DEVELOPMENT

THE CATEGORY ZETTELKASTEN FINDS ITSELF lumped into is called *personal knowledge management* (PKM). PKM is a disciplinary subfield of *knowledge management* concerned with the personal collection, organization, storing, and sharing of digital information.

As it applies to the Antinet, I dislike the categorical term PKM for several reasons. First off, notetaking systems do not exclusively contain knowledge; they contain information, which helps one develop knowledge. In addition, the entire point of Luhmann's Antinet centered on the *development* of knowledge (not *management* of knowledge).

Luhmann's Antinet is not seen as a memory tool, but a *thinking tool.* It's a thinking tool that aims to develop one's thoughts. It's a very active system, not something that is properly encompassed by the term *management.* Because it requires action, a better term for it is *development.* The goal of the Antinet is to develop one's *thoughts* (revealed in the notes you create), as well as your own *thinking* (revealed in how your brain works to link together ideas). For this reason, I encompass both *thoughts* and *thinking* under the umbrella term *knowledge.* In turn this gives us the label in which I categorize the Antinet: a *knowledge development system.*

TWO PROCESSES OF KNOWLEDGE DEVELOPMENT

As Johannes Schmidt observes, there are two processes of the Antinet as a knowledge development system. The first process involves developing thought through the practice of writing by hand. The second process involves interacting with the Antinet as a communication partner.[1]

PROCESS I: SHORT-TERM KNOWLEDGE DEVELOPMENT

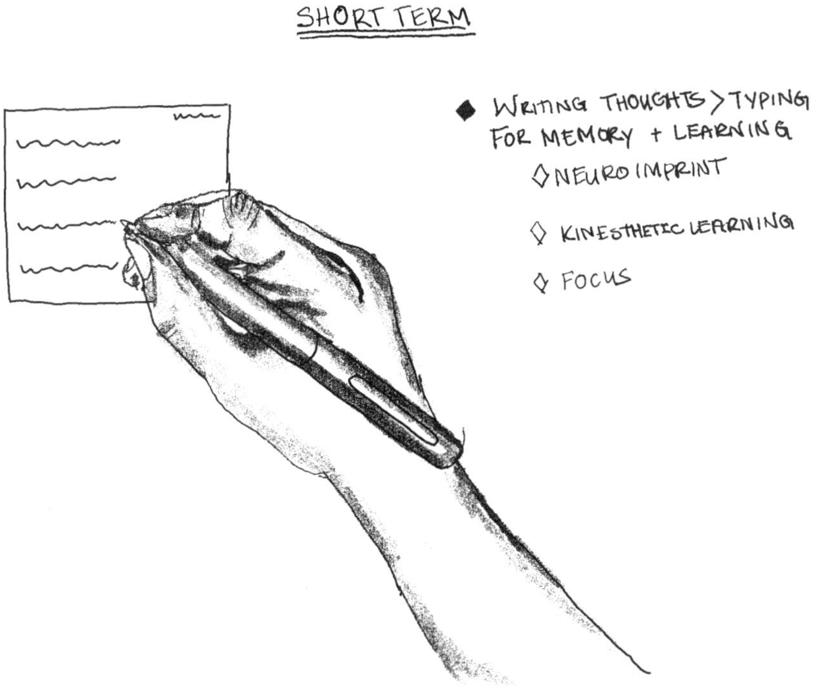

In Luhmann's own Antinet, one finds the following handwritten note: "Underlying the filing technique is the experience that without writing, there is no thinking."[2]

---

1 Johannes Schmidt, "Niklas Luhmann's Card Index: Thinking Tool, Communication Partner, Publication Machine," Forgetting Machines. Knowledge Management Evolution in Early Modern Europe 53 (2016), 309.

2 "ZK II: Paper 9/8g—Niklas Luhmann Archive," accessed April 18, 2022, https://niklas-luhmann-archiv.de/bestand/zettelkasten/zettel/ZK_2_NB_9-8g_V.

In the short term, the Antinet enables users to develop thought through the practice of writing by hand. As I've illustrated throughout this text, I contend that this practice develops thought better than digital systems because of the deliberate attention required. As Schmidt observes, "writing things down enables disciplined thinking in the first place."[3] I also contend that the analog nature of the Antinet develops one's *thinking* better because it neuroimprints ideas on the mind far more effectively than digital tools.

PROCESS II: LONG-TERM KNOWLEDGE DEVELOPMENT

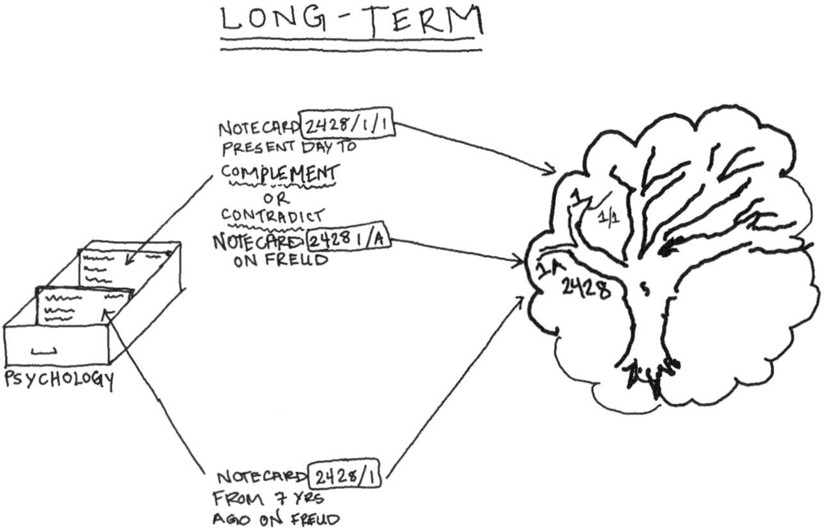

As Schmidt highlights, the second process of knowledge development centers on the Antinet emerging as a *communication partner* during research. This happens by way of the tree structure of the Antinet *evolving* your thoughts over the long term.

3 Johannes Schmidt, "Niklas Luhmann's Card Index: Thinking Tool, Communication Partner, Publication Machine," Forgetting Machines. Knowledge Management Evolution in Early Modern Europe 53 (2016), 309.

When you begin exploring your notes as you prepare to write a manuscript, a communication experience emerges. For instance, you first come upon a note written seven years ago. Following this note is a newer note recently added which seemingly contradicts the first note. What happens next illustrates the internal dialogue that takes place: you question *why* the notes contradict one another, and then you begin investigating the sources of the notes. You begin investigating your chain of thoughts that resulted in coming away with a different understanding from what you now hold as true.

This is an instance that exemplifies the long-term thought development that takes place while using an Antinet. Thoughts are developed both in the short term as well as the long term.

Before we get into the four specific phases of knowledge development, let's first take a step back into the abstract land of information science.

THE NATURE OF KNOWLEDGE AND INFORMATION

In order to better understand knowledge, we need to distinguish it from its close relatives: *data, information,* and *wisdom.* This brings us to the *DIKW pyramid.*

THE DIKW PYRAMID

A convenient model that emerged within the information science field is called the DIKW pyramid.

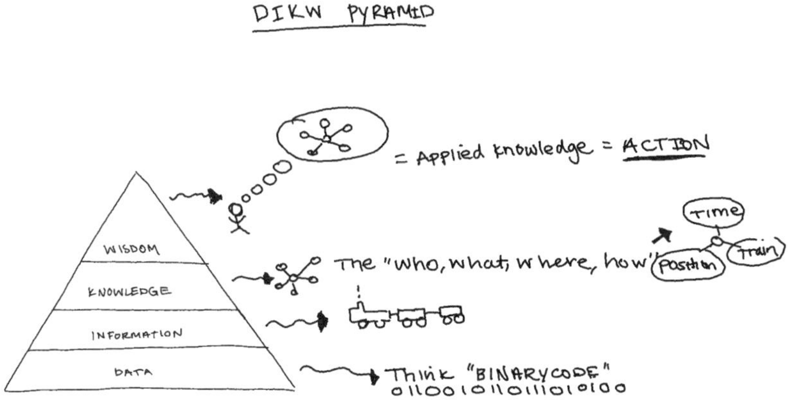

Like all models of reality, the pyramid is fuzzy and imperfect. Every scholar in information science seems to have their own interpretation of the four components of the pyramid. For instance, one paper contains 130 different definitions of *data, information* and *knowledge* from 45 different scholars. The paper was created because it recognized that an issue with information science revolves around the lack of clarity on these fundamental concepts.[4]

The different components of the DIKW pyramid get so fuzzy that I almost scratched this entire section when I started to second-guess whether or not I was getting things right. I would read one scholar's explanation and come away with an understanding of *information* only to find another scholar classifying the same thing as *knowledge*!

Regardless, I've assembled the following explanations, which are more than sufficient for our purposes.

Data

Data is raw, unprocessed stimuli from the universe. The raw material can be physical in nature or metaphysical in nature. Data is raw material, like the universe's energy waves and particles: light, heat, sound, force, and electromagnetic components. Think of data as sound wave represented in computer symbols like *010110100011011*. We cannot understand what this data means at this point.

Information

> *"To be informed is to know simply that something is the case."*
> –Mortimer Adler[5]

Before data can be converted to information, it undergoes a phase transition. The phase transition is the *interpretation phase*. This phase involves our

4 Chaim Zins, "Conceptual Approaches for Defining Data, Information, and Knowledge," Journal of the American Society for Information Science and Technology 58, no. 4 (2007): 479–93.

5 Mortimer Jerome Adler and Charles Van Doren, How to Read a Book, Rev. and updated ed (New York: Simon and Schuster, 1972), 11.

sensory system (sight, smell, sound, taste, touch, balance). For example, our ears receive data, and then interpret the data. We then transcribe the data into forms we can comprehend.

In brief, information is data we can comprehend. For instance, the sound wave data from the previous example (*01011010001101l*) is interpreted through one's ears. It is then transitioned into a comprehensible sound: *the sound of a train,* which is information.

Knowledge

> *"To be enlightened is to know, in addition, what it is all about: why it is the case, what its connections are with other facts, in what respects it is the same, in what respects it is different, and so forth."*
> –Mortimer Adler[6]

Knowledge is information multiplied by *meaning*. Knowledge is *useful* information. I also like to think of knowledge as *structured information*. Knowledge integrates, correlates, and collects several pieces of information.[7] Say, for instance, we have the information that the sound we just heard is that of a train. Knowledge assembles and structures other *useful* pieces of information onto this: the information comprising the *who, what, where,* and *when* properties attached to data.[8] For instance, we know what we heard sounds like a train (what). Yet we piece this information together with other properties: it involves you and the train (who), its general direction (where), and how recently we heard it (when).

Knowledge enables us to connect and structure these disparate pieces of information together to create meaning. It tells us, *holy crap, I'm on the train tracks right now and I just heard a train.* This brings us to *wisdom.*

---

6 Mortimer Jerome Adler and Charles Van Doren, How to Read a Book, Rev. and updated ed (New York: Simon and Schuster, 1972), 11. Emphasis added.

7 "Data, Information, Knowledge, & Wisdom," accessed April 18, 2022, https://www.systems-thinking.org/dikw/dikw.htm.

8 "Data, Information, Knowledge, & Wisdom," accessed April 18, 2022, https://www.systems-thinking.org/dikw/dikw.htm.

Wisdom

"Intelligent action depends on knowledge."
–Mortimer Adler[9]

Wisdom is knowledge multiplied by *action*. When you take action after the information phase, that's *intuitive action*. However, when you take action after the knowledge phase, you're taking *wise action*. You're making a decision based on multiple pieces of information. This doesn't mean you're necessarily taking the *right* action; however, it does mean you have a higher likelihood of taking the right action. Knowing things only gets one so far; wise action stands as a critical phase.

Formulaic Summary

Here's a formulaic summary of what we just covered:

Data = Raw Stimuli

Information = Comprehension x *Data*

Knowledge = Information x *Meaning*

Wisdom = Knowledge x *Action*

KNOWLEDGE CREATION AND SHARING IS THE GOAL

With the Antinet, the goal is to create *knowledge*, not information. Information is a means to an end. We don't just want to collect facts and material we can comprehend; we want to create *knowledge*.

This is why I routinely advise against wasting your time with things like publishing your notes. When it comes to sharing publicly, err on the side of publishing knowledge over information.

9 Mortimer Jerome Adler and Charles Van Doren, How to Read a Book, Rev. and updated ed (New York: Simon and Schuster, 1972), 65.

When you possess information, you're informed. When you possess knowledge, you're enlightened. The difference between being informed and being enlightened is the difference between being able to recite something vs. being able to teach it.[10]

Do not discount the importance of being informed, however, for being informed is a prerequisite for enlightenment.[11] This is why the practice of taking excerpt notes is helpful. It enables one to better comprehend material. However, excerpt notes are only a precursor for the next phase: turning the information into knowledge by way of reformulation and reflection notes.

Within your Antinet, you'll find a mix of knowledge and information. The knowledge it contains isn't fully processed until it makes its way into your creative output.

Again, this emphasizes the point that the Antinet is a *means* to the end (the end being creative output). The Antinet helps you process and create knowledge; however the most important part is that you actually share it. As the philosopher Hans-Georg Moeller points out, "knowledge only counts if it is exchanged and thus given away or spent."[12]

MEANING AND THE INTRAPERSONAL NATURE OF THE ANTINET

As we learned previously, knowledge is information multiplied by *meaning*. However, we never addressed the concept of meaning. The question is, *where does meaning come from?*

According to Alberto Cevolini, "The only operations that can reproduce and manage *meaning* are communication and consciousness."[13] The nature of the

10 Mortimer Jerome Adler and Charles Van Doren, How to Read a Book, Rev. and updated ed (New York: Simon and Schuster, 1972), 11.

11 Mortimer Jerome Adler and Charles Van Doren, How to Read a Book, Rev. and updated ed (New York: Simon and Schuster, 1972), 11.

12 Hans-Georg Moeller, The Radical Luhmann (New York: Columbia University Press, 2011), 108.

13 Alberto Cevolini, ed., Forgetting Machines: Knowledge Management Evolution in Early

communication experience (with your own past self's consciousness) that arises in the course of working with an Antinet helps create *meaning*. It helps you transform information into knowledge that you can share with the world.

Knowledge development is a fluid process that transitions through different states. From complex to simple, and back to complex again. The nature of this process is what we'll cover next.

COMPLEXITY TO SIMPLICITY TO COMPLEXITY

Even though I refer primarily to *reading* throughout this book, what I'm really referring to is more broad. I'm really referring to any *communication experience*. Any time you engage with a *source* of knowledge, you're undertaking a communication experience. As the scholar, Alberto Cevolini states, "Knowledge is socially managed through *communication*, although at least one consciousness is required to perpetuate communication."[14] The source of the communication experience can be a book, podcast, YouTube video, research paper, lecture, one-on-one meeting, group meeting, or any other communication media.

When you engage with a source of knowledge, you're undergoing a process, making a complex entity simple, in order to then convert it back into complexity—your own complexity—your Antinet (see following page).

In the first part, there's the *author of a given text*. The author has spent time forming thoughts and presenting them to you. The thoughts often make sense in the author's mind; yet, the knowledge contained may indeed be complex. It pulls from many experiences and refers to material from different areas the author has engaged with throughout his or her life. If the author has done a good job, they package their complex knowledge into a book that presents the complex ideas in a simplified way. The simplified container of

---

Modern Europe, Library of the Written Word, volume 53 (Leiden ; Boston: Brill, 2016), 13.

14 Alberto Cevolini, ed., Forgetting Machines: Knowledge Management Evolution in Early Modern Europe, Library of the Written Word, volume 53 (Leiden ; Boston: Brill, 2016), 12.

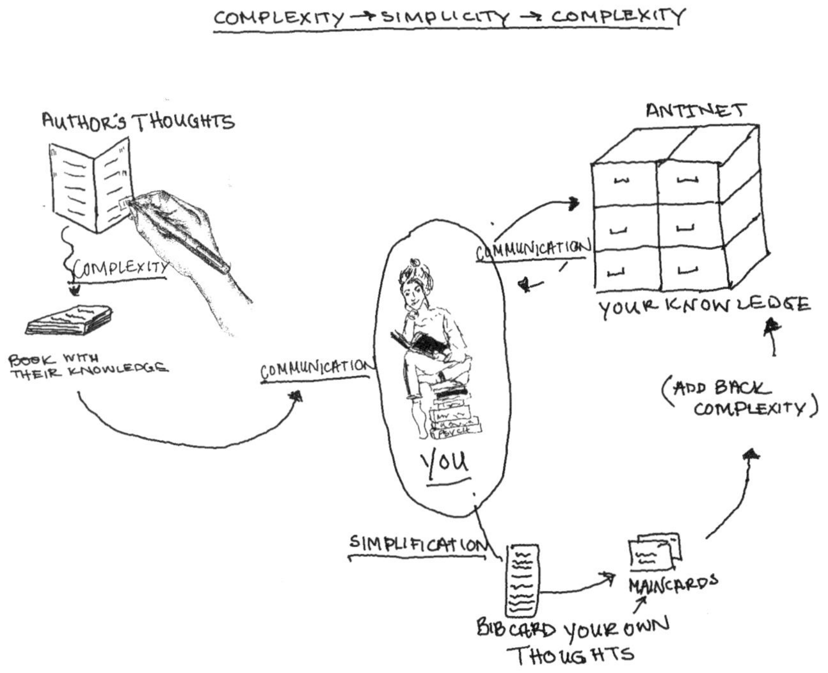

complex knowledge is what composes a book. When you read a book, the book *communicates* with *you*.

Under the diagram of the character of *you*, you'll find a dotted line with the term *communication* next to it. The dotted line refers to the communication that takes place in your mind while you are reading. While you're reading you think of keyterms and thoughts stored in your Antinet. This is the communication experience the dotted line is referring to.

Next, there's a phase that occurs wherein you must *simplify* the material enough to *comprehend* it. You then must *select* from the material the thoughts you find irresistible. With the knowledge that you *select* you then add your own *complexity* by transforming it into notes. The Antinet stores an associative chain of this complexity, which *you* then can communicate with forever.

The communication experience that you have with the Antinet is a bit simpler than reading a book, in part because you've written it down by hand.

As a result, you process the information in a slower, more deliberate way. You make that information more comprehendible later on. Why? Because you've written it out in your own words.

The entire process involves a phase transformation between *complexity* and *simplicity*.

One scholar observes the following of Luhmann's system: "The outcome is the reproduction of complexity by means of selection, that is, the paradoxical reproduction of complexity through a reduction of complexity."[15]

Essentially, you simplify a book's contents by selecting and extracting its most irresistible parts. Then, you create knowledge by adding your own *reformulations* or *reflections* of that content. In turn, you add your own experiences and ways of viewing the world. You then *install* that knowledge in the Antinet, thereby creating a *complex* entity that you can communicate with perennially.

Luhmann confirms this cycle, stating: "In a way, the [Antinet Zettelkasten] is a reduction to build complexity."[16]

ROBERT BOYLE'S KNOWLEDGE DEVELOPMENT PROCESS

Robert Boyle's knowledge development process is similar to what I've just outlined. Boyle specifies three elementary steps that can be extrapolated to the Antinet.[17]

The first step is "careful *selection* of materials." That is, carefully selecting books worth reading.

---

15 Alberto Cevolini, ed., Forgetting Machines: Knowledge Management Evolution in Early Modern Europe, Library of the Written Word, volume 53 (Leiden ; Boston: Brill, 2016), 27.

16 Niklas Luhmann, Niklas Luhmann Short Cuts (English Translation), 2002, 22.

17 Richard Yeo, *Notebooks, Recollection, and External Memory: Some Early Modern English Ideas and Practices* (Brill, 2016), 142.

Second in Boyle's process: "Repeated reflection on key themes." In other words, figuring out what to select, and extract onto cards.

Third is: "Rehearsal of a skeletal direction of meditation." By this, Boyle means reviewing and doing maintenance rehearsal on the cards you've created.

Boyle's process is similar to the model we'll use in this section. Our model has four phases, which I'll introduce to you shortly. But first, let's talk *analog vs. digital* with regards to knowledge development.

ANALOG VS. DIGITAL KNOWLEDGE DEVELOPMENT

One of the reasons the analog component of the Antinet is so important is because of how it affects knowledge development.

To put it simply, knowledge development is different for analog systems and digital systems. The very same principles I teach in this book cannot be perfectly copied to digital workflows, in part because of the time investment analog systems require. The time it takes to slow your mind down and record your thoughts is a hidden advantage of analog systems.

To illustrate this, it's helpful to view knowledge development by revisiting the input-output model (shown previously):

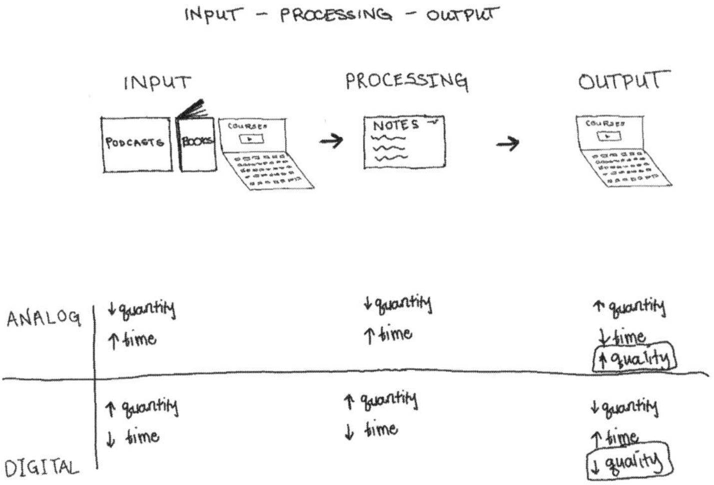

In the *input phase* of an analog workflow, it takes more time to ingest information. With the *priming* practice I'll be teaching you, you'll spend more time actually engaging with the sources you select. However, as a result, you'll be reading less sporadically. With digital workflows, readers navigate sporadically from article to article. Even with a digital e-reader like a Kindle, one ingests information more rapidly than they do when reading physical materials. With bookmarking tools you simply click a button on any web page you visit to remind yourself to read something later. As a result you end up collecting way more material in less time. As you'll soon find out, this isn't a good thing.

Now, let's consider the *processing phase*. "Information processing is the fundamental activity of the brain," Steven Pinker writes.[18] When it comes to processing information, the tradeoff of analog vs. digital is very much the same as the input phase. Analog workflows take more time and energy to process inputs. It takes more time to actually write notes by hand. It's a deliberate process that requires the mind to slow down and think. You think with your pen forming thoughts across the paper. With digital, it's faster—especially if you know how to type without looking down at the keyboard! As a result, you are able to create significantly more notes. In brief, a greater quantity of notes can be written in less time with digital systems.

To recap, digital systems allow you to ingest more information and process more information in less time. However, a great paradox occurs. You see, there is another variable we didn't mention in the previously model. That variable is *quality*.

Sure, digital systems enable the ingesting and processing of a greater quantity of information. However they also result in lower quality ingestion and processing of information. Because analog workflows take more time to absorb and comprehend information, you must be much more selective about what you read. In addition, you will be more selective in *how you pay attention* while you read. The analog workflow also forces you to be selective in what you choose to process. Because analog takes more time,

---

18 Steven Pinker, How the Mind Works, Norton pbk (New York: Norton, 2009), 83.

you are less tempted to create useless notes and are more incentivized to say more with fewer words. As a result, a paradox emerges. Analog systems enable users to produce more output in less time. Furthermore, the quality of the *output* is higher.

This effect derives from several factors. First off, you create less trash in analog systems. Because of the time and energy investment required for ingesting and processing information, there's less trash as a result. In turn this helps during the creation process. It's much easier to create more with less. The reason for this is that notes act largely as *cues*. They stamp knowledge onto your mind, allowing your mind to run with it during the creation process.

For instance, in writing this section right now, the only *cue* I had was a notecard of the diagram shown previously. Everything else consisted simply of me typing my explanation of the diagram. All I needed was a diagram of this idea to serve as a cue for me to write and explain this model.

In addition, stumbling upon the card of the diagram was a structured accident. While writing another section of this book, I stumbled upon the model. When I happened upon it, I set it aside for the knowledge development chapter.

Had I been using a digital workflow, this type of material would have been crowded out by a colossal number of other digital notes. In turn, I might not have even written about this model at all. And even if I had, I would probably have had less time and energy to write about it because more time would have been spent parsing the mountain of digital notes I had. It may seem contradictory, but with analog systems, your energy is stored and saved for the actual process of writing. With analog, you've spent more time producing fewer notes such that, when it comes time to write, it's like being shot out of a cannon.

The section you're reading right now is a little over eight hundred words. It took me about a half-hour to write. This serves as an example of the analog workflow: *more content written, in less time, and at higher quality*. This is why the analog nature of the Antinet is so important. It served as a critical piece that helped Luhmann become "a publication machine."[19]

THE FOUR PHASES OF KNOWLEDGE DEVELOPMENT

I like to think of knowledge development as consisting of four phases.

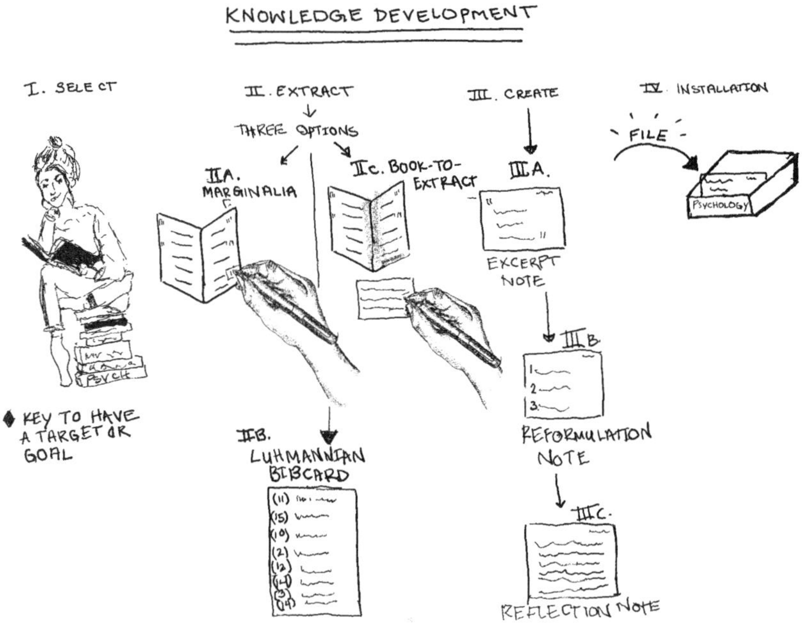

The first phase is *selection*. This pertains to selecting irresistible pieces of information found while engaging with external sources (books, podcasts, videos, etc.). Selection takes place in your own mind. It involves the internal voice in your head. You, and only you, can decide which information is worth selecting. It's an incommunicable process that involves your consciousness and self-awareness. It is indistinguishable from the concept of attention.[20] It requires being in tune with your own internal experience.

---

19 Johannes Schmidt, "Niklas Luhmann's Card Index: Thinking Tool, Communication Partner, Publication Machine," Forgetting Machines. Knowledge Management Evolution in Early Modern Europe 53 (2016), 311.

20 Michael Jacob Kahana, Foundations of Human Memory. (New York: Oxford University

The second phase is *extraction*. This encompasses the actual action of writing down the thoughts and observations you have while reading. There are several workflows to choose from in this phase.

The third phase is *creation*. This describes the process of creating notes. This mean either *excerpting* notes, *reformulating* notes, or elaborating on the notes by *reflecting* on ideas.

The fourth phase is *installation*. This describes both *where* to install the cards you've just created, and *how* to actually install them. This relates to the index keyterms you will assign (if any).

In the following chapters, we'll explore each of these phases in detail. Let's go.

Press, 2014), 26.

CHAPTER THIRTEEN

SELECTION

"We read a lot. I don't know anyone who's wise who doesn't read a lot. But that's not enough: You have to have a temperament to grab ideas and do sensible things. Most people don't grab the right ideas or don't know what to do with them."

–Charlie Munger[21]

IT COULD BE ARGUED THAT SELECTION is *the most* important process when working with an Antinet.

Fiona McPherson, a cognitive scientist specializing in the study of notetaking, agrees that the "most crucial" part of notetaking revolves around *selection*. Specifically this means selecting what information is important, and just as critically, *not selecting information that is not important.*[22]

This introduces the tradeoff between *selection* and *exclusion*. "To select everything would mean to exclude nothing," as the scholar Alberto Cevolini puts it. Or, as Jeremias Drexel (1581—1638) puts it, "to read without selecting means to be negligent."[23]

---

21 Charles T. Munger, Poor Charlie's Almanack: The Wit and Wisdom of Charles T. Munger, Expanded Third Edition, ed. Peter D. Kaufman, 3rd edition (Walsworth Publishing Company, 2005).

22 Fiona McPherson, Effective Note-taking, revised edition (Wellington: Wayz Press, 2018), 13.

23 Alberto Cevolini, Storing Expansions: Openness and Closure in Secondary Memories (Brill, 2016), 185.

In brief, the relationship between what to select and what to exclude from what you read is an important skill—a skill which we will discuss in this chapter.

SELECTION IN THE BRAIN

I like the illustration given by cognitive scientist William K. Estes who posited that human memory can be likened to a computing system. A computing system takes inputs, runs them through a process, and then produces outputs.[24] Here's a diagram of how it works:

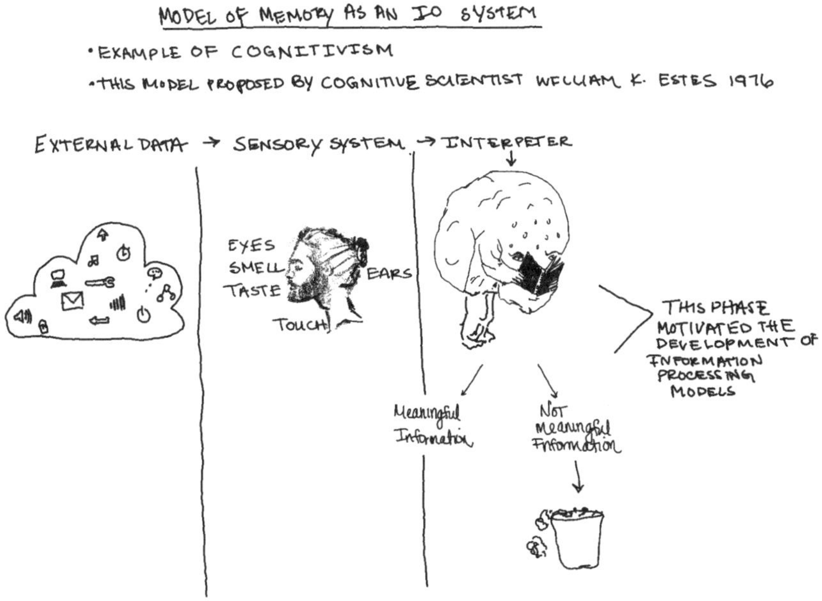

External data comes from the environment. It's essentially the world, the ecosystem we encounter.

Our *sensory system* consists of our senses of sight, hearing, touch, taste, smell, and balance. Our sensory system operates like an *interpreter* as understood in the context of the computer language Python. The interpreter deciphers the input data and transforms it into *information* that the computer can

24 Michael Jacob Kahana, Foundations of Human Memory. (New York: Oxford University Press, 2014), 25.

understand. With our sensory system, it's much the same. It deciphers the data and turns it into information our brains can understand.

From there the brain must make a decision: is the information *meaningful* or is it *not meaningful*? If the information is not meaningful we ignore it. We do not pay attention to it. If it is meaningful we *select* that information. With that information selected we run it through another process. We determine to what *degree* the item is meaningful.

The study of this process is actually what ended up motivating the development of the science of information processing models.[25] This decision between meaningful and non-meaningful information is indistinguishable from the concept of *attention*.[26] Brought back to the process of working with an Antinet, when you are reading, it's an active process that requires full attention. The concept of selection is entrenched in this process.

THE TROUBLE OF SELECTION: FEEDBACK

Here, *selection* refers to the entire process of thinking that takes place in your mind when you encounter a new idea. It refers to the process involved in determining what *thought* generated by a text should be (1) *extracted* onto a card by writing it out by hand to ruminate on or elaborate on; (2) *stored* in the Antinet by installing it in the position most similar and most closely associated with it; or (3) *discarded* entirely because it's not worth the time investment of extracting or storing the thought.

This process occurs very quickly in the mind. It's also not trivial. Consider what Alberto Cevolini observes: "Troubles arise when one wonders about the criteria according to which one should select, store, or discard."[27]

---

25 Michael Jacob Kahana, Foundations of Human Memory. (New York: Oxford University Press, 2014), 26.

26 Michael Jacob Kahana, Foundations of Human Memory. (New York: Oxford University Press, 2014), 26.

27 Alberto Cevolini, ed., Forgetting Machines: Knowledge Management Evolution in Early Modern Europe, Library of the Written Word, volume 53 (Leiden ; Boston: Brill, 2016), 31.

The notion of *troubles arising* with regard to the information one should select or not select while reading is echoed by other scientists. Cognitive scientist, Fiona McPherson, holds selection as the most critical skill you can master. It is the foundation upon which others skills rest. Yet "no-one has yet to come up with an effective way of teaching this skill," observes McPherson. However, there is some good news: what McPherson meant is that there's no universal one-size-fits-all way of teaching this. Each person will pick up the skill of selection in a different way. It is a skill that can indeed be taught. However, certain people may require more practice than others.[28]

Developing the skills of selection requires one thing: *feedback.*

Feedback equals growth. In a classroom setting, you can quickly tell how well your notetaking is working from the feedback you receive in form of test scores. Yet in creative work with long timelines (like one or two years), feedback is a bit more difficult to receive in a timely manner. Sönke Ahrens makes such an observation in his book *How to Take Smart Notes.* "The linear model of academic writing comes with few feedback opportunities," Ahrens writes.[29] Yet he makes an interesting assertion that, by choosing to reformulate or reflect on your reading, you're essentially testing yourself on whether or not you understand the material well enough to explain it in your own words. You're testing yourself to see if you even know it well enough to reformulate the material. You're also testing yourself whenever you attempt to write a reflection note. Do you truly understand it well enough that you'll be able to reflect on what you've selected?

However, receiving feedback is tricky when it comes to *selection.* Whenever you attempt to write notes on something, you receive feedback on how well you understand the material. Yet, this does not provide feedback on whether or not you should have selected the material in the first place.

---

28 Fiona McPherson, Effective Note-taking, revised edition (Wellington: Wayz Press, 2018), 13.

29 Sönke Ahrens, How to Take Smart Notes: One Simple Technique to Boost Writing, Learning and Thinking: For Students, Academics and Nonfiction Book Writers (North Charleston, SC: CreateSpace, 2017), 54.

The question is: *How do we gain feedback from the notes we create?*

One argument is to just publish your notes. In other words, create a so-called 'digital garden' or a personal website which shares your notes so that others can provide feedback. Not surprisingly, this is something I do not advise for a number of reasons. In brief, when you publish your notes, you're publishing information. This is less useful to people than publishing knowledge. With knowledge, you've contextualized and further processed that information. As a result your knowledge provides the reader with much more value than unprocessed information. In turn, if you do indeed receive feedback from such notes, the feedback will be misguided. To a large degree, it will be a waste of time, which is why I advise against it.

In sum, perhaps there are no shortcuts here. The best way to select material is to do so with a clear understanding of why you're reading the source you've selected. It also requires that you have a clear understanding of your audience.

I'll offer a few suggestions for getting better at *selection*:

First, create a profile of your dream reader. Search photos online and cut out a stock photo of him or her. Paste the image on a notecard and write down a made-up name for the person. They're your dream reader, your dream avatar whom you wish to serve. Ideally, create a male and female avatar (unless you're specifically targeting a gender). Write down a one-to-three sentence profile on them, detailing what their interests are, what they like, or dislike, etc. Heck, your avatar could even be your professor if you're a student. Place the picture(s) on your wall or some place you'll see regularly. Whenever you're reading a book, read with your dream reader in mind. This is another reason why it's helpful to adopt a *contribution* mindset (as opposed to a personal *growth* mindset).

Second, I recommend publishing short pieces of your work or material as you're writing. Instead of publishing under-processed notes, I recommend that you give readers chapter samples and tastes of your writing. Do this by publishing short pieces or blog posts online. This is something I've done myself over the course of writing this book.

Later, I'll be introducing you to something called *priming*, which promotes more effective reading. You'll end up selecting information aligned with *why* you've set out to read a book.

"Selection is a highly personalized activity," writes scholar, Alberto Cevolini.[30] In other words, every person is unique, and everyone will spot unique material that speaks to them. Your job is to channel your internal voice and select the material that uniquely resonates with you, plain and simple.

Selection doesn't just mean "gathering," it means "making a judgement."[31] However, what then follows is the question of what you should even make a judgement about! From here, we can rely on the wisdom of early modern literature: *select only what is considered to be of future utility*.[32] That is, select what will be of future utility to you, and through you, what will be of future utility to others.

Selection helps form the uniqueness of your second mind. If you fit an entire library into your Antinet, it would demolish the unique personality you've injected into it by way of *selection*. Digital apps like *Pocket* or *Read Later* or *Evernote* do not create a second mind. They are mere repositories of quotes, articles, and material from others. As scholar, Richard Yeo holds, a second mind is *selected material* (from books, a library, articles, etc.) that you capture through creating notes which then are installed in your Antinet. This entity works in tandem with your internal biological memory to create an internal dialogue, and what results serves as your second mind.[33]

You don't want your Antinet to embody characteristics of just any library. Rather, you want it to be a *personal* library. As one scholar observes, one of

30 Alberto Cevolini, ed., Forgetting Machines: Knowledge Management Evolution in Early Modern Europe, Library of the Written Word, volume 53 (Leiden ; Boston: Brill, 2016), 4.

31 Helmut Zedelmaier, Christoph Just Udenius and the German Ars Excerpendi around 1700: On the Flourishing and Disappearance of a Pedagogical Genre (Brill, 2016), 84.

32 Alberto Cevolini, Storing Expansions: Openness and Closure in Secondary Memories (Brill, 2016), 186.

33 Richard Yeo, *Notebooks, Recollection, and External Memory: Some Early Modern English Ideas and Practices* (Brill, 2016), 130.

the most impressive aspects of the process in building an Antinet is that it builds *a universal personal library out of a universal library*.[34] "Such re-arising of the world (of learning) inside the world (of learning)," Alberto Cevolini writes, "*is possible through selection*, and in turn selection is the crucial operation for begetting *complexity*, that is, an excess of possible combinations, links, or references among meaningful data."[35]

Think of it like this: *reality* is equal to all data in the cosmos. *Science* is the study of reality. Yet science proceeds very slowly and selectively in advancing our understanding of reality. We extract only strands of reality and do our best to provide theories and experiments that clearly explain this slice of reality. Luhmann makes mention of science and reality never being *whole*. They're never equal. Why? Because science proceeds "*selectively*, because this is the only way to bring order and comprehensibility."[36]

In brief, you don't want all the data in the universe in your Antinet. Nor do you want tools that bring you closer to this non-ideal maximum. Digital tools have the tendency to do just that. They have the tendency to create *overselection* (something I'll cover shortly). You simply want to select the most important information from the sources you engage.

As Fiona McPherson writes, "Anything that helps you select the most important information is good."[37] Only you, yourself, can determine what strategy works best for you in selecting material that resonates with you.

In the next chapter I'll teach you some different *extraction methods*, which will make selecting material easier for you. But until then, let's continue our journey through *The Matrix* (that is, *selection*).

---

34 Alberto Cevolini, ed., Forgetting Machines: Knowledge Management Evolution in Early Modern Europe, Library of the Written Word, volume 53 (Leiden ; Boston: Brill, 2016), 29.

35 Alberto Cevolini, ed., Forgetting Machines: Knowledge Management Evolution in Early Modern Europe, Library of the Written Word, volume 53 (Leiden ; Boston: Brill, 2016), 29.

36 "ZK I: Zettel 28,4,8c—Niklas Luhmann-Archiv," accessed August 14, 2021, https://niklas-luhmann-archiv.de/bestand/zettelkasten/zettel/ZK_1_NB_28-4-8c_V.

37 Fiona McPherson, Effective Note-taking, revised edition (Wellington: Wayz Press, 2018), 13.

SELECTION UNDERLIES COMMUNICATION

Communication was a critically important area in Luhmann's research; likewise, for the Antinet, it also stands as a critical component. We'll detail the concept of communication later in this book. However, for now, it's interesting to note one peculiar thing involving Luhmann's concept of communication: it's founded on *selection*.

According to Luhmann, communication is an *emergent* reality that emanates from three different *selections*: (1) selection of information, (2) selection of the message of this function, and (3) selective understanding (or misunderstanding) of the message and its interpretation.[38]

The concept of *selection* is critically important pragmatically, as well as theoretically, for the Antinet. For this reason, we shall spend time on both the theoretical and practical matters of selection.

KNOWLEDGE SELECTION AS NATURAL SELECTION

In natural selection, the environment essentially *selects* organisms that have qualities that are best adapted for it to survive and reproduce. The process of selecting information and turning into knowledge is not much different.[39]

The first step in *knowledge selection* is actually *information selection*. Knowledge is created from information. As found in nature, reproduction (generally) involves an individual selecting a mate with corresponding genetic information. With an Antinet, you select information from *sources* that you read. The *sources* are analogous to a mating partner.

Selected information is then processed into knowledge by reformulating or reflecting on the information, to which you add your own experiences and understanding, anchored by your own unique perspectives (and the context in which you've experienced life). When you create a reformulation note or reflection note, you essentially create a new entity altogether:

---

38 Niklas Luhmann, Niklas Luhmann Short Cuts (English Translation), 2002, 28.

39 Cf. Steven Pinker, How the Mind Works, Norton pbk (New York: Norton, 2009), 169ff.

you create knowledge. In evolutionary terms, you give birth to a child—a new, living organism (after exchanging information in the form of genetic code). In knowledge-science terms, you give birth to a book or other creative work (after exchanging information in the form of reading other authors' works).

Your (intellectual) environment is populated by your audience of readers. If the knowledge you create (your book) resonates with your audience exceptionally well, it will be selected. It will be selected apart from other competing books, to rise in popularity and essentially reproduce.

For your work to survive, it doesn't necessarily need to be the best ever. It doesn't necessarily need to be the most *optimal* piece of work. Rather it must be sufficiently better than the other pieces of work competing for your reader's attention. In turn, your work will rise in popularity and reproduce itself.

This highlights some important points:

1. The success of the knowledge you produce is very much a function of: (a) the source material you select. This means the books, articles, podcasts, lectures, videos, or other media you select; (b) what genes (or ideas) that you select from your mate (or book); and (c) how you then process that information and its genes to produce a new creation (a baby, or a book); and (d) how you then organize that creation (by deciding where to file it, or how to raise it).

2. The output of this process that is best adapted to its audience of readers (that is, its environment), will survive and reproduce more successfully than less adapted output.

THE LEVELS OF SELECTION

The Antinet can be thought of as a system containing *relations of relations of relations*. Encompassed in this model are three levels of selection: (1) selecting what source to engage with (choosing what books to read), and (2) selecting what material to extract, and (3) selecting where in the Antinet to install and link to the selection(s).

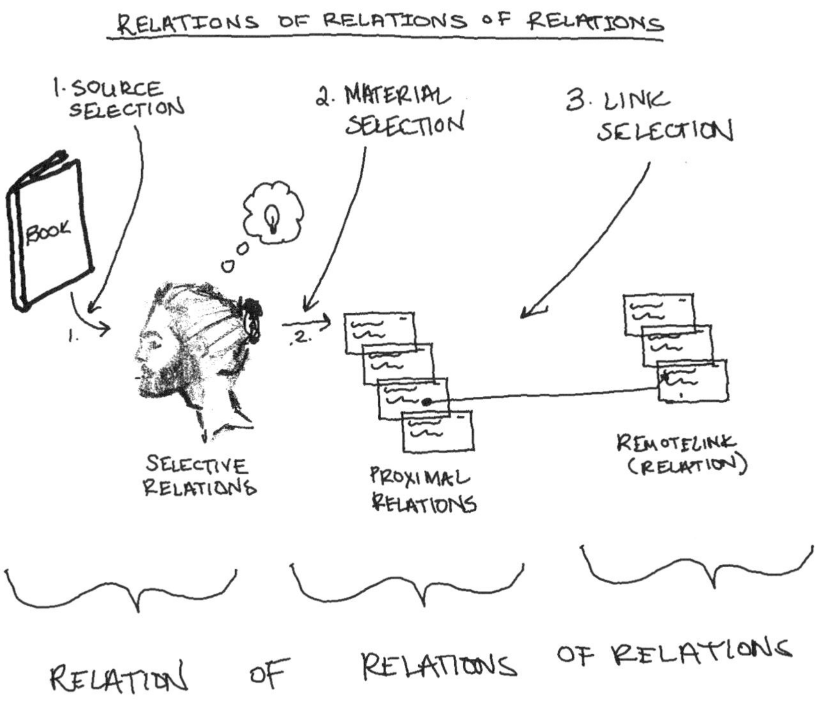

Let's explore each of these levels of selection now.

SOURCE SELECTION

Before embarking upon the process of determining which material to select from the books you read, there is an even more critical challenge: selecting which books are even worth reading in the first place!

As the Catholic intellectual, Antonin Sertillanges writes, the process of selection is prepended with an important stage: "to choose books and to choose *in* books."[40]

40 OP A. G. Sertillanges, The Intellectual Life: Its Spirit, Conditions, Methods, trans. Mary Ryan, Reprint edition (Washington, D.C.: The Catholic University of America Press, 1992), 150. Emphasis added.

Here are some guidelines for selecting which books to read in the first place. These guidelines are not set-in-stone rules. Nor are they comprehensive; yet, I think they're helpful enough to keep in mind as a guideline for selecting books.

Guideline #1: Do Not Trust Bestsellers with Catchy Titles

> *"Do not trust interest[ing] advertising and catchy titles."*
> –Antonin Sertillanges[41]

Even non-sponsored books on Amazon are suspect these days. Major publishers with *big idea* hardbound books produce some of the biggest horse-shit out there. Ghost writers are behind more books than you'll ever know. Big publishing houses thrive on publishing crap. I've been behind the scenes during this process and witnessed how it plays out. The New York Times Best Sellers list is really a list of synthetically engineered crap.

Guideline #2: Do Not Trust Popular Channels That Books are Advertised Through

If you heard about a book because the author was featured on a popular podcast, be suspicious. Such authors are backed by a publishing house. They're backed by a public relations circuit that swaps in their latest figurehead. I know this because (again) I've been behind the scenes and have seen it firsthand. In some cases, there's a lot of pressure for show-hosts to accept guests, regardless of their quality. Why? First, shows need content. Second, the publishing house probably did the show-host "a solid" recently. For instance, a publishing house may have gotten a movie star on their show recently during the star's book tour of their memoir. The show-host may then feel a sense of obligation to return the favor. How do they return the favor? By saying yes to whichever guest the publishing house proposes to feature on their next show (regardless of guest quality). The guest then proceeds to hype-up whatever new (rehashed) book they're launching.

41 OP A. G. Sertillanges, The Intellectual Life: Its Spirit, Conditions, Methods, trans. Mary Ryan, Reprint edition (Washington, D.C.: The Catholic University of America Press, 1992), 150.

Guideline #3: Go to The Original Source

"The majority of writers only edit and publish other writers' thoughts," Sertillanges writes. "Read only those books in which leading ideas are expressed at *first hand*."[42]

When you read this book, you are reading the first-hand account of the Antinet. You are reading of my experiences building an analog knowledge machine—a second mind—using the principles of Niklas Luhmann's Antinet. My primary source *is the* primary source (*Communication with Noteboxes*). Yet I'm not just regurgitating his paper. I'm sharing my knowledge and my first-hand experiences in developing knowledge with such a system. You're reading about my experiences from thousands of hours of using the system. You're learning my nuances and ways of teaching the system. You're reading the primary source of the Antinet.

Many books are secondary sources. They're merely edited curations of the primary source. This includes books like *The Complete Idiots Guides*. Don't read these books. Read a Wikipedia article instead. Do your own research. Soon, you'll spot recurring themes and sources that are regularly cited. These are the original sources, the primary sources. Go to these sources. They're a must.

Of course, secondary sources can be helpful as well. Specifically, they can be helpful in spotting *how* the secondary sources got certain things right and certain things wrong. In addition, the secondary sources may point out the things you missed when reviewing the primary source(s).

Secondary sources are also useful in helping you compile a repository of frequently cited works or authors.

In my readings, there are certain thinkers who are mentioned over and over and over. These people include Immanuel Kant, Voltaire, René Descartes, John Locke, Francis Bacon, Gottfried Wilhelm von Leibniz, and more.

---

42 OP A. G. Sertillanges, The Intellectual Life: Its Spirit, Conditions, Methods, trans. Mary Ryan, Reprint edition (Washington, D.C.: The Catholic University of America Press, 1992), 150. Emphasis added.

The main take-away from this guideline is this: primary sources are a requirement, secondary sources are not.

LINK SELECTION

Another level of selection within the Antinet is selecting *where* to connect the idea (i.e., where to install the card within the Antinet).

Selective Relations

> *"The communication with the second mind becomes fruitful only at a high level of generalization, namely that of establishing communicative* relations of relations."
>
> –Niklas Luhmann[43]

It's not the *relations* between notes that make the Antinet a powerful system; rather it's the *selective relations* that do so.

Johannes Schmidt specifically calls attention to the importance of selective relations near the end of his paper, where he points out that the specific readings and the material one selects from the readings are important to the Antinet. However, what is also critical is found in Luhmann's case with "(selective) relations established between his notes by means of his referencing technique."[44] That is, you must also be selective in linking your selections to certain cards and ideas.

Note how Schmidt encloses the word *selective* in parentheses in the passage. He did this to call out the implicit truth that Luhmann's links were *selective* in nature. When Luhmann used the phrase *communicative relations of relations,* there was no need for him to specify that he meant *selective* relations.

43 Niklas Luhmann, "Communication with Noteboxes (Revised Edition)," trans. Manfred Kuehn, https://daily.scottscheper.com/zettelkasten/. Emphasis added.

44 Johannes Schmidt, "Niklas Luhmann's Card Index: Thinking Tool, Communication Partner, Publication Machine," Forgetting Machines. Knowledge Management Evolution in Early Modern Europe 53 (2016), 309.

For Luhmann, relations (or links) between notes were, by nature, selective. They were not trivial to create. They could not be bulk-applied to digital files using templates, regular expressions (regex), and tags. Links were hard-coded into one's Antinet, and as previously indicated, they were neuroimprinted onto one's mind. This network of highly selective links is a result of the analog nature of the system, the benefit of which we touched on in the analog chapter of this book.

In other words, the magic of the Antinet doesn't revolve around *links*. Rather it involves being very *selective* in what you link cards to. Whenever you install a card in the Antinet, you link by (1) chaining or connecting the card behind another card, and (2) using remotelinks. Due to the analog nature of the Antinet, you are forced to be very selective about what you link to, and to think hard about where a card ought to go, before installing it. With digital notetaking apps, it's simple. You simply start typing in words for tags or wikilinks. The tool then begins auto-populating terms you can link to. Before you know it, you have numerous things you're linking to which you otherwise wouldn't have. With the Antinet, you're usually choosing one, or *maybe* two cards to link to. This creates *selective relations* instead of an overabundance of *hyper relations*. This element serves as a critical factor in transitioning your Antinet into a *second mind*, as well as allowing for *structured accidents*, which I'll detail later in the book.

A LINK IS NOT A LINK (IF IT'S A HYPERLINK)

A notecard link is hard. It's hard-earned. It's deliberate. It's selective. It's a hard link. This is part of what inspired the term I use for linking cards. They're *cardlinks* (because it rhymes with *hard links*).

Cardlinks are not the equivalent of hyperlinks. Hyperlinks are *not* selective. The Antinet is based around being selective. Antinet users are selective about (1) the books they read, (2) the material they extract from those books, and (3) the selective links they create within the Antinet.

Cardlinks are of superior impact compared to wikilinks and hyperlinks. Digital links are whittled down by synthetic features like auto-complete, regex, or retroactive search. Cardlinks are superior to digital links not only because they are not diluted by bloatware. In addition, the power of cardlinks are unleashed when you begin taking advantage of the tree structure of the Antinet. When you follow a cardlink in the Antinet, you're taken down a journey of stems, leaves and other branches of thought that are also linked together.

This results in structured accidents and surprises (like walking down the row of a section in the library that interests you). This accidental discovery happens in a way that is almost incommunicable. Why? Because you follow the path that is made possible thanks to the Antinet's tree structure.

This is a glimpse into the magic of the Antinet as a *thinking tool* and a *second mind*. The magic does not stem from just one thing alone, and it doesn't come about through creating trivial easy links (aka, wikilinks). It's a combination of the four principles of the Antinet that creates its magic:

The "special filing technique," refers to the tree structure which unlocks *infinite internal branching*. The "(selective) relations" between notes (made possible through numeric-alpha addresses).[45] These, combined with the index which neuroimprints keyterms on the mind. These are tied together with the analog component of the Antinet, which forces higher quality *selections*. All of these combined creates the emergent magic of the Antinet.

As Johannes Schmidt points out, this structure *demonstrates how quickly* the Antinet sets users on a path away from what one would normally deem *ordered* and *taxonomically sound*. Although the Antinet's inner logic might appear nonsensical to an outsider, to the creator—that is, to you, the person creating the system—the Antinet is perfectly natural and understandable.[46]

Through exploration of your Antinet, you are *led away* from the original topic and to a variety of other subjects—ones that you would not have ini-

45 **Johannes Schmidt, "Niklas Luhmann's Card Index: Thinking Tool, Communication Partner, Publication Machine," Forgetting Machines. Knowledge Management Evolution in Early Modern Europe 53 (2016), 309.**

46 **Johannes Schmidt, "Niklas Luhmann's Card Index: Thinking Tool, Communication Partner, Publication Machine," Forgetting Machines. Knowledge Management Evolution in Early Modern Europe 53 (2016), 309.**

tially associated with one another. This, in turn, results in unconventional interactions, surprises, and breakthrough insights that otherwise would not have occurred.

This entire process is made possible thanks to linking not being *too easy*. It's thanks to the nature of hard links. It's thanks to the nature of *cardlinks*.

DIGITAL CREATES OVERSELECTION

As I've previously illustrated, it's not just about what material to select. It's also about what material *not* to select.

For this reason, tools that help you *not* select as much information (due to the considerable time and effort required in extracting them), end up increasing your focus. It increases one's proficiency in selecting valuable and irresistible material.

With digital tools, selection is trivial. It's all-too-easy to capture, copy, paste, write, and accumulate an abundance of digital information. This is a downside, not a strength. This is yet another reason why analog outperforms digital. Digital collection results in over-saturation, both in terms of material and the information the material includes.

MATERIAL SELECTION

Thus far we've talked about *source selection* (i.e., what books to select for reading). We also discussed *link selection* (where in your Antinet to install ideas). The last level of selection concerns what material *within a book* one should select.

The Four Quadrants of Ideas

I think it's helpful to think of ideas falling into four quadrants. This concept is inspired by a model introduced to me by Stephen Covey.

Covey proposes four quadrants for managing time by looking at the intersection of four variables: *important, not important, urgent,* and *not urgent.*[47]

47 Stephen R. Covey, The 7 Habits of Highly Effective People: 30th Anniversary Edition, 4th

With regards to selecting material from the books you read, I propose this model helps tremendously. One is left with selecting *Bad Ideas, Good Ideas, Excellent Ideas,* and *Irresistible Ideas.*

Here's a diagram of the model:

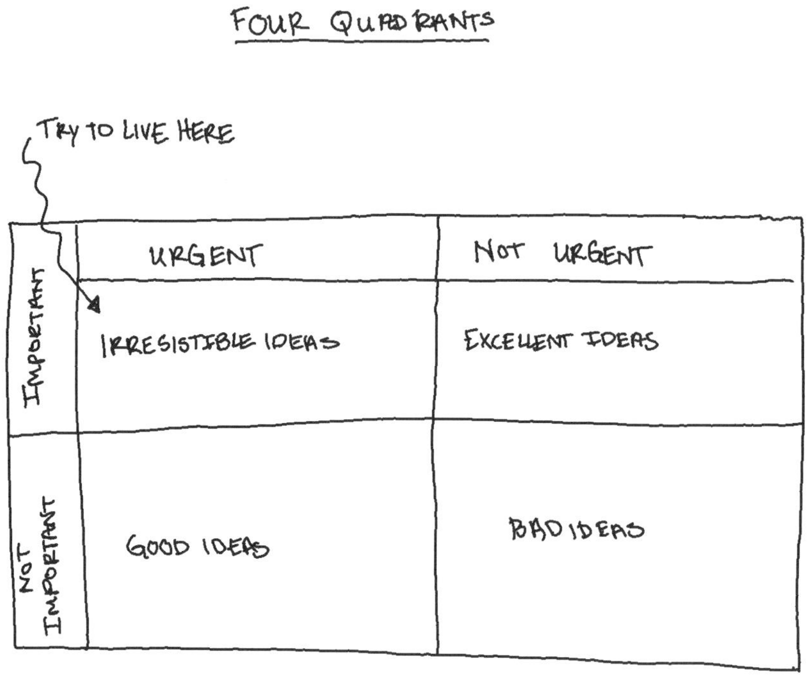

Let's go through each of these now.

BAD IDEAS

Don't select bad ideas or pay attention to them. It's pretty simple. If the idea is irrelevant to what you're working on *and* if the idea isn't even that important, then don't think twice about it. Even if you're unsure, err on the side of the idea being a waste of time. We need to move fast. Time is short. Have the confidence that truly valuable ideas will take hold of you later on.

---

edition (New York: Simon & Schuster, 2020).

GOOD IDEAS

These are ideas that could very well be timely and applicable to what you're working on, yet they don't add much value. If the idea doesn't add much value to your project, or if the information is redundant, then forego selecting them for your project.

For instance, I could bog myself down for a year reading scholarly literature on the history of notetaking systems. I could fill your mind with mountains of seemingly relevant details pertaining to early notebox systems. I could tell you about how there's a debate as to whether the *Josephinian catalog* of the late 1700s was the first card catalog in library history or if Konrad Gessner's of the 1500s actually was.[48]

But in reality, that information isn't *that* important. The matter at hand is this: (1) you want to know *why* the Antinet is the best knowledge development system out there; (2) you want to know the theory behind why it's better than digital; (3) you want to know *how* you can build an Antinet; and (4) you want to know what positive effects you can expect by committing to the Antinet (surprise, creative insights, breakthroughs, etc.). You *do not* need to know every single detail about the history of notetaking. That's for a different book.

In brief, don't feel the need to select material that is related to what you're doing, but is *not that* important. Avoid selecting good ideas. It's OK to note them in your mind and find them interesting and amusing, but that's all they deserve. A grunt of amusement.

EXCELLENT IDEAS

Deciding whether to select or ignore excellent ideas is tricky. These ideas are important, yet they are not relevant to the project or goal you're working on.

48 Markus Krajewski, Paper Machines: About Cards & Catalogs, 1548-1929, trans. Peter Krapp, History and Foundations of Information Science (Cambridge, MA, USA: MIT Press, 2011), 38-9.

I realize it may be difficult, but you want to err on the side of skipping these ideas. Granted, there's a spectrum to the degree of *importance*. If the idea ranks at least 96 out of 100 on the *importance spectrum*, it's OK to select the idea.[49] However, you should only *extract* the idea onto your bibcard (which you'll learn more about soon). You do not want to spend time *processing* these ideas by converting them into maincards (by way of *excerpt, reformulation,* or *reflection* notes). You'll want to create an ExRef for excellent ideas, but that's all.

IRRESISTIBLE IDEAS

You want to spend almost all of your time living for the *irresistible ideas*. These are ideas that are both timely *and* important. Think of these as ideas that truly resonate with you. When you encounter one of these ideas, you simply *just know*. These ideas can be something that *you (and only you)* can see. These ideas are influenced by your own perspectives and unique experiences in life (both good and bad). These ideas collide with truths you've been contemplating that are reverberating in your mind. These are usually things that only you can see and connect.

Time is scarce. This is why you shouldn't care to bother with any of the other quadrants. You want to reserve as much time as possible to select and develop irresistible ideas.

Do not feel obligated to write down excellent ideas. A good chunk of them will be relegated to good ideas in a month. *The ideas you want to write down are the irresistible ideas.*

Make Ideas Prove Themselves

Oftentimes, I'll make an idea *prove* itself. I'll make it prove that it's irresistible. For instance, I'll read something I feel is irresistible on page 100. But I won't

---

49 **I like to view life through a unique value scale. I find using a pre-defined set of values simplifies the complexity of life. I don't believe in something being a 100% yes, or a 0% no. I find that to be too dogmatic. We don't know what we don't know, even when we're certain we do know. Therefore, I like to use the following scale to value things. 4%, 20%, 50%, 80%, 96%. This scale is inspired by the Pareto principle (the 80-20 rule). Yet it also applies a fractal of that principle. We get 4% from 20% of 20%. We get 96% from 20% more than 80%.**

decide immediately whether to select it. I won't extract it immediately onto a bibcard. I'll simply say to myself, *Hmm! That's really interesting!* I note it in my mind and let it ruminate for some time. And then I continue reading. By the time I get to page 150—even if it's several days later—if I still find the idea irresistible, I'll extract it by writing it down on my bibcard.

What Should and Shouldn't You Select?

One author, who, to a large degree, regurgitates Sönke Ahrens's material, puts forth a good question that Ahrens never answers clearly. The question is, *What should, and shouldn't, be noted down?*

Ahrens is rather vague in answering this question, but he at least advises the reader what *not* to do. This other author advises: don't write down anything you already know by heart. Yet, he qualifies this maxim by saying it's OK to write down something you already know—if, that is—you intend to connect it to related thoughts.[50] Such advice is problematic, however, because *everything* is related to something in the cosmos. Even *nothing* can be related by describing it. How does one describe nothing? By stating it's *not nothing*, and linking it to *not nothing* in your Antinet. Everything can be connected to related thoughts by way of inversion.

In brief the advice that you shouldn't write down anything you know by heart—unless you wish to relate it to something else—is rather vague. I also believe it's too simplistic.

The question remains, *What types of things should you write down?*

A better way of asking this is, *What types of material should you select while reading?* Here's why this is an improved question: the material you *select* doesn't necessitate that you'll *extract* that knowledge. You're *selecting* material to determine if it's appropriate to actually extract.

So back to the question, *What types of material should you select while reading?*

---

50 David Kadavy, Digital Zettelkasten: Principles, Methods, & Examples (Kadavy, Inc., 2022), 30.

Here's my take:

1. Adhere to the rule of selecting only irresistible things from your readings. Irresistible things are those things that only you can determine. Irresistible encompasses those things you find to be *genius*, or that you find you simply just *resonate* with in a way that's difficult to explain in words. It must be true. Only you can determine if something is *truly* irresistible.

2. Select irresistible *patterns* that you've noticed from reading across different disciplines. Also select patterns you've noticed from your unique life experiences.

3. Select irresistible ideas that are brand new to you. Granted, if you're reading in a new field, many of the ideas you encounter will be brand new. That's fine. Write them down, especially if they resonate with you.

4. Select hard or challenging ideas that you find irresistible. Say you encounter an idea that you find irresistible. Say it resonates with you. Yet, say you find it hard or challenging to decipher. Select that material with the expectation that you'll be creating an *excerpt* note of it, or a *reformulation* note of it in order to better understand it.

5. Select as if you'll be *teaching* the material. Even if you're in a state of mind where you're focused on *growing* your knowledge, adopt the mindset of a teacher. Operate as if you're selecting the material in order to teach the material. This is the *contribution* state of mind. The great paradox is that if you adopt the mindset of *contribution*, you'll experience more *growth*. When you select material as if you'll be teaching it, you'll focus on extracting the truly helpful and insightful pieces of knowledge.

6. Select material that deeply affects you. There may be certain passages or compositions of prose that move you. Remember that emotions can actually be felt in the body (so pay attention to your responses to the material you read). Fundamentally, emotions can be rolled up into five categories.[51]

---

51 **Jim Dethmer, Diana Chapman, and Kaley Klemp, The 15 Commitments of Conscious**

The five emotions are: anger, sadness, fear, joy, and creative feelings. Material which generates deep experiences involving these emotions ought to be selected.

Now that you know what to select, let's address the material you should definitely *not* select while reading.

This question is simpler. There are two types of material you should not select:

1. Do not select information that is not irresistible. Do not select material that is *bad, good,* or even *excellent.* If it's not irresistible, don't waste your time. You'll have barely enough time to elaborate on and develop irresistible material. Why waste your life energy trying to develop less than irresistible material? The correct answer is: you shouldn't!

2. Do not write something down that you've already written down. In the *knowledge creation* phase I'll introduce a process that helps ensure you don't waste your time developing content you've already written down by hand. In brief, it involves reviewing your Antinet *before* you commit to creating a new note. The directive of not writing down something you've already written down applies mainly to *excerpt* notes. Say you come across Robert Frost's famous poem, *The Road Not Taken* ("Two roads diverged in a yellow wood…"). If you find that poem irresistible, yet you've already written it down, then don't write it down again! Don't select the material again. If you make a mistake and forget that you've already written it down—and if you end up creating an excerpt note for it—make sure you install the note in your Antinet anyway. That way, you'll have a record of your mistake. Remember: don't erase mistakes! Don't delete material in your Antinet.

Now that we have a good grasp of what material to select while reading a book, let's talk about one final concept before moving on: the concept of *priming.*

Leadership: A New Paradigm for Sustainable Success (United States: Conscious Leadership Group, 2015), 84ff.

Priming

The process you must complete before reading even the first page of any book is called the *priming phase*.[52]

The priming phase entails reading related material, relevant background material, even dissecting the book's table of contents, and other techniques (for instance, designing a quiz about the book for yourself).

According to one cognitive psychologist, priming "really does help, especially when the subject matter is difficult or unfamiliar."[53]

I have a specific process that I encourage you to do before reading any book. It works best with a certain knowledge extraction strategy called the *Luhmannian bibcard method*. I'll detail that method in the next section. For this, however, all you'll need is a 4 x 6 inch blank white notecard.

On the front-side of the bibcard you will write three items: (1) the *bibliographic details* of the source, (2) your *goal* in engaging the source, and (3) an *overview* of the source if available (i.e., a *brief* overview of its table of contents).

This becomes your bookmark as you read the book.

Here's a picture of one of my bibcards. The front can be thought of as the *priming* area:

52 Fiona McPherson, Effective Note-taking, revised edition (Wellington: Wayz Press, 2018), 2.
53 Fiona McPherson, Effective Note-taking, revised edition (Wellington: Wayz Press, 2018), 2.

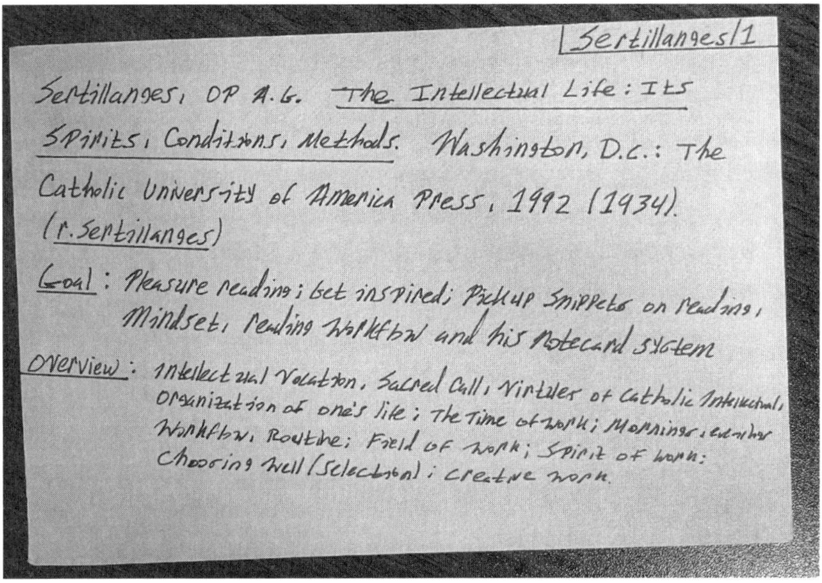
Sertillanges/1

Sertillanges, OP A.G. The Intellectual Life: Its Spirits, Conditions, Methods. Washington, D.C.: The Catholic University of America Press, 1992 (1934).
(r.Sertillanges)

Goal: Pleasure reading; get inspired; Pickup snippets on reading, mindset, reading workflow and his notecard system

Overview: Intellectual Vocation, Sacred Call, Virtues of Catholic Intellectual, Organization of one's life; The Time of work; Mornings, evening workflow, Routine; Field of work; Spirit of work; Choosing well (Selection); Creative work.

CREATING AN OVERVIEW

Note that the overview section isn't a word-for-word copy of the table of contents. It's brief. It forces you to take the deliberate time to read the table of contents and get a general idea of what you're about to read.

This practice was inspired by Mortimer Adler's classic book titled *How to Read a Book*. In this book he introduces the practice he calls X-raying a book. He uses this analogy to illustrate that one ought to get a sense of a book's skeleton—its structure—before reading it.

This practice is also supported by a cognitive scientist who specializes in notetaking. She advises that one ought to analyze a book's table of contents as an important first step before reading any book.[54]

SETTING A GOAL

Being intentional with your reading is a game-changer, plain and simple. Luhmann always had an intentional goal with his readings. He used short-term projects (research papers) that enabled him to immediately apply many

---

54 Fiona McPherson, Effective Note-taking, revised edition (Wellington: Wayz Press, 2018), 3.

of his ideas, and if those ideas weren't immediately useful, to place ExRefs in their appropriate place to ruminate on and be used when the time came.

Luhmann published 550 research papers during his academic career. Two hundred more papers were found among his belongings after he passed away. This comes out to 750 papers. Let's not even take into consideration the seventy books he also published during this period. If we just look at the papers, he was working on roughly two papers per month. Luhmann, ultimately, was always reading with a specific project in mind.

As Antonin Sertillanges advises, your reading should be influenced by a definite idea—a clear goal and purpose. "Let it take account not only of your vocation and your personality, but of their immediate application."[55]

In other words, read specifically with an eye for *immediately applying* the knowledge you encounter.

For the knowledge you encounter that is irresistible yet not immediately applicable, simply create an ExRef for the material in your Antinet. In brief, your time creating main notes—specifically *reflection notes*—should be for material that is immediately applicable.

CONCLUSION

We covered a lot of important material in this section. We outlined the importance of taking *selection* seriously. That is, the importance of selecting books carefully, selecting the material in them carefully, and selecting *where* to install those ideas within the Antinet carefully.

Selection is a vague and fuzzy area of knowledge development. If things are still a bit unclear, rest assured that your selection skills will improve with practice. Thankfully, analog knowledge development helps in this regard.

---

55 OP A. G. Sertillanges, The Intellectual Life: Its Spirit, Conditions, Methods, trans. Mary Ryan, Reprint edition (Washington, D.C.: The Catholic University of America Press, 1992), 191.

You'll quickly learn that you're selecting *way too much* material when it takes you seemingly forever to get through a book!

If you only take one thing from this chapter, let it be this: *select only the most irresistibly important books, and the most irresistibly important ideas within those books, which are immediately applicable to your project or goal.*

Now that you know about selection, it's time to embark upon the next phase of knowledge development: *Extraction.*

CHAPTER FOURTEEN

EXTRACTION

THE *EXTRACTION* PHASE OF KNOWLEDGE development concerns itself with the actual *action* of pulling out material from the sources with which you engage. *Selection* entails the internal experience of taking notice of certain thoughts or ideas, after which you face a yes-or-no question. Are you going to extract the material by writing it down?

If you determine that yes, you're going to convert the material into a note, you then proceed into the extraction phase. The extraction phase is a process that exists *before* you actually create the main note. But in this phase you actually take deliberate action by *marking* the material to be extracted. Within this phase, there are several methods you can use to *extract* material. Before we dive into the explicit methods, let's first survey the different types of strategies involved in reading a book (or engaging with a knowledge source).

INTENTIONAL VS. EXPLORATORY STRATEGIES

Some books may require a more *intentional* extraction strategy and others a more *exploratory* strategy.

As Antonin Sertillanges advises, "One will have recourse to other books for *information*, not for *formation*."[1] In other words, when you are new to material and you're in the exploratory phase, you're reading for *formation*. Your

---

1 OP A. G. Sertillanges, The Intellectual Life: Its Spirit, Conditions, Methods, trans. Mary Ryan, Reprint edition (Washington, D.C.: The Catholic University of America Press, 1992), 154.

primary extraction strategy should consist of comprehending the material you're reading. Your content should consist of *reformulating* the material in your own words.

Once you have developed the foundation of knowledge in a field, you can begin reading *intentionally*. You can begin looking for information to evolve ideas. You begin looking for information that supports your current theories, which are incubating in your Antinet. You begin reading for the purpose of finding material that yields more granular distinctions relative to your theories. You further elucidate these new thoughts by way of *reflection* notes.

Let's consider both intentional extraction and exploratory extraction in detail.

INTENTIONAL EXTRACTION

An *intentional extraction strategy* should be employed when you're already familiar with the material you're reading. If you're pressed for time, or if you are working with a singular project in mind, you'll also want an intentional extraction strategy.

When reading intentionally, you'll be reading for material to enrich your project. The important thing here is that you do not get "bogged down," as Luhmann would say.[2] You want to spend less time writing down *excerpt* and *reformulation* notes, and more time writing *reflection* notes.

The two extraction methods best for this are the *2-step marginalia method*, and the *2-step Luhmannian bibcard method*. These enable you to quickly identify material you find irresistible; but, instead of getting bogged down, and developing them right then and there, you delay the processing. After you're done reading, you can determine how to efficiently process the material. This gives you more time to elaborate on the most important irresistible ideas.

2 "ZK II: Sheet 9/8d—Niklas Luhmann Archive," accessed March 4, 2022, https://niklas-luhmann-archiv.de/bestand/zettelkasten/zettel/ZK_2_NB_9-8d_V.

In the next section, we'll cover the specific extraction methods just outlined in more detail. Before that, however, let's quickly cover the concept of exploratory extraction.

EXPLORATORY EXTRACTION

An *exploratory extraction strategy* should be employed for books that are more difficult to parse. Much of the time this applies to books in fields that are new to you. As Mortimer Adler writes,

> If you are reading in order to become a better reader, you cannot read just any book or article. You will not improve as a reader if all you read are books that are well within your capacity. You must tackle books that are beyond you, or, as we have said, books that are over your head. Only books of that sort will make you stretch your mind. And unless you stretch, you will not learn.[3]

Let's take an example from my own experience. Sometime back I was reading a book called *Book of Proof*. It's an introduction to the world of mathematical proofs (think a bunch of Greek symbols, equations, and numbers. This field was completely new to me. I was attracted to it because of the challenge. In order to understand the text, I had to take diligent notes. Taking notes in margins wasn't effective, as there was not enough space. Taking bullet point notes on a bibcard wasn't the best option either. On average, each of the notes would take up an entire card anyway. It didn't make sense to constrain myself, or have them run across several bibcards.

The method I employed for this book was the *1-step book-to-maincard method*. This method entails stopping while reading, pulling out a notecard and writing down the note immediately (I prefer 3 x 5 inch because the constraints breed focus). The notes you write in this method are either *excerpts* or *reformulations*. The purpose of writing these notes is to better understand the new material. If you proceed through challenging books

3 **Mortimer Jerome Adler and Charles Van Doren, How to Read a Book, Rev. and updated ed (New York: Simon and Schuster, 1972), 330.**

without first understanding the elementary material that came first, you're in for a difficult ride. You need to understand the elementary, fundamental concepts before you understand the more complex concepts.

The book-to-maincard method enables you to proceed through difficult texts, though the downside, of course, is getting bogged down. It's counter-intuitive, but reading using an exploratory 1-step strategy ends up taking more time than 2-step intentional strategies.

Let's cover the extraction methods in detail now.

KNOWLEDGE EXTRACTION METHODS

With notetaking and reading, the method you use to extract knowledge is of paramount importance.

Certain extraction methods work for reading new books with unfamiliar ideas, whereas they fail for other types of books. For this reason you must "understand why and how and when" to use different extraction methods.[4]

When choosing an extraction method, it's important that you not simply choose the one you're "most comfortable with."[5] That is, don't merely choose a strategy that is most compatible with how you're feeling that day. Oftentimes, the best strategy is not the one you're initially comfortable with. Research supports this, as well. [6]

You also should not feel obligated to be married to an extraction method forever. You must have, at your disposal, several extraction methods to choose from. As cognitive scientist Fiona McPherson observes, there's "no one 'best' strategy for taking notes."[7]

---

4 Fiona McPherson, Effective Note-taking, revised edition (Wellington: Wayz Press, 2018), 2.

5 Fiona McPherson, Effective Note-taking, revised edition (Wellington: Wayz Press, 2018), 7.

6 Fiona McPherson, Effective Note-taking, revised edition (Wellington: Wayz Press, 2018), 7.

7 Fiona McPherson, Effective Note-taking, revised edition (Wellington: Wayz Press, 2018), 7.

In my own case, I employ the *2-step Luhmannian bibcard method* the majority of the time (think 96%). However, for books in fields that are completely new to me, or ones that are challenging, I sometimes use the *1-step book-to-maincard method.*

THE 1-STEP BOOK-TO-MAINCARD METHOD

The book-to-maincard method is quite simple. There's a good chance you already do this. You simply read a book with pen and notecards at hand. When you come across a key concept or passage, you stop reading and make a note for it on a dedicated card. Typically the note is either an *excerpt* (i.e., a word-for-word copy of the quote), or a *reformulation* of the concept in your own words. It can also be a *reflection* note; however I find this kind of note to be briefer than the reflection notes I create using the Luhmannian bibcard method. Why? Because you don't have enough time to let the idea ruminate on a staging card (i.e., a bibcard). When writing *reflection* notes using the book-to-maincard method, they seem to embody briefer (and less deep) ideas. I like to think of these as *observations* (which are similar to the concept of *bibnotes,* which you'll learn soon).

Book-to-Maincard Notes in Practice

I like to place my book-to-maincard notes on 3 x 5 inch cards. This prevents me from getting bogged down. Typically my book-to-maincard notes are *excerpts.* Limiting myself to the 3 x 5 inch space prevents me from excerpting quotes or ideas that are too large. In addition, when using 4 x 6 inch cards I frequently experience an unsettling urge to fill up the entire card. If I use only a few lines, it feels much more like I'm wasting paper. Using 3 x 5 inch cards helps me avoid this feeling, and in turn, it helps me avoid getting bogged down in a book by stopping every few pages to write out long excerpts.

On the next page is a picture of a book-to-maincard note I took.

THE 2-STEP MARGINALIA METHOD

Marginalia refers to making notations or other marks in the margins of the books you read. This is something Niklas Luhmann never did.

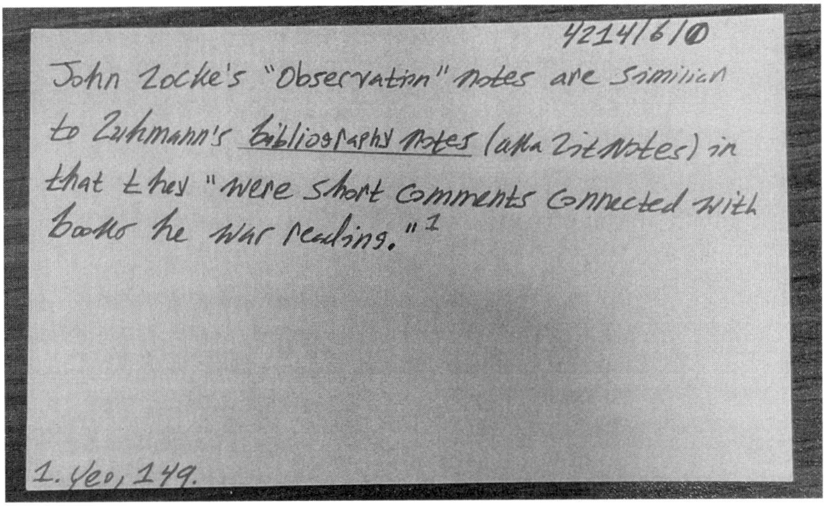
4214/6/10
John Locke's "Observation" notes are similar to Luhmann's bibliography notes (aka LitNotes) in that they "were short comments connected with books he was reading." 1
1. Yeo, 149.

One could argue that the reason Luhmann never wrote in books was because he actually mostly read in libraries.[8] Yet Luhmann did indeed own many books. Among his possessions were 5,000 books, 1,400 journal issues, 300 special journal issues, 1,600 offprints, and other material. Johannes Schmidt observed that they hardly showed any underlining or margin notes. He states, "Luhmann almost always made notes on slips of paper while reading."[9]

Regardless, marginalia remains a popular practice. It's a practice adhered to by many readers and writers, including Cal Newport, Charlie Munger, David McCullough, Ryan Holiday, and countless others.[10]

8 Undisciplined, Archiving Luhmann w/ Johannes Schmidt, 2021, https://www.youtube.com/watch?v=kz2K3auPLWU, 25:40; "Niklas Luhmann-Archiv," accessed April 11, 2022, https://niklas-luhmann-archiv.de/nachlass/uebersicht.

9 "Niklas Luhmann-Archiv," accessed April 11, 2022, https://niklas-luhmann-archiv.de/nachlass/uebersicht.

10 "How I Read When Researching a Book - Study Hacks—Cal Newport," accessed April 11, 2022,https://www.calnewport.com/blog/2017/08/14/how-i-read-when-researching-a-book/; "David McCullough on Reading," accessed April 11, 2022, http://northmainbooknotes.blogspot.com/2017/05/david-mccullough-on-reading.html; Ryan Holiday, "The Notecard System: The Key For Remembering, Organizing And Using Everything You Read," RyanHoliday.Net (blog), April 1, 2014, https://

I've employed the marginalia practice, as well. However, I do not think you should follow this practice.

Here's why: Because marginalia suck.

Yes, marginalia suck. They suck compared to the Luhmannian bibcard practice I'll teach you next.

That said, I foresee many of you not believing me. You may have some sacred scheme or practice such as making notes and dog-earing pages.

I've decided to at least outline the marginalia schemes available. That way you can observe the practices I've found to be inferior so that you can potentially skip having to learn the hard way yourself.

The CVP Marginalia Scheme

During the short period of time I employed a marginalia method, I used a scheme I found quite convenient. Upon coming across a passage I found irresistible, I would place either a C, V, or a P next to it. The C meant *Concept*. The V meant *vocab*. The P meant *prose*.

Whenever I read something with an irresistible *concept, vocab* word, or great *prose*, I would note down either C, V, or P in the margin.

In the beginning this was nice. However, I encountered problems with this method. The barrier to selecting material became too low. It was too easy to *select* any and every thought. It resulted in my selecting way too much material for extraction. This created an over-abundance of homework.

When reading the book *Cataloging the World*, I employed this method. As a result, the material I've selected from this book remains underdeveloped. I have indeed used material from it; however I've had to spend more time developing the material. Additionally, because I never took the time to

---

ryanholiday.net/the-notecard-system-the-key-for-remembering-organizing-and-using-everything-you-read/.

deliberately process the material by writing it down by hand, I find myself relating it to other parts of the book less frequently.

Here you can see a picture of one section of the book. Note how I placed way too many C's in the margin.

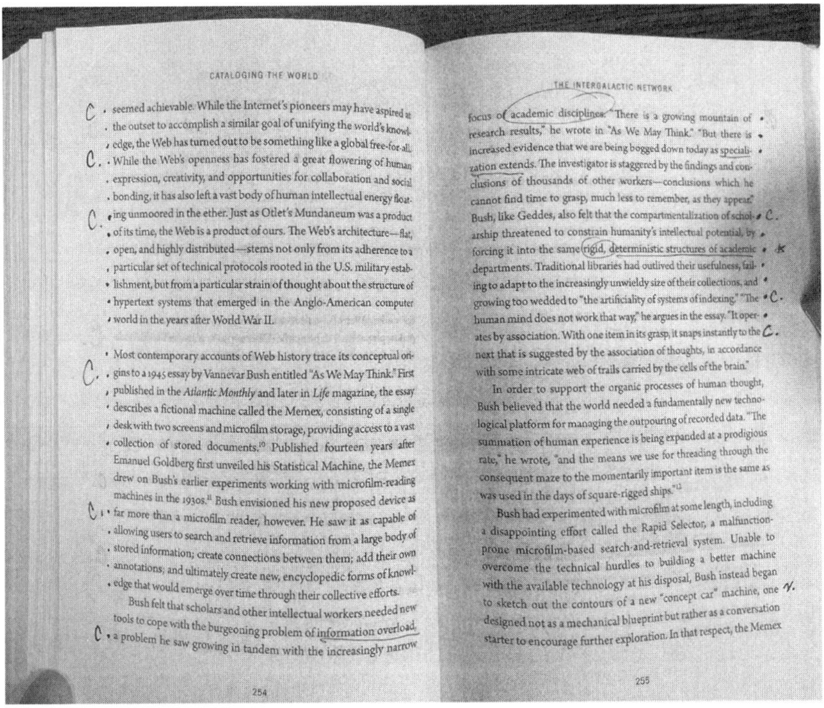
CATALOGING THE WORLD

seemed achievable. While the Internet's pioneers may have aspired at the outset to accomplish a similar goal of unifying the world's knowledge, the Web has turned out to be something like a global free-for-all. While the Web's openness has fostered a great flowering of human expression, creativity, and opportunities for collaboration and social bonding, it has also left a vast body of human intellectual energy floating unmoored in the ether. Just as Otlet's Mundaneum was a product of its time, the Web is a product of ours. The Web's architecture—flat, open, and highly distributed—stems not only from its adherence to a particular set of technical protocols rooted in the U.S. military establishment, but from a particular strain of thought about the structure of hypertext systems that emerged in the Anglo-American computer world in the years after World War II.

Most contemporary accounts of Web history trace its conceptual origins to a 1945 essay by Vannevar Bush entitled "As We May Think." First published in the *Atlantic Monthly* and later in *Life* magazine, the essay describes a fictional machine called the Memex, consisting of a single desk with two screens and microfilm storage, providing access to a vast collection of stored documents.[10] Published fourteen years after Emanuel Goldberg first unveiled his Statistical Machine, the Memex drew on Bush's earlier experiments working with microfilm-reading machines in the 1930s.[11] Bush envisioned his new proposed device as far more than a microfilm reader, however. He saw it as capable of allowing users to search and retrieve information from a large body of stored information; create connections between them; add their own annotations; and ultimately create new, encyclopedic forms of knowledge that would emerge over time through their collective efforts.

Bush felt that scholars and other intellectual workers needed new tools to cope with the burgeoning problem of information overload, a problem he saw growing in tandem with the increasingly narrow

254

THE INTERGALACTIC NETWORK

focus of academic disciplines. "There is a growing mountain of research results," he wrote in "As We May Think." "But there is increased evidence that we are being bogged down today as specialization extends. The investigator is staggered by the findings and conclusions of thousands of other workers—conclusions which he cannot find time to grasp, much less to remember, as they appear." Bush, like Geddes, also felt that the compartmentalization of scholarship threatened to constrain humanity's intellectual potential, by forcing it into the same rigid, deterministic structures of academic departments. Traditional libraries had outlived their usefulness, failing to adapt to the increasingly unwieldy size of their collections, and growing too wedded to "the artificiality of systems of indexing." "The human mind does not work that way," he argues in the essay. "It operates by association. With one item in its grasp, it snaps instantly to the next that is suggested by the association of thoughts, in accordance with some intricate web of trails carried by the cells of the brain."

In order to support the organic processes of human thought, Bush believed that the world needed a fundamentally new technological platform for managing the outpouring of recorded data. "The summation of human experience is being expanded at a prodigious rate," he wrote, "and the means we use for threading through the consequent maze to the momentarily important item is the same as was used in the days of square-rigged ships."[12]

Bush had experimented with microfilm at some length, including a disappointing effort called the Rapid Selector, a malfunction-prone microfilm-based search-and-retrieval system. Unable to overcome the technical hurdles to building a better machine with the available technology at his disposal, Bush instead began to sketch out the contours of a new "concept car" machine, one designed not as a mechanical blueprint but rather as a conversation starter to encourage further exploration. In that respect, the Memex

255

When you use a marginalia technique like this, you end up selecting way too much material for extraction. That's my experience, at least. You're welcome to test yourself, and learn the hard way!

The Dot Marginalia Scheme

After some time employing the CVP marginalia scheme, I began using something I call the *dot marginalia scheme*. In this method you simply read a book, and whenever there's an irresistible idea, you place a simple dot (·) next to it. When you go back to read through your selections, you can usually tell why you selected that material (i.e., whether it's a *concept, vocab* term, or *prose*). Therefore, in theory, it saves time.

Again, like the CVP method, it results in an overabundance of selections. You create a ton of homework for yourself. The material you select tends to include many *good* ideas and *excellent* ideas instead of exclusively containing *irresistible* ideas.

Here's an example of the dot marginalia scheme. I used this while reading the book *The Hero with a Thousand Faces*.

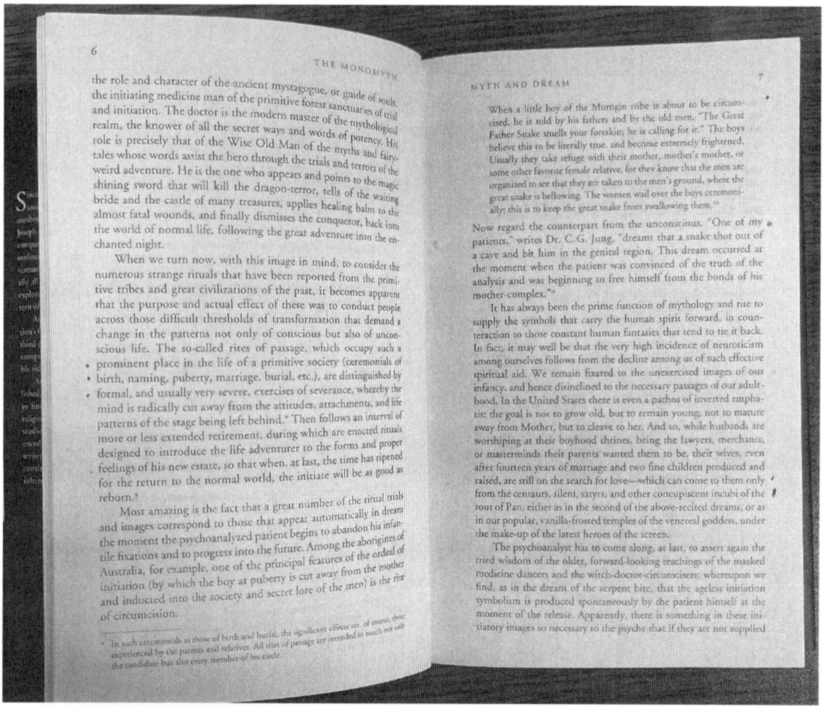

6 THE MONOMYTH

the role and character of the ancient mystagogue, or guide of souls, the initiating medicine man of the primitive forest sanctuaries of trial and initiation. The doctor is the modern master of the mythological realm, the knower of all the secret ways and words of potency. His role is precisely that of the Wise Old Man of the myths and fairy-tales whose words assist the hero through the trials and terrors of the weird adventure. He is the one who appears and points to the magic shining sword that will kill the dragon-terror, tells of the waiting bride and the castle of many treasures, applies healing balm to the almost fatal wounds, and finally dismisses the conqueror, back into the world of normal life, following the great adventure into the enchanted night.

When we turn now, with this image in mind, to consider the numerous strange rituals that have been reported from the primitive tribes and great civilizations of the past, it becomes apparent that the purpose and actual effect of these was to conduct people across those difficult thresholds of transformation that demand a change in the patterns not only of conscious but also of unconscious life. The so-called rites of passage, which occupy such a prominent place in the life of a primitive society (ceremonials of birth, naming, puberty, marriage, burial, etc.), are distinguished by formal, and usually very severe, exercises of severance, whereby the mind is radically cut away from the attitudes, attachments, and life patterns of the stage being left behind.* Then follows an interval of more or less extended retirement, during which are enacted rituals designed to introduce the life adventurer to the forms and proper feelings of his new estate, so that when, at last, the time has ripened for the return to the normal world, the initiate will be as good as reborn.[9]

Most amazing is the fact that a great number of the ritual trials and images correspond to those that appear automatically in dream the moment the psychoanalyzed patient begins to abandon his infantile fixations and to progress into the future. Among the aborigines of Australia, for example, one of the principal features of the ordeal of initiation (by which the boy at puberty is cut away from the mother and inducted into the society and secret lore of the men) is the rite of circumcision.

* In such ceremonials as those of birth and burial, the significant effects are, of course, those experienced by the parents and relatives. All rites of passage are intended to touch not only the candidate but also every member of his circle.

MYTH AND DREAM 7

When a little boy of the Murngin tribe is about to be circumcised, he is told by his fathers and by the old men, "The Great Father Snake smells your foreskin; he is calling for it." The boys believe this to be literally true, and become extremely frightened. Usually they take refuge with their mother, mother's mother, or some other favorite female relative, for they know that the men are organized to see that they are taken to the men's ground, where the great snake is bellowing. The women wail over the boys ceremonially; this is to keep the great snake from swallowing them.[10]

Now regard the counterpart from the unconscious. "One of my patients," writes Dr. C.G. Jung, "dreamt that a snake shot out of a cave and bit him in the genital region. This dream occurred at the moment when the patient was convinced of the truth of the analysis and was beginning to free himself from the bonds of his mother-complex."[11]

It has always been the prime function of mythology and rite to supply the symbols that carry the human spirit forward, in counteraction to those constant human fantasies that tend to tie it back. In fact, it may well be that the very high incidence of neuroticism among ourselves follows from the decline among us of such effective spiritual aid. We remain fixated to the unexercised images of our infancy, and hence disinclined to the necessary passages of our adulthood. In the United States there is even a pathos of inverted emphasis: the goal is not to grow old, but to remain young; not to mature away from Mother, but to cleave to her. And so, while husbands are worshiping at their boyhood shrines, being the lawyers, merchants, or masterminds their parents wanted them to be, their wives, even after fourteen years of marriage and two fine children produced and raised, are still on the search for love—which can come to them only from the centaurs, sileni, satyrs, and other concupiscent incubi of the rout of Pan, either as in the second of the above-recited dreams, or as in our popular, vanilla-frosted temples of the venereal goddess, under the make-up of the latest heroes of the screen.

The psychoanalyst has to come along, at last, to assert again the tried wisdom of the older, forward-looking teachings of the masked medicine dancers and the witch-doctor-circumcisers; whereupon we find, as in the dream of the serpent bite, that the ageless initiation symbolism is produced spontaneously by the patient himself at the moment of the release. Apparently, there is something in these initiatory images so necessary to the psyche that if they are not supplied

Like the CVP marginalia scheme, this one resulted in too many selections.

The Note Marginalia Scheme

One of the more popular marginalia schemes involves writing brief notes in the margins. These notes are typically your own thoughts and observations that relate directly to the passage you've read.

I used this scheme when reading a book on memory science. Here's a picture from a section of the book:

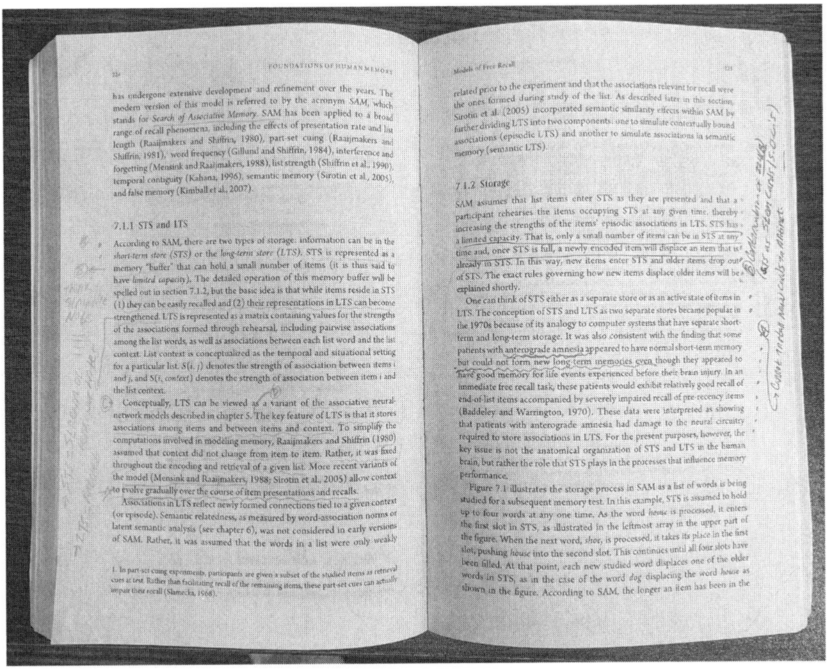

FOUNDATIONS OF HUMAN MEMORY

has undergone extensive development and refinement over the years. The modern version of this model is referred to by the acronym *SAM*, which stands for *Search of Associative Memory*. SAM has been applied to a broad range of recall phenomena, including the effects of presentation rate and list length (Raaijmakers and Shiffrin, 1980), part-set cuing (Raaijmakers and Shiffrin, 1981),[1] word frequency (Gillund and Shiffrin, 1984), interference and forgetting (Mensink and Raaijmakers, 1988), list strength (Shiffrin et al., 1990), temporal contiguity (Kahana, 1996), semantic memory (Sirotin et al., 2005), and false memory (Kimball et al., 2007).

7.1.1 STS and LTS

According to SAM, there are two types of storage: information can be in the *short-term store (STS)* or the *long-term store (LTS)*. STS is represented as a memory "buffer" that can hold a small number of items (it is thus said to have *limited capacity*). The detailed operation of this memory buffer will be spelled out in section 7.1.2, but the basic idea is that while items reside in STS (1) they can be easily recalled and (2) their representations in LTS can become strengthened. LTS is represented as a matrix containing values for the strengths of the associations formed through rehearsal, including pairwise associations among the list words, as well as associations between each list word and the list context. List context is conceptualized as the temporal and situational setting for a particular list. $S(i, j)$ denotes the strength of association between items i and j, and $S(i, context)$ denotes the strength of association between item i and the list context.

Conceptually, LTS can be viewed as a variant of the associative neural-network models described in chapter 5. The key feature of LTS is that it stores associations among items and between items and context. To simplify the computations involved in modeling memory, Raaijmakers and Shiffrin (1980) assumed that context did not change from item to item. Rather, it was fixed throughout the encoding and retrieval of a given list. More recent variants of the model (Mensink and Raaijmakers, 1988; Sirotin et al., 2005) allow context to evolve gradually over the course of item presentations and recalls.

Associations in LTS reflect newly formed connections tied to a given context (or episode). Semantic relatedness, as measured by word-association norms or latent semantic analysis (see chapter 6), was not considered in early versions of SAM. Rather, it was assumed that the words in a list were only weakly

1. In part-set cuing experiments, participants are given a subset of the studied items as retrieval cues at test. Rather than facilitating recall of the remaining items, these part-set cues can actually impair their recall (Slamecka, 1968).

Models of Free Recall

related prior to the experiment and that the associations relevant for recall were the ones formed during study of the list. As described later in this section, Sirotin et al. (2005) incorporated semantic similarity effects within SAM by further dividing LTS into two components: one to simulate contextually bound associations (episodic LTS) and another to simulate associations in semantic memory (semantic LTS).

7.1.2 Storage

SAM assumes that list items enter STS as they are presented and that a participant rehearses the items occupying STS at any given time, thereby increasing the strengths of the items' episodic associations in LTS. STS has a limited capacity. That is, only a small number of items can be in STS at any time and, once STS is full, a newly encoded item will displace an item that is already in STS. In this way, new items enter STS and older items drop out of STS. The exact rules governing how new items displace older items will be explained shortly.

One can think of STS either as a separate store or as an active state of items in LTS. The conception of STS and LTS as two separate stores became popular in the 1970s because of its analogy to computer systems that have separate short-term and long-term storage. It was also consistent with the finding that some patients with anterograde amnesia appeared to have normal short-term memory but could not form new long-term memories even though they appeared to have good memory for life events experienced before their brain injury. In an immediate free recall task, these patients would exhibit relatively good recall of end-of-list items accompanied by severely impaired recall of pre-recency items (Baddeley and Warrington, 1970). These data were interpreted as showing that patients with anterograde amnesia had damage to the neural circuitry required to store associations in LTS. For the present purposes, however, the key issue is not the anatomical organization of STS and LTS in the human brain, but rather the role that STS plays in the processes that influence memory performance.

Figure 7.1 illustrates the storage process in SAM as a list of words is being studied for a subsequent memory test. In this example, STS is assumed to hold up to four words at any one time. As the word *house* is processed, it enters the first slot in STS, as illustrated in the leftmost array in the upper part of the figure. When the next word, *shoe*, is processed, it takes its place in the first slot, pushing *house* into the second slot. This continues until all four slots have been filled. At that point, each new studied word displaces one of the older words in STS, as in the case of the word *dog* displacing the word *house* as shown in the figure. According to SAM, the longer an item has been in the

There are several problems with this scheme. You end up selecting too much material and you end up leaving less time for the irresistible ideas. Furthermore you experience a tendency wherein you write too much, with the result being that you end up wasting time. What you've written down in the book must then be duplicated and written down on a note. This is fine when using a very limited space (such as a single line on a bibcard); however, the space in marginalia often can stretch vertically. This leaves you more space to expand your writing. Often, what you end up writing down in the margin is something you shouldn't have even wasted energy writing down in the first place.

Your Own Marginalia Scheme

As noted, I contend that the marginalia method is inferior to the Luhmannian bibcard method. If you still insist on marking up book margins, though, then chances are you'll use your own marginalia scheme. I've observed that a lot of people like placing little sticky notes or post-it tabs in their books. While I don't recommend any of this, I won't slam you for adding your own flavor to your knowledge extraction process. Each person is different.

Since I do not recommend marginalia notes and I opt for the ultimate strategy that Luhmann used, I'll introduce it to you shortly.

But first, let me cover a few other extraction methods very quickly.

OTHER EXTRACTION METHODS

Cognitive scientist, Fiona McPherson, outlines three other extraction methods: (1) highlighting, (2) headings, and (3) summaries.[11] I'll cover them now.

Highlighting and headings aren't really pure, stand-alone, extraction methods. They're more like pre-extraction methods. They're essentially *selection* methods for noting which items you intend to extract. They're used primarily to help you *comprehend* information and then convert such information into deeper knowledge. You convert the information into deeper knowledge by creating a note for it and elaborating on the material.

Let's talk about highlighting first.

HIGHLIGHTING

Highlighting is not a good method for dense, complex, and challenging information. For that type of material it's best to employ the 1-step book-to-maincard method.

While highlighting does not possess the cognitive development power, it is not "completely pointless," as it does help you actually pay attention to the words on the page.[12] Generally, I'd advise you to stay away from highlighting. If the material is familiar to you, or even if it's complicated, highlighting won't help much. There's even research indicating highlighting may harm one's ability to learn and recall information.[13] Highlighting steals time and energy away from more effective learning practices.

---

11 Fiona McPherson, Effective Note-taking, revised edition (Wellington: Wayz Press, 2018), 14.

12 Fiona McPherson, Effective Note-taking, revised edition (Wellington: Wayz Press, 2018), 17.

13 James H. Crouse and Peter Idstein, "Effects of Encoding Cues on Prose Learning," Journal of Educational Psychology 63, no. 4 (1972): 309–13; Fiona McPherson, Effective Note-taking, revised edition (Wellington: Wayz Press, 2018), 23; R. Barker Bausell and Joseph R. Jenkins, "Effects on Prose Learning of Frequency of Adjunct Cues and the Difficulty

As one cognitive scientist observes, the main value of highlighting does not intrinsically add much value to your understanding of the material; its benefit (if any) stems from *its ability to motivate you to spend more time with the material.* Yet as we've found, writing by hand and spending the time elaborating on material by writing reflection notes is even more motivating and fun—especially if you're only elaborating on the material you find irresistible.

In brief, I'd recommend you stop the practice of highlighting.

HEADINGS

Headings that you write are brief sentences outlining what the following paragraph intends to cover. They do not summarize or spoil what is written in the paragraph; rather they help organize its content.

Headings have been shown to produce better summaries, outlines, and reformulation of material. This in turn helps enhance your recall of the material you read.[14]

Headings are classified as *organizational signals,* and have demonstrated a tendency to improving a reader's recall of information (unlike highlighting).[15]

Headings are usually provided in texts whose author is awesome (like me), and who put the work in to organize their material into chunks with a heading attached.

However, so-called "learned" authors (scientists and scholars, like Luhmann) may forgo such niceties. In such a case it may be a useful practice to create your own headings. I don't recommend doing this directly in the book (i.e., marginalia). Rather, I recommend using your bibcard for this practice.

---

of the Material Cued," Journal of Reading Behavior 9, no. 3 (September 1, 1977): 227–32; John Dunlosky et al., "Improving Students' Learning With Effective Learning Techniques: Promising Directions From Cognitive and Educational Psychology," Psychological Science in the Public Interest 14, no. 1 (January 1, 2013): 4–58.

14 Fiona McPherson, Effective Note-taking, revised edition (Wellington: Wayz Press, 2018), 35.

15 Fiona McPherson, Effective Note-taking, revised edition (Wellington: Wayz Press, 2018), 35-6.

The third extraction method is that of *summaries*. This is analogous to creating a *reformulation* note, which is covered in detail in the next chapter. These are best for tackling difficult material. If tackling difficult material, I recommend creating reformulation notes using the 1-step book-to-maincard method. In brief, you go straight from book to creating an entire notecard dedicated to reformulating the difficult idea you just read.

Let's now turn to the grand-daddy of all the extraction strategies: the *two-step Luhmannian bibcard method.*

THE TWO-STEP LUHMANNIAN BIBCARD METHOD

A phase transition took place in the eighteenth century during the enlightenment wherein the reading styles of scholars changed. "An enlightened reader was no longer supposed to collect and memorize 'factoids' that he found in the texts of others," observed scholar, Fabian Krämer.[16] In the sixteenth and seventeenth centuries, when scholars read, their focus centered on *collecting bits of knowledge* (excerpting). During the enlightenment, scholars began to read by recording their own thoughts (observations).[17] Essentially, reading and observing became "closely intertwined."[18] The observations one made while reading could then be used to process an idea more fully. This could be done by way of (1) creating reflection notes on the material in order to integrate ideas into one's own theories and creative work, (2) testing an author's conclusions by way of experiment, and (3) writing critical reviews of books (which became a popular practice during the enlightenment).

These deeper ways of processing texts begins with recording one's *observations*. The container with which one records such observations is that of the *bibcard*. This is what we'll be covering in this section.

In the course of using the Antinet, I've tried out all of the methods mentioned previously. I've come to conclude that the best method in the majority of cases is what you're about to learn now: *The 2-step bibcard method.*

---

16 Fabian Krämer, Albrecht von Haller as an 'Enlightened' Reader-Observer (Brill, 2016), 224.
17 Fabian Krämer, Albrecht von Haller as an 'Enlightened' Reader-Observer (Brill, 2016), 233.
18 Fabian Krämer, Albrecht von Haller as an 'Enlightened' Reader-Observer (Brill, 2016), 241.

In Luhmann's first Antinet, he primarily adopted the 1-step book-to-maincard method. As Johannes Schmidt observes, "the early notes from the 1950s and 1960s frequently tended to be more of the running-text kind and more closely reflected the original readings."[19]

In Luhmann's second Antinet, his method changed.

Here's an overview of this process:

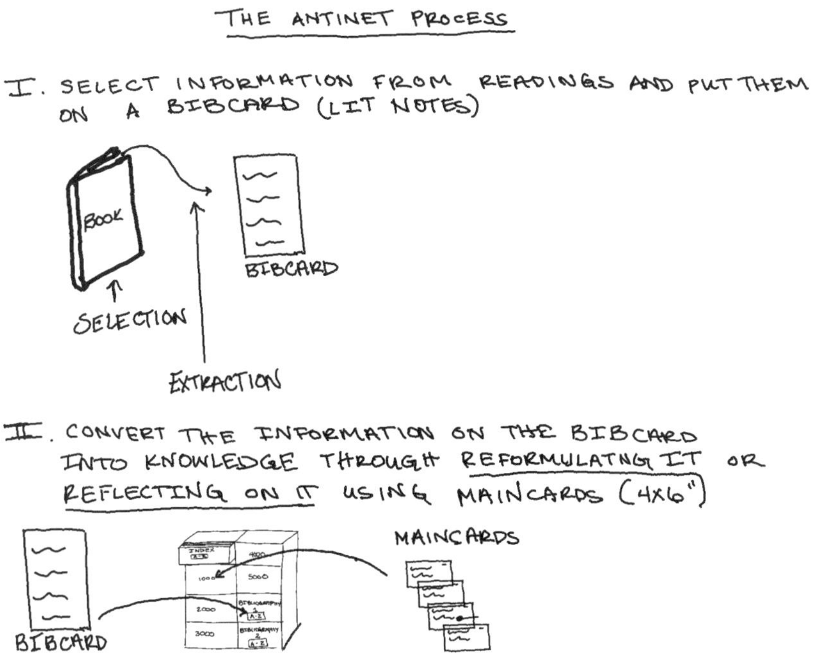
THE ANTINET PROCESS
I. SELECT INFORMATION FROM READINGS AND PUT THEM ON A BIBCARD (LIT NOTES)
BOOK
BIBCARD
SELECTION
EXTRACTION
II. CONVERT THE INFORMATION ON THE BIBCARD INTO KNOWLEDGE THROUGH REFORMULATING IT OR REFLECTING ON IT USING MAINCARDS (4x6")
MAINCARDS
BIBCARD

This method entails extracting knowledge from external sources by placing it on a bibcard.

On the front-side of the bibcard, are three items: (1) the *bibliographic details* of the source, (2) your *goal* in engaging the source, and (3) an *overview* of

19 Johannes Schmidt, "Niklas Luhmann's Card Index: Thinking Tool, Communication Partner, Publication Machine," Forgetting Machines. Knowledge Management Evolution in Early Modern Europe 53 (2016), 292-3.

the source if available (such as a brief overview of its table of contents). This is already covered in the chapter on *selection.*

On the back-side of the bibcard, are the bibnotes. The bibnotes are the *observations* you have while reading. These are the internal thoughts and ideas you wish to select from the material. With these items, you'll either: (1) convert them into main notes by excerpting them, reformulating them, or reflecting on them, or (2) forego elaborating on the items by storing them as ExRefs. By foregoing elaboration, you allow the items to ruminate until the time wherein you're working on a relevant project which will benefit from including the material.

Here's a picture of a bibcard:

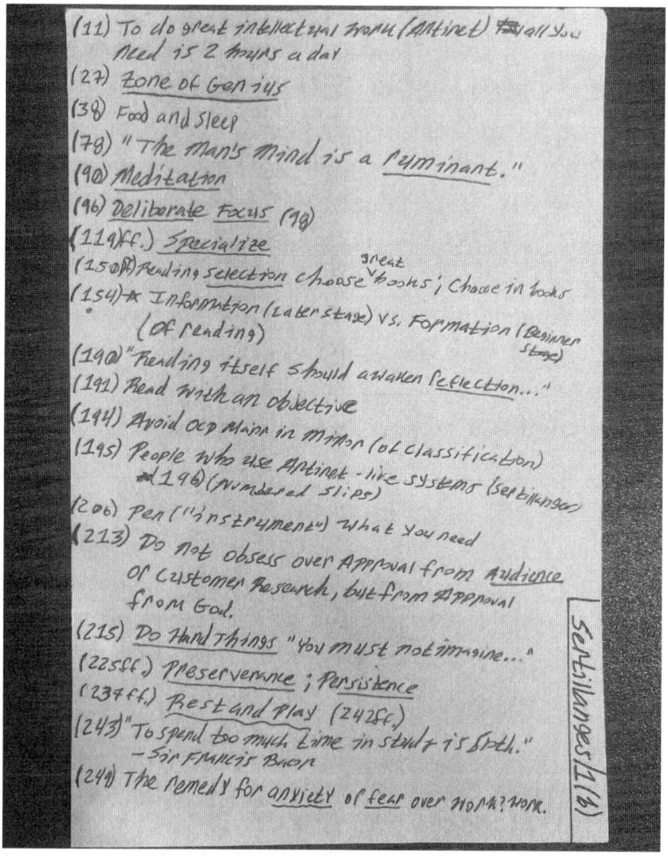

How to Read with a Bibcard

Reading using the bibcard method typically involves three items: (1) a physical book, (2) a pen, and (3) the bibcard.

Ideally I recommend physical books (as opposed to reading digital versions). For almost a decade, I read with a Kindle; however a few years ago I transitioned back to using physical books because I felt a stronger spiritual, even sacred, connection to physical books. Reading physical books also seemed more effective in helping me comprehend what I was reading. Research now backs my observations. Recently, a scientific study found that "reading comprehension is reduced when reading from an electronic device."[20]

The bibcard method works better with physical books than digital books. You simply place the bibcard in any location at the back of the book. When you finish your reading session, place it where you left off, using the bibcard as a bookmark.

In addition, you'll want a pen available at the ready. I like to clip the pen onto the back cover of the book.

Here's how it looks:

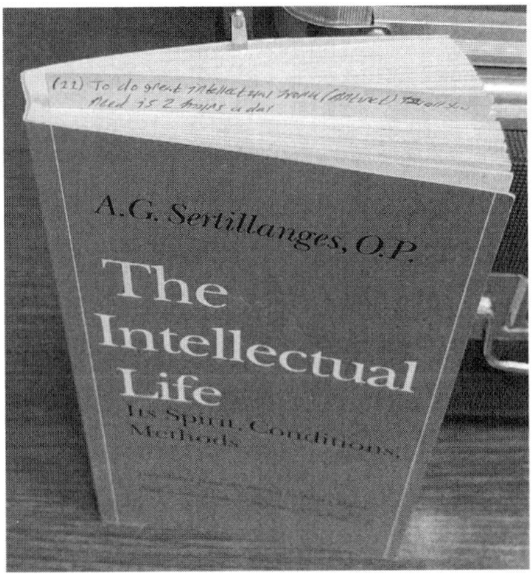

20 Motoyasu Honma et al., "Reading on a Smartphone Affects Sigh Generation, Brain Activity, and Comprehension," Scientific Reports 12, no. 1 (January 31, 2022): 1589.

Inside the book you'll see the bibcard, which acts as a bookmark, and clipped onto the book's back cover is a pen.

I've tried a lot of reading setups. A lot of them have pluses and minuses. Certain ones are fine; however, in unusual situations, like while reading in bed or on a sandy beach, they fail miserably. For instance, reading with a Moleskine notebook while lying in bed isn't something that works for most people. With the bibcard reading method, one can read in bed on their back right before falling asleep and still have everything they need to extract a key idea.

Reading outdoors is also more supported by physical books. Luhmann once said, "I like working in the sun."[21] For those who like reading outside, this is also a great setup because it requires minimal supplies and isn't subject to the limitations some screens have when used in bright direct light.

Here's a photo of Luhmann reading in the sun using this method. Note what looks like a bibcard sticking out of the book.

PHOTO CREDIT: Niklas Luhmann—Theory of Society 4_13 by Schwumbel; philomag, "Niklas Luhmann Und Die Aufrichtigkeit," Philosophie Magazin, accessed April 26, 2022, https://www.philomag.de/artikel/niklas-luhmann-und-die-aufrichtigkeit.

Bibnotes

A bibnote is what Sönke Ahrens refers to as a *literature note*, even though it doesn't make sense to call them literature notes (as that indicates the notes are

21 Niklas Luhmann, Niklas Luhmann Short Cuts (English Translation), 2002, 31.

from literature). For several reasons, I prefer the term *bibnote*. A bibliography is a collection of the works you cite in your research, it's not just composed of literature. The notes one takes can certainly be from a medium beyond literature. You can take notes from YouTube videos, lectures, podcasts, you name it. Furthermore, it can be argued that readers should not confine themselves to reading only literature. In the words of John Aubrey, a fellow of the Royal Society, "material gathered should not be confined to that offered in books."[22]

Since the notes you take while engaging with your sources emanate from your "bibliography" (your list of references), I like to refer to these notes as bibnotes.

Bibnotes are made in bullet-point format. The briefer they are, the better. They begin with a page number in parentheses, and then list out the thought or observation.

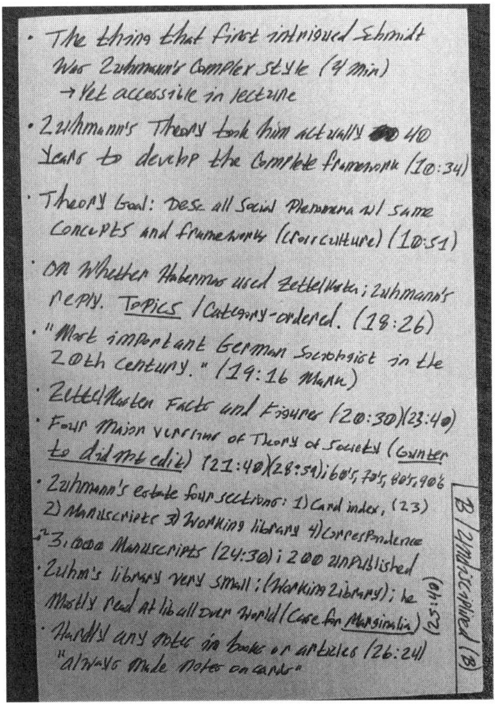

• The thing that first intrigued Schmidt was Luhmann's complex style (4 min) → yet accessible in lecture
• Luhmann's Theory took him actually 40 years to develop the complete framework (10:34)
• Theory Goal: Desc. all Social Phenomena w/ same concepts and frameworks ([illegible] culture) (10:51)
• On whether Habermas used Zettelkasten; Luhmann's reply. Topics / Category-ordered. (18:26)
• "Most important German Sociologist in the 20th century." (19:16 Mann)
• Zettelkasten Facts and Figures (20:30)(23:40)
• Four major versions of Theory of Society (Gunter [illegible] did not edit) (21:40)(28:59); 60's, 70's, 80's, 90's
• Luhmann's estate four sections: 1) Card index, 2) Manuscripts 3) Working library 4) Correspondence (23)
• 3,000 Manuscripts (24:30); 200 unpublished
• Luhm's library very small; (Working Library); he mostly read at lib all over world (Case for Marginalia) (25:10)
• Hardly any notes in books or articles (26:24) "always made notes on cards"

B / [illegible] (B)

For instance, here's a bibcard with bibnotes I took while listening to a podcast.

NOTE: I put timestamps of the ideas in parantheses. I placed them after the bibnote; however I now typically place the timestamp or page number on the left-hand side before the bibnote.

22 Richard Yeo, *Notebooks, Recollection, and External Memory: Some Early Modern English Ideas and Practices* (Brill, 2016), 138.

I like to think of the nature of these individual bibnotes as *observations*. They're observations that you have as you engage with a *source*. By source I mean a book, podcast, lecture, YouTube video, etc.

John Locke's notes were of kindred nature and were referred to as "observation" notes. The scholar, Richard Yeo, refers to them as "short comments connected with books [Locke] was reading."[23]

Much of the time your bibnotes don't even have to be a short comment. They can be condensed even more by simply writing a keyterm.

As Johannes Schmidt observes, bibnotes are "not simply excerpts," and that Luhmann "jotted down only a few keywords in the course of his reading along with the respective page numbers."[24]

I do the same by simply writing a page number down, and then the keyterm. I signal it's a keyterm by underlining it. For instance, see this bibcard:

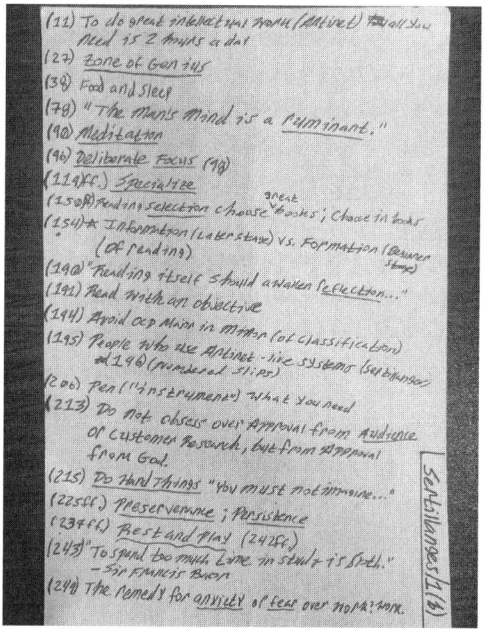

23 Richard Yeo, *Notebooks, Recollection, and External Memory: Some Early Modern English Ideas and Practices* (Brill, 2016), 149.

24 Johannes Schmidt, "Niklas Luhmann's Card Index: Thinking Tool, Communication Partner, Publication Machine," Forgetting Machines. Knowledge Management Evolution in Early Modern Europe 53 (2016), 293.

The bibnote (27) Zone of Genius signals to me that on page 27, there is material relating to the concept of sticking within your "Zone of Genius." In other words, sticking with your core competency and focusing on your gifts. Because *Zone of Genius* is underlined, it indicates that it's a keyterm pertaining to a core idea, which already has an entry in my index box.

Here is a picture of page 27 in *The Intellectual Life*:

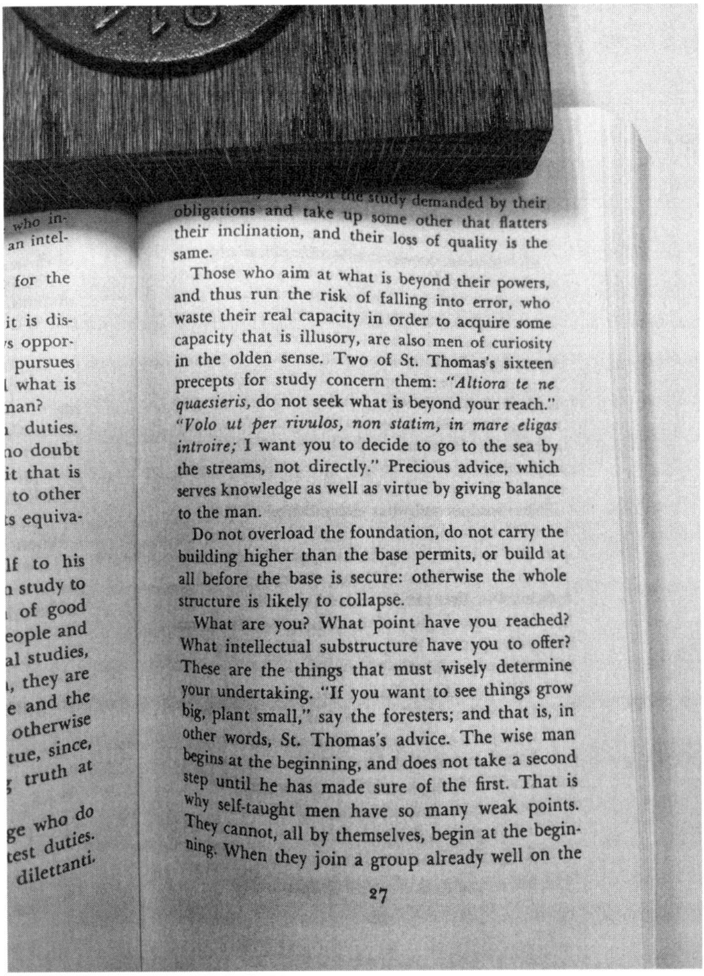
the study demanded by their obligations and take up some other that flatters their inclination, and their loss of quality is the same.

Those who aim at what is beyond their powers, and thus run the risk of falling into error, who waste their real capacity in order to acquire some capacity that is illusory, are also men of curiosity in the olden sense. Two of St. Thomas's sixteen precepts for study concern them: "*Altiora te ne quaesieris*, do not seek what is beyond your reach." "*Volo ut per rivulos, non statim, in mare eligas introire;* I want you to decide to go to the sea by the streams, not directly." Precious advice, which serves knowledge as well as virtue by giving balance to the man.

Do not overload the foundation, do not carry the building higher than the base permits, or build at all before the base is secure: otherwise the whole structure is likely to collapse.

What are you? What point have you reached? What intellectual substructure have you to offer? These are the things that must wisely determine your undertaking. "If you want to see things grow big, plant small," say the foresters; and that is, in other words, St. Thomas's advice. The wise man begins at the beginning, and does not take a second step until he has made sure of the first. That is why self-taught men have so many weak points. They cannot, all by themselves, begin at the beginning. When they join a group already well on the

27

When I thought of the keyterm *Zone of Genius,* it was in regards to the idea that one should not "aim at what is beyond their powers, and thus run the risk of falling into error, [and of those] *who waste their real capacity in order to acquire some capacity that is illusory...*"[25]

In this instance, I didn't have immediately relevant use for this idea, and therefore I didn't develop a maincard for it. Instead, I created an ExRef. Here's a picture of it in the area of my Antinet pertaining to *Zone of Genius*. Within this area there's a card of *Zone-of-Genius-related* ExRefs:

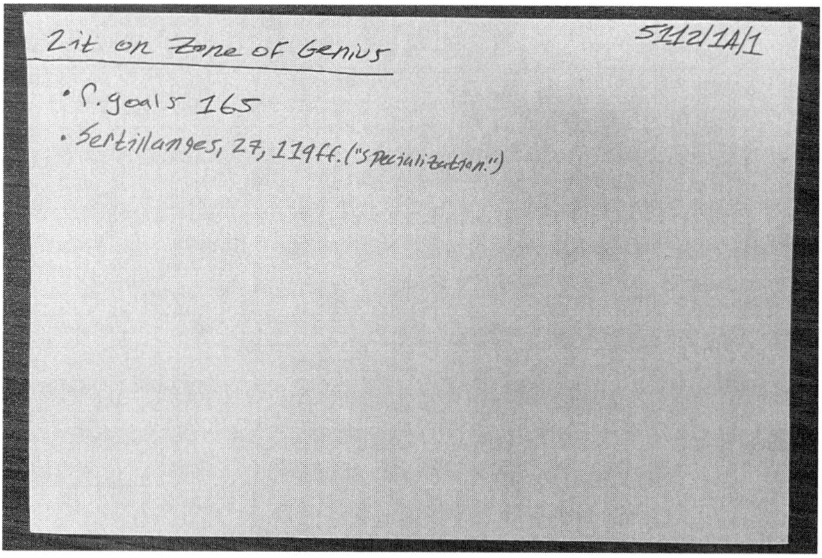

The concept of *Zone of Genius* is important to me; yet I decided it's not immediately applicable to my current project—that project being the book you're reading right now. I mean, *Zone of Genius* technically *could be* relevant to this book, and I could dedicate a section of the book to it (which I guess, indirectly I'm kind of doing right now). However, you have to draw a line in the sand and focus on the most pertinent material for your task at hand. And right now, we have our hands full enough with the material covered in this book. Simply creating an ExRef allows me to delay processing until I have use for it (which will probably be for a future project).

---

25 OP A. G. Sertillanges, The Intellectual Life: Its Spirit, Conditions, Methods, trans. Mary Ryan, Reprint edition (Washington, D.C.: The Catholic University of America Press, 1992), 27. Emphasis added.

This gives you a glimpse into one of my bibcards. Let's now turn our attention to one of Luhmann's bibcards:

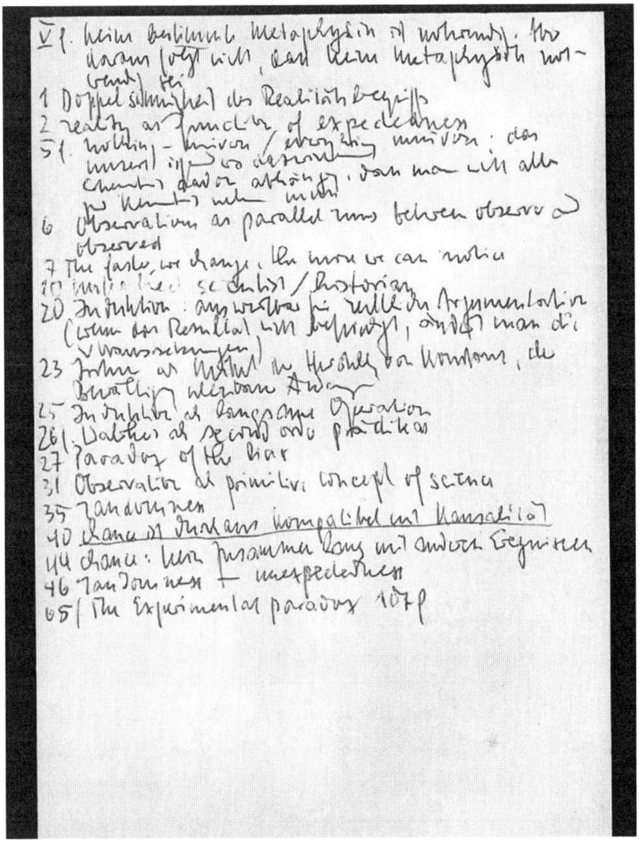

I enlisted the help of the Antinet's Reddit community to help translate this card.[26] Luckily, a community member answered the call and provided a translation despite the fact that Luhmann's handwriting has been called *abysmally bad* and *hideous*.[27] As such, some of the bibnotes are completely indecipherable (designated by [...]). Here is the translation:

---

26 sscheper, "Help Translating Luhmann's Bibcards into English," Reddit Post, R/Antinet, April 12, 2022, www.reddit.com/r/Antinet/comments/u1lqzz/helptranslatingluhmanns bibcardsintoenglish/.

27 BrainOfALion, "You're Welcome! The...," Reddit Comment, R/Antinet, April 12, 2022, www.reddit.com/r/Antinet/comments/u1lqzz/helptranslatingluhmannsbibcardsintoenglish/i4gyjdy/; "Help Translating Luhmann's Bibcards into English," Zettelkasten Forum,

V1. No specific metaphysical theory is necessary. But from this follows not, that no metaphysical theory is necessary

1 Ambiguity of the concept or reality

2 reality as function of expectedness [Original in English]

51 nothing-universe / everything universe, ours somewhere in between [...] depends on, that we all must take note of [...]

6 Observations as parallel runs[...] between observer & observed [Original in English]

7 The faster we change, the more we can notice [Original in English]

10 inferred[...] scientist / historian [Original in English]

20 Induction: evaluable for legal argumentation (if the result doesn't satisfy, one changes the premises)

23 Error as [...] Coping [...]

25 Induction as slow operation

26 W[...] als sec[...] [...] prädikas [...]

27 Paradox of the liar [Original in English]

31 Observation as primitive concept of science [Original in English]

35 randomness [Original in English]

40 Chance is definitively compatible with causality [Underlined]

---

accessed April 12, 2022, https://forum.zettelkasten.de/discussion/2235/help-translating-luhmanns-bibcards-into-english.

44 Chance: not connection to [or: relation with] other events

46 randomness [Original in English]

65 The Experimental paradox 107p [Original in English]

There are several patterns we can glean from this translation. First, note how Luhmann simply jotted down keyterms like *randomness*. Second, he also wrote down terms in the following way {keyterm} as {supporting context}. In essence, Luhmann stated the keyterm first, and then inserted the phrase *as*. After *as* Luhmann would provide a snippet of detail that would contextualize the keyterm. For instance, we see the phrase *reality as function of expectedness*. This method of creating bibnotes stands as both a way of thinking and a practice one should experiment with. It results in building knowledge around the keyterm (not around the supporting context, which sits in a subordinate position to the main idea of the keyterm).

The Bib Box

Luhmann's bibliography box (aka, the *bib box*) was a critical component of his Antinet. The cards in this section show Luhmann's thoughts before they were processed fully into main notes. Luhmann's second Antinet contained 67,000 cards, with 15,000 (roughly 22%) of them bibcards.

Given how large a portion of Luhmann's second Antinet was devoted to bibcards, you would think these would be outlined in Sönke Ahrens's book *How to Take Smart Notes*. Yet this component of Luhmann's system is almost completely omitted in Ahrens's tutorial. His instructions for how to create this critical component of the Antinet is basically: "I strongly recommend using a free program like Zotero."[28]

The bib box stores your bibcards in alphabetical order. It's where you place your bibcards after you finish the book.

---

28 Sönke Ahrens, How to Take Smart Notes: One Simple Technique to Boost Writing, Learning and Thinking: For Students, Academics and Nonfiction Book Writers (North Charleston, SC: CreateSpace, 2017), 30

ONE READS DIFFERENTLY WITH AN ANTINET

Written on a card in Luhmann's own Antinet we find a card on how one "reads differently" when using an Antinet.[29] Johannes Schmidt notes that Luhmann read "with an eye to the notes already contained in his file."[30]

This phenomenon is something other scholars have confirmed: "it is indisputable that in books [he read], Luhmann searched for information or ideas that could be linked to the content of his own card index."[31]

With enough practice with an Antinet, there is a phase transition that occurs whereby you begin to read in such a way that you no longer get "bogged down" by writing out full-excerpts.[32]

If we look at Luhmann's second Antinet and its 15,000 bibcards, most of which referenced books, we can make some calculations (without accounting for titles which span multiple bibcards, which indeed occurred, but not too frequently). Luhmann worked with his second Antinet from roughly 1963 to 1997, which comes out to thirty four years. We can make some calculations (without accounting for titles which span multiple bibcards, which indeed occurred, but wasn't too frequent). If we divide 15,000 bibcards by thirty four years, this gives us 441 titles per year; 37 titles per month; or roughly one title per day.

In other words, on average Luhmann read roughly one book or journal article per day… for thirty four years.

---

29 "ZK II: Sheet 9/8d—Niklas Luhmann Archive," accessed March 4, 2022, https://niklas-luhmann-archiv.de/bestand/zettelkasten/zettel/ZK_2_NB_9-8d_V.

30 Johannes Schmidt, "Niklas Luhmann's Card Index: Thinking Tool, Communication Partner, Publication Machine," Forgetting Machines. Knowledge Management Evolution in Early Modern Europe 53 (2016), 293.

31 Alberto Cevolini, ed., Forgetting Machines: Knowledge Management Evolution in Early Modern Europe, Library of the Written Word, volume 53 (Leiden ; Boston: Brill, 2016), 27.

32 "ZK II: Sheet 9/8d—Niklas Luhmann Archive," accessed March 4, 2022, https://niklas-luhmann-archiv.de/bestand/zettelkasten/zettel/ZK_2_NB_9-8d_V.

There's no way to do this by reading the way normal people read (slowly, sounding out every word in their head). The nature in which Luhmann read was *selective*. I call it *selective reading*. You ingest books at a phenomenal rate, like a reading machine, thanks to the *priming* step we covered in the previous chapter. I suggest this is a hybrid between skimming and reading every sentence. Instead of reading every word, you read every paragraph of the book. You don't try to comprehend each individual word, or each sentence even. Your goal is to comprehend the paragraph quickly, and move on. When you spot an intriguing idea you slow down. At that point your brain undertakes a communication experience in order to draw up concepts from your Antinet. You then run the new material through a filter: *is this idea bad, good, excellent, or irresistible?* If it's irresistible, you extract it onto your bibcard.

As Mortimer Adler advises, reading should not be thought of as a passive activity.[33] It's an *active* process. When employing the bibcard extraction method it's an even faster, more alert process.

SLOWLY CHEWING ON BOOKS

There will be books that are worth chewing on (reading them slowly and deliberately). Typically, these will be the books you read when you're in *exploratory* mode; when you have yet to develop a rough skeleton to serve as the foundation of your project. In this mode, you ought to employ the book-to-maincard method. You also must shift your mindset. You must slow down your thinking and not worry about processing books efficiently.

In this mode you ought to adopt the advice of people like David Deutsch, a great copywriter. Deutsch famously emphasized that it was better to read one great book ten times, instead of ten good books one time.[34] In this mode you should opt to be well-read, not widely read. As Mortimer Adler puts it:

33 Mortimer Jerome Adler and Charles Van Doren, How to Read a Book, Rev. and updated ed (New York: Simon and Schuster, 1972), 4.

34 Ben Settle, "The 10-Minute Workday," https://www.awai.com/members/10-minute/, Unit 12, 4.

> There have always been literate ignoramuses who have read too widely and not well. The Greeks had a name for such a mixture of learning and folly which might be applied to the bookish but poorly read of all ages. They are all sophomores.[35]

SYNTOPICAL READING

If you already have a base-level structure for what you're working on, then it's safer to adopt swifter extraction methods. There are certain books that are so dense, widely-cited, and profound that you just *know* they deserve a slower read. And there are certain books that are suited for swift *selective reading.*

One of the more enjoyable ways to partake in selective reading is to employ a process called *syntopical reading.*[36] With syntopical reading, you read several books on the same subject, at the same time. This is something Luhmann did, as well. In a short piece Luhmann wrote on reading, he states: "Another possibility is to read texts [across] certain topics."[37]

In order to read syntopically, Luhmann writes, "You have to be able to read highly *selectively* and pull out widely interconnected references."[38] Basically you must train your mind to spot certain patterns. This is something neuro-imprinting keyterms on your mind helps with (by way of the index).

Here, Luhmann's referring to storing ideas in long-term memory in the Antinet, such that they evolve and you do not waste your time relearning what you already know.

According to Luhmann, the key to reading scientific texts revolves around this act. You must read selectively, and not waste time relearning what you already know. The key piece in this process relates to *long-term memory* and

---

35 Mortimer Jerome Adler and Charles Van Doren, How to Read a Book, Rev. and updated ed (New York: Simon and Schuster, 1972), 11.

36 Mortimer Jerome Adler and Charles Van Doren, How to Read a Book, Rev. and updated ed (New York: Simon and Schuster, 1972), 301.

37 Niklas Luhmann, Niklas Luhmann Short Cuts (English Translation), 2002, 82.

38 Niklas Luhmann, Niklas Luhmann Short Cuts (English Translation), 2002, 83.

the necessity to distinguish the "essential from the non-essential and the new from the merely repetitive."[39] In other words, you want a system where you can refresh your recollection of your notes and evolve your current ideas with new ideas; you don't want to waste time relearning things you already know.

I like to do this in the following manner: I carve out two hours of back-to-back reading. For the first hour I read one book within one topic. In the next hour I read a different book within that same topic. For example, several years ago I read two books predicting what the future would look like and the technologies that would shape it. The first book I read was *The Industries of the Future;* the book I read was *The Inevitable.* By reading syntopically, I spotted interesting patterns—things that they both agreed upon and the contradictions between them. In addition, I noticed that each of them omitted something which served as an important piece of the other's book.

Again, reading this way usually comes *after* the exploratory phase. It comes after you've gained a sense for what you actually wish to create. However, when you're ready for this type of reading style, the bibcard extraction method, as well as the Antinet as a whole, takes the experience to a whole new level.

In brief, you'll read differently with an Antinet because you've been training and exercising your *neuro-associative recall* muscle. You see, even before reading the first page of a book, you'll have primed your mind to detect certain keyterms and ideas by way of creating index entries of keyterms. The Antinet, with its neuroimprinting process of writing by hand, develops your neuro-associative recall ability. When reading, you'll find yourself thinking of keyterms in your index. This is hugely beneficial because it saves you time. You can simply jot keyterms down on a bibcard, instead of having to write out lengthier notes.

---

39 Niklas Luhmann, Niklas Luhmann Short Cuts (English Translation), 2002, 83.

CONCLUSION

Now you have an idea for the process of extracting material from the sources you engage with. We outlined several strategies (the best one being the 2-step bibcard method). We now turn to the next critical phase of knowledge development: *Creation*.

CHAPTER FIFTEEN

CREATION

THE CREATION PHASE OF KNOWLEDGE development is where the magic really starts to happen. In this phase you begin adding your own *meaning* to the information you extract from the sources you choose to communicate with. In this phase, you begin injecting your own *personality* into the information. As a result, you create knowledge with your own unique perspective with the potential of making an impact on the world.

We're going to survey a large swath of material in this section. The best place to start is exploring the nature of notes.

THE NATURE OF THE NOTES

What are notes? I think there are several ways to answer this question. One helpful way to understand the nature of notes is to use some metaphors. In this section I'll present three illustrations: (1) notes as thoughts, (2) notes as leaves, and (3) notes as neurons.

NOTES AS THOUGHTS

At this point it's helpful to refresh our memory of what a *thought* actually is.

A thought is a metaphysical representation of reality. This reality can be external reality (such as things you see), or internal reality (such as your internal experience, intuition or feelings). The reality can be true in nature or true in fiction (as Hemingway emphasized, each novelist should write the truth). A thought is also shaped by several dimensions, which are represented in the following diagram:

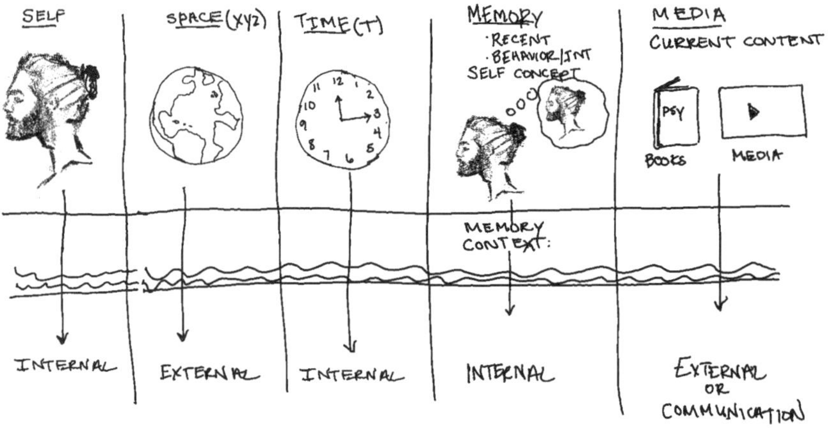

A thought is shaped by one's *self.* You have your own concept of a self (ego, persona or identity). You think of yourself in a certain way that shapes your thoughts. Your experiences, stories, trials, tribulations, and past serve as a background context for your self. Your *self* shapes your thoughts. Your self also embodies the unique ways your brain works based on its biochemical arrangement. Based on your DNA, based on *how you're wired.*

A thought is also shaped by *space:* where you are in space, your latitude, longitude, and altitude. You've heard the phrase, *you are your environment.* It's really: your thoughts are your environment—or at least, your thoughts are shaped by your environment. Your thoughts would be different if you lived in Bangladesh (assuming you're not already living in Bangladesh). In brief, where you reside right now in space shapes your thoughts.

A thought is also shaped by *time.* How you think of something today is drastically different from how you'd have thought of it ten years prior. It's also drastically different from how you'll think of the same thing ten years from now. We're always changing, and our thoughts change with us. Yet it's not only our *selves* changing that shapes thoughts. It's also the world around us. The thoughts you have today would be drastically different if you were suddenly transported two thousand years into the past or future—even if you were to remain the same age, in the same physical body, and at the same physical location. Your own place in time, as well as your own world's place in time, has a significant impact on which thoughts you experience.

A thought is also shaped by *memory* (or *reverberation*). This is closely related to the concept of *self*, but it's more specific. It's related to our short-term concept of self. We have a memory that fades over time. Our recent actions and things we've read—say in the past month—are still reverberating through our minds. Our recent behavior, our recent purchases, the books, TV shows and movies we've seen recently shape our thoughts. After some point, however, these memories fade. Every single day we enter a new state wherein some thoughts will arise, and other thoughts simply will not. This is shaped by our memory which is almost like a rolling wave of reverberation.

A thought is also shaped by *content*. The current content that has our attention and what we're consuming shapes our thoughts. The TV show you're watching or book you're reading shapes thoughts. While you're ingesting the sources of content, you're relating the concepts to what you already know. You're trying to comprehend the concepts and either accepting or rejecting them. When you're consuming content, you're *selecting* which information resonates with you. After reading this book, you're hopefully learning to *select* only irresistible material. As you continue with your Antinet, whenever you engage with content, you're writing down your observational thoughts (onto bibcards).

All of these dimensions (self, space, time, memory, content) shape the phenomena that is a thought. The thoughts can be voluntary or involuntary. Regardless, the metaphysical phenomenon that is a thought is then the raw unit captured and immortalized by way of being written down on paper in the form of a notecard. A note, then, is essentially a container of thought. Or, more succinctly, a *thought container*.

Thought Containers

I think it's helpful to think of notes as a mechanism, or a container of thought. The scholar, Markus Krajewski, likens notes to "Denk-zettel," which is a German term translating roughly to "thought-notes."[1] These are the "units" that stand as the raw material of the Antinet.

---

1 **Markus Krajewski, *Note-Keeping: History, Theory, Practice of a Counter-Measurement against Forgetting* (Brill, 2016), 319.**

There are four components of notes as thought containers. First, notes are containers that develop one's short-term thoughts. They are a mechanism for thought that enables one to reflect and actually instantiate the phenomenon going on internally in one's mind.

Second, notes are containers for developing one's long-term thoughts. If structured properly, notes can serve as a container to collect and evolve thoughts over the long term. This is thanks to the nested tree structure of the Antinet.

Third, notes serve as prompts to help the mind *recollect* knowledge.[2] In digital Zettelkasten systems, many people have a tendency to view notes as an all-encompassing document. In digital systems, users regularly tend to their notes, constantly updating and deleting text. Yet truly powerful note systems are not like this. They simply serve as a cue or a prompt to trigger neurons in your brain to fire and connect. As a result you end up grasping an idea that is often incommunicable. You then use your manuscript or project to make the incommunicable knowledge lucid and clear. The notes within the Antinet are a means to the end (the end being your creative output). This is something that will continually arise throughout this section.

Fourth, notes are a container encompassing different types of thoughts. As one scholar puts it, notes are "free-floating *staging posts of thought,* which record all manner of remarkable things, excerpts and quotes in the permanence of script."[3] Notes serve as a container for *observing* what the material you're reading relates to. Notes serve as a container for thoughts which encapsulate what an author is saying (*excerpt* notes), as a container for learning material by summarizing concepts in your own words (*reformulation* notes), and as a container for *reflecting* on what material means to you, particularly within the context of a current project you're working on.

---

2 Richard Yeo, *Notebooks, Recollection, and External Memory: Some Early Modern English Ideas and Practices* (Brill, 2016), 154.

3 Markus Krajewski, *Note-Keeping: History, Theory, Practice of a Counter-Measurement against Forgetting* (Brill, 2016), 319. Emphasis added.

Notes as Memories

Given that a note can be thought of as a thought (pun intended), it can also be thought of as a *memory*. Why? Because a memory is a stored representation of a thought.

Think of a note as a thought, an abstraction, and as a memory. The problem with digital notes is that they are unidimensional rather than multidimensional. They are virtual; they live in a man-made dimension. Physical thoughts present in space and time have more dimensionality than purely metaphysical systems. This is something digital will have to overcome if it wishes to have the potency of analog knowledge systems.

A thought gets stored and represented as a *memory*. It's therefore important to note—again, pun intended—that how human memory works *is not* unidimensional. Rather, human memory is like a matrix. A memory is a combination of multiple *attributes* and *contexts*. A well-developed hypothesis posits that individual memories are distributed over multiple attributes, features, elements, or dimensions.[4]

Let's translate this into something practical: the notecard that I've written on the topic of *love* is easy to spot. Why? Because I decided to write it on an actual leaf!

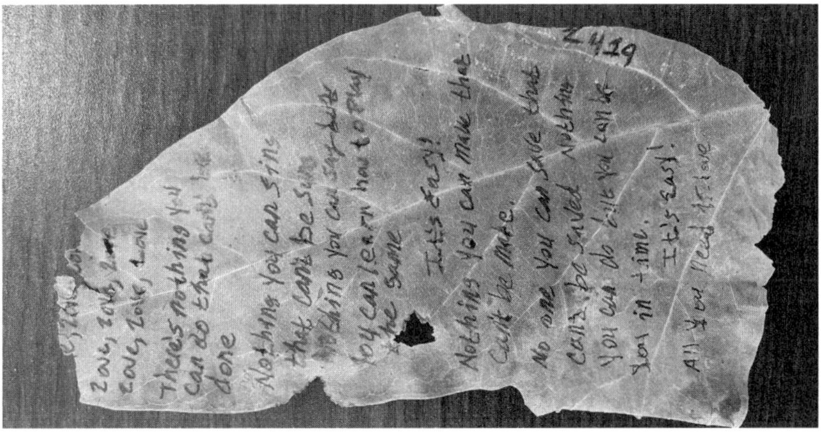

4 Michael Jacob Kahana, Foundations of Human Memory. (New York: Oxford University Press, 2014), 85.

The words on the leaf are the lyrics of *All You Need Is Love* by the *Beatles*.

This is an example of the multi-dimensionality of notes.

You see, early on into a relationship with my now fiancé, I asked her to pick out a leaf for me when she was with our daughter on a hike. This card is packed not only with intriguing features, but with an entire background story as well. The character of this note is also represented by the style of my handwriting, as well as its content.

Human memories function much like this. They are multidimensional objects and not merely digital texts or even digital pictures or diagrams.

The Antinet as a Perfect System of Thought

The Antinet is constructed in a way that emphasizes the two laws that govern thought. The concept that thought is governed by two laws derives from British philosophers John Locke, David Hume, George Berkeley, David Hartley and John Stuart Mill who suggested that thoughts are governed by two components. [5]

1. Contiguity: the notion that ideas that are frequently experienced together become closely associated in one's mind. In the Antinet, the sequence of notes results in closely associated streams of thoughts. These streams of thought are thereby organized closely together in a sequence. This is made possible by the numeric-alpha card addresses and tree structure.

2. Similarity (resemblance): when two ideas are similar, whatever has been closely associated with the first idea (thereby starting the flow of thought) automatically also becomes associated with the following thoughts. The following thoughts are those that then branch downward from the initial thought.

5 Steven Pinker, How the Mind Works, Norton pbk (New York: Norton, 2009), 113.

NOTES AS LEAVES

Another helpful metaphor is to think of notes as *leaves*. The tree metaphor for the Antinet serves as a perfect illustration due to its branching nature. A core component of this metaphor is the leaves on a tree.

The leaves on a tree are (relatively) uniform, yet there's variation between leaves, as well. Some leaves are withered, some have holes in them, and some grow old and dry up. This also happens with notes in the Antinet. Some have holes of logic in them, and some grow old because they're unlinked.

In addition to this, a note-as-a-leaf cannot be simply encapsulated by a short, condensed title. You must view the entire leaf to understand it. When viewing a notecard, you must view the note in its entirety to understand it. On the other hand, with digital notetaking apps, one is forced to squeeze the material of each note into a brief title. This dilutes the material found in the note. For instance, a note that contains profound ideas on the concept of a *thought* is titled *Definition of a Thought*. However, this is not the nature of particular leaves. There's no title for each leaf. To understand the nature of any given leaf you must view the entirety of the leaf. This is the same for notes.

The practical lesson is this: Do not weaken your notes by assigning a human-readable title to them. Respect your thoughts by having the thought contain itself (instead of being contained in a catchy title).

NOTES AS NEURONS

Another way to think of notes is to liken them to neurons in the human brain.

As I detail in a later section on human memory, the neural networks we think of today as *legitimate* are, in reality, merely artificial abstractions, with the result being that the models researchers use to study human memory "bear only a faint resemblance to real biological neurons: they are highly simplified computational 'units' that integrate and transmit information."[6] This description seems to perfectly encapsulate what a note is. Most of what

6 Michael Jacob Kahana, Foundations of Human Memory. (New York: Oxford University Press, 2014), 152.

people think of when they hear the term *neural network* isn't actually a real thing—it's artificial. It's an abstraction. Yet this abstraction nonetheless made it a very useful system in the real world. The same holds true for the Antinet.

Neurons are the perfect stand-in for the concept of notes. Notes fit the definition of "*highly simplified computational 'units' that integrate and transmit information,*" which is one reason why the Antinet works so well—or at least better than information stored in silos of commonplace books.

Niklas Luhmann was familiar with how human memory worked and also deliberate in his design of the Antinet. It's no coincidence that he built his system based on the idea of connections (inspired by connections of neurons in the human brain).

Luhmann pointed out how human memory does not *function as a sum of point-by-point access locations* (such as sequentially moving through notes).[7] Rather your brain utilizes internal links and connections. It's helpful when thinking about a note to view it as a raw unit, as a neuron. The neuron gains its value when it is connected to other notes by way of installing the note under or behind its most similar idea. The neuron is further enriched by connecting to other neurons in your tree of knowledge. This is done by creating remotelinks to other cards on more distant branches of your Antinet.

The latest research in human memory also supports this, revealing evidence for something termed the *distributed representation* of memory.[8] This idea holds that a memory is represented by not merely one notecard (or one neuron), but by an interaction between a large set of neurons.

7 Niklas Luhmann, "Communication with Noteboxes (Revised Edition)," trans. Manfred Kuehn, https://daily.scottscheper.com/zettelkasten/.

8 Michael Jacob Kahana, Foundations of Human Memory. (New York: Oxford University Press, 2014), 26.

THE PROBLEMS WITH THE CURRENT DEFINITIONS OF NOTES WITHIN ZETTELKASTEN LITERATURE

THE PROBLEM WITH THE TERM ZETTEL

The German term *Zettel* translates into "note" in American English. However, in European English it has been translated into "slip," and denotes a slip of paper of A6-size as defined by ISO standards (roughly the size of 4 x 6 inch notecards). Regardless of the slight difference in terms (*note* vs. *slip*), it's become conventional for so-called followers of Zettelkasten to throw around the term *Zettel*. For instance, they ask for critiques on the *Zettels* they've created.

There's one issue, however. Many Zettelkasten enthusiasts use the term Zettel as the equivalent of a *reflection note*. They think of Zettels as some type of evergreen, atomic, permanent note. However, roughly seventeen thousand out of Luhmann's ninety thousand notes were not so-called "Zettels" as these enthusiasts would define it. They were observation notes written down on Luhmann's bibcards. Of the remaining notes, there were many that were just hub notes containing links to other cards (Collectives), or external references (ExRefs). For this reason, I've decided to ditch the whole convention of calling notes Zettels because the term implies that Luhmann had one main type of note. In reality, his so-called "permanent notes" contained several different types of notes. Using the inaccurate and vague term Zettel isn't helpful. It doesn't make sense to obfuscate this system even more than it already has been. For this reason, I hereby sentence the term *Zettel* to death!

Unfortunately Zettel isn't the only term that's unhelpful in the currently confused land of Zettelkasten. Let's go through the other unhelpful terms now.

THE PROBLEM WITH FLEETING NOTES

Fleeting notes is a term coined by Sönke Ahrens in his book, *How to Take Smart Notes*. Ahrens calls fleeting notes those notes that "are only reminders of information [that] can be written in any kind of way and will end up in the trash within a day or two."[9]

The problem with such a concept is that we have zero evidence of Luhmann actually using such a technique. Why? Because they would end up in the trash within a day or two. Quite frankly, I'm not sure why Ahrens includes the concept. My best guess is that this practice is something Ahrens himself uses and decided to prescribe for his readers.

I personally don't have a need to use fleeting notes. I take notes on my bib-cards and then spend my energy processing them by creating main notes. I'm very disciplined and strict about this process. My bib notes and main notes are all I need. If I have a thought that continually arises, I'll wait until I get to my office with my Antinet. If the thought is truly important I'll explore my Antinet and review the stems that the new thought relates to. If the thought is truly important, I'll develop it into a main note.

I think the concept of fleeting notes stems from a place of fear—the fear of a good idea escaping you, never to return. However, I've found that the analog nature of the Antinet has trained my mind and memory to be more disciplined and less sporadic. According to some, we have over six thousand thoughts per day.[10] You have to trust the truly important ones will recur again and again. When they do, don't waste time creating fleeting notes; just create a main note for it, if it's truly relevant.

Luhmann himself was pressed for time and I wouldn't be surprised to learn that he never took fleeting notes, either. He was very disciplined and deliberate in his thinking, and it's probable that his bib notes acted as his fleeting notes—as a place to jot down ideas as they first occurred to him

---

9 Sönke Ahrens, How to Take Smart Notes: One Simple Technique to Boost Writing, Learning and Thinking (2nd Edition), Kindle, 2022, 53.

10 Julie Tseng and Jordan Poppenk, "Brain Meta-State Transitions Demarcate Thoughts across Task Contexts Exposing the Mental Noise of Trait Neuroticism," Nature Communications 11, no. 1 (July 13, 2020): 3480.

while he was reading. Therefore, it makes the whole concept of fleeting notes redundant and unhelpful.

With that said, I do not discount the idea of fleeting notes being valuable for some people. I will grant that the idea of writing down thoughts as they come up is a potentially useful practice. Indeed, writing fleeting thoughts down has been a practice used by some of our greatest thinkers. Nietzsche observed that some of the best ideas are born out in the open (on hikes in nature). Gottfried Wilhelm Leibniz always carried paper with him, as well.[11]

However, I don't think fleeting notes are something that need to be elaborated on too much in the context of knowledge development. It's an obvious practice if you want to function as an adult. It's kind of like keeping track of reminders and appointments. In the rare case I need to capture a fleeting note, I use a weekly paper planner placed in my fanny pack (yes, I rock a fanny pack). I've found a pen and paper planner to be more useful and less distracting than using a to-do app, note app, or calendar app on my phone. There are rare occasions where I'll want to remind myself of a fleeting thought, and in that case I'll write it down in my weekly planner. However, I've noticed a pattern whenever I do this. When it comes time to create a main note for the thought, I usually find that the idea isn't really even valuable or useful.

Again, the whole concept of fleeting notes isn't that important in the workflow of using an Antinet. The important pieces are the bib notes and main notes. For all of these reasons, I opt to drop the whole concept of fleeting notes altogether.

THE PROBLEM WITH PROJECT NOTES

Another term Sönke Ahrens introduced is that of *project notes*. Ahrens explains these are notes which are "kept within a project-specific folder and can be discarded or archived after the project is finished."[12] This whole

---

11 Markus Krajewski, *Note-Keeping: History, Theory, Practice of a Counter-Measurement against Forgetting* (Brill, 2016), 313.

12 Sönke Ahrens, How to Take Smart Notes: One Simple Technique to Boost Writing, Learning and Thinking (2nd Edition), Kindle, 2022, 53.

concept is another Ahrensian invention. One of the most powerful aspects of the Antinet is that the projects you work on will *compound*. Why? Because they're installed in the Antinet. This enables the project you work on for one paper to be potentially used later on in a completely different project. As Johannes Schmidt writes of Luhmann's Antinet, "The bulk of the collections (approximately 75,000 cards) consists of notes documenting the results of Luhmann's readings, his own thoughts, and ideas for *publication projects*."[13] In brief, Luhmann stored the material he worked on for projects inside his own Antinet, not in folders. This can be observed in the notes he created for his paper *Communication with Noteboxes,* as well.[14]

In brief, do not store notes you create for a project in some folder outside the Antinet. Store them in your Antinet so that they can be developed and used for another project in the long term. You'll be surprised how much you end up using from previous material. You may end up stumbling upon the material by accident at the perfect time when you'll need it most.

THE PROBLEM WITH LITERATURE NOTES

Literature note is another term introduced by Ahrens. He writes, "Whenever you read something, make notes about the content."[15] These notes are what he calls *literature notes.*

Yet there's a problem with the term literature notes. First off, it's vague. What are literature notes? They're brief *observations* of what you have read. They also are placed on a bibcard. For this reason, I prefer the term bib notes (or observation notes). Second, as mentioned elsewhere, the term literature notes implies one takes these notes from the literature one reads. However, this is not the case. These types of notes can and should be drawn from many sources (podcasts, videos, lectures, and more). In the words of John Aubrey,

13 Johannes Schmidt, "Niklas Luhmann's Card Index: Thinking Tool, Communication Partner, Publication Machine," Forgetting Machines. Knowledge Management Evolution in Early Modern Europe 53 (2016), 292. Emphasis added.

14 "ZK II: Sheet 9/8—Niklas Luhmann Archive," accessed April 20, 2022, https://niklas-luhmann-archiv.de/bestand/zettelkasten/zettel/ZK_2_NB_9-8_V.

15 Sönke Ahrens, How to Take Smart Notes: One Simple Technique to Boost Writing, Learning and Thinking (2nd Edition), Kindle, 2022, 34.

a fellow of the Royal Society, "material gathered should not be confined to that offered in books."[16]

For these reasons, I suggest dropping the term *literature notes* and instead using *bib notes* (short for *bibliography notes*). In cases in which you're using a 1-step book-to-maincard method, then it's more appropriate to refer to them as *observation notes.*

THE PROBLEM WITH PERMANENT NOTES

Permanent note is yet another Ahrensian term that has become part of the Zettelkasten canon. Ahrens defines permanent notes as those "which will never be thrown away and [that] contain the necessary information in a permanently understandable way."[17]

There are several problems with this term.

First off, the term *permanent* is redundant. Every note you install in the Antinet is permanent. The cards you place in the main box of your Antinet are permanent, and so are the cards you install in the bibliography and index box. Calling a note permanent doesn't differentiate it from the many different types of permanent notes that Luhmann, for example, created.

What's even more perplexing is that the idea of permanent notes seems primarily geared toward digital Zettelkasten practitioners. The idea behind permanent notes is that they permanently define a concept and are then referenced (without being deleted or updated). However, this is problematic for digital notetaking apps. Why? Because digital notes are anything but permanent! Their contents are constantly being refactored, updated, deleted and rearranged. For this reason a new term was invented called *evergreen* notes. According to the inventor of the term, evergreen notes are "written and organized to evolve, contribute, and accumulate over time, across proj-

---

16 Richard Yeo, *Notebooks, Recollection, and External Memory: Some Early Modern English Ideas and Practices* (Brill, 2016), 138.

17 Sönke Ahrens, How to Take Smart Notes: One Simple Technique to Boost Writing, Learning and Thinking (2nd Edition), Kindle, 2022, 53.

ects."[18] The coiner of this term differentiates it from another coined term: *transient notes.* The idea of these notes centers around the idea of notes just being stored in containers and never evolving.

All of this stuff is just confusing gibberish. It's a case of people trying to invent terms to encompass what Luhmann's Antinet really was. Luhmann's notes were indeed permanent. They were not edited. Using such a system, one's thinking is thereby stamped in history. Yet the notes also evolved thanks to the tree structure of the Antinet. This concept isn't really captured in the terms permanent notes or evergreen notes.

For these reason I drop the term permanent notes altogether (same goes for evergreen notes). A better way of thinking about notes is in the terminology I'll be introducing soon. But before I introduce the four types of notes, let's first talk about the art of note creation.

THE ART OF NOTE CREATION

The following section may create endless suffering for computer scientists, engineers, and especially digital notetaking junkies (the ones with one-hundred-point checklists and templates for creating notes). Here's the truth: the Antinet may not be the right tool for those focused on optimization and strict adherence to protocol.

NOTES ARE A MEANS TO AN END

The Antinet—and any knowledge development system for that matter—is not *the end*. It's not the output. It's not the destination. Knowledge development should not be beautiful; it should be messy, drenched in sweat, ink, coffee stains and some loops that are never closed. Knowledge development contains notes which are raw products. The materials serve as products of your thinking. This raw product doesn't happen before or after you think, it happens *as you think*. The symbols on physical paper represent the truest and closest representation of your thinking.

18 "Evergreen Notes," Andy's working notes, accessed April 21, 2022, https://notes.andymatuschak.org/Evergreennotes.

The goal is for your creative output, not your notes, to be beautiful and profound.

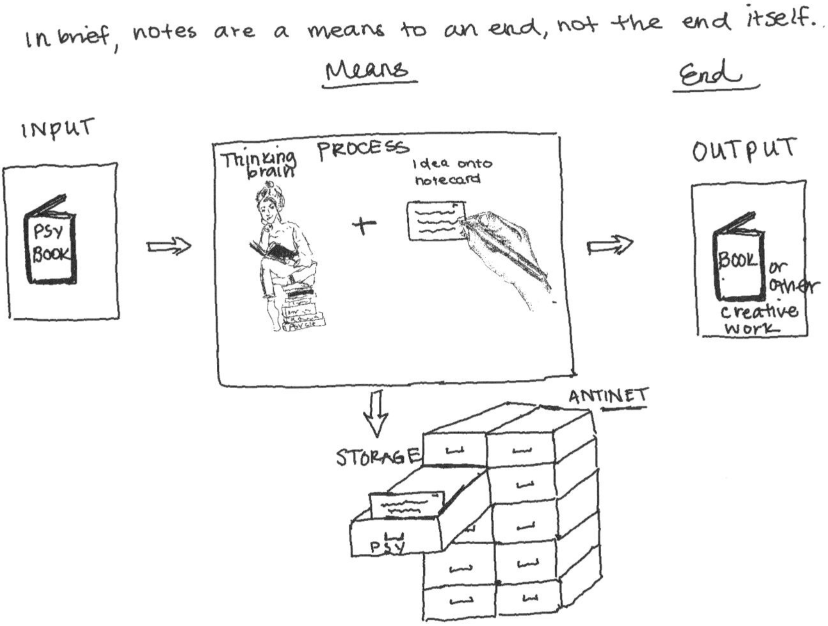

In brief, *notes are a means to an end, not the end itself.* The goal is for the *output phase* to be deeply developed and ordered. It's OK for the *process phase* to be seemingly chaotic.

NOT EVERY NOTE WILL BE USED

Another thing to keep in mind is that you should not put pressure on yourself to only produce notes that end up getting used.

When writing notes, according to Luhmann, "the first thing one does is produce a lot of waste."[19] If you don't anticipate this, you may find yourself discouraged; this is why many people burn out on personal knowledge management systems, and digital Zettelkasten with which it's all-too-easy to create mountains of information. You hit a certain point where you've created so

19 **Niklas Luhmann, Niklas Luhmann Short Cuts (English Translation), 2002, 83.**

much information such that seemingly none of it will ever be used. This can lead to despair and to people giving up knowledge development altogether.[20]

As Luhmann acknowledges, "We are educated to expect something useful from our activities and otherwise quickly lose encouragement."[21] However, with the Antinet, I've found that since it takes longer to produce material, you're incentivized to produce less waste. In addition, you produce less overall. This results in *more* of the material and notes you create being used (in comparison to digital workflows that distract you with the labeling, organizing, and reworking of notes).

The good news about the Antinet, and one of its invaluable features, is that it forces users to "prepare their notes in such a way that they are available for later access."[22] If not easily findable, every note you take is a candidate for an unexpected and invaluable insight if you happen to stumble upon it. Even if you don't stumble upon a particular card, it creates what Luhmann deems, "a consoling illusion" that mitigates against the risk of discouragement during the knowledge development process.[23]

In brief, think of knowledge development with the Antinet like exercising the mind. Exercise is good for you. Creating notes and installing them into the Antinet is good for you. It's a process. It's a workout for your mind. You'll start seeing results in the short term, yes. However, it's something you ought to strive to keep up as a long-term practice.

PRESS ON

When using an Antinet for knowledge development, you must remind yourself to do one thing: *press on*. Prepare yourself to take notes by hand. You must train yourself to slow down and pause to think. Reformulating the author's words with your own voice is very hard work.

---

20 "Rank and File," Real Life, accessed January 14, 2022, https://reallifemag.com/rank-and-file/.

21 Niklas Luhmann, Niklas Luhmann Short Cuts (English Translation), 2002, 83.

22 Niklas Luhmann, Niklas Luhmann Short Cuts (English Translation), 2002, 83.

23 Niklas Luhmann, Niklas Luhmann Short Cuts (English Translation), 2002, 83.

Luhmann's advice on how to read scientific literature echoes this advice. He says it's best to take reformulation notes—and continue to do so—even if it means you must "postpone the hope of scientific productivity for a while."[24] For challenging texts, this is how you level up in your reading. It's how you level up your intellect. Slowing down is how you get to the point where you can take reflection notes on advanced texts.

THE PROCESS IS MORE IMPORTANT THAN THE RESULT

As Richard Feynman explained, his notes were not a record of his thinking; they *were* his thinking. "They are my thinking process," Feynman says.[25]

The goal of creating notes is *not* to provide you with a written record of information. Rather, it's to develop your mind—it's to develop your thoughts.[26] This is one reason why I don't lose sleep at night. I don't fear the prospect of my Antinet catching on fire. The transformation within one's brain (using an Antinet) is more valuable than undeveloped information stored on a computer (which doesn't face the same risk of destruction in terms of fire or flood).

As one cognitive scientist puts it, "research reveals the main value of note-taking is through its effect on how you encode the information in your brain." In other words, she continues, "the *act* of note-taking is more important than the result."[27] I agree.

THE TWO CLASSES OF NOTES

There are two types of note creation: Notetaking and *notemaking*.[28]

24 Niklas Luhmann, Niklas Luhmann Short Cuts (English Translation), 2002, 83.

25 "How Writing Improves Our Thinking," Residential Systems, June 15, 2020, https://www.residentialsystems.com/blogs/how-writing-improves-our-thinking.

26 Fiona McPherson, Effective Note-taking, revised edition (Wellington: Wayz Press, 2018), 6.

27 Fiona McPherson, Effective Note-taking, revised edition (Wellington: Wayz Press, 2018), 6.

28 Fiona McPherson, Effective Note-taking, revised edition (Wellington: Wayz Press, 2018), 5.

Notetaking

Notetaking refers to the process of recording your own *observations* that you have while engaging with a source such as a book. For instance, let's talk about what occurs when you use the 2-step Luhmannian bibcard method. When you record individual bibnotes on a bibcard, the nature of the notes are *observations*. You're recording the thoughts you have while reading the text. In essence, you're taking notes directly influenced by the source.

Notemaking

With notemaking, you're a step beyond notetaking and are actually creating a standalone note from the observations you've made while reading. You *make* a main note from the observations you've recorded on your bibcard. The main notes are either *excerpts, reformulations,* or *reflections* of the material. The difference between *notetaking* and *notemaking* is a little fuzzy—especially with regards to *excerpt notes* (as they're a direct copy of the source material). Yet, because excerpt notes are installed and applied to a specific area or line of thought within the branches or stems of your Antinet, it's defensible that they be classified as part of the *notemaking* process. When you cut the umbilical cord of the material that directly connects to a book, and instead connect the material to a chain of concepts in your Antinet, you're partaking in notemaking.

Notetaking vs. Notemaking

In summary, notetaking is a process enacted through creating bibcards which contain observations during your readings. Notemaking is a process enacted through main notes which contain excerpt notes, reformulation notes, and reflection notes. The differences will start to make sense where it truly matters: in practice. Let's now talk about the four main types of notes in practice.

YOUR NOTE-CREATION REPERTOIRE

You must have multiple note-creation strategies in your repertoire when creating knowledge. There's "no one 'best' strategy for taking notes," states one cognitive scientist.[29]

---

29 Fiona McPherson, Effective Note-taking, revised edition (Wellington: Wayz Press,

The strategy you choose for creating knowledge depends on several factors.[30] What type of note you decide to create depends on your *working memory capacity*. As you use the Antinet over time, your working memory capacity will improve. Yet sometimes you don't have enough bandwidth to simply *reflect* on notes. Sometimes you need to first create a full *excerpt* note in order to construct several cards to express your thoughts. This is one factor that has an impact on which type of note you create during knowledge development.

Another factor that affects note creation is *external distraction*. We already know how distracting the digital environment can be. Research shows us how often people are distracted and pulled into checking communication apps. For 50% of people, it's every six minutes![31] Yet even following an analog workflow, your environment may provide distractions. If you're crammed onto a plane, it's a lot easier to use the 2-step Luhmannian bibcard method, for instance, than it would be trying to manage fifteen different notecards on your tray table.

Not only do external distractions affect your workflow, but *internal distractions* do so as well. When you practice the 1-step book-to-maincard method, it requires a lot of focus. You must be in a very present state of mind to have the self-awareness to know when you're getting unnecessarily bogged down in material. If your internal life is in a state of distress and you're facing many internal distractions, your note creation method should accommodate that state.

The last factor that affects how you should create notes is the *difficulty* of the material. If you're tackling a challenging text, understanding the material is a prerequisite for reflecting on the material. How well you understand what you're reading shapes how you should go about creating notes. In many cases you must first either excerpt or reformulate the material.

2018), 10.

30 Fiona McPherson, Effective Note-taking, revised edition (Wellington: Wayz Press, 2018), 10.

31 Cal Newport, A World Without Email: Reimagining Work in an Age of Communication Overload (New York: Portfolio, 2021), 11.

It's important to know about these factors when deciding *what* type of note to create, and *how* to create them. However don't worry yourself about trying to hold the types in mind during the note creation process. The understanding of these factors, and what process works best for you will come with time and practice.

Let's now get into the four types of notes.

The Four Types of Notes

There are four types of notes:

1. Observation notes
2. Excerpt notes
3. Reformulation notes
4. Reflection notes

Observation notes are traditionally recorded on bibcards (vertical 4 x 6 inch notecards used while reading or engaging with a source), whereas the other three notes (excerpt, reformulation, and reflection notes) are created on maincards (which are horizontal 4 x 6 inch notecards).

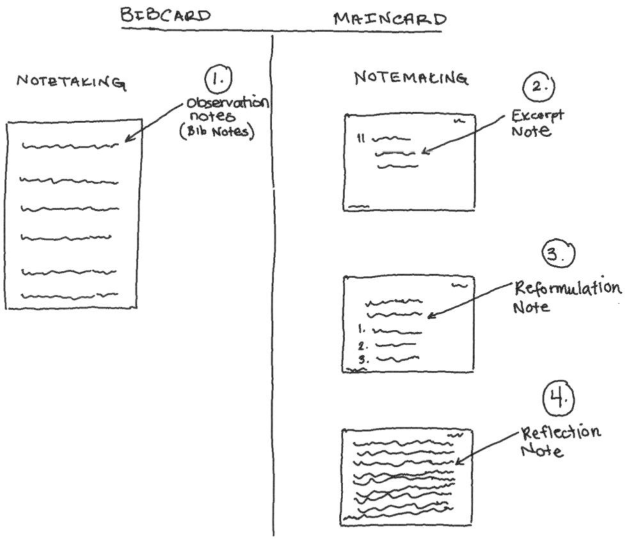

Let's go through each of these in detail now.

OBSERVATION NOTES

John Aubrey, a fellow of the Royal Society, once likened the taking of notes to being a traveller. You don't want to merely copy down a diagram of the map, he said. Rather, you want to explore the land or territory and record your own *observations*.[32] In other words, you want to record your own thoughts. These types of notes are observation notes. John Locke took these types of notes, as well. One scholar referred to Locke's notes as "observations and thoughts."[33] Another scholar refers to observation notes as "one's own comments or annotations on individual textual passages."[34]

Where Observation Notes Live

I teach Antinetters to employ the 2-step Luhmannian bibcard method, with the notes written down on the bibcard being observation notes. While I hold that bibcards are the best medium for capturing observation notes, they're not the only place observation notes can live. As previously mentioned, some users jot down observation notes in book margins. Some may even extract observation notes onto individual (non-bibcard) notecards while reading a text. In fact, I've done such on 3 x 5 inch notecards before.

Observation Notes vs. Reflection Notes

The main characteristic that differentiates an observation note from a reflection note is that observation notes are very short. They're brief pieces of text that represent the brief thought you have immediately in the moment of reading a text.

EXCERPT NOTES

Excerpt notes are notes in that you copy down word-for-word from a text as a direct quote. Here's an example:

32 Richard Yeo, *Notebooks, Recollection, and External Memory: Some Early Modern English Ideas and Practices* (Brill, 2016), 138-9.

33 Richard Yeo, *Notebooks, Recollection, and External Memory: Some Early Modern English Ideas and Practices* (Brill, 2016), 149.

34 Markus Krajewski, *Note-Keeping: History, Theory, Practice of a Counter-Measurement against Forgetting* (Brill, 2016), 322.

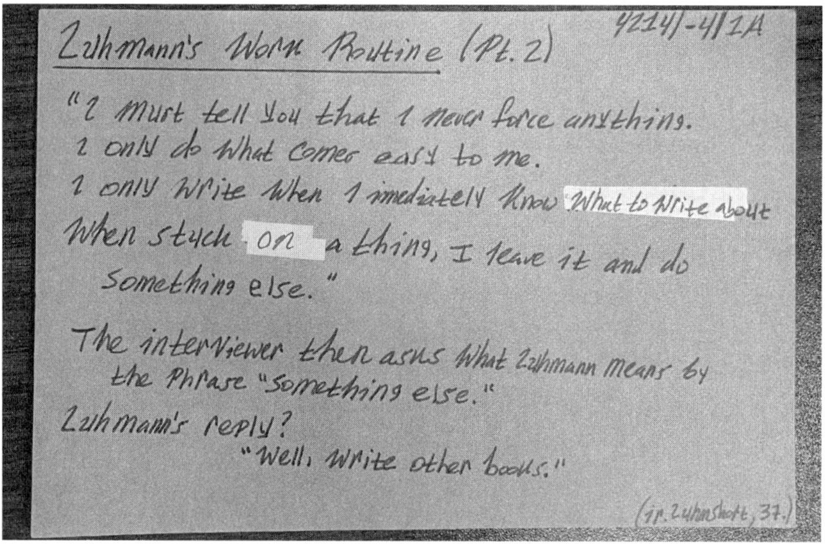

According to one scholar, excerpts do the following things: (1) they capture a text's "train of thought"; (2) they capture the structure of a text's argument; and (3) they contain the worthwhile details of a text and its references to secondary literature.[35] These serve as a few reasons why one should opt to excerpt texts.

However, I think there are other reasons to employ excerpt notes. First, sometimes the prose of a text is so commanding that it's worthwhile to excerpt the entire quote. It's worth excerpting in order to use the quote in your creative output. It's also worth excerpting in order to neuroimprint the prose onto your mind so that you can refine and develop your own writing skills.

"Sometimes a mere recital of facts can itself lead to a greater understanding," Mortimer Adler writes.[36] In other words, the practice of writing down an important snippet of text that you don't quite understand can actually lead to more understanding. Elsewhere in this book I mentioned that in the late

---

35 Markus Krajewski, *Note-Keeping: History, Theory, Practice of a Counter-Measurement against Forgetting* (Brill, 2016), 322.

36 Mortimer Jerome Adler and Charles Van Doren, How to Read a Book, Rev. and updated ed (New York: Simon and Schuster, 1972), 10.

seventeenth century at Harvard College, students were taught from textbooks bought in England. How were they taught specifically? By having students write down the material contained in the texts by hand.[37] Harvard implemented this practice because it worked. It may not be the most engaging way to teach; however the solitude and time spent rehearsing the words in one's mind, by excerpting them down on paper, ends up leading to greater understanding of the material.

I advise the use of excerpt notes when you're trying to really stretch your mind. When you're tackling a challenging text and you encounter a critical part, it may be wise to excerpt the section or concepts. When engaging with a challenging text, it's also recommended to employ the 1-step book-to-maincard method.

If you're engaging with a not-so-challenging text, there are still several instances in which you ought to excerpt material. For instance, if you wish to use the excerpt to support your argument, it's often useful to quote the author directly. It's also advisable to use a direct quote when your goal is to *refute* an argument.

REFORMULATION NOTES

Luhmann was adamant in his views that one should not get bogged down with excerpt notes. Yet he seemed to follow the *do as I say, not as I do* principle in this regard. We know this because he took extensive excerpt notes. Regardless, Luhmann does instruct us in the taking of a special type of note called *reformulations*. "Perhaps the best method is to take notes—not excerpts, but condensed *reformulations* of what has been read."[38]

Reformulation notes entail summarizing and creating a form of the idea *in your own words* so that, as Luhmann put it, you are creating a "re-description of what has already been described."[39]

---

37 Ann Blair, *Early Modern Attitudes toward the Delegation of Copying and Note-Taking* (Brill, 2016), 278.

38 Niklas Luhmann, Niklas Luhmann Short Cuts (English Translation), 2002, 83. Emphasis added.

39 Niklas Luhmann, Niklas Luhmann Short Cuts (English Translation), 2002, 83.

Why Reformulations?

According to Luhmann, reformulation notes automatically train one's mind in such a way that it creates a lens or "frame of mind" for spotting patterns.[40] This process operates in the same way the index does. Reformulation notes enable you to neuroimprint ideas so that you can observe and read literature differently.

Reformulation notes force you to question why the author uses certain words. You're able to pay attention to vocabulary and usage. How? Because you're investing the additional time necessary in understanding a text well enough to re-describe the concept; you're forced to spot "conditions that lead to the text offering certain descriptions and not others," Luhmann says.[41]

Reformulating an author's ideas in your own words forces you to *slow down* and *chew on* the material. This practice forces you to think.

Fiona McPherson, who specializes in the field of notetaking, echoes Luhmann's advice. She asserts, "Note-taking is effective to the extent that you paraphrase, organize and make sense of information while taking notes."[42] Essentially, one of the most effective forms of notetaking is that of reformulation notes.

Like Luhmann, McPherson goes on to warn against excerpt notes. She refers to excerpt notes as "verbatim notes," asserting they're of "minimum value" unless they are used as a staging post, or as "stepping stones" to later paraphrase and then turn into reformulation notes. With this, I partly agree, however I urge one to not overlook the power of excerpt notes in neuroimprinting valuable ideas onto your mind.

McPherson holds a very strong opinion on the importance of reformulation notes, stating that reformulations are "the most important" Notetaking

---

40 Niklas Luhmann, Niklas Luhmann Short Cuts (English Translation), 2002, 83.

41 Niklas Luhmann, Niklas Luhmann Short Cuts (English Translation), 2002, 83.

42 Fiona McPherson, Effective Note-taking, revised edition (Wellington: Wayz Press, 2018), 6.

skill.[43] While I think this may be an overstatement (each type of note has its utility), I won't disagree with her on the potency of reformulations.

Good reformulations extract the meaning of what the author says. The goal centers on creating reformulations that are short, relevant, and in your own words.[44]

Types of Reformulation Notes

There are several types of reformulation notes. The following collection is by no means comprehensive, and the lines get fuzzy when you zoom in with a microscope around their borders; the types of reformulations listed will certainly give you some idea and a feel for their nature. Let's go through them now.

TOPICAL REFORMULATIONS

Topical reformulations are text-based summaries of content. The goal here is quite simple. Instead of excerpting an entire passage, you want to explain the idea in your own words. Topical reformulations "summarize the main points without adding any new information or offering a new perspective."[45]

Here's an example of a topical reformulation:

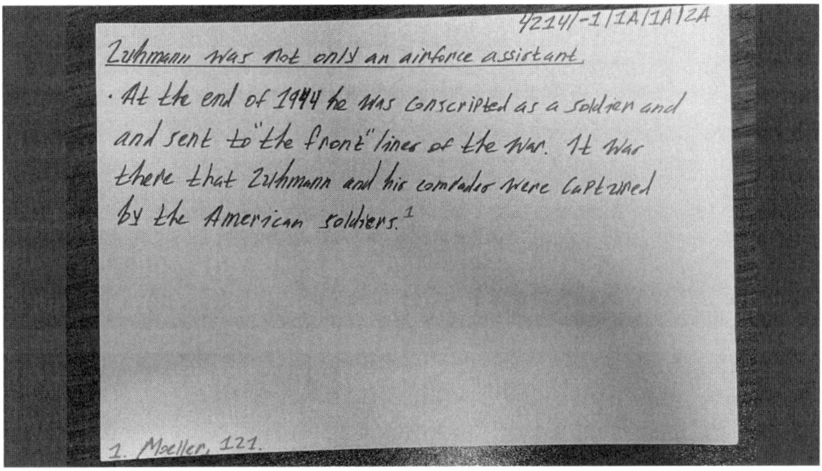

43 Fiona McPherson, Effective Note-taking, revised edition (Wellington: Wayz Press, 2018), 60.
44 Fiona McPherson, Effective Note-taking, revised edition (Wellington: Wayz Press, 2018), 67.
45 Fiona McPherson, Effective Note-taking, revised edition (Wellington: Wayz Press, 2018), 66.

OUTLINE REFORMULATIONS

Outline reformulations refer to the process of breaking down material into a series of steps. For instance, if faced with a daunting wall of text, it's helpful to break apart the material into steps. Here's an example of this:

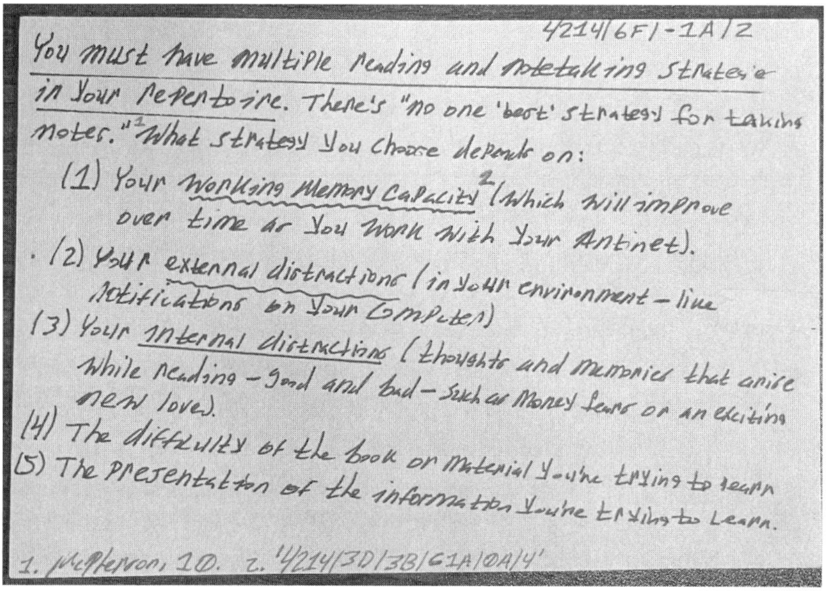

4214/6F1-1A/2

You must have multiple reading and notetaking strategies in your repertoire. There's "no one 'best' strategy for taking notes."[1] What strategy you choose depends on:

(1) Your working memory capacity[2] (which will improve over time as you work with your Antinet).

(2) Your external distractions (in your environment—like notifications on your computer)

(3) Your internal distractions (thoughts and memories that arise while reading—good and bad—such as money fears or an exciting new love).

(4) The difficulty of the book or material you're trying to learn

(5) The presentation of the information you're trying to learn.

1. McPherson, 10. 2. '4214/3D/3B/61A/0A/4'

This outline reformulation will look familiar to you. It's what I used to assemble the section several pages back on having a note creation repertoire.

There are several scenarios in which outline reformulations prove to be the best reformulation strategy. Here are such instances:

1. If the text is simple and based primarily on facts, it's a good idea to use outline reformulations.

2. If you're limited on time, then it's a good idea to use outline reformulations (instead of diagram reformulations, which will be explained shortly).

3. If the material will not represent a major framework in what you intend to teach, then it's a good idea to opt for an outline reformulation (instead of a diagram reformulation).

4. If the information is more hierarchical in nature, then it's a good idea to employ an outline reformulation. Where outline reformulations really shine is in conjunction with texts presenting hierarchical material. Indeed, perhaps "they're only good for displaying hierarchical information."[46]

DIAGRAM REFORMULATIONS

Diagram reformulations are doodles, graphics, illustrations or drawings that represent an idea. You've seen such diagram illustrations throughout this text. The pretty drawn illustrations in this text were made by my lovely fiancé. However they initially began as notecards drawn by myself.

For instance here's one of my diagram reformulations:

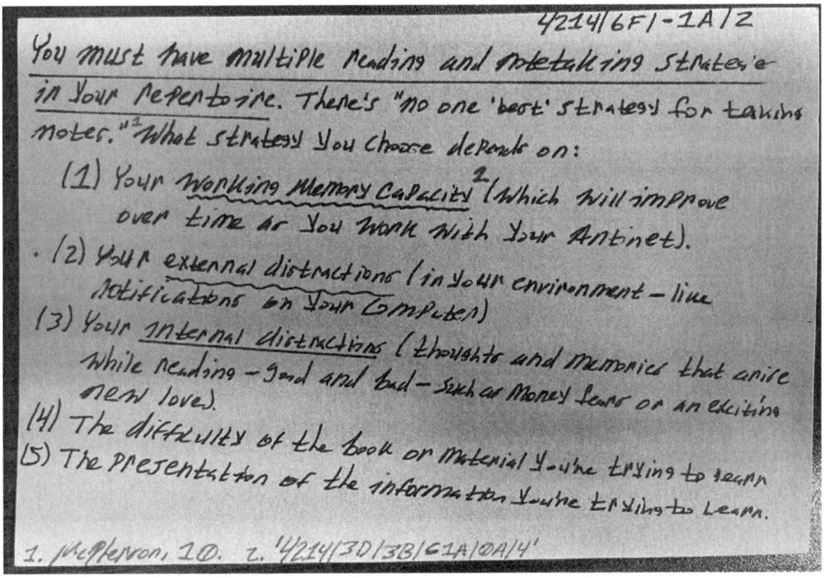

After my fiancé drew it up, it turned out like this:

46 Fiona McPherson, Effective Note-taking, revised edition (Wellington: Wayz Press, 2018), 91.

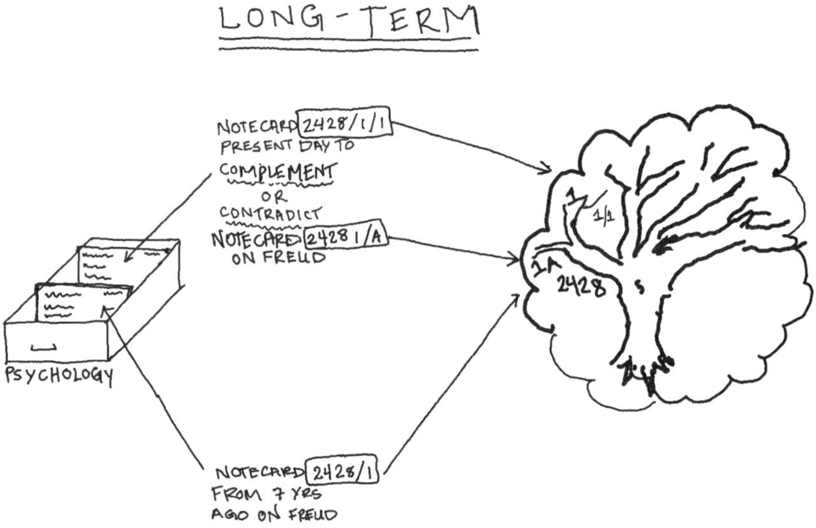

These are diagram reformulations, and I believe they contain the most untapped potential for the Antinet. It's truly remarkable how much understanding and knowledge can be communicated through simple diagrams. It's a practice I've never seen Luhmann himself do, yet it's something I highly recommend integrating into your own repertoire.

The earliest human communication through time, using physical representation, was expressed not in words, but in pictures—using pictographs and cave paintings.[47]

According to some research, diagram reformulations are more effective in procuring long-term recall of material, and they have been shown to greatly facilitate many forms of learning.[48] The biggest limiting factor of diagram reformulations is the *time* they require to make.[49]

---

47 "Ancient Cave Art May Be Origin of Modern Language," Science & Research News | Frontiers (blog), March 7, 2018, https://blog.frontiersin.org/2018/03/07/language-cave-art-mit/.

48 Allan Paivio, Mental Representations: A Dual Coding Approach, Oxford Psychology Series (New York: Oxford University Press, 1990).

49 Fiona McPherson, Effective Note-taking, revised edition (Wellington: Wayz Press, 2018), 89-90.

Not only do Diagram reformulations require more time to create, often, they also require more time to comprehend. With complex diagrams, it's almost easier to comprehend something by simply ingesting a page of text. This is why it's helpful to adhere to a few best practices and guidelines when creating diagrams.

BEST PRACTICES FOR DIAGRAM REFORMULATIONS

Research holds that the best diagrams "portray a series of steps, in a cause-and-effect chain, with explanatory text that is integrated with the illustrations." Research studies also suggest diagrams are "more effective than a purely verbal summary."[50] However, again it's important to note the importance of creating cause-and-effect chains in your diagrams because cause-and-effect chains are more effective representations than a mere listing of facts.

The best diagrams have two traits. They are *concise* and *coherent*.[51] In exhibiting concision, they are simple illustrations with labels one to four words in length. Coherence is manifested when the elements are relevant and connected and show a simple cause-and-effect chain. The label corresponds congruently with the illustration or graphic it's paired with.

REFLECTION NOTES

In teaching about the types of notes used in an Antinet, I've tried my best to simplify things as much as possible. If I wanted to simplify the four types of notes even further, I'd find myself tempted to figure out a way to combine observation notes into reflection notes. However, this simply does not reflect reality. Observation notes and reflection notes are two distinct types of notes.

Antonin Sertillanges points out, "Reading itself should awaken *reflection*."[52] Yet readers cannot expect to simply stop every time they have a thought and reflect deeply on it. Reflection requires some time to ruminate and think about material. Reflection first requires a thought or observation about the

---

50 Fiona McPherson, Effective Note-taking, revised edition (Wellington: Wayz Press, 2018), 95.

51 Fiona McPherson, Effective Note-taking, revised edition (Wellington: Wayz Press, 2018), 96.

52 OP A. G. Sertillanges, The Intellectual Life: Its Spirit, Conditions, Methods, trans. Mary Ryan, Reprint edition (Washington, D.C.: The Catholic University of America Press, 1992), 190.

material being read, and then it requires some time to ruminate and think about it. This is why it's helpful to first extract observations onto bibcards during reading. This enables you to let the thought ruminate and then to allocate time later to reflect on it.

Robert Boyle seems to support this notion, as well. Boyle argued that while reading, our thoughts must be analyzed so "our *reflections* on what we have *observ'd,* improves it into consequences new Axioms and Uses."[53] Boyle points to the process of turning your observation notes into well-developed reflection notes later on.

So what are reflections?

Reflections are notes in which you apply your own experiences, meaning, interpretations, opinions, conclusions, and decisions to material. It's where you begin to inject your own theory into units of knowledge. The Antinet process is founded on taking complex sources of knowledge, and simplifying them into understandable units. From there you begin assembling more complexity into those units of knowledge again. This is done by way of creating reflection notes.

One of the areas where Ahrens and I seem to agree is in the area of *elaborative rehearsal.* This involves thinking about the *meaning* of an idea and explaining the concept in your own words.[54] This type of process encapsulates what takes place within reflection notes. Awareness of the power of elaborative rehearsal is not new. It's an ancient notion expressed by classical scholars in the motto *notae propriae, notae optimae,* meaning "your own notes are the best notes."[55]

---

53 Richard Yeo, *Notebooks, Recollection, and External Memory: Some Early Modern English Ideas and Practices* (Brill, 2016), 142. Emphasis added.

54 Michael Jacob Kahana, Foundations of Human Memory. (New York: Oxford University Press, 2014), 246-7.

55 Alberto Cevolini, ed., Forgetting Machines: Knowledge Management Evolution in Early Modern Europe, Library of the Written Word, volume 53 (Leiden; Boston: Brill, 2016), 5.

So what do reflection notes look like? They are longer in nature than observation notes, typically filling up an entire 4 x 6 inch notecard. Think of reflection notes as medium-sized paragraphs.

Here is an example of a reflection note:

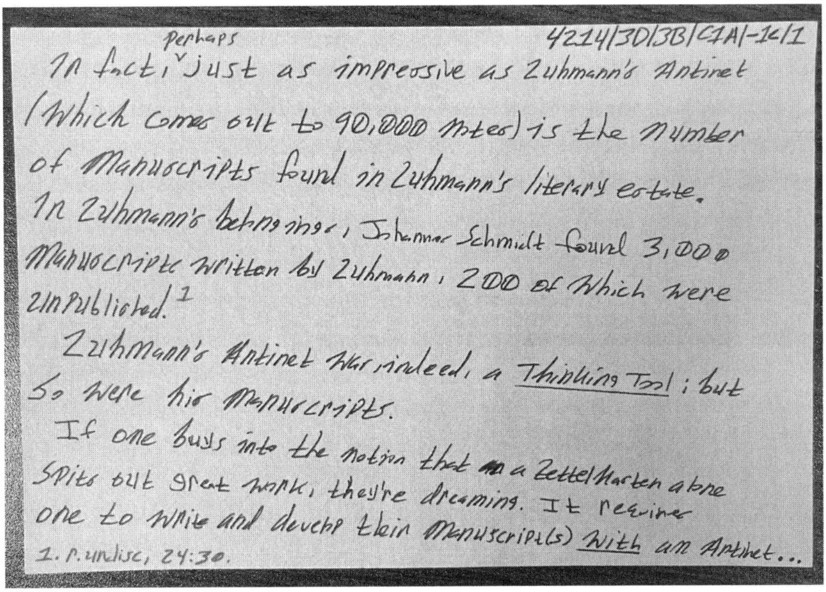
4214/3D/3B/C7A1-1c/1

In fact, perhaps just as impressive as Luhmann's Antinet (which comes out to 90,000 notes) is the number of manuscripts found in Luhmann's literary estate. In Luhmann's belongings, Johannes Schmidt found 3,000 manuscripts written by Luhmann, 200 of which were unpublished.[1]

Luhmann's Antinet was, indeed, a Thinking Tool; but so were his manuscripts.

If one buys into the notion that a Zettelkasten alone spits out great work, they're dreaming. It requires one to write and develop their manuscript(s) with an Antinet...

1. P. undisc, 24:30.

In this note I am reflecting on an observation I made while listening to a podcast on Luhmann's Antinet.[56] At roughly the twenty-four minute and thirty second mark in the video, Johannes Schmidt shared something I found irresistible. I decided to *select* this observation as important and then *extract* the observation onto my bibcard. The observation was simply that three thousand manuscripts were found in Luhmann's literary estate after he passed away. I found this to be a shockingly large amount of material. Imagine what three thousand drafts of papers you're working on would look like! I then decided to *reflect* on this idea, which made me realize that Luhmann's thinking *did not* exclusively take place in his Antinet alone.

---

56 Undisciplined, Archiving Luhmann w/ Johannes Schmidt, 2021, https://www.youtube.com/watch?v=kz2K3auPLWU.

It may have originated in the Antinet. However, at least some of his thinking was extended by writing out his ideas in the manuscripts.

Here's the important part: this reflection did not happen in my mind *before* I wrote the reflection note. Rather it happened *as* I wrote the reflection note. This reflection note *is* my thinking. This reflection note *is* where the idea came from. It did not happen as a pre-conceived step that occurred in my mind before I actually sat down to write it. This, my friend, shows the true power of the Antinet. It expresses the power of writing by hand. The act of writing by hand enables you to *reflect* more effectively than you would by typing on a keyboard like a hyperactive monkey (one that deludes itself into thinking it forms thoughts exclusively in the mind). Thinking can certainly happen by way of keyboard; however, I contend the best ideas emerge by way of reflection with only pen and paper at hand. After which, keyboards should serve as the place to revise, edit and clarify your thoughts.

Here is an example of Luhmann's reflection notes:

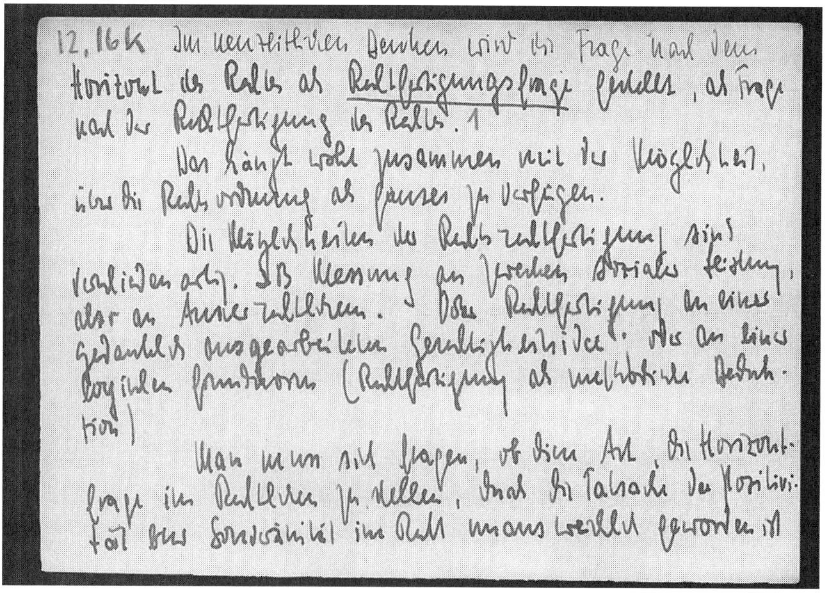

PHOTO CREDIT: "ZK I: Zettel 12,16k—Niklas Luhmann-Archiv," accessed April 21, 2022, https://niklas-luhmann-archiv.de/bestand/zettelkasten/zettel/ZK_1_NB_12-16k_V.

Here's the English translation of the note:

> 12.16k In modern thinking, the question of the horizon of law is posed as a question of justification, as a question of the justification of law.
>
> This probably has something to do with the possibility of disposing of the legal system as a whole.
>
> The possibilities of justification are varied; Eg measurement based on the purpose of social performance, i.e. on the extra-legal. Or justification based on a mentally worked out idea of justice; or a basic logical norm (justification as methodical deduction).
>
> One has to ask oneself whether this way of posing the horizon question in legal matters has become unavoidable due to the fact of positivity or sovereignty in law.

Note how Luhmann makes a statement or observation ("*In modern thinking…*"). Yet he then begins reflecting on this observation ("*This probably has something to do with…*").

This gives you a glimpse into the nature of reflection notes. The lines between different note types get blurry when you zoom in: sometimes your reflection notes will need to contain an excerpt, or you may use an excerpt before you begin to reflect on the author's point. You may also desire to use an excerpt in your reflection note to prove your point or to first reformulate material before you reflect on it. Again, every category gets fuzzy when you zoom in close enough. The main characteristic that differentiates a reflection note from the others, however, is that you write the note as if it will be used as a paragraph or section in the project you're actively working on.

This brings us back to the whole notion of *growth* vs. *contribution*. In brief, focus on contribution so that you can grow more.

Write Reflection Notes as If You're Teaching

One individual who has taught me a lot in regards to entrepreneurship and marketing is Russell Brunson. I don't relate to Brunson on all levels (as I'm not a Mormon with five children, nor do I look like a fifteen year-old boy); still, I greatly admire his enthusiasm and knowledge when it comes to marketing and entrepreneurship.

Brunson has built a multi-hundred million dollar company with over five hundred employees. What's more, he runs it while regularly putting out great content for entrepreneurs. One of Brunson's practices centers on the idea of getting an immediate return on investment (ROI) out of every one of his activities.

During one period, Brunson got sucked into reading the 1,168 page book, *Atlas Shrugged.* He had decided to read it because he had heard it mentioned over and over throughout his life. Now, this is a very long book that took him many months to read; it took him away from the time he would have otherwise allocated to his company and his family. *Atlas Shrugged* has many deep philosophical lessons that can serve as important frameworks to holds in one's mind for life; yet its ideas are not *immediately* practical.

Therefore, because the book has a long-term ROI, instead of a short-term, immediate ROI, what Brunson decided to do was turn the experience of reading the book into a three-part series on his popular podcast. In effect he was able to get an immediate ROI out of reading a behemoth-sized book.

Because he focuses on sharing what he learns while he's still growing, he was then able to teach the book *Atlas Shrugged* to his audience, leading him to attain a richer understanding by teaching it. "If you really want to learn something, write a book on it," Brunson says.[57] In turn, he got an immediate ROI out of the book by providing his audience with valuable content, keeping his community engaged and growing.

---

57 Russell Brunson, "Outwitting The Devil with Josh Forti," Marketing Secrets Podcast.

The lesson here is that the process is not about constant, never-ending *growth*; it's about constant, never-ending *contribution*.

Write your reflection notes as if you're *teaching* an audience. Through teaching, we gain a deeper understanding of material. Strive to make the material something you could share with your audience as quickly as is feasible. Even if you don't end up sharing the content, when you stumble upon the note several years later, you'll find the material easier to understand.

Reformulation vs. Reflection

Sometimes people get confused about the difference between reformulation notes and reflection notes. One of the best ways to think of this relates to differences in the nature of *comprehension* vs. *understanding*.

Comprehension is the process of grasping the meaning of something. The particular emphasis of comprehension focuses on the phase transition from not understanding something at all to having a basic-level understanding of what something is.

Understanding, on the other hand, is the process of grasping something fully via *both* comprehension and also experience. When you understand a concept you possess deeper-level knowledge of the material. You both comprehend the material theoretically, but you also understand the deep *meaning* of the material because you've experience it—you've lived it.

When you employ reformulation notes, you're aiming for comprehension. You're aiming to grasp a basic-level comprehension of a concept. Your goal is to capture the essence of the concept in your own way.

When you employ reflection notes, you're aiming for understanding. You're aiming to add your own experiences to the material. With reflection notes you add your own perspective, experiments, conclusions, opinions, and decisions on the material. Your goal with reflection notes is to achieve not comprehension, but *understanding*.

GUIDELINES FOR MAIN NOTES

I lump the notes written on maincards (excerpts, reformulations, and reflections) under the category of *main notes*. We'll now cover some very important guidelines to follow *before* creating main notes.

BEFORE YOU BEGIN WRITING A MAIN NOTE

Before you even create a main note, you must complete an important step. You must first review your Antinet and determine *where* you want the maincard (that you're about to create) to go. This forces you to review previous lines of thinking and, more importantly, it helps you avoid wasting life energy in re-writing something you've already written.

After reading and creating bibnotes, Luhmann states: "After finishing the book I go through my notes and think how these notes might be relevant for already written notes in the [Antinet]."[58]

What Luhmann highlights is that before actually writing the main note, he goes through his Antinet and figures out where the note will be placed. At this point he still has not even turned the observation note into a main note.

DON'T CREATE A MAINCARD FOR EVERY IDEA ON YOUR BIBCARD

Luhmann didn't develop every idea into a main note. He would let some ruminate and prove themselves useful. They would prove themselves useful if he ever decided to work on a book or paper publication relevant to the material.[59]

For instance, let's say Luhmann already had a note that outlined the *difference between knowledge and information*. If he came across a discussion of *knowledge vs. information* and, if he wasn't sure he would use the card, he would not create a new dedicated main note for it. He wouldn't spend the time

---

58 Niklas Luhmann, Dirk Baecker, and Georg Stanitzek, Archimedes und wir: Interviews (Berlin: Merve Verlag, 1987), 150.

59 Undisciplined, Archiving Luhmann w/ Johannes Schmidt, 2021, https://www.youtube.com/watch?v=kz2K3auPLWU, 33:05.

creating an excerpt note, reformulation note, or reflection note. Rather, he would simply create an external reference (ExRef) for it. For instance, here's one of Luhmann's notes on the concept of *function* (the idea that each part of society has a specific role or function).

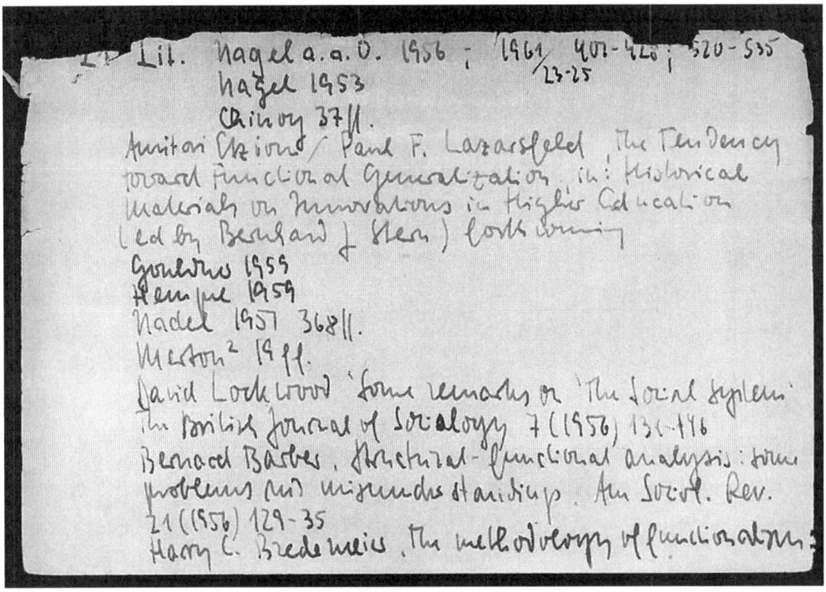
Lit. Nagel a.a.O. 1956 ; 1961 401-420 ; 520-535
23-25
Nagel 1953
Chinoy 37ff.
Amitai Etzioni / Paul F. Lazarsfeld, The Tendency toward Functional Generalization, in: Historical Materials on Innovations in Higher Education (ed by Bernhard J. Stern) forthcoming
Gouldner 1959
Hempel 1959
Nadel 1957 368ff.
Merton² 19ff.
David Lockwood 'Some remarks on 'The Social System'' The British Journal of Sociology 7 (1956) 134-146
Bernard Barber, Structural-functional analysis: some problems and misunderstandings. Am Sociol. Rev. 21 (1956) 129-35
Harry C. Bredemeier, The methodology of functionalism:

PHOTO CREDIT: "ZK II: Zettel 21 (1) - Niklas Luhmann-Archiv," accessed April 22, 2022, https://niklas-luhmann-archiv.de/bestand/zettelkasten/zettel/ZK_2_NB_21_1_V.

On this card are a list of ExRefs to pages in books. Luhmann lists the authors' last name, the year the book was published, and the page numbers.

If the page ends in ff this connotes the Latin term *folio* which means "and the following pages". Therefore, Merton 19ff translates to page 19 and the following pages in the book by Merton.

In Luhmann's second Antinet, he had sixty-seven thousand maincards (mostly of reformulations and reflections of what he had read).[60] He had

60 **Johannes Schmidt, "Niklas Luhmann's Card Index: Thinking Tool, Communication Partner, Publication Machine," Forgetting Machines. Knowledge Management Evolution**

fifteen thousand bibcards which were filled with brief observations he had made while reading different works (with corresponding page numbers). These bibcards usually contained ten to thirty observations notes.

So let's recap: Luhmann's second Antinet contained sixty-seven thousand maincards and fifteen thousand bibcards. This means that for every bibcard, there were four or five maincards. In effect, this means Luhmann did not turn every observation note on a bibcard into a maincard. Much of the time he would just create ExRefs for the idea.

OTHER TYPES OF NOTES

What you have just learned about are the four main types of notes in an Antinet. I wish it was as simple as that—actually, I wish it was even simpler than that! However, there are a few other types of notes that are useful in the system.

COLLECTIVES

In Johannes Schmidt's categorization of the types of links in Luhmann's Antinet, there is one type that he calls "collective references."[61] In network-theory terms, this kind of linked "array" is referred to as a *hub*. In some Zettelkasten circles, these are called *hub notes*.[62] Personally, I like referring to these cards as *collectives*.

Collectives are types of notes that contain a collection of items.

There are several different types of collectives. Let's briefly go through each of them now.

Cardlink Collectives

Cardlink collectives are simply notes that contain a list of links to other cards. These help group cards together based on a specific idea.

---

in Early Modern Europe 53 (2016), 292. https://pub.uni-bielefeld.de/record/2942475.

61 Johannes Schmidt, "Niklas Luhmann's Card Index: Thinking Tool, Communication Partner, Publication Machine," Forgetting Machines. Knowledge Management Evolution in Early Modern Europe 53 (2016), 302. https://pub.uni-bielefeld.de/record/2942475.

62 sascha, "The Money Is in the Hubs: Johannes Schmidt on Luhmann's Zettelkasten," Zettelkasten Method, 19:38 100AD, https://zettelkasten.de/posts/zettelkasten-hubs/.

Here's an example of a cardlink collective from Luhmann:

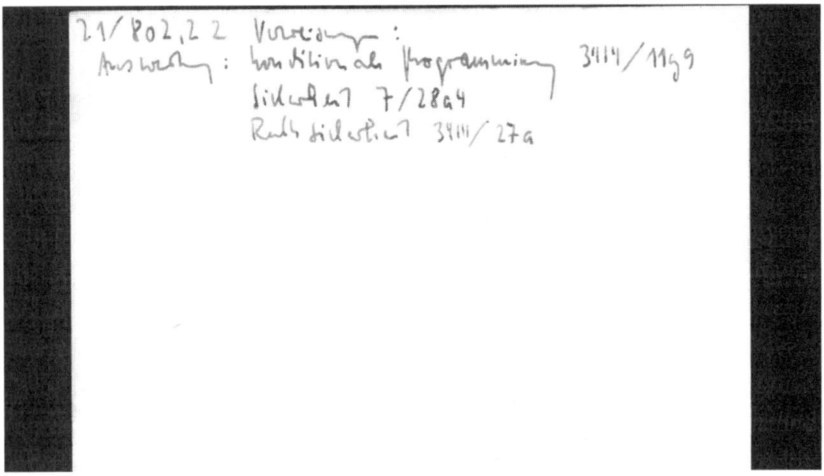

You can see a few keyterms on the left-hand side, followed by some cardlinks (like 3414/11g9).

Here's an example from my own Antinet:

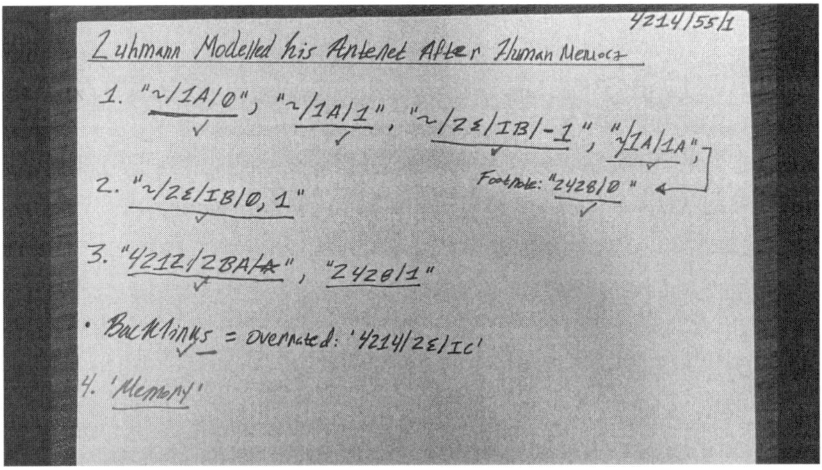

These cardlinks point to notes that support my assertion that Luhmann modeled his Antinet after human memory. Over time, the collective grew as I came upon more examples to support my claim. The green checkmarks under each cardlink indicate that I've integrated the material into this book.

ExRef Collectives

An ExRef collective is a collection of references to external sources. In other words, ExRef collectives reference certain books and their specific page number(s).

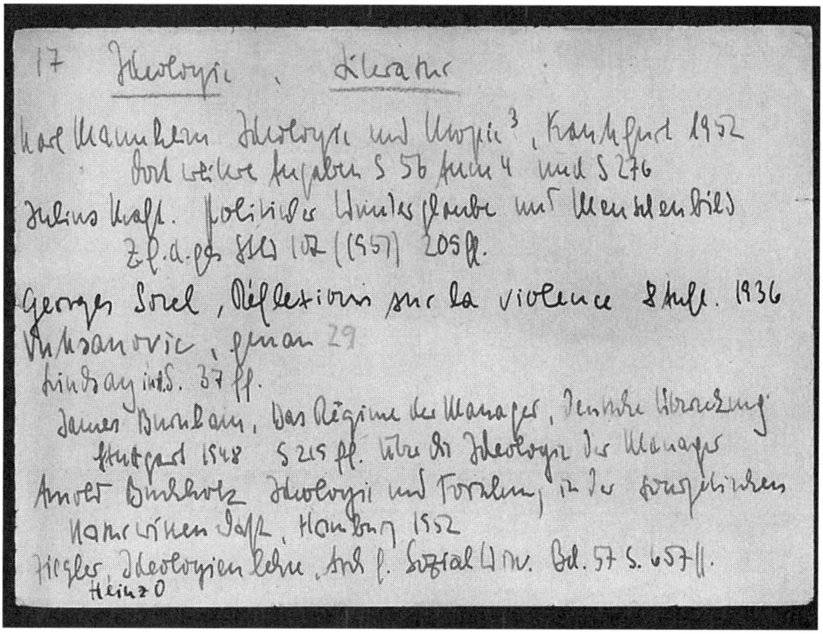
17 Ideologie, Literatur
Karl Mannheim, Ideologie und Utopie³, Frankfurt 1952
Dort weitere Angaben S. 56 Anm. 4 und S 276
Julius Kraft, Politischer Wunderglaube und Menschenbild, Z.f.d.ges. StW 107 (1951) 205 ff.
Georges Sorel, Réflexions sur la violence 8 Aufl. 1936
Vuksanovic, german 29
Lindsay insb. 37 ff.
James Burnham, Das Régime der Manager, Deutsche Übersetzung Stuttgart 1948 S 215 ff. über die Ideologie der Manager
Arnold Buchholz, Ideologie und Forschung in der sowjetischen Naturwissenschaft, Hamburg 1952
Ziegler, Heinz O. Ideologienlehre, Arch. f. Sozialwiss. Bd. 57 S. 657 ff.

PHOTO CREDIT: "ZK I: Zettel 17 (1)—Niklas Luhmann-Archiv," accessed April 22, 2022, https://niklas-luhmann-archiv.de/bestand/zettelkasten/zettel/ZK_1_NB_17_1_V.

In this, titled *Ideology Literature* (underlined in red), there is a list of books with the bibliographic information and page numbers. This is a collective of external references related to ideology. Luhmann typically placed his ExRef collectives near the beginning of his section for the topic to which it related. For instance, this is the second card found in the section on *ideology*.

Branch Collectives

In the beginning branch of each of Luhmann's main section, he included a collective of cardlinks. These collectives were specifically designed to provide links to other areas of interest related to the branch. I call these types of collectives, *branch collectives.* As an example, upon navigating to Luhmann's branch on *ideology,* one is presented with this branch collective:

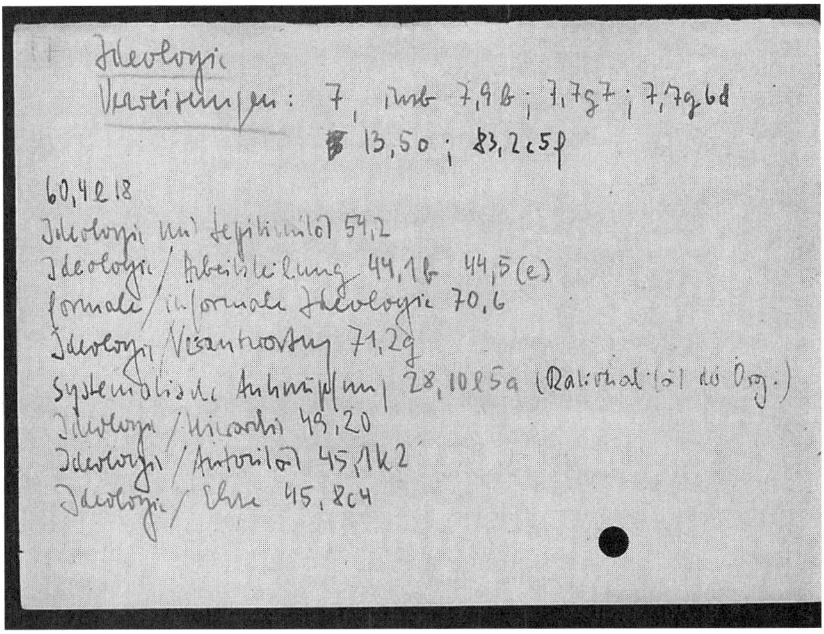

PHOTO CREDIT: "ZK I: Note 17 (2)—Niklas Luhmann Archive," accessed July 13, 2021, https://niklas-luhmann-archiv.de/bestand/zettelkasten/zettel/ZK_1_NB_17_2_V.

Here's the translation:

17 ideology

Links: 7 , especially 7.9 ; 7.7g7 ; 7.7g6d 13.50 ; 83.2c5f

60.4l18

ideology and legitimacy 54.2

ideology / division of labor 44.1b ; 44.5(e)

formal / informal ideology 70.6

ideology / responsibility 71.2g

systematic connection 28.10l5a (rationality of the org.)

ideology / hierarchy 49.20

ideology / authority 45.1k2

ideology / honor 45.8c4

Here is a picture of one of my own branch collectives:

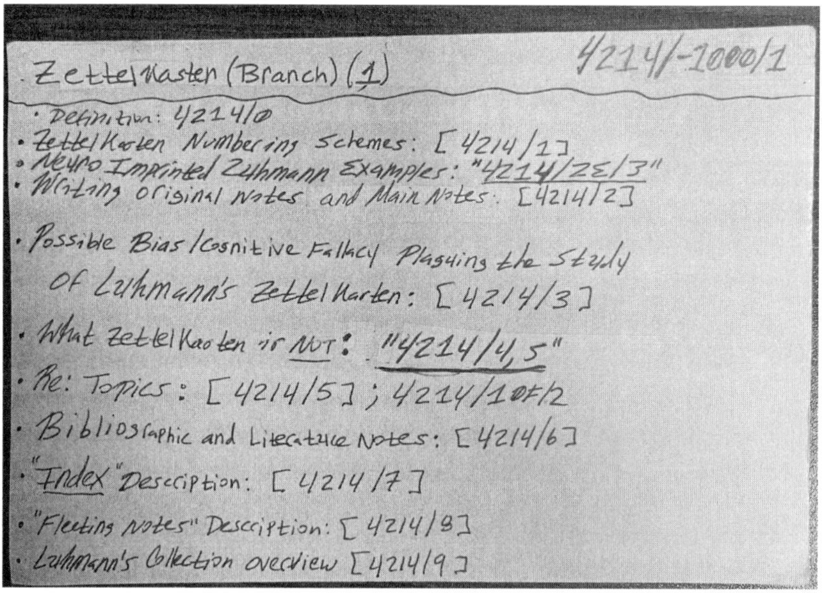

This branch collective is for my content related to *Zettelkasten*. At the time it was created I was still referring to the system as Zettelkasten because I hadn't yet conceived of the term Antinet! This goes to show how knowledge evolves in the Antinet. My own Antinet developed the term Antinet. It doesn't get more meta than that!

Outline Collectives

There's one more type of collective it's important to introduce: I like to refer to these as *outline collectives.*

The book you're reading right now was organized using outline collectives. Think of these as a table of contents for a book or project you're working on.

Each card is dedicated to a certain topic or idea. Accommodating the idea is a list of cardlinks where you can find the material pertaining to the idea.

Unlike cardlink collectives or branch collectives, these types of collectives are more likely to be prearranged and planned. Whereas branch collectives are typically grown over a longer timeframe, outline collectives are created in a short time window in order to outline a project.

The best way to explain this is to see pictures of my outline collective for this book:

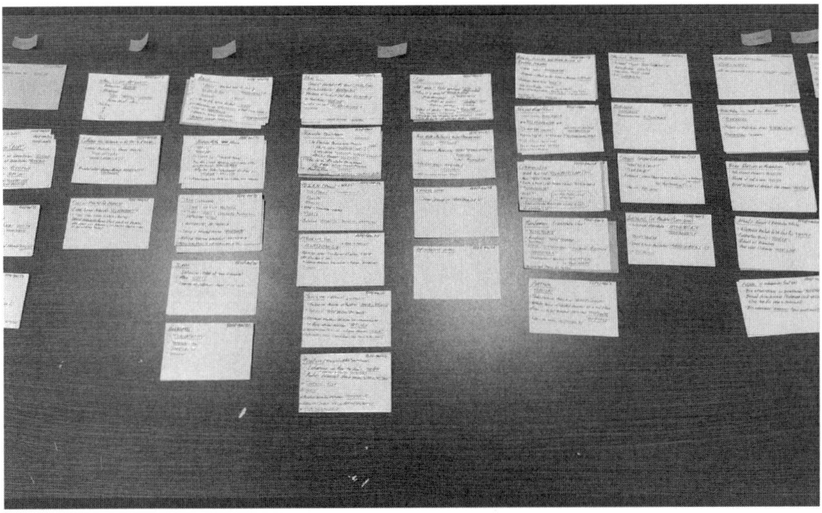

This shows an outline of the main sections of this book.

Here's a closer look at outline collectives:

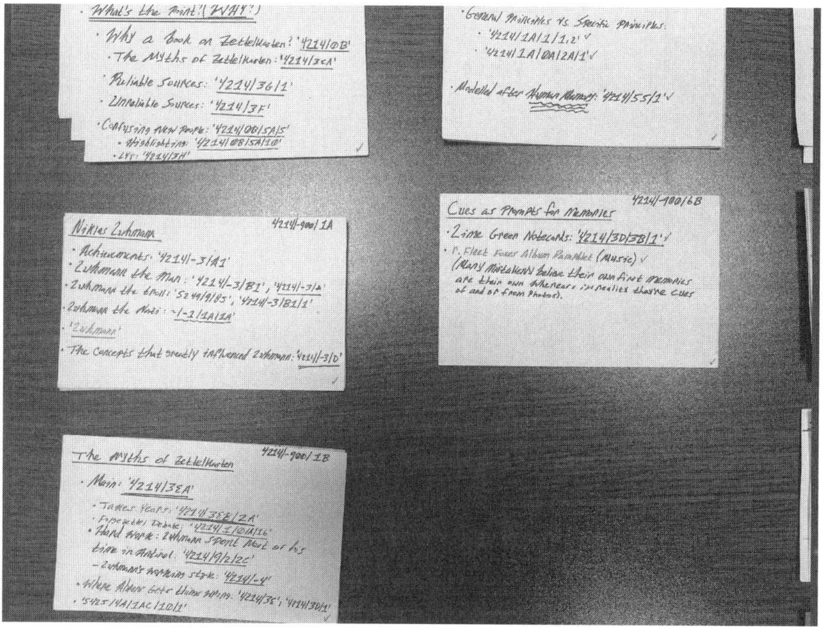

My outline collectives not only include cardlinks, they contain ExRefs as well. See the pink card containing ExRefs pointing to sources I needed to research when writing the section:

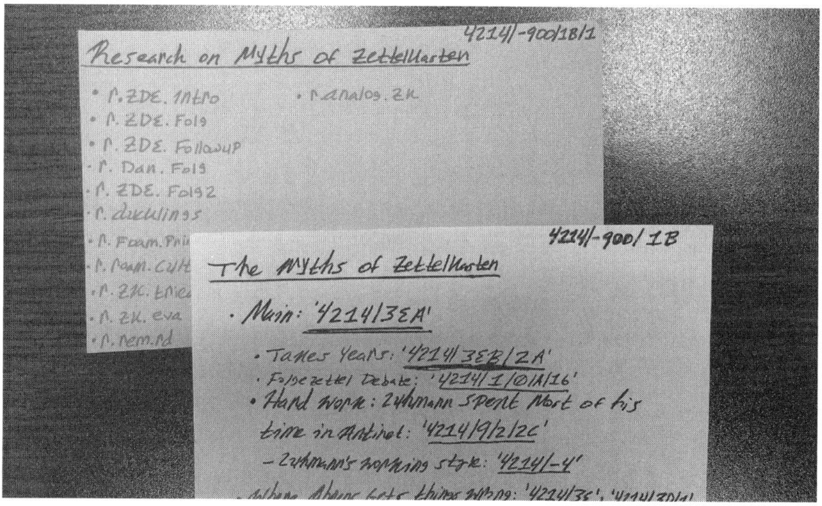

In brief, outline collectives are quite useful when using an Antinet. I recommend using branch collectives to allow your research to build itself from the bottom-up. When it comes time to working on your project or book, then it's time to create outline collectives. At that phase you simply review the material that has been growing in your branch collectives and then build out some logical groups for the content.

Building out projects using outline collectives is where the analog nature of the Antinet truly begins to shine. You lay out each outline collective card on a table and rearrange them until it forms the perfect outline for your project or book.

From there, you fire up a word editor and begin typing out each section. Contrary to what you might think, it's not a boring process to type each note out word-for-word. Rather it's engaging because it's collaborative in nature. And here's the best part: most of the hard work has already been done for you. This is precisely what Luhmann meant when he said his books wrote themselves.[63]

Keyterm Indexcards vs. Collectives

In a way, keyterm indexcards are also a type of collective. For instance, here's a picture of a keyterm indexcard:

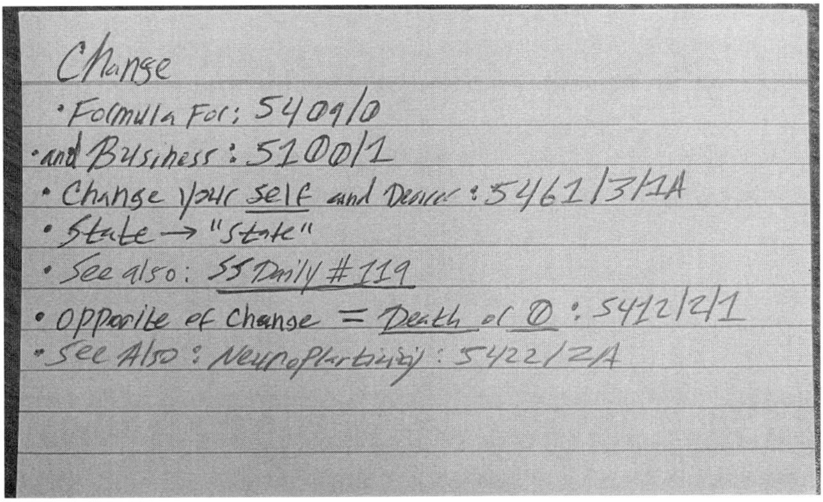

63 Niklas Luhmann, Niklas Luhmann Short Cuts (English Translation), 2002, 17.

However, there are some distinctions between collectives and keyterm indexcards. The more obvious difference is that collective cards are contained in the main box (and keyterm indexcards are contained in the index box). Keyterm indexcards are organized by keyterm, whereas collectives have a numeric-alpha address.

Both types of cards have their own distinct uses. Keyterm indexcards are often quicker to look up (as you only have to think of the keyterm). However, cardlink collectives inside the main box of your Antinet are useful as well. While surfing through a stem of thought, cardlink collectives connect you to a bunch of other vines and areas in your tree of knowledge. This oftentimes proves useful when you're in a more *exploratory mode* (sifting through cards).

HOPLINK CARDS

The last type of note is what I call a *hoplink card*. These are very straightforward, essentially containing a brief snippet of text that says *For more on x concept, see cardlink 'xxxx/xx/x'.*

Here's an example hoplink card:

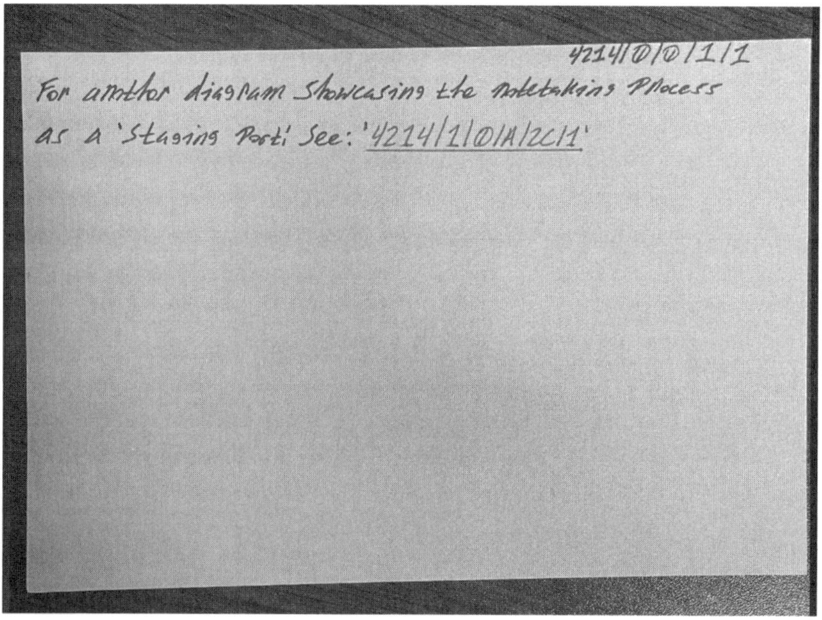

Here's one from Luhmann's Antinet:

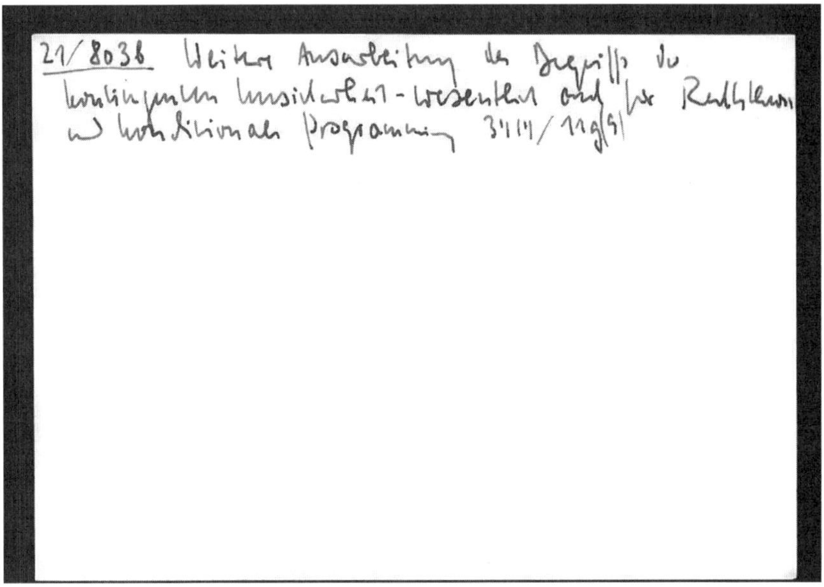

PHOTO CREDIT: "ZK II: Zettel 21/8o3b - Niklas Luhmann-Archiv," accessed April 22, 2022, https://niklas-luhmann-archiv.de/bestand/zettelkasten/zettel/ZK_2_NB_21-8o3b_V.

Hoplinks are useful for breaking up certain stems of thought by linking to another relevant area in the Antinet.

CONCLUSION

The creation phase is perhaps the most enjoyable, yet one of the hardest phases of knowledge development. In this phase you're actually forced to think deeply. This isn't easy work, though for some reason the nature of writing by hand makes this difficult process more enjoyable.

We've covered a lot in this chapter. My advice is to not get overwhelmed. Don't worry about the other notes for the time being. Just focus on the four big boys: observations, excerpts, reformulations, and reflections.

The best style is no style, as Bruce Lee would say. What you've been introduced to in this chapter serves as a framework to get you started. Do not be afraid to add your own creativity and tweaks to the system. The most important thing is that you start. Start creating and building. How do you eat an elephant? One bite at a time. How do you create something great? One note at a time.

CHAPTER SIXTEEN

INSTALLATION

COMPARED TO THE OTHER CHAPTERS in this section on knowledge development, this chapter will be brief.

As you may recall from the previous chapter, I advise you to first review your Antinet to determine where to install a card *before* you begin writing a main note. This is an important step. This step prevents you from rewriting knowledge you've already written. It also enables you to evolve your thinking from where you last left off. In essence, you're evolving the branch or stems of thought in your tree of knowledge.

Due to this prerequisite, figuring out where to install your cards becomes a more manageable endeavor.

In the beginning stages of working with my Antinet, I found myself creating fifteen or so maincards without first figuring out where they should go. This left me with a pile of maincards which made things challenging. It became difficult to go back through my Antinet and figure out where they should go. Moreover, this ended up feeling like tedious homework. It left me wanting to get through the pile as quickly as possible. As a result, I was left with less time and energy to make sure I installed the cards in the best place possible.

Reviewing your Antinet and determining where you'll install the card before you write your main notes results in two things: First, the process of creating and installing notes becomes a lot more fun. And second, the cards end up being installed in more fitting places.

One more important reminder: the name of the game is *similarity*. Your goal is to install the card (or sequence of cards) under or behind its most similar neighbor.

When you're reviewing your Antinet before writing the main note, think of the most similar idea already in the Antinet that it relates to.

Finding the most similar idea, of course, is dependent on one more critical factor: the index. Let's talk a bit about that now.

DETERMINING HOW AND WHEN TO INDEX

When you're installing a note into a sequence of cards within the Antinet, the best case scenario is that you already have the stem of thought indexed.

For instance, say in my research I happen upon an idea relating to *randomness*. The idea discusses how randomness serves as an important function within evolution. Let's also say I already have a keyterm created in my index for randomness. This makes installing this new idea easy. All I have to do is look up "randomness" in my index. I then navigate to the cardlink it points me to and begin exploring the cards. I then spot the one that's closest to my new idea and add it under or behind the most similar card.

However what if *randomness* was not already a keyterm in my index? What would I do then? The first thing I would do is start thinking of what randomness is most similar to. I would think of other concepts such as *accidents, change, chaos, entropy, impermanence*. Chances are I'd have a keyterm already created for such concepts.

In the case I didn't have keyterms created for closely related concepts, I would create a new stem or a new branch.

Now, here's where we have a decision to make. Here's where things get interesting.

There are two scenarios:

The first scenario is that I'm creating a new maincard on randomness *within the context of relating it to how Luhmann's Zettelkasten works.* My branch on the Zettelkasten and Antinet material is 4214. In this scenario, I would either find the most similar stem of cards within 4214, or just create a new stem for it. For instance, I would create the stem 4214/15 and in my index, I would create the entry: Randomness (Zettelkasten): 4214/15.

The second scenario is that I'm creating a new maincard for randomness *within the context of evolution.* In this case, I would consult Wikipedia's *Outline of Academic Disciplines.* I would then search the keyterm *evolution* and place it under the branch of evolution. For instance, I would create a branch for *Evolutionary Biology* and assign it to the branch 3511. I would then create an entry in the index: Randomness (Evolutionary Bio): 3511/1.

Chances are, I would choose the first scenario because I find the Antinet works best if I'm actively using it for a project. That is I find it best if I adopt a *contribution* approach to using it (instead of a personal *growth* approach to using it).

In the beginning, you will find yourself needing to create a lot of index keyterm entries. I must caution you not to burn yourself out! In the very beginning, you risk *index fatigue.* Do not create too many index entries. If you ever have issues finding a maincard, then you know to create an index entry for it (whenever you find it). That way, you won't waste time having to explore the entirety of your Antinet next time.

That's really all there is to discuss on the installation phase of knowledge development. If you follow my advice laid out in the creation phase, the installation phase will be a breeze (or at least easier than it otherwise would)!

CHAPTER SEVENTEEN

MINDSET

In this section we're going to be covering some of the "softer skills" in regard to working with an Antinet. We'll be covering different work routines, and we'll cover the mindset one ought to adopt when working with an Antinet. A variety of such lessons are already dispersed throughout this book in relevant sections; yet I think it's helpful to discuss these lessons in a dedicated place. That's what this chapter is for.

ANTINET WORK ROUTINE

THE THREE STATES OF ANTINET WORK

Deep work sessions are a prerequisite for creating knowledge using an Antinet. Using an Antinet requires a focused environment. However there are three distinct *working states* involved in this work: (1) an emergence state, and (2) an evolutionary state, and (3) a producing state.

I call these *states* (instead of *phases* or *stages*) for a reason. A state is something you switch back and forth between. One hour you may be in an emergence state of mind. The next hour you may be in a producing state of mind. The next, you may be in an evolutionary state. This is fine. It's a natural part of how knowledge development works. It's not so much a process of sequential phases as it is a dance. Creating knowledge is an asynchronous process where different thoughts are developed concurrently. If you get stuck in one spot, you can easily switch to a different project (or branch of knowledge) and begin developing other thoughts from there. Remember what Luhmann said, "I only write when I know immediately how to do it. If it stops for a moment, I put the thing aside and do something else."[1]

Emergence State

"Traveler, there is no path, the path must be forged as you walk."

–Antonio Machado[2]

When in an emergence state, your work is more exploratory. You're looking for your theories to *emerge* from the sources you engage with. You're in research mode. Reading is your primary intellectual activity. In this state, you're taking many reformulation and excerpt notes. You're employing the *book-to-maincard* extraction method. That is, you're stopping at challenging sections in books and creating a maincard immediately for it. You do this in order to comprehend the material so that you can continue reading the text and understand the rest of the book.

From this state, theories start to emerge. This is what Brené Brown refers to as *emergence* and *grounded theory* research. Brown explains, "Initially I set out, on what I thought was a well-traveled path, to find empirical evidence of what I knew to be true." Brown then shifted to employing the *grounded theory* methodology. She shifted to an exploratory way of researching—an *emergent* way of researching. In this state, she writes, "there is no path and, certainly, there is no way of knowing what you will find."[3]

Taking a bottom-up approach to research takes courage. It takes courage to trust that the Antinet will somehow bring theories to the surface. It requires courage to let go and let the readings spark ideas you never predicted. It takes courage to let go of your preconceived notions.

---

1 Niklas Luhmann, Niklas Luhmann Short Cuts (English Translation), 2002, 19.

2 Brené Brown, Daring Greatly: How the Courage to Be Vulnerable Transforms the Way We Live, Love, Parent, and Lead, Reprint edition (New York, New York: Avery, 2015), 251.

3 Brené Brown, Daring Greatly: How the Courage to Be Vulnerable Transforms the Way We Live, Love, Parent, and Lead, Reprint edition (New York, New York: Avery, 2015), 251.

When you use an Antinet, you let your readings create your theories from the bottom-up rather than predetermining them in a top-down approach. You don't go into your research with an already finished theory. You go in with a general intuition and sense, and then let your research make the discoveries for you. This type of research is what the Antinet is built for.

To cultivate the emergence state, I like to allocate two hours in the mornings to reading. I do this as the very first thing I do when I get to the office. I use a block timer that has a one-hour countdown. After the one-hour timer runs out, I reset the timer for another hour. Sometimes, of course, I'll take a fifteen or so minute break in between the hours.

After these two hours of reading, I'll typically allocate the rest of the day to further development and installing the material from these readings.

I like to install the material from the readings into my Antinet that same day. Otherwise I find that notes pile up and installing becomes almost like homework (or something I dread doing).

Evolutionary State

In the evolutionary state, you're looking to *evolve* the ideas that have *emerged* during your research. You'll be evolving the ideas by finding material that supports or challenges your emerging theories.

For instance, in my experience researching Luhmann's Antinet, one theme that I noticed was the importance of the function of *surprises* and *accidents*. In creating any piece of work, surprises and accidents are actually hugely beneficial. Luhmann spoke of this, and it was emphasized in Johannes Schmidt's writings.[4] I was not anticipating this concept when I began researching Luhmann's Antinet. After I extracted this theory onto maincards, I then created

---

4 Niklas Luhmann, "Communication with Noteboxes (Revised Edition)," trans. Manfred Kuehn, https://daily.scottscheper.com/zettelkasten/. "One of the most basic presuppositions of communication is that the partners can mutually surprise each other."; Johannes Schmidt, "Niklas Luhmann's Card Index: Thinking Tool, Communication Partner, Publication Machine," Forgetting Machines. Knowledge Management Evolution in Early Modern Europe 53 (2016).

a keyterm entry for the concepts (*surprises* and *accidents*). I then continued reading more books on knowledge science and human memory. Frequently I would come upon additional material on *surprises* and *accidents*. I would then *evolve* the concepts by adding my reformulations and reflections of the new material. In essence, the ideas that emerged through research continued to then *evolve* by additional research of other literature.

Let's once again talk about Brené Brown and *grounded theory*. At the end of her book *Daring Greatly*, Brown dedicates an entire section to discussing her research method. She highlights the idea of two different states involved in research. The first state "allows the research problem to emerge from the data." The second state conducts "a full review of the significant literature." The literature review served to support the theories she discovered during the emergence phase.[5]

I like to think of the second stage as the evolutionary stage. It seems better than the *literature review* stage. One reason being that sometimes research isn't actually literature.

Anyway, after you've extracted a working set of theories and concepts during the *emergent* phase of your research, your reading style changes (as Luhmann himself pointed out).[6] In the evolutionary phase you're capable of quickly spotting, selecting and extracting ideas that are related to the theories you've already unearthed. At this point, you've already neuroimprinted keyterms on your mind. You are capable of reading differently because any time you spot a related idea, all you need to do is write down the page number and keyterm of the idea on your bibcard.

As a result of doing this, you begin accumulating material that supports the theories and concepts that were unearthed during the emergent state. In brief, you begin *evolving* your ideas.

---

5 Brené Brown, Daring Greatly: How the Courage to Be Vulnerable Transforms the Way We Live, Love, Parent, and Lead, Reprint edition (New York, New York: Avery, 2015), 258-9.

6 "ZK II: Sheet 9/8d—Niklas Luhmann Archive," accessed March 4, 2022, https://niklas-luhmann-archiv.de/bestand/zettelkasten/zettel/ZK2NB9-8dV.

Producing State

Once I've done a sufficient amount of research and the material has evolved, I'll enter the producing state of work. Producing can be creating a podcast episode, a YouTube video, an online course, a song, software, a book, or whatever your craft is. For myself, it's writing. And the most applicable output for most, is writing. So I'll talk primarily about that. If I'm writing a book, I'll aim for an entire drawer full of notecards. If I'm writing a paper, I'd want at least a one-inch pinch of notecards. The material may come from a variety of branches in the Antinet.

When I'm in producing state, I get to the office in the morning and I write until three or four in the afternoon. Basically, I write all day. I use my notecards to write, and I type in what's on the notecards. Again, I don't type the material on the notecards word-for-word. I *start* typing word-for-word (which kills writer's block), yet I then expand and clarify the idea I'm trying to convey. I elaborate on the notecard and also add new ideas I've since realized.

This process is of course broken up by several trips to Starbucks located in the lobby of my building.

MY WORK ENVIRONMENT

My work environment is primarily analog. I have a private office where I cannot be disturbed. I put my phone on *Do Not Disturb Mode* and leave it across the room on the floor where it charges. In addition to this, I place lime green earplugs in my ears to block out external noise (lime green is my favorite color).

I have an analog dictionary and analog thesauri. There's no excuse for me to use a computer unless I'm writing. When in this state, I use the Ulysses app for writing (Mac only).

NIKLAS LUHMANN'S ANTINET ROUTINE

Luhmann's Antinet was actually located at his home. Luhmann lived in Oerlinghausen, which is about a half-hour drive from Bielefeld University where he worked.

Luhmann loved to read outdoors in the sun. He also loved to read at libraries. He would give conferences at various universities on the basis of there being a good library on campus.[7] Perhaps Luhmann would read at Bielefeld's library during the day. In the evenings he would bring home the bibcards from his readings and transform them into main notes. After this he would file the main notes and bibcard in his Antinet in his home office.

Here's a photo of Luhmann reading in the sun (with a bibcard hanging out of the book):

PHOTO CREDIT: Niklas Luhmann—Theory of Society 4_13 by Schwumbel; philomag, "Niklas Luhmann Und Die Aufrichtigkeit," Philosophie Magazin, accessed April 26, 2022, https://www.philomag.de/artikel/niklas-luhmann-und-die-aufrichtigkeit.

---

7 Undisciplined, Archiving Luhmann w/ Johannes Schmidt, 2021, https://www.youtube.com/watch?v=kz2K3auPLWU, 25:40.

In a biographical interview, Luhmann detailed his routine. We can presume this took place on days where he works from home (which were most days, according to Luhmann's son, Clemens):[8]

> If I have nothing else to do, then I write all day: in the morning from 8:30 a.m. to lunchtime, then I go for a short walk with my dog, then I have time again in the afternoon from 2:00 p.m. to 4:00 p.m., then it's the dog's turn again. Sometimes I also lie down for a quarter of an hour, I have gotten into the habit of resting in a very concentrated way, so that I can get back to work after a short time. Yes, and then I usually write in the evening until around 11:00 p.m. At 11:00 p.m. I usually lie in bed and read a few more things that I can still digest at that time.[9]

Here are some photos of Luhmann's office. These photos are taken from a video tour of Luhmann's office in 1989.[10]

Luhmann's literary collection, comprising approximately eleven thousand titles. There were rarely any marks or marginalia notes in the books. He took his notes on bibcards. Note the chaise lounge chair. This was Luhmann's favorite spot, where he both read and took fifteen minute power naps!

8 Clemens Luhmann, Interview by Scott P. Scheper, April 27, 2022.

9 Niklas Luhmann, Niklas Luhmann Short Cuts (English Translation), 2002, 19.

10 holgersen911, Niklas Luhmann—Beobachter Im Krähennest (Eng Sub), 2012, https://www.youtube.com/watch?v=qRSCKSPMuDc.

The floor in front of one of Luhmann's bookshelves. Knowledge work isn't the most orderly process—even for organized Germans.

Luhmann works at his desk. Note the massive red typewriter, and the tea kettle. On the right-hand side of the photo, resting on the floor, is Luhmann's Zettelkasten (not pictured).

Luhmann reviews some of his main notes. At the top of the photo is Luhmann's Antinet Zettelkasten with a pile of papers resting on top.

Luhmann reviews his maincards. Resting on the desk is a bibcard from his most recent reading.

Luhmann navigates his Antinet. He's exploring the contents and refreshing his memory of the material (creating reverberation in his mind).

One other thing of note: Luhmann did not have labels on the outside of his Antinet. He knew his way around the Antinet so well, that he had various branches memorized. The following photo shows Luhmann's Antinet, which resided on the floor to the left of his desk. Note how there are no labels on the outsides explaining the contents of the drawers:

PHOTO CREDIT: "Niklas Luhmann—Archiv," accessed April 26, 2022, https://niklas-luhmann-archiv.de/nachlass/zettelkasten.

THE ANTINET MINDSET

"That is the only way. Without external help of any sort, you go to work on the book. With nothing but the power of your own mind..."

–Mortimer Adler[11]

I've said it elsewhere, and I'll say it here again: getting started with an Antinet isn't the easiest process. You'll have to create a lot of keyterms in the index and you have to write a lot of cards. Later on, you won't have to create as many keyterms, though you'll still be adding cards to your Antinet. At the beginning, you're like an airplane taking off. At some point you'll hit cruise control mode, but it'll take some effort to get to that point.

Luhmann held that it will take a number of years before the payoffs become clear. Until then the Antinet will function merely as a container you put cards into.[12] I don't think it will take a number of years. It could be only a few months before you begin to see the value. However you should go into this with a long-term mindset.

CONSISTENCY OVER THE LONG TERM

Focus on consistency instead of working away all day like a maniac. Even though I advise this, I'll admit that when I got my Antinet up and running, I spent a lot of time working away like a maniac. In the beginning, I spent months integrating my previous notes and journals into the Antinet. I even spent many nights printing out my notes from the digital notetaking app I was using for a time. I would print out, and the cut out those digital notes into 4 x 6 inch size cards. As of now, I have maybe a third of my legacy notes installed in the Antinet. However, I stopped after a while because it was taking too much time and the value wasn't clear. I instead shifted my focus to developing knowledge for my current undertaking and haven't looked

---

11 Mortimer Jerome Adler and Charles Van Doren, How to Read a Book, Rev. and updated ed (New York: Simon and Schuster, 1972), 7.

12 Niklas Luhmann, "Communication with Noteboxes (Revised Edition)," trans. Manfred Kuehn, https://daily.scottscheper.com/zettelkasten/.

back since. That said, I've seen the value of the notes I installed—in fact, I've used a bit of the legacy material for this book!

The bottom line: focus mainly on the future. Don't get too hung up on trying to integrate your old (digital) notes into the Antinet. I have thousands of digital notes. It doesn't matter that they're not in my Antinet. They're underdeveloped compared to notes you write by hand. You shouldn't lose sleep over your digital notes being ported to your Antinet. However, if you do really want to retain your old notes, you can always set aside an hour a day for printing out notes and filing them. Be sure to try and make your life suck less while you're doing it. When I was doing this, I would blast *Pink Floyd* and sip a nice glass of wine.

Again, consistency over the long term is the goal. As I've mentioned before, two hours per day is enough to produce great intellectual work. Don't take my word for it, take the word of the revered intellectual, Antonin Sertillanges.[13] If you work full-time, aim to carve out two hours every day before work. When I worked full-time I would sit down with a cup of coffee every day and go through challenging texts. I read while sitting on a cushion on the floor (as it helps me focus better).

IF IT AIN'T EASY, IT AIN'T FUN

Luhmann worked roughly twelve hours a day. To him, his vocation was his vacation. He didn't really perceive his work as *work*.

In an interview discussing the beginning of his career, an interviewer asked about Luhmann's early life. This was during the period where he worked as a legal clerk for the German Ministry of Culture. It was absolutely boring and Luhmann hated his job. When asked what he did after work, he did not respond with something like *I blow off steam at the local Biergarten*. Instead, he told the interviewer that as soon as the clock struck five, he would race

13 OP A. G. Sertillanges, The Intellectual Life: Its Spirit, Conditions, Methods, trans. Mary Ryan, Reprint edition (Washington, D.C.: The Catholic University of America Press, 1992), 11.

home and "read a lot." He wasn't a drinker, anyway. As he points out, he had just recently started his Zettelkasten at that point in his life.[14]

The same interviewer seemed puzzled when talking to Luhmann. He was trying to figure out what motivated this great intellectual mind; yet he wasn't getting a clear answer. Luhmann asserted that he found it difficult to have wishes or "desires." The only thing, Luhmann said, that he daydreamed about was having more time—like thirty hours in a day, instead of twenty-four. With thirty hours a day, how would he spend it? It's simple, Luhmann said, he would spend it working with his Antinet more, and "study other things, for example mathematics and economics."[15]

In brief, it's helpful to view the Antinet as a vacation, not as a vocation. Using the Antinet won't always be easy, but it will be worth it. The number one thing that will help your chances in making the Antinet a part of your life (long term) is this: make sure it's fun.

CONCLUSION

In this chapter we covered a nice amount of material with regards to working with an Antinet. We discussed the three states one operates in during knowledge development. We also got a glimpse into Luhmann's work routine with his Antinet. Last, we capped off this chapter with some philosophical advice centering around making the Antinet fun. Consistency over the long term is key. In the next chapter, we'll dive into one of the most important metaphysical aspects of the Antinet: the Antinet as a *second mind*. Get ready.

---

14 Niklas Luhmann, Niklas Luhmann Short Cuts (English Translation), 2002, 11.

15 Niklas Luhmann, Niklas Luhmann Short Cuts (English Translation), 2002, 16.

CHAPTER EIGHTEEN

COMMUNICATION WITH YOUR SECOND MIND

"Ghost in the box?

Spectators come. You get to see everything and nothing but that —like porn movies. And so is the disappointment."

–Niklas Luhmann, on communicating with his Zettelkasten[16]

COMMUNICATION WITH THE ANTINET is the most important aspect of the system. There's a reason Luhmann titled his paper *Communication with Noteboxes*. It stands as the key descriptor of what it's like to write and collaborate with an Antinet. Yet, for some reason, this phenomenon is completely omitted when reading about Zettelkasten today. When you research what a Zettelkasten is online, you'll find every descriptor *besides communication partner*. Zettelkasten is described as a system of linking notes, and there are the Ahrensian terms like *fleeting notes, literature notes,* and *permanent notes*.[17] Yet we find no mention of the Zettelkasten as a *com-*

16 "ZK II: Note 9 / 8.3—Niklas Luhmann Archive," accessed January 11, 2022, https://niklas-luhmann-archiv.de/bestand/zettelkasten/zettel/ZK_2_NB_9-8-3_V.

17 "A Beginner's Guide to the Zettelkasten Method," Zenkit (blog), April 29, 2021, https://zenkit.com/en/blog/a-beginners-guide-to-the-zettelkasten-method/. "In short, a Zettelkasten is simply a framework to help organize your ideas, thoughts, and information. By relating pieces of knowledge and connecting information to each other (by way of hyperlinking), you are replicating a train of thought."; "A Beginner's Guide to the Zettelkasten Method," Zenkit (blog), April 29, 2021, https://zenkit.com/en/

munication partner. You would have to do a lot of digging to discover how Luhmann actually viewed his Zettelkasten: as a *second mind*, a *ghost in the box*, or an *alter ego* with whom he *communicated*.

In this chapter, we'll discuss this most powerful part of the Antinet, and explore the concept of *communication* with one's past self—that is, communication with one's second mind.

THE ORIGINS OF COMMUNICATION WITH A SECOND MIND

One interesting parallel with the origins of this idea involves the origins of the Zettelkasten itself.

According to Clemens Luhmann (the youngest child of Niklas Luhmann), the Zettelkasten originated through a communication experience with Luhmann's best friend, Friedrich Rudolf Hohl (1916–1979), whom Luhmann and the rest of the family called *Bruder* (meaning brother). Bruder was Luhmann's closest friend. They shared a love of art, philosophy and other intellectual matters. They were seen almost as if they were the same person. Clemens referred to Hohl as his father's "alter ego."[18]

The origins of the Zettelkasten came by way of letters and notecards exchanged between Hohl and Luhmann. Luhmann would write letters to Hohl about his readings and include his own notecards in the envelope. The letters would elaborate on the ideas contained in the notes. They would discuss various interpretations. Hohl would do the very same thing in his replies.

This was a communication experience between two close friends. It was a communication experience with Luhmann's real-life alter ego.

---

blog/a-beginners-guide-to-the-zettelkasten-method/. "Zettelkasten method comprises of three main types of notes: (1) Literature Notes, (2) Reference Notes, (3) Permanent Notes. Each note has a distinct objective and serves a specific function. Other types of notes include fleeting notes and hub notes."

18 Clemens Luhmann, Interview by Scott P. Scheper, April 27, 2022.

Unfortunately, Luhmann's best friend and "alter ego" Friedrich Rudolf Hohl passed away only two years after Luhmann's wife Ursula. They were the only two people who ever got dedications in Luhmann's books: Ursula and Friedrich Rudolf Hohl (in *Love as Passion*).

A few years later, in 1981, Luhmann published his paper *Kommunikation mit Zettelkästen* ("Communication with Noteboxes"), in which he talked about a second mind arising from his Zettelkasten; he described it as "an alter ego with whom we can constantly communicate."[19]

There exists a parallel between the communication experience of Luhmann and his real-life alter ego, Friedrich Rudolf Hohl, and Luhmann and his metaphysical alter ego: his Antinet Zettelkasten.

LUHMANN'S THEORETICAL VIEW OF COMMUNICATION

> *"Humans cannot communicate; not even their brains can communicate; not even their conscious minds can communicate. Only communication can communicate."*
>
> –Niklas Luhmann[20]

There are a few major concepts that at the cornerstone of Luhmann's theoretical work. The first is general systems theory, which involves the concepts of *cybernetics* and *self-referential systems*, and *autopoiesis* (wherein a system recreates itself).[21] The other concept that is critical to Luhmann's theoretical work is *communication*. In fact, Luhmann uses a communication theory as the starting point for describing his Antinet.[22]

---

19 Niklas Luhmann, "Communication with Noteboxes (Revised Edition)," trans. Manfred Kuehn, https://daily.scottscheper.com/zettelkasten/.

20 Hans Ulrich Gumbrecht and Karl Ludwig Pfeiffer, Materialities of Communication (Stanford University Press, 1994), 371.

21 Niklas Luhmann, Niklas Luhmann Short Cuts (English Translation), 2002, 26.

22 Niklas Luhmann, "Communication with Noteboxes (Revised Edition)," trans. Manfred Kuehn, https://daily.scottscheper.com/zettelkasten/.

According to Luhmann, communication is an *emergent* reality that emanates from three different selections.[23]

1. The "selection of *information*"

2. The "selection of the *message* of this function"[24]

3. The "selective *understanding* or *misunderstanding* of the message and its interpretation"

Luhmann holds that none of these components can occur on their own. Only when they are combined together can communication occur.

Let's break down what Luhmann means by these three concepts in relation to working with an Antinet.

First, Luhmann is referring to the process of how we select information, including choosing the *sources* we wish to engage with in order to ingest information. In other words: what books, articles, podcasts, YouTube videos, or other media we select information from.

The second component Luhmann is referring to is the *message*. This is the material within a source (such as a book) that we select and decide to interpret.

The third component is the *understanding* or *misunderstanding* of the message. Luhmann makes a good point in that we have a choice of whether to understand (or misunderstand) the message we receive. For example, we humans have a phenomenal ability to delude ourselves by way of *confir-*

---

23 Niklas Luhmann, Niklas Luhmann Short Cuts (English Translation), 2002, 28. "Similar to life and consciousness, communication is an emergent reality, an issue sui generis. She is concluded by a synthesis of three different selections—that is, selection of an information, selection of the message of this function, and selective understanding or misunderstanding of the message and its interpretation. None of these components can occur on their own. Only together do they generate communication."

24 This is also termed as "announcement." See: Hans-Georg Moeller, The Radical Luhmann (New York: Columbia University Press, 2011), 133.

mation bias. That is, we may choose to interpret information in such a way to confirm our already-held preexisting beliefs (and filter our messages which conflict with these beliefs).

All three components are required for communication.

Interestingly enough, all three components serve as critical aspects of the knowledge development process of the Antinet.

Again, communication was a core tenet of Luhmann's theoretical work. In fact, he proposed a solution to the classic philosophical mind-body problem by converting it to a triad: *mind-body-communication*.[25] In Luhmann's view, communication serves as the missing link for solving this most ancient philosophical puzzle. If you want to understand what it's like working with an Antinet, you must remind yourself that it's a *communication* experience.

COMMUNICATION IS THE SECRET INGREDIENT FOR GENERATING SURPRISES

One of the key functions of the Antinet is its ability to *surprise*. Johannes Schmidt describes the Zettelkasten as a "surprise generator."[26] The precursor for generating surprises is communication.

As Luhmann writes, "One of the most basic presuppositions of communication is that the partners can mutually surprise each other."[27]

On a more general level, communication surprises. For instance, for the past several years I've been working primarily by myself. However, in the process of writing this book, I've published and shared a lot of material on

25 Hans-Georg Moeller, The Radical Luhmann (New York: Columbia University Press, 2011), 56.

26 Johannes Schmidt, "Niklas Luhmann's Card Index: Thinking Tool, Communication Partner, Publication Machine," Forgetting Machines. Knowledge Management Evolution in Early Modern Europe 53 (2016), 295.

27 Niklas Luhmann, "Communication with Noteboxes (Revised Edition)," trans. Manfred Kuehn, https://daily.scottscheper.com/zettelkasten/.

my social media channels.[28] In doing so I've opened up many more channels of communication with people so that it's no longer just me communicating with my Antinet. I've gained a lot of knowledge by communicating with others, but on top of that, I constantly receive links and ideas that surprise me and generate breakthrough ideas for my research.

Likewise, when you work with an Antinet as a communication partner, you're having a conversation. A conversation emerges in your own mind wherein you're trying to re-understand your own thoughts. You're essentially having a conversation with your old self (that is, your past self).

This communication experience relates to that described in Mortimer Adler's *How to Read a Book*, in which Adler describes the experience of reading a book as an *active process* that he compares to the game of baseball.[29] There's the pitcher (the author of a book), who throws a baseball (the message, material, or an idea contained within the book), and the catcher (you, the reader). The position of catcher is not passive. A catcher is not a lazy inanimate object who does nothing. The catcher is moving, shifting, and anticipating both the pitcher (author) and the pitch (message). It's a communication experience—a very active communication experience.

This type of communication experience mirrors what it's like working with your Antinet. It's an active, creative, collaborative communication experience. One that generates many surprises.

This communication experience is also significantly *deeper* than you might realize. When you are communicating with an author through reading their book, you're not just reading the words written by that one author. As Kate Turabian puts it, when you read a book, "you silently converse with its authors—and through them with everyone else they have read."[30] With

---

28 https://www.youtube.com/channel/UCnvMBVMXMPKA4Lmy5Ihd-FQ; https://twitter.com/ScottScheper; https://www.reddit.com/r/antinet/.

29 Mortimer Jerome Adler and Charles Van Doren, How to Read a Book, Rev. and updated ed (New York: Simon and Schuster, 1972), 5.

30 Kate L. Turabian, Manual for Writers of Research Papers, Theses, and Dissertations,: Chicago Style for Students and Researchers, 9th edition (Chicago ; London: University of

your Antinet, you're creating a deeply evolved and deeply linked communication partner with whom you communicate.

AN EXAMPLE OF THE ANTINET COMMUNICATION EXPERIENCE

As previously discussed, with the Antinet, there is no full-text search. There is no safety net, and this fact underlies the entire experience of using an Antinet. When you begin searching for something, you begin a journey. You undertake an exploration of your mind. During this exploration you're undertaking a communication process with your past self.

During the journey of finding thoughts in your Antinet, all you have is your index and cardlinks. The index sets you out on the journey, and the cardlinks swing you along across different branches and stems of thought in your tree of knowledge.

Creating cardlinks is not easy. They are created at the time you create the notecard, or shortly thereafter when you stumble upon the notecard (and have a related idea reverberating in your mind). Cardlinks are hard to create (unlike digital wikilinks). They cannot be mass-created on a whim and they require life energy to create. It's a deliberate act that requires you to think of truly related ideas.

As a result of cardlinks being harder to create, they also require you to be more *selective*. Since there are fewer cardlinks in analog systems, you have more energy to follow them and you end up taking them more seriously. In contrast, when you encounter links and tags in a digital system, there may be five, ten, or fifteen links associated with a single note. Not to mention that there are backlinks that you can feasibly follow. In effect this dilutes the power of the relations because there are so many of them.

Within an analog system you're dealing with *selective* relations. The entire system is *relations of relations of selective relations*. Whenever you come across a *selective relation*, you're more motivated to take it seriously and actually

---

Chicago Press, 2018), 8.

follow the cardlink. If you're on a tree with fifteen vines, it's less likely you'll explore all fifteen. If you're on a tree with one vine, you'll hop on and continue your exploration with vigor.

Let's walk through a more practical example, an example from Luhmann's Antinet.

Let's say in your index, you look up the keyterm *risk*. When you look up *risk*, it links you to *transformation of risk* (which is at card address 21/3d18c6009).[31] You think to yourself, *Hmm, this is interesting… Risk is within the branch of Systems Theory (21/3d18) and within that, the branch of Complexity (21/3d18c).* Suddenly a secondary conversation takes place in your mind. A dreamlike memory emerges that takes you back to the period in your life when you wrote about *complexity* within *systems theory*. Perhaps you wrote about it that time you travelled to Paris and spent the time in a great Parisian library reading (which is what Luhmann did once, according to Clemens Luhmann).[32] You are suddenly transported back to the setting of that time in the library in Paris. You remember how it was a gray November day in that Paris library. You recall reading about *complexity*, which led you to write about *risk*.

When you begin moving down the stem of *risk* you're soon met with a cardlink collective (21/3d18c6009,1):

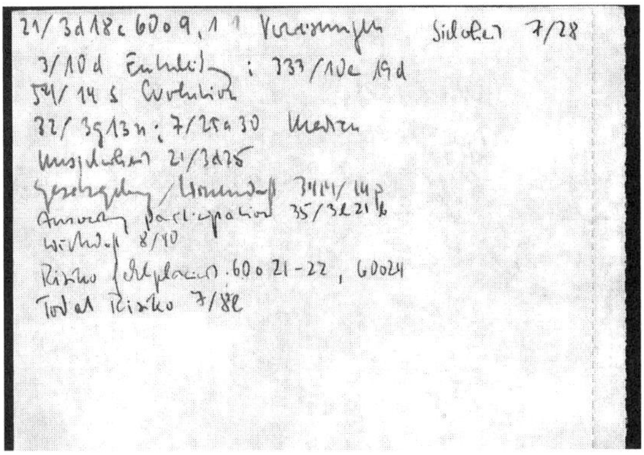

PHOTO CREDIT: "ZK II: Zettel 21/3d18c60o9,1—Niklas Luhmann-Archiv," accessed April 28, 2022, https://niklas-luhmann-archiv.de/bestand/zettelkasten/zettel/ZK_2_NB_21-3d18c60o9-1_V.

31 "ZK II: Zettel 21/3d18c6009—Niklas Luhmann-Archiv," accessed April 28, 2022, https://niklas-luhmann-archiv.de/bestand/zettelkasten/zettel/ZK_2_NB_21-3d18c6009_V.

32 Clemens Luhmann, Interview by Scott P. Scheper, April 27, 2022.

It lists out several concepts related to *risk*. The concepts are as follows:[33]

- *Safety/security: 7/28*
    * *Absorption of uncertainty: 34/4*
    * *Responsibility: 333/10e*
- *Uncertainty as an information variable: 44/2d5*
    * *Money/power as absorption of uncertainty: 352/16a6*
- *Liquidity: 532/4a5fa13a*
    * *Process of education: 7/25g58*
- *Safety/work atmosphere: 532/5d3j2b*
    * *Legal certainty: 3414/27*
- *Certainty/truth/science: 7/25b30k*
    * *Uncertainty: 21/3d25*
    * *Legislation/science: 3414/14p*
    * *Economy: 8/40*
    * *Death as a risk: 7/8l*

You think to yourself *'Death as a risk' what on earth does that have to do with risk?* You then realize, death has *everything* to do with risk. It relates to *Certainty/truth/science* in that death is the ultimate form of *uncertainty* that underlies society and drives human behavior. At the core foundation of *risk* resides the ultimate fear: *risk of death.*

This illustrates the communication experience in working with the Antinet. There are several dialogues taking place concurrently. First, we have the dialogue of recalling the memory of writing and researching *risk* (in the Parisian library). Then, we have the dialogue of actually conversing with the Antinet: *What does the concept of death have to do with risk?*

This example shows how the dots begin to connect over time. When you first wrote about *risk*, you did not write about *death*. Over time, the concept of *death* emerged and was added to the branch collective for *risk*

---

33 **Johannes Schmidt, "Niklas Luhmann's Card Index: Thinking Tool, Communication Partner, Publication Machine," Forgetting Machines. Knowledge Management Evolution in Early Modern Europe 53 (2016), 308.**

(21/3d18c6009,1). These concepts and links needed time to synthesize and grow. Continuing the metaphor of the Antinet as a tree, photosynthesis needed to take place. This area of your tree needed sunlight to synthesize. The structure grew organically over time in a natural way. It creates an antifragile structure (compared to a dynamic digital structure with hyperactive edits and bulk edits).

This example gives you a glimpse into the communication experience that is an outcome of working with the Antinet. It shows you the internal dialogue that takes place. It also shows you how a system of both order *and* chaos works.

You started by looking up *risk*, and then are taken on a journey that brings forth concepts related to *Certainty/truth/science*, *Uncertainty*, and more. This communication experience takes you on a journey that generates breakthrough surprises, leading "to a variety of other subjects that the user initially would not have associated with the first one," as Johannes Schmidt observes. "It also shows how potential relationships between these topics may not have come to mind in the absence of such a chain of references."[34]

When you use an Antinet, you're forced to create *abstractions* of ideas. You're forced to *generalize* ideas and relate them to one another. "Communication," Luhmann says, "becomes fruitful only at a high level of generalization, namely that of establishing communicative relations of relations."[35]

Luhmann gives an example wherein he observes, "Why on the one hand museums are [generally] empty, while on the other hand exhibitions of paintings by Monet, Picasso, or Medici are too crowded."[36] Instead of creating the keyterms *Monet*, *Picasso*, or *Medici*, he instead does something else. He *generalizes* and *abstracts* the idea to get at the core essence. The reason

---

34 Johannes Schmidt, "Niklas Luhmann's Card Index: Thinking Tool, Communication Partner, Publication Machine," Forgetting Machines. Knowledge Management Evolution in Early Modern Europe 53 (2016), 309.

35 Niklas Luhmann, "Communication with Noteboxes (Revised Edition)," trans. Manfred Kuehn, https://daily.scottscheper.com/zettelkasten/.

36 Niklas Luhmann, "Communication with Noteboxes (Revised Edition)," trans. Manfred Kuehn, https://daily.scottscheper.com/zettelkasten/.

why Monet, Picasso, and Medici exhibits are so crowded is because they're temporally limited. That is, they are only available to be viewed at a certain place and for only a short period of time. In this instance, Luhmann created the index keyterm or branch collective card with the following concept: "preference for what is temporally limited."[37] From there he linked to the card that talks about Monet, Picasso, or Medici exhibits being overcrowded. Over time, more and more examples of *preferences for temporally limited* items were added to the collective.

In effect, Luhmann has created a high-level generalization. He points out that communication with the Antinet becomes more valuable when you create such generalizations (instead of merely creating a keyterm for the mention of *Picasso*). Yet there's one final piece of this communication experience: the "moment of evaluation."[38]

Luhmann writes that communicating with the Antinet "becomes productive only at the moment of evaluation, and is thus bound to a certain time and is to a high degree accidental."[39]

In other words, when it comes time to writing, you end up stumbling upon valuable cards. Let's say you stumble upon the branch collective of items for *preferences for temporally limited*. As a result of this, you are reminded that art exhibits serve as an example of people tending to prefer something that is temporally limited. In a card nearby, you then stumble upon a card-link pointing to the concept of *scarcity*. This opens up a whole new stem of thought, and an idea sparks in your mind. Humans are not just driven by things that are temporally scarce, but by *anything* that is scarce. You can then write about how museums leverage the tendency of humans to be motivated by *scarcity* (whether that be time-based scarcity or space-based scarcity), as do retailers, with phrases such as *Only 2 items left!* (when shopping online).

---

37 Niklas Luhmann, "Communication with Noteboxes (Revised Edition)," trans. Manfred Kuehn, https://daily.scottscheper.com/zettelkasten/.

38 Niklas Luhmann, "Communication with Noteboxes (Revised Edition)," trans. Manfred Kuehn, https://daily.scottscheper.com/zettelkasten/.

39 Niklas Luhmann, "Communication with Noteboxes (Revised Edition)," trans. Manfred Kuehn, https://daily.scottscheper.com/zettelkasten/.

These connections are not made at the time they're created, Luhmann points out, but are made at the time of evaluation—at the time you sit down to actually write about them. In effect, you're working with your Antinet as a *communication partner* during the time of writing, and doing so helps you generate breakthrough insights and ideas.

Welcome to the Antinet. Using it sets off the incommunicable experience of a communicable experience (with a notebox). It's filled with order, chaos, and surprises.

INTELLECTUAL EVOLUTION DEPENDS ON COMMUNICATION WITH EXTERNALIZED ARTIFICIAL CONSCIOUSNESS

Something I discuss early on in this book relates to how intellectual evolution relies on communication with an externalized artificial consciousness. I hold that the Antinet serves as a better container of external artificial consciousness than any digital notetaking app (thus far).

Akin to the concept of human evolution happening through the use of *externalizing* tools (like axes and spears), intellectual evolution relies on the "exteriorization" of one's individual memories. This served as a very successful and intriguing idea in the second half of the twentieth century.[40]

To evolve intellectually, we must first externalize our individual memories. Recall, a memory is a representation of a thought. A thought is a representation of reality. Paradoxically, we must externalize our metaphysical thoughts by inserting them into physical reality. When you use an Antinet, you do this by way of writing your thoughts by hand on notecards; in the digital realm, you really aren't participating in the same process because you're externalizing metaphysical thoughts by injecting them into metaphysical reality (on a computer screen).

---

40 Alberto Cevolini, ed., Forgetting Machines: Knowledge Management Evolution in Early Modern Europe, Library of the Written Word, volume 53 (Leiden ; Boston: Brill, 2016), 12.

As a result, digital may fail to make a key step in procuring intellectual evolution. Here's why: intellectual evolution will emerge from shifting from the structural coupling of *communication* and *consciousness* to a structural coupling of *communication* and *artificial consciousness.* In other words, the most advanced communication today happens with conscious entities. Of course communication occurs with unconscious entities as well. After all, when two computers connect, they communicate, though they are unconscious of themselves. They are deterministic agents in a network operated by conscious entities. The next big intellectual evolution will emerge from the communication between conscious entities and artificially conscious entities. Many quickly jump to thinking of robots as the best candidate for becoming the world's first artificially conscious entity; however some hold that, "Artificial consciousness is impossible due to the extrinsic nature of programming which is bound to syntax and devoid of meaning."[41]

In brief, are we wasting our time in holding that the next intellectual advancement will arise by way of an impossible idea (artificial consciousness)? I think it's quite possible we are wasting our time. Yet I don't think this means we ought to cast aside the idea. Instead I think it wise to explore the next best thing to artificial consciousness: creating our own very close versions of artificial consciousness. This is where the Antinet comes into play.

The best tools for intellectual advancement are those which embody the properties of artificial consciousness: a *communication partner* that seems to have its own externalized *personality*. Thus far, computers and digital notetaking apps have outshone analog tools for storing data and information. However, they have not outshone analog tools in one area: storing one's consciousness; one's deepest thoughts and ideas; one's personality. I hold that the analog medium—by way of containing your own handwriting—provides a better mechanism to act like a *cue* or *prompt* for generating an internal dialogue in your mind. More on this will be discussed shortly. But for now, know that the analog medium serves as a better vehicle of artificial consciousness than does a computer.

---

41 David Hsing, "Artificial Consciousness Is Impossible," Medium, March 28, 2022, https://towardsdatascience.com/artificial-consciousness-is-impossible-c1b2ab0bdc46.

Even though the Antinet isn't actually aware of itself and is not alive (and thus not fully artificially conscious), it is composed of (many iterations of) your past self, which was aware of itself at the time of the note's creation. Every note you observe in an Antinet is a containerized capsule of your own consciousness. This is why noteboxes have been described as a view into another's life and mind. This is something Johannes Schmidt touches on when he refers to Luhmann's Antinet as "the backstage of his theory and therefore as Niklas Luhmann's intellectual autobiography."[42] Our consciousness is indeed captured in external memory devices. Paradoxically, communication with such devices is an incommunicable truth.[43] It's impossible to describe to others the internal experience of working with your own artificial consciousness.

COMMUNICATION WITH YOU AND YOUR PAST SELF

The Antinet is a true communication relationship with you and your past self. When I read my handwritten notes and papers from fifteen years ago, it's *me* I'm interacting with. It's my thoughts—even if they're excerpts or reformulations of what I was reading at the time. It signals to me that my past self resonated with whatever idea the note contains. I see myself in my handwriting. I see how much I've grown, and also how much I've stayed the same. There are feelings of both respect, and also feelings of shame and regret when I review old notes. When I come upon handwritten notes of relationship advice, it makes me a little sad to realize those were written during my first marriage. Yet it also makes me laugh, seeing the irony of relationship advice that wasn't effective. When I come across other writings from that time, it makes me feel a certain love and reverence and respect for myself during that period.

---

42 Johannes Schmidt, "Niklas Luhmann's Card Index: Thinking Tool, Communication Partner, Publication Machine," Forgetting Machines. Knowledge Management Evolution in Early Modern Europe 53 (2016), 310.

43 Joseph Campbell, The Hero with a Thousand Faces, 3rd ed, Bollingen Series XVII (Novato, Calif: New World Library, 2008), 25. "Whereas the truths of science are communicable, being demonstrable hypotheses rationally founded on observable facts..." The Antinet almost requires some spiritual, metaphysical experiences to be fully understood. In brief, first-hand personal experience is required to understand it as a communication partner.

This type of stuff may sound sappy and unscientific; however, I assure you it's not. The Antinet contains your personality, and this is a very important feature in interacting with your own thoughts. As previously mentioned, scholars, including Luhmann, are aware of the idea of a *ghost in the box*.[44] One scholar concludes that "Luhmann did not regard his filing cabinet as a simple slip box, rather he interacted with it as if it were a true communication partner."[45]

One way the Antinet serves as a communication partner is in the form of asking it questions and "making queries."[46] This relates to the concept of asking a book questions, which was nicely outlined by Mortimer Adler. "If you ask a living teacher a question, he will probably answer you... If, however, you ask a book a question, *you must answer it yourself*. In this respect a book is like nature or the world. When you question it, it answers you only to the extent that you do the work of thinking and analysis yourself."[47]

Asking a book a question is similar to communicating with an Antinet, except that the Antinet contains a massive store of knowledge from the many books you've read. It's not like the process of hyperactively searching Google. You must *do the work of thinking and analysis yourself*—with whatever knowledge you have at your disposal.

The Antinet is not some "rhetorical storehouse," observes one scholar. It's not a tool for capturing unprocessed information and storing it for a later period of time. You can certainly do this by using ExRefs—however, hyperactive digital tools are much better for collecting unprocessed information. The true value is the Antinet's ability to turn information into knowledge by injecting your own personality to it. "The card index preserves a knowl-

---

44 "ZK II: Note 9 / 8.3—Niklas Luhmann Archive," accessed January 11, 2022, https://niklas-luhmann-archiv.de/bestand/zettelkasten/zettel/ZK_2_NB_9-8-3_V.

45 Alberto Cevolini, ed., Forgetting Machines: Knowledge Management Evolution in Early Modern Europe, Library of the Written Word, volume 53 (Leiden ; Boston: Brill, 2016), 26. Emphasis added.

46 Niklas Luhmann, "Communication with Noteboxes (Revised Edition)," trans. Manfred Kuehn, https://daily.scottscheper.com/zettelkasten/.

47 Mortimer Jerome Adler and Charles Van Doren, How to Read a Book, Rev. and updated ed (New York: Simon and Schuster, 1972), 14.

edge—*we could also say, a past*—that not only continually changes but also can be recalled in a highly *selective* manner."[48]

The *ghost in the box* factor stems from writing by hand. Handwriting seems to containerize consciousness better than standardized digital fonts. Developing true knowledge, filled with *meaningful* information, relies on internal dialogue (i.e., *intrapersonal* communication) with your past self's consciousness.[49] Analog systems with handwriting seem to retain this consciousness better than standardized digital schemes. Your own handwriting is unique—especially when you view it yourself.

THE PHASE TRANSITION FROM ANTINET TO SECOND MIND

Luhmann's thinking evolved with his Antinet, as did his process of taking notes. His early notes from the 1950s and 1960s contained more excerpts and long-passages that flowed across several notecards.[50] At a certain point, Luhmann's process went through a change that perhaps relates to his statement that the Antinet "needs a number of years in order to reach critical mass. Until then, it functions as a mere container from which we can retrieve what we put in."[51] By reaching critical mass, Luhmann was referring to how the Antinet becomes its own *mind*—an independent entity with whom you can communicate.[52]

---

48 Alberto Cevolini, ed., Forgetting Machines: Knowledge Management Evolution in Early Modern Europe, Library of the Written Word, volume 53 (Leiden ; Boston: Brill, 2016), 32. Emphasis added.

49 Alberto Cevolini, ed., Forgetting Machines: Knowledge Management Evolution in Early Modern Europe, Library of the Written Word, volume 53 (Leiden ; Boston: Brill, 2016), 13. "The only operations that can reproduce and manage meaning are communication and consciousness."

50 "ZK I: Zettel 7,9—Niklas Luhmann-Archiv," accessed July 14, 2021, https://niklas-luhmann-archiv.de/bestand/zettelkasten/zettel/ZK_1_NB_7-9_V; Johannes Schmidt, "Niklas Luhmann's Card Index: Thinking Tool, Communication Partner, Publication Machine," Forgetting Machines. Knowledge Management Evolution in Early Modern Europe 53 (2016), 293.

51 Niklas Luhmann, "Communication with Noteboxes (Revised Edition)," trans. Manfred Kuehn, https://daily.scottscheper.com/zettelkasten/.

52 Niklas Luhmann, "Communication with Noteboxes (Revised Edition)," trans. Manfred

Being that the Antinet *is* a cybernetic network, I find network science to be an excellent field from which to glean lessons. There's an emerging area of study within network science called *percolation theory*, which nicely describes the transition from Antinet to *second mind*.

Percolation theory studies the phenomenon in networks wherein a phase transition takes place. This phase is the result of a very small change in the composition of the network (such as adding a certain number of notes to your Antinet, thus meeting a specific *threshold*). Think of boiling water on a stove. At 99°C something is happening, but you're still staring at water. Yet after an increase of one single degree Celsius, a specific threshold is met. Meeting this threshold triggers the entire entity of water to transition into an entirely different substance (gas). This is what is meant by *phase transition*.

The same transformation that occurs during a phase transition when a minimum threshold is met exists within networks, and is studied in a branch of mathematics that studies percolation theory. It is a compelling field because of its utility in studying digital networks on which the success of certain commercial products rely—especially products which rely on mesh networks. Businesses can find significant value in understanding the nature of the networks they have built and what the minimum threshold number of nodes needs to be in order to undergo a phase transition from a disconnected network to a connected one.

As far as the Antinet goes, the matter of importance is to understand the minimum threshold of notes and keyterms needed to undergo a phase transition (from Antinet to second mind). Luhmann never specified this number, other than stating it *takes a number of years*.

Whatever this threshold happens to be is of little value to the more interesting occurrence: the fact is that Luhmann did indeed observe a phase transition with his Antinet when, at some point, his Antinet transitioned from an analog brain that simply stores notes, to a completely different entity entirely.

Kuehn, https://daily.scottscheper.com/zettelkasten/. "If you wish to educate a partner in communication, it will be good to provide him with independence from the beginning."

Just like water turning into gas when it hits 100°C, the Antinet turns into a second mind after reaching a certain number of notes (say one thousand).

In Luhmann's notes on the nature of his Antinet, he talks about having an "impression of a mentally muscular overall personality."[53] What I hold this to mean is that the Antinet develops its own unique, rough personality after it undergoes this phase transition into a second mind. The entity becomes an alter-ego with whom you can communicate. It becomes a research assistant who you can collaborate with. It becomes a true second mind.

We've thus far talked primarily about communication. Understanding this concept is critical in grasping the nature of working with an Antinet. We've also touched upon the entity we communicate with when working with an Antinet—the second mind. Let's now take a deep dive into exploring this entity, the second mind.

SECOND BRAIN VS. SECOND MIND

Second brain is a term that has become popular within productivity and personal knowledge management circles. Also, digital Zettelkasten systems have been *linked* to this term (pun intended). You'll find popular software used for digital Zettelkasten systems described as a second brain.[54] Personally, I find this term lacking. The term *second brain* has been used primarily to refer to technologies that are for collecting and storing information. The information, however, is essentially a disconnected blob of unprocessed material.

In reality, you don't want a second brain; instead you want a *second mind.* A brain is just biological wetware. It, in itself, is nothing without its other interconnected systems functioning together. A second mind describes the occurrence of the *whole becoming greater than the sum of its parts.*

People are intrigued with the Zettelkasten because it's not just an information storage container. If it were a container, people would opt for simpler

---

53 "ZK II: Zettel 9/8f - Niklas Luhmann-Archiv," accessed April 30, 2022, https://niklas-luhmann-archiv.de/bestand/zettelkasten/zettel/ZK_2_NB_9-8f_V.

54 "Obsidian," accessed May 2, 2022, https://obsidian.md/. "A second brain,for you, forever."

notebox systems which merely store thoughts. In contrast, the notecard systems others have shared haven't created a whole niche within knowledge management. The Zettelkasten has indeed created excitement. Why? Because of its promise to not just be a memory storage system, but a thinking system—it is a true *knowledge development system.*

People are also intrigued with the Zettelkasten because of the results it produced for Luhmann. His prolific work—seventy books and 550 published articles over a thirty year timeframe—was achieved through interacting with his system as if it were a communication partner—a second mind.

A second brain is an information store, or information database.

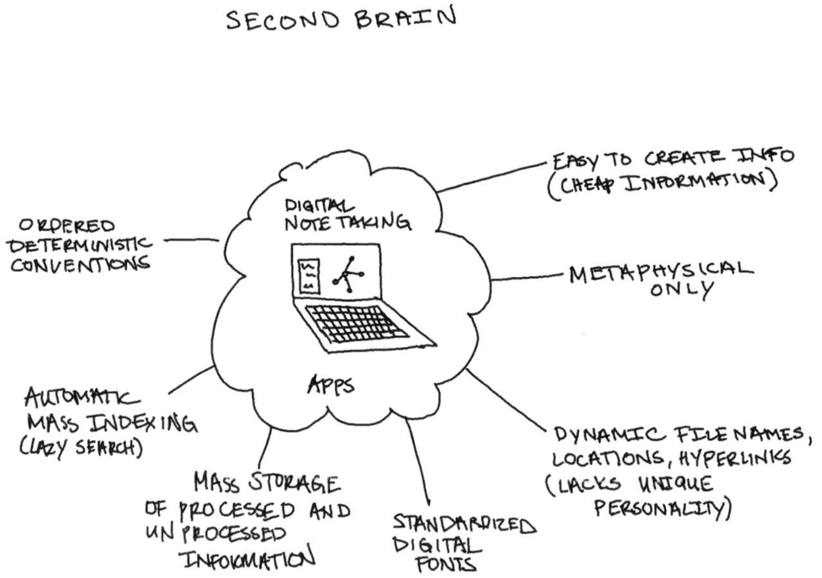

A second mind is a communication partner that forces you to think, to develop ideas (by hand, the old way, the hard way), and later to argue with your ideas. It forces you to see inconsistencies in your old thoughts and evolve them.

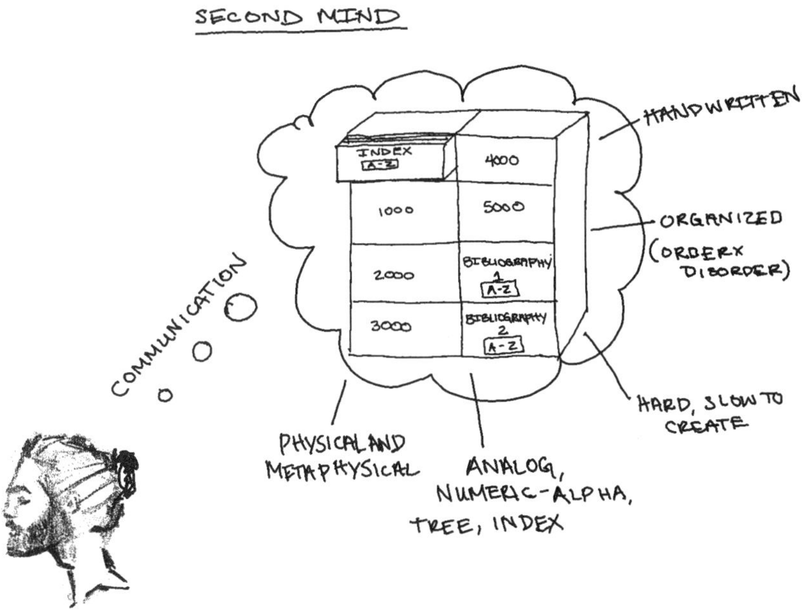

AN ARGUMENT FOR SECOND MIND OVER SECOND MEMORY

Luhmann's description of the communication relationship he had with his Zettelkasten was summed up as follows: "As a result of prolonged work with this technique, a kind of second memory emerges, an alter ego with which one can constantly communicate."[55]

The phrase he used to describe the entity he was communicating with was *eine Art Zweitgedächtnis, ein alter Ego*. This is a second memory type of entity, or an alter ego. Here, *zweit* translates to "second," and *Gedächtnis* to "memory." If we look into the word *Gedächtnis,* we find some interesting origins: its root stems from *gedacht, which is the past participle of denken, meaning* "to think, *call to mind,* conceive."[56] In other words, a *Zweitgedächtnis* is a second-memory entity, an alter ego.

---

55 Niklas Luhmann, "Kommunikation mit Zettelkästen," in Öffentliche Meinung und sozialer Wandel / Public Opinion and Social Change, ed. Horst Baier, Hans Mathias Kepplinger, and Kurt Reumann (Wiesbaden: VS Verlag für Sozialwissenschaften, 1981), 225.

56 "Gedächtnis," in Wiktionary, February 1, 2021, https://en.wiktionary.org/w/index.

The entity Luhmann was referring to involves a communication experience in which you're *calling to mind* a *second part of yourself* (an alter ego). Furthermore, we see Luhmann referring to this entity as a "*Geist*" in his notes written in preparation for the paper.[57] I hold that a better term for this entity involves combining Luhmann's term *Geist* with the concept of *Zweitgedächtnis.* As a result we end up with *Zweitgeist,* which translates to "second mind." Thus, the term for *second mind* is born.[58]

A similar type of evolution from the term *second memory* to *second mind* is something that recently occurred within knowledge science. The term secondary memory is now referred to as "early modern terminology." The newer and more popular term is *extended mind.* Proposed by Andy Clark and David Chalmers, the concept of *extended mind* holds that the mind resides not only in the brain, but also outside of it. One's mind is stored in the external representations of the human body. While I think there's truth in their thesis, there are problems with the term extended mind. Several scholars point out that there exists a failure to explain what aspect of the mind is *extended.* Is it the entire mind that is extended or just cognition? Furthermore, the definition of *extended* is not made clear.[59] This is another reason we'll be sticking to the term *second mind.*

---

php?title=Ged%C3%A4chtnis&oldid=61707257; "Denken," in Wiktionary, May 17, 2021, https://en.wiktionary.org/w/index.php?title=denken&oldid=62540453;Friedrich Kluge, "Denken," in An Etymological Dictionary of the German Language, D (London: George Bell & Sons, 1891). Emphasis added.

57 "ZK II: Note 9 / 8.3—Niklas Luhmann Archive," accessed January 11, 2022, https://niklas-luhmann-archiv.de/bestand/zettelkasten/zettel/ZK_2_NB_9-8-3_V.

58 "What Is the Difference between 'Geist' and 'Verstand. Sie Werden Beiden Als "Mind" Uebersetzt' ? 'Geist' vs 'Verstand. Sie Werden Beiden Als "Mind" Uebersetzt'?," HiNative, accessed June 2, 2021, https://hinative.com/en-US/questions/15369673; "Translation—What Is the German Word for 'Mind'?," German Language Stack Exchange, accessed June 2, 2021, https://german.stackexchange.com/questions/27210/what-is-the-german-word-for-mind. The German language has several terms for "mind." The term "verstand" is used primarily to refer to "understanding" and "intelligence." Whereas "geist" refers to more of the philosophical, spiritual, or abstract reference to the concept of "mind."

59 Alberto Cevolini, ed., Forgetting Machines: Knowledge Management Evolution in Early Modern Europe, Library of the Written Word, volume 53 (Leiden ; Boston: Brill, 2016), 12.

So, the entity one communicates with when the Antinet reaches a critical threshold is the second mind.

There's only one question left. What the hell is a mind?!

What a Mind Is

The mind is a metaphysical entity. It has never been identified. As far as we can tell, it may just be a bunch of neurons connecting to other neurons in the brain. A reductionist approach is to just get rid of the concept altogether.[60] Yet I think this a bit premature. It's simply that, as cognitive psychologist Steven Pinker points out, "we don't understand how the mind works."[61] For a long period of time humankind didn't understand gravity; yet we had a sense that there was something to the phenomenon of objects falling. We just couldn't explain it yet. Aristotle thought it had something to do with elements wishing to return to their natural place.[62] Just because we didn't understand gravity, didn't mean we should have cast aside the concept of something causing the effects we now recognize as being a result of gravity. Just because we don't understand something fully yet doesn't mean we should delete the placeholder term and stop asking questions about it. The mind is a metaphysical entity that we don't fully understand yet. Like human memory, the mind remains one of the last great mysteries in science.

I like to think of the mind as a product of the brain which is a product of evolution.[63] "The mind is not the brain but what the brain *does*," as Pinker puts it.[64] Again, this is why you want a second mind, not a second brain. You don't just want an inanimate jumble of wetware. You want an active, holistic system that becomes greater than the sum of its parts. The system itself

---

60 Yuval Noah Harari, Homo Deus A Brief History of Tomorrow. (New York: HarperCollins Publishers, 2017), 114ff.

61 Steven Pinker, How the Mind Works, Norton pbk (New York: Norton, 2009), xv.

62 "Gravity: From Apples to the Universe | Britannica," accessed May 2, 2022, https://www.britannica.com/story/gravity-from-apples-to-the-universe.

63 Steven Pinker, How the Mind Works, Norton pbk (New York: Norton, 2009), vii.

64 Steven Pinker, How the Mind Works, Norton pbk (New York: Norton, 2009), 24. Emphasis added.

is inanimate; however when all four components of the Antinet interact, a second mind emerges.

THE PERSON INSIDE THE ANTINET

People seem to overlook the fact that the Antinet filled the role of being an actual *person* for Luhmann.

To Luhmann, the Antinet was not just a thinking tool, it was a person. The concept of viewing the Antinet as a person might be seen as similar to the concept of animism, the way of what we in the modern West call "objects" as possessing person-like qualities. For example, in Japanese Shinto culture, it is believed that a soul lives within all matter; every-day things are thought of as being deities.[65] This is perhaps why you'll often find Japanese embracing the idea of robots being companions, nurses and caretaking companions for the elderly.[66] In a similar vein, this might be one reason the pocket-sized digital pets called Tamagotchi first emerged in Japan, though they quickly spread to Western countries, as well. Several studies have analyzed how the Tamagotchi toys changed human behavior with digital devices. "Tamagotchi convinced consumers to willingly dedicate their time, attention, and emotions to the virtual pet."[67]

The phenomenon wherein we experience a deep connection when interacting with certain physical objects is widespread. With the Antinet it becomes even easier to experience this because you're viewing your own thoughts, your own spirit, and your own soul within the handwritten cards of your Antinet. The entire system enables you to *communicate* with such an entity.

---

65 Larissa Hjorth, "In Japan, Supernatural Beliefs Connect the Spiritual Realm with the Earthly Objects around Us," The Conversation, accessed May 1, 2022, http://theconversation.com/in-japan-supernatural-beliefs-connect-the-spiritual-realm-with-the-earthly-objects-around-us-125726.

66 Jon Emont, "Japan Prefers Robot Bears to Foreign Nurses," Foreign Policy (blog), accessed May 2, 2022, https://foreignpolicy.com/2017/03/01/japan-prefers-robot-bears-to-foreign-nurses/.

67 Laura Lawton, "Taken by the Tamagotchi: How a Toy Changed the Perspective on Mobile Technology," The IJournal: Student Journal of the Faculty of Information 2, no. 2 (March 30, 2017), https://theijournal.ca/index.php/ijournal/article/view/28127.

Even though Luhmann was an avid advocate of systems theory, stating, "it is easy to think of systems theory," in trying to describe the Antinet he went a different direction when he opted for communication theory to explain it; but this was because the system revolves around communication with the second mind.[68]

The idea of a notebox emerging into an external instantiation of one's own mind did not originate with Luhmann, but dates back to a situation described by Heinrich Von Kleist in 1805. He remarked upon the phenomenon of something like the second mind emerging in his analysis of the "midwifery of thought."[69]

The reason it was useful for Luhmann to create an actual (metaphysical) person to collaborate with centered around funding difficulties. In brief, Luhmann found that hiring research assistants and employees was too expensive. He needed a communication partner on whom he could rely (for at least thirty years). His Antinet proved to be not only reliable, but also an entity that inspired breakthrough insights in a way that would have been nearly impossible for even the best research assistant to produce.

When Luhmann first began building the Antinet it was seen as a memory aid; however in 1981, when he wrote his paper describing the Antinet, he knew it to be much more than just a memory tool.

The Antinet is not an analog note database. It's not necessarily even about notes. *Its primary nature concerns itself with the dualistic emergence of the second mind.* Again, this dualistic emergence of the second mind relies upon the four principles of the Antinet. I make no claim that the emergence of a second mind is exclusive to the Antinet (perhaps others who have analog noteboxes also experience this phenomenon). However the type of second

68 Niklas Luhmann, "Communication with Noteboxes (Revised Edition)," trans. Manfred Kuehn, https://daily.scottscheper.com/zettelkasten/.

69 Markus Krajewski, *Note-Keeping: History, Theory, Practice of a Counter-Measurement against Forgetting* (Brill, 2016), 325.

mind Luhmann experienced relies upon adhering to the four principles of the Antinet.

In brief, what we're talking about here is truly something special. When I think of the Antinet, I don't think about some tool in the notetaking app market. It's not something that can be compared to whatever digital note-taking app is popular by the time you read this. The Antinet is in a different category altogether. It belongs in a class of tools which induce an intrapersonal dialogue that is helpful during creation.

Modern day scientists agree with Luhmann's notion of a *ghost in the box* emerging from Antinets. One scholar confirms that it would be misleading to classify the Antinet as something which simply stores notes.[70] Here's why: when you peruse and read the thoughts written by someone who has passed—you feel this ghost-like internal presence. You begin to insert yourself in their shoes while they were writing down the thoughts on the card.

With the Antinet, this *ghost in the box* factor is experienced in a slightly different manner. You yourself are viewing your own thoughts. You communicate with your own internal ghost and embark upon an internal dialogue that happens during the act of creation.

Because the Antinet possesses the properties of both short-term thought development, and long-term thought development, it morphs into a unique metaphysical entity. The entity it becomes is beyond your control. You cannot preconceive how it will look in the future. This is oftentimes what people struggle with in the beginning. We're so used to molding our knowledge using digital tools. Digital information is very malleable. We can refactor and reorganize our knowledge on a whim. Whatever cool new convention or idea emerges, can set you out on a months-long quest to reorganize your digital knowledge repository. With the Antinet this is not the case. You must submit yourself to the rigid organic structure that emerges over years of building out your knowledge one notecard at a time, one branch at a time.

---

70 Alberto Cevolini, ed., Forgetting Machines: Knowledge Management Evolution in Early Modern Europe, Library of the Written Word, volume 53 (Leiden ; Boston: Brill, 2016), 19.

This chaotic and evolving structure of the Antinet makes it more fun to engage with. You're always in for a surprise when creating with your Antinet.

One reason why communicating with a second mind is unique centers around the limitations of each individual note. Within digital tools notes can be extensive in nature—seemingly all-encompassing for an idea.

With the Antinet, the notes are constrained by the size of each individual notecard. They're also constrained by the difficulty and time-intensity of writing by hand. As a result of these constraints, the notes are more prompt-like in nature. They are units that prompt one's internal dialogue to internally fire off the remaining details of the idea. Antinet notes communicate the idea without belaboring and over-communicating the idea. As a result of this under-communication of the idea, the rest of the communication takes place in the mind.

This concept of under-communication triggering an internal dialogue has been observed by scholars. It's the result of one's *external memory* interacting with one's *internal memory*. After studying John Boyle, John Locke, and Robert Hooke, one researcher observed how their notes were useful in the way they prompted recollection. The notes weren't valuable in themselves; they were valuable in the way they triggered an internal dialogue within their creator.[71]

The notes in your Antinet set off a chain reaction in your mind. Your notes serve as a *cue* for starting the recall process in your mind. Digital notes, on the other hand, tend to take different form. They tend to include too much detail. They tend to over-communicate the idea. This robs the creation process of much of its magic. Furthermore, the additional detail is unnecessary. It also ends up snowballing and creating an overabundance of information.

---

71 Alberto Cevolini, ed., Forgetting Machines: Knowledge Management Evolution in Early Modern Europe, Library of the Written Word, volume 53 (Leiden ; Boston: Brill, 2016), 12.

THE PERSONALITY OF YOUR SECOND MIND

The power of your second mind relies on its unique *personality*. There are several ways a unique personality is incorporated into the system. Again, the unique personality of the system relies on the core principles of the Antinet: Analog, Numeric-alpha Addresses, Tree Structure, Index. In particular, the numeric-alpha addresses are critical. They enable the system to become self-referential, and thus develop a "self" in the first-place.

Another way the system gains a personality involves how you use the index. Specifically, this relates to what unique keyterms you use to describe concepts. Certain terms you use to describe a concept might make complete sense in your mind, but another person might prefer a different term. You add personality to your system by using terms that make sense in *your* mind. For instance, I have a stem in my Antinet related to the concept of *power law* and the *Pareto principle*, the idea that 80% of something comes from 20% of the participants. For instance, 80% of a nation's wealth comes from 20% of the population. It exemplifies that a small number of people (or objects) can generate a big result. In my index I have created keyterms for *power law*, as well as the *Pareto principle*. However the main term that comes to mind when I think of this principle is *big impact*, due to the idea that a few things can have a big impact on the whole. I've built out a section around instances of "big impact" phenomena in the world. Whenever I come across something related to this in my reading, I write Big Impact on the bibcard and underline it. This unique way of terming something is one way I've injected personality into my Antinet.

It's not only the unique keyterms you use that give the second mind its personality; it's also the way in which you structure those keyterms. For instance, Luhmann observed how museums are frequently empty, while short-term art exhibits are completely packed.[72] I've talked about this concept before; however it's worth bringing up again to show how it affects the personality of one's second mind. Instead of creating the keyterms *Monet*,

---

72 Niklas Luhmann, "Communication with Noteboxes (Revised Edition)," trans. Manfred Kuehn, https://daily.scottscheper.com/zettelkasten/.

Picasso, or *Medici*, Luhmann created the keyterm in his index for *Preferences (For Temporally Limited Events)*. In my Antinet I would create a keyterm for this under *Scarcity*. My keyterm would be: *Scarcity (Examples of It Motivating People)*. It would then link to the card address of the note.

This gives a glimpse into how keyterms inject a unique personality into your Antinet. Both the specific keyterms you use, as well as how you structure them adds a unique personality to your second mind.

CONCLUSION

In this chapter, we covered a very important aspect of the Antinet. Actually two aspects. *Communication*, and the concept of the *second mind*. These concepts are a very real aspect in working with an Antinet. In the next section we'll dive into the science backing the Antinet, and its relation to concepts from the science of human memory.

CHAPTER NINETEEN

HUMAN MEMORY AND THE ANTINET

IN THIS CHAPTER WE'LL EXPLORE how the Antinet mirrors several aspects of human memory, including a look at the neuroscience behind why the Antinet is a helpful structure, and a deep dive into the concept of *context* within the Antinet.

HUMAN MEMORY AND THE ANTINET

Luhmann was not forced into the structure of the Antinet due to the limitations of technology. He could have chosen a *commonplace book*, or a categorical notecard system (organized by human-readable subjects). In fact, Luhmann tried several methods for managing his thoughts from readings. His first attempt was to take notes on notecards and stick them into the book once he had finished. However, this caused the bindings of the books to fray and break.[1]

After that failed experiment, he tried another technique, placing the notecards his readings generated into folders. Yet, as these notes increased, Luhmann complained of no longer being able to find anything in them.[2] He could have

1 Johannes Schmidt, "Niklas Luhmann's Card Index: Thinking Tool, Communication Partner, Publication Machine," Forgetting Machines. Knowledge Management Evolution in Early Modern Europe 53 (2016), 290.

2 Johannes Schmidt, "Niklas Luhmann's Card Index: Thinking Tool, Communication Partner, Publication Machine," Forgetting Machines. Knowledge Management Evolution in Early Modern Europe 53 (2016), 290.

even switched to using a computer later in his life, but he did not choose any of these routes.

These false starts helped Luhmann design the perfect system that served him for over forty years.

Luhmann could have switched to using a computer later in his life. However, Luhmann did not choose those routes. The structure of the Antinet, according to one scholar, was not haphazard, but *was a deliberate choice arising out of Luhmann's familiarity with how human memory worked.*[3] This familiarity also allowed Luhmann to understand how computer memory would work in the future (which emphasized the benefits of multiple storage).[4]

The scholar, Johannes Schmidt, points out that Luhmann's decision to use hard-coded, non-changing numeric-alpha addresses is the essential prerequisite for creativity in his system.[5]

Luhmann was likely aware of the issue with multiple storage: the fact that the computer science conception of it is *grossly misleading* due to it being overly abstract (and thus synthetic). Instead of a computer science concept of multiple storage, Luhmann preferred a more organic version based on the science of human memory.

In a card on the parent stem of Luhmann's Antinet located two cards before Luhmann mentions "multiple storage," we find him citing the following

---

3 Johannes Schmidt, "Niklas Luhmann's Card Index: Thinking Tool, Communication Partner, Publication Machine," Forgetting Machines. Knowledge Management Evolution in Early Modern Europe 53 (2016), 300. When one analyzes the sources of Luhmann's notes created, in preparation of his paper *Communication with Noteboxes,* we find references to W. Ross Ashby's survey of the brain and human memory.

4 "ZK II: Zettel 9/8b2—Niklas Luhmann-Archiv," accessed March 10, 2022, https://niklas-luhmann-archiv.de/bestand/zettelkasten/zettel/ZK_2_NB_9-8b2_V.

5 Johannes Schmidt, "Niklas Luhmann's Card Index: Thinking Tool, Communication Partner, Publication Machine," Forgetting Machines. Knowledge Management Evolution in Early Modern Europe 53 (2016), 299.

reference: "Ashby 1967, p. 103."[6] Luhmann references this, implying that it's noteworthy because it provides a "general structure of memories."

I did some digging and, after some time, was able to get my hands on the source Luhmann referenced. Here is the pertinent quote:

> At the moment, our scientific thinking tends to be grossly misled by the example of the big digital computer. It has a big memory store, kept far from the working parts, which send recordable facts to special places, and then later go back to exactly the same places to regain the information.[7]

"Such a method," Ashby continues, "can hardly be achieved in biological machinery," and he points to biological *noise* in such systems, such as injury, starvation, and infection.[8] Ashby is reflecting on the mechanistic problems found in digital systems. There's no *reality* built into them (like the reality of human memory decaying given any injury, starvation, or infection a person experiences).

Ashby also states something interesting: "More likely is it that most of the brain's memory traces occur, and are retained, at the site of their action."[9] What Ashby means by this is that thoughts are created in the context in which they are developed and are retained within that context. In the case of the Antinet, structured as it is to function akin to human memory, when developing a thought within one branch (like branch 4212, for instance), the memory of that thought is retained in that branch. It's not something that is freely floating around in a context-free graph (which is reflective of how digital notetaking apps operate).

---

6 "ZK II: Sheet 9/8b—Niklas Luhmann Archive," accessed March 17, 2022, https://niklas-luhmann-archiv.de/bestand/zettelkasten/zettel/ZK_2_NB_9-8b_V.

7 W. Ross Ashby, "The Place of the Brain in the Natural World," Biosystems 1, no. 2 (May 1, 1967): 95–104, 103.

8 W. Ross Ashby, "The Place of the Brain in the Natural World," Biosystems 1, no. 2 (May 1, 1967): 95–104, 103.

9 W. Ross Ashby, "The Place of the Brain in the Natural World," Biosystems 1, no. 2 (May 1, 1967): 95–104, 103.

Memories, Ashby observes, are "widely scattered," yet they also retain the context (in the Antinet, it's the branch) in which they were originally developed.[10]

Each component of a memory contains its own context and branches, and this is reflected in how the Antinet works. In the following illustration, a memory (or thought) that is recorded in the Antinet is composed of two other memories, represented by a sequence of cards that are branched (parts A and B).

Ashby likens this to how "animal heat" is understood as having two sub-components, *metabolism* and *oxidation*.[11]

So to reiterate, Ashby argues that the concept of memory is "grossly misled by the example of the big digital computer" (which stores information in mechanistic, discrete places), because this is not how human memory works, since it is "more likely ...that most of the brain's memory traces occur, and are retained, at the site of their action."[12]

In other words, memory is not some simple, perfectly ordered, deterministic, and consistent system. It's not built on a clean binary system (of 1s and 0s). Rather it is a distributed system requiring chains of relationships based within their *context*.

Unlike digital computers, the programs we execute are subject to *noise*. The Antinet, like human memory, is truly a *communication* system, as Ashby alludes to.[13]

---

10 W. Ross Ashby, "The Place of the Brain in the Natural World," Biosystems 1, no. 2 (May 1, 1967): 95–104, 103.
11 W. Ross Ashby, "The Place of the Brain in the Natural World," Biosystems 1, no. 2 (May 1, 1967): 95–104, 103.
12 W. Ross Ashby, "The Place of the Brain in the Natural World," Biosystems 1, no. 2 (May 1, 1967): 95–104, 103.
13 W. Ross Ashby, "The Place of the Brain in the Natural World," Biosystems 1, no. 2 (May 1, 1967): 95–104, 102.

Luhmann's approach to the Antinet structure appeared to opt for the *mereological* interpretation of human memory. As a social scientist capable of applying systems theory to sociology, it comes as no surprise that he would favor a systems-based view (mereology), rather than a computation-based view.

The mereological approach views memory as a system made up of subsystems. The environment in which memory operates is provided by other systems. The computational approach to human memory views memory as an algorithm, with a focus on mathematical equations and quantitative experiments to study the *encoding, storage,* and *retrieval* building blocks of human memory.[14]

Immediately following Luhmann's reference to Ashby, he states, "you do not have to rely on a vast number of point-by-point accesses."[15] What he means is that you don't need a robust list of keyterms that point to every single card. Rather you may *explore* and navigate your Antinet given just a general keyterm in your index. Due to the branched tree structure, you will be able to navigate and uncover genius-level insights and surprises along the way.

It's not a stretch to imagine how Luhmann approached the design and architecture of his Antinet, likely taking a systems-science approach to devising what he initially thought of as his "second memory."[16] Later on, of course, this system evolved, thanks to the unique architecture and design of the Antinet, into a *second mind.*

Luhmann did this by first breaking apart the components that create human memory. After this, he created abstracted instantiations of the components.

You can see such in the architecture of how cardlinks mirror key functional aspects of human memory.

---

14 Michael Jacob Kahana, Foundations of Human Memory. (New York: Oxford University Press, 2014).

15 "ZK II: Zettel 9/8b—Niklas Luhmann-Archiv," accessed March 10, 2022, https://niklas-luhmann-archiv.de/bestand/zettelkasten/zettel/ZK_2_NB_9-8b_V.

16 "Communicating with Slip Boxes by Niklas Luhmann," accessed May 4, 2021, https://luhmann.surge.sh/communicating-with-slip-boxes.

After studying how human memory works, one can begin to see the brilliance in Luhmann's design of the Antinet.

Take, for instance, an Antinet with the following numeric-alpha addresses:

- 4212/1
- 4212/2
- 4212/3
- ...
- 4214/1
- 4214/1A
    * 4214/1A/1
    * 4214/1A/2
    * 4214/1A/3
- 4214/1B
- 4214/2
- 4214/3
- ...
- 5425/1

The branch is expressed by the four-digits at the beginning of the numeric-alpha address. For instance: 4212, 4214, 5425.

The stems are things like: 4214/1, 4214/1A, 4214/2, 4214/3. From this, there are relative stemlinks like 4214/1A/1, 4214/1A/2, 4214/1A/3. These stemlinks are essentially linked to 4214/1A (they've "stemmed down" from 4214/1A). These are analogous to forward and backward associations in human memory.[17]

Because the Antinet is based on similarity by way of proximity, it mirrors human memory in that the further away two memories or thoughts are, and more memories in between them, the more the association decreases.[18] The closer the items and memories are, their greater the association is.

---

17 Michael Jacob Kahana, Foundations of Human Memory. (New York: Oxford University Press, 2014), 11.

18 Michael Jacob Kahana, Foundations of Human Memory. (New York: Oxford University

Yet, from experience, we know this isn't necessarily always the case. There are some ideas located in some contextual branches that are very closely related to an idea in a branch or discipline located far away from it.

For such instance, *remote associations are part of human memory.*[19] These are essentially cardlinks that link to a branch or a card in a remote part of the Antinet. For instance, say the card 4214/1A/2 contains a sentence at the bottom: For more on the subject of the power of writing by hand, see '5425/1'. This is an instance of a remote cardlink (i.e., a *remote association* in the terminology of human memory).

THE NEUROSCIENCE BEHIND THE ANTINET

Another analogy of the Antinet comes from neuroscience. Think of notecards as *neurons*, and the cardlinks as *connections*.

The idea of likening notecards to neurons may seem farfetched at first. However, it's really not. The neural networks we think of today as *legitimate* are artificial abstractions. In fact, they're perhaps even *abstractions of abstractions.* The reason why is simple. The models researchers use to study human memory "bear only a faint resemblance to real biological neurons: they are highly simplified computational 'units' that integrate and transmit information."[20]

Most of what people think of when they think of *neural networks* aren't actually *real*; they're *artificial.*

You see, many people think neural networks are part of natural science. They're abstractions. When people think of neural networks they're usually thinking of *artificial neural networks*. However, there are three types of neural

---

Press, 2014), 11.

19 Michael Jacob Kahana, Foundations of Human Memory. (New York: Oxford University Press, 2014), 7, 11.

20 Michael Jacob Kahana, Foundations of Human Memory. (New York: Oxford University Press, 2014), 152.

networks: (1) biological neural networks, (2) artificial neural networks, and (3) haptic neural networks.

Haptic neural networks are artificial yet not digital; they can be touched and worked with in physical reality. The Antinet is an example of a haptic neural network.

Notecards serve as a wonderful physical world abstraction for neurons—at least the neurons modeled by psychologists, computer scientists and neuroscientists.

Notecards fit the definition of "highly simplified computational 'units' that integrate and transmit information."[21] Another good analogy for a neuron is a tweet (perhaps that's why Twitter, with its character-limited nature, has done so exceptionally well). The simplicity of such containers representing a neuron actually mirrors a natural reality quite well.

There's one difference between the Antinet and the human brain, and the difference centers around one thing: vastness. The sheer size of neurons and connections in the human brain are staggering. The human brain possesses one hundred billion neurons, and two hundred trillion connections.[22] If we were to take the neuroscience analogy of the Antinet seriously, you would need to compile one hundred billion notecards and create two hundred trillion cardlinks between them. From the Antinet Niklas Luhmann worked on from 1951 to 1997, he was only able to create a *measly* seventy-five thousand cards (maincards).[23] That's a lot fewer than one hundred billion.

Yet, I say all of this with a tongue-in-cheek attitude. Of course one shouldn't intend to create 100 billion notecards, with 200 trillion cardlinks. I chose to

21 **Michael Jacob Kahana, Foundations of Human Memory. (New York: Oxford University Press, 2014), 152.**

22 **Michael Jacob Kahana, Foundations of Human Memory. (New York: Oxford University Press, 2014), 30.**

23 **Johannes Schmidt, "Niklas Luhmann's Card Index: Thinking Tool, Communication Partner, Publication Machine," Forgetting Machines. Knowledge Management Evolution in Early Modern Europe 53 (2016), 292.**

illustrate this comparison just to show how powerful this structure can be. With a database of 75,000 notecards one creates a communication partner that proves itself to be quite powerful.

Niklas Luhmann was familiar with how the brain was structured. It's no coincidence that he built his Antinet around the concept of *connections*.

Luhmann points out how memory does not function as a sum of point-by-point accesses[24] (i.e., like sequentially moving through your notes or just navigating *wikilinks* in a digital notetaking app). Rather, your brain needs just a starting direction of access points. From there the brain uses internal links by way of the sequential notes, and the internal links and connections (made possible by *remote cardlinks*).

AN ANTINET REPRESENTATION OF HOW HUMAN MEMORY ACTUALLY WORKS

The latest research on human memory reveals evidence for something termed the *distributed representation* of memory. The idea holds that memory is represented not merely by one notecard (neuron), but an interaction between *a large set of neurons.*[25]

For instance, in one piece of writing, I used the following distributed representations of memories (representations of thought) to form an article: 2428/1, 2428/1/0, 2428/1/1, 2428/1A, 2428/1B, 3535/2, 4212/2BA, 4214/1A/1A, 4214/2E/1B/1. Combined, these created a distributed representation of a memory.

---

24 **"Communicating with Slip Boxes by Niklas Luhmann," accessed May 4, 2021, https://luhmann.surge.sh/communicating-with-slip-boxes. "Memory does not function as the sum of point by point accesses, but rather utilizes internal relationships and becomes fruitful only at this level of the reduction of its own complexity."**

25 **Michael Jacob Kahana, Foundations of Human Memory. (New York: Oxford University Press, 2014), 26.**

THE CONTEXTS OF THE ANTINET

Context can be thought of as a base layer protocol in the Antinet. In other words, context is a foundational component for how thoughts are developed in an Antinet. The importance of context cannot be overstated.

Think of *context* as the branch or stem in which an idea or thought is contained. For instance, my branch on information science is 4212. The thoughts that I develop in this branch are developed within the context of information science.

Early memory scientists thought of context as a fixed container (thus, *4212* would always be known as the information science branch). However, more recent findings in the study of human memory have led to this model being revised. Today it is believed that such context gradually evolves over time.[26] In other words, what starts out as the information science branch can evolve to become the Antinet branch. Paradoxically, the *context* evolves based on its *content*, and the *content* evolves based on its *context*. This *fuzzy* occurrence serves as another illustration as to why the Antinet is built on a *rough* structure with *fuzzy categories*. Such a system mirrors how human memory works.

Digital Zettelkasten systems exhibit fewer properties of *rough* structures and *fuzzy categories*; they're locked into the strict binary world of 1s and 0s.

One scientist specializing in the field of memory writing about what takes place when learning suggests that *one forms associations* not only based on the actual *content* encountered, but actually on three things.[27]

First, of course, is the actual *content*. When you read a book, you're forming associations based on the content of what you read. Content can include other media (music, articles, podcasts, etc.). In other words, when you're

---

26 Michael Jacob Kahana, Foundations of Human Memory. (New York: Oxford University Press, 2014), 224.

27 Michael Jacob Kahana, Foundations of Human Memory. (New York: Oxford University Press, 2014), 12.

reading a biography about F. Scott Fitzgerald, and you read about *The Great Gatsby* selling fewer than five hundred copies in the *entire* decade of the 1930s, you might associate the content (the information) with the principle of *failure*, or with *things taking time to blossom*.[28] The association emerges from the content itself.

Second, associations are formed based on the *external context* of the item that is encountered (for example, the environment or setting, or the tactile dimension of the material one is learning about). More on this will be discussed shortly.

Third, associations are formed based on the *internal context* at the time one is processing the content. For instance, the internal thoughts and ideas taking place in your mind while reading an article today vs. those you had while reading the same article ten years prior; the same content results in a drastically different experience depending on the internal context. In other words, the associations you form based on reading the same content at different periods of your life, will yield different ideas.

AN ILLUSTRATION OF CONTEXT VS. CONTENT

When you learn an idea in a given context (for example, the concept of *asynchronicity* while studying *web development*), the *context* is web development; the *content* is the concept of asynchronicity. Within the context of web development, asynchronicity refers to the loading of web assets in a parallel fashion. There are other contexts for the concept of asynchronicity, for instance *asynchronous learning*. Essentially, this points out the fact that the same *content* can have different meaning given a different *context*. Likewise, this is how human memory is structured and (not surprisingly) it's how the Antinet is structured.[29]

---

28 David S. Brown, Paradise Lost: A Life of F. Scott Fitzgerald, Illustrated edition (Cambridge, Massachusetts ; London, England: Belknap Press: An Imprint of Harvard University Press, 2017), 101.

29 Michael Jacob Kahana, Foundations of Human Memory. (New York: Oxford University Press, 2014), 98.

INTERNAL CONTEXT IS A VERY POWERFUL THING

Around 2010, I recall a conversation with an investor in one of my past companies who was one of the top-level team members at Google's advertising technology division. He told me that Google was currently facing a crisis—a threat to their business. Up to that point, its technology had revolved around *content*. That is, the search term one finds in front of them on the search results page and the ads the user experiences when browsing a web page. The ads and the search terms were based on the *content* of the page. For instance, if you were on a website about cats, you would get ads about cat food. Google's ad technology was built around the *content* the user was currently accessing at the time.

However, a new technology emerged in ad targeting known as *remarketing* or *retargeting*. This technology targeted users based on their recent patterns and habits. This meant, whatever website they recently visited, would be affixed to the profile of that user. The way these profiles were built relied on website cookies (which you've probably now heard of, since almost every website prompts you to accept being tracked with cookies). As a result, when you're viewing a website about cats, you'd start seeing ads for the website of the clothing store you visited yesterday.

Google quickly adapted to this new ad technology and implemented it in their own products. They even went a step further and enabled advertisers to not only target users based on recent websites they had visited, but also on the recent keywords they searched on Google.

Remarketing effectively led to a way of targeting people based on their search terms or the websites they had visited recently (the advertiser could define how recently). Users were essentially grouped into buckets based on their *internal context*. It started with targeting people who visited any given website, but later on became more abstracted. Google enabled audience targeting based on interests, affinity groups, and whether a person was *hot* and in the market to buy certain products (part of what's called an *in-market audience*). For instance, advertisers could target people who were actively shopping for a new car (indicated by their having visited a number of car websites and navigated to the pricing pages).

INTERNAL CONTEXT IN THE ANTINET

Internal context in relation to the Antinet refers to your internal monologue and the internal thoughts that arise while reading a text or engaging with a piece of content.[30] Your internal context is affected by whether or not thoughts are consciously accessible at the time you're engaging with content.

The experience of internal context can be illustrated in an experience you might have had in which you have a completely different opinion of a book you read ten years ago, compared with your opinion after reading it in the present.

For instance, I recall being forced to read *The Great Gatsby* in high school. I found myself bored out of my mind. I didn't retain much. The only thing I remember was some stupidly named place the book was set in, called West Egg and East Egg. Ten years later I read the same book and was captivated. It became one of my favorite books of all time. My mindset was different when I read it the second time. I was interested and intrigued by the prose and writing style. I also understood more background about its author, and was more fascinated with the book because of this.

With non-fiction books the power of different contexts is even more prevalent. For instance, reading the book *How the Mind Works* by Steven Pinker was an interesting experience. I would have probably found it more impactful if I hadn't already read the book *Sapiens* by Yuval Noah Harari. In Pinker's book, he introduced some very intriguing ideas; however they were ideas I was already familiar with thanks to reading *Sapiens*. The internal monologue in my mind was like, *This is interesting. This reminds me of the section in Sapiens about the cognitive revolution.* As a result, while reading *How the Mind Works*, I would simply write down the keyterm *cognitive revolution* on my bibcard. I then would create an external reference to the card on cognitive revolution that was already installed in my Antinet.

30 Michael Jacob Kahana, Foundations of Human Memory. (New York: Oxford University Press, 2014), 12.

In brief, the internal context in which I read the book was quite different than what it would have been if I hadn't read *Sapiens* first. I probably would have been more impressed with Pinker's book if that had been the case, too!

When presented with a concept (or a thought) today, the concept activates related information *internally* in your mind.

For another simple example, imagine you were tasked with memorizing the following list: *house, shoe, pig*. Let's hone in on the item *pig*. You probably imagine an abstract representation of a pig (like a pig emoji). I, myself, on the other hand have a completely different representation of pig. Why? Because for about a six month period while writing this book, I owned a pet pig named Garth. When I think of the word *pig*, I think of Garth (and the many times he pissed on my carpet).[31]

So what does this mean? In brief, even *prior* to the experiment taking place, I had a different internal context than you when beginning to memorize the list. As you can imagine, having certain internal representations could be quite advantageous for memorizing certain things.[32]

A *thought*, which is the raw material of an Antinet, is much like an *experience*. As scholars have long recognized, an experience cannot be repeated exactly on two separate occasions.[33] Every thought is experienced in a somewhat different context. Context can include *surrounding thoughts* you've just had (and that are *reverberating* in your mind), or the *setting* in which you have the thought (the *external context*), or the *time* of occurrence.[34]

---

31 Pigs are, let's just say, "challenging." Garth would get bored during the day and eat the covers off my books at home. That's when I drew the line.

32 Michael Jacob Kahana, Foundations of Human Memory. (New York: Oxford University Press, 2014), 249.

33 Michael Jacob Kahana, Foundations of Human Memory. (New York: Oxford University Press, 2014), 12.

34 Michael Jacob Kahana, Foundations of Human Memory. (New York: Oxford University Press, 2014), 12.

Let's revisit the diagram showing the different variables which shape a thought:

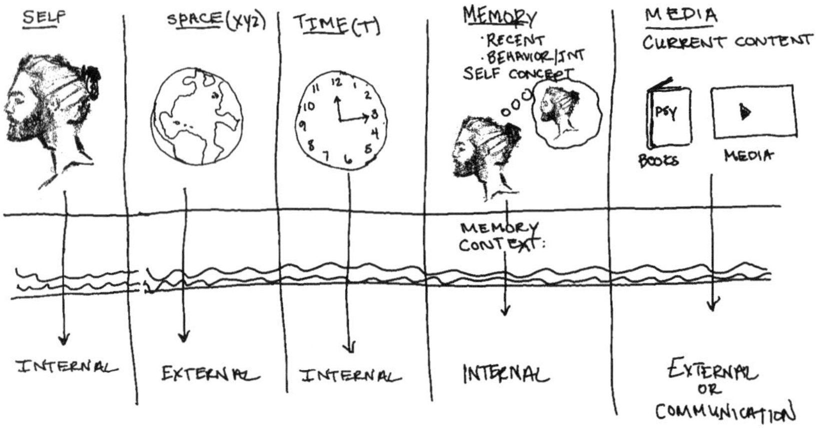

Every thought is shaped by *internal context*. The Antinet captures the *internal context* of one's mind quite effectively, and it locks it in time. It does this in a more effective way than digital systems. I contend this is because digital systems are always updating themselves. They're too fluid and they do not show the internal context of your mind at the time you created a note. For instance, in one of the cards I was referring to when I wrote this section, there was a note that explained internal context, and then said, See '4214/3D/3B/2'. I have no idea or recollection of making this note, nor did I have any idea what note 4214/3D/3B/2 was. It turned out to be a card about *external context*. Essentially, when I was creating this card about *internal context* I mentioned something that had to do with *external context* and decided to create a cardlink to that card (which at the time was something I was closely familiar with). This communicates to me where my mind was during the time I created the card. When I created the card about *internal context*, my past self wanted to make sure I differentiated it from *external context* and I provided a link to *external context* in order to view the differences between the two. It stamps the state of my mind at that time, in a static place in (remembered) time.

With digital notetaking tools, such a note describing a topic would likely be a bullet point list, and would continually grow, only to be edited, rearranged, modified, or deleted. By the time I was ready to actually begin writing the section I would no longer see the original internal context and internal life of that note stamped in time. This is not ideal. You want to see an original track-record and a snapshot of the original state your mind was in when it created the note. Granted, I could update the card and add more links later on; however, to maintain this time connection, I suggest changing ink color for later additions so that you know it was updated later on.

This may seem like we're getting into the weeds here; however, it's something you'll come to realize and recognize the benefits of when you work with your Antinet in practice.

For now, that's enough on *internal context*. To truly understand how the Antinet locks in *internal context* better than digital systems, you'll need to try it out for yourself.

THE PHYSICAL NATURE OF THE ANTINET ENGENDERS MEMORY PROCESSES NOT FOUND IN DIGITAL SYSTEMS

The eponymous album by the band *Fleet Foxes* includes a letter written by lead singer Robin Pecknold that serves as an illustration of the experience of using an Antinet. Pecknold writes:

My first memory has always been of me and my mom on a cold grey day down at some beach in Washington, along the Puget Sound somewhere near Seattle. I would be around two or three years old and we're with a friend of mine from the neighborhood and his mom, walking around among the driftwood looking for crabs. Even now, I can remember the smell and temperature of the air, the feeling of the sand and the swaying tall grass. I can even remember looking over at my friend and how his face looked when he smiled back at me. Another memory that I'll sometimes recall as my first memory is dressing up in the dead of winter as Jack London, with tennis rackets on my feet and wearing my dad's hiking pack, in the middle of summer after seeing Disney's (terrible) version of White Fang. Or there's the memory of stealing my neighbor's big wheel and riding it halfway down the block before getting caught and having to turn around defeated, or of wearing a fireman's outfit while washing my parent's car, or eating an orange popsicle from the ice cream truck.

These are and have always been some of my most distinct and persistent memories of childhood, so it came as a disappointment to me when one day as a teenager, I opened up a photo album and found pictures of each and every one of those memories. I didn't have a single memory that didn't belong to or somehow grow from pictures my parents had taken of me when I was growing up. Even the scenes I remember so clearly in my head are from the same angles as those photographs, and I don't really know what to make of it. I'm going to guess that I'd seen all these photographs at some point, forgotten they were just photographs, and over time made them into my most tangible memories. That's scary to me in a way.

This leads me to something weird about the power that music has, it's transportive ability. ***Any time I hear a song or record that meant a lot to me at a certain moment or I was listening to at a distinct time, I'm instantly taken back to that place in full detail.***

The phenomenon of feeling like you are "instantly taken back to that place in full detail" is something that doesn't just occur with music: it happens in the Antinet.

After I had spent four years developing "critical thinking" skills in college, I determined two things: first, it'd be wise for me to record the very best concepts I learned during my undergraduate studies (so that I could have them for life). And, second, for some reason I determined the best mechanism for storing the best concepts would be 3 x 5 inch lime green notecards. Yes, lime green notecards.

Although the bright colors of these lime green notecards render my thoughts barely legible today, when I happen upon such cards, they're amazingly valuable.

You see, the lime green notecards contain not only ideas written on them, but they transport me back in time. For myself, I'm transported back inside the room I lived in at the time. The Antinet, with its reliance on notecards, serves as a powerful mechanism for capturing and reminding one of certain internal contextual experiences. This derives from the different colors of notecards you choose to use. It also derives from the different diagrams, drawings and even the style of your handwriting at that point in time. This is very powerful when it comes time to writing and creating. This experience leads to potentially insightful breakthroughs that may not otherwise come about from digital notetaking systems (which possess weaker faculties for inducing internal contextual memories).

EXTERNAL CONTEXT IN THE ANTINET

Color is an important attribute of human memory. We can observe this from our own personal experiences (for me, the lime green notecards taking me back in time). We can find such illustrations of this fact in novels.[35] Or, we can refer to the field of human memory studies, which lumps this into a category called *external context*.[36]

External context refers to the physical environment and physical traits involved in learning something. This includes location, environment, and personal perspective. Your perspective derives from your position in the setting in the memory. External context also includes other parts of your sensory system—sounds, smells, tastes, textures, and other sensations.[37]

External context is an important functional memory input, as recent science reveals: what one learns in one environment is better recalled later on in that or a similar environment.[38]

In the digital-focused age of today, far too many people overlook the concept of external context, even though this component is critical for building memory and the mind.

---

35 Lawrence Block, Hit Man, Reissue edition (HarperTorch, 2002), 280.

36 Michael Jacob Kahana, Foundations of Human Memory. (New York: Oxford University Press, 2014), 98.

37 Michael Jacob Kahana, Foundations of Human Memory. (New York: Oxford University Press, 2014), 12.

38 Michael Jacob Kahana, Foundations of Human Memory. (New York: Oxford University Press, 2014), 12.

POSITIONAL CODING IN THE ANTINET

Related to the notion that backs up my use of lime green notecards is the usefulness of notes built using other odd formats. As I've previously mentioned, in my Antinet I have a notecard about *love* written on an actual leaf that my fiancé picked out for me. Whenever I come across this note, it cues the unique external context that generated or embeds the note.

A note such as this inhabits physical space in the Antinet, and also in one's mind. The physical location of items that prompt memory is explained in human memory studies by the notion of *positional coding*. In this case, I know that the position of the leaf notecard is in the middle of the drawer of the 2000 branch of my Antinet. Whenever I wish to navigate to the subject of *love*, I simply navigate to that area without having to look up the keyterm *love* in my index. Whenever I'm reading a book, and the concept of *love* appears, I make a quick observation note of it on my bibcard, and then quickly install the idea near the leaf notecard in my Antinet.

With the Antinet, positional coding blends with spatial memory to create spatial encoding. That is, you know where to look for certain pieces of knowledge based on its spatial position.

Spatial memory is sometimes mentioned in self-help books and programs that promise to teach one how to develop a super memory.[39] The basic premise of spatial coding involves assigning particular words (or concepts) to particular objects in the room you're currently in. That is, readers are instructed to imagine "the items arrayed before them on a table or perhaps imagining themselves learning each item at a different sequential location along a familiar route."[40]

---

39 Jim Kwik, Limitless: Upgrade Your Brain, Learn Anything Faster, and Unlock Your Exceptional Life, Illustrated edition (Carlsbad, California: Hay House Inc., 2020); Kevin Trudeau, Kevin Trudeau's Mega Memory (Niles, IL: Nightingale Conant Corp, 1990).

40 Michael Jacob Kahana, Foundations of Human Memory. (New York: Oxford University Press, 2014), 294.

The earliest reference to this practice was in 88 BC and is referred to as the *method of loci*. People who used this practice include Aristotle, Cicero, and Quintilian. Cicero referred to it as *artificio memoria*.[41] These thinkers assigned to the thoughts that backed their arguments items situated in rooms and gardens in order to facilitate their recall.[42]

The spatial memory of the *method of loci* operates differently than the spatial memory of the Antinet. With the Antinet, one isn't so fixated on assigning thoughts to objects (such as assigning the thought about *consciousness* to a plant in the room). That said, properties of spatial memory do indeed surface when using an Antinet (like me knowing generally where to find the leaf notecard for *love*).

The reason for this occurring can be traced to "Neurons in the hippocampus [which] have been shown to be selective to one's location in space."[43]

The importance of external context and external memory, in which various objects in our physical environment is not foreign to scholars.[44] This may be why many are hesitant to discard physically-dependent knowledge systems that have been actively evolved for over 2,500 years. These important features are not so easily replaced in the latest switch to using digital tools to manage our memory externally.

THE EXPLICIT NATURE OF LUHMANN'S ZETTELKASTEN

It's important for you to understand these components of the Antinet to gain a sense for why each individual principle of the Antinet is important. The

---

41 Richard Yeo, *Notebooks, Recollection, and External Memory: Some Early Modern English Ideas and Practices* (Brill, 2016), 136.

42 Alberto Cevolini, ed., Forgetting Machines: Knowledge Management Evolution in Early Modern Europe, Library of the Written Word, volume 53 (Leiden ; Boston: Brill, 2016), 7.

43 Michael Jacob Kahana, Foundations of Human Memory. (New York: Oxford University Press, 2014), 31.

44 Alberto Cevolini, ed., Forgetting Machines: Knowledge Management Evolution in Early Modern Europe, Library of the Written Word, volume 53 (Leiden ; Boston: Brill, 2016), 129.

Antinet was not designed with little thought or care. It very much mirrors how human brain and memory work. Furthermore, the importance of *context* in the Antinet and how thoughts are developed within contexts (branches) is another component that should not be overlooked.

With the conclusion of this chapter you now have more than enough theoretical understanding of the Antinet's nature to complement your own empirical experiments. As usually, the only right answer is to test the system for yourself, and experience the Antinet's glory (for yourself)!

CHAPTER TWENTY

EVOLUTION, PERCEPTION, PERSPECTIVE AND RUMINANTS

IN THIS CHAPTER WE'LL BE discussing the concept of long-term evolution in the Antinet. We'll also be diving into the concepts of perception vs. perspective, and how the Antinet locks these elements into each notecard. We'll cap this chapter off with the concept of the Antinet as a ruminant.

EVOLUTION

In his paper *Communication with Noteboxes,* Niklas Luhmann talks about the "inner life" of the Antinet. He touches upon its "mental history," which evolves through time.[45] The inner life and mental history of the Antinet are brought forth by its unique structure. Specifically, it's brought forth by the numeric-alpha addresses. Luhmann refers to the fixed positioning of order (*Stellordnung*), which is created through unique card addresses. This property enables the Antinet to evolve over time in such a way that it's possible to view the mental history of your thoughts; with the numeric-alpha addresses and the tree structure, you can observe your mind's evolution.

Viewing the evolutionary history of your thoughts proves useful for certain types of activities. Take, for instance, the activity of reading scientific literature. According to Luhmann, the key to reading scientific texts centers on long-term memory. According to Luhmann, long-term memory is more crucial than short-term memory for reading scientific texts because it is

---

45 Niklas Luhmann, "Communication with Noteboxes (Revised Edition)," trans. Manfred Kuehn, https://daily.scottscheper.com/zettelkasten/.

necessary to distinguish the "essential from the non-essential and the new from the merely repetitive."[46] In other words, you want a system where you can refresh your memory of your notes and evolve your current ideas with new ideas. You don't want to waste time relearning what you already know.

The Antinet's workflow involves noting down observations on a bibcard. Then, before actually developing a main note, you review the Antinet. You figure out *where* a card will be placed before dedicating the time to reformulate or reflect on the material. This is an important step as it prevents you from spending too much time on writing about the *non-essential* or *repetitive* material that you already know.

When you review this material you're not only reducing the risk of getting bogged down on things you already know; there's another useful feature. As Markus Krajewski observes, "The reader is not only reading his own memory, but rather also his *shifting frame of reference over time*."[47] In other words, when you review your Antinet, you're seeing your shifting frame of references over time. You're seeing your different *perspectives* and your different interpretations of ideas based on communication with different sources you've engaged with. It's possible to view how your thoughts have developed, changed, and internally evolved over time.

Oftentimes, the most surprising finds are the links you stamp onto the cards. These shed light into what the idea reminded you of at the time and shed light on your own internal reverberation of ideas at a given time. The cards that these links point to serve as the source material of your own internal perspectives and context. When viewing Luhmann's system, this is something Krajewski confirmed as well: "What is more surprising are the references listed."[48]

---

46 Niklas Luhmann, Short Cuts (English Translation) (Frankfurt am Main: Zweitausendeins, 2002), 83.

47 Markus Krajewski, *Note-Keeping: History, Theory, Practice of a Counter-Measurement against Forgetting* (Brill, 2016), 331.

48 Krajewski, Note-Keeping: History, Theory, Practice, 331.

This relates to something in human memory called *temporal context.*[49] Memories and thoughts that occur around the same time are essentially *linked* together.[50] Temporal context can be thought of as a function of time, external context, and internal context. In essence, your thoughts are a function of the period of time in which you had them. They're shaped by your own internal dialogue at that specific time, as well as the external context in which you have the thought. As a result, you link together a unique set of other ideas at the time of creation. These unique associations of other ideas are represented in the form of cardlinks in your Antinet.

These cardlinks are way more valuable and effective than things like *wikilinks* in digital systems. The reason is that notecards in the Antinet are updated and changed less frequently than in digital systems. Notes in digital systems are constantly being updated, rearranged, deleted, and added onto. Within the Antinet, notecards are locked in time once they're created. This then locks in a view of the temporal context of your ideas over time.

COMPOUNDING OF IDEAS

Albert Einstein considered *compound interest* to be the eighth wonder of the world. Warren Buffett has said his financial success is simply "a product of compound interest."[51] Simple things compound into complex things. Luhmann himself experienced this first hand with his Antinet. The little, simple, everyday commitment to building and evolving your Antinet results in genius-level thought. Over time your ideas evolve and snowball into things you never could have planned. This happens in an organic way, slowly, one notecard at a time. Thought-by-thought, branch-by-branch, stem-by-stem, link-by-link, your Antinet evolves into a complex entity, experiencing the magic of compound interest. Yet it's not easy. You have to earn it. This is

49 Michael Jacob Kahana, *Foundations of Human Memory.* (New York: Oxford University Press, 2014), 14.

50 Mostafa M. El-Kalliny et al., "Changing Temporal Context in Human Temporal Lobe Promotes Memory of Distinct Episodes," *Nature Communications* 10, no. 1 (January 14, 2019): 203.

51 "Compoundingquotes," Investment Masters Class, accessed July 18, 2021, http://mastersinvest.com/compounding.

often seen as a negative aspect of the Antinet (writing things by hand is hard); yet it pays off in the end.

Markus Krajewski observes, "Whoever sets about ongoing work (or communication) with such a secondary memory can not only count on the fact that the apparatus will faithfully reproduce everything which has been shared with it, they can also trust that, with the information successively provided over time, future knowledge will be enriched."[52] In essence, the individual notes you provide to the Antinet will be enriched over time. The individual pieces of information compound and collide with one another to form rich pathways of knowledge. When it comes time to write, your cognitive energy is freed up to collaborate with this entity. You're left with a very rich, interconnected store of knowledge with which you can creatively reinterpret that knowledge and tie it into the paper or creative work you're actively building.

The idea of notes becoming a rich store of value is certainly not a new one. John Aubrey (1626–1697), a fellow of the Royal Society, once said that habitual notetaking creates "'nest eggs' for the future."[53]

The bottom line is this: The entity you're creating with the Antinet is a complex one. It's a product of compounding the interest of your ideas. The result is something magical: it morphs into an entity that you (and only you) can truly understand.

PERCEPTION AND PERSPECTIVE

Perception and *perspective* derive from similar etymological roots. These terms are often confused with one another, even though they're different.

Perception comes from the Latin term *percipere*. Let's break this apart. *Per* means "fully." *Cipere* means "to grasp" or "to take." Combined, *percipere* means to fully grasp, understand or interpret the meaning of something.

52 Markus Krajewski, *Note-Keeping: History, Theory, Practice*, 326.

53 Richard Yeo, *Notebooks, Recollection, and External Memory: Some Early Modern English Ideas and Practices* (Brill, 2016), 138.

Perspective comes from the Latin term *perspecere*. *Per* means the same thing as it does in *percipere* ("fully"). *Specere* means "to observe" or "to spectate." Combined, *perspecere* means to fully observe and to see and spectate.

Think of perception as applying your own *interpretation* of some observations. Perception uses *interpretation* to help us derive *meaning* out of an observation. The meaning you assign to an observation shapes your thoughts, which shape your reality.

Think of perspective as your *point of view*. Perspective is your vantage point. It's a function of space and time. Where you are in the world, and at what time you observe an event shapes your perspective.

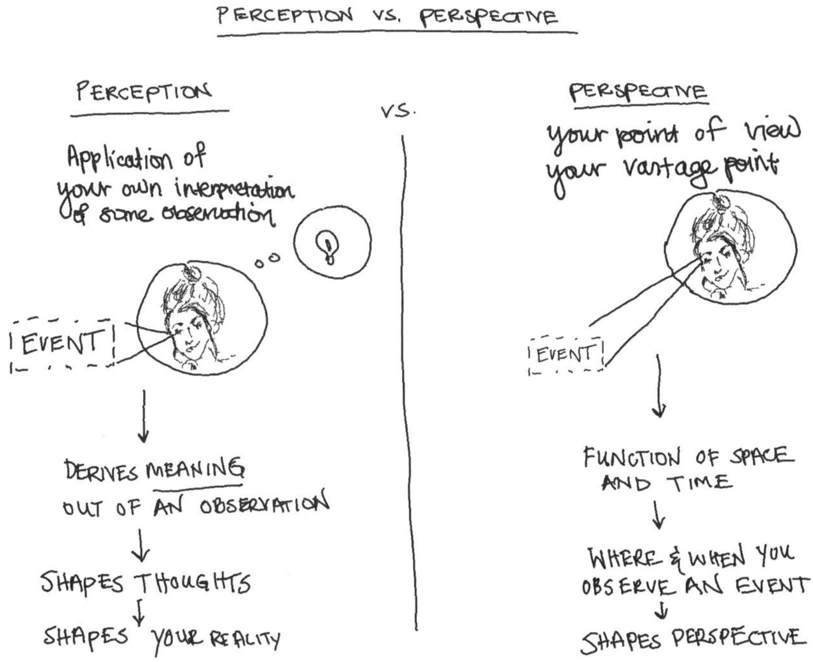

When you use an Antinet your notes contain both your perspective and your perceptions of ideas. When you create reformulation notes, you're summarizing ideas based on your perspective at the time. You're shaping your ideas by your current point of view. When you create reflection notes, you're adding your own *interpretations* of the ideas you encounter. You're stamping your own perceptions of ideas onto your notes. These are locked in time. They are not updated, overwritten or edited (like they often are in digital tools).

It's very important that both your perspectives and perceptions be locked in time. This provides the raw material for the communication experience that makes the Antinet so valuable. When you go back and review old notes, you're having a communication experience. You're viewing ideas containing your second mind's perspectives and perceptions. You're then comparing these with your own present-day perspectives and perceptions. This creates the valuable internal dialogue we've touched upon throughout this book. You begin seeing your perspectives and perceptions *evolve* over time. This proves to be an invaluable interaction during the creation process.

RUMINANTS

Ruminants are a type of mammal that acquire nutrients from eating grass. They first ferment the grass in a specialized stomach called a *rumen*. After the grass is fermented in the rumen, it is then digested.

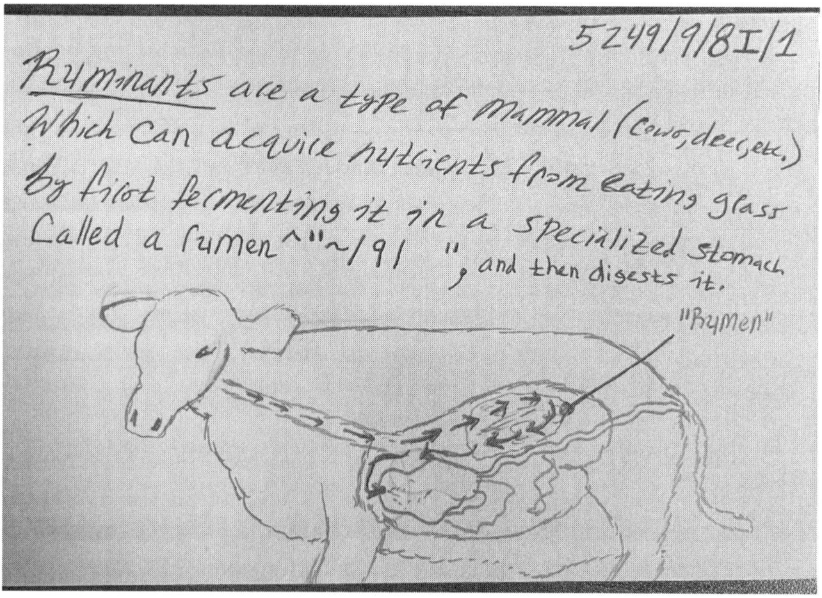

The word ruminant comes from the Latin term *ruminare,* which means "to chew slowly." This is where the term *rumination* derives from.

Here's why I'm even talking about this: in Luhmann's own Zettelkasten, he describes his system by calling it a *ruminant.*

> *"The Zettelkasten is like the complicated digestive system of a ruminant. All arbitrary ideas, all coincidences of reading, can be included. It is then the internal connectivity that decides."*
>
> –Niklas Luhmann, Zettelkasten II: 9/8i[54]

By calling it a ruminant, Luhmann is referring to the idea that some pieces of knowledge need time to be digested. The technique of using external references (ExRefs) helps with this. Sometimes you come across interesting material; however you don't yet know whether the idea is worth fully processing yet. In this case you create ExRefs for the material and thus enable the material to ruminate in the Antinet. If the time comes wherein the material will become useful, you can then digest the material by converting it into a main note. Or, you can digest the material by using it while writing your manuscript.

The idea of the mind as a ruminant is not a new concept. The French Catholic philosopher Antonin Sertillanges writes:

> Man's mind is a ruminant. The cow looks away into the distance, chews slowly, bites off here a tuft and there a twig, takes the whole field for her own, and the horizon as well, producing her milk from the field, feeding her dim soul on the horizon.[55]

What this involves is *reverberation* as understood in the study of human memory. I talk about the concept of reverberation throughout this text.

---

54 "ZK II: Zettel 9/8i—Niklas Luhmann-Archiv," accessed May 4, 2022, https://niklas-luhmann-archiv.de/bestand/zettelkasten/zettel/ZK_2_NB_9-8i_V.

55 OP A. G. Sertillanges, The Intellectual Life: Its Spirit, Conditions, Methods, trans. Mary Ryan, Reprint edition (Washington, D.C.: The Catholic University of America Press, 1992), 78.

The idea involves "just-experienced" ideas and associations reverberating in one's mind.[56] Reverberation is most often associated with short-term memory. However, with the Antinet, you can lock in reverberation over a longer period of time. Reverberation over the long term reflects the concept of rumination.

The idea of rumination doesn't just have important implications in the Antinet. Rather the way you approach books involves rumination as well.

As Francis Bacon once pointed out, "Some books are to be tasted, others to be swallowed, and some few to be chewed and digested."[57] Some books are to be read only in parts; others should be skimmed, some few should be read wholly, and others should be read with deliberate attention. Mortimer Adler asserted: "Reading a book analytically is chewing and digesting it."[58]

Yet without the Antinet, the knowledge one gains during analytical reading is lost. The Antinet captures the insights from deep analytical reading and stores them for the long term. In the Antinet these deep insights collide with other ideas and compound.

The point in all of this is reflected in the following suggestion: view the Antinet as a *ruminant of your mind*. Store all of your material there that you wish to evolve. Store both your fully developed thoughts, as well as thoughts that need more time to sprout.

---

56 Kahana, *Foundations of Human Memory*, 9.

57 Mortimer Jerome Adler and Charles Van Doren, *How to Read a Book*, revised and updated edition (New York: Simon and Schuster, 1972), 19.

58 Adler and Van Doren, *How to Read a Book*, 19.

CHAPTER TWENTY-ONE

RANDOMNESS, SURPRISES AND ACCIDENTS

As we've learned, one of the more overlooked benefits of the Antinet is its ability to foster randomness, thanks to its tree structure. This structure generates invaluable surprises and accidents, allowing users to encounter ideas they would otherwise not have reviewed had they been using digital systems. When you work with an analog system, you're exploring and sifting through your previous thoughts. This ignites a reverberation of ideas that circulate in your mind, causing a crucial "collision" of ideas in your mind during the writing process.

RANDOMNESS

Here, randomness is a feature, not a bug. A key property of a living, evolving, anti-fragile system is its unorthodox structure. The perfectly normalized structures we find in digital notetaking systems are synthetic. They're fragile. They're overly malleable and they rarely retain a unique character. As one scholar points out, "Evolution always occurs through the selection of accidental differences without a design."[1]

It doesn't seem intuitive, but here's the reality: randomness doesn't come from chaos alone. Randomness actually relies on order. As Luhmann states, "even the creation of random suggestions requires organization."[2]

1 Alberto Cevolini, ed., Forgetting Machines: Knowledge Management Evolution in Early Modern Europe, Library of the Written Word, volume 53 (Leiden ; Boston: Brill, 2016), 11.

2 Niklas Luhmann, "Communication with Noteboxes (Revised Edition)," trans. Manfred

When I first began using notecards to store my thoughts in 2006, I would simply take notes about a book on 3 x 5 inch cards. Each card contained one idea. These notes were primarily *reformulation notes*. They summarized individual concepts I learned while reading the book. By the time I finished reading the book, I would have about twenty or thirty new 3 x 5 inch cards. I would then wrap a rubber band around them and throw them in a shoebox. From time to time I would then review the notecards.

However, this isn't the most *ordered* structure. It's seemingly random. The Antinet, on the other hand, introduces an ordered structure (numeric-alpha addresses and the tree-like branching architecture). As a paradoxical result, the structure induces more useful random features.

SURPRISES

The tree structure of the Antinet encourages the asking of unique questions that are less commonly asked when one uses digital systems, since those systems are fully indexed with full text search. Upon encountering a new idea while using an Antinet, you ask yourself questions like *What is the name of that concept*. You're then prompted to ask what other terms live near that concept if you can't find its location. It requires finding alternative ways to think about the concept and to essentially re-imprint the pathways that led you to the idea. This practice is a fun way to approach knowledge. Embarking upon an associative-thinking process brings about fascinating surprises along the way. Your current mind (with its own active memory) has a dialogue with your past self (your second mind), and this dialogue often results in amazing surprises. If nothing else, the core output of the Antinet is one thing: it's a "surprise generator."[3]

Kuehn, https://daily.scottscheper.com/zettelkasten/.

3 Johannes Schmidt, "Niklas Luhmann's Card Index: Thinking Tool, Communication Partner, Publication Machine," Forgetting Machines. Knowledge Management Evolution in Early Modern Europe 53 (2016), 295.

As one scholar observes of Luhmann's system: "a true communication process is triggered that exploits the machine's ability to *surprise*, i.e., to produce information."[4]

The same scholar observes how a true secondary memory arises when the questions one asks triggers a network of associative references and links. These links then give birth to "collaborative" reasoning *that was not intentionally designed*.[5] The network of associative references refers both to the concept of *forward associations* and to *remote associations*. Here we see that the tree structure, with the continuous flow of cards as well as the remote cardlinks, helps create a *collaborative* communication relationship with the second mind. It also serves as the core component for creating surprises (realizations that are a result that *had not been intentionally designed*).

Again, the network structure of the Antinet is similar to *associationism*.[6] The association of nodes in the network is based on contiguity. The continuous flow of notes (containing thoughts) is augmented by insertions of similar material later on. Thoughts grow contiguously from previous branches and are grouped together with similar thoughts over time. These two components (*contiguity* and *similarity*) are the very components which govern thought in general, and that is used to the Antinet's advantage.

THE NATURE OF SURPRISES

Isaac Asimov once observed that great ideas and breakthroughs begin not with *Eureka!* but with *Hmm, that's funny*.[7] While using the Antinet, you'll come across many instances where you think to yourself *Hmm, that's funny!* Take note of these instances and create links between them.

---

4 Alberto Cevolini, ed., Forgetting Machines: Knowledge Management Evolution in Early Modern Europe, Library of the Written Word, volume 53 (Leiden ; Boston: Brill, 2016), 15. Emphasis added.

5 Alberto Cevolini, ed., Forgetting Machines: Knowledge Management Evolution in Early Modern Europe, Library of the Written Word, volume 53 (Leiden ; Boston: Brill, 2016), 20.

6 Steven Pinker, How the Mind Works, Norton pbk (New York: Norton, 2009), 113.

7 Adam Grant, Think Again: The Power of Knowing What You Don't Know (New York, New York: Viking, 2021), 59.

Keep in mind, though, that in the spirit of good science, you should not let your guard down. When you say to yourself, *that's funny*, that doesn't mean the idea is true. It could merely mean that the idea is interesting. Ideas have a tendency to survive not necessarily because they're true, but because they're interesting.[8] In the name of good science, you ought to search for surprises that excavate *truth*. Your goal should not center on excavating stuff that's merely interesting—that's pop science gibberish.

In some ways, the Antinet helps mitigate against getting carried away by interesting but unfounded insights. It does this by collecting *contradictions*. Surrounding the leaves and stems of cards that generate surprises it's likely that one will find thoughts that contradict the surprise. This is only possible thanks to the principle of not erasing anything in your Antinet. The fact that contradictory ideas remain for you to find helps you filter out ideas which are merely interesting in order to find insights that are both interesting *and* true.

In addition to this anti-self-deception mechanism, the fact that you're neuroimprinting ideas enables you to call to mind the contradictory ideas by attending to the reverberation achieved through writing by hand and sifting through your notes. In brief, you're less likely to deceive yourself when working with the Antinet. Why? Because you can think of examples that contradict insights you might otherwise be charmed by.

THE ANTINET IS BUILT FOR SURPRISES

Thanks to the Antinet's structure, surprises are achieved by giving the Antinet "autonomy."[9] This autonomy is created by the commitment to never change card addresses. Unlike digital files with their dynamically updating links, the Antinet's card addresses never change. Likewise, aside from editing marks or additions made directly on a card (that leave a trace of the change in

8 Adam Grant, Think Again: The Power of Knowing What You Don't Know (New York, New York: Viking, 2021), 59.

9 Johannes Schmidt, "Niklas Luhmann's Card Index: Thinking Tool, Communication Partner, Publication Machine," Forgetting Machines. Knowledge Management Evolution in Early Modern Europe 53 (2016), 295.

thinking), any future changes made to the information on a card can only occur by adding related, child-like nodes underneath it.

The commitment to never change card addresses is pretty easy and doesn't require willpower (unlike the temptation to change card addresses in a digital system). Thanks to the analog nature of the Antinet, it's just completely impractical to change the addresses of many cards!

This is a good thing. If constant changing, deleting, or updating of the system were possible, it would rip out the unique personality of that system. Because of this, complementary and contradictory thoughts are gathered in an essentially "locked" system that then generates surprise combinations.

AN EXAMPLE OF A SURPRISE

Something interesting happened a few months into building out my Antinet. I was going through the process of installing my legacy notecards when I came upon a card pertaining to something called *cluster analysis*. In machine learning, cluster analysis involves using algorithms to classify data patterns into groups or clusters. The clusters are then analyzed to determine which features and properties make the groups alike.

When I went to create a keyterm for *cluster analysis* I was surprised by the fact that I already had a keyterm for the term *cluster*! What I found was that the keyterm linked to something in the cognitive biases branch of my Antinet (address 2431/18). When I traveled to that card, I found a concept outlining something called *clustering illusion*. Suddenly I recalled this concept that refers to a cognitive fallacy by which humans see patterns in data—even if the data is completely random. This tendency usually happens when the data is composed of a small random sample.

As a result of this, in my section for cluster analysis, I included a disclaimer for my future self: *Before beginning any significant time investment in cluster analysis, be wary of falling into the trap of clustering illusion (See '2431/18').* In brief, I've created a link across two branches of knowledge that have very important implications for each other.

These types of surprises occur frequently in the Antinet because the keyterms and links are created deliberately. When you see a surprising occurrence (like the shared term *cluster* which points to concepts which may contradict each other), you pay closer attention to them. You appreciate the surprise more and you use the surprise by creating relevant links between the two ideas.

If I were using a digital system, I believe it would have been less likely that I'd have realized the same relationship between the two ideas. If I had searched the term *cluster*, I'd likely have found myself bombarded with dozens, if not hundreds, of notes containing the term *cluster*. My state of mind would have been one of *I want to find the file I'm looking for as quickly as possible, which* is not an *explorer mindset* exhibiting curiosity and pattern-seeking). I would have quickly passed over the commonality of these two concepts because they would have been crowded out by too much information.

HETEROGENOUS RELATIONS

Luhmann points out that the most fruitful types of surprises within the Antinet happen by way of relating "heterogeneous things with each other." He holds that it's more valuable to associate patterns between ideas that otherwise would not be associated with one another.[10]

One interesting way to facilitate these *heterogenous relations* is to group ideas around certain *polarizing* keyterms.

For instance, in my index I've created the keyterm *Most,* and some interesting concepts have grown around it.

For example, there's the idea stemming from life philosophy: ***Most*** *Important Variable for Success in Life*. This keyterm entry points me to card 2460/2/0, which contains an idea from the book *How to Get Rich* by Felix Dennis. The idea centers on the concept that *self-belief* is the most important variable for success in life and suggests that we lack self-belief because we do not

10 Niklas Luhmann, "Communication with Noteboxes (Revised Edition)," trans. Manfred Kuehn, https://daily.scottscheper.com/zettelkasten/.

yet have confidence. One way to develop this confidence is to retrain your mind through the use of self-affirmations, a (positive) form of self-deception.

Now, when I navigate to another keyterm relating to *Most,* I find the following entry: *Most Important Variable for Success in Science.* Cardlink 2431/1/1 points out that avoiding *self-deception* is the key to success in science. Richard Feynman points out that, "The first principle is that you must not fool yourself, and you're the easiest person to fool."

It seems we have an interesting paradox here. The key to success in life is *self-belief,* which may involve self-deception. Yet the key to success in science is avoiding *self-deception.* This creates an opportunity to explore this conflict in greater detail to determine how one can cultivate healthy self-belief, without falling prey to the downsides of self-deception.

This is just one example of how heterogenous relations can emerge around certain keyterms in an Antinet.

Heterogenous Relations by Way of Proximity

Another example of heterogenous relations happens naturally thanks to the tree structure of the Antinet.

As you've learned, *associations* are a fundamental building block of human memory. Yet, rather than liken associations to simply links between related items, associations have an additional function: they create new entities altogether. Some types of associations collide and create new ideas. In human memory studies this is called a *holistic association.*[11] For example, take the following sequence of items: *horse* and *house.* When one thinks of those items together, they may think of a new entity altogether: a *barn.* Essentially the proximity of those two items creates a new holistic entity.

Luhmann would regard these associations as fruitful instances of surprise and accident. They are the result of seemingly heterogenous ideas forming

11 Michael Jacob Kahana, Foundations of Human Memory. (New York: Oxford University Press, 2014), 12.

around a certain area that, when viewed together as a *whole*, create a new entity altogether. Ultimately, these heterogenous relations create a new form of understanding that otherwise would not have existed.

Bisociation

Recall that Luhmann devised the Antinet because, in his words, he "wanted to accumulate knowledge and open up a *combination of possibilities*."[12] Thus, using heterogenous relations to effect bisociation—which refers to the simultaneous mental association of an idea or object across two fields that are not normally regarded as related—Luhmann did in fact create combinations of possibilities.[13] Furthermore, he did this by first reducing the complexity of books he read by extracting irresistible material. He then added back complexity by way of bisociating the material using links. "In a way," Luhmann said, "the [Antinet Zettelkasten] is a reduction to build complexity."[14]

In brief the Antinet is one big network which enables one to create bisociations by way of linking ideas across different branches of knowledge. As you've seen, this is something that can happen in several ways using an Antinet, at the core of which is randomness, surprise, and accidents.

ACCIDENTS

Like randomness, accidents are a feature, not a bug. Accidents play a most crucial part in advancing the evolution of organisms. Likewise, they play a most crucial part in advancing thinking. Luhmann understood this as well. "The role of accidents," he wrote, "in the theory of science is not disputed. If you employ evolutionary models, accidents assume a most important role."[15]

---

12 Niklas Luhmann, Niklas Luhmann Short Cuts (English Translation), 2002, 22. Emphasis added.

13 "Definition of BISOCIATION," accessed January 20, 2022, https://www.merriam-webster.com/dictionary/bisociation; For a nice summary of the concept as found in Arthur Koestler's *The Act of Creation* , see: Maria Popova, "How Creativity in Humor, Art, and Science Works: Arthur Koestler's Theory of Bisociation," The Marginalian (blog), May 20, 2013, https://www.brainpickings.org/2013/05/20/arthur-koestler-creativity-bisociation/; Koestler's work is not without its critics and critiques. See also: Steven Pinker, How the Mind Works, Norton pbk (New York: Norton, 2009), 549ff.

14 Niklas Luhmann, Niklas Luhmann Short Cuts (English Translation), 2002, 22.

15 Niklas Luhmann, "Communication with Noteboxes (Revised Edition)," trans. Manfred

How does one unleash the power of accidents? First, you must understand what is meant by the term *accident*. We're not trying to create *needless* accidents. We're trying to create *useful* accidents. Useful accidents are those which are usually *surprising* in nature. In the section on surprises we explored the types of accidents that are useful. Accidents that involve interesting heterogenous relations and fascinating bisociations are the accidents we're aiming for with the Antinet.

One way the Antinet generates the accidents we're looking for comes from its analog nature: when surfing through the Antinet and shuffling through cards, one increases the probability of useful accidents.

Some of the best advice from scholars and researchers focuses on this act. While doing online research is faster, it misses out on the serendipity of physical exploration. An excellent library encompasses such features. It possesses journals, books, and librarians who are shockingly helpful and more knowledgeable than we give them credit for. Accidents emerge from "prowling the stacks" of books related to the field you're interested in.[16]

The power of *prowling the stacks* of books also applies to notecards. The power of sifting through notecards, and in turn, yielding fruitful accidents, is something scholars have known for quite some time. This powerful feature of card indexes first became recognized by scholars in the seventeenth and eighteenth centuries. Scholars noted that Antinet systems, with their structural decoupling of knowledge into individual notecards, ends up producing "a substantial number of combinations and insights that otherwise might not have existed."[17]

Kuehn, https://daily.scottscheper.com/zettelkasten/.

16 Kate L. Turabian, Manual for Writers of Research Papers, Theses, and Dissertations,: Chicago Style for Students and Researchers, 9th edition (Chicago ; London: University of Chicago Press, 2018), 31.

17 Alberto Cevolini, Storing Expansions: Openness and Closure in Secondary Memories (Brill, 2016), 158.

MOVEMENT OVER MEDITATION

> *"I do not believe in coincidence. I believe that if you keep moving, you expose yourself to a better chance of accidents happening, some good and some bad."*
>
> –Travis McGee, in *A Purple Place for Dying*[18]

Accidents don't come solely from the unique tree structure of the Antinet, however. One other thing is required: movement.

One of my mentors, Sir Gary Halbert, preached *movement over meditation*. In essence, the more you move, the more success you have. The more you create and learn from mistakes, the luckier you'll get. Luhmann himself was tirelessly curious. He kept moving, kept reading, and kept uncovering useful accidents.

This flies in the face of the conventional and popular wisdom today. The advice we hear centers on meditating and sitting under a tree. The advice we hear is that *stillness is key*. Yet on the other end of the spectrum (literally) we have people moving constantly. They're the ones who are going to put the human race on Mars.

Of course, it's a balancing act (like everything). However, if you want to create useful accidents with your Antinet, you need to keep moving. You need to keep creating and learning.

Even if the knowledge you create isn't useful immediately, there's a good chance it will be useful later on. During the writing of this book, I've used material and notecards written from many years ago. I had no idea they would be used for a project when I created them. It's something you'll experience as well.

---

18 John D. MacDonald and Lee Child, A Purple Place for Dying: A Travis McGee Novel, Reprint edition (Place of publication not identified: Random House Trade Paperbacks, 2013), 128.

When Luhmann was working on a new publication he would document and record how his thought process evolved.[19] He would take on publication requests and work on articles that would later prove very useful in other areas. Over the course of producing these developments, Luhmann's theories compounded and evolved. By moving, he created more material which proved useful for other areas of his work. His movement to constantly take on publication projects allowed him to create useful accidents which compounded his actions. It created the rich material that would form his "super theory" of society.

While accidents, and randomness are the key components we're speaking of, the question then becomes: in what spirit of mind does one best cultivate useful accidents? That question is what we'll answer next.

PLAYFULNESS, CURIOSITY, AND TINKERING

Halfway through the month of June in 1749, all of Britain was buzzing with excitement. Things were especially abuzz in Surrey County, which borders London. The excitement revolved around one thing: a matchup between two of Britain's cricket clubs, the All England and the Surrey Cricket Clubs. The cricket teams were viewed as the titans of those times. "The match excited considerable interest and was attended by a very numerous body of spectators," wrote one who attended.[20]

The match between the two clubs was intense. The score was close; however in a wild upset victory, Surrey came away with the win. The best player in the match, Henry Venn, was exhausted. The other players on the team looked up to Henry. He was bold, disciplined, resolute, passionate, and very (very) intense.

---

19 Johannes Schmidt, "Niklas Luhmann's Card Index: Thinking Tool, Communication Partner, Publication Machine," Forgetting Machines. Knowledge Management Evolution in Early Modern Europe 53 (2016), 311.

20 John Venn, Annals of a Clerical Family: Being Some Account of the Family and Descendants of William Venn, Vicar of Otterton, Devon, 1600-1621 (Macmillan and Company, 1904), 70ff.

After Surrey came away with the victory Henry's teammates crowded around him. They gathered to celebrate the upset victory. Yet the excitement came to a stop and things quickly settled down. The fans stopped celebrating and fell quiet.

Everyone was looking at Henry whose face was red, as if he was angry. He threw down his bat and declared, "*Whoever wants a bat, then here! Take it. I have no further occasion for it!*"[21]

His teammates were shocked. Their hero was quitting on the spot! One of his teammates bravely asked Henry why he was quitting, and Henry replied, "Because I am to be ordained on Sunday." Henry explained he was quitting the game of cricket for God. He feared a member of his church remarking to him, "Nice game yesterday, Reverend!"

Henry intended to be a man who was taken seriously. To his mind this meant he must take life seriously, and this meant one thing: cutting out all forms of play.

Sadly, what followed was all but fulfillment and respect for Henry. His health quickly declined by "a sudden transition from a course of most violent exercise to a life of comparative inactivity."[22] Yet Henry pushed through the health issues and stuck with a strict regimen. He would wake up at five in the morning and preach ceaselessly all day. This continued on until he had a breakdown at age forty-nine. Henry burnt himself out and was relegated to a small country parish where he lived for another twenty six years.

Two generations of protestant missionaries followed in their forebear's footsteps. Both his son (John) and his grandson (also named Henry) became Anglican clergymen.

---

21 John Venn, Annals of a Clerical Family: Being Some Account of the Family and Descendants of William Venn, Vicar of Otterton, Devon, 1600-1621 (Macmillan and Company, 1904), 71.

22 John Venn, Annals of a Clerical Family: Being Some Account of the Family and Descendants of William Venn, Vicar of Otterton, Devon, 1600-1621 (Macmillan and Company, 1904), 71.

Yet Henry's physical and mental breakdown hung over the family. It was an unspoken yet very present tension, a tension between work for God vs. play (in the form of cricket).

This tension was present during the upbringing of Henry Venn's great grandson, John Venn.

John was a bright young man. Despite his strict Anglican upbringing, he became interested in mathematics and philosophy. In spite of his interests, John gave in to the religious indoctrination and ended up following in his family's footsteps, becoming ordained as an Anglican priest in 1859.

Unlike his great grandfather, however, John didn't wish to give up his other interests in his life. He loved cricket and outdoor activities like mountain climbing and he did not want to give his interest up as had his great grandfather.[23] Instead of giving up his interests in mathematics and philosophy, John continued his studies, and, in 1883, he resigned from the clergy after concluding that his religion was incompatible with his philosophical beliefs.

John continued to pursue life with a playful spirit. His passions ranged from mathematics, probability theory, and philosophy, to tinkering with inventions and machinery. He would go on to create the first cricket machine in history. It bowled cricket balls and is said to have struck out the leading batsman of the Australian cricket club four times in a row.[24]

Now, the reason you probably know John Venn stems from the following diagram (see following page):

---

23 Patrick J. Hurley and Lori Watson, A Concise Introduction to Logic (Cengage Learning, 2016), 284.

24 "John Venn | Biography, Inventions and Facts," accessed May 3, 2022, https://www.famousinventors.org/john-venn.

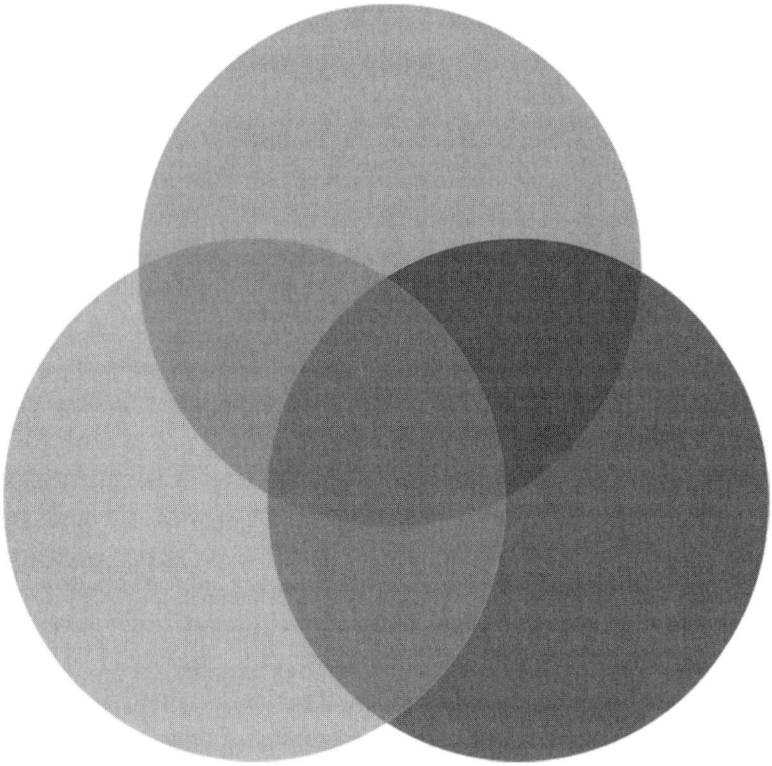

The Venn Diagram

All of John Venn's wide-ranging interests ironically led him to create a diagram in symbolic logic. This diagram is widely used and bears his name to this day.

This breakthrough in symbolic logic was not unearthed in the same manner John's great grandfather operated. It was not unearthed through rigid routine and workaholism. John was playful in spirit, he was a tinkerer, and he was curious.

Those who love order and structure may at first have trouble adopting the philosophy of the Antinet. In the land of binary, the world is perfectly ordered. This (0), or not this (1) underlies the language of digital systems. Binary logic makes life quite simple. But that's not reality. There's entropy and chaos in reality.

You must be willing to submit to randomness. You must be willing to submit to the mess of knowledge development, and to adopt and appreciate the value of randomness, embracing odd structures and surprises along the way. It involves adopting a playful mindset when working with your knowledge. Hopefully this story about John Venn will remind you of this.

To make sure I don't forget the lesson of John Venn, I purchased a cricket ball online which I keep in my office. Whenever I see it, I'm reminded to adopt the playful tinkering mindset of John Venn. This is the spirit I believe best suited for working with an Antinet. A playful, curious spirit.

In my YouTube videos I teach the Antinet from my office. Using my iPhone camera, I navigate around and teach certain aspects. Some viewers have commented, asking why there's a cricket ball sitting around. Now you know why. It's a great reminder. Adopting playfulness, randomness, and curiosity into your knowledge workflow is something one should not forget.

Now, as we end this book, I'd like to invite you to adopt this same spirit. Take it with you into the world. The spirit of playfulness, randomness, and curiosity.

I had no idea I'd be ending this book with this seemingly random story of John Venn. His story relates to the playful intellectual human spirit. This is but another example of randomness and accidents being brought forth by the Antinet. Quite frankly, it serves as a fitting end for such a book.

I wish you enjoyment in your journey. The journey of getting in touch with that deep, internal voice inside of you. I wish you luck in your intellectual pursuits and the things you will create (with the help of your Antinet).

Please keep in touch and share your own Antinet Zettelkasten journey with me. You can keep in touch by visiting my website: https://scottscheper.com.

Stay crispy, my friend.

AFTERWORD

What you have read in this book contains both everything and nothing you need to know about building an Antinet Zettelkasten. That's how you know the material is true. I believe the most *truthful* knowledge resembles that of a paradox. It simultaneously tells you everything and nothing about the nature of something. It's kinda like learning about Einstein's theory of relativity. It tells you everything and nothing about how the universe works. It just is what it is.

What I've laid forth in this book is the theory, practice, and history of working with the Antinet. I've also done my best to describe the more metaphysical features of the system—the Antinet as a communication partner and second mind. Interspersed between this is the science of human memory and the science of knowledge.

However, in the end, the only right answer is: test.

To experience the power of the Antinet, you must experiment with it yourself. You must commit to it. You must invest in it. Commit yourself to the work. Commit yourself to the time and the energy required to build your own second mind.

I hope you've enjoyed reading this book. I've had a wonderful time creating it. Stewie and I have been through a lot together in the year we spent writing it. We've been through several lives together. We have seen our personalities change drastically throughout the process. We've been through many rearrangements of my office here in downtown San Diego. We've been through many different arrangements of my Antinet. During the writing of this book I've gone from a single dude with one cat (Brodus); to a single dude with two cats (Brodus and Fiona); to an engaged dude with two cats, a soul-daughter, and a pig (Garth); to an engaged dude with two cats and a soul-daughter (sorry, Garth). Throughout all phases of this journey, one thing has been the same, actually two: first, I've continued to be a badass (in my own mind), and second, Stewie has been by my side.

I hope you get to enjoy the fullness of creating and evolving your own thoughts using an Antinet. If you do, please share your story and experiences in our Antinet Zettelkasten community on Reddit: https://www.reddit.com/r/antinet/

Warm regards,

And always remember...

...to stay crispy, my friend.

Scott P. Scheper
Downtown San Diego, CA
Tuesday 10:12 AM

APPENDIX A: LUHMANNIAN TREE STRUCTURE (ZETTELKASTEN I)

THE FOLLOWING CONTAINS THE LUHMANNIAN tree structure of his first Zettelkasten. There are 108 top-level categories, which branch internally from there. The list is translated into English and comes from the Niklas Luhmann Archive.[1]

- 1: Unity and Unification of the Group in General
- 2: State as Idea
- 3: Legal Method in the Application of Constitutional and International Law
- 4: Right of Veto
- 5: Control
- 6: Equality
- 7: The Value of Organization
- 8: The System as a Research Tool
- 9: State as an Organization in Principle
- 10: Organization as Imagination and as Reality
- 11: Individual/Community Problem
- 12: Organization and Law
- 13: Unification of Will
- 14: Politics
- 15: Structural Homogeneity
- 16: Sovereignty
- 17: Ideology
- 18: Political Party
- 19: Limits of Organization and Organizational Theory

1 "Inhaltsübersicht ZK II—Niklas Luhmann-Archiv," accessed March 31, 2022, https://niklas-luhmann-archiv.de/bestand/zettelkasten/inhaltsuebersicht.

- 20: Planning
- 21: Statesman
- 22: Exception
- 23: Formal Sociology (Relationship Theory)
- 24: Competition
- 25: Suggestion
- 26: Power
- 27: Constitution
- 28: The Nature of the Organization Fundamentally
- 29: Organization Theory: General and Methodical
- 30: Revolution
- 31: Terminology
- 32: Method
- 33: Theory / Practice
- 34: State of Emergency
- 35: National Territory
- 36: Government
- 37: Mediation / Mediator
- 38: Historical Foundation of the Theory of the State as a Science
- 39: Identity
- 40: Welfare State
- 41: Majority Principle
- 42: Line
- 43: Coordination
- 44: Division of Labor
- 45: Authority
- 46: Discipline
- 47: Command
- 48: Centralization / Decentralization
- 49: Hierarchy
- 50: Representation
- 51: Adequacy of Organization
- 52: Organization and People
- 53: Masked Relationships
- 54: Legitimacy

- 55: Technique
- 56: Organization and Size
- 57: Science
- 58: The Problem as a Research Category
- 59: Rewards as Performance Incentives and Other Performance Drives
- 60: The Process of Decision-Making
- 61: Measurement of Social Performance / Of Organizational Performance / Of Government Performance
- 62: Role
- 63: Lot as a Decision-Making Mechanism
- 64: Probability
- 65: Bureaucracy
- 66: The "Spirit" of Institutions
- 67: Establishment of Organizations
- 68: Communication in the Organization
- 69: Integration
- 70: Informal Organization
- 71: Responsibility
- 72: Permission
- 73: State
- 74: The Post
- 75: Office
- 76: Causality
- 77: Concept of the World
- 78: Philosophical Concepts: History of Dogmas and Intentions of Meaning
- 79: Conflicts and Their Solution
- 80: Balance
- 81: Status Naturalis
- 82: Sanctions
- 83: Performance Increase
- 84: Regulation (Rules of Human Behavior)
- 85: The Historical Conception of the State
- 86: Delegation

- 87: Legislation
- 88: Institutions
- 89: Separation of the State from the Public Order of the Middle Ages
- 90: Success
- 91: Administrative Science, Administrative Reform
- 92: State Science Funding
- 93: Political Pedagogy
- 94: Political Science
- 95: Information
- 96: Poster
- 97: Promises
- 98: Separation of Powers
- 99: Collegiality
- 100: On the Religious Foundation of the Social Order
- 101: Art
- 102: Initiative
- 103: Modern Social Order
- 104: Constituency
- 105: Feedback
- 106: Installments (Advice)
- 107: Family
- 108: Advertisement

APPENDIX B: LUHMANNIAN TREE STRUCTURE (ZETTELKASTEN II)

THE FOLLOWING CONTAINS THE LUHMANNIAN tree structure of his second Zettelkasten. There are 11 top-level categories, which branch internally from there. The list is translated into English and comes from the Niklas Luhmann Archive.[1]

- 1: Introduction to Modern Administrative Science
- 2: Basic Terms and Method
- 3: General Decision Theory
- 4: Office (Offices and Their Order)
- 5: Organization and Living Environment
- 6: Sovereignty / State
- 7: Single Terms, Single Problems
- 8: Economy
- 9: Ad Hoc Notes
- 10: Archaic Societies: Generalizable Main Features
- 11: Civilizations

1 "Inhaltsübersicht ZK II—Niklas Luhmann-Archiv," accessed March 31, 2022, https://niklas-luhmann-archiv.de/bestand/zettelkasten/inhaltsuebersicht.

APPENDIX C: DIGITAL ANTINETS

SOMETIMES PEOPLE CONTACT ME and write *Scott, thank you! I finally understand how the Zettelkasten is supposed to work!* These reactions are typically found in the YouTube comments on my videos. Yet every so often I get people who follow up this praise with some excuse. They insist analog won't work for them. For instance, they complain about their bad handwriting. Or they object to keeping a notebox due to their work environment.[1] Naturally, they follow this up with the question of *How can I implement the Antinet digitally?*

In brief: you can't.

Well, you can't without sacrificing various benefits, that is.

But...

If you put a gun to my head and told me to build a digital Antinet, here's what I would do:

First, I wouldn't do it.

Now with that out of the way, we can move on to the second thing I'd do.

The second thing I would do would be to add a character limit to notes. I did a rough count of the character space on 4 x 6 inch notecards (or the equivalent, A6 paper). I estimate the character space to be roughly 825 characters.

Here's one of my notecards, word-for-word:

---

1 **I address these objections in the chapter on Analog.**

> When you strip away "contiguity" in the system, thus leaving a pile of leaves, you dismantle the mind of the system. You destroy the system's memory and its unique way in understanding things. You've turned your communication partner into a pile of leaves! See: '4212/2B5'
>
> "Shared meaning" of items that are also located nearby one another (forward associations, backward associations, and nearby associations) "play a crucial role in the function of human memory," according to one scholar who specializes in the field.
>
> In other words, note the important distinction: it's the stemlinks & branchlinks which play a crucial role in how human memory works—not just remote links. Digital Zettelkastens do not possess the first two.
>
> (Kahana, 11)

Here's a photo of it:

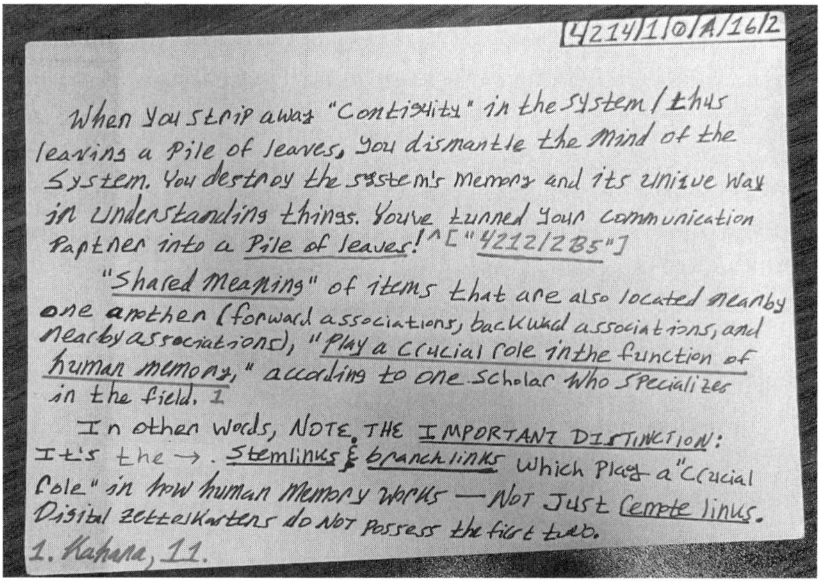
4214/1/0/A/16/2

When you strip away "Contiguity" in the system, thus leaving a pile of leaves, you dismantle the mind of the system. You destroy the system's memory and its unique way in understanding things. You've turned your communication partner into a pile of leaves! ^["4212/2B5"]

"Shared meaning" of items that are also located nearby one another (forward associations, backward associations, and nearby associations), "play a crucial role in the function of human memory," according to one scholar who specializes in the field. 1

In other words, NOTE THE IMPORTANT DISTINCTION: It's the →. Stemlinks & branchlinks which play a "crucial role" in how human memory works — NOT just remote links. Digital Zettelkastens do NOT possess the first two.

1. Kahana, 11.

This card comes out to 738 characters (excluding the card address). Also there's some extra room at the top.

Here's one of Luhmann's notecards, word-for-word:

> Im Grunde führt also die Als-Struktur des Erkennens auf das System. Denn etwas kann nur erkannt werden durch Hinweis auf ein anderes, das wiederum in weiteren Zusammenhängen bedeutsam ist. Und das Gewicht, das die Feststellung von etwas als etwas hat, empfängt sie von diesen anderen Zusammenhängen her, auf die sie verweist. Sobald solches Feststellen begrifflich wird, wird es daher auch systematisch.
>
> Vgl. auch Schlick, S. 62: "Das Erkenntnisurteil ist einen neue Kombination von lauter alten Begriffen. Die letzteren kommen in zahllosen anderen Urteilen vor, von denen uns einige (z.B. ihre Definitionen) schon vorher bekannt sein mussten; sie bilden die Verbindungsglieder, durch die das Neue in das grosse System der bekannten Urteile eingeordnet wird, welches den Bestand unserer Erfahrungen

Here's a picture of this card:

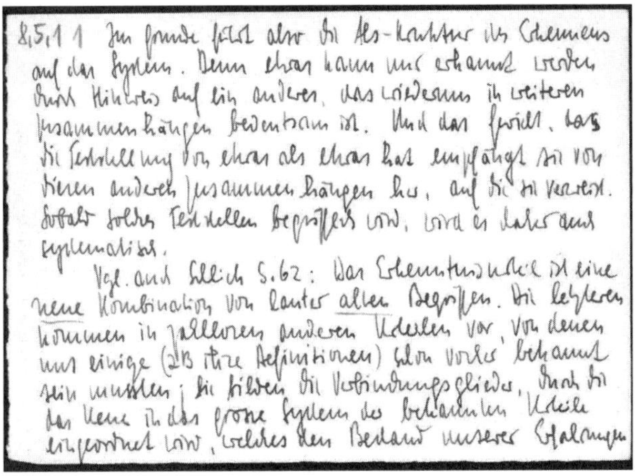

PHOTO CREDIT: "Niklas Luhmann-Archiv," accessed May 5, 2022, https://niklas-luhmann-archiv.de/bestand/zettelkasten/zettel/ZK_1_NB_8-5-1_V.

This comes out to 797 characters.

Again, there's some white space in both of these cards. Plus, I'm not counting the card addresses. For these reasons, I think a character limit of 825 is a good guesstimate.

If I were forced to build a digital Antinet, the third thing I'd do is this: I'd disable editing and deleting. Once a note is created it should not be edited or deleted. Yet, appending other ideas onto the note is fine. Such additions can be in the form of adding text to any blank space. For example, adding *'See Also'-cardlinks*. This would be like a pop-up bubble seen when hovering your mouse over an image. For instance, there are design collaboration apps that allow designers to add pop-out text over areas of the design as a comment bubble over the image.

The fourth thing I'd do if forced to build a digital Antinet relates to the directory structure. There would be three top level structures, corresponding to the three boxes of an Antinet: (1) Bibliography Box, (2) Index Box, and (3) Main Box). It would be look like this:

- Bib
    * Adams, Scott—*God's Debris*
    * Adler, Mortimer—*How to Read a Book*
    * Ahrens, Sönke—*How to Take Smart Notes*
    * ...
    * Zlotnik, Gregorio—*Memory: An Extended Definition*
- Index
    * bstraction
    * Abundance
    * Accounting
    * ...
    * Zone of Genius
- Main
    * 1000
    * 1100
    * 1100.1
    * 1100.1.1
    * 1100.1.1A

* 1100.1.2
* ...
* 5999

The fifth thing I would do if forced to build a digital Antinet would be to eliminate the ability to copy and paste.

The sixth thing I would do would be to delete tags and backlinks from the system.

The seventh thing I would do is delete the search box. This forces users to deliberately create keyterms in the index. It also forces one to navigate the Antinet in a more exploratory way.

The final thing I would do would be to delete the whole digital repository and get back to creating knowledge the analog way!

Ironically, one of the individuals who, early on, claimed analog wasn't an option for them ended up changing their stance. They tried building out the Antinet the right way (the analog way), and they've since come to see the light.

I believe the majority of those who claim that analog isn't for them simply possess false beliefs. If they would only test it first themselves, they'd come to realize the advantages of analog.

Still, everyone's different. I'm not some analog luddite. Try both for yourself. If you decide analog doesn't do it for you, then hopefully the guidelines I've laid forth in this section will be of service to you.

Oh, and one last thing: don't do digital.

GLOSSARY

ANALOG KNOWLEDGE DEVELOPMENT ("AKD"): A term for those who *develop* knowledge using analog tools. Knowledge development refers to four phases: (1) *selecting* sources of knowledge and the material within those sources; (2) *extracting* interesting thoughts from books, podcasts, videos, and other media; (3) *creating* notes that elaborate on the thoughts one extracts from knowledge sources; (4) *installing* those thoughts into a long-term storage structure so that the thoughts may evolve (the Antinet Zettelkasten being the ultimate storage structure).

Antinet: A notebox containing four core properties (or principles): Analog, Numeric-Alpha Card Addresses, a Tree Structure, and an Index. Together, these four principles create a cybernetic thinking network. *Variant terms: Antinet Zettelkasten, Analog Zettelkasten, Luhmannian Zettelkasten.*

Antinetter: Those who develop knowledge using the Antinet. These are the crazy ones, the crazy few. Those who know, deep-down, that developing their thoughts using analog tools (and specifically the Antinet Zettelkasten) is the most magical, powerful, intimate way of creating meaningful output.

Bibliography Box ("Bib Box"): A box in the Antinet which stores all of your bibcards (notes from the books you read). These bibcards are stored alphabetically by author's last name.

Bibliography Card ("Bibcard"): A 4 x 6 inch notecard oriented vertically. This card is used to store observational thoughts with a corresponding page number while reading (or engaging with other sources like podcasts, videos, lectures, etc.). Also useful as a bookmark. *Variant terms: Staging Card, Literature Notes.*

Bibliography Notes ("Bib Notes"): These are short, observational notes from readings (or other media), which are placed on bibcards. They begin with a page number, and then a very brief observation or thought. The bib notes are then transformed into more in-depth notes (called main notes).

Bubble Graph Boiz: Digitally-obsessed PKM individuals who spend their days majoring in the minor. These folks obsess over metadata tags, and creating interesting templates for creating notes. The one thing they do not prioritize is knowledge development. Nor do they prioritize output. You can find these individuals hanging out in your favorite PKM software's forums. *Variant terms: Workflow Warriors, Digital notetaking Junkies, Hotkey Addicts, Plugin Perverts.*

Card Address: The numeric-alpha notecard address affixed to the top-left or top-right of each notecard (e.g., 4214/5a/1).

Cardlink: Within a notecard, when you reference another card address in your Antinet, you're effectively creating a cardlink. For instance, when you find the following card address placed within the main area of a notecard (not in the top-left or top-right), you're creating a cardlink (e.g., 4214/14). Cardlinks aren't like digital links. They're hard to create. Cardlinks are hardlinks (this is a good thing)!

Collectives: A notecard with a list of keyterms, phrases or cardlinks to other cards in the Antinet. *Variant terms: Hubs, Hub Notes, Structured Notes, Maps of Content.*

External References (ExRefs): References to external sources outside of the Antinet. For instance, a reference to a specific book and page number (*Scheper, Scott. Antinet Zettelkasten, p. 122*). *Variant Terms: External Links.*

Hoplink Cards: Very simple cards that contain a brief snippet of text that say something like: *For more on x concept, see cardlink 'xxxx/xx/x'.* These cards enable one to quickly hop to other relevant places in the Antinet.

Index: A box within the Antinet containing keyterms and corresponding cardlinks in the Antinet. *Variant Terms: Index Box, The Index, Register, Keyword Register.*

Indexcards: Notecards placed in the index, which enable you to navigate to different areas of the Antinet (by way of cardlinks and a human-readable keyterm).

Keyterm:A human-readable concept that points you to a numeric-alpha address (cardlink) in the main box of your Antinet.

Keyterm Indexcards: A keyterm indexcard, as opposed to a list indexcard, is a dedicated card listing multiple links or external references for a given keyterm. Whenever a keyterm entry in a list indexcard accumulates multiple cardlinks, you'll want to create a dedicated keyterm indexcard for it.

List Indexcards: Indexcards filed alphabetically, each pertaining to one letter of the alphabet (*A*, *B*, *C*, etc.). Under the assigned alphabetical character is a list of keyterms that begin with the letter affixed to the card.

Main Box: The main part of your Antinet containing the main types of notecards with numeric-alpha addresses affixed to them. These cards follow the tree-like branching structure of the Antinet.

Maincards ("Cards"): The main types of notecards stored in your Antinet (in the main box). Maincards are 4 x 6 inch (or A6) horizontal notecards (preferentially white and blank). They contain a numeric-alpha card address affixed to the top-left, or top-right, of the notecard. Maincards contain one of the four types of main notes. *Variant terms: Cards, Notecards.*

Main Notes: The types of notes you'll find on maincards. These four note types are observation notes, excerpt notes, reformulation notes, and reflection notes.

Neuroimprinting: The concept of more effectively stamping an idea onto your mind for later recall done by way of writing by hand.

Personal Knowledge Management ("PKM"): A *Personal Information Storage System* used by digital apps, which enables one to link documents (of typically low-processed information). Otherwise known as a procrastinator's wet dream.

Remotelinks: Say you're writing a note within the card 4214/5A/2 and you create a link to the card 1334/2A/4. What you have just created is a *remotelink*. You're linking to a remote area of a card in your tree of knowledge (your Antinet). Remotelinks are essentially the full card address of another card that reside in a more remote part of your Antinet (relative to the location of the card referencing it).

"See Also" Cardlinks: Oftentimes, you don't need to create a dedicated hoplink card to navigate around your Antinet. You can just append relevant cardlinks to already developed cards. This is where *"See Also" Cardlinks* come in handy. These are snippets of text at the bottom of cards that say something like, *See also: "xxxx/xx/x."*

Wikilinks: Cheaply created digital links to other notes (usually markdown files). Wikilinks are typically created with text enclosed in two square brackets (e.g., [[I'm a Useless Link to a Digital Note]]).

ACKNOWLEDGMENTS

SPECIAL THANKS TO THE FOLLOWING people who helped me make this book a reality: First and foremost, thank you to my lovely fiancé, Arianna Zabriskie-Scheper. The diagrams in this book were hand-drawn by her (you can blame her for the illustrations containing the man with a man-bun). My copyeditor, Wendy Smyer Yu (aka, "Wendy The Wonderful"). My writing coach, Ross Hartmann, who I worked with only briefly, yet he had a big impact in getting me started on the actual writing process. Thank you to Chris Aldrich, who reviewed the *Preface,* and provided other invaluable feedback. Chris is an infinite well of knowledge when it comes to the history of analog notetaking systems. He is also less of a knucklehead than Moe, Larry, and Curly. Last, but not least, I would like to thank all of my Antinetters who supported me (by way of my YouTube channel and Reddit and my private email list). Also a very special thank you is deserved for my Antinetters who wrote to me by physical mail very early on in this process. This book is for those who are committed to growth and learning.

ABOUT THE AUTHOR

SCOTT P. SCHEPER, aka "*The Analog Knowledge Revolutionary,*" is a writer, copywriter and marketer residing in San Diego, California. When not communicating with his Antinet ("Stewie"), one may find Scott communicating with an actual human being. Actually, probably not. One is more likely to find Scott reading a book with a bibcard sticking out of it. Keep in touch with Scott, and join his highly entertaining private email list, by visiting his website: https://scottscheper.com.